Sun® Certified Web Component Developer Study Guide

(Exam 310–081)

David Bridgewater

McGraw-Hill/Osborne
New York Chicago San Francisco Lisbon London Madrid
Mexico City Milan New Delhi San Juan Seoul Sydney Toronto

The McGraw·Hill Companies

The McGraw Hill Companies
McGraw-Hill/Osborne
2100 Powell Street, 10th Floor
Emeryville, California 94608
U.S.A.

To arrange bulk purchase discounts for sales promotions, premiums, or fund-raisers, please contact **McGraw-Hill**/Osborne at the above address.

Sun® Certified Web Component Developer Study Guide (Exam 310–081)

1234567890 CUS CUS 0198765

Book p/n 0-07-225882-9 and CD p/n 0-07-225883-7
parts of
ISBN 0-07-225881-0

Acquisitions Editor
Tim Green

Production Coordinator
Azadeh Poursepanj

Project Manager
Jody McKenzie

Acquisitions Coordinator
Jennifer Housh

Technical Editor
Karen Tegtmeyer

Copy Editor
Donald Pharr

Proofreader
Kathy Finch

Indexer
Marilyn Augst

Composition
G&S Book Services

Illustration
G&S Book Services

Series Design
Roberta Steele and Peter Hancik

Cover Series Design
Peter Grame

This book was composed with Abode Indesign®.

To my mother, Kay Bridgewater

CONTENTS

ABOUT THE CONTRIBUTORS

About the Author

David Bridgewater has a long career in application development and spent some of his happiest professional years helping a large UK retail company to embrace Java technologies. Now he works as freelance Java/WebSphere trainer, author, and consultant. He is a regular contributor to technical journals and web sites (such as IBM DeveloperWorks), focusing on web application development with Java and J2EE and supporting IBM technologies. He can be reached at dbridgewater@jbridge.co.uk.

About the Technical Editor

Karen Tegtmeyer has over 15 years of software development experience and works as a consultant and independent software developer. She specializes in Java and J2EE and has worked on numerous domestic and also international projects. She can be found on the Internet at www.javadiva.com. She is a Sun Certified Programmer, Sun Certified Web Component Developer, and IBM Certified Developer—XML and Related Technologies. She lives in Des Moines, Iowa. She can be reached at karen@javadiva.com.

About LearnKey

LearnKey provides self-paced learning content and multimedia delivery solutions to enhance personal skills and business productivity. LearnKey claims the largest library of rich streaming-media training content that engages learners in dynamic media-rich instruction complete with video clips, audio, full motion graphics, and animated illustrations. LearnKey can be found on the Web at www.LearnKey.com.

ACKNOWLEDGMENTS

I would like to thank the following people:

- Tim Green, Acquisitions Editor for the McGraw-Hill/Osborne Certification Series, for having faith in me and the book over the long haul of its preparation.
- All the other staff at McGraw-Hill/Osborne who had a hand in the book, especially Jessica Wilson and Jennifer Housh for their skill and diplomacy in keeping the book on track.
- Karen Tegtmeyer, Technical Editor for this book, for her pragmatic and astute advice on improving the book—a Java Diva in talent only, never in tantrums.
- Donald Pharr, Copy Editor for this book, for his astute eye.
- Azadeh Poursepanj and the other hardworking staff at G&S Book Services for translating plain text and drawn-on-cigarette-packet diagrams into a professional and aesthetic layout.
- The original project team at Arcadia who embraced Java in its early days and whose enthusiasm and immense hard work have been an inspiration to me ever since. Scattered as you are now—Tony Cracknell, Peter Thomas, Mark Campbell, Steve Pratt, Malcolm Watts, Ian Seckington—I salute you. Et in Arcadia Java!
- The staff at IBM ITES for giving me the opportunity to teach Java to others.
- Benedict Heal for an inspiring introduction to Java and for expanding my mind beyond its limited horizons.
- Last and most, to my immediate family—Francesca, Sally, and Jess—who have supported me even at my most demented while writing this book.

PREFACE

In This Book

This book is organized in such a way as to serve as an in-depth review for the Sun Certified Web Component Developer Exam both for experienced Java web developers and for those at an earlier stage of experience with Servlet and JavaServer Page technologies. Each chapter covers a major aspect of the exam, with an emphasis on the "why" as well as the "how to" of working with and supporting J2EE web applications.

On the CD

For more information on the CD-ROM, please see Appendix A.

Exam Readiness Checklist

At the end of the Introduction, you will find an Exam Readiness Checklist. This table has been constructed to allow you to cross-reference the official exam objectives with the objectives as they are presented and covered in this book. The checklist also allows you to gauge your level of expertise on each objective at the outset of your studies. You can check your progress and make sure you spend the time you need on more difficult or unfamiliar sections. References have been provided for the objective exactly as the vendor presents it, the section of the study guide that covers that objective, and a chapter and page reference.

In Every Chapter

We've created a set of chapter components that call your attention to important items, reinforce important points, and provide helpful exam-taking hints. Take a look at what you'll find in every chapter:

- Every chapter begins with the **Certification Objectives**—what you need to know in order to pass the section on the exam dealing with the chapter topic. The objective headings identify the objectives within the chapter, so you'll always know an objective when you see it!

- **Exam Watch** notes call attention to information about, and potential pitfalls in, the exam. These helpful hints were written by authors who took the exams and received their certification—who better to tell you what to worry about? They know what you're about to go through!
- **Practice Exercises** are interspersed throughout the chapters. These are step-by-step exercises that allow you to get the hands-on experience you need in order to pass the exams. They help you master skills that are likely to be an area of focus on the exam. Don't just read through the exercises; they are hands-on practice that you should be comfortable completing. Learning by doing is an effective way to increase your competency.

- **On the Job** notes describe the issues that come up most often in real-world settings. They provide a valuable perspective on certification- and product-related topics. They point out common mistakes and address questions that have arisen from on-the-job discussions and experience.
- **Inside the Exam** sidebars highlight some of the most common and confusing problems that students encounter when taking a live exam. Designed to anticipate what the exam will emphasize, getting inside the exam will help ensure you know what you need to know to pass the exam. You can get a leg up on how to respond to those difficult-to-understand questions by focusing extra attention on these sidebars.
- **Scenario and Solution** sections lay out potential problems and solutions in a quick-to-read format:

SCENARIO & SOLUTION	
You have information retrieved from a database, which is required for a one-off web page and isn't part of a longer transaction.	Store the information in a request attribute. If the information truly isn't needed beyond one production of one HTTP response, then don't keep it around cluttering up the web application JVM memory.
You have some XML files that store essential information about the way your web application works: perhaps some information about table headings and columns. This information changes only when the web application undergoes development changes and is redelivered.	Store the information derived from the XML files in one or more context attributes. The information is then in JVM memory for any web resource to access—no need to keep trawling through the XML file every time a request needs information.

- The **Certification Summary** is a succinct review of the chapter and a restatement of salient points regarding the exam.

- The **Two-Minute Drill** at the end of every chapter is a checklist of the main points of the chapter. It can be used for last-minute review.

Q&A

- The **Self Test** offers questions similar to those found on the certification exams. The answers to these questions, as well as explanations of the answers, can be found at the end of each chapter. By taking the Self Test after completing each chapter, you'll reinforce what you've learned from that chapter while becoming familiar with the structure of the exam questions.
- The **Lab Exercise** at the end of the Self Test section offers a unique and challenging exercise format that requires the reader to understand multiple chapter concepts to answer correctly. These exercises are more complex and more comprehensive than the earlier ones in the chapter, as they test your ability to take all the knowledge you have gained from reading the chapter and apply it to complicated, real-world situations. These exercises are aimed at exercising all the development competencies you need to deal with questions in the exam. If you can do these exercises, you have proven that you know the subject!

Some Pointers

Once you've finished reading this book, set aside some time to do a thorough review. You might want to return to the book several times and make use of all the methods it offers for reviewing the material:

1. *Re-read all the Two-Minute Drills*, or have someone quiz you. You can also use the drills as a way to do a quick cram before the exam. You might want to make some flash cards out of 3 × 5 index cards that have the Two-Minute Drill material on them.
2. *Re-read all the Exam Watch notes*. Remember that these notes were written by authors who took the exam and passed. They know what you should expect—and what you should be on the lookout for.
3. *Review all the S&S sections* for quick problem solving.
4. *Re-take the Self Tests*. Taking the tests right after you've read the chapter is a good idea, because the questions help reinforce what you've just learned. However, it's an even better idea to go back later and do all the questions in the book in one sitting. Pretend that you're taking the live exam. (When you go through the questions the first time, you should mark your answers on a

separate piece of paper. That way, you can run through the questions as many times as you need to until you feel comfortable with the material.)

5. *Complete the Exercises*. Did you do the exercises when you read through each chapter? If not, do them! These exercises are designed to cover exam topics, and there's no better way to get to know this material than by practicing. Be sure you understand why you are performing each step in each exercise. If there is something you are not clear on, re-read that section in the chapter.

INTRODUCTION

The Certification Path

Sun's J2EE Certification Exams

As you will have gathered from its title, this book is all about the Sun Certified Web Component Developer (SCWCD) Exam. It is one of several exams you can take once you have passed your Sun Certified Java Programmer (SCJP) Exam—this book assumes you have already done that. The SCWCD is one among a group of Java 2 Enterprise Edition (J2EE) exams. There are three in all which cover the following J2EE developer areas:

Sun Certified Web Component Developer (SCWCD)

This exam is the subject of this book. It explores the fundamentals underpinning the web side of J2EE: servlets, JavaServer Pages (JSPs), and several related technologies, such as custom tags and expression language.

Sun Certified Business Component Developer (SCBCD)

This exam is all about the development of components that encapsulate the business logic of a J2EE application. You are tested on all aspects of Enterprise JavaBean (EJB) technology.

Sun Certified Developer for Java Web Service (SCDJWS)

This exam concerns the development of web services for the J2EE platform. You have to know all about related XML and Java technologies (like SOAP and JAX-RPC).

All the preceding certifications are similar in format to the SCJP. Each consists of a single exam containing a large number of tricky multiple-choice questions. There are slight variations in the exact number of questions, the pass mark, and the length of the exam.

Apart from these three exams, there is an independent certification strand within J2EE to become a Sun Certified Enterprise Architect (SCEA). You don't have to have taken the Sun Certified Java Programmer exam as a prerequisite for this qualification—you don't even have to be a developer (though it undoubtedly helps if you have some hands-on experience of J2EE development). Don't regard

FIGURE 1

Sun Certification Exams for J2EE

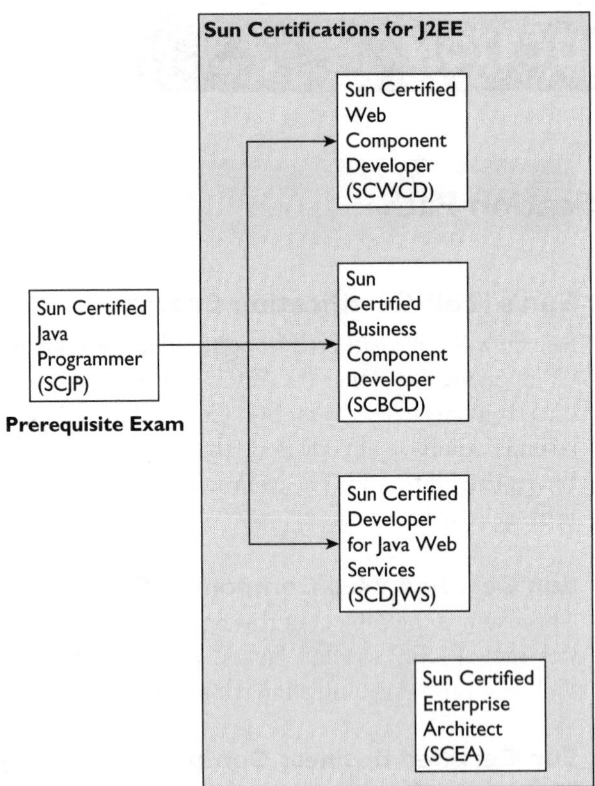

this as a soft option, though. There are three components to SCEA certification: a multiple-choice exam (much like the other exams described), an assignment, and an essay exam.

The range of Sun Certification Exams for J2EE is summarized in Figure 1.

If Enterprise Java isn't enough for you, there are certification paths in standard Java (J2SE) and mobile Java (J2ME). Take a look at the index page for Sun Java Certification to learn more about these certification paths (http://www.sun.com/training/certification/java/index.html), as well as the J2EE options already described.

The SCWCD and Enterprise Java

The current SCWCD exam (310-081) is based on J2EE version 1.4. While the content still focuses on JavaServer Pages and servlets, there has been a lot of change since the (now withdrawn) 310-080 exam based on J2EE version 1.3. The following table summarizes the specification levels for technologies within J2EE that pertain to the exam as it was and the exam now:

	J2EE 1.4 (Current Exam 310-081)	J2EE 1.3 (Obsolete Exam 310-080)
Servlets	2.4	2.3
JavaServer Pages	2.0	1.2
JavaServer Pages standard tag library	1.1	Not featured
Base Java level	J2SE 1.4	J2SE 1.3

On base Java level—note that this exam is still based on J2EE 1.4, which assumes 1.4 of the standard edition of Java. Although the SCJP exam is just beginning to embrace the "Tiger" edition of Java (known as version 5.0 or version 1.5), the SCWCD exam is still firmly anchored to J2SE 1.4. So—perhaps a little disappointingly—you don't get to play with Java's new language features in your preparation for the SCWCD. However, you shouldn't be disheartened by this. If you haven't yet got up to speed with the sea of change between JSP 1.2 and JSP 2.0, you will find a whole wealth of new technologies to learn about. Furthermore, big commercial web application servers (such as IBM's WebSphere) are still at the time of writing only now fully embracing J2EE 1.4 technology. Sensibly, commercial products are cautious in their adoption of the very latest standards. Echoing this, the Sun Certification Exams only test you on technologies that are fully adopted and likely to form a core part of what you are likely to need to know in your current job role.

This book addresses the full exam 310-081. If you have already taken the J2EE 1.3–based web certification exam (the retired 310-080 exam), you can take an *upgrade* exam instead of the full 310-081 exam. The upgrade exam has the code number 310-082. It is based on a subset of the objectives in (and has fewer questions than) the full exam. It concentrates on the new areas that have been introduced with J2EE 1.4, rather than retesting you on topics that haven't changed since J2EE 1.3. This book can be used to study for the upgrade exam as well as the full exam. One option is to follow the full book anyway. Another is to cherry-pick only those sections that relate to the topics you need to know. The Exam Readiness Checklist starting on page xxxvi makes clear which objectives belong to the full exam, which belong to the upgrade exam, and which parts of the book relate to each objective.

Don't Underestimate the SCWCD Exam!

If you are coming to this exam in the aftermath (or afterglow) of taking the SCJP exam, you may be thinking that from now on all will be smooth sailing. Surely nothing could be as tough as a bitwise operator question out of left field! My first word of advice would be: Don't underestimate the SCWCD! It's a longer exam, has more questions, and requires a higher pass grade than the Sun Certified Java Programmer exam (at least when compared with the SCJP 1.4 exam, which readers are likely to have taken; the new SCJP 1.5 exam is a slightly different story). So don't underestimate or rush into the SCWCD exam!

There is also a misconception that the world of servlets and JSPs is the soft and easy underbelly of Enterprise Java development—it's what you do as a developer before you get up to speed with "properly difficult" areas such as Enterprise Java Beans and Web Services. This, I can assure you, is a gross misrepresentation. Certainly, servlets and JavaServer Pages contain a lot of simple and elegant ideas and can quickly be pressed into service by developers with even a minimal amount of knowledge. But the devil, as always, is in the detail—and this being a Sun Certification Exam, you will be grilled broadly and deeply on detail.

There is certainly a danger in the SCJP that you are a good Java developer with plenty of experience, you wander underprepared in to the SCJP . . . and you flunk it because there are areas that you haven't needed before (and even those you have needed you might find you didn't understand quite as deeply as you thought). The same is true for the SCWCD exam, and possibly more so: You may have a lot of experience in Java web development, but simply never get exposure to many topic areas. This will be especially true if you develop in a Struts environment, which insulates you from many dealings with J2EE web APIs that you need to know intimately to pass the SCWCD.

Having said all this, I hope not to have put you off taking the exam. Take heart: You studied and passed the SCJP—the skills and attitude to get the SCWCD are no different. Mere mortals (the author included) can study and get the qualification. It just requires diligence and persistence.

Why Get Certified?

Why go to the pain and trouble of taking this exam? Certainly, there are many more imaginably pleasant ways of spending your precious hours than on preparing for a Sun Certification Exam.

First of all, I would point out that the SCWCD is valuable because it is challenging. The effort required to get this qualification is directly proportional to the esteem in which the exam is held. Anything worth getting requires an effort—and Sun Certifications are all worth getting. The SCWCD is no exception.

Second, employers like this additional qualification. The SCWCD distinguishes you from the (admittedly glorious) crowd of developers who just have SCJP status to their name. I can't point you to statistics that say that someone with an SCWCD certification gets paid better, but it is still likely to be true—just because it demonstrates a true comprehension of a J2EE topic area. No employer is likely to look at this qualification in isolation; your web development experience and other sterling personal qualities must come into play also. However, it is tangible proof of commitment and knowledge.

A third and less tangible benefit: The fact is you really do get to know Java web development much better by going through the certification process. Light is shed on all those gray, unclear, and half-understood areas through countless exposure to certification topics and questions. I can guarantee you will encounter not one, but several examples of ways to do things which represent an improvement over your current practice. These may come in the form of APIs that you were previously unaware of, whole technologies (like EL and JSTL) that didn't seem necessary to you before, or design patterns that shed light on your thinking about the architecture of your web applications. In truth, this is my overriding reason for being enthusiastic about this exam and the entire Sun Certification program. I have found that the more concrete benefits spin out of this one.

You may find some web postings and blogs that suggest that the SCWCD is superseded or irrelevant and that you are better off devoting time to learning technology that lives at a layer "above" the topics tested by the SCWCD. This could mean Struts or (now more fashionably) Java Server Faces. My counter to this is that all these layers require a proper understanding of the lower levels. The latest incarnation of the SCWCD also includes now more than ever topic areas that are complementary to these higher layers: For example, you have to understand the exam topic on JSTL (JavaServer Pages Standard Tag Libraries) as a prerequisite to learning about Java Server Faces. And while fashions change as to the best Java presentation techniques, core J2EE knowledge persists in value. Sure, some of the APIs you learn may go the same way as your SCJP bitwise operator knowledge—but the understanding you gain by using them will remain.

Preparing for the Exam

Practice Questions

Ultimately, the certification requires you to sit down and answer lots of questions. Perhaps it's not so surprising, then, that doing lots of practice questions is a very good way of preparing for the exam.

There is something about the heightened emotional trauma of working through a question and agonizing over the correct answer which serves you well in the process of learning and memorizing. The trick is to keep up the emotional heat when you are reviewing the answers to questions. Don't stop at just marking your work—really commit to understanding why the right answers are right, and the wrong ones wrong.

This book furnishes plenty of review questions at the end of each chapter to practice this art. I have placed a great deal of emphasis on explaining the answers. I recommend having both questions and answers visible when you review the end-of-chapter answers in this book. Much as I'd love you to buy two copies of the book, a more economic approach might be to have the electronic book showing the questions on screen and the paper book with the answers by your side. A lot of the questions (as for the real exam) are code based. Have your coding environment handy so you can copy and paste this code and test it for yourself.

Programming

Java APIs (and their accompanying documentation) are dry and unmemorable when you consider them flatly on the page, as an abstract academic exercise. The only way to bring them to life is to try them out. You *must* program as much as you can; otherwise, the act of memorizing all the SCWCD topics will become overwhelming and meaningless.

To this end, there are structured exercises at the end of each section in the book (typically, there are four sections in each chapter). Nearly all of these lead you to building small but fully functional web applications. Instructions are given in a step-by-step way, but you are not completely spoon fed. The expectation is that you use the material and examples from the accompanying section of the book to supply the right syntax.

If you are foxed by some problems, all the exercises come with solution code (and source). However, it is good to strive and struggle with issues a bit—because when the penny drops and you solve a problem, you have made another emotional connection with some vital piece of SCWCD knowledge and are all the more likely to remember it when it matters to you in the exam.

So these exercises are not optional! Do not be afraid to experiment. Set out to break things on purpose, even if this is not in your nature! Many of the questions in the exam contain deliberately broken code and ask you to predict the outcome. So change return codes to unexpected values, override methods when you shouldn't, and stay curious—set up situations to find out what will happen in different circumstances.

Of course, it goes without saying that if you are doing web development *in addition to* the work in this book, so much the better. The more code you write, the better you get—both in exam preparation terms and in real usefulness as a developer. Don't regard your day-job web development, though, as a *substitute* for exercising all the coding techniques you need for SCWCD exam topics (the exercises give you this coverage).

Memory

Like the SCJP, success in the SCWCD depends to a large extent on memory. You might feel put out by this. Do you need to remember APIs and valid element values to be a successful web developer? Is it ever worthwhile being able to remember things that an IDE can prompt you for? Whatever your feelings on these issues, you can't escape the philosophy of the SCWCD exam which rates memory highly. Relatively few of the questions in this version of the exam are straight memory questions—but practically every question relies on detailed recall of something—be it an API exception, life cycle detail, or XML syntax value.

If it makes you feel any better, I defend the emphasis on memory in this way. You are forced to know the content really well. By internalizing a lot of the detail, you are free to be more creative with the tools at your disposal. It is likely that some of the specifics will fade after you have taken the exam (and you will again be grateful for the code completion features in your IDE), but you will find that you are much better (and quicker) at pinpointing the right web component technology to use to solve a given application problem.

So, more practically: Since you can't avoid the issue of memory, what do you do to help yourself remember things for the exam? The very idea of memorizing things has become almost unfashionable (just compare the amount of poetry your grandparents had to learn by heart at school with your own educational experience). So much so that the prospect of having to remember anything instills fear more than delight.

The good news is that there are plenty of materials and advice at hand for improving your memory—and your attitude to memorizing. The web application you build in the lab at the end of Chapter 4 is a memory game (the application is supplied in the solution code on the CD should you want to use this before building it yourself). You input a list of ten words and then get an opportunity to recollect them—after which you are scored on how well you remembered (marks are given for correct words and correct sequence). You may like to try this with SCWCD exam specifics. You may also like to try the game again after reading some good resources for list memorization: Start with http://www.mindtools.com/memory.html.

Tony Buzan's book *Use Your Head* is a great resource on memory and learning. Furthermore, it introduces the concept of arranging information in the form of a "mind map"—useful for all kinds of applications, including learning, memorization, and revision. The principle of mind maps involves selecting key words and arranging them in a connected hierarchy. I used many mind maps in the design and writing of this book—you can see a fragment of a mind map for Chapter 10 in Figure 2. Most were hand produced, but the mind map presented here was built using a free open source Java tool called FreeMind—a great resource (see http://freemind.sourceforge.net/wiki/index.php/Main_Page).

Memory becomes more effortless the more you do—so again I encourage you: Write code! As you gain in confidence, try writing some code with any of your IDE code completion features switched off. If you're using a straight text editor anyway, so much the better. This is a great test of API knowledge.

FIGURE 2 Part of the Mind Map for Chapter 10

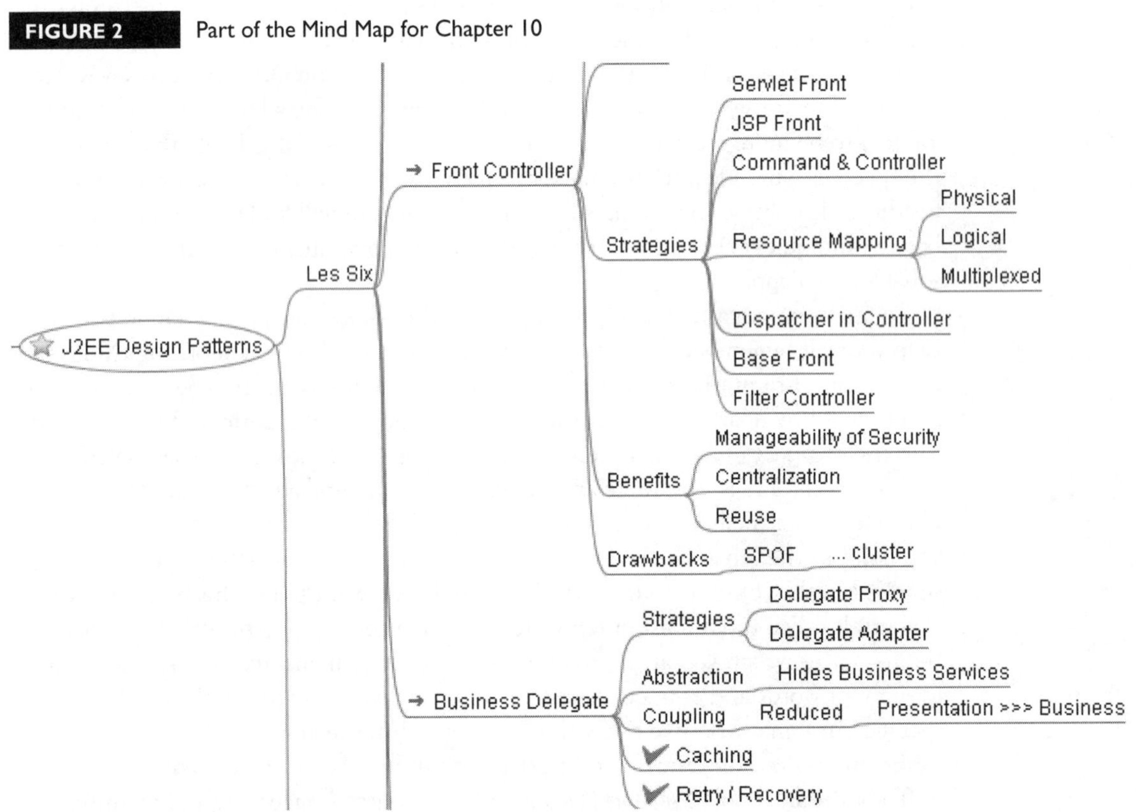

Other Resources

This book aims to be as complete a resource as it can be when it comes to studying for the exam. However, even a book of this magnitude cannot cover everything. There are some other good resources out there which are worth knowing about, especially if you feel compelled to cover every angle from all sides.

A search of the Internet will quickly reveal free sources of test exam questions for the SCWCD. However, many of these are still tied to the old version of the exam. That doesn't make them useless—but you do have to be aware that these sources won't cover many of the new topics in the exam, and occasionally may be based on some aspect of the specification that has changed. If you are prepared to spend money for a commercial resource, the WhizLabs Exam Simulator for SCWCD is useful—and specifically targeted at the latest exam.

The web site http://www.javaranch.com is a great certification resource. Apart from static resources (revision notes, test questions—but again beware those are based on the old specification), there is a forum dedicated to the SCWCD exam. Ask a question there, and you will usually get an expert answer within a few hours (at the most, a day). It's like taking part in a worldwide study group for the exam, and the people in it are very supportive.

Keep the J2EE API documentation for relevant packages (javax.servlet, java .servlet.http, etc.—you'll meet them all in the coming pages) available at all times. No doubt you found the API documentation for J2SE invaluable for the SCJP exam; the same is no less true for the SCWCD. Make sure to download the J2EE 1.4 documentation from the web site. Consider also getting hold of the following specification documents (all available in downloadable PDF format):

- The Servlet 2.4 specification (available from http://jcp.org/aboutJava/communityprocess/final/jsr154/index.html)
- The JSP 2.0 specification (available from http://jcp.org/aboutJava/communityprocess/final/jsr152)
- The JSTL 1.1 specification (available from http://jcp.org/aboutJava/communityprocess/final/jsr052/index2.html; you need to make sure you pick up the maintenance release documentation that relates to version 1.1—not version 1.0)

Specification documents are rarely the most readable in the world—but while these three documents aren't quite in the Dan Brown page-turning category, they are surprisingly lucid. The JSTL specification, in particular, is more like a developer's manual than a set of esoteric definitions. If you want the ultimate authority on any aspect of the certification objectives, these documents deliver it.

You do have to bear in mind that both the API documentation and the specification documents are not written exclusively for web component developers. They are as much (or more) aimed at system programmers who write the middleware: the application servers that actually *run* the servlets and JavaServer Pages you develop. You'll be working with an application server called Tomcat in the course of this book, which is regarded as the reference implementation software for these J2EE web specifications. So you may find some comments that you think might apply to you as a page author, but on closer inspection are more appropriate for a developer of a tool like Tomcat. Take the following scary comment from the API documentation for the class javax.servlet.jsp.tagext.JspFragment:

```
Implementation Note: It is not necessary to generate a separate
class for each fragment. One possible implementation is to
generate a single helper class for each page that implements
JspFragment. Upon construction, a discriminator can be passed
to select which fragment that instance will execute.
```

Actually, the preceding paragraph in the documentation gives you a way out:

```
Note that tag library developers and page authors should not
generate JspFragment implementations manually.
```

In other words, it's the hapless Tomcat developer who has to pay close attention to this part of the documentation.

So my recommendation is to keep the API documentation and the specifications handy, and use them for back-up reference when you feel the need. Just be careful not to get hung up on parts that aren't relevant to your SCWCD study—let this book be your route map!

Taking the Exam

As you've already taken the SCJP, you won't find much new here with regard to scheduling and taking the test. Any good advice you've received in the past about good approaches to the SCJP will serve you just as well in the SCWCD.

One difference you might encounter: If you are coming from an older version of the SCJP (or SCWCD for that matter), there is a slight change to the exam format because of the inclusion of "drag and drop" questions. There is more explanation of these in the section on questions below.

Logisitics

To take the exam, you must first purchase a voucher from Sun. This voucher is valid for one year and currently costs $150. This entitles you to schedule the date, time, and place of your exam. Exams are administered by Thomson Prometric (formerly Sylvan Prometric), which is responsible for the administration of certification tests for many companies as well as Sun (for example, Novell and Microsoft). The company offers an online booking service at http://www.2test.com. Alternatively, this web site has contact numbers for different regions, and you can book by phone.

Thomson Prometric's testing centers are widely distributed worldwide and are often found in the offices of computer training companies. You should be able to find one very local to you. You must schedule your exam to take place before the expiration date on your voucher. You don't normally have to book months ahead; most testing centers can accommodate you within a week of making your request. So don't schedule until you are ready.

On the day of the test, you need to take two forms of identification with you, one containing a photograph. From your SCJP exam, you will have a Prometric User ID—make sure you have this handy as well as your Sun voucher details, as it will expedite administration at the testing center. It's a good idea to turn up early to the testing center, to reduce your stress. You can spend the time before the exam glancing through notes. More often than not, test centers are happy to let you start early, if that's your wish. Arriving late is not a good option, even leaving aside the feverish anxiety you will feel as you travel. The test center is likely to try to accommodate you, but there are no guarantees—in the worst cases, you might be short of time or even forfeit your slot altogether.

You can't take anything with you into the exam—bags, mobile phones, pagers, reference notes, this book or any other. A water bottle is allowed (most test centers will provide drinks). You will be provided with paper and pencil (or wipe-clean scratchpad) for use during the exam. You can't take anything away with you either; any notes you make during the exam must be left behind.

The exam administrator will make sure you are settled in the exam room, which typically contains some computers and chairs and not much else. There are likely to be other candidates, quite probably midway through their own exams—clearly, you mustn't talk to them or otherwise distract them. The exam administrator logs you on to your exam and verifies your ID and that you have the screen for the SCWCD exam and no other. Then you are on your own. You have the option of taking a tutorial to remind you how the exam-taking software works. You are probably familiar with the software from the SCJP anyway and eager to get on with the test, which is fine. My strategy is to do the tutorial anyway, to re-familiarize myself with the nuances of the software as well as calming myself. There is no time pressure at this point; the time only begins when you decide to proceed.

Once you do go ahead, you are presented with a short questionnaire about your abilities and current skills. The clock is ticking at this point, so don't agonize over the answers! Then you get to the questions. Similar to the SCJP, each question occupies one page, and you can navigate forward and backward through the questions. Some questions have an "Exhibit" button that shows supplementary information (usually a code listing) as a pop-up window. Most important, you are able to check off a box to "mark" questions where you are unsure of the answer. You can easily identify and return to the "marked" questions at a later stage. The software also keeps track of unanswered questions.

Once you have answered all the questions (or—more unfortunately, but less likely—you have run out of time), the software presents a screen that indicates your score and whether you have passed or failed. You can look at a percentage breakdown by objective if you wish, but this is printed on a report that the exam administrator will give you. At this point, you will probably be very grateful to get out of the exam room by the shortest route!

Question Format

The SCWCD exam questions used to be multiple choice without stating the number of correct answers (particularly mean questions might have had no correct answers—it takes a lot of courage not to check off any boxes!). Now, in keeping with other Sun Certification exams, SCWCD questions do stipulate the number of correct answers.

The questions come in three forms:

- Multiple choice with a single answer (indicated in the testing software by a radio button for the choices)
- Multiple choice with several answers (indicated by check boxes—the question text tells you the number of boxes to check off)
- Drag and drop

This last category (drag and drop) may be unfamiliar to you if it's been a while since you did the SCJP. You can expect roughly 10% of the questions to be in this form. You are presented with some example or other (often a piece of Java code, or an

XML file, or a JavaServer Page source) with missing segments. You have a list of text items that you can click on and drag to the appropriate gap in the example. The software skillfully arranges the example so you can't infer anything from the length of the gaps (to decide whether you should choose a short or long word).

You'll get plenty of practice with this type of question in the course of the self test questions and the accompanying exams. Obviously, the self test questions printed in the book can't quite simulate drag-and-drop software, but you'll find they are close enough in spirit to give you the right idea.

A couple of tips on questions. The examiners consider it perfectly acceptable to choose words—such as the names of variables or attributes—that run counter to the purpose of the code. Here's an example:

```
<jsp:forward page="included.jsp" />
```

At a quick glance, you jump to the conclusion that the page source here is including another page—because the value for the page attribute is included.jsp. But beware: The action requested here is forwarding (with <jsp:forward>), not including. (Even though these concepts are may be unfamiliar at this stage of your study, you can likely appreciate this type of question-setting snare from this description.)

You may also encounter near-identical questions, often in close proximity on the exam. You may even think that the same question has been asked again by mistake. Be assured, though, that the exam presentation software never makes a mistake of that kind (not in my experience, or that of thousands of others who recollect their experiences in certification forums). There will be a difference between the questions. Often, you can turn this technique to your advantage: Usually a quick comparison of the two questions reveals vital clues that yield answers to both.

You may be unsure of an answer and decide to mark the question for later review. If you have already eliminated some choices, it is worth making a quick note (on paper or your scratchpad) of the options remaining to you (for example—22: A or C). That way, when you return to the question at a later stage, you will have saved yourself time having to completely think yourself back into the question only to eliminate the same wrong choices you identified in the first place. (I'm indebted to Kathy Sierra and Bert Bates for this tip, from their companion volume in this certification series, *Sun Certified Programmer & Developer for Java 2*.)

Sometimes you may think that no answers fit the question properly. This could be your misunderstanding, and if you have the time available, consider revisiting the question later. However, there are a few occasions when a question isn't expressed as precisely or unambiguously as you might like. Under those circumstances, select the most reasonable answer or most probable answer, and realize that we live in a less than perfect world.

A final clichéd word of advice: *Read the question*. It doesn't matter how often this mantra is repeated—candidates often don't read questions properly, whether in Sun Certification exams or other walks of life. If you are asked to identify which of a series of statements are *false*, don't check all the *true* statements. Your reasoning may be perfect—but there's still no prize for a wrong answer.

Exam Techniques and Strategies

The exam takes a traditional form with a set number of questions. It is not "adaptive," as some certification exams are (though not Sun Java certification exams). Adaptive exams tend to be much shorter and adjust the next question based on a correct or incorrect answer to the current question. While "shorter" may be very appealing, the traditional format does give you—the candidate—much more control over your test-taking strategy. This is because you can return to previous questions as well as going forward. There are incidental benefits to this. Because questions are drawn from a random pool, you may well find that some questions provide information that helps you answer previous questions. Exploiting this facet of the exam is not in any sense cheating—it shows how smart you are!

A strategy is very valuable. Decide how you are going to budget your 135 minutes. With 69 questions, you have a little less than two minutes to spend per question. You're likely to find that some questions take less time to answer, and some questions take more. Just don't forget that all questions carry equal weight—so it really isn't worth spending 15 minutes on one question.

You should aim for more than one pass through the test. How many passes is up to the individual: somewhere between two and four is the norm. Here are a couple of variant approaches:

Approach I

First pass: Work through all the questions of the test, reading them rapidly. Answer any questions that are easy and don't require much working out. Spend no more than 25 minutes on this pass. Second pass: Work through all the questions you didn't answer on the first pass, making your best judgment. Mark any questions where you are unsure of the answers. Spend the majority of your time on this pass, but try to leave at least 20 minutes for the third and last pass. Third pass: Return to the marked questions—see if the answer is now clearer (possibly as a result of working out answers to other questions). If there is any time left over, use it to quickly review the answers to as many questions as you can.

Approach 2

First pass: Work through all the questions on the test, answering all of them and marking any where you are unsure of the answer. Be strict on progressing through the questions, as you will want 40 minutes or so remaining for the second pass.
Second pass: Work through all the questions again, starting with the marked ones. Only change answers where you are quite sure you missed the point on the first round—but be alert for clues you missed.

Many test takers favor Approach 1. I prefer Approach 2. There are no absolute rules: Different strategies suit different individuals. The only really important rules are that you should have a strategy and stick to it. Above all, don't get bogged down—keep moving forward through the questions at the rate you need to (which might typically be 10 questions every 15 minutes for your "main" pass through the exam).

A Note on Objectives

I would have liked to write a book that followed each exam objective in order, but decided this wasn't the best approach. The exam objective sequence is not always the ideal way to present the material—especially if you are relatively new to it. Largely, the chapters do follow the major objective headings, and every single objective for the full and upgrade exams is covered. The following Exam Readiness Checklist shows you in detail the part of the book relevant to a particular objective. I would also suggest that you don't get too hung up on exam objectives in isolation; take a holistic approach. The exam throws questions at you in any order and has many questions that demand knowledge cutting across objectives.

Exam Readiness Checklist

Exam 310-081 (The Full Exam)

Official Objective	Certification Objective	Ch #	Pg #	Beginner	Intermediate	Expert
Section 1: The Servlet Technology Model						
For each of the HTTP methods (such as GET, POST, HEAD) describe the purpose of the method and the technical characteristics of the HTTP method protocol, list triggers that might cause a Client (usually a web browser) to use the method, and identify the HttpServlet method that corresponds to the HTTP method.	HTTP Methods	1	2			
Using the HttpServletRequest interface, write code to retrieve HTML form parameters from the request, retrieve HTTP request header information, or retrieve cookies from the request.	Form Parameters, Requests	1	18, 36			
Using the HttpServletResponse interface, write code to set an HTTP response header, set the content type of the response, acquire a text stream for the response, acquire a binary stream for the response, redirect an HTTP request to another URL, or add cookies to the response.	Responses	1	46			
Describe the purpose and event sequence of the servlet life cycle: (1) servlet class loading, (2) servlet instantiation, (3) call the init method, (4) call the service method, and (5) call the destroy method.	Servlet Life Cycle	1	55			
Section 2: The Structure and Deployment of Web Applications						
Construct the file and directory structure of a web application that may contain (a) static content, (b) JSP pages, (c) servlet classes, (d) the deployment descriptor, (e) tag libraries, (f) JAR files, and (g) Java class files and describe how to protect resource files from HTTP access.	File and Directory Structure	2	96			
Describe the purpose and semantics of the deployment descriptor.	Deployment Descriptor Elements	2	101			
Construct the correct structure of the deployment descriptor.	Deployment Descriptor Elements	2	101			
Explain the purpose of a WAR file and describe the contents of a WAR file, how one may be constructed.	WAR Files	2	123			

Exam Readiness Checklist
Exam 310-081 (The Full Exam)

Official Objective	Certification Objective	Ch #	Pg #	Beginner	Intermediate	Expert
Section 3: The Web Container Model						
For the ServletContext initialization parameters, write servlet code to access initialization parameters, and create the deployment descriptor elements for declaring initialization parameters.	ServletContext	3	150			
For the fundamental servlet attribute scopes (request, session, and context), write servlet code to add, retrieve, and remove attributes; given a usage scenario, identify the proper scope for an attribute; and identify multithreading issues associated with each scope.	Attributes, Scope, and Multithreading	3	157			
Describe the web container request processing model; write and configure a filter; create a request or response wrapper; and given a design problem, describe how to apply a filter or a wrapper.	Filters	3	189			
Describe the web container life cycle event model for requests, sessions, and web applications; create and configure listener classes for each scope life cycle; create and configure scope attribute listener classes; and given a scenario, identify the proper attribute listener to use.	Request and Context Listeners	4	256			
Describe the RequestDispatcher mechanism; write servlet code to create a request dispatcher; write servlet code to forward or include the target resource; and identify and describe the additional request-scoped attributes provided by the container to the target resource.	Dispatching	3	175			
Section 4: Session Management						
Write servlet code to store objects into a session object and retrieve objects from a session object.	Attributes, Scope, and Multithreading	3	157			
Given a scenario, describe the APIs used to access the session object, explain when the session object was created, and describe the mechanisms used to destroy the session object and when it was destroyed.	Session Life Cycle	4	238			
Using session listeners, write code to respond to an event when an object is added to a session and write code to respond to an event when a session object migrates from one VM to another.	Session Listeners	4	264			

Exam Readiness Checklist
Exam 310-081 (The Full Exam)

Official Objective	Certification Objective	Ch #	Pg #	Beginner	Intermediate	Expert
Given a scenario, describe which session management mechanism the web container could employ, how cookies might be used to manage sessions, how URL rewriting might be used to manage sessions, and write servlet code to perform URL rewriting.	Session Management	4	250			
Section 5: Web Application Security						
Based on the servlet specification, compare and contrast the following security mechanisms: (a) authentication, (b) authorization, (c) data integrity, and (d) confidentiality.	Security Mechanisms	5	306			
In the deployment descriptor, declare a security constraint, a web resource, the transport guarantee, the login configuration, and a security role.	Deployment Descriptor Security Declarations	5	312			
Compare and contrast the authentication types (BASIC, DIGEST, FORM, and CLIENT-CERT); describe how each type works; and given a scenario, select an appropriate type.	Authentication Types	5	327			
Section 6: The JavaServer Pages (JSP) Technology Model						
Identify, describe, or write the JSP code for the following elements: (a) template text, (b) scripting elements (comments, directives, declarations, scriptlets, and expressions), (c) standard and custom actions, and (d) expression language elements.	JSP Elements	6	376			
Write JSP code that uses the following directives: (a) "page" (with attributes "import," "session," "contentType," and "isELIgnored"), (b) "include," and (c) "taglib."	JSP Directives	6	389			
Write a JSP document (XML-based document) that uses the correct syntax.	JSPs in XML	7	473			
Describe the purpose and event sequence of the JSP page life cycle: (1) JSP page translation, (2) JSP page compilation, (3) load class, (4) create instance, (5) call the jspInit method, (6) call the _jspService method, and (7) call the jspDestroy method.	JSP Life Cycle	6	362			

Exam Readiness Checklist

Exam 310-081 (The Full Exam)

Official Objective	Certification Objective	Ch #	Pg #	Beginner	Intermediate	Expert
Given a design goal, write JSP code using the appropriate implicit objects: (a) request, (b) response, (c) out, (d) session, (e) config, (f) application, (g) page, (h) pageContext, and (i) exception.	JSP Implicit Objects	6	400			
Configure the deployment descriptor to declare one or more tag libraries, deactivate the evaluation language, and deactivate the scripting language.	Tag Libraries	8	534			
Given a specific design goal for including a JSP segment in another page, write the JSP code that uses the most appropriate inclusion mechanism (the include directive or the jsp:include standard action).	JSP Dispatching Mechanisms	7	462			
Section 7: Building JSP Pages Using the Expression Language (EL)						
Given a scenario, write EL code that accesses the following implicit variables: pageScope, requestScope, sessionScope, and applicationScope; param and paramValues; header and headerValues; cookie; initParam; and pageContext.	Expression Language	7	488			
Given a scenario, write EL code that uses the following operators: property access (the . operator) and collection access (the [] operator).	Expression Language	7	488			
Given a scenario, write EL code that uses the following operators: arithmetic operators, relational operators, and logical operators.	Expression Language	7	488			
Given a scenario, write EL code that uses a function, write code for an EL function, and configure the EL function in a tag library descriptor.	EL Functions	8	572			
Section 8: Building JSP Pages Using Standard Actions						
Given a design goal, create a code snippet using the following standard actions: jsp:useBean (with attributes "id," "scope," "type," and "class"), jsp: getProperty, and jsp:setProperty (with all attribute combinations).	JSP Standard Actions	7	444			

Exam Readiness Checklist

Exam 310-081 (The Full Exam)

Official Objective	Certification Objective	Ch #	Pg #	Beginner	Intermediate	Expert
Given a design goal, create a code snippet using the following standard actions: jsp:include, jsp:forward, and jsp:param.	JSP Dispatching Mechanisms	7	462			
Section 9: Building JSP Pages Using Tag Libraries						
For a custom tag library or a library of Tag Files, create the "taglib" directive for a JSP page.	Tag Libraries	8	534			
Given a design goal, create the custom tag structure in a JSP page to support that goal.	Tag Libraries	8	534			
Given a design goal, use an appropriate JSP Standard Tag Library (JSTL v1.1) tag from the "core" tag library.	JSTL	8	547			
Section 10: Building a Custom Tag Library						
Describe the semantics of the "Classic" custom tag event model when each event method (doStartTag, doAfterBody, and doEndTag) is executed, explain what the return value for each event method means, and write a tag handler class.	The Custom Tag Model	8	579			
Using the PageContext API, write tag handler code to access the JSP implicit variables and access web application attributes.	Tags and Implicit Variables	9	644			
Given a scenario, write tag handler code to access the parent tag and an arbitrary tag ancestor.	Tag Hierarchies	9	673			
Describe the semantics of the "Simple" custom tag event model when the event method (doTag) is executed, write a tag handler class, and explain the constraints on the JSP content within the tag.	The Simple Custom Tag Event Model	9	651			
Describe the semantics of the Tag File model, describe the web application structure for tag files, write a tag file, and explain the constraints on the JSP content in the body of the tag.	The Tag File Model	9	664			

Exam Readiness Checklist

Exam 310-081 (The Full Exam)

Official Objective	Certification Objective	Ch #	Pg #	Beginner	Intermediate	Expert
Section 11: J2EE Patterns						
Given a scenario description with a list of issues, select a pattern that would solve the issues. The patterns you must know are Intercepting Filter, Model-View-Controller, Front Controller, Service Locator, Business Delegate, and Transfer Object.	J2EE Patterns	10	719			
Match design patterns with statements describing potential benefits that accrue from the use of the pattern, for any of the following patterns: Intercepting Filter, Model-View-Controller, Front Controller, Service Locator, Business Delegate, and Transfer Object.	J2EE Patterns	10	719			

Exam Readiness Checklist

Exam 310-082 (The Upgrade Exam)

Official Objective	Certification Objective	Ch #	Pg #	Beginner	Intermediate	Expert
Section 1: The Servlet Technology Model						
Using the HttpServletResponse interface, write code to set an HTTP response header, set the content type of the response, acquire a text stream for the response, acquire a binary stream for the response, redirect an HTTP request to another URL, or add cookies to the response.	Responses	1	46			
Describe the purpose and event sequence of the servlet life cycle: (1) servlet class loading, (2) servlet instantiation, (3) call the init method, (4) call the service method, and (5) call the destroy method.	Servlet Life Cycle	1	55			
Section 2: The Structure and Deployment of Web Applications						
Construct the correct structure of the deployment descriptor.	Deployment Descriptor Elements	2	101			

Exam Readiness Checklist

Exam 310-082 (The Upgrade Exam)

Official Objective	Certification Objective	Ch #	Pg #	Beginner	Intermediate	Expert
Section 3: The Web Container Model						
Describe the web container request processing model; write and configure a filter; create a request or response wrapper; and given a design problem, describe how to apply a filter or a wrapper.	Filters	3	189			
Describe the web container life cycle event model for requests, sessions, and web applications; create and configure listener classes for each scope life cycle; create and configure scope attribute listener classes; and given a scenario, identify the proper attribute listener to use.	Request and Context Listeners	4	256			
Section 4: Session Management						
Using session listeners, write code to respond to an event when an object is added to a session and write code to respond to an event when a session object migrates from one VM to another.	Session Listeners	4	264			
Given a scenario, describe which session management mechanism the web container could employ, how cookies might be used to manage sessions, how URL rewriting might be used to manage sessions, and write servlet code to perform URL rewriting.	Session Management	4	250			
Section 5: Web Application Security						
In the deployment descriptor, declare a security constraint, a Web resource, the transport guarantee, the login configuration, and a security role.	Deployment Descriptor Security Declarations	5	312			
Section 6: The JavaServer Pages (JSP) Technology Model						
Write JSP code that uses the following directives: (a) "page" (with attributes "import," "session," "contentType," and "isELIgnored"), (b) "include," and (c) "taglib."	JSP Directives	6	389			
Write a JSP document (XML-based document) that uses the correct syntax.	JSPs in XML	7	473			

Exam Readiness Checklist
Exam 310-082 (The Upgrade Exam)

Official Objective	Certification Objective	Ch #	Pg #	Beginner	Intermediate	Expert
Configure the deployment descriptor to declare one or more tag libraries, deactivate the evaluation language, and deactivate the scripting language.	Tag Libraries	8	534			
Section 7: Building JSP Pages Using the Expression Language (EL)						
Given a scenario, write EL code that accesses the following implicit variables: pageScope, requestScope, sessionScope, and applicationScope; param and paramValues; header and headerValues; cookie; initParam; and pageContext.	Expression Language	7	488			
Given a scenario, write EL code that uses the following operators: property access (the . operator) and collection access (the [] operator).	Expression Language	7	488			
Given a scenario, write EL code that uses the following operators: arithmetic operators, relational operators, and logical operators.	Expression Language	7	488			
Given a scenario, write EL code that uses a function, write code for an EL function, and configure the EL function in a tag library descriptor.	EL Functions	8	572			
Section 8: Building JSP Pages Using Standard Actions						
Given a design goal, create a code snippet using the following standard actions: jsp:include, jsp:forward, and jsp:param.	JSP Dispatching Mechanisms	7	462			
Section 9: Building JSP Pages Using Tag Libraries						
Given a design goal, use an appropriate JSP Standard Tag Library (JSTL v1.1) tag from the "core" tag library.	JSTL	8	547			
Section 10: Building a Custom Tag Library						
Given a scenario, write tag handler code to access the parent tag and an arbitrary tag ancestor.	Tag Hierarchies	9	673			

Exam Readiness Checklist

Exam 310-082 (The Upgrade Exam)

Official Objective	Certification Objective	Ch #	Pg #	Beginner	Intermediate	Expert
Describe the semantics of the "Simple" custom tag event model when the event method (doTag) is executed, write a tag handler class, and explain the constraints on the JSP content within the tag.	The Simple Custom Tag Event Model	9	651			
Section 11: J2EE Patterns						
Given a scenario description with a list of issues, select a pattern that would solve the issues. The patterns you must know are Intercepting Filter, Model-View-Controller, Front Controller, Service Locator, Business Delegate, and Transfer Object.	J2EE Patterns	10	719			
Match design patterns with statements describing potential benefits that accrue from the use of the pattern, for any of the following patterns: Intercepting Filter, Model-View-Controller, Front Controller, Service Locator, Business Delegate, and Transfer Object.	J2EE Patterns	10	719			

1

The Servlet Model

CERTIFICATION OBJECTIVES

- HTTP Methods
- Form Parameters
- Requests
- Responses
- Servlet Life Cycle
- ✓ Two-Minute Drill
- Q&A Self Test

We go to the first topics in the Sun Certification for Web Component Developers. This chapter begins outside the formal world of Java and J2EE, for you're going to need to know something about the primary "inputs" to a web application: HTTP methods. And because the information carried from HTTP methods is mostly carried from web pages, the exam requires you to know a little about HTML syntax, which we'll cover here. Then we'll begin to open up the core exam topics of HTTP requests and responses: how these are decomposed and composed inside a J2EE web application.

CERTIFICATION OBJECTIVE

HTTP Methods (Exam Objective 1.1)

For each of the HTTP Methods (such as GET, POST, HEAD), describe the purpose of the method and the technical characteristics of the HTTP Method protocol, list triggers that might cause a Client (usually a Web browser) to use the method and identify the HttpServlet method that corresponds to the HTTP Method.

Because you are studying for Sun's Web Component exam, it will come as no surprise to you that you need to know something about the main protocol underlying web communication: HTTP. No huge expertise is required. You don't have to be any kind of networking expert or even know what TCP/IP stands for. However, you will need some grasp of the "big seven" HTTP methods—and, in particular, how these relate to J2EE and to the Web. The designers of the exam succeed in targeting just those areas that are also essential for becoming effective in your real-life web application developments.

HTTP

HTTP is a simple request/response protocol. A client—often (but not exclusively) a web browser—sends a request, which consists of an HTTP method and supplementary data. The HTTP server sends back a response—a status code indicating what happened with the request, and (typically) data targeted by the request. Once the request and response have happened, the conversation is over; the client and server don't remain connected. When you use a web browser to fill up your shopping cart, what's mostly happening is a series of lapses in a protracted conversation. This situation makes life much more efficient for the server (it doesn't have to keep its attention focused on you for much of the time); how it manages not to forget your identity is a subject covered in Chapter 4.

An HTTP Request and Response

Let's take a look at an HTTP request at work. There are strict rules about how the request is made up, defined by the World Wide Web consortium in a "Request for Comments" (RFC) document. Actually, the time for commenting on this version of the HTTP standard is long past, so you can regard RFC 2616 (defining HTTP/1.1) as an absolute yardstick.

A request consists of a request line, some request headers, and an (optional) message body. The request line contains three things:

- The HTTP method
- A pointer to the resource requested, in the form of a "URI"
- The version of the HTTP protocol employed in the request

Therefore, a typical request line might look like this:

```
GET http://www.osborne.com/index.html HTTP/1.1
```

A carriage return/line feed concludes the request line. After this come request headers in the form—name: value (the name of the request header, followed by a colon and space, followed by the value). Here are some examples:

```
Accept: image/*, application/vnd.ms-excel, */*
Accept-Language: en-gb
Accept-Encoding: gzip, deflate
User-Agent: Mozilla/4.0 (compatible; MSIE 6.0; Windows NT 5.1)
Host: www.osborne.com
Connection: Keep-Alive
```

We'll explore the meaning of one or two of these headers a bit later. A blank line must follow the last request header and, after that, the request body—if there is one (there doesn't have to be). The request body can contain pretty much anything, from a set of parameters and values attaching to an HTML form, to an entire image file you intend to upload to the target URL.

You won't be tested on the valid construction of HTTP messages, though you might find questions that expect you to know the effect of setting certain request headers. We'll meet these in the "Requests" section of this chapter.

Having sent the request, you can expect a response. The construction of the response is very similar to that of the request. Here's an example:

```
HTTP/1.0 200 OK
Connection: Close
Date: Fri, 02 May 2003 15:30:30 GMT
Set-Cookie: PREF=ID=1b4a0990016089fe:LD=en:TM=1051889430:
LM=1051889430:
S=JbQnlaabQb0I0KxZ; expires=Sun, 17-Jan-2038 19:14:07 GMT;
path=/; domain=.google.co.uk
Cache-control: private
Content-Type: text/html
Server: GWS/2.0
[BLANK LINE]
"<html><head><meta HTTP-EQUIV="content-type" CONTENT="text/html;
 charset=UTF-8"><title>Google Search: MIME </title>
 etc. etc. rest of web page
```

The response line also has three parts. First is the HTTP version actually used, reflected back to the client. Next is a response code (200 denotes success; you'll already know 404, page not found). After that is a brief description of the response code. A carriage return/line feed denotes the end of the response line.

Response header lines follow, similar in format to request headers, although the actual headers themselves are likely to be a bit different. We'll explore some of these later in the chapter. Finally, separated from the headers by a blank line, is the response body. In the example, you can see the beginning of a web page being returned. Figure 1-1 shows the request/response interchange graphically.

The "Big Seven" HTTP Methods

The most fundamental request method is GET, which simply means "I want this resource from this server, so kindly return it to my browser." Whenever you type an address line in your browser and press GO, or click an underlined link on a web page, it's a GET method that is generated in the request behind the covers. However,

FIGURE 1-1

A Request/ Response Interchange

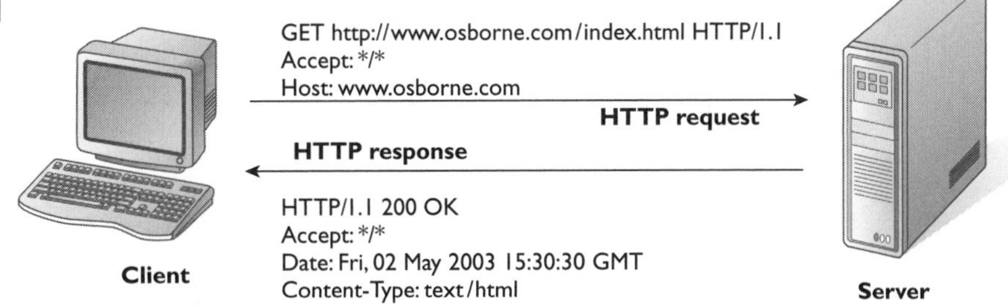
GET http://www.osborne.com/index.html HTTP/1.1
Accept: */*
Host: www.osborne.com
HTTP request
HTTP response
HTTP/1.1 200 OK
Accept: */*
Date: Fri, 02 May 2003 15:30:30 GMT
Content-Type: text/html
<html><head><title>Welcome to Osborne Books</title> etc.
Client
Server

GET is not the only HTTP method. Six others are sanctioned by Internet Standards Bodies: POST, HEAD, OPTIONS, TRACE, PUT, and DELETE—these, together with GET, constitute the "big seven" mentioned in the heading.

There are other pretenders to the ranks of HTTP methods beyond the big seven. CONNECT is officially listed in the RFC, but it is essentially reserved for future use and won't be further discussed in this book. Other methods have some limited support outside the official sanction of the RFC, and these may have full or limited support on some servers. Yet others are defined in other RFCs—for example, RFC2518, which defines HTTP extensions for web authoring (WebDAV). On servers that support this approach, you'll find methods such as PROPFIND, LOCK, and MOVE. However—to come back to basics—methods other than the "big seven" don't impinge on the standard servlet way of doing things and so don't figure on the SCWCD exam.

Let's examine each of the big seven methods in turn.

GET We've already said quite a bit about the GET method. It's meant to be a "read-only" request for information from a server. The server might respond with a static web page, an image, or a media file—or run a servlet and build up a dynamic web page, drawing on database and other information. The three standard triggers for a GET request (in the confines of a standard browser) are

- Typing into the address line of the browser and pressing GO
- Clicking on a link in a web page
- Pressing the submit button in an HTML `<form>` whose method is set to GET

The importance of an HTML `<form>` (this subject gets full treatment in the "Form Parameters" section of the chapter) is the ability to pass parameters along with the request. With a GET requested, these parameters are appended to the URL. Let's look at a true-life example, taken from a well-known dictionary web site (http://www.dictionary.com). On the home page, I type in the word I want to look up ("idempotent") in the one-field form provided, which uses the GET method. Pressing SUBMIT generates and executes the following request on the address line of my browser:

```
http://dictionary.reference.com/search?q=idempotent
```

Everything up to and including the word "search" is the standard URL—I am wanting to run the HTTP method GET for the "search" resource found on the computer hosting the dictionary.reference.com domain. The question mark introduces the query string (in other words, the parameter list). The name of the parameter is *q*, and—separated from the name by the equal sign—is the parameter's value, "idempotent."

POST The next most usual method is POST. This is again triggered from forms in browsers, this time when the form method is itself set to POST. When compared with GET, the main difference with POST is one of intent. Usually, a POSTed form is intended to change something on the target server—add a registration, make a booking, transfer some funds—an action that is likely to result in a database update (or something of equal seriousness). Whereas GET is intended as read-only, POST is for add/update/delete operations.

This discussion leads us to an important word, the one cited in the dictionary example: "idempotent." An idempotent request is meant to have the same result no matter how many times it is executed. So a request to look up a word in a dictionary changes nothing: The request can be executed again and again with the same result. That feature makes it idempotent. However, a request to transfer funds mustn't be repeated casually, for obvious reasons. Such a request can't be classified as idempotent. Each HTTP method is classified as being idempotent or not—and you're probably ahead of me in realizing that GET is supposed to be idempotent, whereas POST most definitely is not. Of course, that's how things are meant to be, but there is no absolute guarantee that any given GET request won't have irreversible side effects. However, the outcome depends on what the server program that receives the GET request actually does with it. Equally, a POST request may not result in an update—though that's generally less serious. However, by and large, GET and POST methods obey idempotency rules, and it goes without saying that your web applications should observe them.

Although as a web surfer you won't typically be aware when you're executing a GET and when a POST, there are some practical as well as philosophical differences.

When there are parameters with a POST request, they are put into the request body, not appended on to the query string of the URL, as for GET. This situation has two benefits:

- A URL is limited in length. The official line of RFC 2616 (the HTTP 1.1 specification) is not to impose a length limit: Servers should be able to handle anything. However, the authors of the specification are realistic enough to declare some caveats, especially with regard to browsers: The specification points out that some older models are limited to 255 characters for URL length. Even at the time of writing, Microsoft's Internet Explorer browser allows only 2,083 characters for the URL—much more generous than 255, but still not limitless. By contrast, the request body is as long as you want it to be (megabytes, if necessary) and is limited in practical terms only by the bandwidth of your Internet connection.
- Putting parameters into the URL is very visible and public and is usually recorded by the "history"-keeping nature of most browsers. It's much more private (though still not wholly secure) to pass parameters in the request body.

Indeed, POST isn't just for passing simple name/value parameter pairs. You can use the POST method to upload whole text or binary files in the request body (in which case, it is acting a lot like the PUT request, which we'll examine a bit later).

HEAD The HEAD method is identical to the GET method except for one important respect: It doesn't return a message body. However, all the response headers should be present just as if a GET had been executed, and these contain a great deal of information about the resource (content length, when the resource was last modified, and the MIME type of the file, to name three of the more straightforward pieces of information available). These data are often called "meta-information." Using the HEAD method is an economical way of checking that a resource is valid and accessible, or that it hasn't been recently updated—if all you're doing is some checking on the state of the resource, why bother to bring the whole thing back to your local machine?

OPTIONS The OPTIONS method is even more minimal than HEAD. Its sole purpose, pretty much, is to tell the requester what HTTP methods can be executed against the URL requested. So, for example, if I target the following URL on the McGraw-Hill web site:

```
http://www.mcgrawhill.com/about/about.html
```

I'm told I can target the GET and HEAD options for this web page. This seems fair—there's certainly no reason to permit the execution of more dangerous methods (such as PUT or DELETE) on this URL. As an aside—the information on allowed methods is squirreled away in the values of one of the *response header* fields, whose key is Allow. This subject will be covered in the "Responses" section of this chapter.

PUT The object of the PUT method is to take a client resource (typically, a file) and put it in a location on a server as specified in the URL of the request. If there's anything already on the server in that location, then tough luck—a PUT will obliterate it, overwriting the current contents of the URL with the file it is uploading. You can determine from the response codes you get back (and more on these later) whether the resource was replaced (typically, response code 200) or created for the first time (response code 201).

I mentioned earlier that a POST can do the same work of uploading a file, and many other things besides. What is the difference between POST and PUT in this capacity? It's the fact that PUT works directly on the URL given in the request. PUT is not supposed to do anything clever, such as put the uploaded file in the request somewhere different. However, that is the prerogative of POST. The object URL of a POST method is usually a clever program (in our case, probably a Java servlet), which can do whatever it pleases with the uploaded resource, including putting it in some other location. Indeed, the program is almost certain to put uploaded files in another location, for to put the file in its own URL slot would mean overwriting itself! So, in summary, a PUT does direct file replacement (and so is rather like using FTP), but a POST can be much more subtle.

DELETE DELETE is the direct counterpart of PUT: It causes the server to delete the contents of the target URL—if not permanently, then by moving the resource there to an inaccessible location. A server has the right to delay its response to a DELETE method, as long as it responds later. A response code of 200 (OK) indicates that the deed has been done; 202 (accepted) means that the request has been accepted and will be acted on later.

TRACE Finally, the TRACE method exists because a request over HTTP is unlikely to go directly to the target host machine that actually holds the resource you require. The nature of the Internet is to pass a request from computer to computer in a long chain. Some request headers may be rewritten in transit along this chain. The purpose of TRACE is to return the request back to the requester in the state it was in at the point where it reached the last computer in the chain. As you might guess, the primary reason for doing so is to debug some problem that you attribute to request header change.

Idempotency and Safety

Let's return to the idea of idempotency, which we first came across on contrasting the scope of the GET and POST methods. We saw that GET requests should be idempotent and that POST methods are not. The other concept to introduce you to is safety. GET, TRACE, OPTIONS, and HEAD should leave nothing changed, and so are safe. Even if a GET request has irreversible side effects, a user should not be held responsible for them. Therefore, from a user perspective, the methods *are* safe. PUT, DELETE, and POST are inherently not safe: They do cause changes, and a user can be held accountable for executing these methods against the server.

What about idempotency? The safe methods are inherently idempotent because they don't (or shouldn't) change anything that would change the results when running the method again. Surprisingly, PUT is considered idempotent as well—because even if you run the same PUT request (uploading the same file to the same URL) repeatedly, the net result is always the same. The same reasoning applies to DELETE. The following illustration shows the methods grouped according to safety and idempotency.

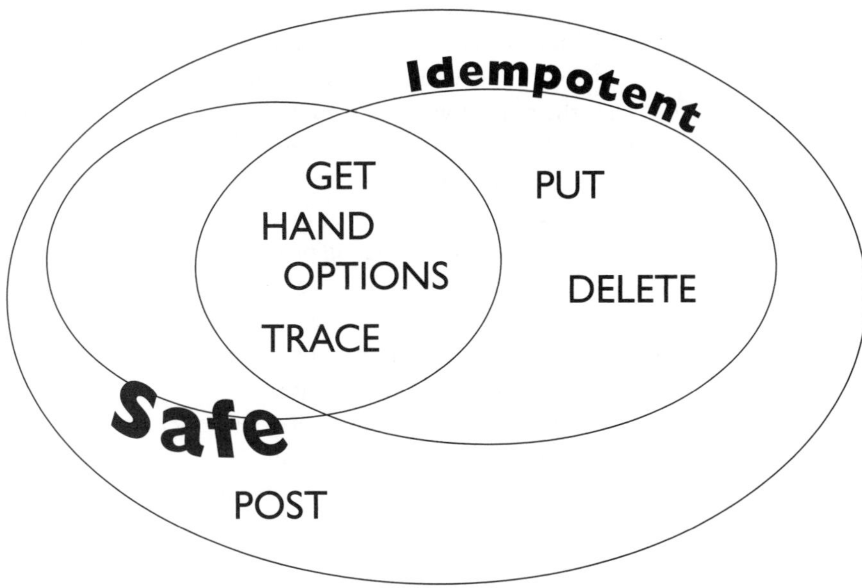

Most web browsers don't have the capability of executing all of the "big seven" methods. Most limit their execution to GET and POST, as directed by the web page currently loaded. However, you'll meet a browser in the first exercise at the end of this section that—although cosmetically challenged—gives you the opportunity to try out all seven methods.

What Does This Discussion Have to Do with Java?

Now that you have a good grasp of HTTP methods, the question is "What does any of this have to do with Enterprise Java?" There is clearly a diverse world of web servers out there that understand HTTP methods and respond to them. For its part, Enterprise Java defines the concept of the *servlet*—a Java program written to a strict (but small) set of standards that can deal with HTTP (and other) requests and send back dynamic responses to client browsers.

Normal web servers are good at dealing with static document requests—web pages, images, and sundry other files that don't change. (Their authors may update the pages from time to time, but the point is that the pages don't change or get created in mid-request.) Web servers didn't take very long to develop dynamic features—capabilities to run programs or server-side scripts on receipt of an HTTP request—rather than simply returning a static document. These techniques frequently came under the heading of "common gateway interface" (CGI).

CGI has been very useful, but not without problems, the greatest of these being performance. The original CGI model demanded a heavyweight process on the web-serving host machine for each request made. Furthermore, this process would die once the request was completed. This was not a sustainable or scalable approach for web applications of any size, as the startup and shutdown of a process are heavy operations for most machines, often outweighing the "grunt" needed to get the real work done! Consequently, better models quickly followed. These included FastCGI, which has the benefit of keeping processes alive—usually, one for each different server-side program that your server supports. And there are many other alternatives—Active Server Pages (ASP), PHP, mod_Perl, and ColdFusion—to name some main players. All vary in their characteristics, such as which web servers support them and how efficient they are.

It's beyond the scope of this book to do any more than take this cursory glance at the differing technologies. After all, we're here to learn the Enterprise Java way of "doing CGI." So I will stop short of claiming that Java is better than the alternatives listed. I'll simply say that it offers a simple and elegant way of getting the job done and that it has other benefits. The structure of a Java web server is shown in

FIGURE 1-2

A Java Web Server

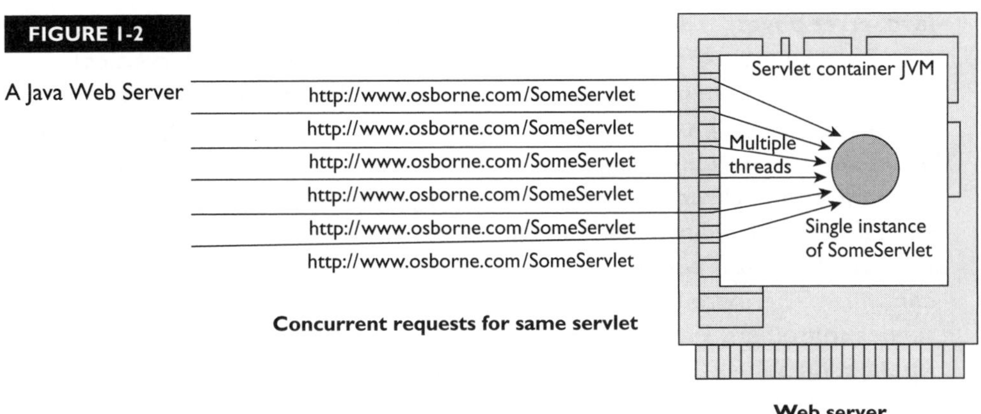

Figure 1-2. You can see that the web server contains a running JVM—a single running process on the host machine. Because Java is a multithreaded language, many threads can be set running within a single process. Many servlet-servicing threads run side by side in a pool. If the request is for a servlet, it doesn't matter which thread is selected—any thread can run any servlet (as well as doing normal web server stuff, such as returning static HTML files). It's not like FastCGI, in which a process is tied to one particular program.

Of course, a web server designed to support servlets is written to stringent specifications in order to provide support for the many things we describe in this book. Tomcat is one such server—an open source Java web server from the Apache Jakarta Project (http://jakarta.apache.org/tomcat). Tomcat is described as the official reference implementation for Java Servlet and JavaServer Page technologies, so it's the one I encourage you to use in the practical exercises and labs throughout this book—you can pretty much guarantee it will do exactly what the specifications say it should do. From the point of view of SCWCD exam readiness, this server is exactly what you require—it's easy to believe something about servlets as true that turns out to be a quirk of a server that doesn't quite support the specification as it should.

Tomcat is perfectly capable of working as a stand-alone web server that happens to run servlets. That's the mode we'll use it in throughout the practical exercises in this book. However, Tomcat doesn't really set itself up to be a "one-stop shop" for all your web serving needs. It describes itself as a servlet and JSP container—that is, a piece of software for running servlets (and

JavaServer pages). The most usual arrangement in a production environment is to have an industrial-strength web server separate from the servlet container. A typical open source combination is the Apache HTTP server (http://httpd.apache.org/), the most popular web server on the Internet, with Tomcat as the servlet container plug-in. The Apache HTTP server is great for serving up static content (such as images from image libraries), as well as being highly configurable for security and robustness. Whenever it encounters a request for a servlet that it cannot deal with, it hands this on to the Tomcat servlet container. There are also many commercial combinations of web servers and servlet containers, such as IBM's HTTP Server together with IBM's WebSphere Application Server. The following illustration shows how a web server and a servlet container cooperate.

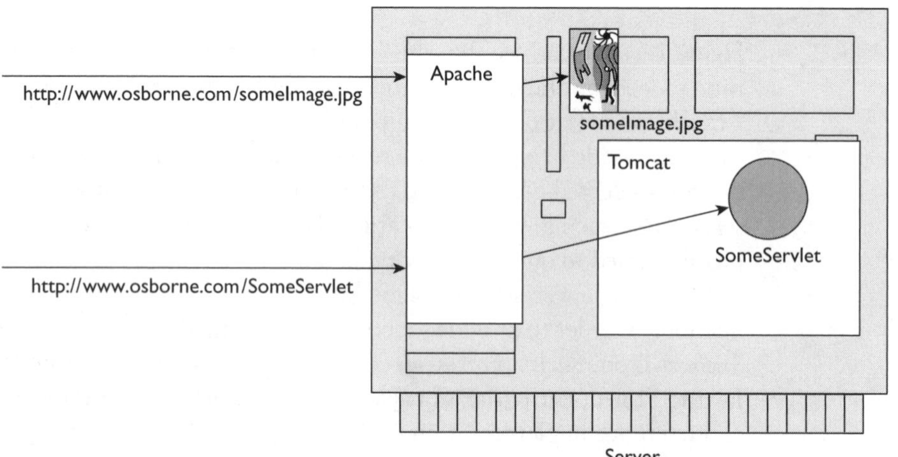

We return to servlets. What happens when a request for a servlet reaches the Tomcat servlet container? That's easy. If the HTTP method is GET, the servlet container will attempt to run a method called `doGet()` in the target servlet. If POST, then the method is `doPost()`. OPTIONS prompts `doOptions()`—it's an easy pattern to grasp.

We'll get to actually writing servlets a bit later in the chapter. Suffice to say two things for now:

1. You typically extend the existing javax.servlet.http.HttpServlet class.
2. You override at least one of the methods we've described: almost always `doGet()`, `doPost()`, or both, and sometimes `doPut()` or `doDelete()`.

If your servlet is hit by an OPTIONS, TRACE, or HEAD request, the existing implementation of the `doOptions()`, `doTrace()`, and `doHead()` methods in HttpServlet should suffice, so you rarely if ever override these methods.

All of these methods receive two parameters—Java objects that wrapper up the HTTP request and response. These are of type javax.servlet.HttpServletRequest and javax.servlet.HttpServletResponse, respectively. These make it easy (in Java terms) to extract information from the request and write content to the response. No low-level knowledge about formatting is required. After doing an exercise on the principles learned in this section of the book, we'll spend the next two sections learning about these two fundamental servlet classes.

EXERCISE 1-1

Custom Browser for Learning HTTP Methods

This exercise uses a browser specifically designed to show the use of the various HTTP methods. Unlike the common full-fledged models (Netscape, Mozilla, Internet Explorer), which render web pages prettily and shield you from so much, my browser exposes you to the dirty underbelly of HTTP.

You won't write any code in this exercise. However, you will deploy a web application (even though you won't officially learn about this until Chapter 2). You'll be doing this a lot through the various exercises—the instructions are in Appendix B. In this case, the web application file is called ex0101.war, and you'll find it on the accompanying CD in directory sourcecode/ch01. The instructions in the appendix also take you through starting up Tomcat, the Java-aware web server that underpins the exercises in this book.

Using the Custom Browser for Learning HTTP Methods

1. Start up a command prompt.
2. Change to directory <TOMCAT INSTALLATION DIRECTORY>/webapps/ex0101/WEB-INF/classes.
3. Execute the command: `java uk.co.jbridge.httpclient.User Interface`. If you get a rude message (such as "java" not recognized as a command), then you need to ensure that the J2SDK commands (in <J2SDK INSTALLATION DIRECTORY>/bin) are in your system path.

4. If successful, you'll see a graphical user interface as illustrated below. There's an area at the top where you can type in a URL—equivalent to the address line in popular browsers. Beneath this is a drop-down list where you can select the HTTP method to execute. Beneath this is a text field where you can type some text to associate with an HTTP POST request. Under that is a display area—by using the browser button to the right of this, you can select a file from your file system and then execute the HTTP PUT method to upload the file to the area of your web server's directory structure targeted by the URL. The button underneath this—Execute HTTP Request—will do exactly that when pressed, using the parameters as you have set them above. The area beneath the button is tabbed, and it displays the result of execut-

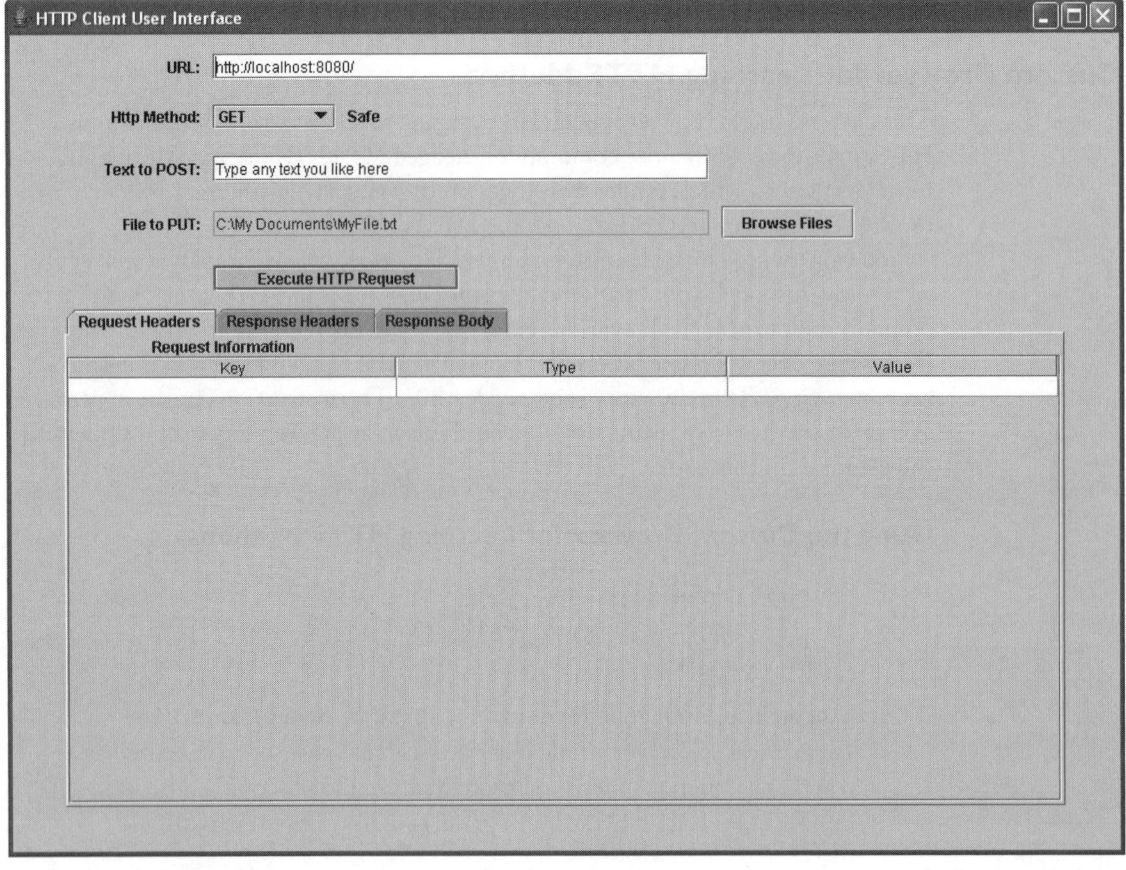

ing the HTTP request. The first tab—Request Headers—shows information sent from the browser to the server (we learn about request headers in the next section). The second tab—Response Headers—shows information sent back from the server to the browser (we explore valid values for these later in the chapter). The third tab shows the response body—the resource retrieved from the server. If this is a web page, it is displayed as the underlying HTML.

5. Note that what you've done here is to start a plain old Java application—using the **java** command on a class with a `main()` method. As it happens, the code resides in the same place as the code for the web application it will communicate with (in a few steps), but that's just a coincidence. If you prefer, place all the classes from the package uk.co.jbridge.httpclient in a completely separate location on your machine and run the browser from there instead.

Executing Safe Methods (GET, HEAD, OPTIONS, TRACE)

6. In the browser, change the text in the URL field to say `http://localhost:8080/ex0101/index.jsp`. Leave the HTTP method as the default GET, and press the Execute HTTP Method button. This will invoke a very simple web page. Take a look at the request headers. The request headers are set up within the user interface program. "User-Agent" describes the type of client—usually one that derives from the Mozilla browser. "Accept-Language" indicates the (human) languages the client would prefer to see in any requested web pages. "Accept" indicates the file types the client can deal with, using standard MIME abbreviations (you learn more MIME in Chapter 2).

7. Now take a look at the response headers. These may vary depending on your server setup—the accompanying illustration shows you what I see.

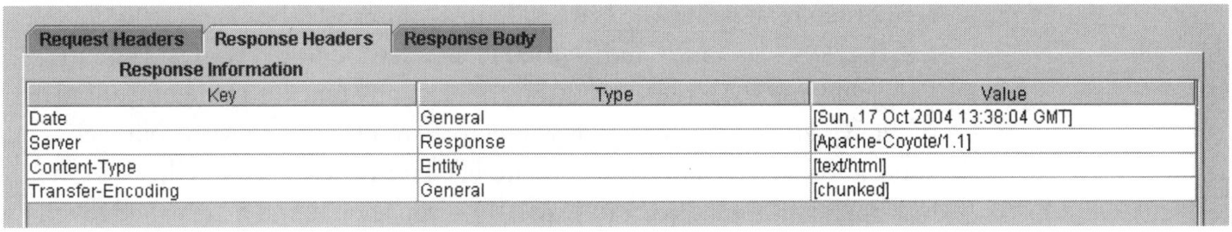

Request Headers | Response Headers | Response Body

Response Information

Key	Type	Value
Date	General	[Sun, 17 Oct 2004 13:38:04 GMT]
Server	Response	[Apache-Coyote/1.1]
Content-Type	Entity	[text/html]
Transfer-Encoding	General	[chunked]

`Date` reflects the date the requested resource was last changed. `Server` shows some version and type information about the web server software, in this case Tomcat. `Content-Type` shows the MIME type of the information returned—in this case, plain HTML text. Finally, `Transfer-Encoding` shows how the response message is parceled up—"chunked"—to help the browser interpret the contents.

8. Repeat the above exercise for the other safe HTTP methods. The browser gives a clear indication about which methods are safe and which are not. Try the safe methods on a range of other public URLs (e.g., http://www.osborne.com—you must type in the complete address). Note the different response headers you get back.

Executing Unsafe Methods (POST, PUT, DELETE)

9. The unsafe methods are POST, PUT, and DELETE. Nearly any browser will POST. This browser is set up to POST a line of text, which you can type into a field. The exercise comes with a corresponding servlet that will accumulate all the lines you type into this field and then display them on a web page.
10. Enter `http://localhost:8080/ex0101/PostServlet` in the browser's URL field. Change the HTTP method to POST, and type any text you like in the Text to POST field. Click the Execute HTTP Request button (which should have turned red to indicate an unsafe method). Click the Response Body tab—you should see some simple HTML with the text you typed in the middle.
11. Write some different text in the Text to POST field, and click the Execute HTTP Request button again. This time, in the Response Body tab you should see both the original text you typed, plus the latest text. (To avoid losing text between HTTP requests, the text is appended to a file called postData.txt—you can find this in the ex0101 context directory for the web application.)
12. Now we'll try using the browser to PUT a file in your web application directory structure. Change the URL field to say `http://localhost:8080/ex0101/myFile.txt`. Change the HTTP method to PUT. In the File to PUT field, use the Browse... button to select any text (.txt) file on your file system (preferably outside of any directory structure to do with your web applications). Now click the Execute HTTP Request button. Check in the web application subdirectory (ex0101)—you should find a file called myFile.txt, whose contents should be the same as the file you selected as the "file to PUT."
13. The above attempt to PUT a file may fail under Tomcat with a 403 response code: forbidden. By default, Tomcat blocks HTTP methods (such as PUT and DELETE) that alter the structure of a web application. Under these circum-

stances, you will need to find the file web.xml in <TOMCAT-INSTALL-DIRECTORY>/conf. Edit this with a text editor, and insert the lines in bold below:

```
<servlet>
  <servlet-name>default</servlet-name>
  <servlet-class>
    org.apache.catalina.servlets.DefaultServlet
  </servlet-class>
  <init-param>
    <param-name>debug</param-name>
    <param-value>0</param-value>
  </init-param>
  <init-param>
    <param-name>readonly</param-name>
    <param-value>false</param-value>
  </init-param>
  <init-param>
    <param-name>listings</param-name>
    <param-value>true</param-value>
  </init-param>
  <load-on-startup>1</load-on-startup>
</servlet>
```

What you have done here is to add an initialization parameter to a servlet, which usefully anticipates the work we'll do in Chapter 2. In this case, you've added an initialization parameter to one of Tomcat's own servlets—the default servlet—which is used to process requests when the URL requested is not otherwise mapped to a resource in a web application. By setting *readonly* to *false*, you are saying that the PUT and DELETE methods will be permitted. You must *restart the Tomcat server* after making this change. If you're using another server to perform the exercises in this book, you're on your own, but be aware that many servers block PUT and DELETE methods by default, and you may have to do some digging in your server documentation to find out how to enable them.

14. Now try using the browser to delete the file you have just PUT in your web application. Leave the URL as is (`http://localhost:8080/ex0101/myFile.txt`), but change the HTTP method to DELETE. Click EXECUTE HTTP REQUEST. You may get a strange response code (204: No Content), but you should find if you look in the web application directory structure that the file has disappeared.

15. That concludes the exercise. Bask in the comfortable knowledge that you have exercised more HTTP methods than most people get to do in a career of working with web servers!

CERTIFICATION OBJECTIVE

Form Parameters (Exam Objective 1.2)

Using the HttpServletRequest interface, write code to retrieve HTML form parameters from the request.

Now that you have seen the connection working between a client and a servlet, we can turn our attention to the Java code. We're going to explore one of the most fundamental aspects: getting information from an HTTP request and using that within our servlet. It's possible to attach parameters to an HTTP request as a series of name/value pairs. These travel in the request body or the URL—it's even possible to type parameter names and values directly into a browser's address line (if you know what you're doing!). More usually, though, information destined for a request is collected in an HTML form embedded within a web page. The user types in data, and the browser sorts out how to format the HTTP request appropriately so that the parameters are included. Consequently, we'll need to explore HTML form construction—for the exam, you'll be expected to understand HTML well enough to predict the parameters that will arise from a given web page. Then we'll see the range of APIs for teasing out the parameters from the request on arrival in the servlet.

HTML Forms

HTML forms are very easy to construct and use. You use the `<form>` tag and place the screen controls you need before the closing `</form>` tag. That said, a range of graphical components (often called form controls, sometimes called "widgets") are supported within a web page, and you need to understand them all. These are mainly provided to allow for the user to input data and then to submit these data to the server in the form of parameter name/value pairs. Most form controls are defined using the `<input>` tag with a variety of attributes, but you'll need to understand the `<select>` and `<textarea>` tags as well.

The Form Itself (<form>)

A form is defined on a web page starting with the opening tag `<form>` and ending with the closing tag `</form>`. The opening tag has a number of attributes, but only two of them have real significance to web application operation. A typical form opening tag might look like this:

```
<form action="someServlet" method="POST">
```

Most browsers tolerate wide syntactic variety—you'll probably find that

```
<form action=someServlet method=POST>
```

or

```
<FORM ACTION = 'someServlet' METHOD = 'POST'>
```

works just as well. The essentials are that

- The tag begins with "<" and finishes with ">."
- The name of the tag is *form* (lowercase preferred), which comes immediately after the "<."
- At least one attribute is present in the tag—*action*—whose value contains some target resource in the web application.
- Each attribute is separated from its neighbor (or the tag name, *form*) by at least one space.
- The attribute name is followed (usually immediately) by the equal sign ("="), which is followed (again, usually immediately) by the attribute value. The correct form is to surround the value with double quotes.

Fortunately, you're not being tested on what constitutes well-formed HTML, which demands a book in its own right. What you really need to know is the interaction between a `<form>` definition and a web application, as determined by the *action* and *method* attributes.

- The value for *action*, as we noted above, denotes some target resource in the web application. This target is most often a dynamic resource, such as a servlet or JSP. However, no rule says that it has to be: Static resources can be the target of an action as well.
- The value for *method* denotes the HTTP method to execute. The default (if this attribute is missed out) is to execute an HTTP GET when the form is submitted. Most typically, you use this attribute to specify that the method is POST (this has advantages for parameter sending, which we will discuss soon).

The path for the *action* parameter obeys the rules that apply for any web page link. Suppose you call the web page containing the form with the following URL:

```
http://localhost:8080/ex0101/index.jsp
```

And the form tag within index.jsp looks like this:

```
<form action="someServlet">
```

Then when you submit the form, the browser will assume that someServlet resides in the same place as index.jsp. So the full URL for the request will be

```
http://localhost:8080/ex0101/someServlet
```

If—on the other hand—your path begins with a slash:

```
<form action="/someServlet">
```

Then the browser will assume the path begins at the root location for the specified host, in this case http://localhost:8080. Hence, the full URL would look like this:

```
http://localhost:8080/someServlet
```

It's important to distinguish this behavior from paths constructed within servlet code, as we'll discover in Chapter 2.

on the job

There can be more than one form on the same web page. However, only one can be submitted at once. This technique can be useful if you are dealing with multiple rows in an HTML table. If your application allows you to operate on only one row at once, it can save a lot of data passing on the network to have a form associated with each row.

FIGURE 1-3

<input> Types for Data Input

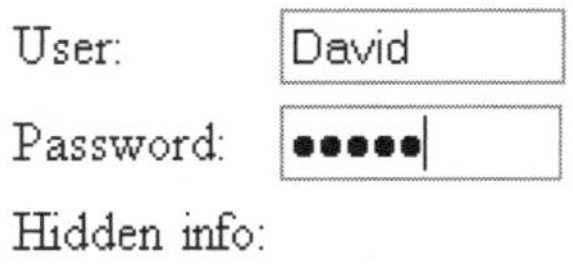

User: David

Password: ●●●●●

Hidden info:

Single Line Form Controls

Most form controls for data input are controlled through HTML's <input> tag. By varying the value for the *type* attribute, a wide range of field types are available. Figure 1-3 shows three of those—those that are dedicated to holding a single line of text. One—being a hidden field—is invisible!

Common to all <input> tags, whatever their type, is the *name* attribute. When form control data are passed to the server, the *name* attribute supplies the parameter name. The *value* attribute supplies the parameter value. This doesn't have to be included in the HTML for the form because whatever the user types in or selects will become the value for a control's *value* attribute. However, it can be used within HTML to supply a default value for a field. You'll see these attributes at work in the following definitions.

<input type="text" /> This control allows a user to input a single line of text. The *size* attribute specifies the width of the text field in characters. The *maxlength* attribute controls the maximum number of characters that a user can type into the text field. The following HTML definition generated the field with the label "User" in Figure 1-3:

```
<input type="text" name="user" size="10" maxlength="5" />
```

This definition sets up a field whose name is "user." The width of the field as displayed is ten characters, but the user will be allowed to input only five characters. Suppose I type "David" into the field; when I press the submit button on my form, a parameter name/value pair will be sent in the form *user=David*.

<input type="password" /> The *password* input type works just like *text*. The only difference is that a browser should mask the characters typed in by the user. The following HTML definition generated the field with the label "Password" in Figure 1-3:

```
<input type="password" name="password" size="10" maxlength="5" />
```

Assuming I type in "wells" as the password, the parameter passed to a server will be *password=wells*.

`<input type="hidden" />` The *hidden* input type is not available for user input. As its name implies, such a form control is hidden—invisible as rendered by the browser. You see only the contents of a hidden field if you view the HTML source of the web page. A hidden form control can be useful in two ways:

1. A servlet can write values to hidden fields. These may not be directly useful (and hence not visible) to the user of the web page that the servlet generates. However, when the user requests the next servlet in the chain (by clicking a button on the web page), these values may be useful as parameters to the next servlet. It's one approach to "session control" (answering such questions as "What's in my shopping cart?").
2. Script running within the web page can set the hidden values. This could be contingent on anything—a mouse movement, a keyboard press, an action taken in an applet or a Flash control, or even the selection of a value in some other control.

The following HTML definition generated the invisibly present "hiddenInfo" field in Figure 1-3:

```
<input type="hidden" name="hiddenInfo" value="Discrete Information" />
```

Parameter construction is no different: *hiddenInfo=Discrete Information* will be passed to the server.

Multiple Choice Form Controls

Often, instead of allowing direct text input, it's better to have groups and lists of predefined choices in your user interface. You have several ways to achieve this—two still using the `<input>` tag and one using the entirely separate `<select>` tag. Figure 1-4 shows each of these in a browser screenshot.

`<input type="checkbox" />` Use *checkbox* to put one or more small boxes on screen. By clicking on these, the user ticks or "checks" the corresponding value to denote that it is selected—so in Figure 1-4, the musicians Beethoven and Schubert are selected. Let's look at the HTML used to set up the fields:

FIGURE 1-4

Multiple Choice Form Controls

Mozart
Beethoven
Schubert

High volume
Medium volume
Low volume

```
<br /><input type="checkbox"
             name="musicians" value="MOZRT" />Mozart
<br /><input type="checkbox"
             name="musicians" value="BTHVN" />Beethoven
<br /><input type="checkbox"
             name="musicians" value="SCHBT" />Schubert
```

Note that all these checkboxes share a name in common: musicians. There is no technical necessity for this—every checkbox can have an independent name. However, it is the usual convention when the checkboxes are closely related.

This is our first example of a parameter with multiple values. If you make the choices shown in Figure 1-4 (and press the submit button on the form), the parameter string generated from this set of checkboxes will look like this:

```
musicians=BTHVN&musicians=SCHBT
```

There are two issues to note: Only the checked values make it to the parameter string (that's how you know which ones are chosen). Also, it's the value of the attribute *value* that is passed through on the right-hand side of the equal sign. That's no different from the way other `<input>` types work—it's just that for regular "text" fields, the *value* attribute isn't necessarily set up in the HTML.

We'll see a bit later in this section that servlet code has no issues when dealing with multiple values for the same parameter name.

Should you wish to set up some of your checkboxes as already selected, you can, using the HTML syntax (in bold) below:

```
<br /><input type="checkbox"
             name="musicians" value="BTHVN"
             checked="checked" />Beethoven
```

It's actually sufficient to write the attribute name (*checked*) alone, but I am giving you the benefit of full XHTML syntax, which you should of course strive for. There's nothing stopping the user unselecting a checkbox defined in this way, which prevents the value being passed through as a parameter.

<input type="radio" /> The construction of radio buttons is very similar. This time, however, the choice made is mutually exclusive. Also, the name attribute is crucial to tying together a group of radio buttons. Here's the HTML that creates the radio button example shown in Figure 1-4:

```
<BR /><INPUT type="radio" name="volume" value="HIGH" />High Volume
<BR /><INPUT type="radio" name="volume"
             value="MED" checked="checked" />Medium Volume
<BR /><INPUT type="radio" name="volume"
             value="LOW" checked="checked" />Low Volume
```

The name attribute is set to "volume" for each of the three choices. The value attribute is set appropriately, and as for checkboxes, you will need to place some adjacent regular text (e.g., "High Volume") to act as a label; otherwise, the radio button appears without any choice description. As shown, there are two radio buttons "preselected" using the *checked="checked"* syntax. However, only one choice is possible. The browser resolves this by letting the last one marked as checked (in this case, "Low Volume") take precedence. So unless the user makes a choice here, the parameter string passed through will be *volume=LOW*.

The <select> tag Finally in this "multiple choice" array of form controls, we consider an entirely separate tag: `<select>`. This control allows you to set up a list of values to choose from in a web page—the style is either a pop-up menu or a scrollable list. There are two "modes" for this control: The user is either restricted to one choice from the list or has multiple choices from the list. Both sorts are illustrated in Figure 1-5. Let's consider the HTML for the single-choice, pop-up menu first:

```
<select name="Countries">
  <option value="FR">France</option>
  <option value="GB" selected>Great Britain</option>
  <option value="DK">Denmark</option>
</select>
```

This time, there is an outer tag beginning with `<select>` and closing with `</select>`. The opening tag has a name attribute, which will form the parameter name—in this case, "Countries." Within the `<select>` are nested the predefined list choices, each in an individual `<option>` tag. The user-visible text goes between the opening `<option>` and closing `</option>`; the value passed in the parameter is expressed as the *value* attribute of the opening `<option>` tag. In order to preselect an item in the list, the attribute *selected* is added to the opening `<option>` tag. So the parameter string looks like this: *Countries=GB*.

The alternative form of `<select>` is very similar, apart from the presence of the attribute name *multiple* in the opening `<select>` tag. It's illustrated in the lower part of Figure 1-5. Here's our list of countries again, but now you can choose more than one:

```
<select name="Countries" size="5" multiple>
  <option value="FR" selected>France</option>
  <option value="GB">Great Britain</option>
  <option value="DK" selected>Denmark</option>
  <option value="BE">Belgium</option>
  <option value="CX">Christmas Island</option>
  <option value="CO">Colombia</option>
</select>
```

This time, France and Denmark are preselected. It's a good idea to use the *size* attribute. At least with the browser I'm using, setting this to the same value as the number of `<option>` elements gives you a box with all the options shown. When the size value is less than the number of options, you get a scrolling region that displays as many rows as you specify in the size attribute. So in the example above, you need to scroll down to see Colombia. Leaving the size attribute out altogether allows the browser to impose its own rules, which may or may not give the effect you want. If the user leaves the above preselections unaltered, the parameter string passed through is *Countries=FR&Countries=DK*.

FIGURE 1-5

Select Tag

Multiple Lines of Text

Should one line of text be insufficient, and should you want your user to be able to type in an essay (or at least a multiline comment), you can resort to the `<textarea>` tag. This has an opening tag and an ending tag—you can put any text you like between the tags. This text will display in the middle of an editing box. The user can overtype or add to any text already there, and this constitutes the value of the parameter passed back to the server. The opening `<textarea>` tag has three attributes of consequence:

- *name*—as elsewhere, the parameter name
- *rows*—the number of visible lines (a scroll bar activates when access to further rows is needed)
- *cols*—the number of characters to displayed across the width of the area (based on an average-width character)

Another attribute—wrap—offers some flexibility in the treatment of carriage return and line feed characters, introduced either by the user pressing the enter key or the browser wrapping the text. There is no HTML standard for this attribute, and implementations vary slightly from browser to browser. All you need to know for practical purposes is that your servlet code should be able to deal with carriage return and line feed characters within the body of the text returned.

Figure 1-6 shows a text area, and below is the HTML that produced it:

```
<TEXTAREA name="notes" rows="5" cols="35">
  This is the area for sleeve notes about the music
  you are listening to.
  Overtype with your own text.
</TEXTAREA>
```

The parameter string passed back from this text area (from Internet Explorer) bears some attention:

```
notes=This+is+the+area+for+sleeve+notes+about+the+music+you+are+listening+to.%0
D%0A%09%09++Overtype+this+area+with+your+own+text.
```

FIGURE 1-6

A Text Area

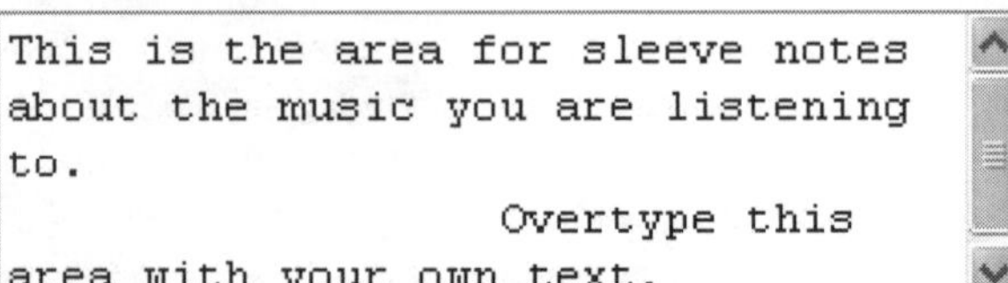

Most browsers have a horror of embedded white space in their parameter strings. Internet Explorer here substitutes a + for the space character (%20 is sometimes seen instead). Substitutes are also made for "non-typeable" characters. %0D and %0A are hex representations of the line feed and carriage return characters, and %09 is the horizontal tab. This reflects the fact that the full HTML source was set up in a text editor that inserted exactly those characters.

exam watch

You've seen how you can get multiple values associated with a related group of form controls—checkboxes all sharing the same name, for example. However, there is nothing illegal about entirely separate form controls sharing the same name. You can have, say, a checkbox, a set of radio buttons, and a text field that all share the same name—and so give rise to multiple values for the same parameter name when retrieved in the target servlet code.

Buttons

Now that we've surveyed all the form controls that allow data input or selection, let's consider other actions you can take with your form. Most especially, we need to know how to submit the data that our user has so generously supplied! For this and other actions triggered by buttons, we return to the `<input>` tag. There are three types: *submit*, *reset*, and *button*. They are no different in appearance; Figure 1-7 shows examples.

`<input type="submit" />` The purpose of an input tag whose *type* is submit is to send the form data to the URL designated by the *action* attribute of the opening `<form>` tag. To define it, no more is required than defining the *type*:

```
<input type="submit" />
```

FIGURE 1-7

Buttons within an HTML Form

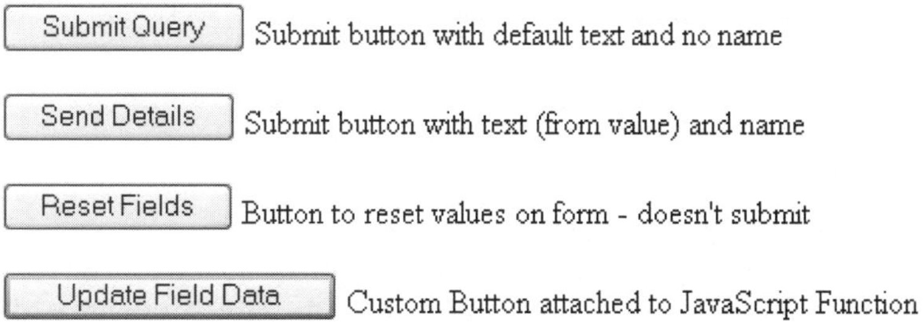

Submit Query	Submit button with default text and no name
Send Details	Submit button with text (from value) and name
Reset Fields	Button to reset values on form - doesn't submit
Update Field Data	Custom Button attached to JavaScript Function

However, it is quite usual to supply the *value* attribute, which allows you to define your own text on the button. If you supply a *name* attribute as well, then the name/value data for the submit button are passed just like any other parameter as part of the submitted form data. The HTML below defines the submit button seen in Figure 1-7:

```
<input type="submit" name="formSubmission" value="Send Details" />
```

It gives rise to parameter data like this: *formSubmission=Send+Details*.

<input type="reset" /> When an input tag is a *reset* type, the resulting button doesn't send form data. No request is made to the server. Instead, it's a request to the client browser to reset all the values within the form to the way they were when the page was first loaded—in other words, to scrap any user input since that point. You can regard it as an all-or-nothing "undo" facility. Again, you can supply a name attribute and have the button name/value passed as a parameter (though it's hard to find a good reason for doing this). The reset button in Figure 1-7 has the following HTML definition:

```
<INPUT type="reset" value="Reset Fields" />
```

<input type="button" /> Slightly confusingly, there is a third type of button whose type is—well—*button*. Surely the other two types were buttons as well? It's best to think of type button as defining a "custom button," which is connected to some sort of script within your page. You typically harness this by defining an *onclick* attribute within the input tag and making the value correspond to some JavaScript function. The JavaScript function can do pretty much anything—up to and including submission of the form. More usually, functions define themselves to effects within the browser, such as changing which form control has focus or validating the contents of a field. Here's a fairly trivial example that uses a custom button to take the contents of a text-type input field and place the contents in a hidden field. It uses a simple message dialog to display the old and new values of the hidden field. Here's the script, contained in the `<head>` section of the enclosing HTML page:

```
<head>
  <title>Welcome</title>
  <script language="JavaScript">
  <!--
    function setAndDisplayHiddenField() {
      hiddenField = document.getElementById("hiddenInfo");
      alert("Current Value Of Hidden Field: " + hiddenField.value);
```

```
      hiddenField.value = document.getElementById("inputToHidden").value;
      alert("New Value Of Hidden Field: " + hiddenField.value);
    }
    -->
  </script>
</head>
```

The button that summons this script is illustrated in Figure 1-7 and has the following HTML definition:

```
<INPUT type="button" value="Update Field Data"
onclick="setAndDisplayHiddenField();" />
```

Note that if you're trying this script for yourself, you'll need a hidden field named "hiddenInfo" and a text field named "inputToHidden" to make it work. Type text into "inputToHidden," press the button, and the value will be transferred to "hiddenInfo"—the message dialogs will prove this to you.

When all is said and done, JavaScript is well "off topic" for the SCWCD but has a nasty habit of creeping into the day-to-day headaches of a web application developer.

Retrieving Parameters

Now that you have mastered HTML form controls, and understand the parameter data generated from them, we can move to the server side. Our first proper look at servlet code will examine the issue of retrieving parameter data. This is usually the first and most vital step in any web application—getting hold of what a user has supplied.

Servlet APIs for Parameters

Parameters are part of an HTTP request. However, they are regarded as so fundamental to servlet workings that the APIs to retrieve them are found on javax.servlet.ServletRequest, the parent interface for javax.servlet.http.HttpServletRequest interface (which you might consider a more likely home). Your servlet engine provides a class implementing the HttpServletRequest interface, and it passes an instance of this as a parameter to whichever of a servlet's `doXXX()` methods is targeted by an HTTP request. The HttpServletRequest object encapsulates information in the request, providing APIs to make it easy to access this information. Since HttpServlet Request inherits from ServletRequest, any implementing class must provide the ServletRequest methods as well, and these include methods for parameter access.

exam watch

In the heat of web application programming, you're unlikely to care very much whether a method originates from HttpServletRequest or the parent ServletRequest interface. Unfortunately, the exam does include questions that target knowledge of origin interfaces—there's no real option but to commit the methods on HttpServletRequest and ServletRequest to memory prior to taking the exam.

When you know the name of a parameter, and can guarantee a single value back from the form, then the easiest API to use is `ServletRequest.getParameter(String parmName)`. This returns a String representing the parameter value, or **null** if the parameter doesn't exist.

However, we've already seen that parameters can have the same name and multiple values. When you are after a specific parameter and know the name, your best bet is to use the `ServletRequest.getParameterValues(String parmName)` method. This returns a String array with all values present, or **null** if no value exists for the parameter name. If this array has a length of 1, this indicates that there was only one value. Can you predict anything about the order of the values? In practice, the order appears to reflect the left-to-right, top-to-bottom occurrence of the values within the form controls. However, the servlet specification is silent on this question. All you can guarantee is that parameters in the query string (associated with the URL) should be placed before parameters in a POST request body. This isn't greatly informative, for mostly you only get one or the other—parameters placed in the query string by a GET request, or parameters embedded in the request body by a POST request. However, you might encounter this sort of form declaration:

```
<form action="servlets/MyServlet?myparm=thisfirst" method="post">
```

This uses the POST method—which will put form parameters in the request body—but also specifies a parameter in a query string in addition.

The one other guarantee on offer is that the parameter value returned by `getParameter()` must be the first value in the array returned by `getParameterValues()`.

When you want to find out about all the parameters in a request, you have two options:

- `ServletRequest.getParameterNames()`, returning an Enumeration of String objects representing the names of all the parameters in the request. There's only one occurrence of any given name; however, many form controls share that name. Should no parameters be passed, the Enumeration is empty. To get hold of corresponding values, each parameter name retrieved from the Enumeration can be plugged into either of the `getParameter()` or `getParameterValues()` methods discussed above.
- `ServletRequest.getParameterMap()`, returning a java.util.Map object, where the keys in the map are of type String (and represent each unique parameter name) and the values in the map of type String array (representing the values for the parameter). Though the API documentation doesn't come clean on what should apply, my Tomcat implementation returns an empty Map if there are no parameters present—which makes sense and matches the behavior of `getParameterNames()`. The map returned is immutable. That means that if you try yourself to `put()` key/value pairs in the Map retrieved from this method, you will be told in no uncertain terms that this isn't appropriate behavior (Illegal StateException for Tomcat 5). This is right and proper—you shouldn't be adding to the list of genuine parameters. There are plenty of other mechanisms for storing data with the request, and other scopes that we meet in Chapter 2.

Getting at Parameters the Hard Way

Actually, there *is* an alternative way to get at POSTed parameters. You can read the request body directly by using `ServletRequest.getReader()` or `ServletRequest.getInputStream()`. It's then up to you to examine the resulting character or input stream for name/value pairs separated by ampersands. This process is not that hard, as you can see from the code below:

```
protected void doPost(HttpServletRequest request,
 HttpServletResponse response)
 throws ServletException, IOException {
  response.setContentType("text/html");
  PrintWriter out = response.getWriter();
  out.write("<html><head></head><body>");
  BufferedReader reader = new BufferedReader(new InputStreamReader(
                        request.getInputStream()));
  String line;
  while ((line = reader.readLine()) != null) {
    StringTokenizer st = new StringTokenizer(line, "&");
```

```
    while (st.hasMoreTokens()) {
      out.write("<br /" + st.nextToken());
    }
  }
  out.write("</body></html>");
}
```

This code uses a BufferedReader to work through the lines in the POSTed body. A StringTokenizer breaks down the input by splitting out the text between ampersands (which should delimit each name/value pair, internally separated by an equal sign). The servlet simply writes out each name/value pair to a new line on the web page. Note in this approach how multivalued attributes are written out many times. Suppose a web page submits a list of countries from a multiselect `<select>` form control named "Countries." The output from the servlet code above might look like this:

```
Countries=GB
Countries=DK
Countries=FR
```

Should you attempt to use `getInputStream()` after you have used `getReader()`, you are likely to get a message such as the one below:

```
java.lang.IllegalStateException: getReader() has already been
 called for this request
```

The reverse holds equally true—don't call `getReader()` after `getInputStream()`. These methods can blow up in other ways: with a straight IOException (if something goes wrong with the input/output process) or—for `getReader()` only—with an UnsupportedEncodingException if the character set encoding used is not supported on the platform, and the text therefore remains un-encodeable.

You won't often want to mess directly with the POST data; after all, it's much easier to use the getParameter* methods. However, there are occasions when you might want or even need to. This is when a POST request is being used to upload a file, usually in conjunction with an HTML `<input>` type we didn't explore in our form control review. The following tag—`<input type ="file" name="fileForUpload" />`—creates a button and a text field in your browser. The button can be used to launch a "choose file" type dialog allowing you to browse your local file system—the result of the choice is stored in the text field. When you submit the form, the chosen file is uploaded in the post body. The servlet code that receives the file (or files—a

single form can have several input elements where the type is "file") and does something with it that is not trivial—you can find a fabulous implementation (complete with source code) at http://www.servlets.com/cos.

exam watch

Conceptually, the data from a POSTed form are transferred to a "parameter set" and, once there, are available to convenience methods such as `getParameter()`***. The conditions for the data to be present in the set are as follows: The request follows the HTTP or HTTPS protocol, using the POST method. The content type for the request (as declared in the Content-Type request header) must have a value of "application/x-www-form-urlencoded." Finally, a call must be made to one of the getParameter* convenience methods: The first such call causes the transfer. Once data have been transferred to the parameter set, you must not use the request's*** `getInputStream()` ***or*** `getReader()` ***to get hold of the parameters. Although you may not get any exception, the servlet specification promises unpredictable results, and this is borne out by practical experimentation. The reverse is also true; a call to a getParameter* method is unlikely to do you much good if the request body has been treated as a raw byte or character stream.***

There's an alternative way to get at parameters that are sent in a GET request. That's with the `HttpServletRequest.getQueryString()` ***method. This returns the raw data following the question mark (if present) in a URL—you'll find a discussion of this in Chapter 3, in the "Forwarding" section.***

EXERCISE 1-2

Form Parameters

In this exercise, you'll construct an HTML form containing a number of controls. Then you'll write a servlet to receive the parameters from the form and display the choices made on a web page.

This exercise is the first of many that follow a similar pattern, described in Appendix B. Most exercises and labs exist as unique "web applications" in their own right. Full instructions are provided in Appendix B, and a solution (which you can deploy and look at independently) is included in the CD supplied with the book. The unique directory for this exercise is ex0102, and you'll need to create that (together with a directory structure underneath it, as described in Appendix B).

The solution is on the CD in the file sourcecode/ch01/ex0102.war—check there if you get stuck. Instructions for deploying the solution WAR file are also in Appendix B.

Write the HTML Form

1. Create an HTML file in directory ex0102 called weather.html.
2. Create a form on the page whose method is POST and whose action is "Weather." All the remaining instructions for the HTML form pertain to controls that should come between the opening and closing `<form>` tags.
3. Create an input field (with a *type* of "text") for the name of the person observing the weather.
4. Create an input field (with a *type* of "password") for the observer's password.
5. Create a hidden input field containing any information you like.
6. Create a series of checkboxes, all with the same name, to record different types of weather observed (rain, sun, snow, fog, and so on).
7. Create a series of radio buttons, all with the same name, for the observer to select a suitable temperature range to reflect the highest temperature achieved today.
8. Create a select box with three options for each of three possible weather stations.
9. Create a text area to hold comments on today's weather.
10. Finally, create a submit button (`<input>` of type *submit*) to send the form data to the servlet that you are about to write.

Write the WeatherParams Servlet

11. You're going to write a servlet that picks up all the parameters from the form and reflects these back on a web page to the user. You need to create a source file called WeatherParams.java, with a package of webcert.ch01.ex0102. Place this in an appropriate directory (webcert/ch01/ex0102) within the exercise subdirectory ex0102/WEB-INF/classes.
12. Following the package statement, your servlet code should import packages java.io, java.util, javax.servlet, and javax.servlet.http.
13. Your WeatherParams class should extend HttpServlet (and doesn't need to implement any interfaces).
14. You will override one method from the parent class, which is `doPost()`. The method signature is as follows:

```
protected void doPost(HttpServletRequest request,
                      HttpServletResponse response)
          throws ServletException, IOException
```

15. Here's some boilerplate code to place at the beginning of the method. This gets hold of a PrintWriter from the response, giving you a slate to write on to create your web page. The code also sets an appropriate MIME type to indicate you're generating HTML from your code, and starts off an HTML page in the right way. You'll learn more about all this in the next section.

```
response.setContentType("text/html");
PrintWriter out = response.getWriter();
out.write("<html>\n<head>\n<title>" +
  "Display Weather Parameters</title>\n</head>\n<body>");
```

16. Here's some boilerplate code to place at the end of the method. This closes off your HTML web page properly and closes the response's PrintWriter:

```
out.write("\n</body>\n</html>");
out.close();
```

17. All your remaining code goes between the two pieces you input above.
18. Your aim now is to write code to retrieve all the parameter names passed to the servlet and to write these as headings for the web page. The heading-writing code will look something like this:

```
out.write("<h4>" + paramName + "</h4>");
```

The variable *paramName* is a String holding each parameter name you've retrieved—in some kind of loop. For each name you retrieve, write out all the parameter values underneath. Here's the code to do the writing so that each value appears on a new line in the web page:

```
out.write("<br />" + paramValue);
```

As for the remaining code to do the parameter name and value retrieval, you're on your own for that. Well, not entirely. Refer back to and adapt the code examples in this section. If you get really stuck, refer to the source in the solution code.
19. Compile your servlet code in the same directory as your source file.

Running Your Code

20. You won't learn about deployment and WAR files until Chapter 2, so for this chapter's exercises we will cheat a bit.
21. Start the Tomcat Server.
22. Deploy the *solution* code WAR file, ex0102.war (follow the instructions for deploying WAR files in Appendix B).
23. Copy weather.html from your directory structure to the <Tomcat Installation Directory>/webapps/ex0102 directory (overwrite the solution version).
24. Copy WeatherParams.class from your directory structure to <Tomcat Installation Directory>/webapps/ex0102/WEB-INF/classes/webcert/ch01/ex0102 (overwrite the solution version).
25. Point your browser to an appropriate URL. For a default Tomcat installation, this will be

    ```
    http://localhost:8080/ex0102/weather.html
    ```

26. Test your code by filling in the parameters and pressing the submit button. If all goes well, you'll get a web page back that tells you the parameters you chose.

CERTIFICATION OBJECTIVE

Requests (Exam Objective 1.2)

Using the HttpServletRequest interface, . . . retrieve HTTP request header information or retrieve cookies from the request.

In this section you will work through the several APIs available on HttpServlet Request that break down the available information on an HTTP request. The APIs are straightforward. You will also encounter several header properties recognized by the HTTP protocol and learn the significance they have for servlet containers. We'll explore some of the more common header properties that sometimes grace the screens of the SCWCD exam.

We'll also look at the question of cookies—those small and useful text files that can be uploaded from browsers (we'll look at downloading to browsers in the next section, on the HttpServletResponse interface). You might regard cookies as a violation of your privacy, but there's no denying their usefulness—and you can't deny their place as a core topic on the exam syllabus!

Request Headers

The HTTP RFC lays out an extensive list of separate pieces of header information that can accompany a request (or a response). These are described as name/value pairs, very much like parameters. There are almost fifty valid named headers. And again very similar to parameters, one named header can have multiple values. Headers can be categorized into four types:

- Request Headers: pertaining strictly to the request—for example, communicating to the server what the client will find acceptable in terms of file formats and encodings.
- Response Headers: pertaining strictly to the response—for example, describing a specific aspect of how the server responded to a particular request.
- General Headers: can occur on either the request or the response. "Date" is a good example—this contains a timestamp for the HTTP message, so it is equally applicable whatever message is under consideration.
- Entity Headers: again, applicable to both request and response. These headers have information about the request or response body (how it's encoded or encrypted, for example).

Within an HTTP message, headers' names are separated from their values by a colon, multiple values are comma-separated, and each header is separated from the next by a carriage return. Here's how an HTTP request line looks with its headers immediately following:

```
GET /search?q=MIME&ie=UTF-8&oe=UTF-8&hl=en&btnG=Google+Search&meta= HTTP/1.0
Accept: image/*, application/vnd.ms-excel, */*
Accept-Language: en-gb
Accept-Encoding: gzip, deflate
User-Agent: Mozilla/4.0 (compatible; MSIE 6.0; Windows NT 5.1)
Host: www.google.co.uk
Connection: Keep-Alive
 [BLANK LINE]
```

A blank line finishes the header section, separating this from any attached request body.

Our interaction with headers is made easier through the provision of five methods on HttpServletRequest. Here they are in summary:

HttpServletRequest Method	Description
String `getHeader(String name)`	Returns the (first or only) value of the specified request header as a String
Enumeration `getHeaders(String name)`	Returns all values of the specified request header as Strings within an Enumeration
Enumeration `getHeaderNames()`	Returns the names of all request headers as Strings within an Enumeration
long `getDateHeader(String name)`	Returns the value of the specified request header as a **long** primitive representing a date
int `getIntHeader(String name)`	Returns the value of the specified request header as an **int** primitive

exam watch

Method families that return Strings and Enumerations have a typical pattern—compare the getHeader* family with getParameter* (on the ServletRequest interface) and getAttribute* (on several interfaces). If there is no header (or parameter or attribute) of the given name, methods returning a String will return null. Methods returning Enumerations will return an instance of an Enumeration object, but it will be empty. (That said, look carefully at the API documentation for `getHeader(String name)` and `getHeaderNames()`).

The simplest method is `getHeader(String name)`, which returns a String—use this when you know the name of the request header you want and you know there will only ever be one value. If the name is not recognized, **null** is returned. Note that with this and the other header methods, you can specify the name in an entirely case-InSensitive manner.

- `getHeaders(String name)` returns all the values for the given request header name, in the form of an Enumeration containing Strings. The Enumeration object will be empty if the header name is not recognized, or simply not present.

- `getHeaderNames()` returns an Enumeration of Strings representing all available request header names, which you will typically feed into successive calls to `getHeader(String name)` or `getHeaders(String name)`. If there are no request headers, this Enumeration will be empty—although it's most unlikely you would ever receive an HTTP request (at least from a conventional browser) that contained no header information at all.

For `getHeaders(String Name)` and `getHeaderNames()`, it's possible for the servlet container to deny access to the request headers. In this case—and only this case—**null** may be returned instead of an Enumeration object.

You can do everything you need to with the methods above. However, there are a couple of convenience methods when you know that the value returned for a specific request header name will represent either a date or an integer. The two methods are `getDateHeader(String name)` and `getIntHeader(String name)`, which return a **long** (representing a date) and an **int**, respectively. These methods perform conversion from the original String representation of the header's value. Of course, there's the possibility of using these methods inappropriately— one way is to supply a header name that doesn't convert to a **long** date or an **int**. In that case, `getDateHeader()` will throw an IllegalArgumentException, while `getIntHeader()` will throw a NumberFormatException. Both methods return a value of −1 if the requested header is missing. There's an assumption there that `getIntHeader()` could never legitimately return a negative value, while any dates sought with `getDateHeader()` are after midnight on January 1, 1970, Greenwich Mean Time!

Here's a short code example that you might embed in a `doGet()` or `doPost()` method to obtain a date header, and write this to a resulting web page ("response" is the HttpServletResponse object passed as parameter to the `doGet()` or `doPost()` method and "request" is the HttpServletRequest object). Of course, the code runs satisfactorily only if an "If-Modified-Since" date header is supplied in the HTTP request.

```
PrintWriter out = response.getWriter();
long aDateHeader = request.getDateHeader("If-Modified-Since");
DateFormat df = DateFormat.getDateInstance();
String displayDate = df.format(new Date(aDateHeader));
out.write("<br>If-Modified-Since Request Header has value: " + displayDate);
```

What you next need to consider is some of the actual HTTP request headers you're likely to deal with. Table 1-1 summarizes these. The table shows the request header name, describes its purpose briefly, shows an example value, and has a column to indicate whether the value is a date or an integer, and therefore amenable to the use of the `getDateHeader()` or `getIntHeader()` convenience method.

TABLE 1-1 Common Request Headers

Request Header Name	Description	Example Value	int (I) or date as long (D)
Accept	MIME types acceptable to client (we'll explore what a MIME type is later: for now, think file formats).	text/html, text/plain, image/*	
Accept-Charset	ISO character sets acceptable to client. ISO-8859-1 is assumed as the default.	ISO-8859-6	
Accept-Encoding	The content encoding acceptable to client—usually associated with compression methods.	gzip, compress	
Accept-Language	The (human) language acceptable to client. ISO codes are used to denote which language.	en, us	
Authorization	Authentication information. Usually provided after the server has returned a 401 response code (indicating that the request requires user authentication).	(at simplest, user ID and password passed with minimum encoding)	
From	The e-mail address of the request sender. The server might use this to log request origins, or to notify the sender of unwanted requests.	zebedee@ magicroundabout.com	
Host	Internet host and port number from the request URL. Mandatory with HTTP 1.1 requests.	localhost:8080	
If-Modified-Since	If the requested resource has not been modified since the date given, it's not returned: A 304 status code is returned instead.	Thu, 07 May 2003 14:01:31 GMT	D
Max-Forwards	The maximum number of interim proxy servers a request can be forwarded to.	5	I
Referer	The URL of the resource that had the link to the resource now being requested. *Note the misspelling*—should be "Referrer," but "Referer" is kept for historical reasons.	http://www.osborne .com/mybookshelf	
User-Agent	Information about the client software (typically, browser) making the request—helpful to the server in tailoring responses to clients or in gathering statistics.	Mozilla/4.0 (compatible; MSIE 6.0; Windows NT 5.1)	

TABLE 1-2 Common General Headers

General Header Name	Description	Example Value	int (I) or date as long (D)
Cache-Contro	Directives that must be followed by all caches in the request/response chain—a complex area and not one you need to understand for the exam.	max-age=10000 (This means that the resource in the cache must not be returned if over 10,000 seconds old.)	
Connection	A directive about the connection (from server to client or vice versa). Typically used to denote that connections cannot be persistent.	close	
Date	Date and time when a message is originated. This is almost always supplied by the server (in a response), but seldom supplied by a client (in a request).	Tue, 15 Nov 1994 08:12:31 GMT (note the Internet standard date format)	D
Transfer-Encoding	The transfer encoding applied to the message (which gives options around the way the message is structured).	chunked	

At the beginning of this section, we noted that request headers are not the only kind of header. There are general headers, entity headers, and response headers as well. We'll defer discussion of response headers until we look in more detail at responses later in this chapter. However, let's devote a couple of tables to common general headers (Table 1-2) and entity headers (Table 1-3) that you might discover in the request (or place in the response).

Remember that the entity headers (listed in Table 1-3) describe things about the request (or response) body, if this is present in the HTTP message.

Cookies

Cookies are small text files passed between client browsers and web servers. They are used in part as an extended parameter mechanism. Although generally limited to a few thousand bytes in length, a cookie can store a great deal of essential information—often enough to identify the client and to store information about choices made. Nearly every sizable commercial web site uses cookies to "personalize" the user's experience. In this section, we're interested in one direction only—intercepting cookies sent from the browser. We'll look at the other direction (setting up cookies

TABLE 1-3 Common Entity Headers

Entity Header Name	Description	Example Value	int (I) or date as long (D)
Allow	HTTP options permitted for the requested resource. This is the value returned by the HTTP OPTIONS method.	GET, HEAD, OPTIONS, TRACE	
Content-Encoding	A modifier to the media type ("Content-Type"), indicating further encoding of the entity. Used mainly to allow a document to be compressed.	gzip	
Content-Language	The natural (human) language for the entity's intended audience.	En	
Content-Length	Length of the entity in bytes.	8124	I
Content-Location	The URI denoting where the requested resource is to be found on the server. Typically the same as the request URI—but can be different (see the discussion of welcome-file-list in Chapter 2 for one reason that this comes about).	http://www.osborne .com/index.html (This might be returned when the request URI was simply http://www .osborne.com.)	
Content-Type	The MIME type of the entitytext/html.		
Expires	Date/Time by which the response—returned from a cache—is considered stale.	Thu, 17 Nov 1994 09:13:32 GMT	D
Last-Modified	Date/Time on which the entity was last modified, as best the server can determine. This is easy for static resources (by using the date of a file on the file system, for example), but is less obvious for dynamic resources.	Thu, 17 Nov 1994 09:13:32 GMT	D

at the server end to send to the browser) when we get around to the HttpServlet Response interface later in the chapter.

Getting Cookies from the Request

Getting cookies passed with the request is easy—you simply use the `HttpServlet Request.getCookies()` method. This returns an array of javax.servlet.http.Cookie objects, or **null** if none are sent with the request.

You'll need to have at least a passing familiarity with the things you can do with a Cookie. It's a very simple class, consisting entirely of data with some getters and setters. The data attributes are shown in Table 1-4.

TABLE 1-4 Cookie Attributes

Attribute	Type	Mandatory?	Description
Name	String	Yes	May contain only ASCII alphanumeric characters; cannot contain commas, semicolons, or whitespace; must not begin with a $ character. The name can't be changed once passed into the constructor—hence, there is no `setName()` method.
Value	String	Yes	A String value. To be compliant with version 0 cookies (see "Version," below), a value can't have any embedded white space, and most punctuation signs are banned: (){}[]=@,:;?"\/ are explicitly outlawed. That does leave a few options for delimiters—* and—and _, for example.
Domain	String	No	The domain to which the cookie is applicable—if visiting that domain, the browser should send the cookie (e.g., google.com). Although not a mandatory attribute, it's hard to imagine a very functional cookie without this attribute set.
Path	String	No	A path for the client to return the cookie to—specifically, this is meant to match the path of the servlet that set the cookie (e.g., ex0101/CookieMakerServlet). This meaning of the path is that this cookie should be visible to resources invoked with this directory path, or to resources held in any subdirectories of it (e.g., ex0101/CookieMakerServlet/chocchip).
Comment	String	No	A comment meant to explain the purpose of a cookie to a user (if the browser is designed to present such comments)—supported at Version 1 only.
MaxAge	int	No	The maximum age of the cookie in seconds. There are two special values: ■ any negative value: denotes that the cookie should be deleted on exiting the browser (a transient cookie) ■ a value of zero: denotes that the cookie should be deleted
Secure	boolean	No	When set to **true**, indicates that the cookie should be passed over a secure transport layer (HTTPS, SSL).
Version	int	No	0 indicates the original cookie specification defined by Netscape. 1 indicates the standard defined by RFC 2109. It's less widely supported—the default is that cookies are created at version 0 for maximum compatibility (so you have to explicitly set Version (1) if that's what you really want).

A Cookie has a two-argument constructor passing in the mandatory name and value—thereafter, you can set any of its attributes except the name, which is treated with the same kind of sanctity reserved for unique keys on database tables. Cookies are transmitted to servers within HTTP request header fields. You can `clone()` a cookie to make a copy of it.

EXERCISE 1-3

Reading HttpServletRequest Headers and Cookies

In this exercise, you'll write and deploy servlet code to display request headers and the details of any cookies passed with the request. This activity follows the same pattern as the previous exercise. The unique directory is ex0103, and the solution is on the CD in file sourcecode/ch01/ex0103.war.

Write the RequestHeaders Servlet

1. You need to create a source file called RequestHeaders.java, with a package of webcert.ch01.ex0103. Place this in an appropriate package directory (webcert/ch01/ex0103) within the exercise subdirectory ex0103/WEB-INF/classes.
2. Following the package statement, your servlet code should import packages java.io, java.util, javax.servlet, and javax.servlet.http.
3. Your RequestHeaders class should extend HttpServlet (and doesn't need to implement any interfaces).
4. You will override one method from the parent class, which is `doGet()`. The method signature is as follows:

```
protected void doGet(HttpServletRequest request,
                     HttpServletResponse response)
            throws ServletException, IOException
```

5. You need code to set the response type to HTML and to start and finish the web page with appropriate HTML syntax. Copy and adapt the boilerplate code you used for this purpose in the Exercise 1-2.
6. Using the content of this section as a guide, find the appropriate method to discover all the request header names. This returns an Enumeration—set

up a loop to process each element in turn. Use `out.write()` to output each header name as an HTML heading.

7. Within the loop, insert the method that pulls back all values for a given header name, again as an Enumeration. Feed each header name in turn as a parameter to this method. Set up an inner loop to process all the elements representing header values. Use `out.write()` to output each value in turn to a fresh line on the web page.
8. After the above code, include the following line of code, which ensures that an HttpSession object is associated with your use of this servlet. You don't formally learn about HttpSession objects until Chapter 4. I'm including it here only because it practically guarantees the creation of a cookie to be passed from client to server.
9. Retrieve the array of cookies from the HttpServletRequest passed as parameter to the `doGet()` method. Assuming this is not **null**, process each cookie in turn, and display each attribute of the cookie as a line of text on the web page. Refer to Table 1-4 for a list of attributes of cookies.

Running Your Code

10. Start the Tomcat Server (if not started already).
11. Deploy the *solution* code WAR file, ex0103.war (follow the instructions for deploying WAR files in Appendix B).
12. Copy RequestHeaders.class from your directory structure to <Tomcat Installation Directory>/webapps/ex0103/WEB-INF/classes/webcert/ch01/ex0103 (overwrite the solution version).
13. Point your browser to the appropriate URL. For a default Tomcat installation, this will be

    ```
    http://localhost:8080/ex0103/RequestHeaders
    ```

    If you don't see any cookie information at first, then refresh the browser page. The second and subsequent accesses to the RequestHeaders servlet in the same session should at least guarantee that you see a cookie whose name is JSESSONID.

CERTIFICATION OBJECTIVE

Responses (Exam Objective 1.3)

Using the HttpServletResponse interface, write code to set an HTTP response header, set the content type of the response, acquire a text stream for the response, acquire a binary stream for the response, redirect an HTTP request to another URL, or add cookies to the response.

We've seen some of the fundamental things we can do with HttpServletRequest. Now we're going to deal with its counterpart, HttpServletResponse, a class that conveniently wrappers up the HTTP message sent back to the requester. It's available as the second parameter in the set of `doXXX()` methods within a servlet.

HTTPServletResponse

We'll explore how to set header fields in the response. Some of these header fields we met already when we looked at how to read them from HttpServletRequest. Now we'll discover how to write header fields, some of which have the same name, and others that are new and unique to the response. Earlier, we were able to read cookies from the request; now we'll see how it's possible to write cookies to the response—and at the same time discover that a cookie is really just a specialized kind of response header. Maybe the servlet we invoke isn't quite what the client needs, so we'll explore how easy it is to instruct the client to redirect itself to a different URL.

There are many possibilities for the material you transmit in the response. You'll see how you can help the recipient client by at least hinting at what type of content is in the HTTP response message. You'll also see how to deal with the two fundamental divisions of content—textual and binary—the response provides both Writer- and Stream-based approaches.

Setting Response Header Fields

For the request, we were interested in reading the values of header fields coming into our servlet. For the response, we are interested in setting the values of header fields to send back to the client. We'll explore in a moment the range of methods available on the HttpServletResponse, which complement the getHeader* methods on HttpServletRequest.

In the previous section, on HttpServletRequest, we looked at most common possibilities for header fields. You'll want to look back at the tables in that section. One table listed header fields that applied only to the request, but Tables 1-2 and 1-3 described general and entity header fields that are just as applicable to the response. Table 1-5 shows the most commonly used header fields that you would expect to find only in a response.

There are two approaches to setting headers on the response field. I'd suggest that you most want to use `addHeader(String name, String value)`. This will keep adding values, even where the name is the same (which is just the effect you want if there are multiple values to add—perhaps on the Accept header, for example).

TABLE 1-5 Response Header Fields

Response Header Name	Description	Example Value	int (I) or date as long (D)
Age	If the server has returned the response from a cache, this figure determines the age (in seconds) of the cached resource—giving an indication of its "freshness."	814487	I
Location	Used to redirect the requester to a URI other than the requested URI. Used "under the covers" by the `sendRedirect()` method.	http://www.osborne.com/altlocation.html	
Retry-After	If a service is unavailable, the time after which a client should try again. Could be a time in seconds *or* an absolute date/time.	180 Thu, 07 May 2003 11:59:59 GMT	I D
Server	Information about the web server providing the response—for example, the product and version number.	Apache 2.0 45-dev (Unix)	
Set-Cookie	Used by a server to ask a client to create a cookie according to the details set in the value. Used "under the covers" by the `addCookie()` method.	(A String—usually fairly long—containing cookie fields. Format varies according to cookie version.)	
WWW-Authenticate	Accompanies a response status code of 401 (unauthorized). This field describes the authentication method required and expected parameters (authentication methods are discussed in Chapter 5).	BASIC	

There's also a `setHeader(String name, String value)` that overwrites existing values.

You may well wonder what happens if you use* `addHeader()` *to add multiple values for the same header name, and then invoke* `setHeader()` *on the same header name. Do all the values you added get obliterated in favor of the single value you have just added with* `setHeader()`*? The API documentation is silent on this point, and the answer appears to be no:* `setHeader()` *just replaces one of the existing values with its own setting—from my testing, the first one added with* `addHeader()`*. My advice would be don't use* `setHeader()` *for multiple value headers; use it only to replace (or add) a single value header field. Otherwise, you will confuse those maintaining your code. You can always use* `HttpServletResponse.containsHeader(String headerName)` *to determine if a value has been set for a given header name already—as you've probably guessed, this returns a boolean primitive.

Most of the art of writing headers has to do with, first, knowing the header name for your purpose and, second, providing appropriate and well-formatted values for the header name. Tables 1-2, 1-3, and 1-5 help you get started with that and give you more than sufficient guidance for the exam. There are two pairs of convenience methods when you know the value you are dealing with is either an integer or a date. Take the case of the header Retry-After—this can accept either an integer (representing a number of seconds) or a date. So you can use

```
response.addIntHeader("Retry-After", 180);
```

to add a header to tell the client to try again in 180 seconds, or

```
Date retryAfter = new Date();
long retryAfterMillis = retryAfter.getTime() + 180000;
response.addDateHeader("Retry-After", retryAfterMillis);
```

to achieve the same effect with dates. There are "set" equivalents of both the above methods to replace values instead of adding to what's already there.

Redirection

HttpServletResponse also provides other methods that don't set headers directly, but instead do this "under the covers." These may set appropriate headers and sometimes do additional work in order to get the job done. A good example is the `sendRedirect()` method. When a client makes a call to a servlet, there is the op-

FIGURE 1-8

Redirection

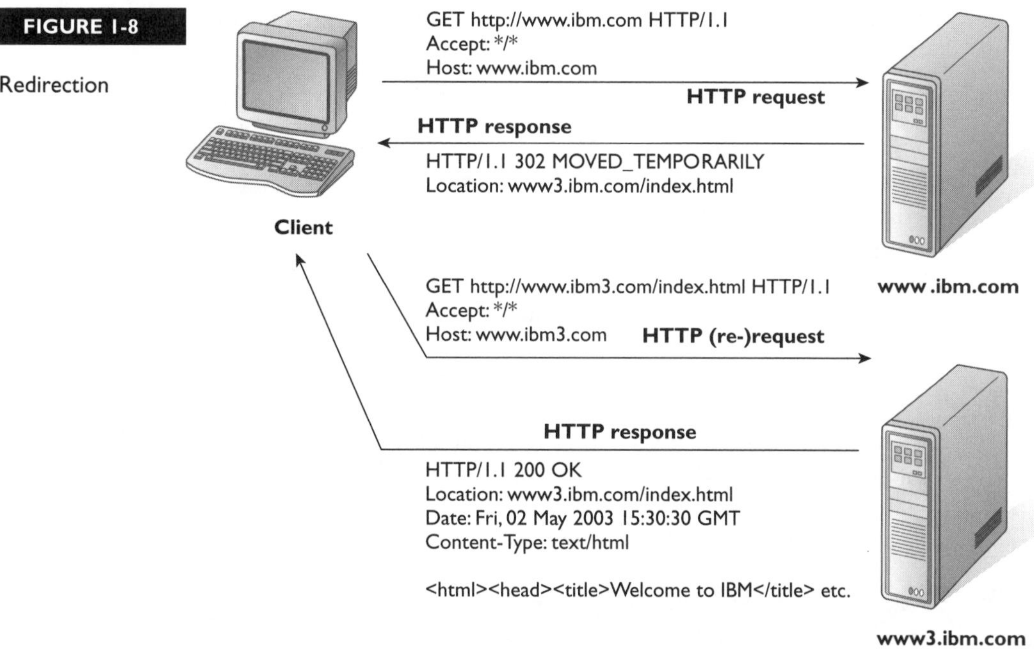

tion to send an alternative URL back—and the client will understand on receiving this URL to look there instead. It works as shown in Figure 1-8.

The redirection is achieved through the `HttpServletResponse.sendRedirect (String pathname)` method. The String parameter in this method is a path capable of conversion to a URL. This can be either relative or absolute. Let's consider a request for a servlet that has a call to this method, which looks like this:

```
http://localhost:8080/ex0104/servlet/RedirectorServlet
```

In this example, `/servlet/RedirectorServlet` is a path to a specific servlet inside the web application `/ex0104`. The servlet container's root is `http://localhost:8080/` (if running under Tomcat, you'll find the main help page at this location).

The RedirectorServlet code might redirect to a completely different domain, with code like this:

```
response.sendRedirect("http://www.otherdomain.com/otherResource");
```

If the parameter begins with a forward slash, this is interpreted as relative to the root of the servlet container. The code might look like this:

```
response.sendRedirect("/otherResource");
```

The servlet container would translate this to the following URL:

```
http://localhost:8080/otherResource
```

If you don't lead with a forward slash, the parameter is interpreted as relative to the path in which the original resource is found. So if you asked for the following address:

```
http://localhost:8080/ex0104/servlet/RedirectorServlet
```

and the code of RedirectorServlet had the following redirection request:

```
response.sendRedirect("subservlet/OtherPlace");
```

then the server would assume that the search for this resource should begin with the same path that found RedirectorServlet and tell the client to redirect to

```
http://localhost:8080/ex0104/servlet/subservlet/OtherPlace
```

exam watch

Redirection achieves roughly the same effect as forwarding, which we meet later. Both effectively divert the request and cause a different resource to be served back to the client. The big difference is that `sendRedirect()` actually sends a message back to the client, so the client makes a re-request for the actual resource required. With forwarding, all the action stays on the server.

What has all this to do with response headers? Well, the call to **`sendRedirect()`** causes the servlet container to fill out a "Location" header with the (full) alternative URL, according to the rules given above. But this isn't quite enough by itself. The servlet container must also tell the client that the resource has been moved temporarily. In technical terms, this is achieved by setting a response status code with the **`setStatus()`** method on response. If you wanted to achieve the same effect as a **`sendRedirect()`**, you could execute code such as the following:

```
response.setStatus(HttpServletResponse.SC_TEMPORARY_REDIRECT);
response.setHeader("Location", "http://www.osborne.com/index.jsp");
```

HttpServletResponse comes loaded with a set of constant values (public static final int variables) to represent different possible values for the response status code.

Setting Cookies on the Response As we learned earlier, cookies are small pieces of textual information sent between server and client. In this case, we're interested in attaching cookies to a response for the browser to receive them—and if not refused, store them. A browser is expected to support 20 cookies for each Web server, 300 cookies total, and may limit cookie size to 4 KB each. The rules on cookie creation and attributes are covered in the earlier section on getting cookies from the request. To attach a cookie to the response, simply invoke the `addCookie(Cookie cookie)` method as many times as you need to add cookies. There is no "remove cookie" method—though `addCookie()` is a convenience method to add a header with the name "Set-Cookie" and a correctly formatted cookie content. In theory, you could use `setHeader("Set-Cookie", newValue)` to change the value of an existing cookie, but then you would have to do the formatting of the value yourself as a String.

Sending Back Content in the Response As you may well ask at this point, "Setting headers and cookies is all very well, but how do I simply send back stuff in the HTTP response message?" We couldn't avoid introducing part of this in the exercises, but now it's time to look at the topic in a little more detail.

The first decision you have to (well, should) make is this: What kind of information am I sending back to the client? This means setting the correct content type with the `ServletResponse.setContentType(String mimeType)` method. Although there's no validation as such on the parameter passed in (beyond the fact that it has to be a String), you should provide information that a browser will understand, in the form of a registered MIME type. MIME stands for Multipurpose Internet Mail Extension, but despite the "mail" component in the acronym, it has become accepted as the universal standard for describing formats (primarily, file formats) for transmission through any Internet protocol (not just e-mail). You can easily find a list of allowed MIME types on the Internet: A good one is at ftp://ftp.isi.edu/in-notes/iana/assignments/media-types/media-types. One of the most common is "text/html," which indicates text using HTML markup. The MIME type "text/plain" denotes text with no markup at all. Generally, a MIME type consists of a top-level classification (text, image, application), followed by a slash, followed by a subclassification (often represented as the typical file extension).

Content type is one thing. The exact encoding you are using for your files is another. This could range from simple ASCII through to full Unicode, with plenty of variants in between. You can, in fact, set the encoding along with the content type as part of the String passed to `setContentType()`. The API documentation tells you how. You can set the encoding separately through the `setCharacterEncoding()`. You don't necessarily have to do this: Often, you can get away with whatever default encoding is supplied on your server (probably ISO-8859-1).

It's all very well defining the type of your content, but at some point you have to produce the content. Your first decision is whether the content is character-based or byte-based, for you have both a PrintWriter and an OutputStream associated with the response, but you can't use both at once. To get hold of the PrintWriter, all you have to do is execute

```
PrintWriter out = response.getWriter();
```

You know this already, as you have had to use this code from the first servlet you wrote in Exercise 1-2. You then have access to all the methods that java.io.PrintWriter allows, though the most convenient is undoubtedly the overloaded `out.write()` method, to which you typically pass a String. This means that if your MIME type is "text/html," you can start writing (preferably well-formed) HTML syntax directly to the Writer—as we have been doing throughout. Writing HTML in Java code seems bizarre when first encountered, but you quickly get used to it, and it's a fine approach for simple, dynamic web pages. You have the option of flushing the PrintWriter (`out.flush()`), which is a pretty good idea if you want to make sure that all the output written has been committed to the response. You can even close the PrintWriter (`out.close()`), though this may not be a good idea unless you know that your servlet is the last thing that will contribute to the composition of the response (as you'll learn later, a servlet may be one small part in a chain of other servlets and/or filters).

If it's a binary file format you want to send in your response, then

```
OutputStream out = response.getOutputStream()
```

is the right choice for you. You'll be expected to know the range of methods for this class and the techniques you learned for the SCJP in mastering the java.io package. At its most basic, you can write each byte individually with out.write (int byteToWrite).

EXERCISE 1-4

Using HttpServletResponse

You'll write two servlets in this exercise: one to return a binary file to the requester, and another to simply redirect to this image-loading servlet. The unique directory for this exercise is ex0104, and the solution is on the CD in file sourcecode/ch01/ex0104.war.

Write the ImageLoader Servlet

1. You need to create a source file called ImageLoader.java, with a package of webcert.ch01.ex0104. Place this in an appropriate package directory (webcert/ch01/ex0104) within the exercise subdirectory ex0104/WEB-INF/classes.
2. You'll need a gif image—any image file will do—placed directly in directory ex0104.
3. Following the package statement, your servlet code should import packages java.io, javax.servlet, and javax.servlet.http.
4. Your ImageLoader class should extend HttpServlet (and doesn't need to implement any interfaces).
5. Override the `doGet()` method. (Refer back to previous exercises if the signature isn't yet familiar.)
6. Set the response content type to "image/gif."
7. Obtain the full path to the example image file with the following line of code (we'll learn more about ServletContext APIs later in the book):

```
String path = getServletContext().getRealPath("exampleimage.gif");
```

8. Use the path so obtained to create a File object.
9. Set the response content length to the size of the File.
10. Wrapper the File object in a FileInputStream, and wrapper that in a Buffered InputStream.
11. Obtain the OutputStream from the response.
12. Write the contents of the BufferedInputStream to the response's Output Stream.
13. Compile the servlet to the same directory as the source.

Write the Redirector Servlet

14. You need to create a source file called Redirector.java, with a package of webcert.ch01.ex0104. Place this in an appropriate package directory (webcert/ch01/ex0104) within the exercise subdirectory ex0104/WEB-INF/classes.
15. Following the package statement, your servlet code should import packages java.io, javax.servlet, and javax.servlet.http.

16. Your Redirector class should extend HttpServlet (and doesn't need to implement any interfaces).
17. Override the `doGet()` method. (Refer back to previous exercises if the signature isn't yet familiar.)
18. Have the servlet accept a parameter called "location"—store the value in a String.
19. Pass the location String as a parameter into the response's redirection method.
20. Compile the servlet in the same directory as the source.

Write redirect.html

21. Create an HTML file called redirect.html directly in directory ex0104.
22. Create a form within the file, whose action is "Redirector" and whose method is GET (you can leave this out—as then the default method for the form will be GET).
23. Create an input text field within the form named "location." You'll use this to type the URL to redirect to (so make it a reasonable size).
24. Create a submit button within the form.

Run the Code

25. Start the Tomcat Server (if not started already).
26. Deploy the *solution* code WAR file, ex0104.war (follow the instructions for deploying WAR files in Appendix B).
27. Copy redirect.html and your image file from your directory structure to the <Tomcat Installation Directory>/webapps/ex0104 directory (overwrite solution versions).
28. Copy ImageLoader.class and Redirector.class from your directory structure to <Tomcat Installation Directory>/webapps/ex0104/WEB-INF/classes/webcert/ch01/ex0104 (overwrite the solution versions).
29. Point your browser to the appropriate URL. For a default Tomcat installation, this will be

    ```
    http://localhost:8080/ex0104/redirect.html
    ```

30. Type in ImageLoader into the text field, for this is the servlet you want to redirect to. Your image should load into the browser.

CERTIFICATION OBJECTIVE

Servlet Life Cycle (Exam Objective 1.4)

Describe the purpose and event sequence of the servlet life cycle: (1) servlet class loading, (2) servlet instantiation, (3) call the init method, (4) call the service method, and (5) call destroy method.

Now that we've seen some of the practicalities of servlets—responding to requests and supplying responses—we'll throw the net a bit wider in the next examination objective. At the end of this chapter, we'll look at the entire lifespan of a servlet and see what support the servlet container is bound to provide and the rules it has to follow.

Life Cycle

So far, we've focused more or less exclusively on overridden `doXXX()` methods in our servlets. We have buried the fact that all these methods are called from the `service()` method in the parent class we override, HttpServlet. There's no need to override `service()` itself, as it already does a splendid job of converting HTTP requests into appropriate `doXXX()` method calls. However, what we do need to take note of is that the `service()` method comes at the center of the servlet life cycle—and that's true not just for HTTP, but in the plain world of GenericServlet as well.

The certification objective asks you to consider the following stages of the servlet life cycle, and it is kind enough to list them in order:

1. Servlet class loading—the point where static data (if any) in your servlet are initialized
2. Servlet instantiation—the point where instance data (if any) in your servlet are initialized, and the no-argument constructor (if present) is called
3. `init()`—the initialization method called when a servlet instance is created
4. `service()`—the method called to perform the work
5. `destroy()`—the method called when a servlet is taken out of service

We need to consider in a bit more detail when each of these milestones occurs, and what they are good for. To set the stage, Figure 1-9 shows the five stages in pictures.

FIGURE 1-9

The Servlet Life Cycle

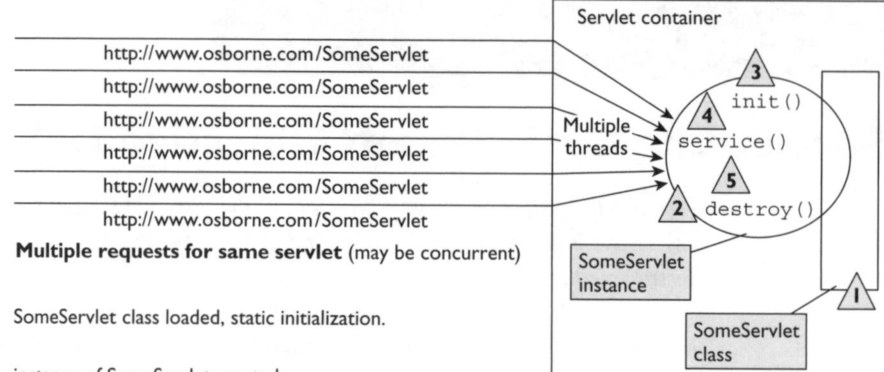

1 SomeServlet class loaded, static initialization.

2 instance of SomeServlet created

3 `init()` called

Requests to SomeServlet processed by calling `service()` method. May occur in multiple concurrent threads.

Servlet taken out of `service()`:
- `destroy()` called
- instance of SomeServlet garbage collected.

Servlet Class Loading and Servlet Instantiation

You are bound to be asked about when servlets are loaded and instantiated; it's a classic exam topic. There'll be questions that lead you astray by talking about events that are always linked to servlet creation. Actually, there is only one rule to remember: The servlet must be loaded and instantiated before the first request for it is processed. It's pretty obvious that the servlet must be there to service the request! The implication of the rule, though, is that it doesn't matter when instantiation happens. It might be "just in time"—the servlet is loaded at the point where a request comes through for it (which might lead to a performance penalty for the first user to access the servlet). Or it might happen as soon as the servlet container is started up. Or it might happen at any point in between, according to the servlet container's whim.

For any given declaration of a servlet (and what that means we learn in Chapter 2), there will—normally—be one instance. That's not to say the servlet can deal with only one request at a time. Again—normally—the same servlet instance can be used by multiple Java threads to maximize throughput. It's a very efficient model. However, it does mean that servlet instance data can be accessed by any of those threads at any time, so the best approach is to avoid using servlet instance data al-

FIGURE 1-10

The Deprecated SingleThread Model

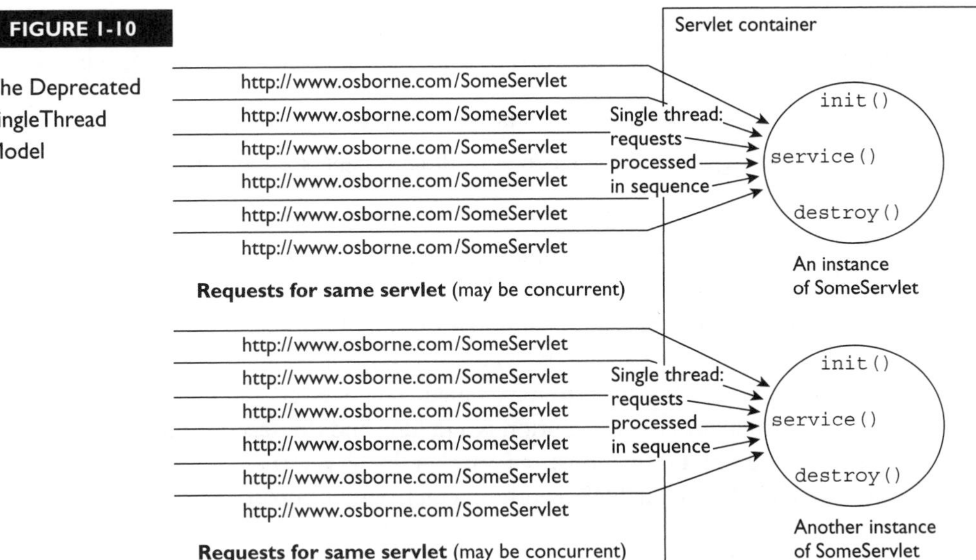

together. You can get around the problem by having your servlet implement the (now deprecated) SingleThreadModel interface. It's a marker interface—no methods to implement—but it's a sign to the servlet container to ensure that any one instance of the servlet has only one request accessing it at a time. To avoid a single-instance bottleneck, servlet containers can instantiate multiple instances of a servlet (as a less efficient but bearable alternative to having multiple threads going through a single instance). Figure 1-10 shows how it looks.

But the good news (for exam purposes, especially) is that you should need to know about this interface only for historical reasons. Its use is heavily discouraged, and it's deprecated: Servlet containers probably still support it for backward compatibility, but its time has come and gone. And any mention of it has been removed from the exam syllabus.

In the next chapter, you'll learn that a servlet can be set to "load on startup." The only way in which this affects the process is that the servlet is loaded and instantiated on startup of the web application.

The `init()` Method

Initialization code for a servlet could go in the constructor. There's nothing wrong in having a zero-argument constructor for a servlet, but it's more usual to override the `public void init()` method and place initialization code there. The servlet container is guaranteed to call this method once—and only once—on instantiation of the servlet. Here are the sorts of things you might do in this method:

- Set up expensive resources (database connections, object pools, etc.)
- Do one-off initialization (such as reading configuration files into Java objects in memory)

The `init()` method must complete successfully before the servlet container will allow any requests to be processed by the servlet. Two things might go wrong. The method might throw a ServletException, or it might run out of time. Dealing with out of time first: A server should provide its own means of setting a default time beyond which `init()` is deemed to have failed. The ServletException is a little more complex. A straight ServletException is a failure, and the servlet container can abandon this instance and try to construct another. However, there is a subclass of Servlet Exception called UnavailableException, which can be constructed in two ways:

- With a message—this denotes permanent unavailability. The servlet container should log the fault and not necessarily try to create another instance. The nature of the error is likely to require some operator intervention—changing some configuration information, perhaps.
- With a message *and* a time limit (in seconds)—this denotes temporary unavailability. There's no absolute definition of what the servlet container should do under these circumstances. A sensible resolution would be to block requests to the

exam watch

You might get questioned about the parentage of the `init()` method. The `init()` method is a convenience method in the GenericServlet class. The servlet container actually calls `Servlet.init(ServletConfig config)`, passing in a servlet configuration object (we'll learn more about that in the following chapters). This method does some essential initialization of its own, including loading any initialization parameters associated with the servlet. The no-parameter `init()` saves you the bother in your servlets of overriding `init(config)` and then having to remember to call `super(config)` before adding your own initialization. The servlet container actually calls `init(config)`—which is found in GenericServlet—and this calls `init()` after completing its own work. If you have overridden the no-parameter `init()`, your version of the method will be found polymorphically.

servlet until the time limit has expired, then allow them through if the `init()` method has successfully completed.

The `service()` Method

Let's review the key points about this method, some of which we've met already:

- The method is called by the servlet container in response to a client request.
- The method is defined in the Servlet interface.
- The method is implemented in the GenericServlet and HttpServlet classes.
- The method accepts a ServletRequest and ServletResponse as parameters.
- There is an overloaded version of the method in HttpServlet that dispatches to the appropriate `doXXX()` methods. The overloaded version accepts an Http ServletRequest and HttpServletResponse as parameters.
- If there are multiple requests, these may come through on multiple threads. So multiple threads may simultaneously access the `service()` method for a single servlet instance.
- There may be no client requests at all, and that means the `service()` method may never get executed.

The `destroy()` Method

When a servlet instance is taken out of service, the `destroy()` method is called—only once for that instance. It's an opportunity to reclaim all the expensive resources that may have been set up in `init()`.

What prompts a servlet container to take a servlet out of service is, like startup, somewhat arbitrary. Clearly, this method should be called if the web application or entire web server is closed down. However, there may be more transient reasons for taking a servlet out of service: to conserve memory, for example (you get the feeling that a web server would be have to be in a pretty bad way to undertake this sort of reclamation, but it's possible).

There are some conditions that dictate whether or not `destroy()` can be called:

1. All threads executing a `service()` method on this instance must have ended—or if not ended, gone beyond a server-defined time limit.
2. `destroy()` is never called if `init()` failed. It's inappropriate to call a method to tear down what was never set up in the first place.

EXERCISE 1-5

Exploring the Servlet Life Cycle

In this exercise, you'll write a servlet that tracks its own life cycle. You'll be able to tell when the class loads, when an instance is made, and when the life cycle methods are called. The unique directory for this exercise is ex0105, and the solution is on the CD in file sourcecode/ch01/ex0105.war.

Write the LifeCycle Servlet

1. Create a source file called LifeCycle.java, with a package of webcert.ch01.ex0105. Place this in an appropriate package directory (webcert/ch01/ex0105) within the exercise subdirectory ex0105/WEB-INF/classes.
2. Following the package statement, your servlet code should import packages java.io, javax.servlet, and javax.servlet.http. (Note: Future exercises won't mention a list of imports—you're ready to handle this yourself!)
3. Your LifeCycle class should extend HttpServlet (and doesn't need to implement any interfaces). Again, future exercises won't repeat this information.
4. You will override the `init()`, `destroy()`, and `doGet()` methods in your servlet. Also, you will supply a zero-argument public constructor.
5. In each of the above methods, output some text to indicate what method is being executed. Don't try to write this to the response (which in any case is only available in the `doGet()` method)—go for something simple, such as `System.out.println()`, to put text on the server's console. For a more advanced approach, use Java's native logging facilities.
6. Also include "static initializer" code. This is code between curly braces within the class but outside any method. It will be called at the point where the class is loaded. This code should also do a `System.out.println()` to indicate that the class is being loaded.

Run the Solution Code and Your Code

7. Start the Tomcat Server (if not started already).
8. Deploy the *solution* code WAR file, ex0105.war (follow the instructions for deploying WAR files in Appendix B).

9. Copy LifeCycle.class from your directory structure to <Tomcat Installation Directory>/webapps/ex0105/WEB-INF/classes/webcert/ch01/ex0105 (overwrite the solution version).
10. This time, restart (or stop and start) the Tomcat Server.
11. Check to see if there is any output from the LifeCycle servlet already on the console (is the class loaded on server startup?).
12. Point your browser to the appropriate URL for the servlet. This is likely to be

    ```
    http://localhost:8080/ex0105/LifeCycle
    ```

13. Note any additional messages on the console. Refresh the browser page a few times to ensure that you enter the `doGet()` method without going back through `init()`. Remember that the `doGet()` method is called from `service()`, in case you were wondering where `service()` fitted into the picture. My Tomcat console is shown below, from my run of the exercise (don't be alarmed by the Exception: I print a stack trace to the console specifically to show that `doGet()` is called from `service()`).

14. Finally, recompile your version of LifeCycle.java, such that your compiled class file replaces the existing servlet class solution file LifeCycle.class. See if Tomcat picks up the change to the class file—you should see a call to the `destroy()` method as the old class is unloaded. Call your own version of LifeCycle by pointing to the appropriate URL as at step 10 above, to check that it works OK.

CERTIFICATION SUMMARY

This chapter has discussed the certification objectives that are really fundamental to the way servlets work. You started off by learning about the seven HTTP methods—GET, POST, HEAD, OPTIONS, TRACE, PUT, and DELETE. You saw that HTTP (hypertext transfer protocol) is a high-level protocol built on top of TCP/IP and used for the transfer of messages across the Internet between client and server machines.

You looked at HTTP messages in some detail and saw that they contain three components: an initial line, some headers, and an (optional) body. You learned that this structure holds true for both requests and responses, though clearly the exact content of requests and response differs a little. You learned that a request line consists of the method itself (one of the seven), the target URI, and an HTTP version. You saw a number of request headers following this request line, some typical ones being Accept (to indicate what file formats the client can cope with), User-Agent (to describe the client software), and Host (to state which server the client is targeting). You learned that the request body might contain parameters (name/value pairs) when the HTTP method is POST.

Regarding the seven methods, you saw that GET generally obtains a resource, while POST may get a resource but is more intended for sending data to the server. You learned that HEAD does everything that GET does, short of retrieving the resource itself. You saw that OPTIONS told you what you could do with a target resource. You found out that PUT and DELETE are much more rarely used, but serve to place resources at or remove resources from a given URL. You learned that POST, PUT, and DELETE are "unsafe" methods in that they can cause a permanent change to server state. Also, all the methods except POST are idempotent—that is, you can repeat them over and over again, yet expect no difference to occur just because you repeat the method call to the same URL.

Most importantly, you learned how the servlet world relates to HTTP. You saw that a J2EE servlet container will take the raw HTTP request and translate this to a method call within a servlet. A GET method is translated to a `doGet()` call, a POST to a `doPost()`, and so on. Each of these methods receives two parameters—an HttpServletRequest object (representing the HTTP request) and an HttpServlet Response object (representing the HTTP response).

From there, you went on to look at HTML forms because you need to learn how parameters generated from such forms could be made available to your servlets. You saw that the form itself began with a `<form>` opening tag, whose `action` attribute targets the servlet you want to execute. You also learned that `<form>` has an optional method attribute, which you often want to set to POST, and when left out defaults to GET. Within the opening and closing form tags, you saw that you could create several sorts of form controls. You learned that most of these are controlled by the `<input>` tag, which has numerous values for the attribute `type`. A `type` of `text`, `password` or `hidden`, creates a straight line of text—visible, concealed when typed, or hidden altogether. You saw that you are not restricted to straight text—a `type` of `checkbox` or `radio` creates tick boxes and mutually exclusive radio buttons, respectively. You learned that for form controls to be passed as parameters, they must have their `name` attribute set—and where the value isn't directly input by the user, the `value` attribute also.

You went on to learn about the `<select>` tag, which allows the user to define from a predefined list of options defined within individual `<option>` subelements. You saw that this could work in two modes—for selection of a single value or of multiple values (achieved by including the "multiple" attribute within the opening `<select>` tag). You also met the `<textarea>` element, for input of multiple lines of text in a single control.

Finally, on form controls, you saw how to create different sorts of buttons—again through use of the `<input>` element. You met the `types` of `submit`, `reset`, and `button`. As you found, pressing on a submit type actually sends the form data to the target of the action, along with the named parameters. You saw that the reset type keeps the action on the client browser and simply restores the values in form controls as they were before any user input took place. You finally saw that the button type is meant for connection with custom scripting (for example, with JavaScript) and that, again, all the action stays within the client browser.

You saw that when parameters are submitted, they are passed as name/value pairs separated by ampersands—for example, *user=David&password=revealed*. You learned that multiple parameters with the same name could be passed, simply by repeating the name with a fresh value—for example, *country=DK&country=GB*. You saw parameters passed in the URL when the HTTP method is GET and didn't see parameters passed when the HTTP method is POST, for they are then concealed in the request body.

You then met the servlet APIs for intercepting parameters. You saw that the ServletRequest object had useful methods for this—`getParameter()` to get hold of the first value from a named parameter, `getParameterValues()` to get hold of all values for a named parameter as a String array, and `getParameterNames()` to get an Enumeration of Strings with all parameter names present in the request. You also met `getParameterMap()`, which returns an Enumeration of all keys and their values. You also learned that you could get at parameters the hard way through a request's InputStream—and also never to mix and match the two approaches (APIs vs. InputStream).

You went on to look at more methods on the HttpServletRequest object, passed as the first parameter into `doXXX()` methods. This first of these concerned request headers—each a piece of information within the request consisting of a name with single or multiple values. You met APIs for getting hold of the headers within the request, such as `getHeader()` returning a single value for the supplied name. You saw that you could get all values as an Enumeration for a given header name using `getHeaders()`—and that if you needed to find out the names themselves, you could use `getHeaderNames()`, also returning an Enumeration. You saw that there were also convenience methods—the `getDateHeader()` and `getIntHeader()` methods—specifically for headers whose values are dates or integers. You then met the `getCookies()` method, which returns an array of javax.servlet.http.Cookie objects. You saw that cookies come in two versions—0 or 1—and that the only mandatory attributes in both cases are a name and a value. Other attributes include a domain, a path, a maximum age, and a comment. You learned that you could create a cookie with a two-parameter constructor, accepting the mandatory attributes of `name` and `value`, and attach this to the HttpServletResponse object with the `addCookie()` method.

There were several more things you learned about the HttpServletResponse object. You saw that just as you can read headers from HttpServletRequest, so you can write headers to HttpServletResponse. You saw that there are add* and set* methods to do this, with each call to an add* method for the same-named header placing an additional value against the header, and with each call to a set* method replacing a value already there (if any). You were warned against the use of set* methods for multiple value headers. Like the request methods, there are convenience methods for integers and dates: an `addIntHeader()`, `setIntHeader()`, `addDateHeader()`, and `setDateHeader()`.

You also learned how to achieve redirection using the `HttpServletResponse.sendRedirect()` method. You saw that this can accept a String representing a complete or partial URL—partial URLs being interpreted as relative to the web server's root (when beginning with a forward slash) and relative to the location of the redirecting resource (when not beginning with a forward slash). You learned that the server converts a partial URL to a full URL, then transmits this back to the client with an appropriate response code, so it's up to the client to re-request the suggested URL. You also learned that the mechanics of this (setting a Location header and an appropriate response code) are concealed within the `sendRedirect()` method.

Finally, you met the methods you are likely to use most often in HttpServlet Response: those to do with setting a content type and with actually writing content. You saw that you should use the `setContentType()` method to supply a suitable MIME type for the content, represented by a String such as "text/html." You learned that you can supply an optional character encoding at the same time, or set this separately. You then saw that you can obtain a PrintWriter or OutputStream from the response, using `getWriter()` and `getOutputStream()` respectively—but that you should never mix and match the two within the same response. You saw that you can use the regular java.io methods on these classes (most typically, `write()`) to place content in the response.

In the final section of the chapter, you learned about the servlet life cycle. You learned that the web container generally makes only one instance of a servlet class (though there was a mysterious sentence about "if the class is declared only once," which will make sense when we look at the deployment descriptor in Chapter 2). You learned that the web container does any static class initialization, then calls the no-argument servlet constructor (if there is a bespoke one in your servlet), and then calls the `init(ServletConfig config)` method—and you are guaranteed that the `init(ServletConfig config)` method will only ever be called once for any given instance of a servlet. You learned that this whole initialization process can take place any time before the first request to the servlet is processed. You saw then that if the servlet received any requests (and it might not), the web container calls the `service()` method—which in the case of HTTP servlets, dispatches to the appropriate `doXXX()` method. Finally, you learned that when a web container takes a servlet out of service, it calls the servlet's `destroy()` method (just once) before that instance of the servlet is garbage collected. You learned that for `destroy()` to be called, certain conditions have to be true: (1) initialization must have completed successfully, and (2) all requests against the servlet must be complete *or* some server-defined time limit must have expired.

You briefly met the SingleThreadModel, which keeps requests unique to particular instances of servlets. However, you learned that knowledge of this is required only for legacy code you maintain and that the interface has been deprecated and dropped from the exam syllabus.

TWO-MINUTE DRILL

HTTP Methods

- HTTP is a simple request/response protocol underpinning most web applications on the Internet, regardless of whether they are written in Java.
- J2EE servlet containers provide a Java "superstructure" built around the HTTP protocol.
- HTTP works through seven methods, supplied with the request. These are GET, POST, HEAD, OPTIONS, TRACE, PUT, and DELETE.
- GET is used to obtain a web resource, usually in a "read only" fashion.
- POST is used typically to send data to a web server, but is also frequently used to return web resources in addition.
- HEAD is equivalent to GET except that it doesn't return the web resource—only meta-information about the resource.
- OPTIONS lists which of the seven methods can be executed against a target resource.
- TRACE is for debug purposes and reflects a client request back from the server to the client (to check how it might have changed en route).
- PUT places a resource at the URL that is the target of the HTTP request.
- DELETE does the opposite of PUT—it removes a resource from the URL that is the target of the HTTP request.
- PUT and DELETE are disallowed on most web servers. They are "unsafe" methods. POST is also deemed an "unsafe" method. "Unsafe" means that the client may be held accountable for the action.
- By contrast, GET, OPTIONS, HEAD, and TRACE are "safe" methods that should never execute anything for which the client can be held to account.
- The HTTP specification defines most methods as "idempotent," which means that if you execute them more than once, the result is the same as executing them only once (in terms of the state the web server is left in).
- Of the seven methods, POST is the only one that is not considered "idempotent."
- HTTP requests consist of a request line, some headers, and an (optional) message body.

- HTTP responses are similar: response line, some headers, and message body.
- The seven HTTP methods map on to servlet methods of the same name with a "do" in front (e.g., POST maps on to `doPost()`).
- The `doXXX()` methods receive two objects as parameters—the first representing the HTTP request and the second the HTTP response.

Form Parameters

- The primary means by which user input is made available to a web application is through an HTML form.
- An HTML `<form>` element consists of an opening and closing form tag, containing other elements representing user interface elements on the form (form controls).
- The opening `<form>` tag has two crucial attributes: *action* (used to target a resource in the web application—typically a servlet or JSP) and `method` (to denote the HTTP method).
- If the *method* attribute is left out, the default method invoked is an HTTP GET.
- It's more usual to set method="POST."
- Many form controls are created using the `<input>` element.
- The `<input>` element has three crucial attributes: *type*, *name*, and *value*.
- The type attribute determines what sort of user interface component should be drawn by the browser within the web page (e.g., text field, checkbox, radio button).
- If `<input>` elements have a `name` and `value` set, these are passed in the HTTP request as parameters, separated by an equal sign. Each name/value pair is separated from the next by an ampersand. Example: *user=david&password=indiscrete*.
- Parameters are attached to the URL when the HTTP method is GET, separated from the rest of the URL by a question mark (e.g., `http://localhost:8080/login?user=david&password=indiscrete`).
- Parameters are passed in the request body when the HTTP method is POST.
- An input element doesn't necessarily have the value attribute set when this is supplied by direct user input. A text field (`type="text"`) is a good example—by typing into the field, the browser knows to associate the value with the named form control.

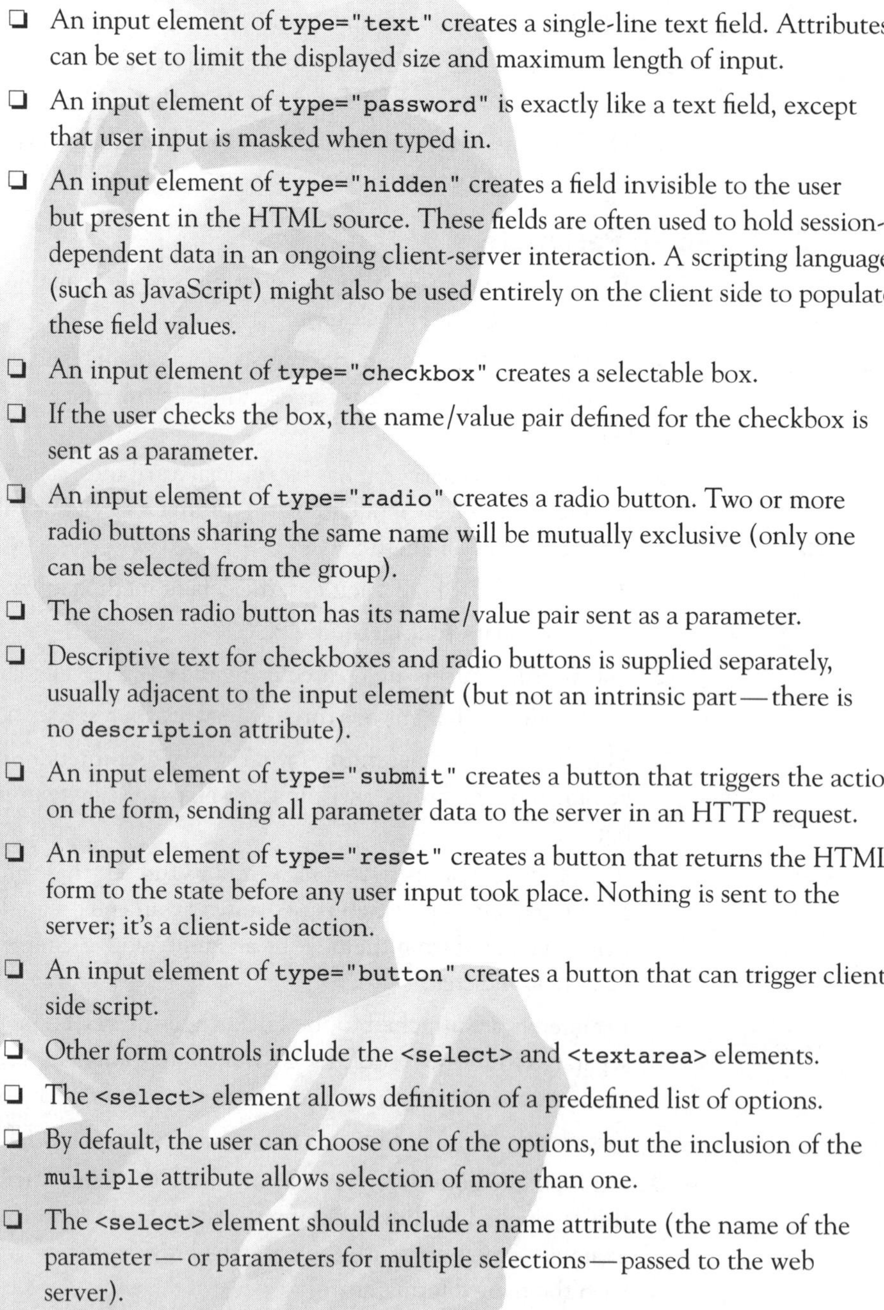

- An input element of `type="text"` creates a single-line text field. Attributes can be set to limit the displayed size and maximum length of input.
- An input element of `type="password"` is exactly like a text field, except that user input is masked when typed in.
- An input element of `type="hidden"` creates a field invisible to the user but present in the HTML source. These fields are often used to hold session-dependent data in an ongoing client-server interaction. A scripting language (such as JavaScript) might also be used entirely on the client side to populate these field values.
- An input element of `type="checkbox"` creates a selectable box.
- If the user checks the box, the name/value pair defined for the checkbox is sent as a parameter.
- An input element of `type="radio"` creates a radio button. Two or more radio buttons sharing the same name will be mutually exclusive (only one can be selected from the group).
- The chosen radio button has its name/value pair sent as a parameter.
- Descriptive text for checkboxes and radio buttons is supplied separately, usually adjacent to the input element (but not an intrinsic part—there is no `description` attribute).
- An input element of `type="submit"` creates a button that triggers the action on the form, sending all parameter data to the server in an HTTP request.
- An input element of `type="reset"` creates a button that returns the HTML form to the state before any user input took place. Nothing is sent to the server; it's a client-side action.
- An input element of `type="button"` creates a button that can trigger client-side script.
- Other form controls include the `<select>` and `<textarea>` elements.
- The `<select>` element allows definition of a predefined list of options.
- By default, the user can choose one of the options, but the inclusion of the `multiple` attribute allows selection of more than one.
- The `<select>` element should include a name attribute (the name of the parameter—or parameters for multiple selections—passed to the web server).

- The `<select>` element can restrict the number of visible rows using a *size* attribute (e.g., `size="3"`). Remaining rows are generally accessible with a scroll bar.
- The `<select>` element contains `<option>` elements, which should have a *value* attribute included (for the value of the parameter passed back to the server—if this item in the list is selected).
- The `<textarea>` element has a `name` attribute, whose function is the same as for other form controls.
- Generally, you should define `rows` and `cols` attributes, which define the number of visible rows and columns (imposing—usually—scrollbars for rows and wrap-around for columns).
- Text typed into the text area is passed back as the *value* parameter. This may contain special characters to denote white space, tabs, line feeds, and carriage returns.
- On the receiving end, a servlet can use a number of methods through the interface ServletRequest to get at request parameters.
- The simplest is `getParameter(String parmName)`, which returns the (first) value for a given parameter name.
- `getParameterValues(String parmName)` returns all values for a given parameter name—as a String array (**null** if no values present).
- `getParameterNames()` returns an Enumeration of String objects containing all parameter names. The Enumeration will never be **null**, but there may be no Strings within it.
- Finally, `getParameterMap()` returns a java.util.Map object with all the parameter names (the keys of the Map, of type String) and all the parameter values (the values in the Map, of type String array).
- You can get at parameters directly through the Reader associated with the request (`ServletRequest.getReader()`).However, this approach should not be used in conjunction with the APIs already described—unpredictable results occur.

Requests

- Request header information can be obtained using APIs available in the HttpServletRequest interface.

- `getHeader(String headerName)` returns the (first or only) value for the specified header name. This can return **null** if the named header is not present.
- `getHeaders(String headerName)` returns an Enumeration of all values for the specified header.
- `getHeaderNames()` returns an Enumeration of all header names present in the request.
- The Enumerations returned by the above two methods can be empty but are—in general—never **null**, unless the web container imposes security restrictions on the availability of some or all request headers.
- `getIntHeader(String headerName)` returns a primitive **int** for the specified header name.
- If the requested header isn't present, this method returns −1.
- If the request header is present but isn't numeric, this method throws a NumberFormatException.
- `getDateHeader(String headerName)` returns a **long** representing a date for the specified header name.
- If the requested header isn't present, this method returns −1.
- If the requested header is present but can't be interpreted as a date, this method throws an IllegalArgumentException.
- Common request headers are Accept, Accept-Language, Host (compulsory in HTTP version 1.1), and User-Agent.
- There are other headers used in the request that aren't tied to request messages. They may be generally used in HTTP messages or describe the entity attached to either a request or a response.
- Cookies are small text files attached as request or response headers.
- When present in the request, the HttpServletRequest method `getCookies()` can be used to return a javax.servlet.http.Cookie array.
- Cookies have two compulsory attributes: *name* and *value*.
- Optional attributes of cookies are *domain*, *path*, *comment*, *maximum age*, *version*, and a flag denoting whether the cookie has been passed over a secure protocol or not.

Responses

- ❑ HTTP responses can be manipulated using APIs in the HttpServletResponse interface.
- ❑ `addHeader(String name, String value)` adds a header of a given name and value to the response.
- ❑ If a header of that name already exists, `addHeader()` simply interprets this as an additional value to add to the existing response header.
- ❑ `setHeader(String name, String value)` also adds a header of a given name and value to the response; however, it replaces a value already given if the header is already present.
- ❑ `addIntHeader(String name, int value)` can be used to add a header whose value is known to be an integer.
- ❑ `addDateHeader(String name, long value)` can be used to add a header whose value is known to be a date.
- ❑ There are `setIntHeader()` and `setDateHeader()` counterpart methods.
- ❑ Common response headers include Date (the date the message was returned), and most usually have to do with the entity returned, such as Content-Type, Content-Encoding, and Content-Language.
- ❑ HttpServletResponse has some convenience methods that mask the underlying setting of response headers. These include `sendRedirect(String path)`, which sets the Location header with an alternative URL and sets a response code to tell the client to make a request to the alternative URL.
- ❑ `addCookie(Cookie aCookie)` is used to attach a Cookie to the response.
- ❑ Under the covers, a Set-Cookie response header is written.
- ❑ `setContentType(String MIMEtype)` sets the Content-Type header to an appropriate value (which should be chosen from the list of defined MIME types—such as "text/html").
- ❑ Content itself is written to the response through a PrintWriter (for characters) or OutputStream (for binary data).
- ❑ Either (but not both) can be obtained using the HttpServletResponse methods `getWriter()` or `getOutputStream()`.

Servlet Life Cycle

- ❑ Servlets can be instantiated at any point before processing their first request (server startup, at the point where the first request is received, or somewhere in between).
- ❑ In general, there is only one instance of a servlet per servlet class.
- ❑ The same servlet class can have more than one declaration in the deployment descriptor; in that case, the servlet may have one instance per declaration.
- ❑ Multiple request threads may access this one instance (hence, servlets are not thread-safe).
- ❑ Servlets have their own creation and instantiation rules over and above obeying standard rules for Java class loading and object instantiation.
- ❑ First, the class is loaded, and any static initialization is done (obviously not repeated for any subsequent servlet instance—if there is one).
- ❑ Second, the no-argument constructor on the servlet is called (you can supply one in your own servlets).
- ❑ Third, the `init(ServletConfig config)` method is called—once only for the given instance.
- ❑ In general, you should place initialization code in the `init(ServletConfig config)` method rather than in the constructor.
- ❑ Now the servlet is instantiated, its `service()` method is called for every request made—probably in multiple threads if there are many concurrent requests.
- ❑ `service()` dispatches to `doXXX()` methods in HTTP servlet implementations—there is no need to override `service()` in HttpServlet.
- ❑ `service()` may never be called; there may be no requests.
- ❑ Servlets can be taken out of service at any point the web server sees fit (closed down, running out of memory, not used for a long time, . . .).
- ❑ The servlet container must wait for all threads running `service()` methods on a servlet to complete before taking the servlet out of service.
- ❑ The servlet container can impose a time limit on this waiting period.
- ❑ Before the servlet container takes a servlet out of service, it must call the servlet's `destroy()` method.

- The `destroy()` method can be used to cleanly close down expensive resources probably initialized in the servlet's `init()` method.
- `destroy()` is never called if the servlet fails to initialize.
- Failure to initialize is denoted by `init()` not completing properly.
- `init()` may throw a ServletException to denote not completing properly.
- `init()` may throw a subclass of ServletException called Unavailable Exception.
- UnavailableExceptions can be temporary or permanent; the servlet container has the right to treat these differently or treat everything as a permanent error.
- `init()` may simply run out of time (as determined by a web server specific configuration parameter).
- With most of the preceding failures of `init()` the servlet container dereferences the failing servlet instance and allows it to be garbage collected.
- If the failure is not permanent (i.e., a temporary UnavailableException), the servlet container may try again to make another instance of the servlet.
- If the failure is permanent, the servlet container must return an HTTP 404 (page not found) error.

SELF TEST

The following questions will help you measure your understanding of the material presented in this chapter. Read all the choices carefully because there might be more than one correct answer. The number of correct choices to make is stated in the question, as in the real SCWCD exam.

HTTP Methods

1. Which of the HTTP methods below is not considered to be "idempotent"? (Choose one.)

   A. GET
   B. TRACE
   C. POST
   D. HEAD
   E. OPTIONS
   F. SERVICE

2. Which of the HTTP methods below are likely to change state on the web server? (Choose three.)

   A. DELETE
   B. TRACE
   C. OPTIONS
   D. POST
   E. PUT
   F. CONNECT
   G. HEAD
   H. SERVICE

3. Which of the following are valid servlet methods that match up with HTTP methods? (Choose four.)

   A. `doGet()`
   B. `doPost()`
   C. `doConnect()`
   D. `doOptions()`
   E. `doHead()`
   F. `doRequest()`
   G. `doService()`

4. What is the likely effect of calling a servlet with the POST HTTP method if that servlet does not have a `doPost()` method? (Choose one.)

   A. If the servlet has a `doGet()` method, it executes that instead.

   B. 404 response code: SC_NOT_FOUND.

   C. 405 response code: SC_METHOD_NOT_ALLOWED.

   D. 500 response code: SC_INTERNAL_SERVER_ERROR.

   E. 501 response code: SC_NOT_IMPLEMENTED.

5. What is the likely effect of calling a servlet with the HEAD HTTP method if that servlet does not have a `doHead()` method? (Choose one.)

   A. 200 response code: SC_OK

   B. 404 response code: SC_NOT_FOUND

   C. 405 response code: SC_METHOD_NOT_ALLOWED

   D. 500 response code: SC_INTERNAL_SERVER_ERROR

   E. 501 response code: SC_NOT_IMPLEMENTED

Form Parameters

6. What will be the result of pressing the submit button in the following HTML form? (Choose two.)

```
<form action="/servlet/Register">
  <input type="text" name="fullName" value="Type name here" />
  <input type="submit" name="sbmButton" value="OK" />
</form>
```

   A. A request is sent with the HTTP method HEAD.

   B. A request is sent with the HTTP method POST.

   C. A request is sent with the HTTP method GET.

   D. The parameter *fullName* is the only parameter passed to the web server in the request URL.

   E. The parameter *fullName* is the only parameter passed to the web server as part of the request body.

   F. The parameters *fullName* and *sbmButton* are passed to the web server in the request URL.

   G. The parameters *fullName* and *sbmButton* are passed to the web server as part of the request body.

   H. No parameters are passed to the web server.

7. Consider the following form and servlet code. Assuming the user changes none of the default settings and presses SUBMIT, what will the servlet output in the response? (Choose one.)

```
<form action="PrintParams?param1=First" method="post">
    <input type="hidden" name="param1" value="First" />
    <input type="text" name="param1" value="Second" />
    <input type="radio" name="param1" value="Third" />
    <input type="submit" />
</form>
protected void doPost
  HttpServletRequest request,
  HttpServletResponse response)
  throws ServletException, IOException {
  response.setContentType("text/html");
  PrintWriter out = response.getWriter();
  out.write("<html>\n<head>\n<title>Print
    Parameters</title>\n</head>\n<body>");
  String[] param1 = request.getParameterValues("param1");
  for (int i = 0; i < param1.length; i++) {
    out.write(param1[i] + ":");
  }
  out.write("\n</body>\n</html>");
  out.close();
}
```

A. First:Second:Third

B. First:Second:Second

C. First:Third:Third

D. Second:Third:First

E. First:First:Second

F. No response—servlet will not compile.

G. No response—ServletException occurs.

8. (drag-and-drop question) The following illustration shows a form in an HTML page and also the `doPost()` method of the servlet that is the target of the form's action attribute. Match the hidden lettered values from the HTML form and the servlet code with numbers from the list on the right.

```
protected void doPost(
  HttpServletRequest request,
  HttpServletResponse response)
  throws ServletException, IOException {
  response.setContentType("text/plain");
  PrintWriter out = response.getWriter();
  out.write("<HTML>\n<HEAD>\n<TITLE>Parameters
as    Map Servlet</TITLE>\n</HEAD>\n<BODY>");
  Map params = request.get[    A    ]();
  Set s = params.[  B  ]();
  Iterator it = s.iterator();
  while (it.hasNext()) {
   [   C   ] entry = ([   D   ]) it.next();
   [   E   ] value = ([   F   ])
entry.getValue();
    out.write(value[0]);
  }
  out.write("\n</BODY>\n</HTML>");
  out.close();
}
```

```
<form action="Question8?param1=First"
  [     G     ]>
  <input type="hidden" [ H ]="param2"
      value="Second" />
  <input [      I      ] />
</form>
```

1	name
2	ParameterSet
3	ParameterValues
4	getParams
5	ParameterMap
6	type="submit"
7	value
8	Map.Entry
9	method="head"
10	String[]
11	Parameters
12	entrySet
13	values
14	Object[]
15	method="post"

9. What is the maximum number of parameter values that can be forwarded to the servlet from the following HTML form? (Choose one.)

```
<html>
  <body>
    <h1>Chapter 1 Question 9</h1>
    <form action="ParamsServlet" method="get">
      <select name="Languages" size="3" multiple>
        <option value="JAVA" selected>Java</option>
        <option value="CSHARP">C#</option>
        <option value="C" selected>C</option>
        <option value="CPLUSPLUS">C++</option>
        <option value="PASCAL">Pascal</option>
        <option value="ADA">Ada</option>
      </select>
      <input type="submit" name="button" />
    </form>
  </body>
</html>
```

A. 0
B. 1
C. 2
D. 3
E. 4
F. 5
G. 6
H. 7

10. What request header must be set for parameter data to be decoded from a form? (Choose one.)

A. EncType: application/x-www-urlencoded
B. Content-Type: application/x-www-form-urlencoded
C. Content-Type: multipart/form-data
D. Encoding-Type: multipart/form-data
E. Accept-Encoding: application/www-form-encoded
F. Encoding-Type: multipart/www-form-data

Requests

11. Which of the following are likely to found as request header fields? (Choose three.)

    A. Accept

    B. WWW-Authenticate

    C. Accept-Language

    D. From

    E. Client-Agent

    F. Retry-After

12. What is the most likely outcome of running the following servlet code? (Choose one.)

```
long date = request.getDateHeader("Host");
response.setContentType("text/plain");
response.getWriter().write("" + date);
```

    A. A formatted date is written to the response.

    B. −1 is written to the response.

    C. Won't run because won't compile.

    D. IllegalArgumentException

    E. NumberFormatException

    F. DateFormatException

13. What is the likely outcome of attempting to run the following servlet code?

```
String[] values = request.getHeaders("BogusHeader");
response.setContentType("text/plain");
response.getWriter().write(values[0]);
```

    A. IllegalArgumentException

    B. NumberFormatException

    C. Won't run: 1 compilation error.

    D. Won't run: 2 compilation errors.

    E. Nothing written to the response.

    F. *null* written to the response.

14. What is the likely outcome of attempting to compile and run the following servlet code, assuming there is one cookie attached to the incoming request?

```
11 Cookie[] cookies = request.getCookies();
12 Cookie cookie1 = cookies[0];
13 response.setContentType("text/plain");
14 String attributes = cookie1.getName();
15 attributes += cookie1.getValue();
16 attributes += cookie1.getDomain();
17 attributes += cookie1.getPath();
18 response.getWriter().write(attributes);
```

A. Compilation error at line 11
B. Compilation error at line 16
C. Output to the response including at least the name and domain
D. Output to the response including at least the name and value
E. Output to the response including at least the name, value, and domain
F. Output to the response including all of name, value, domain, and path

15. Under what circumstances can the `HttpServletRequest.getHeaders(String name)` method return *null*? (Choose one.)

A. If there are no request headers present in the request for the given header name.
B. If there are multiple headers for the given header name.
C. If the container disallows access to the header information.
D. If there are multiple values for the given header name.
E. If there is only a single value for the given header name.
F. There is no such method on HttpServletRequest.

Responses

16. Which of the following methods can be used to add cookies to a servlet response? (Choose two.)

A. HttpServletResponse.addCookie(Cookie cookie)
B. ServletResponse.addCookie(Cookie cookie)
C. HttpServletResponse.addCookie(String contents)
D. ServletResponse.addCookie(String contents)
E. HttpServletResponse.addHeader(String name, String value)
F. ServletResponse.addHeader(String name, String value)

17. What is the outcome of running the following servlet code? (Choose two.)

```
public void doGet(
  HttpServletRequest request,
  HttpServletResponse response)
  throws ServletException, IOException {
  response.setContentType("text/plain;charset-UTF-8");
  PrintWriter out = response.getWriter();
  out.flush();
  out.close();
  System.out.println(response.isCommitted());
  response.setContentType("illegal/value");
}
```

A. An IllegalArgumentException is thrown.

B. A blank page is returned to the client.

C. A 500 error is reported to the client.

D. "true" is output on the server's console.

E. "false" is output on the server's console.

18. What will be the outcome of executing the following code? (Choose one.)

```
public void doGet(
  HttpServletRequest request,
  HttpServletResponse response)
  throws ServletException, IOException {
  response.setContentType("text/plain");
  response.setContentLength(4);
  PrintWriter out = response.getWriter();
  out.write("What will be the response? ");
  out.write("" + response.isCommitted());
}
```

A. Won't execute because of a compilation error.

B. An IllegalArgumentException is thrown.

C. An IllegalStateException is thrown.

D. A blank page is returned to the client.

E. "What" is returned to the client.

F. "What will be the response?" is returned to the client.

G. "What will be the response? true" is returned to the client.

H. "What will be the response? false" is returned to the client.

19. (drag-and-drop question) Consider the following servlet code, which downloads a binary file to the client. Match the concealed (lettered) parts of the code with the (numbered) possibilities. You may need to use some possibilities more than once.

```
protected void doPost(
  HttpServletRequest request,
  HttpServletResponse response)
  throws ServletException, IOException {
  response.setContentType("text/plain");
  PrintWriter out = response.getWriter();
  out.write("<HTML>\n<HEAD>\n<TITLE>Parameters
as     Map Servlet</TITLE>\n</HEAD>\n<BODY>");
  Map params = request.get[     A     ]();
  Set s = params.[  B  ]();
  Iterator it = s.iterator();
  while (it.hasNext()) {
   [   C   ] entry = ([   D   ]) it.next();
   [   E   ] value = ([   F   ])
entry.getValue();
    out.write(value[0]);
  }
  out.write("\n</BODY>\n</HTML>");
  out.close();
}
```

```
<form action="Question8?param1=First"
 [     G     ]>
 <input type="hidden" [ H ]="param2"
      value="Second" />
 <input [     I     ] />
</form>
```

1	name
2	ParameterSet
3	ParameterValues
4	getParams
5	ParameterMap
6	type="submit"
7	value
8	Map.Entry
9	method="head"
10	String[]
11	Parameters
12	entrySet
13	values
14	Object[]
15	method="post"

20. Which of the approaches below will correctly cause a client to redirect to an alternative URL? (In the code fragments below, consider that "response" is an instance of HttpServletResponse.) (Choose two.)

A. `response.sendRedirect("index.jsp");`

B. `response.setLocation("index.jsp");`

C. `RequestDispatcher rd = response.getRequestDispatcher("index.jsp");`
`rd.sendRedirect();`

D. `response.redirect("index.jsp");`

E. `response.setHeader("Location", "index.jsp");`

F. `response.setStatus(HttpServletResponse.SC_TEMPORARY_REDIRECT);`
   `response.setHeader("Location", "index.jsp");`

Servlet Life Cycle

21. Identify statements that are always true about threads running through the `service()` method of a servlet with the following class declaration. (Choose two.)

```
public class MyServlet extends HttpServlet { // servlet code }
```

A. The `destroy()` method never cuts short threads running through the `service()` method.
B. Threads running through the `service()` method must run one at a time.
C. There could be anything from zero to many threads running through the `service()` method during the time the servlet is loaded.
D. If the `init()` method for the servlet hasn't run, no threads have yet been able to run through the `service()` method.
E. At least one thread will run through the `service()` method if `init()` has been executed.

22. Under which of the following circumstances are servlets most likely to be instantiated? (Choose four.)

A. During web application startup
B. If there are insufficient instances of the servlet to service incoming requests
C. On a client first requesting the servlet
D. At the same time as a different servlet is instantiated, when that different servlet makes use of the servlet in question
E. After the servlet's `destroy()` method is called, dependent on the server's keep-alive setting
F. At some arbitrary point in the web application or application server lifetime
G. After the time specified on an UnavailableException has expired

23. Which of the following are true statements about servlet availability? (Choose two.)

A. If a servlet is removed from service, then any requests to the servlet should result in an HTTP 404 (SC_NOT_FOUND) error.
B. The `init()` method must not throw an UnavailableException.

C. If permanent unavailability is indicated via an UnavailableException, a servlet's `destroy()` method must be called.

D. Servlet containers must distinguish between periods of temporary and permanent unavailability.

E. If a servlet is deemed temporarily unavailable, a container may return an HTTP 503 (SC_SERVICE_UNAVAILABLE) message on receiving requests to the servlet during its time of unavailability.

24. Under what circumstances will a servlet instance's `destroy()` method never be called? (Choose two.)

A. As a result of a web application closedown request

B. When `init()` has not run to completion successfully

C. If no thread has ever executed the `service()` method

D. After `destroy()` has already been called

E. During servlet replacement

25. Given the following servlet code, identify the outputs that could not or should not occur during the lifetime of the web application housing the servlet.

A. init:destroy:

B. init:destroy:init:destroy:

C. init:init:init:

D. destroy:service:

E. init:service:service:service:service:service:

F. init:service:init:service:

```
public class Question25 extends HttpServlet {
  public void init() {
    System.out.print("init:");
  }
  public void destroy() {
    System.out.print("destroy:");
  }
  protected void service(HttpServletRequest arg0,
     HttpServletResponse arg1)
     throws ServletException, IOException {
     super.service(arg0, arg1);
     System.out.print("service:");
  }
}
```

LAB QUESTION

Here is your turn to put together the skills you've learned in this first chapter. You'll write the servlet that you used at the start of this chapter in Exercise 1-1. Your servlet is going to do several things: (1) accept posted data from a request parameter, then (2) append this data to the end of a text file, and finally (3) read the entire text file and return this in the web page response.

Use PostServlet as the name and webcert.lab01 as the package. Use the web.xml file from the solution file, lab01.war—place this in your lab01/WEB-INF directory. To operate the servlet, write a basic HTML page with a form and an appropriate action and text field— or series of input fields, depending on how adventurous you are feeling.

This and future labs have solution code on the CD—you'll find the references to this in the Lab Answer after the Self Test Answers in each chapter.

SELF TEST ANSWERS

HTTP Methods

1. ☑ **C** is correct. Idempotent methods should behave the same however many times they are executed against a particular resource. The POST method doesn't offer that guarantee.
   ☒ **A**, **B**, **D**, and **E** are incorrect because all these methods (GET, TRACE, HEAD, and OPTIONS) are the personification of idempotency. **F** is incorrect because SERVICE is not an HTTP method at all.

2. ☑ **A**, **D**, and **E** are correct. The methods DELETE, POST, and PUT are all liable to change state on the web server—DELETE by removing a resource at the specified URL, PUT by placing one there, and POST by doing whatever it pleases.
   ☒ **B**, **C**, and **G** are incorrect because all these methods (TRACE, OPTIONS, and HEAD) are enquiry methods that should change nothing on the server. **F** and **H** are incorrect because these are not HTTP methods at all.

3. ☑ **A**, **B**, **D**, and **E** are the correct answers. `doGet()` matches HTTP GET, `doPost()` HTTP POST, `doOptions()` HTTP OPTIONS, and `doHead()` HTTP HEAD.
   ☒ **C**, **F**, and **G** are incorrect. CONNECT is a method reserved for future use in the HTTP RFC and has no servlet method counterpart. Although the concepts of request and service play a part in the servlet response to HTTP messages (you receive a request as a parameter into the `doXXX()` method family, and a servlet's `service()` method dispatches to the correct `doXXX()` method), there are no REQUEST or SERVICE HTTP methods.

4. ☑ **C** is the correct answer: 405, SC_METHOD_NOT_ALLOWED. If your servlet doesn't provide a `doPost()` method (overriding the one in HttpServlet), the default behavior is to reject the POST method request in this way.
   ☒ **A** is incorrect—there's no automatic substitution of a `doPost()` with the next-best method. **B** is incorrect, as the resource is actually there. **D** is incorrect—a 500 error is reserved for the servlet failing with some kind of exception. **E** is plausible because the method is indeed not implemented—but this isn't the response code returned. Try it!

5. ☑ **A** is correct. Your own servlet should rarely or never override the `doHead()` method—the default implementation for this is fine. The default `doHead()` method will return all response headers, but no body—and the likelihood is a normal (200) response code as well.
   ☒ **B** is incorrect because the resource is found in the scenario described. **C** is incorrect because the method is allowed through a servlet container's default implementation. **D** is incorrect in that you could get a 500 error if the servlet goes wrong—but that will be for some other

reason, not the absence of a `doHead()` method (which is what the question is driving at). Finally, **E** is incorrect—a "not implemented" error is very unlikely.

Form Parameters

6. ☑ **C** and **F**. In the absence of specifying a method parameter on the `<form>` opening tag, an HTTP GET is the default. This means that parameters from the form are passed within the query string of the URL.
   ☒ **A** and **B** are incorrect because an HTML's default method is GET—you are likely to explicitly specify POST instead with method="post," but this happens only if you are explicit. You would never use HEAD in a form—GET and POST are the only valid methods. **D** is incorrect because *sbmButton* is passed as a parameter as well as *fullName*: As long as a field in a form has a name, its value will be passed as a parameter (even if there may seem no point in passing the submit button as a parameter). **E** is incorrect for the same reason as **D**, and because form parameters get passed in the request body only when the method is POST. **G** is incorrect—right parameters, wrong place for them when the method is GET. Finally, **H** is incorrect because parameters are passed to the server—there's nothing in the HTML that would indicate this wouldn't happen.

7. ☑ **E** is correct. The servlet writes out the value of param1 in the query string of the form's action, then the value of param1 in the hidden field, and then the value of param1 in the text field. It doesn't print out the value of param1 in the radio field: The user doesn't select it, nor is it preselected with the "checked" attribute in the HTML.
   ☒ **A**, **B**, **C**, and **D** are incorrect according to the reasoning for the correct answer. The servlet compiles fine, so **F** is incorrect—and there's no reason for it to throw a ServletException; hence, **G** is incorrect.

8. ☑ **A**, 5; **B**, 12; **C**, 8; **D**, 8; **E**, 10; **F**, 10; **G**, 15; **H**, 1; and **I**, 6. There are a few things thrown in here that rely on your knowledge of the map interface—and that's fair game for the exam. The key thing is that each entry in the map is a Map.Entry object. Beyond that, you have to know that the values part of the Map.Entry will be held as a String array, even though the parameters concerned have only a single value.
   ☒ All other combinations are incorrect, as dictated by the right answer above.

9. ☑ **H** is the correct answer. Seven parameter values may be returned by the form by selecting all six of the language options in the select (it's a multiple selector), and you get an additional parameter value for free with the named `<input>` submit button.
   ☒ **A** through **G** are incorrect, according to the reasoning in the correct answer. Issues you might have thought that limited the number of parameters: Does the size attribute for the

`<select>` limit the number of choices? No, only the number of visible rows. Does the fact that two of the options are already selected make a difference? No, the user can select all the others in addition to the ones already selected. Does the button have an associated parameter value, as it lacks a value attribute? Yes it does—because the `<input>` button has a name attribute, a default value will be passed (something like "Submit Query"—matching the default text on the button).

10. ☑ **B** is correct. You just have to know this one.
    ☒ **A** is incorrect—EncType is not a proper request header name, and the value is mangled. **C** is incorrect: Content-Type is the correct request header names, and *multipart/form-data* is a valid value—but you use it when posting complete data files from an HTML form rather than simple parameters. **D**, **E**, and **F** are incorrect—Encoding-Type and Accept-Encoding are correct request header names, but not applicable to this situation—and the values are mangled in different ways.

Requests

11. ☑ **A**, **C**, and **D**. Accept describes the MIME types acceptable to the client, and AcceptLanguage describes the human language preferred for the response. From has the e-mail address of the client.
    ☒ **B** is incorrect because WWW-Authenticate is returned as a response header, to indicate that authentication details are required from the client. **E** is incorrect— Client-Agent is made up. (User-Agent is a real request header, however, and describes the type of client making the request.) **F** is incorrect—Retry-After is returned as a response header, not a request header, to indicate that a service is unavailable and the client should retry after the suggested time or time interval.

12. ☑ **D** is the correct answer—the most likely outcome is an IllegalArgumentException. This occurs because the request header "Host" is almost certainly present in the request (it's mandatory with HTTP 1.1) but patently doesn't contain a date (it holds the domain that is the target of the request). Since the header value can't be formatted as a date, the exception results.
    ☒ **A** is incorrect—even if a date was returned from `getDateHeader()`, the code makes no attempt to format it. **B** is incorrect, though close—if the header requested *didn't exist*, then `getDateHeader()` would indeed return −1. The code compiles just fine, ruling out **C**. **E** is incorrect: A NumberFormatException is, however, a possible outcome from `getIntHeader()`. Finally, **F** is incorrect: There's no such thing as a DateFormatException.

13. ☑ **D** is the correct answer—there are two compilation errors, both relating to the first line of code. For one thing, `HttpServletRequest.getHeaders()` returns all request header names,

so you don't specify any parameter to the method to narrow down the range. Second, the method returns an Enumeration, not a String array.

☒ A and B are incorrect—`getHeaders()` doesn't give rise either to an IllegalArgument Exception or a NumberFormatException. C is wrong because there are two compilation errors, not one. E and F—to do with writing to the response—are incorrect because you'd never reach that point. Furthermore, you would need code to extract the Strings from the Enumeration returned to actually write header names to the response.

14. ☑ D is the correct answer—you will get output to the response including at least the name and value.

    ☒ A is incorrect—there is no compilation error in the call to `getCookies()`. You may have thought this returned an Enumeration, as do many other get* methods in the servlet API (especially when getting a plural number of things). However, a Cookie array is indeed what's returned. B is incorrect—you may have thought that `getDomain()` did not exist in the Cookie class, but it does. C is incorrect—as a cookie's value is a mandatory attribute, that should be present in the list. E and F are incorrect—both answers are perfectly possible (as domain and path, though optional attributes, are regularly set), but as statements they are not as accurate as the correct answer.

15. ☑ C is the correct answer—the one circumstance where `HttpServletRequest.getHeaders(String name)` would return *null* is if the servlet container disallows return of values.

    ☒ A is incorrect—if there are no request headers for the given name, this method returns an empty Enumeration. B is incorrect—multiple headers for the given header name don't make sense. D is incorrect—the whole point of the method is to return multiple values for the given header name. E is incorrect—if there is only a single value for the given header name, you still get an Enumeration back containing one String value. F is incorrect because there is such a method on HttpServletRequest—it returns all the values for a given request header name.

Responses

16. ☑ A and E are the correct answers. A is correct, for the `addCookie()` method is part of HttpServletResponse, not ServletResponse—and accepts a Cookie object as a parameter. You can also add cookies the hard way, using the `addHeader()` or `setHeader()` methods also on HttpServletResponse—making E correct as well. You pass in a header name of Set-Cookie, and a formatted String as the value, with the cookie fields formatted according to the version of the cookie standard used.

    ☒ B, D, and F are incorrect, for there are no methods on ServletResponse (the generic servlet response interface) that have to do with cookies—it's most definitely an HTTP thing. C is incorrect—there is no overloading on the `addCookie()` method to allow passing in of a String directly.

17. ☑ **B** and **D** are the correct answers. A blank page is written to the client (nothing is written to the PrintWriter, although it's obtained from the response); "true" is output to the console: once the PrintWriter is flushed and closed, the response is committed.
☒ **A** is incorrect, for there is no IllegalArgumentException. You can put any rubbish into the parameter of setContentType, but nothing will go wrong in the server code. (However, you may confuse the client—though again, most browsers are built to be fairly robust faced with incorrect content types. Some even ignore what's set and do their own interpretation of the response.) **C** is incorrect. You might have thought that the call to `setContentType()` after the response was committed would cause an exception resulting in a 500 error code to the client, but this call is simply ignored. Finally, **E** is incorrect—"false" isn't shown on the server console because the response has been committed at this point.

18. ☑ **E** is the correct answer: "What" is returned to the client. The response is committed once the content length (of 4 bytes) is reached.
☒ **A** is incorrect—there's nothing wrong with the code that will prevent compilation. **B** and **C** are incorrect—there's nothing in the code to cause IllegalArgumentException or Illegal StateException (you might have thought that exceeding the content length would do this, but additional content is simply ignored). **D** and **F** are wrong because the output is as described in the correct answer. **G** and **H** are wrong for the same reason, but as a point of interest, the output of `response.isCommitted()` in the output would be "true" at this point.

19. ☑ **A** matches to **5**: The content type here should be "image/gif." **B** matches to **6**: This is java.io revision—the size of a file is returned as a **long**. **C** matches to **4: `HttpServletResponse.setContentLength()`** is the method for setting the length of the response, here to match the size of the file. As this method accepts an **int**, **D** matches to **7**: We have to convert the **long** returned from inspecting the file length to an **int**. **E** also matches to **7**: A Reader reads an **int** representing a byte from the file. Finally, **F** matches to **9**: The OutputStream method is `write()` for writing an **int** (representing a byte) to a file.
☒ Other matches are wrong, according to the correct answer. It's worth mentioning that some other contenders for content type (such as "image/mime") are made up. "text/plain" exists—but we're clearly dealing with a binary file here.

20. ☑ **A** and **F** are the correct answers. **A** shows the easy way to do it: simply invoke the `sendRedirect()` method on the response. The code in answer **F** shows what `sendRedirect()` does under the covers—sets an appropriate status code, then sets the Location header with the URL to redirect to (the container must translate this to a complete URL).

☒ B is incorrect—there is no `setLocation()` method on HttpServletResponse. C is incorrect—we will encounter the RequestDispatcher class later in the book, but it has no `sendRedirect()` method, and doesn't perform redirection (as such). D is incorrect—the method name on HttpServletResponse is not `redirect()`; it's `sendRedirect()`. E is incorrect—when redirecting the manual way, it's insufficient to set the Location header only: You have to set an appropriate response status as well, as per the correct answer.

Servlet Life Cycle

21. ☑ C and D are the correct answers. There can be any number of threads active at one time in a `service()` method—it just all depends on the number of client requests and how the servlet container manages those requests.

    ☒ A is incorrect, though there's room for some discussion. `destroy()` should not be run until all the threads in the `service()` method end. However, there is a let-out clause that allows a servlet container to impose a time-out for threads in `service()` to end. If they are not complete by the end of this time, then `destroy()` will be called. So it's fair to say that `destroy()` should not cut short `service()` threads if at all possible, but not fair to say that it will never cut them short. B is incorrect—only if the servlet implements the deprecated SingleThread Model interface should threads be single-queued through an instance. We can see from the declaration that it doesn't implement this interface (nor should it, being as it's deprecated). E is incorrect—even if the servlet is initialized, there is no guarantee that any thread will run through the `service()` method. Of course, it's likely—especially if servlets are lazily initialized at the point of a user first requesting them—but it's not always true.

22. ☑ A, C, F, and G are the correct answers. A servlet is very likely to be instantiated on web application startup (especially if `<load-on-startup>` is specified—we learn about this in Chapter 2). If servlet instantiation doesn't happen, then it must happen when a client first requests a servlet. The server may also start and stop servlets on a whim (maybe for memory management reasons), so a servlet may start at a seemingly arbitrary point. Finally, some servlet containers will attempt to reinitialize a servlet that first failed with an UnavailableException (if this is of a temporary nature).

    ☒ B is incorrect. A servlet container just starts up more threads on the same instance. Only if the servlet container was supporting servlets implementing the deprecated SingleThreadModel interface could it possibly work as described. D is incorrect—there is no check on servlet dependencies at instantiation stage, and consequent loading of "chains" of servlets. E is incorrect—there's no such thing as a server's keep-alive setting for servlet instances.

23. ☑ **A** and **E** are the correct answers, being true statements. A servlet container should return an HTTP 404 error when a servlet is not in service, and can return an HTTP 503 error during a period of unavailability.
☒ **B** is incorrect, for an error can occur during initialization and cause an Unavailable Exception (subtype of ServletException). **C** is almost correct—if an UnavailableException occurs during a run of a servlet's `service()` method, then the `destroy()` method must be called, true enough—but not if the exception occurs in the `init()` method. Finally, **D** is incorrect: The servlet specification allows containers to treat temporary and permanent unavailability in the same way (removing a servlet from `service()`; returning HTTP 404 errors).

24. ☑ **B** and **D** are the correct answers. When `init()` does not complete successfully, the container deems this an initialization error, so it's not appropriate to call `destroy()`. Also, once `destroy()` has been called on a servlet instance, the servlet should be made available for garbage collection; hence, `destroy()` cannot be called again on the same instance.
☒ **A** is incorrect, for `destroy()` is very likely to be called on all servlet instances as a result of web application closedown. **C** is incorrect—the number of threads that have executed the `service()` method (including zero) has no bearing on whether `destroy()` is called or not. Finally, **E** is incorrect—"hot" replacement of servlet classes very often results in `destroy()` being called on the running instance, where the servlet container supports this.

25. ☑ **D** and **F** are the correct answers, for the methods should not be executed in the immediate sequence shown. In **D**, if a servlet is destroyed, then the next instance of the same servlet should not show output from the `service()` method before `init()` is called. In **F**, a "destroy:" is missing. `init()` cannot be called again on the same instance, so the implication is that the same servlet must have been taken out of service; hence, there should be a "destroy:" between the first "service:" and the second "init:."
☒ **A**, **B**, **C**, and **E** are incorrect, for they are all perfectly feasible outputs. **A** ("init:destroy:") occurs if a servlet is put into service, then taken out again at some later stage—though no requests are directed to it. **B** ("init:destroy:init:destroy") is an extension of the same idea—just that after the servlet was taken out of service, it was put back into service again. **C** ("init:init:init:") might occur if a servlet stalls on initialization and the servlet container tries to start it again. **E** ("init:service:service:service:service:service:") is a snapshot of business as usual for a servlet (prior to destruction)—initialization followed by five requests.

LAB ANSWER

You'll find the solution file lab01.war on the CD, in the /sourcecode/chapter01 directory. Deploy this according to the instructions in Appendix B. The initial web page to call is postData.html, so for me, running the Tomcat server at port 8080 on my local machine, a URL of `http://localhost:8080/`

`lab01/postData.html` works well. Enter some data in the text field, and press the "Submit Query" button. You should see what you just typed displayed on a web page. Press the "back" button on your browser, and repeat the exercise. Now you should see what you typed before as well as what you just typed on the web page. If you inspect the postData.txt file (for me, at <Tomcat Install Directory>/webapps/lab01), then all the text you typed in should also be saved there.

2

Web Applications

CERTIFICATION OBJECTIVES

- File and Directory Structure
- Deployment Descriptor Elements
- WAR Files

 Two-Minute Drill

Q&A Self Test

In Chapter 1 we saw how J2EE gave us a coding framework for our web applications. But J2EE also has plenty to say about how to package and deploy applications—nothing is left to chance! In this chapter you'll see how to design the correct directory structure for a J2EE web app, and which files go where. You'll learn about the "deployment descriptor" file, web.xml, which tells any self-respecting J2EE web container all it needs to know about your web app. Finally, you'll get to bundle up all the files making up your application into a single "web archive" or WAR file, making deployment that much easier.

Do not think there is anything optional about these topics, either in the real world or in the exam! You can't wash your hands of your web app as soon as the code is written—you have to package and deploy with the best of them. The good news is that any decent J2EE IDE does practically all the packaging and deployment as you code. But because you need to understand what you're doing, we'll keep things explicit and hands-on in this chapter.

CERTIFICATION OBJECTIVE

File and Directory Structure (Exam Objective 2.1)

Construct the file and directory structure of a Web Application that may contain (a) static content, (b) JSP pages, (c) servlet classes, (d) the deployment descriptor, (e) tag libraries, (f) JAR files and (g) Java class files; and describe how to protect resource files from HTTP access.

One of the many goals outlined in the J2EE specification is the "portable deployment of J2EE applications into any J2EE product." A logical consequence of this goal is that any one J2EE application should have a structure broadly identical to any other J2EE application. Sun has standards for this. Although a J2EE web container is free to impose its own structure, it rarely makes sense for it to do so. And more to the point, the standard structure is something you are expected to know for the exam.

A Place for Everything and Everything in Its Place

Generally, servers (with J2EE web containers) have a preferred location for web applications—sometimes more than one. You should generally abide by preferred locations, but most servers provide a facility to specify any directory whatsoever as a home for web application contexts. The Tomcat server prefers `<TOMCAT`

INSTALLATION DIRECTORY>/webapps—you'll see this in action in the chapter exercises.

Whether or not there is a preferred location, each web application needs its own home directory, which generally means a directory immediately beneath the preferred location. All the resources a web application needs go inside this home directory, or subdirectories beneath it. Once the web application is placed there, how can we get at those resources? Typically, we point toward them with a URL, usually (but not exclusively) entered in the address line of a browser, such as

```
http://host:port/webappcontext/resourceIneed
```

Let's look at what different parts of the URL equate to (always assuming that a J2EE web application is the target):

- **host:port**—directly or indirectly, this identifies a running instance of an application server hosting a J2EE web container.
- **webappcontext**—this part of the URL uniquely identifies a particular web application running within the server. This is the "context root," and it identifies the home directory for the web application.
- **resourceIneed**—any resource available in the web application. This could be a simple static web page or a servlet returning complex dynamic content; the request mechanism (resource name in URL) is the same.

In a production environment, the host:port part of the URL rarely points directly to an application server running a web container. More usually, the host:port combination identifies an industrial-strength web server, such as Apache. The web server works out—from the rest of the URL—which requests are appropriate to hand off to the web container.

For web applications running under the same server to be distinguished from one another, the context root must be unique. There's no requirement that the context name match the home directory name, though this is often the case—for one thing, it keeps organization simple, and for another, many deployment tools actively encourage this behavior.

HTTP Accessible Resources

Any files directly within the context root are meant to be available to users of your web application: They are there for the requesting. Here's a nonexhaustive list of resources we might expect to find there:

- Static HTML files
- Dynamic JavaServer Page (JSP) files
- Images
- Media clips
- Stylesheets
- Java applets (and their supporting classes and JARs)

Nothing in the rules says you can't define your own directories off the context root. So if you want a directory to store JPEGs and GIFs, create an "images" directory. If you want another directory to store stylesheet files, create one called "style." The process is no different from defining a typical directory structure for a regular web site.

Special Directories Beneath the Context Root

What do we do, though, with all those files that support the operation of the web application but that have no business being the direct target of a user request? These might include (but are not limited to)

- Servlet class files
- Other class files that support the work of your servlets
- Whole libraries of support code in JAR files
- Configuration files—your own, or those mandated by the servlet specification

The servlet specification strongly recommends that you have a directory called WEB-INF for these files. The directory is called WEB-INF: capitalized WEB, hyphen, capitalized INF. Other variants don't count (Web-Inf, WEB_INF, web-inf—none of these will do). There are a standard set of directories defined within WEB-INF:

- /WEB-INF/classes—for classes that exist as separate Java classes (*not* packaged within JAR files). These might be servlets or other support classes. Of course, because your classes are likely to live in packages, the directory structure should normally reflect that: for example, /WEB-INF/classes/webcert/chapter2/WellLocatedServlet.class.
- /WEB-INF/lib—for JAR files. These can contain anything at all—the main servlets for your application, supporting classes that connect to databases—whatever.
- /WEB-INF itself is the home for an absolutely crucial file called web.xml, the deployment descriptor file. You'll learn much more about this in the "Deployment Descriptor Elements" section of the chapter.

FIGURE 2-1

A Web Application Directory Structure with Typical Contents

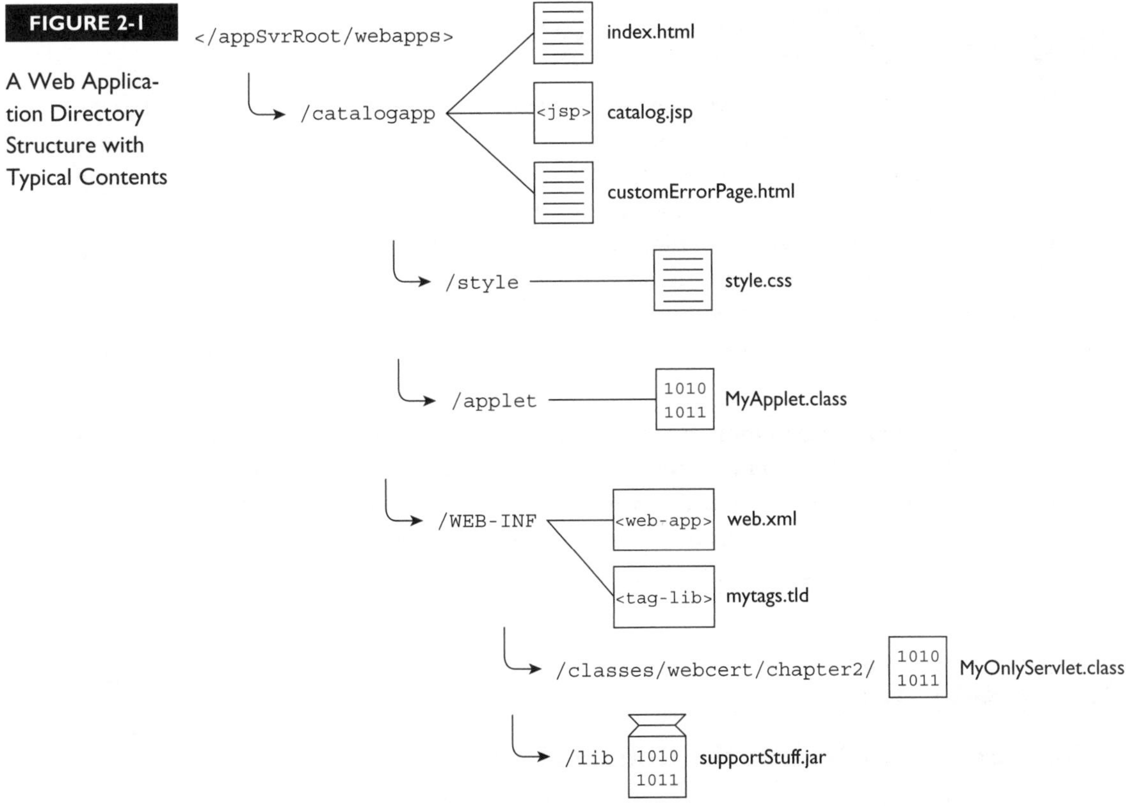

Again, there is nothing wrong with defining your own directories (or directory structure) under WEB-INF. You might have, perhaps, a /WEB-INF/xml directory to house a bunch of XML configuration files that support your application. The point—especially for exam purposes—is that you can distinguish between the Sun-specified directories and any other sort.

Two special rules apply to files within the /WEB-INF directory. One is that direct client access should be disallowed with an HTTP 404 (file not found) error. The second regards the order of class loading. Java classes in the /WEB-INF/classes directory should be loaded before classes resident in JAR files in the /WEB-INF/lib directory.

Before doing the exercise at the end of this section, take a look at Figure 2-1, which shows a web application directory structure. Although sparsely populated, you can see a selection of different sorts of files and where they belong.

exam watch

Having a directory called WEB-INF is a strong recommendation, but not an absolute obligation. Look out for questions that ask you to say whether a web application must have particular directories. The correct answer is "no"! More usually, though, questions will be phrased to allow for this loophole in the specification. So if you see a question along these lines—"Should a servlet class live in the WEB-INF/classes directory?"—you are safe to answer "yes." The expectation is that files normally do live in the recommended file structure.

on the job

If you are designing a web container, or working with one that allows flexibility over the name of the WEB-INF directory, you should still support the usual naming convention. You may not like the standard, but practically all of the Java web application universe abides by it. So you're very much on your own if you go your own way.

EXERCISE 2-1

Using a Servlet to Look at the Context Path

In this exercise we are going to deploy a small web application containing a single servlet. By running the servlet, we will see details of the web application's home directory and context.

Install and Deploy

1. Start the Tomcat server.
2. In the book CD, find file sourcecode/ch02/ex0201.war.
3. Copy this file to <Tomcat Installation Directory>/webapps.
4. Observe the messages on the Tomcat console—make sure that it finds ex0201.war and installs it without error messages.

Explore Directories and Run Servlet

5. Use your file system facilities to confirm that a new directory has been created: <Tomcat Installation Directory>/webapps/ex0201.

6. Check under this directory for files in the right places: a couple of JSPs in the context root and a servlet class file under /WEB-INF/classes.

exam watch

You are very likely to get questions that require you to spot a misplaced file, such as a jsp in the WEB-INF directory or a class file in a subdirectory that isn't WEB-INF/classes.

7. Now run the servlet. The default URL will be http://localhost:8080/ex0201/ShowContext. Study the output carefully. Look at the source code (which is listed to the web page, but you may find the original file easier to work with—look under /WEB-INF/src). Work out which parts of the code produce which parts of the web page.

CERTIFICATION OBJECTIVE

Deployment Descriptor Elements (Exam Objectives 2.2 and 2.3)

Describe the purpose and semantics of the following deployment descriptor elements: error-page, init-param, mime-mapping, servlet, servlet-class, servlet-mapping, servlet-name, and welcome-file.

Construct the correct structure for each of the following deployment descriptor elements: error-page, init-param, mime-mapping, servlet, servlet-class, servlet-mapping, servlet-name, and welcome-file.

Proper file structure is an important part of web application packaging, but the story does not end there. As we have seen, each web application contains a deployment descriptor file called web.xml in the WEB-INF directory. We need to start exploring the semantics of this file in gory detail. Again, your IDE will do you no favors. Chances are your IDE builds the WEB-INF file as you build each web component. As the IDE fills in deployment descriptor details from wizards or through intelligent guesswork, you are left in happy ignorance of web.xml detail. The exam, though, expects you to have developed deployment descriptors from childhood. You need to memorize the elements, the elements that go inside the elements, and sometimes the element order. Time to put aside that IDE and go to your text editor!

This section of the book is the first (but not the last) to examine web.xml elements. We'll start with some of the more fundamental ones, pertaining to servlets or the web application as a whole. As we look at different facets of web applications throughout the rest of the book, their associated deployment descriptor elements will be introduced.

Overall Structure of the Deployment Descriptor

The first thing to note about the deployment descriptor file is that it's an XML file. Given that the name is web.xml, you were probably ahead of me on that one. You might find it reassuring (or disappointing!) to know that next to no XML knowledge is required for the exam, but we will start this part of the chapter by giving you enough knowledge to tackle deployment descriptor semantics. With that foundation, we can go on to explore the seven specific deployment descriptor elements mentioned in the exam objective above.

The Least You Need to Know about XML

If you're reading this book, it's hard to believe that you have not been exposed to XML at some point in your development career. However, it can't do any harm to pin down some essentials about XML format that assume no previous knowledge and that will aid your efforts in deconstructing deployment descriptor files.

Let's start by looking at a minimalist deployment descriptor file, just for the purpose of picking out the XML features. The lines are numbered for ease of reference, as they might appear in some text editors, but the numbers are not part of the syntax.

```
01 <?xml version="1.0" encoding="UTF-8"?>
02 <web-app version="2.4" xmlns=http://java.sun.com/xml/ns/j2ee
03   xmlns:xsi="http://www.w3.org/2001/XMLSchema-instance"
04   xsi:schemaLocation="http://java.sun.com/xml/ns/j2ee
05  http://java.sun.com/xml/ns/j2ee/web-app_2_4.xsd">
06
07   <welcome-file-list>
08     <welcome-file>index.jsp</welcome-file>
09   </welcome-file-list>
10
11 </web-app>
```

Line 1 This line tells us that the file is an XML file, which version of XML is used, and what character set is used for encoding the file contents.

Lines 2–5 and Line 11 These lines define the start and end tags of the root element `<web-app>`, together with a number of attributes that define aspects of the entire document. Every XML document must have a root element to enclose its contents. So in the case of web.xml, the start tag `<web-app>` is closed off with `</web-app>` on line 11. The start tag contains some attributes (name/value pairs). For example, the version attribute (*version*="2.4") marks the document version being used and matches the version number of the servlet specification. (A short digression on versions: The exam you are studying for pertains to the J2EE 1.4 standard. However, J2EE 1.4 embraces a whole range of technologies, each with an associated version number. So J2EE 1.4 has embraced version 2.4 of the servlet specification, which is what's reflected in the deployment descriptor document.) The remaining attributes all have to do with defining an associated "schema" document. The software, which reads an XML file (an XML Parser), has the option of validating the document contents against rules defined in the schema document.

on the job

Schemas are not the only mechanism by which XML documents can be validated. Up to and including J2EE 1.3 and version 2.3 of the servlet standard, web.xml was validated against something called a DTD—or document type definition. The heading material of the XML file looks slightly different, as you can see:

```
<?xml version="1.0" encoding="UTF-8"?>
<!DOCTYPE web-app PUBLIC "-//Sun Microsystems, Inc.//DTD Web Application 2.3//EN"
"http://java.sun.com/dtd/web-app_2_3.dtd">
```

However, the intention is the same—to have a means of validating the deployment descriptor. If you have worked on web applications prior to J2EE 1.4, the good news is that the actual rules for element validation have changed very little, even if the mechanism has. We'll examine the few subtle version differences as we encounter them in the discussion.

Lines 7 and 9 These lines define the start and end tags for `<welcome-file-list>`, one of the many immediate children of the root tag `<web-app>`. XML works by having pairs of tags nested inside each other, to any depth you like. We'll defer talking about what `<welcome-file-list>` actually does for you until later in the chapter; at the moment, we'll stick with XML syntax features.

Line 8 This line defines the start and end tag for `<welcome-file>`, child of `<welcome-file-list>` and grandchild of the root element `<web-app>`. The start and end tags enclose some character data: `index.jsp`.

In terms of content, this very brief deployment descriptor tells us that there is one welcome file, called index.jsp, defined in the welcome file list for this web application. Of course, we have many more options available to us for the information we record about our web application in the deployment descriptor. The next section opens up the possibilities.

Anatomy of web.xml

The deployment descriptor has, in fact, 27 top-level elements, shown in Figure 2-2. These top-level elements each contain — on average — a half dozen or so elements, at various levels of nesting, ranging from the very simple (e.g., `<distributable>`, with no nested elements) to `<servlet>` (with 9 nested elements, some containing more nested elements).

FIGURE 2-2

The Full List of Top-Level Elements in the Deployment Descriptor web.xml

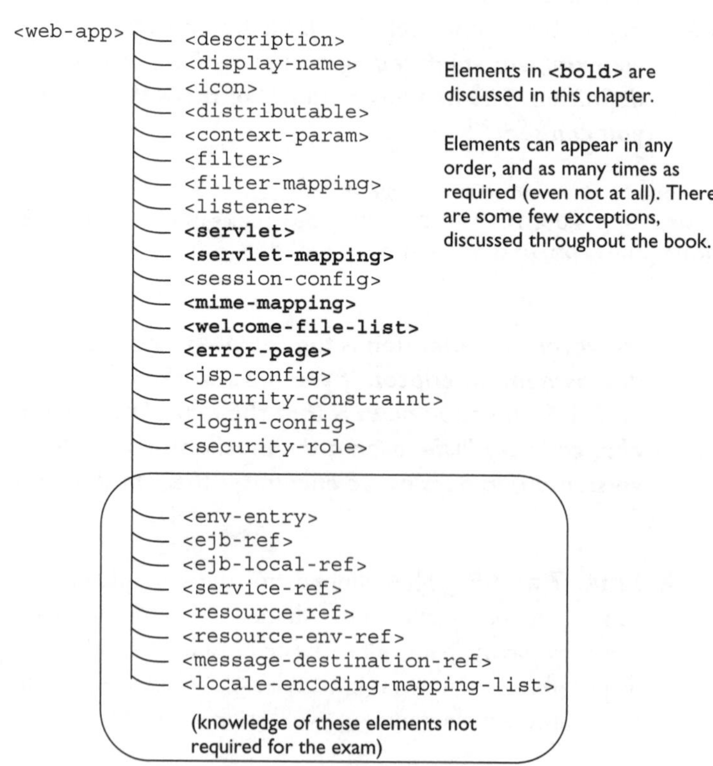

exam watch ***A traditional type of "gotcha" exam question asks you to identify which of a list of elements within root element web-app are mandatory. None of them are! A web.xml file that contains only an empty root element (<web-app></web-app>) is perfectly legal.***

Differences from Previous Servlet Specification

Good news for examinees: Top-level elements can now appear in any order! For an earlier version of the exam, I spent a lot of time memorizing sequence. Having said that, you are probably well advised to follow the order shown in Figure 2-2. People are very used to the order from previous versions of the servlet specification, so they might be thrown by placement of elements radically different from the established norm.

watch ***Sequence still matters within the elements inside the top-level elements—`<servlet>`, for example.***

Some elements that used to be optional or appear once are now optional and can (according to schema validation) appear many times. This doesn't make a lot of sense in some circumstances. For example, the `<distributable>` element need only appear once for the application to be marked distributable—repeating the element ten times doesn't make the application any more distributable! The servlet specification tells you what containers are supposed to do when there is more than one occurrence of an element that formerly could only appear once, and we'll draw attention to the rules in subsequent chapters.

Deployment Descriptor Elements for Servlets

One of the top-level elements in the deployment descriptor is `<servlet>`. This is a "complex type" of element because it contains several other elements within itself. For the exam and for real-life development, it isn't sufficient just to know the top-level elements—you'll need to know the contents as well.

There are several characteristics you can define for a servlet, beyond a simple name. We'll need to give the deployment descriptor the fully qualified name of the actual Java class for a start. Other optional subelements control whether the servlet is loaded when the web container starts, and any security rules in force.

And we'll find that <servlet> is a slight misnomer. Not only can you use the element to define plain servlets; you can also use it to define a reference to a JSP (JavaServer Page). (However, as we'll see later, JSPs are converted to servlets by the web container, so perhaps the element name isn't such a misnomer after all.)

A separate element called <servlet-mapping> gives you flexibility over which URLs are used to access servlet resources, and we'll talk about that too.

<servlet> and Its Important Subelements

Figure 2-3 shows the <servlet> element expanded so that you can see how the sub-elements nest within one another, which ones are optional, and how many times each can appear. You can see that only the <servlet-name> and <servlet-class>/<jsp-file> elements are mandatory and that these elements can appear only once within the <servlet> element. Other elements, such as <load-on-startup>, are entirely optional. You don't have to have any <init-param> elements, or you can have as many as you like. The figure indicates that if you do include an <init-param>, it must house one <param-name> and one <param-value>.

The ordering of subelements within <servlet> is crucial. We've already noted that the top-level elements within the root element <web-app> can come in any order. However, the deployment descriptor schema validates that when it comes to the elements in <servlet>, then (for example) <servlet-name> must come before <servlet-class> (and after <icon>, if you choose to include an <icon> element).

FIGURE 2-3 The Servlet Element Expanded

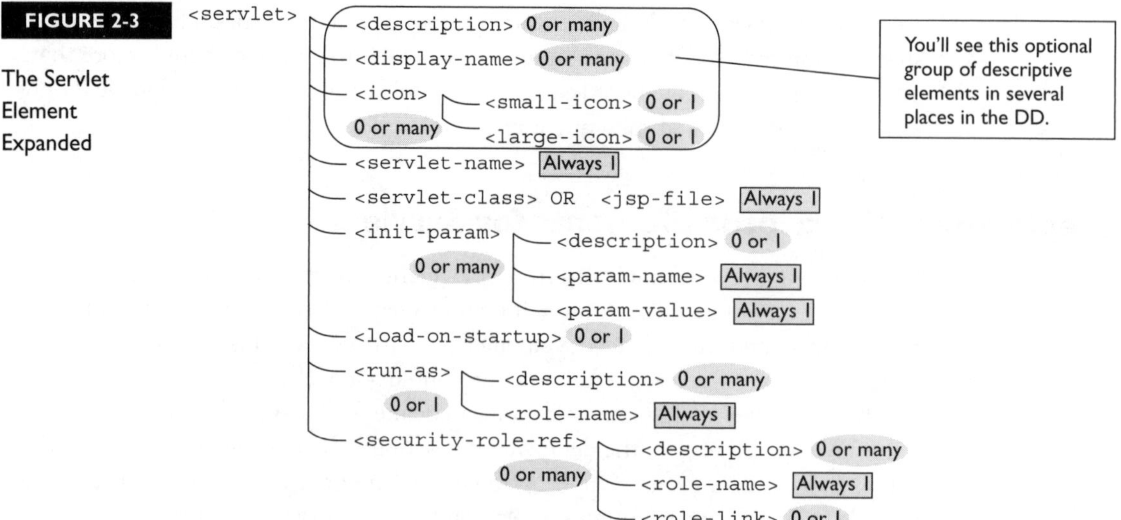

FIGURE 2-4 An Example <servlet> Declaration in the Deployment Descriptor

```
<web-app>
  <servlet>
    <description>A servlet for predicting the future</description>
    <description xml:lang="fr">une servlette pour prédire l'avenir</description>
    <display-name>Future Predictor</display-name>
    <display-name xml:lang="fr">Pour Prédire L'avenir</display-name>
    <icon>
      <small-icon>/images/futurep.gif</small-icon>
    </icon>
    <servlet-name>FutureServlet</servlet-name>
    <servlet-class>com.osborne.c02.FutureServlet</servlet-class>
    <init-param>
      <description>The number of months ahead to predict: default value</description>
      <param-name>months</param-name>
      <param-value>3</param-value>
    </init-param>
    <init-param>
      <description>How wild to make the prediction: default adjective</description>
      <param-name>wildness</param-name>
      <param-value>exaggerated</param-value>
    </init-param>
    <load-on-startup>1</load-on-startup>
  </servlet>
</web-app>
```

Fully qualified name of class—NB: don't add .class to the end!

run-as and security-role-ref omitted—these make a comeback in Chapter 5, on web security.

Figure 2-4 completes the picture by showing servlet deployment definitions in practice: a mostly complete servlet definition for a web.xml file. The more important start and end tags are in boldface. Just note for now that the servlet is called Future Servlet and that it maps to the Java class com.osborne.c02.FutureServlet. There are two initialization parameters, one called *months* and the other *wildness*, with values of 3 and "exaggerated," respectively.

Let's take a look at the more important subelements in a bit more detail.

<servlet-name> This subelement defines a logical name for the servlet. There aren't many rules for this element, but you should know them. The name must be unique within the web application. Any string for the name will do, provided it's at least one character long. There's no obligation to make this name the same as the Java class to which it relates (though people often do use the Java class name stripped of the fully qualified package parts).

Why do we want to name a servlet anyway? There are many other possible resources in a web application that don't boast a specially defined name in the deployment descriptor. However, here are at least a couple of reasons:

- Servlets are normally a protected resource, kept in the WEB-INF/classes directory, so that direct URL access to the servlet won't work. The servlet name is part of the mechanism by which controlled access to servlets is allowed (you'll learn more about this when we look at `<servlet-mapping>`).

- A logical, unique name for the servlet is a deal less cumbersome than always referring to a servlet, say, by its fully qualified Java class name. You'll find that you can reference a servlet name at various points from elsewhere in the deployment descriptor.

Should you want to access the servlet name within your own code, you can. There is a `getServletName()` method defined in the ServletConfig interface (which is implemented by GenericServlet, so any inheriting servlet will have the method available). Here's a code listing showing how a servlet's `doGet()` method can print the servlet name on the server console:

```
protected void doGet(HttpServletRequest request, HttpServletResponse response)
  throws ServletException, IOException {
  System.out.println(this.getServletName());
}
```

exam watch

You may think I'm very pedantic in pointing out which interface defines the `getServletName()` method (ServletConfig). You might encounter questions that ask you to distinguish whether a method originates from, say, the ServletConfig or the Servlet interface. Helpful hint: Three of the four methods on ServletConfig have to do with extracting information from the deployment descriptor (all of which you meet in this section); Servlet has no methods of this kind; its methods are mainly to do with servlet life cycle, which we meet in Chapter 3. However you do it, though, you need the methods of Servlet memorized for the exam, together with the interfaces from which they originate.

`<servlet-class>` This subelement defines the fully qualified name of a Java servlet class. You'll want this class to be a descendant of GenericServlet or HttpServlet. Your XML validation software won't tick you off if you violate this rule, but your web container will choke when it tries to run a nonservlet defined as a servlet class here. Separate parts of the package name should be separated with dots (nothing unusual there). On no account put ".class" at the end of the value you enter.

Although the names of servlets (defined in `<servlet-name>`) have to be unique, there is no such constraint on servlet classes. You can define the same servlet class against two or more names, as shown in the deployment descriptor extract below:

```
<servlet>
 <servlet-name>MyServletHere</servlet-name>
 <servlet-class>webcert.chapter2.MyServlet</servlet-class>
</servlet>
<servlet>
 <servlet-name>MyServletThere</servlet-name>
 <servlet-class>webcert.chapter2.MyServlet</servlet-class>
</servlet>
```

Why would you want to do this? Although not shown, it's the only way of supplying separate sets of initialization parameters to the servlet, for starters. It's also a way of ensuring a separate running instance of the servlet. Normally, a web container would deal with any number of requests for the servlet logically known as My ServletHere by instantiating only one object of the MyServlet type. However, as soon as the web container received a request for MyServletThere, it would be forced to instantiate another separate object of MyServlet type. If it's important, you can use the `getServletName()` method to determine which instance you are running.

... or `<jsp-file>` We don't meet JSPs (JavaServer Pages) for another few chapters. When we do, you'll see that—unlike servlets—they are normally located in the HTTP-accessible regions of a web application. So users typically request a JSP directly from the web application context root (or a suitable subdirectory).

However, suppose we want a JSP that is not directly accessible, which we keep in some directory of WEB-INF—for example,

```
/WEB-INF/secure/concealed.jsp
```

The direct approach—say, http://localhost:8080/mywebcontext/WEB-INF/secure/concealed.jsp—rightly results in an HTTP 404 (page not found) error. However, the following deployment descriptor entries give a means of access:

```
<servlet>
  <servlet-name>ConcealedJSP</servlet-name>
  <jsp-file>/WEB-INF/secure/concealed.jsp</jsp-file>
</servlet>
<servlet-mapping>
  <servlet-name>ConcealedJSP</servlet-name>
  <url-pattern>/allIsRevealed</url-pattern>
</servlet-mapping>
```

The full chapter and verse on `<servlet-mapping>` will follow very soon. Suffice to say for the moment that the user can now type http://localhost:8080/mywebcontext/allIsRevealed into her browser and have the JSP returned. One possible reason for doing this is to conceal the usage of JSPs in the application: The URL gives nothing away. Another is to support existing links that are converted from static pages to JSPs (so . . . /index.html finds a JSP file). There is no necessity to keep the JSPs under WEB-INF for this purpose; just set up an appropriate servlet mapping.

`<init-param>` We saw in Chapter 1 how we can get parameters to a servlet from the web page `<form>`, which has the servlet as the subject of its action. `<init-param>` gives another means of priming a servlet, but this time the information is recorded directly in the deployment descriptor file. We saw in Figure 2-4 the full deployment descriptor details for the FuturePredictor servlet. Here's the deployment descriptor for the initialization parameters alone:

```
<init-param>
  <description>The number of months ahead to predict: default value</description>
  <param-name>months</param-name>
  <param-value>3</param-value>
</init-param>
<init-param>
  <description>How wild to make the prediction: default adjective</description>
  <param-name>wildness</param-name>
  <param-value>exaggerated</param-value>
</init-param>
```

The `<init-param>` envelope can repeat as many times as you want parameters for the servlet. Inside the envelope, we always find two subelements: `<param-name>` and `<param-value>`. These are mandatory, and they represent a key/value pairing: You use the key of the name to return the value. There can only be one `<param-name>/<param-value>` pairing for each `<init-param>` (if you want another pairing, use a fresh `<init-param>`). Should you wish, you can place a `<description>` before `<param-name>`.

All we need now is the means of retrieving the information, which is very easy. The code below uses two servlet methods (originating from the ServletConfig interface, implemented in the GenericServlet class) to get at the initialization information. `getInitParameterNames()` returns an Enumeration of all the parameter names available to the servlet. Armed with a parameter name, you can use `getInitParameter(String paramName)` to return an individual parameter value.

```
protected void doGet(HttpServletRequest request,
  HttpServletResponse response) throws ServletException, IOException {
  /* Local variables to hold parameter values */
  int months = 0;
  String wildness = "";
  /* Iterate through all the initialization parameters */
  Enumeration e = getInitParameterNames();
  while (e.hasMoreElements()) {
    String parmName = (String) e.nextElement();
    if (parmName.equals("months")) {
      months = Integer.parseInt(getInitParameter(parmName));
    }
    if (parmName.equals("wildness")) {
      wildness = getInitParameter(parmName);
    }
  }
  /* Return a page showing the values discovered */
  response.setContentType("text/plain");
  PrintWriter out = response.getWriter();
  out.write("Intialization parameters were 'months' with a value of "
    + months + ' and 'wildness' with a value of '" + wildness + "'");
}
```

Because `getInitParameter(String paramName)` returns a String value, you have to write your own parsing code to coerce numeric values to their right type—as is the case with the *months* parameter.

Finally, there's no servlet API to get at the optional `<description>` element of an initialization parameter. That's there for the benefit of those responsible for maintaining the deployment descriptor, and it might show up in a graphical administrative console.

exam watch

`<init-param>` appears elsewhere in the deployment descriptor—not just as a nested element within `<servlet>`. Watch out for its very similar use as a nested element in `<filter>`, which makes its appearance in Chapter 3. And the trio of subelements—`<description>`, `<param-name>`, `<param-value>`—also crop up inside the `<context-param>` element.

The <servlet-mapping> element

Although we've defined a number of key aspects of the servlet, we haven't yet given users of our application any means of getting at it as a URL resource. That's what the <servlet-mapping> element is for. You might find it surprising that <servlet-mapping> is not another subelement of <servlet>; instead, it lives as a top-level element directly off the root <web-app>. Perhaps the designers of the deployment descriptor thought the <servlet> tag was already too overloaded. You can see in the following illustration expanding <servlet-mapping> and its subelements that it's considerably simpler than the related <servlet> element.

```
<servlet-mapping>
    <servlet-name>
    <url-pattern>
```

The subelement <servlet-name> should tie back to a <servlet-name> defined in a <servlet> element. The <url-pattern> subelement specifies what the user can expect to type into the URL after the context name and have her request find the associated servlet. So if the deployment descriptor has the following servlet mapping defined:

```
<servlet-mapping>
  <servlet-name>FutureServlet</servlet-name>
  <url-pattern>/myfuture</url-pattern>
</servlet-mapping>
```

And the user types something like the following URL:

```
http://localhost:8080/webappcontext/myfuture
```

Then the servlet (or JSP) defined in a corresponding <servlet> tag with a <servlet-name> of FutureServlet will execute.

exam watch

What values are allowed for the URL pattern? You can use almost any characters you like. Two things to note: First, carriage returns and line feeds are not allowed. No real surprise there. What is more surprising is that white space is legal—a URL pattern such as `<url-pattern>My Servlet</url-pattern>` is legal and works. You'll probably find that your browser substitutes a hexadecimal representation of the white space character in the address line (%20).

INSIDE THE EXAM

URL Mapping Strategies

Actually, we're not quite done with servlet mapping. The servlet specification builds in a deal of flexibility into URL patterns, which you need to know for the exam. There are four kinds of mapping you can specify. There are also rules which dictate—in the case of more than one matching mapping for a URL—which mapping should take precedence. Let's look in more detail.

Exact Path Mapping The URL content following the context path exactly matches the URL pattern in the servlet mapping.

Longest Path Prefix The URL content following the context path is tested against partial paths specified in URL patterns. The longest match wins.

Extensions If the last part of the request URL is a file with an extension (e.g., the .jsp in /index.jsp), the extension is matched against any extension-type URL patterns.

Default Servlet If the above mapping methods have failed, the server may have one ace left up its sleeve: the default servlet.

The following table shows how to specify the URL patterns to indicate which of the four match methods is intended, and gives some examples of URLs that would cause a match.

Rule	URL Pattern	How to Form the URL Pattern	URLs That Would Match
Exact match	/findthis	Any string—must begin with "/."	/findthis
Path match	/findthat/here/*	String must begin with "/" and end in "/*."	/findthat/here /findthat/here/quickly /findthat/here/quickly/index.html
Extension match	*.jsp	String must begin with "*."	/index.jsp/any directory/index.jsp
Default	/	Single forward slash only: "/."	(any URL that fell through all other matching attempts)

Once a match is found according to the rules above, no further matching is attempted. And whereas these rules were merely "recommendations" in past versions of the servlet spec, web containers are now "required" to support them.

INSIDE THE EXAM (continued)

Two things to remember: URL patterns are case sensitive. A URL of /findthis would match a pattern of /findthis, but not /FindThis. Second, servers may have some implicit mappings already set up outside of web .xml—for example, something to trap a ".jsp" extension, for JSP files can't be served directly. If you specify your own extension match for ".jsp" or an alternative to the default servlet, then you will override what the server does: It's then your web application's responsibility to deal with the request.

on the job

Do you need a `<servlet-mapping>` to execute a servlet? The answer is "not necessarily." Many web servers have the capability of "serving servlets by name." There is nothing particularly magical about this, and it does—in fact—involve servlet mappings. Imagine your server had a `<url-pattern>` set up of /servlet/*, which mapped on to a servlet called ServletExecutor. This means that a request such as mycontext/servlet/SomeServletOrOther will invoke the ServletExecutor servlet. The ServletExecutor servlet determines that SomeServletOrOther is indeed a servlet within this web application, and it redirects control to the SomeServletOrOther servlet—even though there is no mapping necessarily set up for SomeServletOrOther. Convenient as such a facility is, you will want to switch it off in production environments for security reasons! This approach may be convenient for development and test environments, however; it saves some setup in the deployment descriptor. That said, you will probably be working with an IDE that sets up the deployment descriptor servlet mappings as part of the servlet creation process. In such circumstances, the usefulness of serving servlets by name dwindles somewhat. Added to this, you could argue that it's not a proper test of your servlet except in the context of mappings correctly set up in the deployment descriptor.

Other `<servlet>` Subelements

There are other elements embedded in the `<servlet>` tag that we haven't yet discussed. Some of these will return in future chapters and objectives. Others aren't explicitly mentioned in the exam objective, but your knowledge of the `<servlet>` tag wouldn't be complete without them.

We'll start with the trio of `<description>`, `<display-name>`, and `<icon>`. This is a standard grouping of elements that occurs several times in the deployment descriptor. For example, these three elements are actually the first three top-level elements under `<web-app>` (see Figure 2-2). In that case, they apply to the entire web application. As subelements of `<servlet>`, they apply to a particular servlet. As you might hope, though, they are functionally equivalent wherever they appear.

We'll end this section with elements that are entirely specific to `<servlet>`.

<description> Optionally, you can enter descriptive text for your servlet in this tag. There is no API in the servlet packages to retrieve this description. It's not for the consumers of your web application; it's for the benefit of administrators. So a web container might have an administrative console that chose to display this text for a deployed web application, for example.

You can include as many descriptions as you want (i.e., separate occurrences of the description element). What's wrong with just one, you ask? The reason is to accommodate multiple languages. You can qualify each description element with the *xml:lang* attribute, giving a valid two-character country code. If you omit *xml:lang*, then a default of *xml:lang="en"* is presumed. Here's an extract from a longer web.xml file, which shows both an English and a French description:

```
<description>A servlet for predicting the future</description>
<description xml:lang="fr">une servlette pour prédire l'avenir</description>
```

<display-name> The function of `<display-name>` is very similar to the `<description>` element. It's also meant for use in web container administrative user interfaces in order to provide a short descriptive name—perhaps less cryptic than the servlet name, but less expansive than the description text. However, you can provide any string you want, of course. The same rules apply about language: You can have as many display names as different languages. Here's an example:

```
<display-name>Future Predictor</display-name>
<display-name xml:lang="fr">Pour Prédire L'avenir</display-name>
```

<icon> This subelement is the last of the descriptive trio. As with the others, it is entirely optional, and you can have many occurrences. Within the icon element you can embed a `<small-icon>` and a `<large-icon>` element (one, both, or neither). The element describes a path (from the context root) to an image file (JPG and GIF are the permitted formats) that might be used by your web container administrative GUI to display next to your servlet. Example:

```
<icon>
  <small-icon>/images/futurep.gif</small-icon>
</icon>
```

That concludes the "descriptive trio" of elements. There are three remaining subelements of `<servlet>`: `<load-on-startup>`, `<run-as>`, and `<security-role-ref>`. Actually, we're going to postpone the last two until we discuss security in Chapter 5, leaving just `<load-on-startup>`.

`<load-on-startup>` A web container's usual practice is to load a servlet at the point where it is first accessed. In fact, the web container is free to load the servlet at any point it regards as suitable. However, by defining the `<load-on-startup>` element, the servlet is loaded at the point when the web container starts. Furthermore, you can control the order in which servlets load by the integers you specify as the values of the `<load-on-startup>` tags:

- A servlet with a lower number will be loaded before a servlet with a higher number.
- If the numbers are the same, you're in the lap of the web container designers—there are no guarantees on which servlet starts first.
- If the number is negative, the web container can do whatever it pleases regarding loading the servlet: It's as if the `<load-on-startup>` element wasn't there at all.

If a `<jsp-file>` is specified rather than a `<servlet-class>`, a `<load-on-startup>` setting ensures that the JSP is pre-compiled (turned into a servlet), then loaded as any other servlet would be.

Before you individually register hundreds of JSPs from your web-app in web .xml just to force pre-compilation, check out the facilities of your application server. These days, almost every application server has an option for pre-compiling JSPs at the point of deploying the application into the server.

Other Deployment Descriptor Elements

Now we'll turn our attention to some of the deployment descriptor elements that affect the web application as a whole, as opposed to individual servlets.

Welcome Files: <welcome-file-list>

There have probably been many occasions in your life where you have typed in a web site address into your browser—such as www.osborne.com—and, owing to some magic in the target web server, you are taken to the resource for a specific URL, say http://www.osborne.com/index.html. If a J2EE web application is the object of your request, the chances are that this behavior comes about through the specification of a welcome file list in the deployment descriptor. Here's an example:

```
<welcome-file-list>
  <welcome-file>index.html</welcome-file>
  <welcome-file>index.jsp</welcome-file>
  <welcome-file>mainlibrary/catalog.jsp</welcome-file>
</welcome-file-list>
```

To see how this works, we need a set of files and a directory structure for the corresponding web application. We're imagining a library application with a host of mylibrary.com and a context of catalogapp. Here we see the visible (HTTP-accessible) directories and files from context root downward.

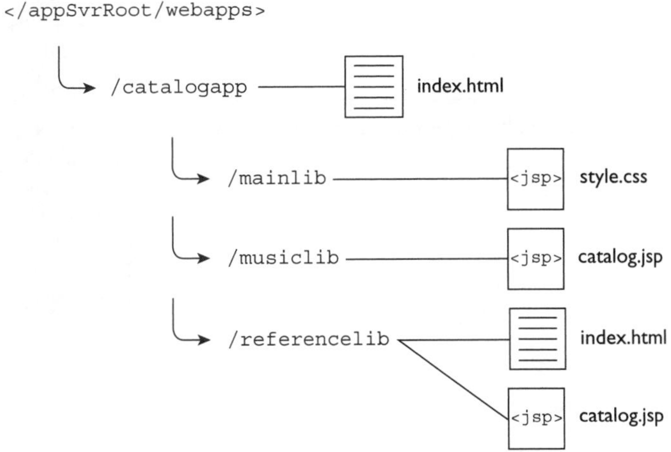

Now we need to consider what happens when you request a URL that falls to the web container to deal with but that doesn't immediately match a specific resource. A trailing slash is appended to the URL if not already present. Then each entry in the welcome file list is appended—in turn—to this URL and tested for a match against a specific resource. If the resource is present in the directory, it's returned to the requester. Here are some examples:

http://mylibrary.com/catalogapp	■ "/" appended to URL. ■ "index.html"—first welcome-file—appended to URL. ■ catalogapp directory checked for index.html—found! ■ index.html returned to requester.
http://mylibrary.com/catalogapp/mainlib/	■ "index.html"—first welcome file—appended to URL. ■ mainlib directory checked for index .html—not found. ■ "index.jsp"—second welcome file—appended to URL. ■ mainlib directory checked for index .jsp—found and returned!
http://mylibrary.com/catalogapp/musiclib/	■ "index.html"—first welcome file—appended to URL but not found in musiclib directory. ■ "index.jsp"—second welcome file—appended to URL but still no match in musiclib directory. ■ "catalog.jsp"—third welcome file—appended to URL. Found and returned!
http://mylibrary.com/catalogapp/referencelib/	■ "index.html"—first welcome file—appended to URL. Found and returned! ■ *Even though catalog.jsp—the third welcome file—is present in the referencelib directory, it won't be returned by the welcome file mechanism, which will always find index.html first.*

The rules in the servlet specification state that welcome-file entries must describe a partial URL with *no leading and no trailing slashes*. This makes sense when you consider that the entries are appended to a URL that has a trailing slash (either because the user typed it into the browser or the web server put it in implicitly) and should match up to a specific resource (not a directory).

exam watch

It's very easy to be caught out on the exact wording and nesting of the tags. Look out for questions that get the element order inside out (`<welcome-file-list>` nested under `<welcome-file>`) or that introduce subtle and incorrect variant spellings (`<welcome-files>`). Remember also that the direct parent of `<welcome-file-list>` is `<web-app>`, the root element.

Error Files: <error-page>

In Chapter 1 we examined the world of HTTP requests, including the error codes that crop up when requests go bad. The `<error-page>` element in the deployment descriptor gives you customized control over the web page displayed to the user in the event of requests going wrong. Let's suppose you have the following set up in your deployment descriptor:

```
<web-abb>
  <error-page>
    <error-code>404</error-code>
    <location>/customErrorPage.html</location>
  </error-page>
</web-app>
```

Your context root contains your customErrorPage.html file and a couple of other files.

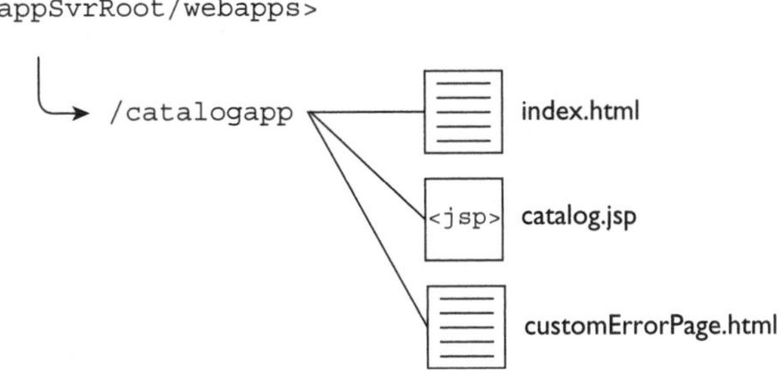

A user means to request catalog.jsp but erroneously enters the following in his browser:

```
http://mylibrary.com/catalogapp/qatalog.jsp
```

The request correctly routes to the web application because the context is correct, but it doesn't find the specific resource qatalog.jsp. The result is an HTTP 404 error code, page not found. Instead of returning the standard web server page for this error, the web container looks for a matching error code in the deployment descriptor's list of error codes. A match is found, so the custom error page customErrorPage.html is set up instead.

There are some important things to note about the deployment descriptor construction:

- `<error-page>` has `<web-app>` as its immediate parent.
- `<error-code>` and `<location>` both have `<error-page>` as their parent.
- The resource specified in `<location>` *must* start with a "/." The path described is from the context root.

exam watch

It's very easy to get the rules for `<location>` in `<error-page>` confused with `<welcome-file>` in `<welcome-file-list>`. Resources specified in `<location>` must begin with an "/," whereas those in `<welcome-file>` must not begin with an "/." Neither should end with an "/," of course, because they specify particular resources—files and servlets—not directories.

The web container is perfectly capable of generating HTTP status codes when the conditions are right (or should I say wrong!). We can—in servlet code—generate our own status or error codes, using the `sendError()` and `setStatus()` methods on HttpServletResponse. So servlet code like this (to generate a "404" error):

```
response.sendError(HttpServletResponse.SC_NOT_FOUND);
```

would cause the error page mechanism to kick in just as effectively as the user typing error we saw a few moments ago. And so would

```
response.setStatus(HttpServletResponse.SC_NOT_FOUND);
```

However, it is a *bad thing* to use `setStatus()` for anything other than normal conditions.

You are not limited to specifying static html pages as the location for an error page. You can specify a servlet to perform any dynamic processing you like. Just make sure that you specify a location value that will chime in with the servlet mapping for your dynamic error servlet.

That's not the end of the story for <error-page>. HTTP status codes are not the only error page mechanism at your disposal. You can also map plain old Java exceptions to particular error pages. In that case, you substitute the <exception-type> tag for <error-code>:

```
<web-abb>
  <error-page>
    <exception-type>javax.servlet.ServletException</exception-type>
    <location>/customErrorPage.html</location>
  </error-page>
</web-app>
```

If you have a servlet that happens to throw a ServletException at runtime, the web container will return the custom error page as specified. Take care to specify the full qualified name of the exception (e.g., *javax.servlet.*ServletException), though, or the mechanism will not be triggered, and you'll get some standard application server error page instead.

Mime-mapping: <mime-file>

MIME (Multipurpose Internet Mail Extensions) is an Internet standard for describing media types. By "media," understand "file"—which could be anything from plain text to images to movies. Don't be fooled by the "Mail" part of the MIME acronym: The standard has been embraced by web servers, application servers, and web browsers everywhere. See http://www.iana.org/assignments/media-types/ for the official list of MIME types.

We already saw in Chapter 1 how you could set the MIME type of a servlet response programmatically. That's fine and appropriate when the object of your request is a servlet. However, your web application may serve up other types of resources. Some are likely to be understood. If I set up plain text files with a .txt extension in my web application, my web container serves them up to my browser without difficulty. What if I wanted to serve up my own brand of XML files, though, with an .xmldavid extension? My application server returns them happily enough, but with no mime-type, the browser has to do the best it can to figure out the response. However, if I set up a <mime-mapping> entry in the deployment descriptor as follows:

```
<web-app>
  <mime-mapping>
    <extension>xmldavid</extension>
    <mime-type>text/xml</mime-type>
  </mime-mapping>
</web-app>
```

The client has an opportunity to process the file as an XML file, despite the unusual extension. I say "opportunity," because browsers may ignore the MIME-type set in the response and apply their own rules on processing the content.

EXERCISE 2-2

Defining Deployment Descriptor Elements

In this exercise we are going to deploy a small web application containing a single servlet. The servlet isn't very useful because the supplied deployment descriptor file is minimal (`<web-app></web-app>`). You will complete the deployment descriptor in the course of the exercise and run the servlet.

Install and Deploy

1. Start the Tomcat server.
2. In the book CD, find file sourcecode/ch02/ex0202.war.
3. Copy this file to <Tomcat Installation Directory>/webapps.
4. Observe the messages on the Tomcat console—make sure that it finds ex0202.war and installs it without error messages.
5. Delete ex0202.war.

Adjust the Deployment Descriptor

6. Find the deployment descriptor file, web.xml (in <Tomcat Installation Directory>/webapps/ex0202/WEB-INF).
7. Using your favorite text editor, amend the file to have a `<welcome-file-list>` pointing to index1.jsp, and an `<error-page>` pointing to error.jsp for an HTTP status code 404 error.
8. Restart Tomcat.
9. Check that index1.jsp displays for URL http://localhost:8080/ex0202/. (Hint: If this—or any other page—fails to display, first make sure you *clear your*

browser cache by hitting the refresh button. This applies throughout this and future exercises!)

10. Check that error.jsp displays for URL http://localhost:8080/ex0202/notfound.html. (You may have a problem seeing this page—some browsers have a habit of substituting their own 404 "page not found" error page instead of deferring to the server's page.)
11. Stop Tomcat.
12. Re-edit web.xml. Add a servlet definition for servlet class webcert.ch02.ex0202.ShowInitParms. Give the servlet any number of initialization parameters you like. Don't forget to add a servlet mapping for the servlet.
13. Restart Tomcat, and call the servlet using your mapping details.
14. If you are really stuck (and only if!), check out the web.solution.xml file in the /WEB-INF directory of the web application.

CERTIFICATION OBJECTIVE

WAR Files (Exam Objective 2.4)

Explain the purpose of a WAR file and describe the contents of a WAR file, how one may be constructed.

Web applications get chock-full of directories and files in even the most unambitious of projects. If you are happy to deploy and manage all those directories and files individually, you have more of a taste for configuration management than I do. Fortunately, the J2EE providers thought of that and provided a standard for packaging all web application components into a single zip-format file whose format is known as the web archive—or WAR, for short.

Packaging Your Web Application

Provided you have abided by the file and directory naming rules outlined in the first section of this chapter, packaging your web application is no big deal. You simply take the contents beneath the context path and zip up the whole structure into one file. The context path itself is not part of the WAR. WARs are designed to be unzipped into a context path of the deployer's choosing.

The structure of a WAR file is exactly the same as a Java archive (JAR), which is in turn the same as a ZIP file. So on a Windows system, a tool such as WinZip is very useful for interrogating the contents of a WAR file. A zip-type tool is all that's required to package and unpackage a WAR file, and, of course, the J2SDK comes with one supplied in the shape of the "jar" tool.

A WAR Is Not a JAR

Although a WAR file can be produced in the same way as a JAR file, and has the same underlying file format, it is different. The most obvious difference is the file extension naming convention: .jar for Java ARchive, and .war for Web (Application) ARchive.

JARs are packaged in a particular way to make it easy for a running JVM to find and load Java class files. WARs are packaged for a different purpose: to make it as easy as possible for a web container to deploy an application.

Several web containers have automatic deployment mechanisms. The server recommended for this book—Tomcat—has a "webapps" directory. Place a WAR file in this directory, and Tomcat (by default) will un-jar the contents into the file system under the webapps directory. It provides a context root directory with the same name as the WAR file (but without the .war extension)—then makes the application available for use. The interesting contrast here is that WAR files are not *necessarily* "un-jarred" for use; some web containers run web applications directly from the WAR file itself. For example, the Sun application server that comes with the J2EE 1.4 download has an "autodeploy" directory. Placing the WAR file there causes the server to load the constituent parts of the application into memory and available for use—but doesn't unzip them.

Either way, I hope you are beginning to see the point of having the WAR file standard. When it comes to deployment, life is very easy. Get the packaging wrong, however, and your web container will disown the WAR file in no uncertain manner.

Just before we move on to methods for making WAR files, we need to consider one last required directory for our web application: META-INF.

The META-INF Directory

In the beginning, WARs were intended to be completely self-contained. Everything a web application relied on would be packaged in the WAR. This setup was convenient, but it overlooked the fact that many web applications deployed on the same server might make use of many common libraries of code. Including these as JAR files in every WAR seemed wasteful; if nothing else, it led to huge inflation of WAR file size. Configuration management was potentially an issue, for updating a common library JAR file meant duplicating it to every web application that used it.

The solution was to allow web containers to provide a common repository for code. How and where the web container defines this common repository is specific to the web container; it may have several. It's quite a complex business that demands associated rules to do with class loading. For a good explanation on how one web container does this—Tomcat—take a look at

```
http://jakarta.apache.org/tomcat/tomcat-5.0-doc/class-loader-howto.html
```

For exam purposes, though, you don't need to know anything of the detail. All you need is some grasp of the general principle so that the purpose of META-INF is clearer to you.

Although the rules for storing and loading common code are container-specific, the mechanism by which a WAR references such common code is a J2EE standard. Each WAR can now reference the JARs it needs in this common repository by using an existing mechanism: a manifest file. This file is called MANIFEST.MF, and it must be located in the META-INF directory in the WAR file.

The essential content of MANIFEST.MF is a list of JARs under a heading of "classpath." Suppose you wanted to take advantage of a logging library such as log4j in your web server's common repository. You might see an entry in the file such as this:

```
Classpath: log4j.jar
```

Note that only the JAR file name is present; the server knows which specific directories to search.

There is plenty more you can specify about referenced code in MANIFEST.MF, such as version information or the vendor that sold (and digitally signed) a code library. You can find chapter and verse on the standard at

```
http://java.sun.com/j2se/1.4.2/docs/guide/extensions/
```

You have to introduce META-INF only at the WAR-making stage, and then only if you have a need for it. Chances are you will want it available to you in most applications; indeed, most development tools will put it there for you whether you request it or not.

exam watch

When META-INF is present in your web application, the same access rules apply as for WEB-INF. Server-side code is welcome to access resource files in the META-INF directory. However, the web container should reject any attempt at client-side access with the regular "page not found" HTTP error code of 404.

Cross-referencing common code isn't the only purpose for the META-INF directory. If you are signing the WAR file for security reasons, or JARs contained in WEB-INF/lib, the META-INF directory is also the right place to store digital certificates.

Making WARs

Now that we know what a WAR is for and how it's made up, let's look a bit more closely at how we make a WAR. The most obvious method is using the **jar** tool in the J2SDK. For the exam you will be expected to know the basic parameters to provide to **jar**, both for packaging and unpackaging WAR files.

The **jar** tool is not the only game in town, however. We'll touch on some other WAR-making devices that you're more likely to encounter in "real" development than naked use of the **jar** command.

Packaging Your Web Application

To run the jar command, you will want a command line. To make things easier, change directory to the context directory of the web application that you want to package. You'll need to have your <J2SDK>/bin directory in your PATH. Enter the following command (for Windows—UNIX is very similar):

```
jar cvf0 mywarfile.war *.*
```

This creates a WAR file called mywarfile.war in the context directory, containing all the files in the context directory and any subdirectories (/WEB-INF, /WEB-INF/lib, etc.). The following table explains the parameters:

c	Creates the WAR file.
v	Verbose: outputs messages on the command line telling you about every file added.
f	A WAR file name will be specified (*can* be omitted, but you're unlikely to want to go there).
0	Don't compress the file (you would usually omit this).
mywarfile .war	The name of the WAR file to be created. It must follow straight after the "cvf0" group (separated by a space).
.	The files to include in the WAR file: in this case, everything. Must follow straight after the WAR file name (separated by a space).

Unpackaging Your Web Application

Unpackaging looks very similar, and it is not usually something you would do manually anyway, for web servers invariably have their own deployment mechanisms, as previously explained. If you do want to expand a WAR file manually so that you know how to for the exam, here are instructions:

- Create a context directory in the relevant part of your web server's hierarchy.
- Put the WAR file in the context directory.
- Execute the following command (Windows and UNIX are very similar):

```
jar xvf mywebapp.war
```

- Command explanation follows:

x	Extracts the contents of the WAR file.
v	Verbose: outputs messages on the command line telling you about every file extracted.
f	A WAR file name will be specified.
mywarfile .war	The name of the WAR file to be created. It must follow straight after the "xvf" group (separated by a space).

exam watch

Another useful command parameter for the **jar** *command is* t, *to display the contents of a WAR file. The full command might look like this:* `jar tf mywarfile.war`.

on the job

Development Tools (IDEs) often have built-in functionality to export WAR files directly from your web development environment, and most will do more than this. Furthermore, if your IDE is lacking, your web server probably won't be. Most web servers come with some sort of assembly and packaging tool. You specify the files and directories you want to include using the tool's graphical user interface; out pops a WAR file at the other end. These tools tend to more than just package WARs: They have facilities to build the deployment descriptor from graphical dialogs and to cope with other aspects of J2EE: Enterprise Java Beans (EJBs), EAR files, Resource Files . . . the full story belongs in a separate book!

exam watch

In real life, you will use all the packaging support tools you can get hold of. But don't neglect to practice more primitive assembly methods so you really get the structure in your mind. Just as you had to "be the compiler" in the programmer exam, you have to "be the assembler" in the web component exam!

EXERCISE 2-3

Making and Deploying WARs

In this exercise we are going to jar up a web application, then deploy it.

Make the WAR File

1. Stop the Tomcat server.
2. Using your command line facility, navigate to <Tomcat Installation Directory>/webapps/ex0201.

3. Use the **jar** command with appropriate parameters to create ex0203.war, which zips up all the files from Exercise 2-1.

Adjust the Deployment Descriptor

4. Make a directory under <Tomcat Installation Directory>/webapps called ex0203.
5. Move the WAR file you made in step 3 to this directory.
6. Use the jar command to extract the contents of the file.
7. Check that the extraction worked: There should be an error.jsp and index1 .jsp directly in the ex0203 directory, as well as a WEB-INF and META-INF directory.
8. Start the Tomcat server.
9. This application is a clone of Exercise 2-1, deployed to a new context root—ex0203. Check the deployment by running the ShowContext servlet:

```
http://localhost:8080/ex0203/ShowContext
```

CERTIFICATION SUMMARY

In this chapter you have learned a lot about the fundamental structure of web applications. You are now equipped not just to write servlet code but also to structure the code and all other resources that make up a web application—by putting them in the right directory structure and by providing declarative information about them in the deployment descriptor.

You started by looking at directory structure. You learned that web applications have a "context path" at their root. By making up a stub URL from the server details and context path, you saw how you could append a path to find a particular resource in your web application. You learned that resources meant for public HTTP access should be placed directly in the directory matching the context path, or in subdirectories with names of your own choosing off the context root.

You further learned that every web application has a directory called WEB-INF, which must exist directly in the context root. You saw that any resources kept in

WEB-INF are not for direct public HTTP access. You learned that, as a minimum, WEB-INF must contain a file called web.xml—the deployment descriptor for the application. WEB-INF also has two other officially sanctioned directories: WEB-INF/classes (for separate Java class files, typically servlets and other supporting code) and WEB-INF/lib (for JAR files of Java code). You learned that a web container should look for the classes it needs first in WEB-INF/classes, then in WEB-INF/lib.

You went on to learn about the deployment descriptor file. You examined the XML structure and several of the more fundamental elements within the file. In the exercises you set up `<servlet>` elements, logically defining servlet names and their corresponding servlet classes. You examined the deployment descriptor elements and code required to access initialization parameters in servlets, using a combination of `<init-param>` tags and ServletConfig methods such as `getInitParameter(String paramName)` and `getInitParameterNames()`. You learned how to set up corresponding `<servlet-mapping>` elements so that users of your web applications can enter a URL to access a servlet resource. You learned about the four different sorts of URL mappings and the order in which they are processed: exact match, path prefix, extension, and default. You also learned about some of the more esoteric elements affecting servlets—optional `<description>`, `<display-name>`, and `<icon>` elements for the benefit of web server administrators and graphical web server consoles—and the concept of being able to load servlets in a predefined order determined by `<load-on-startup>` elements.

After learning about deployment descriptor elements affecting servlets, you looked at elements that affect the web application as a whole. These include the `<welcome-file-list>`, which gives a web server a possible resource to serve up when the user requests a directory rather than a specific file. You also met `<error-page>`, which allows you to associate customized pages with specific HTTP error codes (such as 404—SC_NOT_FOUND) and/or Java exception types. Finally, you learned about `<mime-mapping>` and saw how you used this to associate an arbitrary file extension with a known file type from a predefined list of MIME file types.

In the last section of the chapter, you turned your attention to web archive (WAR) files. You found out how you could compress your application into a single, ZIP-format file with a .war extension. In the exercises, you experimented with the process of deploying WAR files on to the Tomcat server. You also learned how to handcraft your own WAR files using the **jar** command with appropriate parameters (cf mywar.war *.*), and how to use the **jar** command to reverse the process and extract the files from a WAR into a web application directory structure on the file system. You learned that WAR files may contain a META-INF directory (short for meta-information), which may have a manifest file (MANIFEST.MF) describing dependencies on common code lying outside of the web application context.

TWO-MINUTE DRILL

File and Directory Structure

- ❑ Every web application within a web container has a unique context path.
- ❑ The context path and any directories you choose to create within it contain resources that are accessible through HTTP.
- ❑ HTTP-accessible resources in your context path might include but are not restricted to static HTML files, JavaServer Pages, Java applets and support code (including JARs), JavaScript files, images, media clips, and stylesheets.
- ❑ The context path contains a special directory called WEB-INF, which must contain the deployment descriptor file, web.xml.
- ❑ A client application may not directly access resources in WEB-INF or its subdirectories through HTTP—any attempt to do so results in an HTTP 404 (page not found) error.
- ❑ Server-side web application code is permitted to access files in WEB-INF and its subdirectories, using methods such as `getResourceAsStream(String path)` on the ServletContext interface.
- ❑ The special directory /WEB-INF/classes contains Java class files—servlets and supporting code.
- ❑ The special directory /WEB-INF/lib contains JAR files with supporting libraries of code.
- ❑ You can create your own directories as needed under /WEB-INF.
- ❑ Apart from those already mentioned (web.xml, class files, JAR files), resources that you expect to find under /WEB-INF include tag libraries (.tld files—discussed in Chapter 8), configuration files (typically xml or properties files), and server-side scripts.

Deployment Descriptor Elements

- ❑ The deployment descriptor file is called web.xml, and it *must* be located in the WEB-INF directory.
- ❑ web.xml is in XML (extended markup language) format. Its root element is `<web-app>`.
- ❑ web.xml houses other elements, each with a start and end tag, which in turn may house other elements.

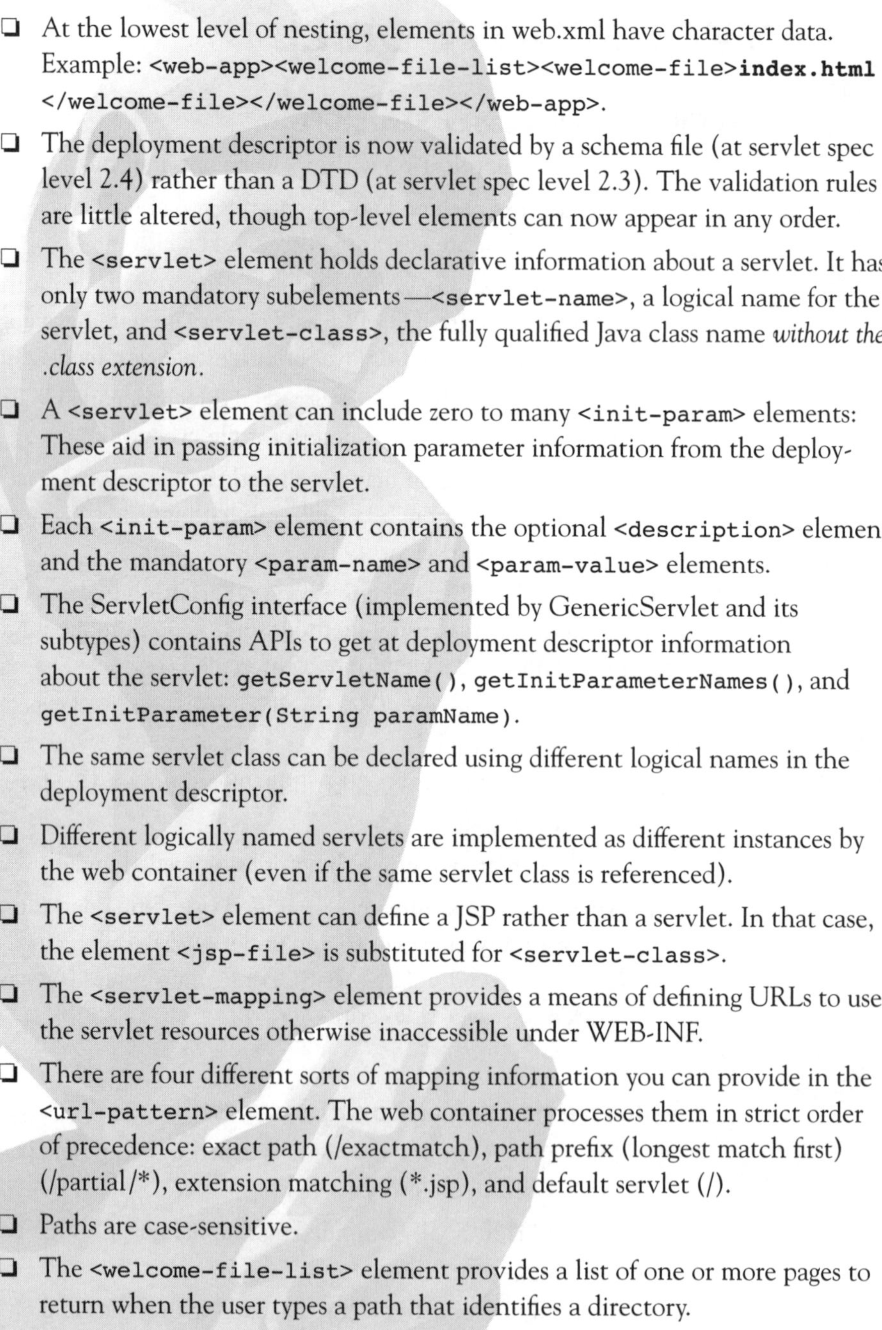

- At the lowest level of nesting, elements in web.xml have character data. Example: `<web-app><welcome-file-list><welcome-file>`**`index.html`**`</welcome-file></welcome-file></web-app>`.
- The deployment descriptor is now validated by a schema file (at servlet spec level 2.4) rather than a DTD (at servlet spec level 2.3). The validation rules are little altered, though top-level elements can now appear in any order.
- The `<servlet>` element holds declarative information about a servlet. It has only two mandatory subelements—`<servlet-name>`, a logical name for the servlet, and `<servlet-class>`, the fully qualified Java class name *without the .class extension*.
- A `<servlet>` element can include zero to many `<init-param>` elements: These aid in passing initialization parameter information from the deployment descriptor to the servlet.
- Each `<init-param>` element contains the optional `<description>` element and the mandatory `<param-name>` and `<param-value>` elements.
- The ServletConfig interface (implemented by GenericServlet and its subtypes) contains APIs to get at deployment descriptor information about the servlet: `getServletName()`, `getInitParameterNames()`, and `getInitParameter(String paramName)`.
- The same servlet class can be declared using different logical names in the deployment descriptor.
- Different logically named servlets are implemented as different instances by the web container (even if the same servlet class is referenced).
- The `<servlet>` element can define a JSP rather than a servlet. In that case, the element `<jsp-file>` is substituted for `<servlet-class>`.
- The `<servlet-mapping>` element provides a means of defining URLs to use the servlet resources otherwise inaccessible under WEB-INF.
- There are four different sorts of mapping information you can provide in the `<url-pattern>` element. The web container processes them in strict order of precedence: exact path (/exactmatch), path prefix (longest match first) (/partial/*), extension matching (*.jsp), and default servlet (/).
- Paths are case-sensitive.
- The `<welcome-file-list>` element provides a list of one or more pages to return when the user types a path that identifies a directory.

- ❑ The `<error-page>` element associates custom error pages with HTTP status codes and/or Java exception types.
- ❑ The `<mime-mapping>` element serves to associate file extensions with officially recognized file types.

WAR Files

- ❑ Web archive (WAR) files provide a convenient means of storing an entire web application in a single, compressed file.
- ❑ WAR files must have a .war file extension.
- ❑ The contents of the context directory and all its subdirectories (including WEB-INF) should be included in the WAR file, but *not the context directory itself*. A WAR file can be installed at any context path.
- ❑ A WAR file can be created with the **jar** command, using *cf* as parameters: `jar cf myapp.war *.*`.
- ❑ A WAR file can be extracted with the **jar** command, using *xf* as parameters: `jar xf myapp.war`.
- ❑ A WAR file must contain a META-INF directory, containing a file called MANIFEST.MF. This lists dependencies on common code JAR files stored outside of the web application context (but available through a web server's own mechanisms).
- ❑ The META-INF directory can also be used to store security-related resources, such as signature files and digital certificates.

SELF TEST

The following questions will help you measure your understanding of the material presented in this chapter. Read all the choices carefully because there might be more than one correct answer. The number of correct choices to make is stated in the question, as in the real SCWCD exam.

File and Directory Structure

1. Which of the following directories are legal locations for the deployment descriptor file? Note that all paths are shown as from the root of the machine or drive. (Choose two.)
   - A. /WEB-INF
   - B. /appserverInstallDirectory/webapps/webappName/WEB-INF/xml
   - C. /appserverInstallDirectory/webapps/webappName/WEB-INF
   - D. /appserverInstallDirectory/webapps/webappName/WEB-INF/classes
2. What would be the best directory in which to store a supporting JAR file for a web application? Note that in the list below, all directories begin from the context root. (Choose one.)
   - A. /WEB-INF
   - B. /WEB-INF/classes
   - C. /jars
   - D. /web-inf/jars
   - E. /CLASSES
   - F. /WEB-INF/lib
   - G. /lib
   - H. None of the above.
3. What's the likely outcome of a user entering the following URL in her browser? You can assume that index.html does exist in /WEB-INF/html, where /WEB-INF/html is a directory off the context root, and that the server, port, and context details are specified correctly. (Choose one.)

   ```
   http://localhost:8080/mywebapp/WEB-INF/html/index.html
   ```

   - A. Because the file is an HTML file, the web application serves it back to the browser.
   - B. An HTTP response code in the 500 range is returned (server error).

C. An HTTP response code of 403 is returned to indicate that the server is not allowed to serve files from this location.

D. An HTTP response code of 404 returned to indicate that the requested resource has not been found.

E. None of the above.

4. (drag-and-drop question) In the following illustration, match the numbered files on the right to the appropriate lettered locations on the left. All files must find a home, so you will have to use some of the lettered locations for more than one file.

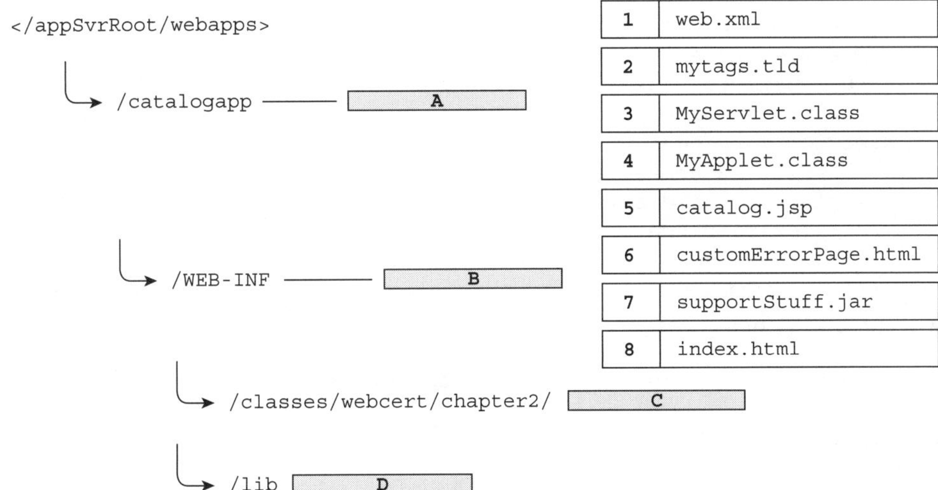

5. Identify which of the following are true statements about web applications. (Choose three.)

A. The only way to access resources under the /WEB-INF directory is through appropriate servlet mapping directives in the deployment descriptor.

B. Server-side code has access to all resources in the web application.

C. Clients of web applications can't directly access resources in /WEB-INF/tld.

D. A good place to keep a .tld (tag library file) is directly in the /WEB-INF directory.

Deployment Descriptor Elements

6. See the extract from web.xml below:

```
<servlet-mapping>
  <servlet-name>ServletA</servlet-name>
  <url-pattern>/</url-pattern>
</servlet-mapping>
<servlet-mapping>
  <servlet-name>ServletB</servlet-name>
  <url-pattern>/bservlet.html</url-pattern>
</servlet-mapping>
<servlet-mapping>
  <servlet-name>ServletC</servlet-name>
  <url-pattern>*.servletC</url-pattern>
</servlet-mapping>
<servlet-mapping>
  <servlet-name>ServletD</servlet-name>
  <url-pattern>/dservlet/*</url-pattern>
</servlet-mapping>
```

Given that a user enters the following into her browser, which (if any) of the mapped servlets will execute? (Choose one.)

```
http://myserver:8080/mywebapp/Bservlet.html
```

A. ServletA

B. ServletB

C. ServletC

D. ServletD

E. The answer is dependent on the web container you use.

F. None of the above: A 404 "page not found error" will result.

7. What is the parent tag for `<welcome-file-list>`? (Choose one.)

A. `<welcome-file>`

B. `<web-app>`

C. None — the tag doesn't exist.

D. `<welcome-files>`

E. `<servlet>`

8. Which of the following are true statements about the deployment descriptor for a web application? (Choose two.)

   A. At least one `<servlet>` element must be present.

   B. `<welcome-file>` is a child element of `<welcome-file-list>`.

   C. `<web-application>` is the root element.

   D. `<servlet>` elements must all be declared before `<servlet-mapping>` elements.

   E. At least one element must be present.

9. (drag-and-drop question) Complete the missing lettered elements from the deployment descriptor in the following illustration, using the numbered choices on the right. You will not have to use all the numbered choices but may have to use some more than once.

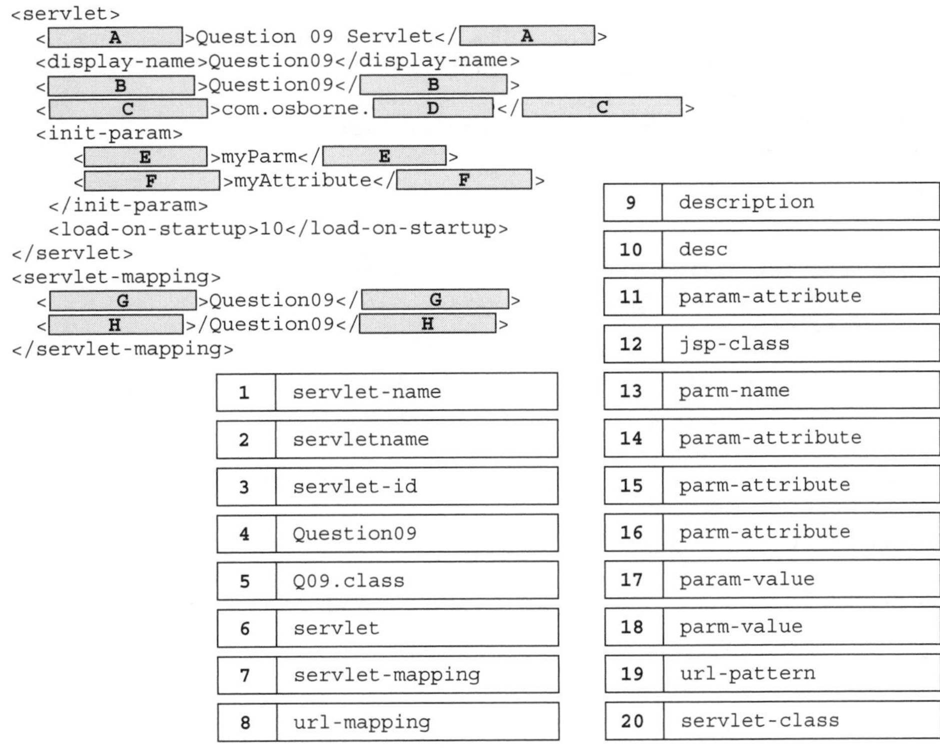

10. What of the following represents a correct declaration of a servlet in the deployment descriptor? (Choose one.)

A.

```
<servlet>
  <servlet-class>MyServlet</servlet-class>
  <servlet-name>MyServlet</servlet-name>
</servlet>
```

B.

```
<servlet>
  <servlet-name>MyServlet</servlet-name>
  <servlet-class>MyServlet.class</servlet-class>
</servlet>
```

C.

```
<servlet>
  <description>My Servlet</description>
  <servlet-name>MyServlet</servlet-name>
  <servlet-class>MyServlet</servlet-class>
</servlet>
```

D.

```
<servlet>
  <servlet-class>MyServlet</servlet-class>
  <jsp-file>index.jsp</jsp-file>
</servlet>
```

11. Given five servlets with `<load-on-startup>` value set as follows, and declared in the following order in the deployment descriptor,

- ServletA: 1
- ServletB: 0
- ServletC: 1
- ServletD: 1
- ServletE: no value set for `<load-on-startup>`

Identify true statements from the list below. (Choose one.)

A. ServletA will load before ServletB.

B. ServletB will load before ServletC.

C. ServletC will load before ServletD.

D. ServletD will load before ServletE.

E. ServletA will load before ServletE.

12. What will be the outcome of compiling and deploying the servlet code below? (You can assume that correct import statements are provided and that the servlet lives in the default package. Line numbers are for ease of reference and are not part of the code.)

```
11 public class NameServlet extends HttpServlet {
12   protected void doGet(HttpServletRequest request,
13     HttpServletResponse response) {
14       out.write(getServletName());
15   }
16 }
```

A. Will not compile because the `doGet()` method doesn't throw the correct exceptions

B. Will not compile for some other reason

C. When run, terminates with a ServletNotFoundException at line 14

D. Outputs "NameServlet"

E. Outputs the contents of the corresponding `<servlet>` element

F. Outputs the contents of the corresponding `<servlet-name>` element

13. Assume that there is a file called secure.txt, located at /WEB-INF/securefiles, whose contents are "Password=WebCert." What statements are false about the result of compiling and running the following code?

```
public class CodeTestServlet extends HttpServlet {
  protected void doGet(HttpServletRequest request,
    HttpServletResponse response) throws IOException {
    ServletContext sc = getServletContext();
    InputStream is = sc.getResourceAsStream("/WEB-" +
      "INF/securefiles/secure.txt");
    BufferedReader br = new BufferedReader(new InputStreamReader(is));
    System.out.println(br.readLine());
  }
}
```

A. The code will not compile.

B. A RuntimeException will occur at lines 15/16.

C. An IOException will occur at line 18.

D. The string "Password=WebCert" will be returned to the requester.

E. A, B, and C above.

F. B, C, and D above.

G. A, B, C, and D above.

14. Given the following deployment descriptor:

```
<web-app>
 <servlet>
   <servlet-name>InitParams</servlet-name>
   <servlet-class>com.osborne.c02.InitParamsServlet</servlet-class>
   <init-param>
     <param-name>initParm</param-name>
     <param-value>question14</param-value>
   </init-param>
  </servlet>
</web-app>
```

What is the outcome of running the following servlet? (Choose one.)

```
public class InitParamsServlet extends HttpServlet {
 protected void doGet(HttpServletRequest request,
   HttpServletResponse response) throws ServletException, IOException {
   ServletContext sc = this.getServletContext();
   PrintWriter out = response.getWriter();
   out.write("Initialization Parameter is: "
     + sc.getInitParameter("initParm"));
 }
}
```

A. A runtime error

B. "Initialization Parameter is: null" written to the console

C. "Initialization Parameter is: question14" returned to the requester

D. "Initialization Parameter is: null" returned to the requester

E. "Initialization Parameter is: question14" written to the console

15. Which of the following methods derive from the ServletConfig interface? (Choose three.)

    A. `ServletContext getServletContext()`

    B. `String getInitParameter(String name)`

    C. `MapEntry getInitParameterEntry()`

    D. `Iterator getInitParameterNames()`

    E. `String getServletName()`

16. Which of the following is a valid way to set up a mime mapping in the deployment descriptor? (Choose one.)

    A.

```
<mime-mapping-list>
  <mime-type>text/plain</mime-type>
  <extension>txt</extension>
<mime-mapping-list>
```

    B.

```
<mime-mapping-list>
  <extension>.txt</extension>
  <mime-type>text/plain</mime-type>
<mime-mapping-list>
```

    C.

```
<mime-mapping>
  <mime-type>txt</mime-type>
  <extension>text/plain</extension>
<mime-mapping>
```

    D.

```
<mime-mapping>
  <extension>txt</extension>
  <mime-type>text/plain</mime-type>
<mime-mapping>
```

17. Which of the following servlet methods can return **null?** (Choose one.)

    A. `getInitParameterNames()`

    B. `getInitParameter(String name)`

    C. `getServletName()`

    D. `getServletContext()`

WAR Files

18. Identify correct statements about the META-INF directory from the list below. (Choose three.)
    - A. META-INF is a suitable location for storing digital certificates.
    - B. META-INF is used as a repository for common code.
    - C. The MANIFEST.MF file is found in the META-INF directory.
    - D. The deployment descriptor file is found in the META-INF directory.
    - E. META-INF is not directly accessible to clients.

19. Identify correct statements about WAR files from the list below. (Choose three.)
    - A. A META-INF directory will be present in the WAR file.
    - B. A WEB-INF directory will be present in the WAR file.
    - C. A web container can't work directly from a WAR file; it must be extracted (unzipped) into the file system.
    - D. A WAR file is in ZIP file format.

20. Consider the following list of files in a web application, where myApp is the context path:

```
/devDir/myapp/index.jsp
/devDir/myapp/WEB-INF/web.xml
/devDir/myapp/WEB-INF/classes/webcert/ch02/SomeServlet.class
```

Which of the following sets of instructions will build a correctly formed web archive file? (Choose one.)

- A. None of the sets of instructions will build a valid WAR file until /webcert/ch02/Some Servlet.class is moved to the WEB-INF/lib directory.
- B. Change directory to /devDir; execute jar tvf myapp.war *.*
- C. Change directory to /devDir/myApp; execute jar cvf myapp.jar *.*
- D. Change directory to /devDir/myApp/WEB-INF; execute jar xvf myapp.war *.*
- E. Change directory to /devDir/myApp; execute jar cvf someapp.war *.*

LAB QUESTION

It's your turn now to develop a web application from scratch! Develop a servlet that displays its name back to the user. Register this same servlet class three times in the deployment descriptor. Prove to yourself (through extra code in the servlet) that by calling servlets with different names, you are genuinely getting different instances of the servlet (i.e., separate Java objects). One way of doing this is to place an instance variable in the servlet that keeps a count of how many times the servlet has been called.

SELF TEST ANSWERS

File and Directory Structure

1. ☑ **A** and **C** are the correct answers. The deployment descriptor file, web.xml, must go directly in the WEB-INF directory. **A** looks strange—it would be peculiar, not to say foolish, to have the context of a web app located in the root directory—but it is still legal.
   ☒ **B** is incorrect; though it's perfectly OK to create a directory called xml within WEB-INF to keep your own configuration files, it is not OK to have web.xml housed there. **D** is incorrect because although WEB-INF/classes is a standard J2EE-defined directory, it's meant for Java classes (such as servlet classes), not web.xml.

2. ☑ **F** is the correct answer. WEB-INF/lib is the right place for supporting JAR files, though you can include JAR files in the META-INF directory as well.
   ☒ The remaining answers are incorrect. Only **A**, **B**, and the correct answer, **F**, define directories found in the servlet specification. **D** is wrong on two counts, one of which is that the case is wrong (the directory is WEB-INF in capitals), and the other is that you're welcome to have a subdirectory called "jars," but there's no standard to say that the web container should look there. **C** and **G** come straight off the context root, which is the publicly accessible area. Finally, **H** is wrong because there is a correct answer!

3. ☑ **D**. A 404 response code should be returned: resource not found. That way, the server masks the fact that a resource even exists at the location specified (as it does in this example).
   ☒ **A** tries to fool you into thinking that certain types of file will be served from WEB-INF and its subdirectories: incorrect. **B** (a 500 range error) is reserved for genuine server problems (uncaught exceptions in servlet code). **C** (a 403 error) sounds reasonable; you might expect a "nonauthorized" type message. But that reveals that there is a resource to get at. **E** is incorrect because there is a correct answer.

4. ☑ **A** is the location for **4**, **5**, **6**, and **8**: static HTML (including custom error pages), Java Server Pages, and applet classes should live in the context directory (or—not shown in the picture—a directory that isn't WEB-INF under the context directory). **B** is the location for **1** and **2**: The deployment descriptor web.xml must be located here, and tag library descriptors (.tld files) can be located here or a subdirectory of WEB-INF. **C** is the location for **3**, a servlet class file: under /WEB-INF/classes, in its own package directory. **D** is the location for **7**: /WEB-INF/lib is for supporting JAR files.
   ☒ Other combinations are ill-advised or won't work at all.

5. ☑ **B**, **C**, and **D**. Server-side code can get at anything in the web application, even resources under the WEB-INF directory. Clients can't directly access resources under WEB-INF/tld (don't be thrown by the fact the WEB-INF/tld isn't an "official" directory; it's perfectly OK to invent a directory called tld, and because it's under WEB-INF, clients can't get at it).
   ☒ **A** is incorrect. The only way for a *client-side* application to access resources under WEB-INF is through a servlet mapping, true enough. But *server-side* code can get directly at those resources through, for example, `ServletContext.getResourceAsStream(String path)`.

Deployment Descriptor Elements

6. ☑ **A** is correct. ServletA—set up for the default mapping of "/"—will execute.
   ☒ **B** is incorrect because BServlet.html does not match the URL pattern for ServletB in terms of case sensitivity. **C** and **D** don't have mappings remotely similar to the URL requested. **E** is incorrect because mapping behavior is not permitted to be server-specific since the 2.4 servlet spec. Finally, **F** is incorrect—because a default servlet mapping is set up, you will never get a 404 error (unless you code the default servlet to return a 404 error).
7. ☑ **B**. `<welcome-file-list>` nests directly under the root element `<web-app>`.
   ☒ **A** is incorrect because `<welcome-file>` is the child of `<welcome-file-list>`. **D** is incorrect because `<welcome-files>` does not exist. Answer **C** tries to persuade you that `<welcome-file-list>` doesn't exist, but it does. **E** encourages you to think that `<welcome-file-list>` is a subelement of `<servlet>`; of course, it's not, as it pertains to the whole application, not just one particular servlet.
8. ☑ **B** and **E**. `<welcome-file>` is the child of `<welcome-file-list>`. And there does have to be one element in web.xml: the root element (`<web-app></web-app>`).
   ☒ **A** is incorrect because you don't have to have a `<servlet>` element, or indeed any element except for the root element. **C** is incorrect because `<web-app>` is the root element, not `<web-application>`. **D** is incorrect because, since servlet spec 2.4 (in J2EE 1.4), order no longer matters: Elements can come in any order. That said, Tomcat (the reference implementation) server objects to referencing the servlet in a `<servlet-mapping>` before it is declared in a `<servlet>` element—you can, however, have the elements alternating so that servlet mappings are kept close to their associated servlets.
9. ☑ **A** maps to **9** (description), **B** to **1** (servlet-name), **C** to **20** (servlet-class), **D** to **4** (Question09—the answer most likely to be a class name without the extension .class), **E** to **16** (param-name), **F** to **17** (param-value), **G** to **1** (servlet-name—again), and **H** to **19** (url-pattern).
   ☒ Other combinations are incorrect.

10. ☑ **C** is the correct answer. All the elements are correctly specified, in the correct order.
☒ **A**, **B**, and **D** are incorrect. **A** reverses the `<servlet-name>` and `<servlet-class>` tags (order does matter within the `<servlet>` element). **B** has correct element order but incorrectly appends ".class" to the servlet name. **D** is almost correct but for the fact that the JSP file should be expressed from the context root and so begin with a leading slash, thus: `<jsp-file>/index.jsp</jsp-file>`.

11. ☑ **B**. The web container must guarantee that ServletB, with a `<load-on-startup>` value of 0, loads before ServletA, with a `<load-on-startup>` value of 1.
☒ **A** is incorrect because servlets with a negative `<load-on-startup>` value have an indeterminate load time—probably on first user access, but not guaranteed. Servlets with no load-on-startup value are indeterminate in the same way; hence, answers **D** and **E** are incorrect. **C** is incorrect because there is no guarantee that servlets with the same `<load-on-startup>` value will load in their declared order in the deployment descriptor.

12. ☑ **B**. It won't compile for other reasons—the reason being simply that the `out` variable is not declared (it's presumably meant to be the PrintWriter obtained from HttpServletResponse).
☒ **A** is incorrect because it's OK to throw fewer exceptions on a method than are in your superclass. **C** is incorrect because the code will never run, and in any case there isn't such a thing as ServletNotFoundException. **D** could be correct if the code compiled: If the servlet isn't registered in web.xml, the class name is returned from `getServletName()`. In the same way, **F** would be correct if code compiled and the servlet was registered. **E** would never be correct; the `<servlet>` element contains a lot else besides the servlet name.

13. ☑ **G** is the correct answer, for all of **A**, **B**, **C**, and **D** are false statements. **A** is false because the code will compile. **B** is false because there's nothing wrong with the method call and the path to the file is correctly stated. **C** is false; although an IOException is always possible from IO-based methods, it mostly won't happen. **D** is false because the string read from the file is not returned to the requester, but output to the server console.
☒ **A**, **B**, **C**, **D**, **E**, and **F** are incorrect answers, following the reasoning in the correct answer.

14. ☑ **D**. Although there is a correctly set up initialization parameter for the servlet in the deployment descriptor, the code is looking for a *context* parameter. There isn't one set up, and **null** is returned.
☒ **A** is incorrect; the code runs fine. **B** and **E** are incorrect, for nothing is written to the console—the output is to the response's PrintWriter, and so it is returned to the requester. **C** would be right if the code was set up to return the *servlet's* initialization parameter.

15. ☑ **A**, **B**, and **E**. All are correct signatures for methods on the ServletConfig interface.

☒ C is incorrect; there's no such method as `getInitParameterEntry()`. D is incorrect: ServletConfig does have a method called `getInitParameterNames()`, but it returns a good old-fashioned Enumeration, not an Iterator.

16. ☑ D is the correct answer. This has the correct element names and sequence and content for a `<mime-mapping>`.
☒ A and B are incorrect because both have the wrong-named outer element, `<mime-mapping-list>`. In addition, A reverses the `<extension>` and `<mime-type>` elements, and B—while getting the order correct—declares the extension content with a "." (it must be specified as "txt," not ".txt"). C is incorrect only in that `<mime-type>` and `<extension>` are reversed.

17. ☑ **B**. If an initialization parameter name does not exist, `getInitParameter(String name)` returns **null**.
☒ A is incorrect because `getInitParameterNames()` returns an empty Enumeration if there are no servlet initialization parameters declared in the deployment descriptor. C is incorrect because `getServletName()` always returns some name or other: Even if the servlet is undeclared, it will return the class name of the servlet. D is incorrect because there must always be a ServletContext to return (no servlet can operate in a vacuum).

WAR Files

18. ☑ **A**, **C**, and **E**. It's the right place for digital certificates and the MANIFEST.MF file. Like WEB-INF, client access to META-INF should be rejected with an HTTP 404 error.
☒ **B** is incorrect because META-INF isn't used to store common code across web applications; the MANIFEST.MF text file within it references common code via classpath entries. **D** is incorrect because the deployment descriptor file web.xml is kept in WEB-INF, not META-INF.

19. ☑ **A**, **B**, and **D**. **A** might surprise you, and there are plenty of WAR files around without a META-INF directory that deploy OK on most web servers. However, the servlet spec section 9.6 does say that META-INF "will be present."
☒ **C** is incorrect. Although most web servers do expand WAR files into the file system (like Tomcat), it's not a requirement. The Sun application server (part of the J2EE 1.4 reference implementation) doesn't expand WAR files, but runs the application directly from the WAR file itself.

20. ☑ **E** is the correct answer. Note that the WAR file name need bear no relation to the context path.
☒ **A** is incorrect, for the servlet class is in entirely the right place. Only if it was in a JAR file should it be present in /WEB-INF/lib. **B** is incorrect because you shouldn't be zipping up the

context directory itself, only the contents of the context directory and below. **C** is incorrect because the file created has a .jar extension, and a WAR file must have a .war extension. **D** is incorrect because you can't just wrap up the WEB-INF directory; you need all the web content in the directory above, the context root.

LAB ANSWER

Deploy the WAR file from the CD called lab02.war, in the /sourcecode/chapter02 directory. This contains a sample solution. You can call the servlets using a URL such as `http://localhost:8080/lab02/ServletA` (or `../ServletB` or `../ServletC`). The source for the servlet is included in the WEB-INF/src directory. If you experience strange behavior even though your code and deployment descriptor look right (counts not incrementing, perhaps), then do make sure you *refresh your browser cache* as you make repeat calls to each servlet URL and after redeployment of the WAR file.

3

The Web Container Model

CERTIFICATION OBJECTIVES

- ServletContext
- Attributes, Scope, and Multithreading
- Request Dispatching
- Filters and Wrappers
- ✓ Two-Minute Drill
- Q&A Self Test

In this chapter we examine more closely that largely overlooked piece of software that looks after your requests, responses, and servlets: the web container. As you'll have gathered from looking at the J2EE API documentation for javax.servlet and related packages, there are a large number of classes and interfaces implicated in web applications. Some you have to write yourself as a developer: implementing interfaces in the API or extending useful base classes (such as Generic Servlet). However, there are many more interfaces that you never have to implement—because your web container provider has done it for you. That's the deal if you are creating a J2EE web container: You have to understand the servlet specifications in detail and provide suitably compliant classes. That's not to mention orchestrating the runtime environment: making sure that instances of servlets are created in the right circumstances and that life cycle methods are called at the right time.

Fortunately, you are a web *component* developer, not a web *container* developer. So you can take for granted much of what is built into the web container (both for the exam and for real development work). You are a consumer of what the web container provides—and have to understand the infrastructure only insofar as it affects your own business applications.

That's the focus of the exam objectives we explore in this chapter. We start with the ServletContext interface. You never build a class implementing this interface, nor do you instantiate such a class at runtime: The web container does that for you. All you have to do is to understand when and why a ServletContext is available—and what you can do with it (attaching initialization parameters for your web application, for example). We go on to dissect three different scopes maintained by the web container—request, session, and context—and examine how you can attach information to these scopes. We'll also see how this information is affected by the multithreaded nature of web containers. The mechanism of request dispatching will be laid bare: how one servlet can take advantage of other servlets and other web resources. And we'll finish the chapter with a look at filters, a way of trapping and processing requests and responses going to and from a target web resource.

CERTIFICATION OBJECTIVE

ServletContext (Exam Objective 3.1)

For the ServletContext initialization parameters: write servlet code to access initialization parameters; and create the deployment descriptor elements for declaring initialization parameters.

We have already met the ServletContext, and in this chapter—describing the web container model—we explore its remaining secrets. The ServletContext most closely represents the web application itself—or, more correctly, provides a set of services for the web application to work with the web container.

We'll start this chapter by looking at one of the fundamentally useful aspects of the ServletContext: the ability to set up initialization parameters that are then available to every servlet and JSP in your web application.

ServletContext Initialization Parameters

What if you want some fundamental information available to all the dynamic resources (servlets, JSPs) within your web application? We've already seen how to provide initialization information for servlets by using servlet initialization parameters in the deployment descriptor and by using the `getInitParameter(String parmName)` method. But a servlet initialization parameter is accessible only from its containing servlet. For web application level, we have ServletContext parameters.

Setting Up the Deployment Descriptor

You can have as many ServletContext initialization parameters as you wish—none, one, fifty, or more. The listing below shows two ServletContext initialization parameters as the only things in the deployment descriptor:

```
<web-app>
  <context-param>
    <param-name>machineName</param-name>
    <param-value>GERALDINE</param-value>
  </context-param>
  <context-param>
    <param-name>secretParameterFile</param-name>
    <param-value>/WEB-INF/xml/secretParms.xml</param-value>
  </context-param>
</web-app>
```

How does this compare with servlet initialization parameters (covered in Chapter 1)? You can see that the `<param-name>` and `<param-value>` tag pairings are identical between Servlet and ServletContext. If you are good at deciphering the XSD used to validate the deployment descriptor—not that you need to be for the exam!—this will come as no surprise, because this "block" of `<param-name>` and `<param-value>` has a unifying element description that occurs wherever a parameter name/value pairing is required. But note that the parent element is not the same.

Whereas a servlet has `<init-param>` to encase the parameter name/value pairing, ServletContext has `<context-param>`. And whereas—for servlets—`<init-param>` has `<servlet>` as its parent, a ServletContext's `<context-param>` elements sit directly in the root element, `<web-app>`. This makes perfect sense, because servlet initialization parameters belong to a servlet, whereas context initialization parameters belong to a web application.

Writing Code to Retrieve ServletContext Initialization Parameters

Furthermore, the coding approach for getting hold of initialization parameters is nearly identical. In fact, the method signatures involved—`getInitParameter (String parmName)` and `getInitParameterNames()`—are identical. Here's servlet code to retrieve the ServletContext parameters we set up in the deployment descriptor in the previous section. (It's a fragment: You'll have to imagine this is part of a `doGet()` method and that the response's PrintWriter has already been retrieved to a variable called `out`.)

```
ServletContext sc = getServletContext();
String database = sc.getInitParameter("machineName");
String secret = sc.getInitParameter("secretParameterFile");
out.write("<BR />The machine name is: " + database);
out.write("<BR />The secret parameter file is: " + secret);
```

This might yield output in the web page looking like the following:

```
The machine name is: GERALDINE
The secret parameter file is: /WEB-INF/xml/secretParms.xml
```

If you wish to recover the names of all the parameters set up for the Servlet Context, then look up the values for those names, the snippet of servlet code below will do the trick:

```
ServletContext sc = getServletContext();
Enumeration e = sc.getInitParameterNames();
while (e.hasMoreElements()) {
  String paramName = (String) e.nextElement();
  out.write("<BR />Parameter name <B>" + paramName
    + "</B> has the value <I>" + sc.getInitParameter(paramName)
    + "</I>");
}
```

When I run this code in Tomcat, I get the following web page output:

```
Parameter name secretParameterFile has the value /WEB-INF/xml/secretParms.xml
Parameter name machineName has the value GERALDINE
```

You might have noticed that this lists the parameters in the opposite order from their setup in the deployment descriptor, where the *machineName* parameter came first. Let this be a warning to you: In this case and many more, you can't rely on deployment descriptor order.

exam Watch

ServletContext initialization parameters are not tricky—it might be hard to imagine any difficult questions arising! Watch out, though, for questions that focus on what you get back from ServletContext methods when the initialization parameters are wrong or missing. `getInitParameter(String parmName)` *hands back a* **null** *String reference if the parameter is not recognized. If there are no context parameters at all,* `getInitParameterNames()` *hands back an empty Enumeration (i.e., a non-***null,** *bona fide Enumeration reference—but the Enumeration has no elements). What you don't get is any kind of exception being thrown from these methods—at least, not under these normal circumstances, where parameters are unrecognized or missing.*

on the job

I don't put all my system parameters and other meta-information in Servlet Context initialization parameters. I put most data of that sort in files on the file system—maybe in simple properties files, or XML files for more sophisticated data. I would locate the files under a directory located within the WEB-INF directory, then use a single ServletContext initialization parameter to hold this location, relative to the web context. For properties files, I would use methods such as `getResourceAsStream()` *to return an InputStream I could* `load()` *into a Properties object. (XML files might need a more handcrafted approach, dependent on the Java classes that will receive the XML-described information.) The properties object itself could be set (and subsequently accessed) as a ServletContext attribute—something we'll learn about in the next section of this chapter. Why do I do this? Because while Servlet Context initialization parameters are a great idea, they're not as flexible as data held in files. Files can be altered in situ—and, if necessary, you can*

arrange a call to a servlet that will reload the file values into Java variables in your web application dynamically, without recourse to closing the application down. A change to a ServletContext parameter necessitates redeploying the deployment descriptor file and restarting the web application to cause the parameters to be re-read.

EXERCISE 3-1

Using the ServletContext to Discover and Read a Properties File

In this exercise, you'll set up a ServletContext initialization parameter that holds the location and name of a file. You'll write servlet code to use this parameter to locate and read the file, holding the individual properties within it as ServletContext attributes (this gives you a taste of what is to come in the next section!). Finally, you'll write more servlet code to access those properties at a later point in the servlet life cycle.

Each exercise from now on will involve a web application of its own. I suggest you work in the following way, as described more fully in Appendix B:

- Create a directory that follows the naming structure of the chapter and exercise number—ex0301 for this exercise.
- Create a web application directory structure underneath this. This structure should contain the /WEB-INF directory, the /WEB-INF/classes directory, and the deployment descriptor file web.xml in the /WEB-INF directory.
- Create a package structure under /WEB-INF/classes of your own (you don't have to put your servlets into packages).
- Create your source files directly in your package directories (or directly in /WEB-INF/classes if there are no package directories).
- Compile the source in place so that the class files appear in the same directories as the source directories.

For this exercise, there's a solution in the CD in the file sourcecode/ch03/ex0301.war—check there if you get stuck.

Set Up the Deployment Descriptor

1. In web.xml, set up two context initialization parameters, one named "propsFileName," with a value of /WEB-INF, and the other "propsFile

Location," with a value of ex0301.properties. Refer to the section above to see how to set up context initialization parameters.

2. Declare a servlet named ContextInitParms, with a suitable servlet mapping. Ensure that it loads on start up of the server. Refer to Chapter 2 to refresh yourself on `<servlet>` element setup if you need to.

Set Up the Properties File

3. Create a file called "ex0301.properties" in the /WEB-INF directory.
4. Use a text editor to put the following contents into the properties file:

```
application_name=EX0301 ContextInitParms
```

Write the ContextInitParms Servlet

5. Create a Java source file ContextInitParms.java in /WEB-INF/classes or an appropriate package directory. Write the class declaration in the source file, extending HttpServlet.
6. In your ContextInitParms servlet, override the `init()` method (inherited from GenericServlet)—that's the `init()` without any parameters.
7. In the `init()` method, return the context initialization parameters you set up in step 1 of the exercise into local String variables.
8. Still in the `init()` method, concatenate the Strings retrieved in step 7, with a forward slash in between. Use this concatenated string as the parameter to `ServletContext.getRealPath()`, which will return the true path on the file system to the properties file.
9. Still in the `init()` method, create a FileInputStream from the true path you calculated in step 8. Create a new Properties object, and use the `Properties.load()` method to load information from the FileInput Stream into your Properties object.
10. Use the `ServletContext.setAttribute()` method to set up the Properties object as an attribute of the ServletContext. You don't meet servlet context attributes until the next section of this chapter, but don't let that worry you—they're simple. They allow you to associate a String name with any object. Make sure the name of the attribute is *properties*. The code you use to do it will probably look very like this:

```
context.setAttribute("properties", properties);
```

11. Now override the `doGet()` method in ContextInitParms.
12. Retrieve the context attribute you set up in the `init()` method. You'll use the `ServletContext.getAttribute()` method with a parameter of *properties*. Since this returns a plain Object, ensure that you cast the result to a Properties type.
13. Obtain the "application_name" property from your properties object with the `getProperty()` method, and display this (it's a String) in the servlet (write it to the response's PrintWriter).

Run the Application

14. Having compiled your code, copy the entire ex0301 directory to your server's web applications directory.
15. Stop and start your server, checking the application log produced. Since you specified that ContextInitParms should load on start up, the `init()` method should run—make sure that there are no problems.
16. If step 15 was successful, point your browser (using the appropriate servlet mapping that you set up in step 2) to the ContextInitParms servlet with a URL such as this one:

```
http://localhost:8080/ex0301/ContextInitParms
```

17. Check that the application name "EX0301 ContextInitParms" appears on the resulting web page. Here's how the solution page looks:

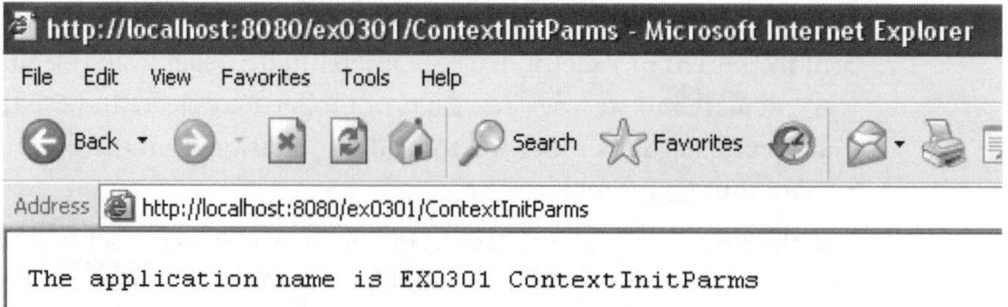

CERTIFICATION OBJECTIVE

Attributes, Scope, and Multithreading (Exam Objectives 3.2 and 4.1)

For the fundamental servlet attribute scopes (request, session, and context): write servlet code to add, retrieve, and remove attributes; given a usage scenario, identify the proper scope for an attribute; and identify multithreading issues associated with each scope.

Write servlet code to store objects into a session object and retrieve objects from a session object.

In this section, we're going to spend some time on attributes. These have a little in common with parameters, but we will explore the difference. Parameters allow information to flow into a web application. We started (in Chapter 1) with request parameters—attaching identifiable data to an HTTP request. In Chapter 2 we met initialization parameters for servlets, and at the beginning of this chapter, we met initialization parameters for the servlet context. Both get information from the web deployment descriptor to web application code. Attributes are more of a means of handling information *within* the web application. They are more of a two-way street than parameters—because you can update attributes in your code, not just read them.

We're also going to consider scope in this section. Web application context (as represented by the ServletContext object) is one of three "scopes" you can use. The other two are session scope (represented by HttpSession objects) and request scope (represented by objects implementing the ServletRequest or HttpServletRequest interfaces). You can attach your attributes to any of these three scopes, and you need to be very familiar with their characteristics for the exam. (Before the end of the book you'll encounter a fourth—page scope—but that needs to wait until we discuss JavaServer Pages more fully in Chapter 6.)

Once you know about scopes, you'll be ready to understand about multithreading issues: questions about the thread safety of different types of attribute—those attaching to request, session, and context. When should you use synchronized blocks for attribute access? Is it ever appropriate to use servlet instance variables instead of attributes? We'll cover these questions and more before the end of the chapter.

Attributes

Attributes are a dumping ground for information. The web container uses attributes (alongside APIs) as a place to

- *Provide information to interested code*. There are a number of standard attributes that a web container should provide as part of the servlet specification, and chances are it will provide a few optional extras of its own. You can regard attributes used this way as a means of supplementing the standard APIs that yield information about the web container.
- *Hang on to information that your application, session, or even request requires later*. These "user-defined" attributes are likely to account for the bulk of attribute usage in your web application.

Attributes are easy to learn for this reason: Whatever scope you are dealing with (request, session, or context), the retrieval and update mechanisms are pretty much identical. The essentials are that you can pick the appropriate object for the scope, then use the appropriate get/set/removeAttribute method.

The thing that takes a little more learning is the idea of "scope." The idea of scope will already be familiar from general Java coding—for example, the idea that a local variable goes out of scope when a method comes to an end. Java coding scope defines how long a variable is available. Web application scope is the same idea on a grander scale—an attribute's scope can span an entire request, web application, session, and even—occasionally—multiple JVMs.

exam watch

Make sure you don't mix up your attributes and parameters! Parameters—whatever scope you find them in—are read-only. They travel one way: perhaps from an HTML form through an HTTP request, or from initialization parameter settings in the deployment descriptor file to the servlet context or individual servlets. You'll find only "getters" for them. Attributes are read/write—you can create, update, and delete them from all the scopes—request, session, or context.

Mechanisms for Manipulating Attributes

For all three scopes—request, session, and context—there are four methods for the manipulation of attributes. If you take any one of those four methods—say, `getAttributeNames()`—you'll find that it has an identical signature (well, nearly identical) across request, session, and context. Input parameters and return types don't vary, nor do the rules governing what type or constant is returned under what circumstances. The only thing that spoils the perfect symmetry is session, whose methods can throw IllegalStateExceptions. No need to worry about why those might occur (it's a topic we cover in Chapter 4)—it's just worth noting that the session methods are the "exception" that proves the rule when it comes to parameter and attribute methods (which in general don't throw exceptions on their signature).

The four methods and the three scopes are shown in Table 3-1, for ease of comparison.

TABLE 3-1 Comparison of Attribute Methods for Different Scopes

Scope	Request Scope	Session Scope	Context (Application) Scope
on Interface	javax.servlet .ServletRequest	javax.servlet.http .HttpSession	javax.servlet .ServletContext
`public void setAttribute (String name,Object value)`	Binds an object to the request, keyed by the String name. If the object passed as a value is **null**, has the same effect as `removeAttribute()`.	Binds an object to the session, keyed by the String name. If the object passed as a value is **null**, has the same effect as `removeAttribute()`. Throws IllegalStateException if invoked when the session is invalid.	Binds an object to the context, keyed by the String name. If the object passed as a value is **null**, has the same effect as `removeAttribute()`.
`public Object getAttribute (String name)`	Returns the value of the named attribute as an Object, or **null** if no attribute of the given name exists.	Returns the value of the named attribute as an Object, or **null** if no attribute of the given name exists. Throws IllegalState Exception if invoked when the session is invalid.	Returns the value of the named attribute as an Object, or **null** if no attribute of the given name exists.
`public Enumeration getAttribute Names()`	Returns an Enumeration containing the names of available attributes. Returns an empty Enumeration if no attributes exist.	Returns an Enumeration containing the names of available attributes. Returns an empty Enumeration if no attributes exist. Throws IllegalStateException if invoked when the session is invalid.	Returns an Enumeration containing the names of available attributes. Because there are some attributes that the web container must supply to the context, this Enumeration should never be empty.
`public void remove Attribute (String name)`	Removes the named attribute.	Removes the named attribute. Throws IllegalState Exception if invoked when the session is invalid.	Removes the named attribute.

exam watch

You have to memorize the material in Table 3-1 for the exam—no way around it! Focus on the similarities and (few) differences between the method calls. There are numerous tricky questions on this content. Be aware that when JavaServer Pages are introduced in Chapter 6, you'll be adding a fourth scope into the mix—page scope—and that exam questions mostly ask you to differentiate among all four scopes, not just the three you have learned so far.

So as you can see, the mechanisms are pretty much identical. There are a few points worth making about the use of these methods:

- *You can choose any String you want for your attribute name.* That said, the servlet specification suggests you follow the "reverse domain name" standard, using names such as "com.mycompany.myattributename."
- *It's impossible to have two or more attributes with the same name.* If you make a call to `setAttribute()` using a name of an attribute that already exists, the existing attribute is replaced with the new value.
- *Session methods are unique among the three scopes in being able to throw exceptions.* This has to do with attempting to use the methods on an "invalid session" and is discussed in detail in Chapter 4.
- *But despite this caveat about session method exceptions, note that* none *of the methods (whatever the scope) throw exceptions just because attributes don't exist.* In this, they are just like parameter methods.
- *Although there is a* `removeAttribute(String name)` *method, you don't necessarily need it.* A call such as this to `setAttribute()` has the same effect:

```
scopeinstance.setAttribute("com.myco.attrname", null);
```

There are some families of attribute names that are reserved for use by Sun Microsystems and the servlet specifiers. Proscribed names begin with

- java.
- javax.
- sun.
- com.sun

This is so that web containers can provide some standard attributes—just like standard properties inside a JVM, retrieved with the `System.getProperty(String propertyName)` static method. A case in point is the ServletContext attribute "javax..servlet.context.tempdir." This is a mandatory attribute that web containers must provide, and it specifies a temporary storage directory unique to a particular web application. This is why—as noted in Table 3-1—you should never have an empty Enumeration returned from `ServletContext.getAttributeNames()`.

So let's look at some code that exercises all these methods for ServletContext (which serves as a guide for all three scopes). The code listing is a fragment from a longer `doGet()` method in a servlet:

```
10 // "out" is the response's PrintWriter
11 out.write("<H2>Context (Application) Scope</H2>");
12 ServletContext context = getServletContext();
13 String myAttributeName = "com.osborne.conductor";
14 context.setAttribute(myAttributeName, "Andre Previn");
15
16 enum = context.getAttributeNames();
17 while (enum.hasMoreElements()) {
18   attrName = (String) enum.nextElement();
19   attrValue = context.getAttribute(attrName);
20   out.write("<BR />Attribute name: <B>" + attrName + "</B>, value: <B>"
21            + attrValue + "</B>");
22 }
23 String conductor = (String) context.getAttribute(myAttributeName);
24 out.write("<BR /> Just used getAttribute() to obtain "
25            + myAttributeName + " whose value is " + conductor);
26
27 context.removeAttribute(myAttributeName);
28 context.setAttribute(myAttributeName, null);
29
30 out.write("<BR />Value of attribute " + myAttributeName + " is now "
31            + context.getAttribute(myAttributeName));
```

The code can be explained as follows:

- Line 12: get hold of a handle to the ServletContext.
- Lines 13–14: add our own attribute (name—"com.osborne.conductor," value—a String object holding the conductor "Andre Previn").
- Lines 16–22: obtain the Enumeration of all context attribute names. Loop around this, using the `getAttribute()` method, to obtain the context value for each name in turn, and output the name and value to the web page.

- Lines 23–24: use `getAttribute()` to get hold of the attribute we added above at lines 13–14, and output the name and value to the web page.
- Line 27 removes this attribute using `removeAttribute()`.
- Line 28 removes this attribute again, using a different technique with `setAttribute()`. This action is completely redundant, for the attribute has already been removed in the previous line, but makes the point that this doesn't matter (no exceptions thrown).
- Line 30: use `getAttribute()` again to prove that the attribute has really gone (**null** is output to the web page, as you can see in the output listing below).

The output from the code (when I run it under Tomcat) is this:

```
Context (Application) Scope
Attribute name: com.osborne.conductor, value: Andre Previn
Attribute name: org.apache.catalina.jsp_classpath, value: /C:/Java/jakarta-
tomcat-5.0.27/webapps/scratchpad/WEB-INF/classes/;C:/Java/jakarta-tomcat-
5.0.27/shared/classes/;<...>
Attribute name: javax.servlet.context.tempdir, value: C:\Java\jakarta-tomcat-
5.0.27\work\Catalina\localhost\scratchpad
Attribute name: org.apache.catalina.resources, value: org.apache.naming
.resources.ProxyDirContext@aa0877
Attribute name: org.apache.catalina.WELCOME_FILES, value: [Ljava.lang
.String;@111ded2
Just used getAttribute() to obtain com.osborne.conductor whose value is Andre
Previn
Value of attribute com.osborne.conductor is now null
```

You can see the context attribute added by our code at the top of the web page—com .osborne.conductor (but do note that there's no guarantee of the order of attributes within the Enumeration returned by the `getAttributeNames()` method). Tucked in the middle of the listing is the compulsory context attribute, javax.servlet.context .tempdir. Sprinkled in between are a few "org.apache.<whatever>" context attributes—these are particular to the Tomcat web container. Some of the outlandish values (e.g., org.apache.naming resources.ProxyDirContext@aa0877) underline the fact that any object of any type can be held as an attribute value—not merely Strings.

Scope

So far in this chapter, I have happily bandied around the term "scope" without attempting to pin down exactly what it means for request, session, and context. I've given you the eagle-level definition: Scope describes the lifetime and availability of web application artifacts (by which I mean attributes, mostly). What we'll do in this section is to go through each of the three scopes in turn, mapping out their extent.

Request Scope

Request scope lasts from the moment an HTTP request hits a servlet in your web container to the moment the servlet is done with delivering the HTTP response. More accurately, the request scope is available from entry into a servlet's `service()` method up to the point of exit from that method. Of course, the default behavior of a servlet's `service()` method—unless you've overridden it to do something unique and strange—is to call a method you're more likely to override—such as `doGet()` or `doPost()`. And here the request is still very much alive and well, and available as a parameter. Now, your `doGet()` or `doPost()` method may in turn make use of other classes, and pass on their HttpServletRequest parameter to those classes' methods. In other words, the whole tree of method calls initiated by the `service()` method—however deep—counts as a single request scope.

The scope is represented by an instance of a request object: most often, one of type HttpServletRequest (it could be of type ServletRequest if we're considering a non-HTTP servlet container—most developers won't meet such a thing, ever). Figure 3-1 shows the progress of a request—possibly not a typical one, for its lifetime is arguably longer than most. You see at (1) in Figure 3-1 a client making a request for a servlet called ServletA. This triggers the web container (at (2) in Figure 3-1) to provide a request object to the servlet's service method. This will—in all likelihood—be passed on as a parameter to the `doGet()` or `doPost()` method (assuming that ServletA is an HttpServlet). ServletA makes use of a helper class (at (3)): We're imagining that the helper class contains a method receiving a Servlet Request as a parameter, so the request object is passed into the helper class. Something more extravagant happens at (4) in Figure 3-1: ServletA decides it needs to make use of ServletB in a separate web application. It can do this by using the RequestDispatcher mechanism—something we learn all about later in this chapter. The reason for its premature inclusion here is to show that a request object's scope can transcend web application boundaries. When you use a RequestDispatcher, you have to pass on the request (and response) objects to the resource to which you are dispatching.

At the end of the request ((5) in Figure 3-1), the request object is placed out of scope. This doesn't necessarily mean that the web container sets its value to **null** and that the JVM garbage collects the object. It's more efficient for a web container to refrain from destroying and recreating request objects—better to throw them back

FIGURE 3-1 Request Scope

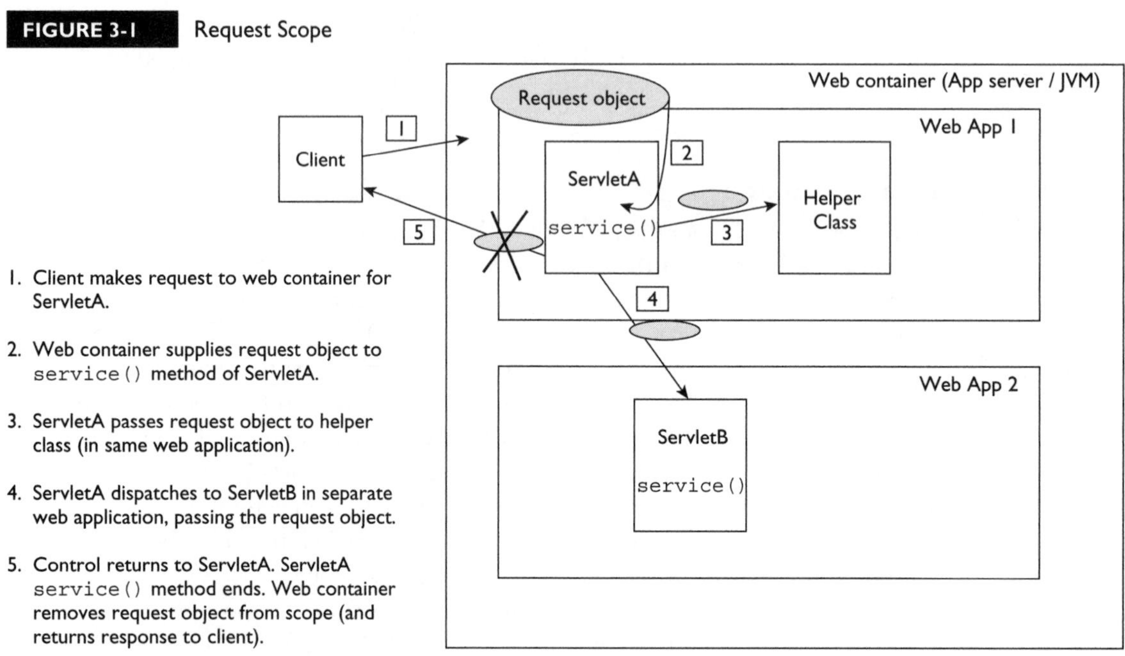
Web container (App server / JVM)
Request object
Web App 1
Client
1
2
ServletA
service()
3
Helper Class
5
4
Web App 2
ServletB
service()
1. Client makes request to web container for ServletA.
2. Web container supplies request object to service() method of ServletA.
3. ServletA passes request object to helper class (in same web application).
4. ServletA dispatches to ServletB in separate web application, passing the request object.
5. Control returns to ServletA. ServletA service() method ends. Web container removes request object from scope (and returns response to client).

into a pool where they can be recycled. You don't have to concern yourself (either for the exam or—usually—in real life) with the mechanism for this: It's up to the web container implementers. What you need to take away is that a request object is no longer any use beyond the scope of a single request. You may wonder how you could ever think otherwise. Well, a misguided move would be to save a reference to the request object—say—as an attribute of your session, then try to recover the request object on the next request to that session. As the servlet specification says, the results could be—well—"unpredictable." As far as the container is concerned, once a request object has passed beyond its rightful scope, the object can be recycled for another request.

Of course, we've accessed the request object for many different reasons already—such as for obtaining header information and retrieving parameters set up on an HTML form. This chapter asks you to consider a new purpose for the request object: as a repository for objects, held as attributes. You might think it hardly worth bothering going to the trouble of attaching and retrieving request attributes. If your request scope comprises a short `doGet()` method in a single servlet, you would be quite right. Why would you set an attribute only to retrieve it a few lines of code later? You might just as well use a local variable in your `doGet()` method instead. However, the moment you involve a couple of resources—a servlet forwarding to a JSP or, indeed, the fuller life cycle shown in Figure 3-1—request attributes can prove a useful way of passing on information.

Note in passing (though it's very unlikely to come up in the exam) that the web container might attach some attributes of its own to the request. Sometimes it's obliged to when the request is transmitted through a secure protocol such as HTTPs. For example, there is an attribute named javax.servlet.request.key_size, which holds an integer object indicating the bit size of the algorithm used to encrypt the transmission (and you might legitimately wonder why this information isn't enshrined in a full-blown HttpServletRequest API—a method such as `getKeySize()`, perhaps).

Attributes aren't the only things of interest in connection with request objects. Request parameters—which we looked at in Chapter 1—are bound by the same scope. Just as for attributes, if you don't strip out parameter values while the request is in scope—and put them somewhere a bit more permanent—they'll be lost. The "more permanent" aspect is something we now go on to consider as we examine session and context scopes.

Session Scope

Session scope is something we are going to skimp on in this chapter. Don't feel cheated, though—Chapter 4 thoroughly revisits sessions. However, it's worth saying a little about session scope here so you can see it alongside the other two scopes.

You are likely to use session scope a great deal in your applications. Loosely speaking, session scope comes into play from the point where a browser window establishes contact with your web application up to the point where that browser window is closed.

On the application server side, the session is represented by an object implementing the HttpSession interface and can be retrieved from the request object using code such as the following:

```
HttpSession session = request.getSession();
```

The idea is that successive requests from the same browser window will each obtain the same session object each time. And that's the whole idea—to provide a scope that allows you as a developer to give a user the feeling of continuity throughout a series of interactions with your web application. So any parameters from web page forms that need to survive beyond single requests—items you add to your shopping cart (the classic, clichéd, and clinching example)—are best served by converting their information to session attributes.

Context (Application) Scope

Let's now deal with context scope, which is the longest-lived of the three scopes available to you. Figure 3-2 shows a web container with two different web applications. On startup of the container, a servlet context is created for each web application (at (1) in Figure 3-2). A client web browser—Client 1—then requests the services of ServletA, which in turn uses the context object—at (2) in Figure 3-2. Client 2 uses both ServletA and ServletB: Both servlets use the same context object ((3) in Figure 3-2).

So far, all the action has taken place inside one web application—Web App 1. Now Client 3 requests the services of ServletB and ServletC. ServletB uses the context object we've already met in Web App 1. However, ServletC—located in Web App 2—uses the separate context object that belongs to Web App 2. The point here is that context objects do not straddle different web applications: There is strictly one per web application.

The loss of context scope is shown at (6) in Figure 3-2. If the web container is stopped, then the web applications die—and this includes the context objects for each web application. If a web application is reloaded, then the context object is

FIGURE 3-2 Context Scope

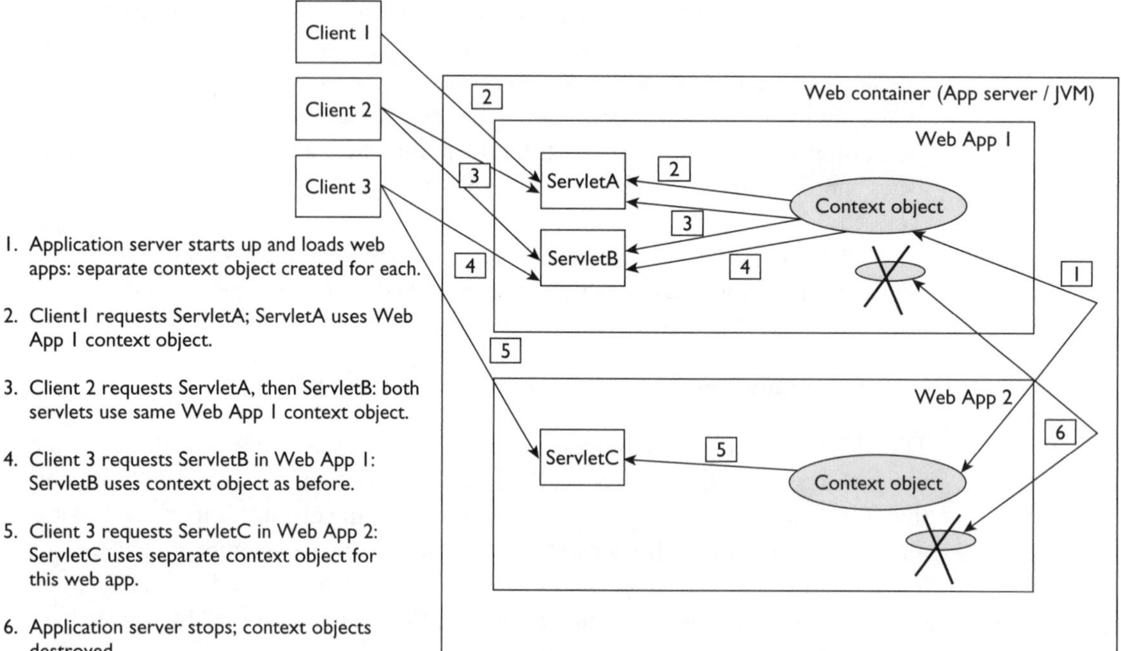
Client 1
Client 2
Client 3
Web container (App server / JVM)
Web App 1
ServletA
ServletB
Context object
Web App 2
ServletC
Context object
2
3
4
5
1
6
1. Application server starts up and loads web apps: separate context object created for each.
2. Client1 requests ServletA; ServletA uses Web App 1 context object.
3. Client 2 requests ServletA, then ServletB: both servlets use same Web App 1 context object.
4. Client 3 requests ServletB in Web App 1: ServletB uses context object as before.
5. Client 3 requests ServletC in Web App 2: ServletC uses separate context object for this web app.
6. Application server stops; context objects destroyed.

destroyed and recreated. And if an individual web application is taken out of service, the context object necessarily dies.

When a web application is distributed across different machines—in other words, different JVMs—you might consider the web application to be logically the same wherever it occurs. Don't fall into the trap of thinking that the context object is therefore the same instance whichever clone of the web application you use. Of course, it can't be literally the same instance because we're talking about different JVMs. But neither is the context object logically the same across the identikit copies of the web application: There is one context object per web application per JVM. If you add an attribute to the context in one web application's JVM, it won't be present in the cloned web application's JVM unless you explicitly add it there as well. This is shown in the following illlustration:

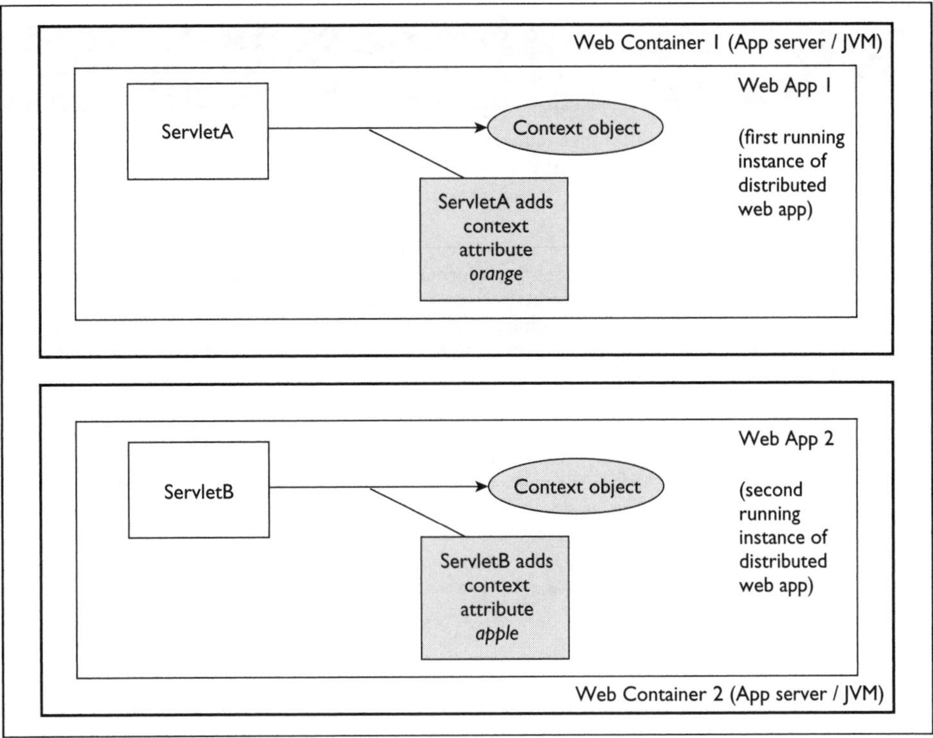

You can see the cloned web application Web App 1 appearing twice, each in a separate JVM. Some overall application server architecture (represented by the outer box) will manage issues such as which requests get routed to which clone of the JVM. You see the different servlets in the separate clones adding different named context attributes to the context object—"apple" in one, "orange" in the other—there is nothing to stop the instances drifting apart and holding different information. If you do need attributes with the same values across JVMs, you need to use session attributes in a distributed web application (see Chapter 4). For distributed sessions, the overall application server architecture is supposed to replicate session information across cloned web applications in different JVMs.

Choosing Scopes

Mostly, you care about scopes for attaching attributes. The question is this: Which is the best scope to use for a given scenario? Should you ignore request attributes because the information placed there evaporates so soon? Should everything go in the context object, because then anything in the web container can access the information? Of course, it depends on circumstances.

SCENARIO & SOLUTION	
You have information retrieved from a database, which is required for a one-off web page and isn't part of a longer transaction.	Store the information in a request attribute. If the information truly isn't needed beyond one production of one HTTP response, then don't keep it around cluttering up the web application JVM memory.
You have some XML files that store essential information about the way your web application works: perhaps some information about table headings and columns. This information changes only when the web application undergoes development changes and is redelivered.	Store the information derived from the XML files in one or more context attributes. The information is then in JVM memory for any web resource to access—no need to keep trawling through the XML file every time a request needs information.
You have information retrieved from a database to a web page in one request. The user makes updates on the web page to the information, and submits the changes, which are subject to some complex, server-side validation. The validation fails, so the user is presented with the changes made and a list of problems that need resolving.	This scenario is a transaction spanning several requests. However, it is information unique to a particular client transaction—not appropriate to attach to the "public" context object. The information that persists across web pages should be held in one or more *session attributes*: more on these in Chapter 4!

Multithreading

Java is a multithreaded language, but you can pursue a viable Java development career without ever attempting multithreaded programming (apart from what you had to do to pass the SCJD exam, anyway!). However, development for the web container model (not to mention the certification exam) requires some knowledge of the way threads work. Although you are not likely to create threads of your own during servlet and JSP programming (some other areas of J2EE programming actively ban you from making your own threads), you need to be aware that the web container has the potential to create many threads of its own. And your developed servlets have to live within this multithreaded model.

The issue—which is no different from any other multithreaded environment—is when you have two (or more) concurrently running threads that require access to the same resource. And in the context of threads and web applications, "resource"—more often than not—means an object that is held as the value of some named attribute in some scope or other—request, session, or context. Is one thread changing an attribute value under the feet of another thread reading that value? Worse, are the threads both trying to update an attribute value at the same time? What we consider in this section is the three scopes again: which are thread safe, which are not, and what you need to do about it as a developer.

Multithreading and Request Attributes

We'll first consider requests. The good news here is that request attributes are thread safe. In fact, everything to do with the request and response objects (results of method calls on these objects, request attributes, request parameters, etc.) will only ever be accessed by one thread and one thread alone. The web container provides a new (or as good as new) instance of the request and response objects whenever a new request is received. Here's how it looks:

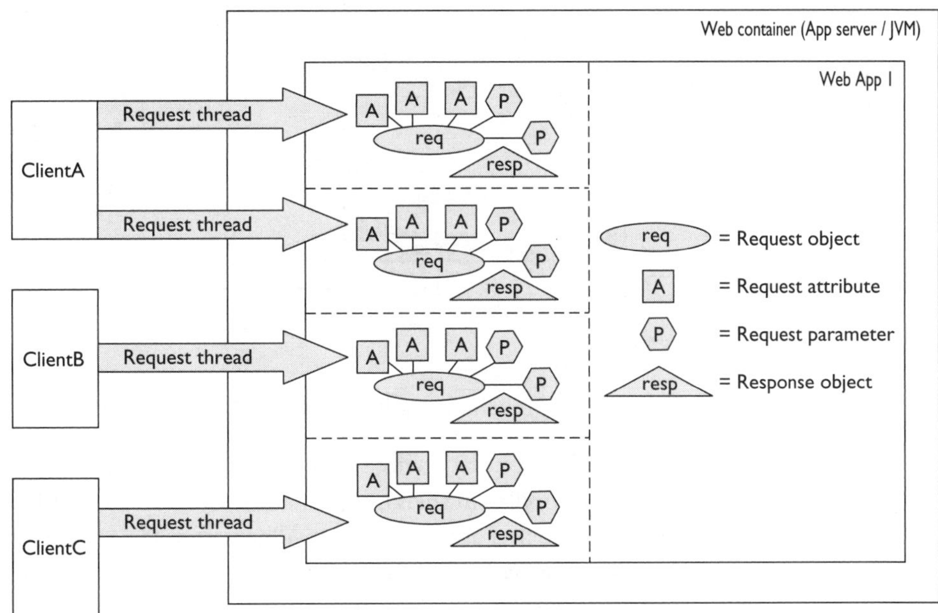

Multithreading and Session Attributes

Again, we're going to defer a full discussion of this until Chapter 4, on sessions. Suffice to say for the moment that session attributes are *officially* not thread safe. For most common web applications, though, you can assume thread safety. But until you've passed your SJWCD exam, assume not (just as you wouldn't cross your hands on the steering wheel until *after* you've passed your driving test).

Multithreading and Context Attributes

The servlet context represents the opposite extreme from the request. The world and his wife have access to the servlet context object. To speak more technically, each and every client requesting thread to a web application can potentially update a servlet context attribute. So you *do* need to worry about thread safety.

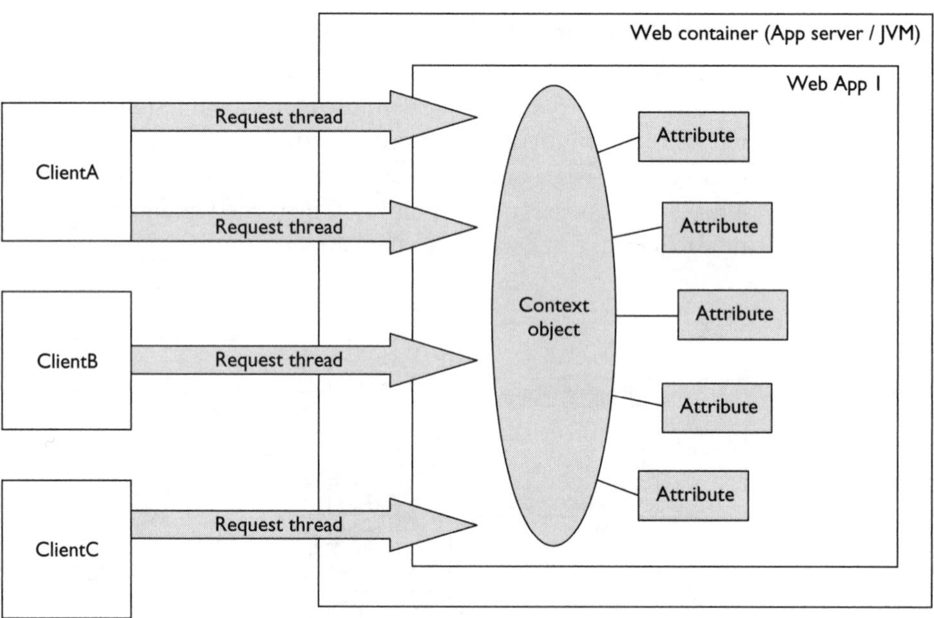

You have two approaches to solve the multithreading dilemma:

1. Treat servlet context attributes like servlet context parameters. Set up servlet context attributes in the `init()` method of a servlet that loads on the startup of the server, and at no other time. Thereafter, treat these attributes as "read only"— only ever call `getAttribute()`, never `setAttribute()`, on the context object.

2. If there are context attributes where you have no option but to update them later, surround the updates with synchronization blocks. If it's crucial that no other thread reads the value of these attributes mid-update, you'll need to synchronize the `getAttribute()` calls as well.

Bear in mind that synchronization—especially on a much-accessed context attribute—might create a huge bottleneck in your application. Keep it to a minimum! Also bear in mind that the recommendations above are not enforced by anything in the web container model. It's down to programming standards to enforce these approaches.

exam watch

As of this version of the exam, you will no longer get questions about the SingleThreadModel interface. This interface is deprecated in the version 2.4 of the servlet specification. The idea was that if a servlet implemented this interface, the web container would guarantee that only one thread at a time would be able to access any given instance of the servlet. Web containers providing this facility paid a high cost in performance terms. And so it was deemed much better to avoid this approach altogether: better to rely on other ways of enforcing thread safety where needed (in general, synchronize what you have to, but keep this to a minimum).

on the job

The old exam syllabus required awareness of thread safety issues regarding types of variables you might use in servlets: local, instance, and class. Although this isn't part of the exam anymore, it's still good to have some knowledge when out in the field.

Local Variables: ***These are either parameters to servlet methods, or variables declared within methods. Just as elsewhere in Java, local variables are completely thread safe: The JVM guarantees that there can be only one thread ever accessing a local variable. Even if the same instance of a servlet is running simultaneously in multiple threads, the*** `service()` ***and other methods are effectively separate.***

Instance Variables: ***These are considered harmful! They are not thread safe, so add your own synchronization if you have to. You never know when there will be more than one thread accessing a single instance of a servlet.***

But more than that, servlet instance variables are not particularly useful. Except for the very specialized case in which you want to keep track of information about individual servlet instances (perhaps to record a usage count per instance), there isn't much you can usefully define as servlet instance information. You can't guarantee that the same client targeting the same servlet URL more than once will get the same instance, so servlet instance information is no substitute for session attributes.

Class Variables: ***Again, these are not thread safe. However, they are potentially a bit more useful than servlet instance variables because the information is shared across all instances of a particular servlet. So a usage counter on a class variable does tell you how many times the actual servlet class was accessed—which is more likely to be something you want to know (as opposed to separate counters for individual instances of the servlet).***

EXERCISE 3-2

Displaying All Attributes in All Scopes

In this exercise, you'll display the attributes available to a web page in all scopes. The context directory for this exercise is ex0302, so set up your web application structure under a directory of this name.

For this exercise, there's a solution in the CD in the file sourcecode/ch03/ex0302 .war—check there if you get stuck.

Set Up the Deployment Descriptor

1. Declare a servlet named AttributesAllScopes, with a suitable servlet mapping. If needed, refer to Chapter 2 to refresh yourself on `<servlet>` element setup.

Write the AttributesAllScopes Servlet

2. Create a Java source file AttributesAllScopes.java in /WEB-INF/classes or an appropriate package directory. Write the class declaration in the source file, extending HttpServlet.
3. Override the `doGet()` method in AttributesAllScopes.

4. Do the necessary preliminaries to obtain the response's PrintWriter, and set the content type to "text/html."

5. Using the request object (of type HttpServletRequest) that's passed as a parameter into the `doGet()` method, retrieve an Enumeration using the `getAttributeNames()` method.

6. Write code to go through all the elements in the Enumeration. For each parameter name retrieved, display the attribute name. Get hold of the corresponding attribute value using the `getAttribute()` method on the request object.

7. Now obtain the session object, using the `getSession()` method on the request object. Repeat steps 5 and 6—getting an Enumeration of parameter names and displaying the attribute names and values—but with the session rather than the request object.

8. Now obtain the context object, using the servlet's `getServletContext()` method. Again, repeat steps 5 and 6 for context attributes.

Run the Application

9. Having compiled your code, copy the entire ex0302 directory to your server's web applications directory. Stop and start your server (if necessary to deploy the application).

10. Point your browser (using the appropriate servlet mapping that you set up in step 1) to the AttributesAllScopes servlet, and check that a web page appears displaying at least some attributes. Here's the URL you are likely to use with the Tomcat server:

```
http://localhost:8080/ex0302/AttributesAllScopes
```

11. It's almost certain you will get some context attributes appearing. However, it's quite likely that request and session scopes will come up blank. Add some request and session attributes to the request and session objects (using the `setAttribute()` method) at the beginning of your `doGet()` method to prove that your retrieval code works. The following illustration shows a screen shot from the solution code.

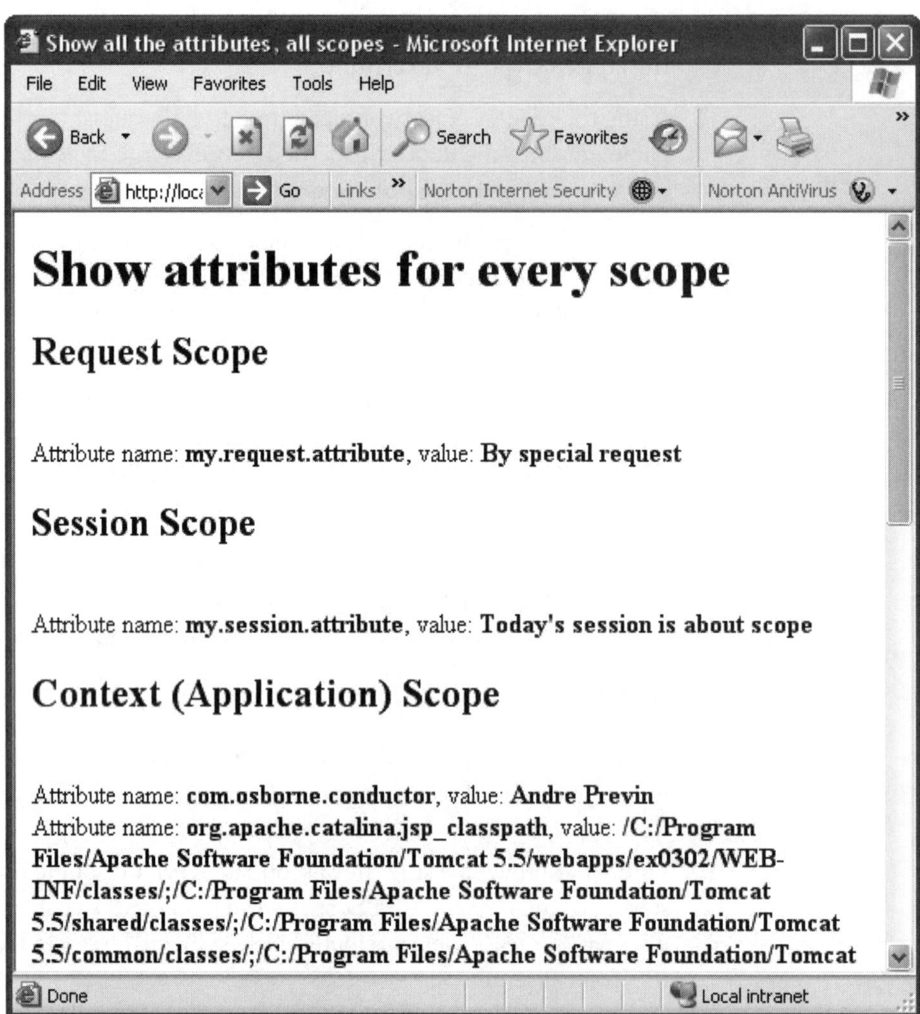
Show all the attributes, all scopes - Microsoft Internet Explorer
File Edit View Favorites Tools Help
Back Search Favorites
Address http://loca Go Links Norton Internet Security Norton AntiVirus
Show attributes for every scope
Request Scope
Attribute name: my.request.attribute, value: By special request
Session Scope
Attribute name: my.session.attribute, value: Today's session is about scope
Context (Application) Scope
Attribute name: com.osborne.conductor, value: Andre Previn
Attribute name: org.apache.catalina.jsp_classpath, value: /C:/Program Files/Apache Software Foundation/Tomcat 5.5/webapps/ex0302/WEB-INF/classes/;/C:/Program Files/Apache Software Foundation/Tomcat 5.5/shared/classes/;/C:/Program Files/Apache Software Foundation/Tomcat 5.5/common/classes/;/C:/Program Files/Apache Software Foundation/Tomcat
Done
Local intranet

CERTIFICATION OBJECTIVE

Request Dispatching (Exam Objective 3.5)

Describe the RequestDispatcher mechanism; write servlet code to create a request dispatcher; write servlet code to forward or include the target resource; and identify and describe the additional request-scoped attributes provided by the container to the target resource.

So far, we've considered the case of calling one single servlet to accomplish a task: request made, servlet executes, response generated—job done. We have also learned about helper classes that a servlet can use. We can include those in the web application's /WEB-INF/classes directory or in a JAR file in /WEB-INF/lib, as we saw in Chapter 2.

What, though, if the servlet we summon wants to call on the services of another servlet within the web application? Or some other web resource, maybe a JSP? Or even hand off all responsibility and let a different servlet handle the work? Enter the RequestDispatcher: a mechanism for controlling the flow of control within the web resources in your web application.

Obtaining a RequestDispatcher

You can obtain a RequestDispatcher either from the request (ServletRequest) or the web application context (ServletContext). ServletRequest has one method for getting hold of a RequestDispatcher, and ServletContext has two—making three possible ways of getting hold of a RequestDispatcher. You can be sure that exam questions will focus on the subtle shades of difference among these three methods!

We'll first of all look at the "how" of getting a RequestDispatcher from the three methods in question.

From ServletRequest

ServletRequest has one method for getting a RequestDispatcher: `getRequestDispatcher(String path)`. Note that the method is part of parent interface ServletRequest. Of course, HttpServletRequest has it too by virtue of inheriting from ServletRequest. But if you're faced with a question about where the method originates, you need to know this information!

The path parameter can be a full path beginning at the context root. This means a path to the resource without naming the context root itself. The following illustration gives some examples.

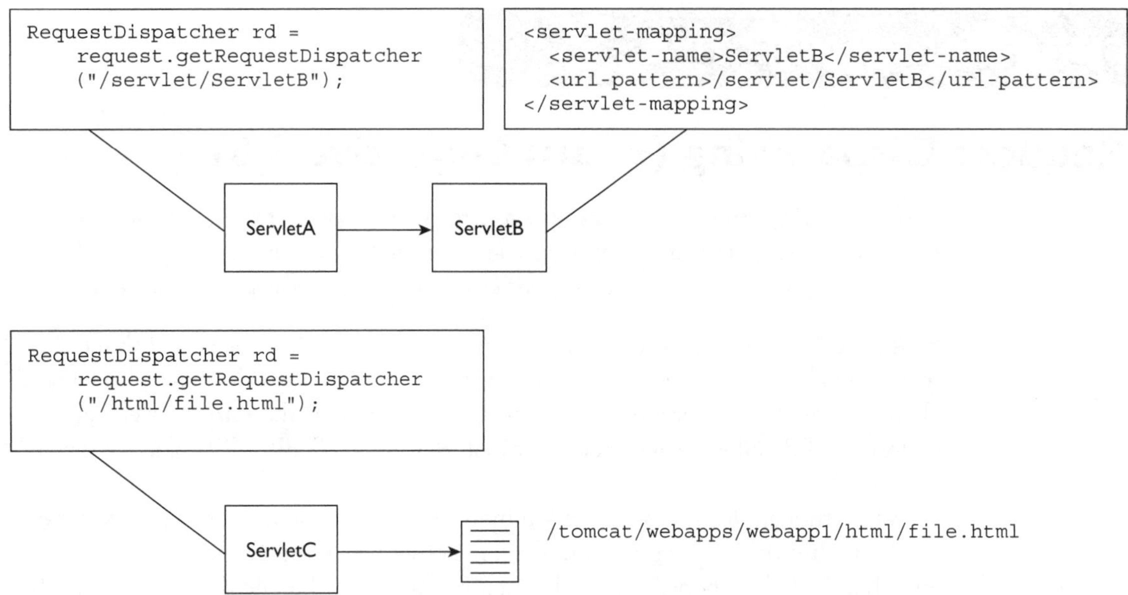

The forward slash ("/") at the beginning of the path denotes the context root. After this, you can append whatever path leads to a web resource—typically a dynamic one (another servlet or JSP), though it doesn't have to be. You can point your RequestDispatcher to a plain old static HTML page if that's your wish. So when ServletA calls ServletB, it uses a matching `<url-pattern>` for ServletB when creating the RequestDispatcher. When ServletC dispatches to a static HTML file (file.html in the html directory of webapp1), it supplies the full path starting from the context root (e.g., "/html/file.html").

There's also the possibility of specifying a path without an initial forward slash to **`ServletRequest.getRequestDispatcher()`**.The following illustration shows how this might work.

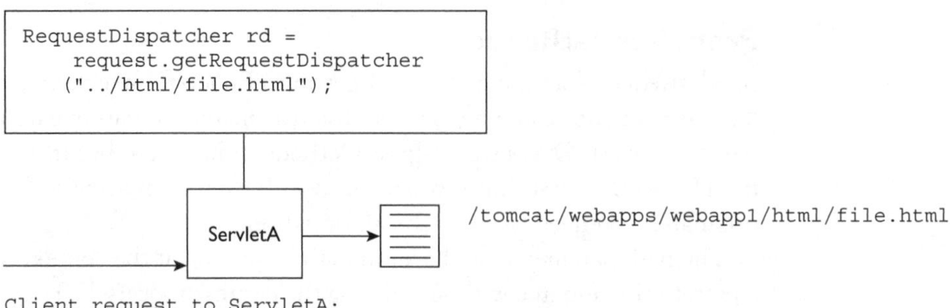

You see how the client request to ServletA—from the web application root—is "/servlet/servletA." The parameter to the `getRequestDispatcher()` method is relative to something—but what? It's not the context root. This time, it's the directory containing the resource requested (ServletA)—notionally the directory /servlet. Yes, I know this may not be a *real* directory—just a logical fiction made up in a servlet mapping—because the real servlet class probably inhabits some more involved location such as "/WEB-INF/classes/com/osborne/servlets." The point is that relative requests are relative to the URL as given. So now the `getRequestDispatcher()` receives the parameter "../html/file.html." The ".." means go up one directory in the request—in other words, from servlet to the root directory of the web app. The rest of the parameter "/html/file.html" now works as if expressed from the root directory of the web app.

So you see that this form of relative path syntax gives considerable flexibility. That said, I try to keep things simple—and favor straightforward full paths from the context root beginning with a forward slash. You can see how the use of ".." to go up to the parent directory is quite vulnerable to later restructuring of resources in the web application (for example, through servlet mapping changes).

From ServletContext

ServletContext has two methods of getting hold of a RequestDispatcher. These are `getRequestDispatcher(String path)` and `getNamedDispatcher(String name)`.

`getRequestDispatcher(String path)` This method works in exactly the same way as the same named method on ServletRequest. There is a restriction: Only full paths are allowed (i.e., paths beginning with a forward slash "/," which denotes the context root). Paths without the initial forward slash will not work. You'll get a runtime exception—IllegalArgumentException—and text along the lines of "Path myPath does not begin with a "/" character."

`getNamedDispatcher(String name)` This method does bring something new to the party. Instead of specifying a path, you supply a name for the resource you want to execute. The name must match one of the `<servlet-name>` values you have set up in the deployment descriptor, so it can refer to a named servlet or a JSP.

You may have idly wondered whether there was any point in setting up a `<servlet>` entry in the deployment descriptor without a corresponding `<servlet-mapping>`. The `getNamedDispatcher()` method is the point—it gives a means of executing a servlet (or JSP) that doesn't have any other means of access. This is potentially very useful. There may be some services within your application that are

exam watch *What happens if an incorrect path is fed to a RequestDispatcher method? Answer: the method returns* **null**. *So that's what your code should test for (you don't attempt to catch any kind of exception).*

available only in particular circumstances, or only internally to your application. You may not want these to be sitting on any kind of public path that can be typed into the address line, and a `<servlet-mapping>` gives just that sort of public access. If you do exploit this technique, make sure to switch off any server loopholes—such as the ability to execute servlets if you happen to know their name. Most servers have such capabilities as a convenience for developers, but they have no place in a production environment.

exam watch *There is no way of escaping a web application context with any of the methods that return a RequestDispatcher. However, there's nothing stopping you from using ServletContext's* **getContext()** *method to get yourself another web application context, then obtaining a Request Dispatcher on that other context.*

Using a RequestDispatcher

Having obtained a RequestDispatcher, your servlet can do one of two things with it. Either it forwards to another web resource (washing its hands of the responsibility of returning a response) or includes another web resource within its own output. The RequestDispatcher interface has only two methods—`forward()` and `include()`—so no surprises there. We'll now look at these methods in some detail.

Forwarding

We'll first consider the case of forwarding. The following illustration gives a graphic account of what happens when a servlet forwards to another servlet.

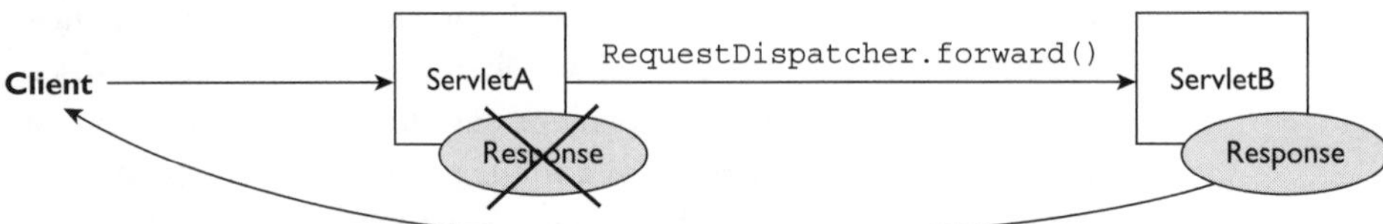

You see that the first servlet is effectively forgotten. Although it can have code that writes output to the response, the contents of the response buffer are lost at the point of forwarding to the second servlet. For this reason, if the first servlet is past the point of no return and has committed any of its response to the client, then a forward call is illegal—and will, indeed, result in an IllegalStateException at runtime.

The forward method accepts two parameters—a ServletRequest and the Servlet Response. All you have scope to do is to pass on the request and response received into the forwarding servlet's `service()` method (which you more likely get hold of in the `doGet()` or `doPost()` servlet method). You mustn't manufacture your own servlet requests and responses and plug these in instead. But then, why would you?

So, let's consider a servlet class that exists solely to forward somewhere else (import statements omitted to save space):

```
public class FlexRequestDispatcher extends HttpServlet {
  protected void doGet(HttpServletRequest request,
                       HttpServletResponse response)
                       throws ServletException, IOException {
    String fwdPath = request.getParameter("fwd");
    System.out.println("The dispatch path is: " + fwdPath);
    RequestDispatcher rd = request.getRequestDispatcher(fwdPath);
    // The following two lines are a waste of effort: the
    // response output will be binned...
    PrintWriter out = response.getPrintWriter();
    out.write("This text will be lost");
    // ...in favor of the response from the resource you are
    // forwarding to...
    rd.forward(request, response);
  }
}
```

The code expects a parameter named *fwd* which contains a String with the path to forward to. So you might call it with a request such as the following:

```
http://localhost:8080/mywebapp/FlexRequestDispatcher?fwd=/AnotherServlet
```

The *fwd* parameter is then translated from the query string, so the *fwdPath* string local variable would have a value of "/AnotherServlet." This is passed into the ServletRequest's `getRequestDispatcher` method. Because the path begins with a forward slash ("/"), it will be interpreted relative to the context root—equivalent to the address

```
http://localhost:8080/mywebapp/AnotherServlet
```

Assuming that "/AnotherServlet" is a valid resource in the web application (presumably a valid servlet mapping), then the RequestDispatcher instance *rd* will have a value. All that remains is to execute `rd.forward()`, supplying the request and response as passed into the `doGet()` method. A well-behaved servlet might first test whether *rd* is **null** before attempting to execute the `forward()` method, to protect against a NullPointerException.

Note the two lines that obtain the PrintWriter from the response and write to it. These are effectively a waste of effort. As soon as the FlexRequestDispatcher servlet forwards to the requested resource, the response of FlexRequestDispatcher will effectively be nullified—only the forwarded-to resource's output will be visible in the resulting response.

Special Attributes for Forwarding

Let's now suppose you've arrived in the "forwarded-to" servlet AnotherServlet, which contains the following code:

```
public class AnotherServlet extends HttpServlet {
  protected void doGet(HttpServletRequest request,
                       HttpServletResponse response)
                       throws ServletException, IOException {
    String servletPath = request.getServletPath();
    System.out.println("The servlet path is: " + servletPath);
  }
}
```

Which servlet path is printed to the server console—that of the *forwarding* servlet FlexRequestDispatcher, or the *forwarded-to* servlet AnotherServlet? The answer is the *forwarded-to* servlet AnotherServlet. So the output in the server console might look like this:

```
The servlet path is: /AnotherServlet
```

This is because a *forwarded-to* servlet has complete control over the request—it's as if the *forwarding* servlet had never been called.

What, though, if you want to get at the original servlet path for the request while within AnotherServlet's code? The web container provides for this. Five special attributes are set up that reflect "original" values about the request path, instead of the request path, which has been modified to fit the forwarded to servlet. To get one of these values, simply use the `request.getAttribute()` method. The following table shows all five attributes, together with a description of what they represent and the request method for which the attributes provide a necessary substitute. Assume that the full URL to the forwarding servlet is

```
http://localhost:8080/myapp/ForwardingServlet/pathinfo?fruit=orange
```

Attribute Name	Description	"Equivalent" Method on ServletRequest
javax.servlet.forward.request_uri	The URI of the original request to the forwarding servlet (e.g., /myapp/ ForwardingServlet /pathinfo)	`getRequestURI()`
javax.servlet.forward.context_path	The context path for the forwarding servlet (e.g., /myapp)	`getContextPath()`
javax.servlet.forward.servlet_path	The servlet path for the forwarding servlet (e.g., /ForwardingServlet)	`getServletPath()`
java.servlet.forward.path_info	The path information for the forwarding servlet (e.g., /pathinfo)	`getPathInfo()`
java.servlet.forward.query_string	The query string attaching to the original request for the forwarding servlet (e.g., fruit=orange)	`getQueryString()`

The web container is contracted (by the servlet specification) to provide these attributes. Of course, the attributes are not present if the value returned by them would be **null** anyway (e.g. you won't find a java.servlet.forward.query_string attribute when there is no query string on the request URI).

The "equivalent" methods shown in the table are not really equivalent at all. The point of supplying the attributes is that they give alternative information that is otherwise invisible through the apparently equivalent method. This is summarized in Table 3-2, after we look at the set of special attributes that arise when a Request Dispatcher is used to include a web resource.

on the job

Forwarding is not so very different from request redirection (`ServletRequest.sendRedirect()`). However, forwarding has an advantage—the request information (parameters and attributes) are preserved. Redirection effectively initiates a new request from the client; the original request parameters and attributes are lost (though you can add new parameters—or preserve existing ones—by adding them to the query string in the URL that is the parameter for `sendRedirect()`). So on the face of it, forwarding is always better—information is preserved, and it's more efficient, for there's no return trip to the client. However, beware of any relative URLs in the response from the servlet to which you forward. The requesting browser will still think it's dealing with the original URL (i.e., of the servlet that did the forwarding). You can generally see this in the address line of the browser: If ServletA did the forwarding, and ServletB is forwarded to, you'll still see http://www.myco.com/webapp/ServletA. If your image links for ServletB's output are relative links, they'll be fine—unless the relative path from ServletB to the images is different from that of ServletA.

exam watch

When you forward to another servlet, you might be tempted to think that control never returns to the servlet you are forwarding from. Not so. Consider the following code, where ServletA forwards to ServletB, but there is code following the `forward()` method in ServletA:

```
public class ServletA extends HttpServlet {
  protected void doGet(HttpServletRequest request,
                       HttpServletResponse response)
                       throws ServletException, IOException {
    String fwdPath = "/ServletB";
    RequestDispatcher rd = request.getRequestDispatcher(fwdPath);
    rd.forward(request, response);
    System.out.println("Back in ServletA");
  }
}
```

```
public class ServletB extends HttpServlet {
  protected void doGet(HttpServletRequest request,
                       HttpServletResponse response)
                       throws ServletException, IOException {
    System.out.println("Now in ServletB");
  }
}
```

When you call ServletA, the output to the server console (note: not the response/web pages!) is as follows:

```
Now in ServletB
Back in ServletA
```

What you can't do in ServletA—after the forward call—is anything that might attempt to affect the response. Well, you can do it—and the lines of code will execute harmlessly, having no effect. But code that does things unrelated to the response (such as outputting text to the console, setting attributes, and writing to logs) will execute as normal.

Including

The alternative to the `forward()` method on RequestDispatcher is the `include()` method. Instead of "passing the buck," an including servlet takes the contents of the included web resource and adds this to its own response. Let's adapt an example from before, now using the `include()` method instead of `forward()`:

```
public class FlexRequestDispatcher extends HttpServlet {
  protected void doGet(HttpServletRequest request,
                       HttpServletResponse response)
                       throws ServletException, IOException {
    String incPath = request.getParameter("inc");
    System.out.println("The dispatch path is: " + incPath);
    RequestDispatcher rd = request.getRequestDispatcher(incPath);
    PrintWriter out = response.getPrintWriter();
    out.write("The output will start with this text, ");
    rd.forward(request, response);
    out.write("and finish with this text.");
  }
}
```

Suppose we fed a parameter such as *inc=/IncludedServlet* to FlexRequestDispatcher, and IncludedServlet includes this code:

```
PrintWriter out = response.getPrintWriter();
out.write("continue with this included text, ");
```

The sum of the output should look something like this in the resulting response:

```
The output will start with this text, continue with this
included text, and finish with this text.
```

exam watch

What if you try to call the `forward()` or `include()` methods when a response has already been committed to the client? The answer is that you get an IllegalStateException for the `forward()` method—as we mentioned before. But you don't get any exception if you call an `include()` after the response is committed. After all, you are not trying to throw away the original response with an `include()`—only augmenting the original response.

Special Attributes and Including

Just as a "forwarded-to" servlet has access to some special attributes, so does an "included" servlet. There are a similarly named set of five attributes, though their significance is almost opposite to the forwarding set. We'll assume a URL this time of

```
http://localhost:8080/myapp/IncludingServlet/pathinfo?fruit=orange
```

and a code snippet from Includ**ing**Servlet that includes Includ**ed**Servlet, as follows:

```
RequestDispatcher rd =
  req.getRequestDispatcher("/IncludedServlet/newPathInfo?fruit=apple");
rd.forward(req, resp);
```

Now the attributes (as you access them in Includ**ed**Servlet) have the following values:

Attribute Name	Description	"Equivalent" Method on ServletRequest
javax.servlet.include.request_uri	The URI of the revised request to the included servlet (e.g., /myapp/IncludedServlet/newPathInfo)	`getRequestURI()`
javax.servlet. include.context_path	The context path for the included servlet (e.g., /myapp)	`getContextPath()`
javax.servlet. include.servlet_path	The servlet path for the included servlet (e.g., /IncludedServlet)	`getServletPath()`
java.servlet. include.path_info	The path information for the including servlet (e.g., /newPathInfo)	`getPathInfo()`
java.servlet. include.query_string	The query string attaching to the *revised* request to the included servlet (e.g., fruit=apple)	`getQueryString()`

It's not an easy picture to grasp! The value derived from the attribute is different from the value returned from the "equivalent" method. When in the *included* servlet, use the method to get information about the *including* servlet, and the attribute to get information about the *included* servlet (i.e., the servlet you are in). Table 3-2 summarizes what servlet you get information about, dependent on (a) what kind of servlet you are in (forwarding, forwarded to, including, or included) and (b) whether you are using request methods, special forward attributes, or special include attributes.

TABLE 3-2 Summary of Information from Request Methods and Special Attributes

In the Code of	Forwarding Servlet	Forwarded to Servlet	Including Servlet	Included Servlet
servlet method call (e.g., `getServletPath()`)	Forwarding	Forwarded to	Including	Including
forward attribute (e.g., javax.servlet.**forward**.servlet_path)	N/A	Forwarding	N/A	N/A
include attribute (e.g., javax.servlet.**include**.servlet_path)	N/A	N/A	N/A	Included

Special Attributes and `getNamedDispatcher()`

One last point about special attributes (both the forward set and the include set, so this is as applicable to javax.servlet.**forward.**context_path as it is to javax.servlet .**include.**query_string): When you use `getNamedDispatcher()` on ServletContext to get hold of a RequestDispatcher (as opposed to `getRequestDispatcher()` on ServletContext or ServletRequest), these special attributes *are not set*. The rationale is that you are not forwarding or including via an external request. Because all these special attributes pertain to features of external requests (mostly URL information), they are not deemed relevant to an internal server call to a named resource.

EXERCISE 3-3

Implementing a RequestDispatcher and Viewing Special Attributes

This exercise will implement two servlets, one that dispatches to the other. By accepting a parameter, we'll make the dispatching servlet behave flexibly so that it may either forward or include the dispatched-to servlet. In either case, we'll display the special attributes that are associated with the forward or include so that these appear on the web page produced by the servlet(s). The context directory for this exercise is ex0303, so set up your web application structure under a directory of this name.

For this exercise, there's a solution in the CD in the file sourcecode/ch03/ex0303 .war—check there if you get stuck.

Set Up the Deployment Descriptor

1. Declare a servlet named Dispatcher, with a suitable servlet mapping. If needed, refer to Chapter 2 to refresh yourself on `<servlet>` element setup.
2. Also declare a servlet named Receiver with a servlet mapping that will trap path information—a `<url-pattern>` of (e.g.) /Receiver/*.

Write the Dispatcher Servlet

3. Create a Java source file Dispatcher.java in /WEB-INF/classes or an appropriate package directory. Write the class declaration in the source file, extending HttpServlet.
4. Override the `doGet()` method in Dispatcher.
5. In the `doGet()` code, retrieve a request parameter whose name is "mode," and hold this in a local String variable.

6. Obtain a RequestDispatcher from the request or context object—set the path parameter to "/Receiver/pathInfo?fruit=orange."
7. Test the value of the "mode" parameter obtained in step 5. If the value is "forward," call the forward method on the request dispatcher object obtained in step 6; if it is "include," call include instead.
8. Write something to the response object so that you know from the web page that this is the Dispatcher servlet (not the Receiver).

Write the Receiver Servlet

9. Create a Java source file Receiver.java in /WEB-INF/classes or an appropriate package directory. Write the class declaration in the source file, extending HttpServlet.
10. Override the `doGet()` method in Receiver.
11. In the `doGet()` code, obtain the Enumeration of parameter names from the request object, and display to the web page all parameter names and values.
12. Do the same for request attribute names and values. This will display the special attributes supplied by the web container for a forwarded or included servlet.

Run the Application

13. Having compiled your code, copy the entire ex0303 directory to your server's web applications directory. Stop and start your server (if necessary to deploy the application).
14. Point your browser (using the appropriate servlet mapping that you set up in step 1) to the Dispatcher servlet, ensuring that you pass the "mode" parameter: Use a URL such as the following:

```
http://localhost:8080/ex0303/Dispatcher?mode=forward
```

15. Compare the outputs you get from forwarding and including. Note that the text output by the Dispatcher servlet is simply not present when you forward. However, when you include, the text of the Dispatcher and Receiver servlets should appear. The following illustration shows the solution code output when mode=forward.

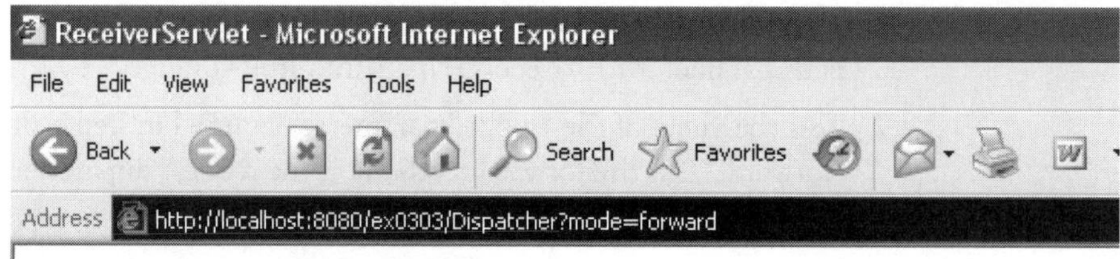

Request Parameters

Parameter name: mode; parameter value(s): forward
Parameter name: fruit; parameter value(s): orange

Request Attributes

Attribute name: javax.servlet.forward.request_uri; attribute value: /ex0303/Dispatcher
Attribute name: javax.servlet.forward.context_path; attribute value: /ex0303
Attribute name: javax.servlet.forward.servlet_path; attribute value: /Dispatcher
Attribute name: javax.servlet.forward.query_string; attribute value: mode=forward
Attribute name: vegetable; attribute value: carrot

Request Method Output for Servlet Receiver

getRequestURI(): /ex0303/Receiver/pathInfo
getContextPath(): /ex0303
getServletPath(): /Receiver
getPathInfo(): /pathInfo
getQueryString(): fruit=orange
End of Receiver Servlet

CERTIFICATION OBJECTIVE

Filters and Wrappers (Exam Objective 3.3)

Describe the web container request processing model; write and configure a filter; create a request or response wrapper; and, given a design problem, describe how to apply a filter or a wrapper.

We're now going to look at the interfaces and classes that make up the filtering mechanism in the web container model. Filters are intriguing beasts. In many respects they are like servlets: They receive requests and responses that they can manipulate, they have access to the servlet context, and (like request dispatchers for the servlet) they have an inclusion mechanism whereby a filter can pass control to another filter or a servlet.

Their main purpose is to intervene before and after a request for a web resource. The web resource itself need not be aware that it has been nested in a filter. An example might help. Suppose you want all the output from your web application to be encrypted. You can write a filter that triggers on any request to your web application (whatever the web resource requested). The filter will trap the response from the web resource, run some kind of encryption algorithm over it, then assume responsibility for returning the response to the requester.

Because you so often use a filter to transform the response—and sometimes the request—you may want specialized request and response objects with their own specialized behavior. There is provision for this in the so-called "wrapper" classes—such as HttpServletResponseWrapper. You can subclass these wrapper classes, then substitute them for the original response (or request) that is passed to the filter. We'll talk about filters and wrappers in some detail.

Filters

The servlet specification gives a useful and fairly comprehensive list of the uses you might find for filters:

- Authentication filters
- Logging and auditing filters
- Image conversion filters

- Data compression filters
- Encryption filters
- Tokenizing filters
- Filters that trigger resource access events
- XSL/T filters that transform XML content
- MIME-type chain filters
- Caching filters

You may gather from this list that filters might be used for pre-processing requests for resources, as would be the case for an authentication filter. If your credentials aren't up to scratch, a filter has the power to deny access to the requested resource. A data compression filter is most likely to kick in on the response, perhaps converting the output to a zipped output stream before allowing the response to return.

Now that we've seen what filters are capable of, let's take a look at what you need to know to write and implement one: which interfaces and classes are involved, and what you need to declare in the deployment descriptor.

Writing the Filter Code

When writing a filter, these are the steps:

1. Write a class that implements the javax.servlet.Filter interface.
2. Implement the three methods of the Filter interface: `init()`, `destroy()`, and `doFilter()`.
3. Optionally, provide a no-argument constructor.

Not much to it, really—but there is a bit of devilry in the detail. Let's consider those three methods further. Together, they constitute the filter life cycle, as shown in Figure 3-3.

`init()` The full signature is

```
public void init(FilterConfig config) throws ServletException.
```

The `init()` method is called once only—when the web container creates the instance of the filter. This could be on server startup, and at latest will occur just before the filter is pressed into service (because someone has requested a web resource

FIGURE 3-3

Filter Life Cycle

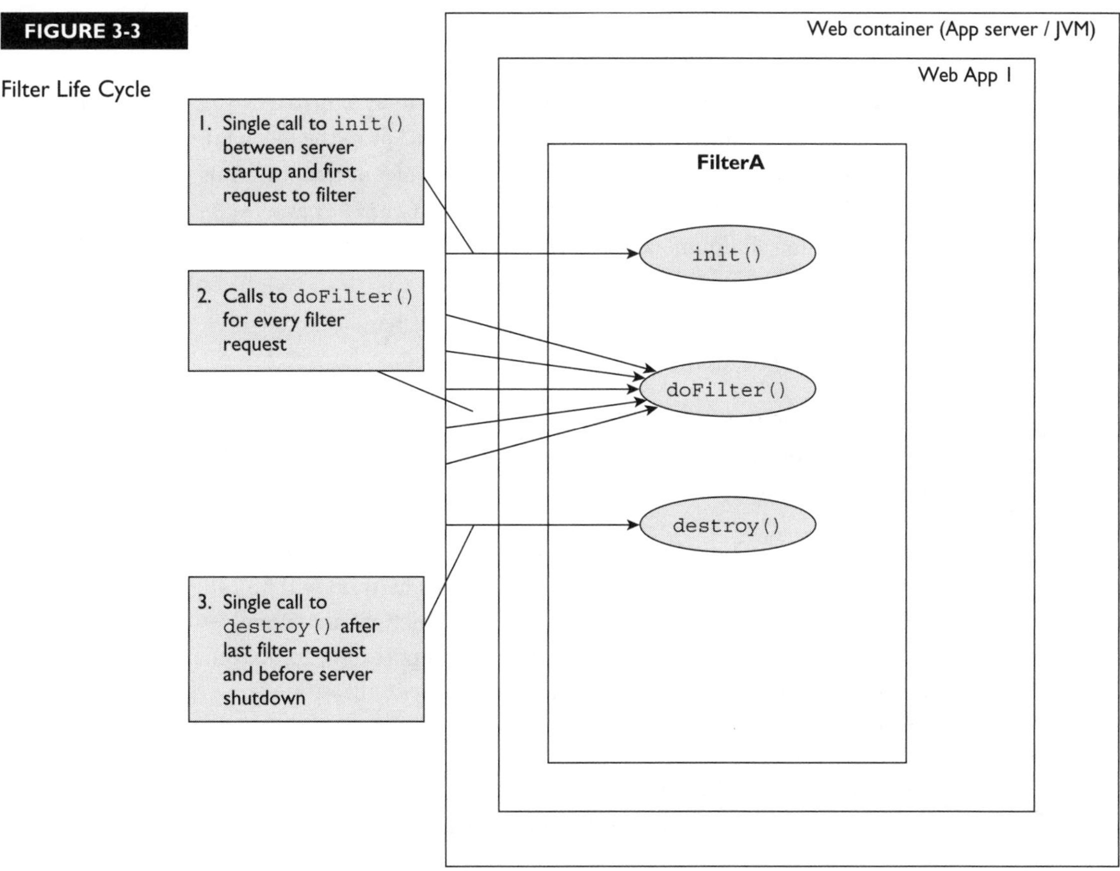

that triggers the filtration). You have one shot at this point to capture the Filter Config object that is passed as a parameter to the method and to keep it available for later use—typically as a private instance variable. Here's an extract from a Filter which does just that:

```
private FilterConfig config;
public void init(FilterConfig config) throws ServletException {
  this.config = config;
}
```

There's no compulsion to do this, but the FilterConfig object has some handy methods that you might want to use later:

- `getFilterName()`, which returns a String returning the name of the filter as defined in the deployment descriptor.
- `getInitParameter(String name)`, which returns a String value for the named parameter. This is identical in concept to the mechanism for setting up ServletContext parameters, which we met at the beginning of this chapter. Unsurprisingly, FilterConfig also has a `getInitParameterNames()` method, returning an Enumeration of the names of all the initialization parameters defined for this filter.
- `getServletContext()`, which returns a handle to the servlet context for the web application.

You can use the `init()` method to do other initialization tasks you deem necessary. You're not restricted in any way as to what these might be: Do whatever the Java language lets you do.

`destroy()` The full signature is `public void destroy()`: no parameters in, nothing returned. You are guaranteed that this method will be called once and once only when the filter is taken out of service, which means, usually, when the web application closes down. This gives you the opportunity to do some cleanup and resource reclamation, typically unpicking the initialization you performed in the `init()` method.

`doFilter()` The full signature is lengthy and is very close to a servlet's `service()` (or `doGet()` or `doPut()`) method.

```
public void doFilter(ServletRequest request,
  ServletResponse response, FilterChain chain)
  throws IOException, ServletException
```

So you can see that—like a servlet—the method accepts a request and a response object. There's another object as well, though—the FilterChain object—and it's this that allows a filter to pass control (or deny access) to other filters and web resources. Here's an abbreviated list of what you generally do in a `doFilter()` method:

1. Look at the request.
2. Wrapper the request and response object—if required.
3. Add or change things about the request, through the wrapper.
4. Call the next filter (or servlet) in the chain (using `doFilter()` on the Filter Chain object passed as a parameter), *or*

5. Block the request by *not* calling the FilterChain's `doFilter()` method.
6. On return from the FilterChain's `doFilter()` method (or even if it wasn't called), amend the response—headers or content—through the wrapper.

Constructor If you wish, you can supply a no-argument constructor (or rely on the default constructor that the Java compiler provides in the absence of other constructors). There's no point at all in providing constructors with arguments: After all, the web application model is the framework that instantiates filters, and the framework is not set up to call constructors with arguments.

An Example Filter

So now let's take a look at an example filter. It's a logging filter that makes no attempt to alter the request and response objects it receives. It simply writes the URL (and other default logging details) to a named log file. Here's the code:

```
import java.io.*;
import java.util.logging.*;
import javax.servlet.*;
import javax.servlet.http.*;
public class LogFilter implements Filter {
  private FilterConfig config;
  private static Logger logger = Logger.getLogger("com.osborne.accesslog");
  public void init(FilterConfig config) throws ServletException {
    // Initialize the logger
    try {
      Handler fh = new FileHandler("C:\\temp\\accessLog.txt");
      logger.addHandler(fh);
    } catch (IOException ioe) {
      throw new ServletException(ioe);
    }
    logger.setLevel(Level.INFO);
    // Capture the config object
    this.config = config;
  }
  public void doFilter(ServletRequest request, ServletResponse response,
    FilterChain chain) throws IOException, ServletException {
    HttpServletRequest httpReq = (HttpServletRequest) request;
    String path = httpReq.getRequestURI();
    logger.info("The following path was requested: " + path);
    chain.doFilter(request, response);
  }
  public void destroy() {
```

```
37      logger = null;
38      config = null;
39    }
40 }
```

Let's talk through some parts of this code:

- Line 14 declares the class—called LogFilter—and shows that it implements the Filter interface.
- Line 15 declares an instance variable of type FilterConfig. We go on to initialize this from the parameter passed to the **init()** method at line 27, just in case we wanted to make use of the FilterConfig object in the filter (which we don't, as it happens—but you might amend this code and choose to do so later!).
- Line 16 declares a static variable of type Logger, from the javax.util.logging package. Space doesn't permit a full explanation of Java logging—take a look at the Java Logging Overview in the J2SDK documentation.
- Lines 17 to 28 encompass the **init()** method. Apart from trapping the Filter Config parameter, as we discussed earlier, the code here is devoted to setting up the Logger: tying this to a file on the file system called accessLog.txt (in directory C:\Temp) and setting it to receive informational (or more serious) messages.
- Lines 29 to 35 make up the **doFilter()** method. At line 29, this accepts a standard parameter: request, of type ServletRequest. Since we know we will be running this filter in an HTTP environment, we know it's safe to cast the parameter to an HttpServletRequest reference at line 31. This enables us to execute the **getRequestURI()** method at line 32 to get a String showing the web resource requested. This we pass as a parameter into the logger's **info()** method at line 33, so it's written to the access log. Finally—at line 34—we simply call the FilterChain's **chain()** method, passing on the request and response entirely unaltered.
- Lines 36 to 40 cover the **destroy()** method, which cleans up by setting references to *null*.

Defining Deployment Descriptor Elements for Filters

So now that we have written our Filter, all we have to do is to ensure that the web container will call it when we require. This is achieved through setting up <filter> and <filter-mapping> elements in the deployment descriptor. Figure 3-4 shows graphically how the <filter> element looks.

FIGURE 3-4

Filter Declaration in the Deployment Descriptor

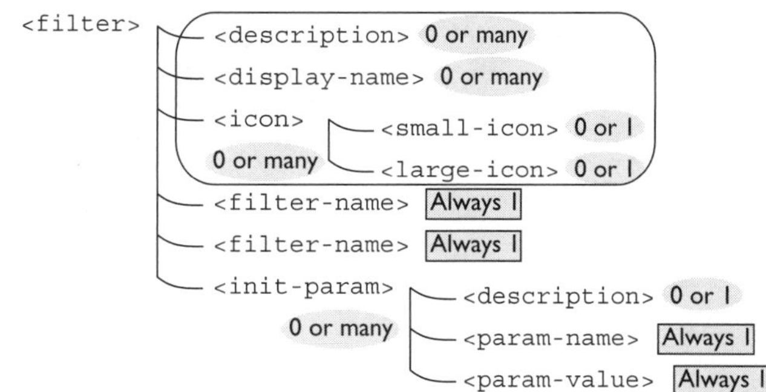

The first three optional trio of elements—**<description>**, **<display-name>**, **<icon>**—are no different in function or form from other places where they occur (see Chapter 2, Figure 2-3, and the accompanying explanation), except, of course, that they apply specifically to the filter you're setting up.

The meat of the **<filter>** element is in the two subelements **<filter-name>** and **<filter-class>**, which are mandatory. Here you give your Filter a logical name (which can be used to tie into later filter mappings) and the full qualified name of your filter's class file.

Optionally, supply as many **<init-param>** elements as you like, and use the FilterConfig's `getInitParameter()` and `getInitParameterNames()` methods to get at them in your Filter code.

Let's now take a look at **<filter-mapping>**, which is shown in Figure 3-5. This is a little more complex than **<servlet-mapping>**, which we met in Chapter 2. You see that it has three subelements, two of them mandatory. The first is **<filter-name>**, which must tie back to a **<filter-name>** specified in a **<filter>** element. The second subelement is also mandatory, but you have a choice: either **<url-pattern>** or **<servlet-name>**. This is the element that actually ties your filter to an incoming request for a web resource.

- **<url-pattern>**: Suppose your client request has a URL that matches the **<url-pattern>** on a particular **<servlet-mapping>**. Suppose then that this same **<url-pattern>** matches a **<filter-mapping>** as well. That's the trigger for the filter to run ahead of the servlet that has been targeted. The rules for legal filter mapping URL patterns are exactly the same as those embedded in servlet mappings: We explored them in Chapter 2. We'll see some example URL patterns for filters a little later in this section.
- **<servlet-name>**: The servlets in your web application have a **<servlet-name>** as a mandatory subelement of **<servlet>**. If the filter mappings's

FIGURE 3-5

Filter Mapping Declaration in the Deployment Descriptor

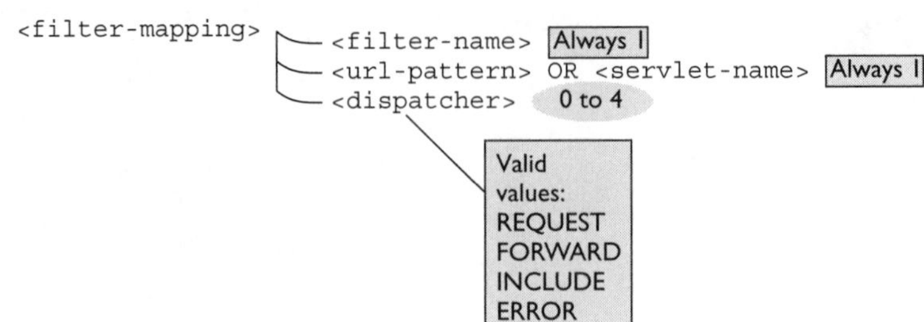

`<servlet-name>` matches a requested servlet's `<servlet-name>`, it's a trigger for the filter to run ahead of the servlet.

The third subelement—`<dispatcher>`—is optional; when you leave it out, though, it's equivalent to explicitly stating `<dispatcher>REQUEST</dispatcher>`. This feature—introduced in servlet specification 2.4—acknowledges that there are many routes into a web resource on your web application. It could well be that you want the filter to kick in dependent on one of these routes. Here are the four valid values for the dispatcher element, with a description of the route:

- REQUEST (the default)—a direct client request for a web resource.
- FORWARD—an internal web server request for a web resource via the `forward()` method on a RequestDispatcher.
- INCLUDE—an internal web server request for a web resource via the `include()` method on a RequestDispatcher.
- ERROR—an internal web application request for a resource that has been set up as an `<error-page>`.

When you supply a `<dispatcher>` value, you are giving permission for a filter to trigger for the route specified. The normal situation is probably that you want your filter to apply only to bona fide external client requests. If a servlet is called internally via a RequestDispatcher, chances are you want that servlet to run without the filter intervening. But if you do want the filter to run even on RequestDispatcher calls as well as client requests, include

```
<dispatcher>REQUEST</dispatcher>
<dispatcher>FORWARD</dispatcher>
<dispatcher>INCLUDE</dispatcher>
```

in your `<filter-mapping>`. Here's an illustration of this. FilterA applies to ServletA, FilterB to ServletB, and FilterC to ServletC.

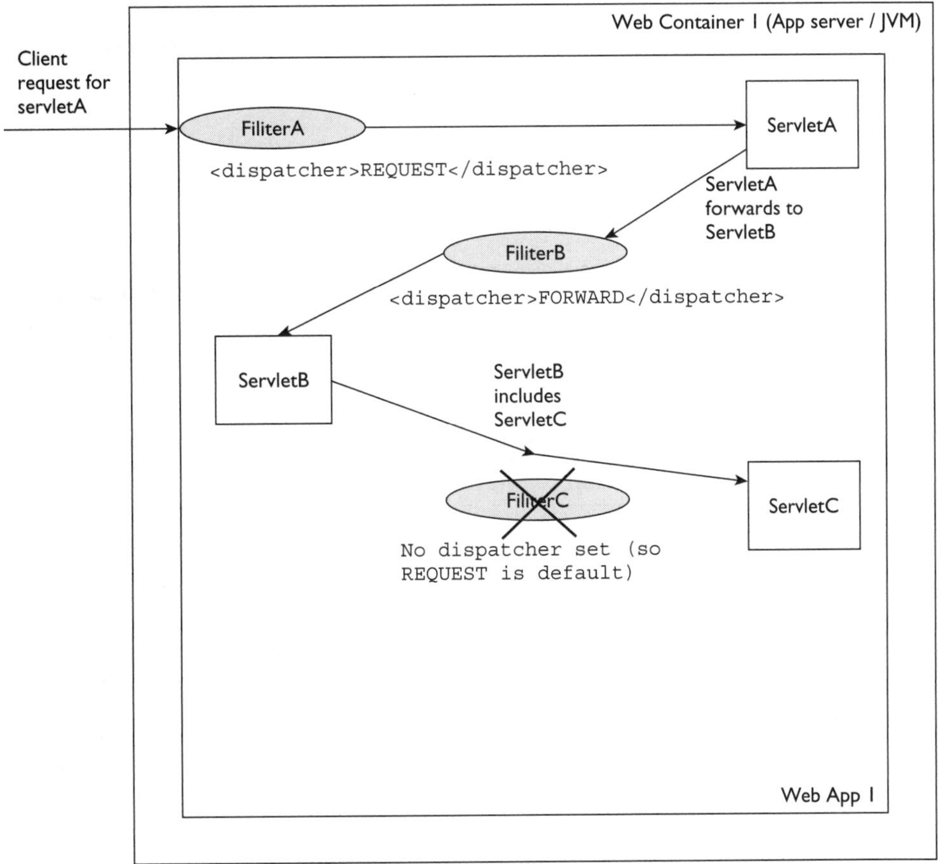

FilterA is explicitly set up to fire when its corresponding ServletA gets a client request, so FilterA runs and calls ServletA. ServletA forwards to ServletB. Because FilterB (attached to ServletB) allows forwarding requests, FilterB runs and calls ServletB as the next item in the chain. Now ServletB includes the output of ServletC. Even though FilterC attaches to ServletC, it won't run—because it will reject "includes" as a valid route in. So FilterC is bypassed, and ServletC is called directly by ServletB.

Here's how a complete deployment descriptor might look for the Log Filter we set up earlier:

```
<filter>
  <filter-name>LogFilter</filter-name>
  <filter-class>com.osborne.LogFilter</filter-class>
</filter>

<filter-mapping>
  <filter-name>LogFilter</filter-name>
  <url-pattern>/</url-pattern>
</filter-mapping>
```

You see how the URL pattern for the LogFilter is "/." This is the catchall: Whatever resource is requested matches this mapping, so the LogFilter will trigger—at least for direct client requests.

Stacking Filters

What if we want to run not just a LogFilter for every request but an Authorization Filter as well? Well, the answer is that we can. Simply stack them up in the deployment descriptor:

```
<filter>
  <filter-name>LogFilter</filter-name>
  <filter-class>com.osborne.LogFilter</filter-class>
</filter>
<filter>
  <filter-name>AuthorizationFilter</filter-name>
  <filter-class>com.osborne.AuthorizationFilter</filter-class>
</filter>
<filter-mapping>
  <filter-name>LogFilter</filter-name>
  <url-pattern>/</url-pattern>
</filter-mapping>
<filter-mapping>
  <filter-name>AuthorizationFilter</filter-name>
  <url-pattern>/</url-pattern>
</filter-mapping>
```

In this case, both filters have the same generic mapping: The URL pattern matches any request that comes in. Which will run first? That's determined by the order of `<filter-mapping>` declarations in the deployment descriptor. Suppose a client requests ServletA in this web application. The "filter chain" formed in this case will be

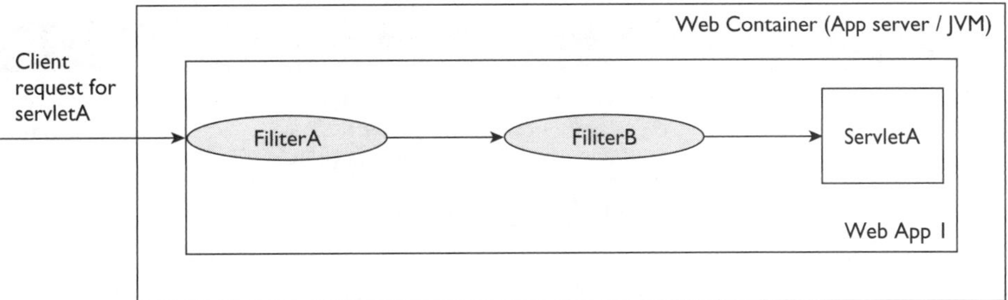

The general case is this: Given a request that matches more than one filter mapping,

- First, all matching filters will run for `<filter-mappings>` with `<url-pattern>` matches, in order of `<filter-mapping>` declaration.
- Second, all matching filters will run for `<filter-mappings>` with `<servlet-name>` matches, in order of `<filter-mapping>` declaration.

exam watch

Note that filters will run equally well in front of (or after) static content (such as a plain-vanilla HTML file); they are not solely for fronting (or backing) servlets and JSPs.

INSIDE THE EXAM

Servlet/Filter Comparison

It's uncanny how many parallels there are between servlets and filters (well, not really—it's the product of intentional design!). For exam purposes, I find it really helpful to explore the similarities and also the nuances of difference: It reinforces my memory of both. The following table should get you started on this process.

INSIDE THE EXAM (continued)

	Servlet	Interface
Type	Typically built by extending the javax.servlet.GenericServlet or javax.servlet.http.HttpServlet class.	Built by implementing the javax .servlet.Filter interface.
Construction	Optional, no-argument constructor (not often used)	Same.
Initialization	Override the `init(ServletConfig config)` method—or the plain init() method.	Implement the `init(FilterConfig config)` method.
Destruction	Override the `destroy()` method.	Same.
Parameters	Can have initialization parameters declared in the deployment descriptor.	Same.
Declaration element in deployment descriptor	Declared in a `<servlet>` element, which contains `<servlet-name>` and `<servlet-class>` elements.	Declared in a `<filter>` element, which contains `<filter-name>` and `<filter-class>` elements.
Mapping element in deployment descriptor	Declared in a `<servlet-mapping>` element, which contains `<servlet-name>` and `<url-pattern>` elements.	Declared in a `<filter-mapping>` element, which contains `<filter-name>` and `<url-pattern>` elements. `<servlet-name>` can be substituted for `<url-pattern>`.
Instantiation	There will be one instance of a servlet per `<servlet>` element in the deployment descriptor. The same actual class may have separate `<servlet>` declarations: Each occurrence will result in a separate instance of this class.	There will be one instance of a filter per `<filter>` element in the deployment descriptor. The same actual class may have separate `<filter>` declarations: Each occurrence will result in a separate instance of this class.
Passing control	Via a RequestDispatcher object that wrappers a target URL, by calling the `forward()` or `include()` method. The servlet code can determine (dynamically, if required) which web resource URL to target.	Calling the `doFilter()` method on the next item in the chain, from the current filter's `doFilter()` method. The next item in the chain is predetermined by the order of filter elements in the deployment descriptor, and can't be changed in the filter code.

exam watch

A Filter can throw an UnavailableException, which is a subclass of ServletException. UnavailableException has an `isPermanent()` method: If this returns `true`, the web container gives up calling the filter; if this returns `false`, the web container will try again after a specified time interval. Whether it will return true or false depends on how the exception is created. If you use the version of the constructor that simply accepts a String message, the exception is construed as permanent. If, however, you use the two-parameter constructor that accepts a String message and an "int seconds," the web container should deem the exception as temporary and try to call the Filter again after the specified number of seconds.

on the job

The drawback with filtering static content is that every request to your web server has to be processed by the web container. Big production applications normally consist of a straight web server (such as Apache) that forward requests to J2EE-aware web containers only when it's necessary. That leaves them free to serve the static content more efficiently: There's no additional "hop" to get the information. If you want all static content to be subject to Filter processing, then there is nothing for it but to make the additional round trip to the J2EE-aware web container. There's nothing wrong with that if you really need the filter processing for every piece of static content you serve up. However, place only the static content you need to under J2EE control: Leave the rest for plain-vanilla web serving.

Filtering vs. Dispatching

You might wonder what the point is of using filters at all. Why not just use a chain of servlets that dispatch from one to another? Before the invention of filters (at servlet specification level 2.3), that's exactly what happened. Methods existed (now deprecated) to construct a servlet chain. Filtering was intended to provide a more flexible replacement. So what advantages are there?

- A filter chain can be reshuffled fairly easily by moving entries up or down in the deployment descriptor. You can easily insert additional filters at a later stage, without any programming required.
- Filters can trap requests for any kind of resource, again with no programming required to forward on the request.

Wrappers

In our LogFilter example, we were only interested in trapping the request to log a URL to an audit file. No attempt was made to change the request or response. Finally in this chapter, we are going to consider how you should program a Filter when you do want to make such an intervention. That's where we need to deftly substitute a wrapper class in the `chain.doFilter()` invocation.

Why We Need a Wrapper

Let's consider the following snippet from a longer `doFilter()` method that doesn't use a wrapper, but nonetheless writes to the response object:

```
chain.doFilter(request, response);
PrintWriter out = response.getWriter();
out.write("<BR />A line of text at the bottom of your web page");
```

If you try out this filter code in front of a servlet of your choosing, it stands a fair chance of working— outputting the line of text promised. However, what if the servlet code that is the target of the `chain.doFilter` call does the following?

```
PrintWriter out = response.getWriter();
out.write("<BR />This is the servlet speaking");
out.close();
```

You don't have to close the PrintWriter, but a scrupulous servlet developer might well do so in the spirit of tidy resource management. In this case, the filter code will run without failing, but the line of text will no longer appear at the bottom of the web page. How can we ensure it does? Use a response wrapper, which in this case will be a class you write that subclasses javax.servlet.http.HttpServletResponse Wrapper.

Four Wrappers from Which to Choose

There are four wrapper classes that you might choose to subclass according to circumstance:

- javax.servlet.ServletRequestWrapper
- javax.servlet.ServletResponseWrapper
- javax.servlet.http.HttpServletRequestWrapper
- javax.servlet.http.HttpServletResponseWrapper

It's self-evident from the names which ones are used to wrapper requests and which ones to wrapper responses, and which ones pertain to HTTP web containers as opposed to plain servlet containers.

So let's return to that problem where we want to prevent the closing of the Print Writer. The solution is a little involved, but not too challenging:

- Write a subclass of PrintWriter called MyPrintWriter. Override the `close()` method—to do nothing. Optionally, write a `trueClose()` method that calls the superclass `close()` method (i.e., the one in PrintWriter that actually does the closing).
- Write a subclass of HttpServletResponseWrapper called MyHttpServletResponse Wrapper. This should contain an instance variable of MyPrintWriter type. Override the `getWriter()` method to return this instance variable. Make sure you reproduce the single-parameter constructor from HttpServletResponseWrapper (which takes an HttpServletResponse as its argument).
- Back in the `doFilter()` method of the Filter class, create a MyHttpServlet ResponseWrapper using the single-parameter constructor. Pass to this the response that comes as a parameter to the `doFilter()` method.
- Call the `chain.doFilter()` method, with the request (unchanged) and the wrappered response.

We'll see the code for this in a moment, but let's briefly reflect on the design pattern in use here, known most often as the "decorator" pattern (if "pattern" is an unfamiliar term, then take comfort that patterns are the subject of Chapter 10). You take a class, then wrap around it another class, which might mimic, extend, or change the functionality. It's exactly the same principle at work as in those java.io classes that you learned about for your SCJP exam, where you used constructors to nest InputStreams in BufferedStreams (one of the myriad possibilities). So you have the genuine response muffled by your own response wrapper class, like this:

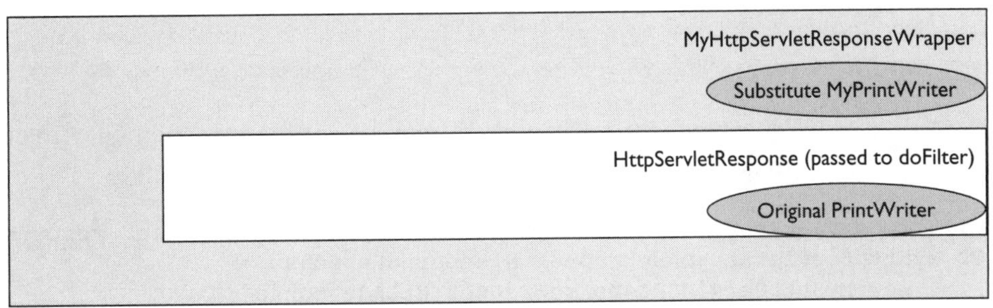

Now we'll see how this looks in code. First MyPrintWriter. This shows the essential "do nothing" `close()` method, and also one constructor. This copies a signature from one of its parent PrintWriter constructors, and simply calls the parent constructor using `super()`.

```
public class MyPrintWriter extends PrintWriter {
  public MyPrintWriter(Writer out) {
    super(out);
  }
  public void close() {
    // do nothing
  }
}
```

More interesting is the MyHttpServletResponseWrapper class. This also calls its superclass constructor because the parent HttpServletResponseWrapper is already set up to do the response wrappering part. Then comes the crafty code to do some more wrappering: creating a new MyPrintWriter object by passing in the writer from the original HttpServletResponse. This is held as an instance variable. Now any unsuspecting call to `getWriter()` will return a MyPrintWriter object—unbeknown to the other servlets and filters using it somewhere down the chain.

```
public class MyHttpServletResponseWrapper extends
HttpServletResponseWrapper {
    private MyPrintWriter out;
    public MyHttpServletResponseWrapper(HttpServletResponse response) {
        super(response);
        try {
        out = new MyPrintWriter(response.getWriter());
        } catch (IOException ioe) {
            ioe.printStackTrace();
        }
    }
    public PrintWriter getWriter() throws IOException {
      return out;
    }
}
```

Now here's the relevant code from the `doFilter()` method of the Filter that wants to do the wrappering.

```
HttpServletResponse httpResponse = (HttpServletResponse) response;
MyHttpServletResponseWrapper wrapperedResponse =
     new MyHttpServletResponseWrapper(httpResponse);
```

```
03 chain.doFilter(request, wrapperedResponse);
04 PrintWriter out = wrapperedResponse.getWriter();
05 out.write("<BR />This was put here by the WrappingFilter");
```

Because the response passed into the `doFilter()` method is a ServletResponse, line 1 does some discrete casting to an HttpServletResponse, for we know that this filter will be used only in an HTTP environment. Line 2 creates the wrapper for the response, by passing in the HttpResponse instance to the constructor of our newly created response wrapper class. Line 3 actually does the call to the next `doFilter()` in the chain—but notice that while the request is left alone, the wrapperedResponse is put in place of the response variable. On return from whatever is invoked by the chain, the filter proves it has worked by adding an extra line of HTML text to the response. Finally, here's some servlet code that won't be able to close the writer when invoked through this filter code:

```
response.setContentType("text/html");
PrintWriter out = response.getWriter();
out.write("<HTML><HEAD><TITLE>ItsAWrap Servlet</TITLE></HEAD><BODY>");
out.write("<H1>This servlet attempts to close the PrintWriter!</H1>");
out.write("<P>But as the response is wrappered, it doesn't succeed.</P>");
out.write("</BODY></HTML>");
out.flush();
out.close();
```

Because the response received by the servlet is a MyHttpServletResponseWrapper object, the PrintWriter obtained by the code is in fact of type MyPrintWriter. So when—at the end—the overridden `close()` method is called, it does nothing. Here's the output as I see it in my browser:

This servlet attempts to close the PrintWriter!

But as the response is wrappered, it doesn't succeed.

This was put here by the WrappingFilter

One thing you might observe about the code above is that it results in improperly formed HTML. The page has already been terminated with `</body>` and `</html>` tags, and then the filter adds an additional line of text. Most browsers are fault-tolerant of such sloppiness, and just display the text anyway. But the real point is that the response wrappers you write should be more sophisticated than this simple example; you should unpick and rework responses as is necessary for well-formedness or other requirements.

EXERCISE 3-4

Using a Filter for Micropayments

This exercise gets you to build a filter that makes micropayments. It's software to support fortune-making referral schemes. You know the kind: If someone makes a request to your web application, the filter will deposit a fraction of a cent in the referrer's PayPal account. We'll set the filter up to make the payment when you invoke a servlet called MicroPaymentServlet in your web application. The context directory for this exercise is ex0304, so set up your web application structure under a directory of this name.

For this exercise, there's a solution in the CD in the file sourcecode/ch03/ex0304.war—check there if you get stuck.

Set Up the Deployment Descriptor

1. Declare a servlet named MicroPaymentServlet, with a generic URL mapping (e.g., "/MicroPayment/*") so that you can trap path information. If needed, refer to Chapter 2 to refresh yourself on `<servlet>` element setup.
2. Declare a filter named MicroPaymentFilter that is tied to the named servlet MicroPaymentServlet in its filter mapping. It doesn't actually matter if the `<filter>` and `<filter-mapping>` elements come before or after the `<servlet>` and `<servlet-mapping>` you have already set up. However, to stay compatible with the old rules, I would be inclined to place filter elements before servlet elements.

Write the MicroPaymentFilter

3. Create a Java source file MicroPaymentFilter.java in /WEB-INF/classes or an appropriate package directory. Write the class declaration in the source file, ensuring that it implements the Filter interface.
4. Override the `doGet()` method in MicroPaymentServlet.
5. Supply "do nothing" `init()` and `destroy()` methods. You may prefer at least to put in some code to hang on to the FilterConfig object even though we won't use it in this exercise, but it gets you into good habits:

```
private FilterConfig filterConfig = null;
public void init(FilterConfig filterConfig)
    throws ServletException {
    this.filterConfig = filterConfig;
}
public void destroy() {
    this.filterConfig = null;
}
```

6. Write a `doFilter()` method. As the first thing you do in this method, take the path information from the request: Use this as the value for a request attribute you set up called "referrer." You may want to strip out the leading slash from the path information.
7. Still in the `doFilter()` method, call the `doFilter()`on the FilterChain object. Pass on the request and response (unwrappered).
8. Still in the `doFilter()` method, and after the chain call in step 7, get the PrintWriter from the response object. Output some text to indicate that the micropayment has been made.

Write the MicroPaymentServlet

9. Create a Java source file MicroPaymentServlet.java in /WEB-INF/classes or an appropriate package directory. Write the class declaration in the source file, extending HttpServlet.
10. Override the `doGet()` method in MicroPaymentServlet.
11. Get hold of the referrer name—this will be the value pulled from the request attribute "referrer" that you set up in the filter during step 6.
12. Write some HTML output (set the response appropriately and obtain the response's writer). It doesn't matter what the web page says, but at least include the referrer name.

Run the Application

13. Deploy and run the application. Use a URL containing appropriate path information such as the one below—in place of "referrerName" at the end of the path, substitute your own first name:

```
http://localhost:8080/ex0304/MicroPayment/referrerName
```

14. Optional: Alter the MicroPaymentServlet so that it closes the response's PrintWriter, and redeploy and run the code again. My findings are that no exceptions are thrown, but the words that MicroPaymentFilter writes to the web page do not appear. This is because the writer is already closed by the time the filter code gets hold of it—and demonstrates why you are better off working with wrapper classes. With a (response) wrapper that is a subclass of HttpServletResponseWrapper, you can substitute your own writer. This writer can override the `close()` method to prevent closing; you can always have a method of a different name that truly closes the writer back in the filter code.
15. Optional: Have the filter operate on any servlet in the web application by changing the `<servlet-name>` element to a `<url-pattern>` of "/" instead. Create another servlet that dispatches to the MicroPaymentServlet. Change the filter so that it comes into play only when another servlet dispatches to the MicroPaymentServlet, but not when the MicroPaymentServlet is requested directly. Hint: You'll want appropriate `<dispatcher>` elements in your filter mapping definition.
16. The following illustration shows how typical output looks with a referrer name (see step 13) of David:

CERTIFICATION SUMMARY

In this chapter we covered a great deal of ground—all under the umbrella subject of the "web container model." We started with an easy topic: how to set up initialization parameters on the ServletContext object. We saw that the process is not dissimilar from setting up servlet initialization parameters. We met a new deployment descriptor element—`<context-param>`—which houses a `<param-name>` and `<param-value>` element pairing and can appear for as many parameters as you need inside the `<web-app>` root element. We covered the two ServletContext methods you can use—`getInitParameter(String name)`, to get hold of individual parameters by name, and `getInitParameterNames()`, to get an Enumeration of all names of context parameters to be found in a web application.

We widened the scope then—in every sense!—by looking at the three scopes available in a web application: request, session, and context. We saw that request scope addresses a single client request to the web application. Request scope begins on entry to a servlet's `service()` method, ends on exit from the method, and lasts through whatever else the servlet might invoke during the `service()` method. We had a tantalizing, pre–Chapter 4 glimpse of session scope, and learned that this offers continuity over a series of requests from the same client. Finally, we discussed context scope, represented by a single ServletContext object, and saw that this object is available during the whole of a web application's life.

We saw that a principal reason for having scopes—and objects representing them—is to hold information important to the application, in the form of attributes. We saw that attribute values aren't restricted to Strings; an object of any type can be held as an attribute. We met the fundamental methods used to manipulate attributes—`getAttribute(String name)`, to get hold of the object value for a single named attribute, and `setAttribute(String name, Object value)`, to put a key/value pairing into a given scope. We also saw `getAttributeNames()`, returning an Enumeration of all the names of attributes for a scope, and `removeAttribute(String name)`, to delete an attribute from a scope. We saw that these four methods are available on each of the three objects representing scopes: ServletRequest (for request scope), HttpSession (for session scope), and ServletContext (for context scope).

We then touched on the web container as a multithreaded environment, able to service many client requests simultaneously. We saw the impact this has on the attributes set up in different scopes. We saw that because a single request is confined to a single thread in the web application, request attributes are thread safe. You took my word for it that session attributes are not quite thread safe and that we would learn more about session scope and multithreading in Chapter 4. You appreciated that context attributes cannot possibly be thread safe, for they are available to any thread running in the web application — or even in other web applications, because one web application can get hold of another's context.

We then moved on to the subject of dispatching. We found that it was possible to use a RequestDispatcher object to obtain the services of some other resource in the web application. We also saw that this could be any resource, static (such as an HTML page) or—more usually—dynamic (another servlet or JSP). You learned that there are two ways of getting a RequestDispatcher object: either through the `getRequestDispatcher()` method on ServletRequest or through the `getRequestDispatcher()` or `getNamedDispatcher()` method on ServletContext. We discussed the nuances of these methods: how the `getRequestDispatcher()` method on ServletRequest is the most flexible because it can accept paths beginning with a forward slash or not, and how the same method on ServletContext can accept only paths beginning with a forward slash. We also saw how `getNamedDispatcher()` on ServletContext is used in an entirely different way — to obtain a servlet or JSP identified by `<servlet-name>` within the deployment descriptor's `<servlet>` elements. We also learned that it might make sense to have a `<servlet>` without a `<servlet-mapping>` so that any access to this can be controlled through the `getNamedDispatcher()` method, while it remains impervious to direct client requests.

We identified that all paths fed to the `getRequestDispatcher()` methods are bound to be inside the web application to which the request dispatcher belongs. Paths beginning with a forward slash ("/") are relative to the context root of the web application. Paths without the initial forward slash are relative to the path of the resource invoking the RequestDispatcher, and can't use "`..`" (double dot: go up to parent directory) to escape the context root. However, we did learn that request dispatchers can come from other web application contexts, if web server security allows access to them through the `ServletContext.getContext(String otherContext)` method.

After a lot of discussion about how to get RequestDispatcher objects, we finally learned how to use them—by invoking the `forward()` or `include()` method. We saw that the `forward()` method effectively hands responsibility to the target of the request dispatcher: The forwarded-to servlet (or JSP) has sole responsibility for producing the response. We learned that the `include()` method does as its name implies—it includes the output of the target inside the response of the servlet doing the including. We saw that the forwarded-to or included servlets have access to special request attributes (such as javax.servlet.forward.context_path and javax.servlet

.include.path_info). We found that the information in these attributes supplements methods on the request, such as `getContextPath()` and `getServletPath()`, because these methods cannot return information both about the request to the dispatching and the request to the dispatched-to servlet at one and the same time. As an aside, we learned that these special request attributes are not present when the dispatcher is obtained as a named dispatcher—because this is seen as an internal request, not properly associated with a request URL. Finally, we saw how important it is not to call `forward()` after a response has been committed, and that doing so leads to an IllegalStateException.

The final topic in this web container model chapter—and the most complex—was about filters and wrappers. We learned how filters can be used to pre-process a request for a web resource, or to completely transform the response, even supplying entirely alternative responses when the need arises. We listed common uses for filters, such as encryption, caching, logging, authentication, and XML transformation. We then looked at the mechanics of filter creation: the classes you have to write and the deployment descriptor elements you have to set up. We saw that a filter is a class that implements the Filter interface, with its three life cycle methods: `init()`, `doFilter()`, and `destroy()`. We learned that `init()` and `destroy()` are called only once apiece: `init()` before the first request for a filter and `destroy()` after the last request has been processed (on web application shutdown). We saw that every request to the filter results in a call to the `doFilter()` method. We learned about the FilterConfig object, passed to the filter's `init()` method, and saw how this can be used to get at the filter name, the servlet context, and information about any initialization parameters set up for the filter.

We then looked at the deployment descriptor requirements for filters, comprising `<filter>` and `<filter-mapping>` elements. We saw that `<filter>` has some minor and some crucial subelements, the mandatory ones being `<filter-name>` (to supply a logical name for the filter) and `<filter-class>` (for the fully qualified class name of the filter); `<init-param>` is a nonmandatory subelement for setting up initialization parameters. We tried out `<filter-mapping>` elements, which have to have a `<filter-name>` subelement matching an existing filter, and most crucially, a `<url-pattern>` or `<servlet-name>` subelement as the means for making a match to the filter. We learned that the rules for a `<url-pattern>` mapping are identical to those for servlets. We saw that multiple filter mappings can match a given request and that the web container assembles these into a chain, with the web container processing matches by `<url-pattern>` first and `<servlet-name>` next—both sweeps based on the order of the matching `<filter-mapping>` elements in the deployment descriptor.

We saw then how the chain is started by the web container calling the first filter's `doFilter()` method, passing in the request, response, and FilterChain object—this last parameter representing the next item in the chain. We learned that this next item can be another filter or the resource targeted by the request when there are no more filters left in the chain. We wrote code that executed `chain.doFilter()` (from within Filter's `doFilter()` method) and learned that only by including this call would the next item in the chain execute.

We learned that when a filter wants to alter the request or response, it should wrapper up the original request and response objects passed as parameters to the `doFilter()` method. We saw how to subclass an appropriate wrapper class and override methods on this class (or add new ones) if we want to customize request or response behavior. We saw how to replace the original request or response with the wrappered class in the `chain.doFilter()` method call.

Finally, we learned that filters will—by default—trigger only on direct client requests. However, we saw that we can make filters trigger through request dispatcher calls to forward or include, and through the error page mechanism. We learned that this can be achieved by adding `<dispatcher>` subelements to `<filter-mapping>`, with appropriate values of FORWARD, INCLUDE, or ERROR. We saw that as a consequence of this, we have a fourth valid value for `<dispatcher>` of REQUEST and that this has to be included whenever one of the other three values is used, if the filter is still to trigger on direct client requests.

TWO-MINUTE DRILL

ServletContext

- The ServletContext is the closest thing your application has to an object that represents the web application itself.
- You can use the deployment descriptor to set up initialization parameters at ServletContext level. Each initialization parameter is housed in a `<context-param>` element; each one of these elements contains a mandatory `<param-name>` and `<param-value>` set of elements.
- The parent element for `<context-param>` is the root element `<web-app>`: This makes perfect sense, for ServletContext parameters belong at the web application level.
- The `getInitParameter(String parmName)` method on ServletContext is used to retrieve a parameter value whose name is known.
- The `getInitParameterNames()` method on ServletContext is used to retrieve an Enumeration of all context parameter names known to the web application.
- You can have as many context parameters as you want (none, one, several, or many).

Attributes, Scope, and Multithreading

- Attributes are a two-way street: You can set them as well as get them in your code.
- The web container can set attributes as well as your code.
- Attributes are not the same thing as parameters. Parameters flow into your application—from the client request or from deployment descriptor elements—and are read-only. Attributes flow within your application and can be read, created, updated, and deleted.
- There are three fundamental scopes—request, session, and context. (There is a fourth scope—page—which you learn about with JavaServer Pages from Chapter 6 onward.)
- Attribute manipulation methods look and behave almost identically, whatever the scope. There are four relevant methods: `getAttribute(String`

name), getAttributeNames(), setAttribute(String name, Object value), and removeAttribute(String name).

- Attribute methods don't throw exceptions (with one small exception for session-related attribute methods).
- A call to getAttribute(String name) can result in a null object reference being returned when the object doesn't exist.
- A call to getAttributeNames() will always result in a valid reference to an Enumeration, though the Enumeration itself may be empty if there are no attributes for the scope.
- You can only have one attribute of a particular name. Subsequent calls to setAttribute(String name, Object value) for the same name will overwrite the previous value. A value of **null** will remove the attribute (having the same effect as a call to removeAttribute(String name)).
- Request scope begins on entry to a servlet's service() method and ends on exit from that method.
- Request scope is bound to a single thread, so it's thread safe.
- Request scope is represented by the HttpServletRequest (or ServletRequest) object.
- Session scope exists across multiple requests from the same client to the same web application.
- Session scope is represented by the HttpSession object, obtainable using the HttpServletRequest.getSession() method.
- There is no "non-HTTP" equivalent of session scope.
- Context scope is sometimes thought of and referred to as web application scope.
- Context scope is represented by the ServletContext object, obtainable through the getServletContext() servlet method.
- The web container provides one ServletContext object per web application per JVM. So if the web application is distributed, the servlet context objects in different clones of the application are separate.
- Context scope lasts from when a web application is put into service to the point where it is removed from service.
- Context attributes are not thread safe: Practically every thread in your web application can access them.

Request Dispatching

- Dispatching is a means of delegating control from one web resource to another.
- You use a RequestDispatcher to represent the web resource to which you want to delegate. A RequestDispatcher can be obtained from one of two places: the ServletRequest or the ServletContext.
- ServletContext has two methods for obtaining a RequestDispatcher: `getRequestDispatcher(String pathFromContextRoot)` and `getNamedDispatcher(String nameOfServlet)`.
- ServletRequest has only one method for obtaining a RequestDispatcher, which is also `getRequestDispatcher(String path)`. The difference from the ServletContext method of this name is that the method will accept a path relative to the context root *or* a path relative to the current resource.
- A path relative to the context root begins with a forward slash ("/") . You don't include the context root name itself when forming a path like this.
- A path relative to the current resource does not begin with a forward slash and is relative to the client request URI within the context. So for a client request to /webappname/servlet/ServletA, a relative path of "ServletB" would translate to a path relative to the context root of /servlet/ServletB.
- Paths used as parameters to the three RequestDispatcher methods are restricted to the context to which the RequestDispatcher belongs. You can't go outside a single web application.
- You can obtain RequestDispatchers for other web applications by obtaining another web application's context and getting a RequestDispatcher from that (but note that your web container's default security settings may prevent you, by causing request dispatchers returned from other contexts to be **null**).
- Having obtained a request dispatcher, you can call either the `forward()` or `include()` methods on it, passing in the ServletRequest and Servlet Response objects.
- The `forward()` method passes responsibility to another web resource. The response will come entirely from the target of the forward. Any work that the *forwarding* servlet has done on the response will be discarded.
- The `include()` method includes the output of the included web resource inside the including servlet. On return from the `include()` call, the including servlet can still add more to the response.

- If a response has already been committed in a servlet, a call to `forward()` will result in an IllegalStateException.
- If a response has already been committed in a servlet, a call to `include()` will still work.
- A forwarded-to servlet has access to five special request attributes, which describe the state of the request in the *forwarding* servlet. The special attribute names all begin javax.servlet.forward.
- An included servlet has access to five different special request attributes, which describe the state of the request in the *included* servlet. The special attribute names all begin javax.servlet.include.

Filters and Wrappers

- Filters are used for pre-processing requests or post-processing responses, before they reach a target resource in a web application.
- Common uses for filters include authentication, logging, data compression, encryption, and caching.
- Filters you write must implement the javax.servlet.Filter interface. This has three methods—`init(FilterConfig config)`, `doFilter(ServletRequest request, ServletResponse response, FilterChain chain)`, and `destroy()`.
- A filter's `init()` method is called only once, at some point between server startup and definitely before the first request is intercepted by the filter.
- A filter's `doFilter()` method is called by the web container whenever it intercepts an appropriate request for the filter.
- A filter's `destroy()` method is called only once, at some point after the last filter request is processed in the `doFilter()` method, and before the web application closes down.
- A typical use of the `init()` method is to capture the FilterConfig object passed in as a parameter and keep this as an instance variable on the filter for later use.
- The FilterConfig object has a `getServletContext()` method to return the current servlet context , a `getFilterName()` method to get the filter name as declared in the `<filter-name>` element in the deployment descriptor, and `getInitParameter(String paramName)` and `getInitParameter`

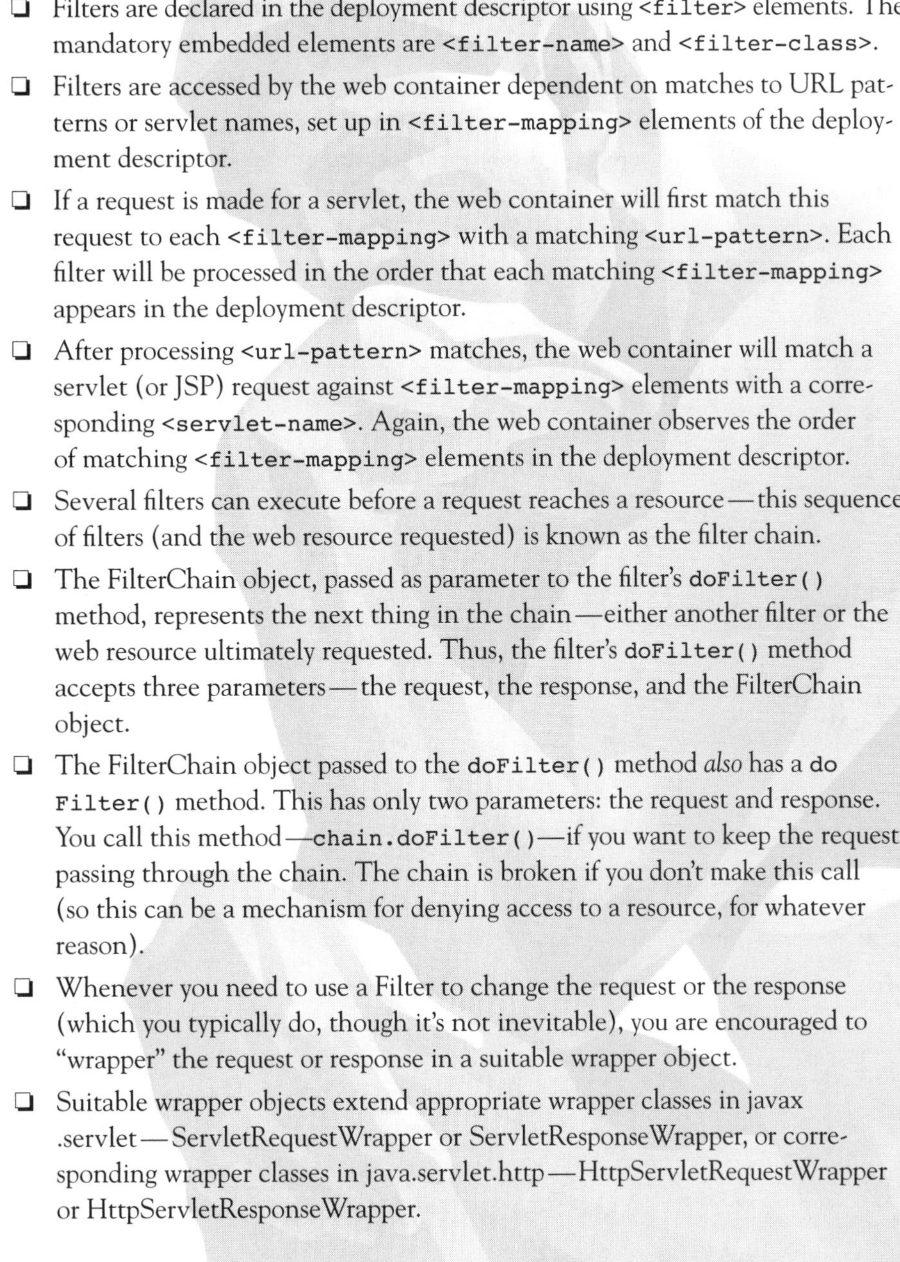

`Names()` methods to return initialization parameters set up as `<init-param>` elements within the `<filter>` element.

- Filters are declared in the deployment descriptor using `<filter>` elements. The mandatory embedded elements are `<filter-name>` and `<filter-class>`.
- Filters are accessed by the web container dependent on matches to URL patterns or servlet names, set up in `<filter-mapping>` elements of the deployment descriptor.
- If a request is made for a servlet, the web container will first match this request to each `<filter-mapping>` with a matching `<url-pattern>`. Each filter will be processed in the order that each matching `<filter-mapping>` appears in the deployment descriptor.
- After processing `<url-pattern>` matches, the web container will match a servlet (or JSP) request against `<filter-mapping>` elements with a corresponding `<servlet-name>`. Again, the web container observes the order of matching `<filter-mapping>` elements in the deployment descriptor.
- Several filters can execute before a request reaches a resource—this sequence of filters (and the web resource requested) is known as the filter chain.
- The FilterChain object, passed as parameter to the filter's `doFilter()` method, represents the next thing in the chain—either another filter or the web resource ultimately requested. Thus, the filter's `doFilter()` method accepts three parameters—the request, the response, and the FilterChain object.
- The FilterChain object passed to the `doFilter()` method *also* has a `doFilter()` method. This has only two parameters: the request and response. You call this method—`chain.doFilter()`—if you want to keep the request passing through the chain. The chain is broken if you don't make this call (so this can be a mechanism for denying access to a resource, for whatever reason).
- Whenever you need to use a Filter to change the request or the response (which you typically do, though it's not inevitable), you are encouraged to "wrapper" the request or response in a suitable wrapper object.
- Suitable wrapper objects extend appropriate wrapper classes in javax.servlet—ServletRequestWrapper or ServletResponseWrapper, or corresponding wrapper classes in java.servlet.http—HttpServletRequestWrapper or HttpServletResponseWrapper.

- You pass the real request or response to the constructor of the wrapper class, hence the wrappering effect (an example of the decorator design pattern).
- The wrapper class may override methods in the request or response and add specialized methods of its own—to transform output to XML, for example.
- The `<dispatcher>` subelement of `<filter-mapping>` can be used to allow filters to trigger on certain routes into the filter: via a client request, through a request dispatcher's forward or include, or as the result of a web container directing to an error page. The valid values are REQUEST, FORWARD, INCLUDE, and ERROR, respectively.

SELF TEST

The following questions will help you measure your understanding of the material presented in this chapter. Read all the choices carefully because there might be more than one correct answer. The number of correct choices to make is stated in the question, as in the real SCWCD exam.

ServletContext

1. What is the result of loading the web-app with the following deployment descriptor and attempting to execute the following servlet? (Choose two.)

```
<web-app>
  <context-param>
    <paramname>author</paramname>
    <paramvalue>Elmore Leonard</paramvalue>
  </context-param>
</web-app>

public class ContextInitParms extends HttpServlet {
  protected void doGet(HttpServletRequest request,
    HttpServletResponse response) throws ServletException, IOException {
    response.setContentType("text/html");
    PrintWriter out = response.getWriter();
    out.write("<HTML><HEAD></HEAD><BODY>");
    ServletContext sc = getServletContext();
    out.write(sc.getInitParameter("auther"));
    out.close();
  }
}
```

A. ParameterNotFoundException is thrown.

B. Some other exception is thrown.

C. "Elmore Leonard" is output on the web page.

D. An application failure occurs.

E. **null** is output on the web page.

F. A 404 error occurs in the browser.

G. Some other error (status code in the 500s) occurs in the browser.

2. What results from a call to the `getInitParameterNames()` method on ServletContext when there are no context parameters set up in the deployment descriptor? (Choose two.)

   A. A NoParametersExistException is thrown.

   B. An empty Enumeration object is returned.

   C. **null** is returned.

   D. An ArrayList object of size zero is returned.

   E. No exceptions are thrown.

   F. An empty Iterator object is returned.

3. Identify true statements about context parameters from the list below. (Choose one.)

   A. The deployment descriptor elements used to describe context parameter names and values are unique to the context parameter element.

   B. Context parameters must be declared in the deployment descriptor before servlets.

   C. Context parameters are available to all web applications loaded by an application server.

   D. In distributable applications, context parameters are duplicated between JVMs.

   E. None of the above.

4. Given a servlet containing the following code, what is the outcome of attempting to compile and run the servlet? (Choose one.)

```
ServletContext context = getServletContext();
String s = context.getAttribute("javax.servlet.context.tempdir");
```

   A. The servlet won't compile.

   B. The servlet won't run.

   C. String *s* has a **null** value.

   D. String *s* has a valid directory as its value.

Attributes, Scope, and Multithreading

5. What is the likely result from attempting to compile and execute the following servlet code? (Choose one.)

```
HttpSession session = getSession();
String s = session.getAttribute("javax.servlet.session.tempdir");
```

A. Won't compile for one reason.

B. Won't compile for more than one reason.

C. Runtime exception when attempting to get access to the attribute.

D. *s* contains **null**.

E. *s* contains a valid String, denoting a temporary directory.

6. Identify true statements from the list below. (Choose two.)

   A. Attribute methods don't throw exceptions.

   B. You cannot remove request parameters.

   C. Attributes can be set by the web container or by application code.

   D. Attribute values are String objects.

   E. "malhereusement" is an illegal name for an attribute.

7. (drag-and-drop question) In the servlet code shown in the following illustration, fill in all the concealed (lettered) parts of the source code with (numbered) choices from the right-hand side, such that the output when the servlet is run is:

```
nulltwothree
```

```
protected void doGet(HttpServletRequest request,
  HttpServletResponse response)
  throws ServletException, IOException {
  PrintWriter out = response.getWriter();
  response.setContentType("text/plain");
  [    A    ] session = request.getSession();
  session.setAttribute("one", "one");
  ServletContext context = getServletContext();
  context.setAttribute("two", "two");
  [  B  ].setAttribute("three", "three");
  [  C  ].[  D  ]Attribute("one", [ E ]);
  out.print(session.getAttribute("one"));
  out.print(context.getAttribute("two"));
  out.print(request.getAttribute("three"));
}
```

1	Session
2	session
3	HttpSession
4	set
5	remove
6	get
7	delete
8	null
9	""
10	request
11	context

8. What is result of attempting to run the following code? (Choose one.)

```
public void doGet(HttpServletRequest request, HttpServletResponse response)
  throws ServletException, IOException {
  request.setAttribute("a", "request");
  System.out.print(request.getAttribute("a"));
  request.setAttribute("a", "2nd request");
  System.out.print(",");
  System.out.print(request.getAttribute("a"));
  request.removeAttribute("a");
  request.removeAttribute("a");
  System.out.print(",");
  Object o = request.getAttribute("a");
  System.out.print(o);
}
```

   A. "request, request, 2nd request, null" written to standard output
   B. NullPointerException at line 22
   C. AttributeAlreadyRemovedException at line 22
   D. NullPointerException at line 24
   E. "request, 2nd request, null" written to standard output
   F. "request, 2nd request" written to standard output
   G. "request, request, 2nd request" written to standard output

9. From the following list, what is a probable outcome from a call to the `ServletContext.getAttributeNames()` method? (Choose one.)
   A. A **null** reference is returned.
   B. An empty Enumeration is returned.
   C. A nonempty Enumeration is returned.
   D. An empty ArrayList is returned.
   E. A nonempty ArrayList is returned.
   F. A NoAttributesFoundException is thrown.
   G. Some other exception is thrown.

10. Identify true statements about scope from the following list. (Choose two.)
   A. Context scope can span JVMs.
   B. Session scope can span JVMs.

C. Requests can span web apps.

D. Sessions can span web apps.

E. Requests can span JVMs.

Request Dispatching

11. What is the outcome of executing ServletA? You can assume that (1) ServletB has a mapping of "/ServletB" and a name of "ServletB," and (2) imports have been omitted from the code for brevity; the code will compile successfully. (Choose one.)

```
public class ServletA extends HttpServlet {
    public void doGet(HttpServletRequest req, HttpServletResponse resp)
            throws ServletException, IOException {
       RequestDispatcher rd = getServletContext().getNamedDispatcher(
              "ServletB");
       rd.forward(req, resp);
    }
}

public class ServletB {
  public void doGet(HttpServletRequest req, HttpServletResponse resp)
            throws ServletException, IOException {
        String attr = (String)
req.getAttribute("javax.servlet.forward.servlet_path");
        PrintWriter out = resp.getWriter();
        out.write("Attribute value: " + attr);
    }
}
```

A. NullPointerException thrown

B. "Attribute value: null" output to the web page

C. A blank web page

D. ServletNotFoundException thrown

E. "Attribute value: /ServletB" output to the web page

F. "Attribute value: ServletB" output to the web page

G. ClassCastException thrown

12. Identify which of the following are names of special attributes associated with the dispatching mechanism. (Choose two.)

    A. java.servlet.include.servlet_name

    B. javax.http.servlet.include.query_name

    C. javax.servlet.include.servlet_path

    D. javax.servlet.forward.request_url

    E. javax.servlet.include.path_info

    F. java.servlet.forward.context_path

13. What are possible outcomes from executing the `doGet` method in ServletC below? (Choose two.)

```
public class ServletC extends HttpServlet {
    public void doGet(HttpServletRequest req, HttpServletResponse resp)
            throws ServletException, IOException {
        RequestDispatcher rd = getServletContext().getRequestDispatcher(
                "ServletB");
        rd.forward(req, resp);
    }
}
```

    A. HTTP 500 error (error in 500s).

    B. NullPointerException.

    C. HTTP 404 error.

    D. Some other exception.

    E. ServletNotFoundException.

    F. ServletB runs.

    G. A file called ServletB is served from the context directory.

14. What is the web page output from executing ServletD with the URL below? (Choose one.)

```
http://localhost:8080/myapp/ServletD?fruit=orange
public class ServletD extends HttpServlet {
   public void doGet(HttpServletRequest req, HttpServletResponse resp)
           throws ServletException, IOException {
```

```
        RequestDispatcher rd = getServletContext().getRequestDispatcher(
                "/ServletE?fruit=pear");
        rd.forward(req, resp);
    }
}

public class ServletE extends HttpServlet {
    public void doGet(HttpServletRequest request, HttpServletResponse response)
throws ServletException, IOException {
        response.setContentType("text/plain");
        PrintWriter out = response.getWriter();
        String[] valueArray = request.getParameterValues("fruit");
        for (int i = 0; i < valueArray.length; i++) {
            if (i > 0) {
                out.write(", ");
            }
            out.write(valueArray[i]);
        }
        String queryString = (String)
request.getAttribute("javax.servlet.forward.query_string");
        int pos = queryString.indexOf("=") + 1;
        String values = queryString.substring(pos);
        out.write(", " + values);
    }
}
```

A. pear, pear

B. pear, orange, orange

C. orange, pear, orange

D. orange, pear, pear

E. orange, pear

F. pear, orange, **null**

G. orange, pear, **null**

H. pear, orange, pear, orange

15. ServletA forwards to ServletB, which includes Servlet C, which forwards to ServletD, which includes ServletE. When ServletA is requested, which servlets might contribute to the final response? (Choose one.)

A. ServletD and ServletE

B. ServletB, ServletC, ServletD, and ServletE

C. ServletD only

E. ServletB only

F. All of them

Filters and Wrappers

16. Identify true statements about filters. (Choose one.)

    A. You cannot work directly with the request object that is passed as a parameter to the filter.

    B. The order of filter processing is arbitrarily determined by the web container.

    C. Only URL patterns can be used by filters to target specific web resources.

    D. You must implement the `doChain(request, response)` method to pass control from filter to filter, or filter to servlet.

17. Which of the following is a legal filter mapping declaration in the deployment descriptor? (Choose one.)

    A.

```
<filter-mapping>
  <filter-name>MicroPaymentFilter</filter-name>
  <servlet-name>MicroPaymentServlet</servlet-name>
  <dispatcher>REQUEST</dispatcher>
</filter-mapping>
```

    B.

```
<filter>
  <filter-name>MicroPaymentFilter</filter-name>
  <filter-class>webcert.ch03.MicroPaymentFilter</filter-class>
  <filter-mapping>
    <url-pattern>/MicroPaymentServlet</url-pattern>
  </filter-mapping>
</filter>
```

C.

```
<filter-mapping>
  <filter-name>MicroPaymentFilter</filter-name>
  <url-pattern>MicroPayment/*</url-pattern>
</filter-mapping>
```

D.

```
<filter>
  <filter-name>MicroPaymentFilter</filter-name>
  <filter-class>webcert.ch03.MicroPaymentFilter</filter-class>
  <filter-mapping>
    <servlet-name>MicroPaymentServlet</servlet-name>
  </filter-mapping>
</filter>
```

18. (drag-and-drop question) In the following illustration, FilterA chains to Servlet1, which extends HttpServlet. Neither of these components is loaded on startup. Imagining that this is the first invocation for each of these components, match the numbered method calls to the lettered sequence if Servlet1 is requested.

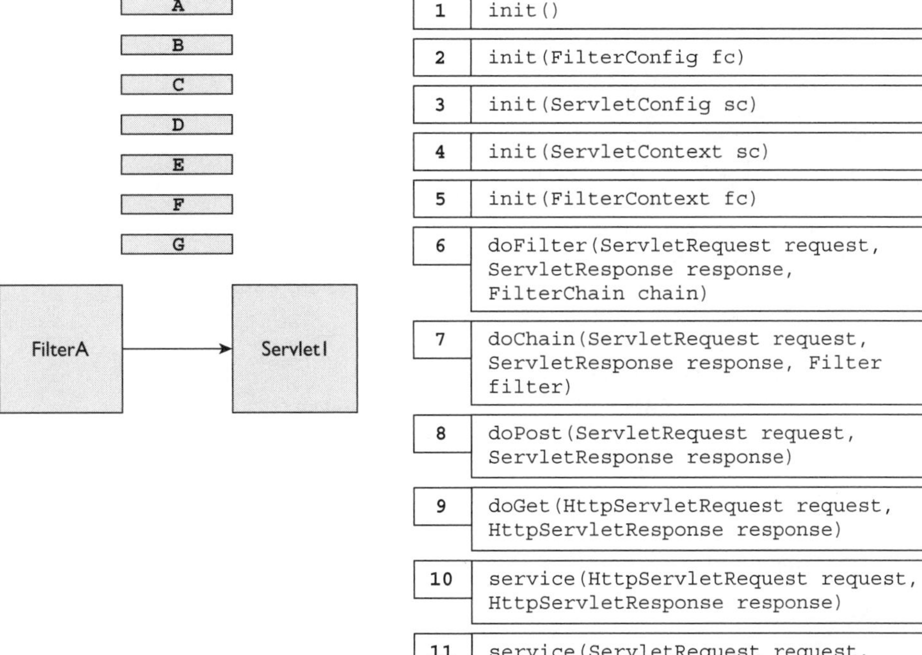

19. From the available options, what is the likely outcome from running the code below? (Choose one.)

```
protected void doGet(HttpServletRequest request,
  HttpServletResponse response) throws ServletException, IOException {
  RequestDispatcher dispatcher =
    getServletContext().getNamedDispatcher("/ServletB");
  dispatcher.forward(request, response);
}
```

A. DispatcherNotFoundException.

B. Runtime error because of incorrectly formed parameter to `getNamedDispatcher()` method.

C. NullPointerException.

D. ServletB can obtain request attribute javax.servlet.forward.request_uri.

20. Given the following deployment descriptor, identify the sequence of filters that execute on a direct client request for ServletA. (Choose one.)

```
<filter-mapping>
  <filter-name>LogFilter</filter-name>
  <servlet-name>ServletA</servlet-name>
</filter-mapping>
<filter-mapping>
  <filter-name>AuditFilter</filter-name>
  <url-pattern>/ServletA</url-pattern>
  <dispatcher>FORWARD</dispatcher>
</filter-mapping>
<filter-mapping>
  <filter-name>EncryptionFilter</filter-name>
  <url-pattern>/*</url-pattern>
</filter-mapping>
<servlet-mapping>
  <servlet-name>ServletA</servlet-name>
  <url-pattern>/ServletA</url-pattern>
</servlet-mapping>
```

A. LogFilter, AuditFilter, EncryptionFilter

B. LogFilter, EncryptionFilter

C. LogFilter

D. EncryptionFilter, AuditFilter, LogFilter

E. EncryptionFilter, LogFilter

F. AuditFilter, EncryptionFilter, LogFilter

LAB QUESTION

We'll use this lab as an opportunity to put together several of the concepts you have encountered in this chapter in order to write a censorship filter. If there are any words in a web page you disapprove of (such as "massive executive pay bonus"), your filter will throw a fit of pique, suppress the response entirely, and substitute an alternative message.

Have an AttributeSetter servlet, which will pick up a properties file name and location from servlet context initialization parameters. AttributeSetter should load the file as a properties object and write each named property as a request attribute. This mainly uses techniques you covered in the first two exercises in this chapter. Then have AttributeSetter forward to another servlet, Attribute Displayer—which simply displays all the request attributes it knows about.

Then write a filter—CensorshipFilter—which triggers on access to the AttributeSetter servlet. The filter should scan the (wrappered) response for any words it doesn't like. If any are encountered, the filter should clear the response completely and write its own response instead. Turn the filter on and off using a filter initialization parameter.

As a more subtle form of censorship, have the CensorshipFilter scan all the request attributes and remove any containing words it doesn't like—before passing control down the chain to Attribute Displayer. Then AttributeDisplayer will display as normal, but of course, the offensive attributes have already been purged.

SELF TEST ANSWERS

ServletContext

1. ☑ **D** and **F**. **D** is correct because the application will not load. The deployment descriptor is incorrectly formed: The element names should be `<param-name>` and `<param-value>`, with hyphens. **F** is also correct. The question says that you attempt to execute the servlet. In the event of the web application simply not being available, a "page not found" (404) error results.
   ☒ **A** is incorrect because you never get any kind of exception (including the made-up ParameterNotFoundException) from the `getInitParameter` method—even though the requested parameter name ("auther") doesn't match what is set up in the deployment descriptor. **B** is incorrect because the servlet code is perfectly fine in all respects and in any case never executes! Because the servlet is never loaded and never executes, **C** and **E** can be discounted (though had the deployment descriptor been correctly formed, **E** would have described the output correctly: null). Finally, **G** is incorrect because an error in the 500s results only when the target resource is actually found, but runs incorrectly.

2. ☑ **B** and **E**. **B** is correct because you do get an Enumeration object returned that has no elements. No exceptions are thrown just because there are no context parameters, so **E** is correct as well.
   ☒ **A** is incorrect because you never get any kind of exception (including the made-up NoParametersExistException) from the `getInitParameterNames` method. **C** is incorrect because you don't get a null object reference; the Enumeration returned has a valid reference, just no elements. **D** and **F** are incorrect because it is an Enumeration that's returned, not an ArrayList or Iterator (or Vector or any other sort of thing from the myriad Collection classes Java has available).

3. ☑ **E** is the correct answer: There are no true statements in the list!
   ☒ **A** is incorrect because `<param-name>` and `<param-value>` are used for servlets' initialization parameters as well as ServletContext initialization parameters. **B** was correct in previous versions of the exam and servlet specification. However, the XSD for servlet specification 2.4 gives you latitude to place context parameters wherever you like in the deployment descriptor (provided, or course, that each `<context-param>` element is bedded directly under the root element `<web-app>`). I have to say that I prefer to respect the old order when setting up the deployment descriptor—for backward compatibility if nothing else. But for exam answer purposes, you should identify answer **B** as false. **C** is incorrect: Context parameters are available only

to the web application to which they belong, no others. **D** is incorrect because an important limitation of servlet context information is that there is no mechanism to duplicate parameter information from one JVM to another in distributed apps. (Of course, chances are you have identical deployment descriptors with the same parameters declared in other JVMs supporting the distributed application—so, effectively, the data are available wherever the application runs. However, that doesn't make answer **D** any truer!)

4. ☑ **A** is the correct answer. The compilation fails with a ClassCastException. The output of the `ServletContext.getAttribute()` method is an object. Since the value of the standard attribute named javax.servlet.context.tempdir is a String, the output is safe to cast to a String.
   ☒ **B** is incorrect because the servlet never gets as far as running, which of course also discounts **C** and **D**. If the ClassCastException were corrected, then **D** should be the correct answer, for this standard attribute should always have a valid value set by the web container.

Attributes, Scope, and Multithreading

5. ☑ **B** is the correct answer. Although this looks like a question about attributes, it is also about session API knowledge. You retrieve a session from a request, not from the servlet itself, so that's one error. Furthermore, whatever scope you use the `getAttribute()` method in (in this case, session scope), you have to cast the object retrieved back to the type of variable you are using in the assignment (in this case, String). So there are two compilation errors.
   ☒ **A** is incorrect because there are two compilation errors. **C** is incorrect because the code never gets to run. If the compilation error were fixed, then **D** is likely to be correct: *s* would be null. The web context shouldn't have set up an attribute of this name, nor should your code (as javax.<anything> is reserved for web container attributes). **E** is incorrect, a deliberate attempt to confuse you with the context attribute javax.servlet.context.tempdir.

6. ☑ **B** and **C** are the correct answers. You can't remove request parameters: There are no methods to do this (don't confuse this with the fact that you can remove attributes). And attributes can be set up in two places: by the web container or in your code.
   ☒ A is incorrect because although most attribute methods don't throw exceptions, session attribute methods can throw an IllegalStateException. **D** is incorrect because you can hold any kind of object as an attribute value, not just Strings. E is incorrect: Although your attribute names should begin with a reverse domain name (e.g., com.myco.malhereusement), they don't have to do so—it's only a suggestion in the servlet specification, not a requirement.

7. ☑ **A** maps to **3** (you retrieve an HttpSession type, not Session), **B** maps to **10** (must be the `request` parameter), **C** maps to **2** (must be the `session` parameter), **D** maps to **4** (must be

setAttribute, for there are two parameters; removeAttribute takes only one), and **E** maps to 8 (**null** literal—so that session.getAttribute("one") will fail to find an attribute and thus return **null**).

☒ There are no other correct combinations.

8. ☑ **E** is the correct answer. The first value of the attribute is printed out, then the changed second value, then **null**, for the attribute has been removed.

   ☒ **A** is incorrect: The answer tries to persuade you that values added to attributes accumulate (a bit like parameters) instead of being totally replaced. **B** and **C** are incorrect—there's no reason for a NullPointerException, and there's no such thing as an AttributeAlreadyRemoved Exception. It doesn't matter how many times you remove the same-named attribute; the code doesn't blow up. **D** is incorrect—you don't get a NullPointerException from passing a null object reference into System.out.print. **F** is incorrect—you might think it was correct if the System.out.print at line 24 did go wrong. **G** is yet another red herring that plays on some of the wrong assumptions already described.

9. ☑ **C** is the correct answer: It's the only probable outcome. There should be at least one context attribute set by the servlet container; hence, the Enumeration is unlikely ever to be empty.

   ☒ **A** is incorrect; you will always get a valid reference. **B** is remotely possible, but not probable (it could occur because your code removed all context attributes, including ones set up by the web container). **D** and **E** are incorrect—you get old-fashioned Enumerations from this method, not any newer collection class such as ArrayList. Finally, the method shouldn't throw any exceptions, so **F** and **G** are incorrect.

10. ☑ **B** and **C** are correct answers. Session scope can span JVMs in a distributable application. Requests can span web applications when a request dispatcher is used from another context.

    ☒ **A** is incorrect; there is one context per web application per JVM. **D** is incorrect; threads dispatching across web applications find themselves dealing with separate session objects in each web application. **E** is incorrect; there is no mechanism to carry requests across JVMs, even in distributable applications.

Dispatching

11. ☑ **B** is the correct answer. The code executes correctly. However, because the method used to obtain a RequestDispatcher in ServletA is `getNamedDispatcher()`, the attribute javax.servlet .forward.servlet_path is not set up in the servlet that is the target of the forward, ServletB.

    ☒ **A**, **D**, and **G** are incorrect, for the code runs perfectly well. In ServletA, the line `rd .forward()` has the potential to throw a NullPointerException—but not when a valid servlet is found. The `getAttribute()` output cast to a String in ServletB is quite correct, hence no

ClassCastException. ServletNotFoundException does not exist. **C** is incorrect because there is output on the web page. **E** and **F** are incorrect—**E** would have been a correct version of the servlet path had the dispatcher used arisen from a `getRequestDispatcher()` method.

12. ☑ **C** and **E** are the correct answers.
   ☒ **A**, **B**, and **F** are incorrect: You can eliminate them immediately, for all the special attributes begin javax.servlet, which is then followed by .forward or .include. **D** is almost right—but the attribute name should end request_uri, not request_url.

13. ☑ **A** and **D** are the correct answers. An IllegalArgumentException occurs because the `getRequestDispatcher` method on ServletContext cannot accept a path that begins from somewhere other than the context root—in other words, the path parameter must begin with a forward slash. As a consequence, a server side error (error in 500s) will be returned to the client.
   ☒ **B** is incorrect. There won't be a NullPointerException from the `rd.forward()` line because it will never be reached. **C** is incorrect because there won't be a search for a file that cannot be found. **E**—ServletFoundNotException—is as made up now as it was in a previous bogus answer. **F** and **G** are incorrect, but would both be possible outcomes if the `getRequestDispatcher()` call were legal.

14. ☑ **B** is the correct answer. The parameter named "fruit" is passed as part of the query string to ServletD, with a value of "orange." When the request path is set for ServletE in the call to `getRequestDispatcher`, the query string contains the same-named parameter with a value of "pear." This doesn't overwrite the original parameter value. You can have multiple parameter values of the same name. Instead, it inserts the "pear" value ahead of the "orange" value, but both are valid parameter values for "fruit." So when the ServletE code prints out the parameter value for "fruit" obtained with request.getParameterValues("fruit"), it outputs "pear, orange" in that order. Then the query string is obtained from javax.servlet.forward.query_string. This contains the query string as it was in the forwarding servlet, ServletD, so fruit=orange. After some judicious string manipulation, the value "orange" is extracted from the query string and added to the response output, so "pear, orange, orange" is the final result.
   ☒ **A**, **C**, **D**, **E**, **F**, **G**, and **H** are all incorrect because of the reasoning above.

15. ☑ **A** is the correct answer. The last servlet in the dispatching sequence that is forwarded to is ServletD, so anything that previous servlets did to the response is ignored. ServletD includes ServletE, so both might contribute to the response.
   ☒ **B** is incorrect because the forward to ServletD obliterates the contribution of ServletB and ServletC, which also excludes answer **D**. **C** is incorrect, for ServletD includes ServletE, so ServletE's work on the response should be taken into account. **E** is incorrect because of the reasoning in the correct answer.

Filters

16. ☑ A is the correct answer (the only true statement). The request object passed as parameter to the filter must be wrappered in a ServletRequestWrapper or HttpServletRequestWrapper object.
☒ B is incorrect because the order of filters is determined by their placement in the deployment descriptor. C is incorrect because filters can target servlets by name as well as by URL pattern. D is incorrect: The thing you are implementing is a chain of filters, but the method used to pass control along the chain is called `doFilter(request, response)`, not `doChain()`.

17. ☑ A is again the correct answer. A filter mapping can be legally expressed with a filter name and a servlet name. Although the dispatcher element with a value of REQUEST is what you get by default when no dispatcher element is specified, there's nothing wrong with explicitly including the element like this.
☒ B is very incorrect; you don't include `<filter-mappings>` within `<filter>` elements. They are separate elements nested in the root element `<web-app>`. This makes answer **D** incorrect as well. **C** is incorrect, not because of incorrectly stacked elements, but because of an illegal value for the URL pattern—which should begin with a forward slash ("/").

18. ☑ **A** maps to **2** (init with FlterConfig parameter), **B** maps to **6** (doFilter method), **C** maps to **3** (init with ServletConfig parameter), **D** maps to **1** (init with no parameters), **E** maps to **11** (service method passing ServletRequest and ServletResponse), **F** maps to **10** (protected service method passing HttpServletRequest and HttpServletResponse), and **G** maps to **9** (`doGet` method). This is as much a question about servlet life cycle as filter life cycle—mean, but you do get questions that cross over different objectives from time to time.
☒ This is the only sequence that can be guaranteed to occur.

19. ☑ **C** is the correct answer from the available options. If the `getNamedDispatcher()` method fails to find the path to ServletB, the dispatcher reference will be null, so a Null PointerException will result on executing the `forward()` method.
☒ **A** is incorrect—DispatcherNotFoundException is made up (dispatcher methods that fail to find a dispatcher simply return null). **B** is incorrect because the parameter to `getNamed Dispatcher()` is legal. The name used begins with a forward slash, so looks more like a servlet name than a servlet mapping. However, while it is inadvisable to have a servlet name in this form, it does work. **D** is incorrect. Although the special attribute is correctly named, it is not available when the forward is on a named dispatcher.

20. ☑ **E** is the correct answer. First, the processing works through the filter-mappings with a matching URL pattern. EncryptionFilter runs because the URL pattern of "/*" matches any request. Then processing works through the filter mappings with matching servlet names.

LogFilter has a matching name, so it executes. Note that filters mapped by URL pattern are executed before filters mapped by servlet name.

☒ **A**, **B**, **C**, **D**, and **F** are incorrect because of the reasoning in the correct answer above. Note that AuditFilter doesn't execute through a direct client request. AuditFilter will only be invoked as the result of calling ServletA via the `forward()` method on a RequestDispatcher object.

LAB ANSWER

Deploy the WAR file from the CD called lab03.war, in the /sourcecode/chapter03 directory. This contains a sample solution. If you look in the deployment descriptor web.xml, you'll find a definition for a filter named CensorshipFilter. This has an initialization parameter named *censorship*. As delivered, this has its value set to "off." When you run the application using the URL

```
http://localhost:8080/lab03/AttributeSetter
```

You should see a list of attributes like this:

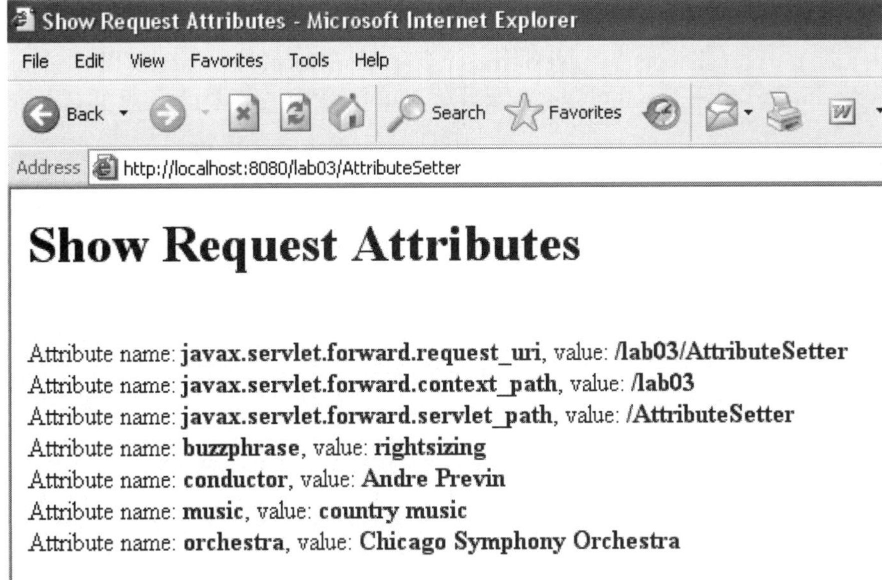

Some attributes arise from container-provided "forwarding" attributes (because AttributeSetter executes a `forward()` method on a request dispatcher object).

It also displays some attributes that originate from the properties file lab03.properties. If you change the *censorship* initialization parameter in web.xml to have a value of "on," restart your server, and call AttributeSetter with the same URL, you should see a screen like this:

This message comes about because the filter class (CensorshipFilter) has logic that discovers "banned words" in the attributes that subsequent servlets would otherwise display, so it suppresses the call to those servlets. If you look in the source of CensorshipWrapper.java, you'll find out what the banned words are. You can change the text of the lab03.properties file (in the /WEB-INF directory) to avoid the banned words—see then if a refresh of your browser will display the properties from the file.

4

Sessions and Listeners

CERTIFICATION OBJECTIVES

- Session Life Cycle
- Session Management
- Request and Context Listeners
- Session Listeners
- ✓ Two-Minute Drill
- Q&A Self Test

If you need a way to associate a series of related requests—and let's face it, most web applications do—then you need a session. Sessions are a central plank in the web container framework. We began to explore them in Chapter 3, but they have enough facets to justify this chapter (almost) to themselves.

We have already learned that sessions provide one of the three principal "scopes" of the web container model, the other two being request and context. We have also seen that (like requests and contexts) an object represents each session and that you can attach attributes to this object representing information of any sort. What we will do in this chapter is to more fully explore the boundaries of session scope and find out exactly what causes the beginning and end of a session. We'll find out when a session is regarded as "new," and what happens to make it lose that newness.

We'll also see what mechanisms a web container might employ to maintain its sessions. The mechanism of choice uses a cookie, a small file traded between the web container and the client browser and containing a unique identifier for the session. A poor man's substitute (in environments where cookies are disallowed or unsupported) is "URL rewriting"—having the session ID embedded in the URL—and we'll explore that also.

Then we'll cover "listeners," an aspect of the web container model deferred from Chapter 3. These are classes with methods called by the web container under particular circumstances—when an attribute is changed, for example, or when a context comes into being. We'll depart from the session focus for a section to find out how listeners pertain to the request and context life cycles. But we then return to session with a vengeance, which boasts the most listeners to support its more complex life cycle. And that will round off the exploration both of sessions and the web container model.

CERTIFICATION OBJECTIVE

Session Life Cycle (Exam Objective 4.2)

Given a scenario, describe the APIs used to access the session object, explain when the session object was created, and describe the mechanisms used to destroy the session object, and when it was destroyed.

In this section, you'll learn what you need to know about session basics for the exam. You'll see how the J2EE spec gets around the fundamental problem of HTTP communication: a series of unconnected requests and responses between client and server, often described as "fire and forget." What if you're the client and you don't want to be forgotten? Or if you're the server, and want to know when the client last got in touch with you? What if the client has finished with you the server: How do you know, and once you do know, how can you gracefully let go of that client knowledge?

The Life History of a Session

Of course, a session isn't just about continuity across a series of requests—though we'll have plenty to say about that. There are good application reasons for wanting sessions—usually to store information to ensure the smooth running of your application. You will often have a transaction running over several requests. Perhaps I set up a new order header on one page but don't want to commit the results until I've set up order lines on a separate page. My application could hold the order header information in attributes attaching to a session. Only after hitting the button on the order line setup page would header and line information be taken out of the session's memory and planted permanently in the database.

And this is mostly what session APIs are about. Besides that, it's about control of a session—dictating when it will end. You have mechanisms to time out a session if no requests are received for a certain time. Or you can use session APIs to apply more stringent timing rules. You might want to ensure that the session will not exceed a certain time limit, regardless of the requests it receives—perhaps in a game application. And you'll see in this chapter that your scope is wider than that: You can invalidate a session for any reason you see fit.

But first we'll explore a fundamental question: How can you get hold of a session in the first place?

Getting Hold of a Session

When a client makes its very first request to a particular web application, neither party knows about each other. How could they? It's as if the client has just rung the doorbell. At this point, there's no session. And there doesn't need to be a session. If the person on the doorstep is merely asking you to sign for a parcel delivery, then it's a one-off request. If he wants you to participate in a survey about your buying habits (and you agree), that requires a series of interactions—in other words, a session.

So a session exists only if your servlet decides it needs one. The servlet gets hold of that session from the HttpServletRequest object. This has a `getSession()` method, which returns an HttpSession object. And the idea is that a series of calls to `HttpServletRequest.getSession()` from a related set of requests (ones emanating from the same client) will always retrieve the same session object, as shown in the following illustration.

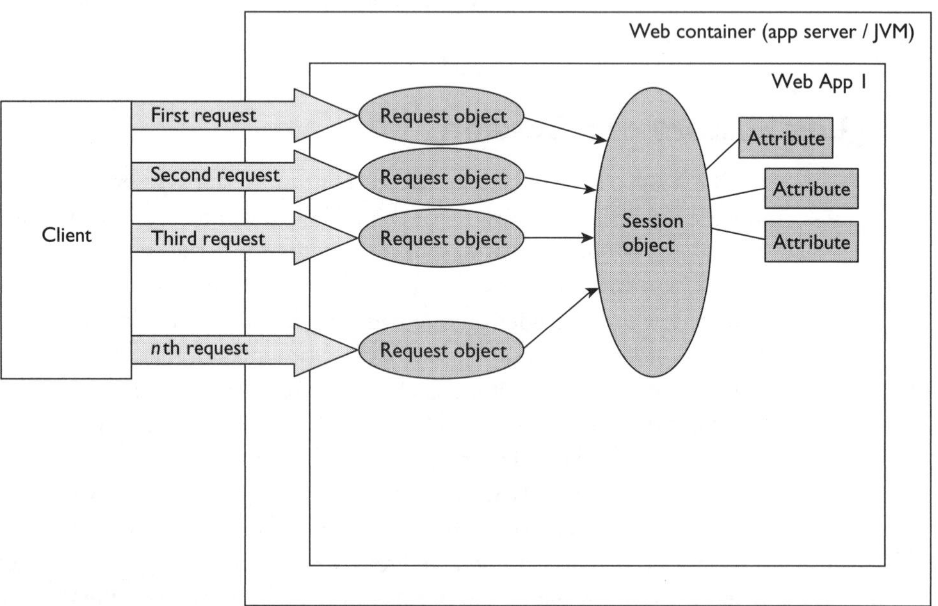

As far as the J2EE servlet API is concerned, sessions and session scope belong to the world of HTTP. HttpSession is an interface that lives in the javax.servlet.http package. You can get HttpSession objects only from HttpServletRequest, not from ServletRequest. There is no equivalent in the non-HTTP servlet world—for example, a Session interface provided in the javax.servlet package. Of course, there's nothing stopping you from providing your own infrastructure, but outside of HTTP, you're on your own.

Actually, `HttpServletRequest.getSession()` is an overloaded method. It exists in the no-argument form, or can accept a single **boolean** parameter: `HttpServletRequest.getSession(boolean create)`. First you should know that

```
HttpSession session = HttpServletRequest.getSession();
```

is a shorthand form of

```
HttpSession session = HttpServletRequest.getSession(true);
```

These two calls are functionally equivalent. These calls will return an HttpSession come what may, returning the existing object if it already exists or *creating a session object if one does not exist already*.

Alternatively, you might call

```
HttpSession session = HttpServletRequest.getSession(false);
```

This call will return a session object, but *only* if one already exists. Why might you want to do this? Perhaps your application is designed so that initial requests should pass through a "Login" servlet, which establishes a session. As a security measure, all other servlets in the application make a `getSession(false)` call when they need the session object. Only if the user has legitimately passed through the "Login" servlet will the other servlets get the session object they need for the application to function.

Session Scope Revisited

Let's now revisit session scope, which we briefly explored in Chapter 2. Figure 4-1 shows a possible session "lifetime." At (1) in Figure 4-1, a client (web browser window) makes its first request to your web application—as it happens, for ServletA. ServletA obtains a session object through the request, supplied by the web container ((2) in Figure 4-1). At this point, the session is deemed to be "new." The client doesn't yet know about the session's existence—after all, it has only just come into being. You can test the session state as follows:

```
HttpSession session = request.getSession();
if (session.isNew()) {
  // Do something conditional on session newness
}
```

At (2) in Figure 4-1, the boolean value returned by `HttpSession.isNew()` will be true. So how does a session lose its newness? Along with the response to ServletA, the web container (at (3) in Figure 4-1) returns some sort of tracking information that uniquely identifies the session that has just been created.

FIGURE 4-1 Session Scope

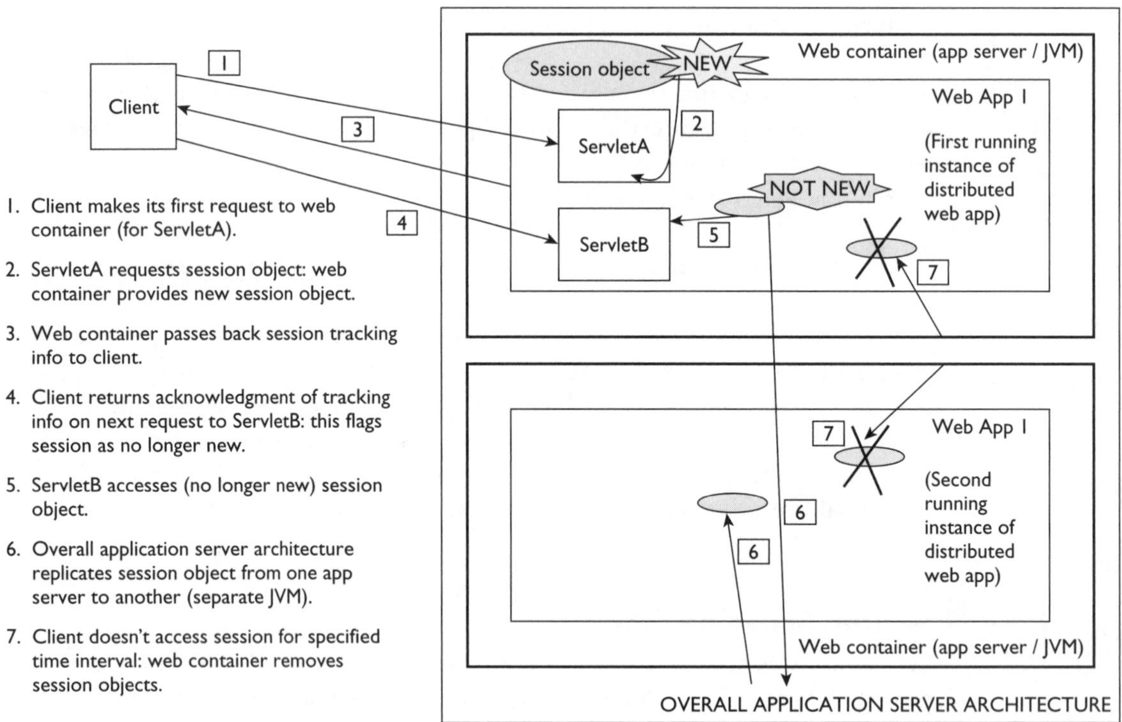
Client
1
2
3
4
5
6
7
Session object
NEW
NOT NEW
ServletA
ServletB
Web container (app server / JVM)
Web App 1
(First running instance of distributed web app)
Web App 1
(Second running instance of distributed web app)
Web container (app server / JVM)
OVERALL APPLICATION SERVER ARCHITECTURE
1. Client makes its first request to web container (for ServletA).
2. ServletA requests session object: web container provides new session object.
3. Web container passes back session tracking info to client.
4. Client returns acknowledgment of tracking info on next request to ServletB: this flags session as no longer new.
5. ServletB accesses (no longer new) session object.
6. Overall application server architecture replicates session object from one app server to another (separate JVM).
7. Client doesn't access session for specified time interval: web container removes session objects.

on the job

What constitutes a "new browser session"? Here's an observation on Internet Explorer's behavior. If you launch Internet Explorer afresh, then access a session-aware servlet—that's a new session. If Internet Explorer itself launches a new Internet Explorer window (e.g., by running File | New Window or by running some appropriate script) and that new window accesses a session-aware servlet—it shares the session object with the Internet Explorer window from which it was launched. This makes reasonable sense, and it's probably not the only browser that exhibits this behavior. I point it out for two reasons. First, for the sake of your application logic, you will need to know what circumstances cause the client software on a particular PC to maintain or drop the session. Second, this behavior makes session attributes officially not thread safe. It is imaginable that your user might toggle between two Internet Explorer windows, one spawned from the other, and set off a long-running request from each. Both these request threads could access the same session object.

exam watch

You will often encounter questions where you need to know the two circumstances whereby sessions remain "new." The first is when the client doesn't yet know about the session because this is a first request to a web application. The second is because a client declines to join the session, which it typically does by refusing to return the session tracking information. Under these circumstances, the web application treats each later request from the client as if it were the first, providing a new session each time.

The client now makes another request (at (4) in Figure 4-1), this time to ServletB (though for the purposes of this account, it wouldn't matter if the request were made to the same servlet again, ServletA). The client has agreed to join the session, which is typically achieved by passing the tracking information (the session key) back to the web container along with the new request. ServletB (at (5) in Figure 4-1) obtains the session from the request. This is exactly the same session object that ServletA had access to, but now—as the client knows about the session and has agreed to join it—the session is no longer new (as tested with the `isNew()` method).

Distributed Sessions

That's normally as far as a session gets. However, it is possible—for the sake of load balancing or fail-over or both—to mark a web application as distributable, if it is supported by your application server. All you need do is place the element `<distributable />` (or `<distributable></distributable>`) somewhere underneath parent element `<web-app>` in your deployment descriptor. Note that this step may have no effect whatsoever: This element works *if and only if* your application server supports distributed applications. If it does, the effect should be as shown in Figure 4-1: The same web application running in two (or more) different JVMs. In Figure 4-1, there are two "clones" of the same web application. The lower half of the figure depicts a second running instance of Web App 1.

Why would you do this? If the first running instance should fail, your architecture might have a fail-over mechanism in place to divert requests to the second running instance. Would this disrupt a client session if the failure came between two requests from a client? Not if the architecture had migrated your session object from one JVM to another. And this is what is shown at (6) in Figure 4-1: The session is replicated from the first running instance of Web App 1 to the second running instance of Web App 1. And with the session go all the objects attaching to the session. The only condition is that the attributes you place in a session should implement the Serializable interface.

The exact mechanism by which this is achieved varies from one application server to another and is beyond the scope of the exam. The phrase in Figure 4-1 "overall application server architecture," is deliberately vague. There might be some direct communication in place between the two application servers shown in Figure 4-1. There might be some additional application server process polling each web application clone, and maybe a database that stores session objects. You don't need to care at this point—all that's required is that you understand the implications for sessions when a web application is marked distributable.

exam watch

A session is available to be shared between web resources in a single web application. Note I say a single web application: A session cannot cross web application boundaries. If you use the RequestDispatcher mechanism to get at a servlet in another web application and that servlet accesses the session object, it will be a different session object, as shown in the following illustration.

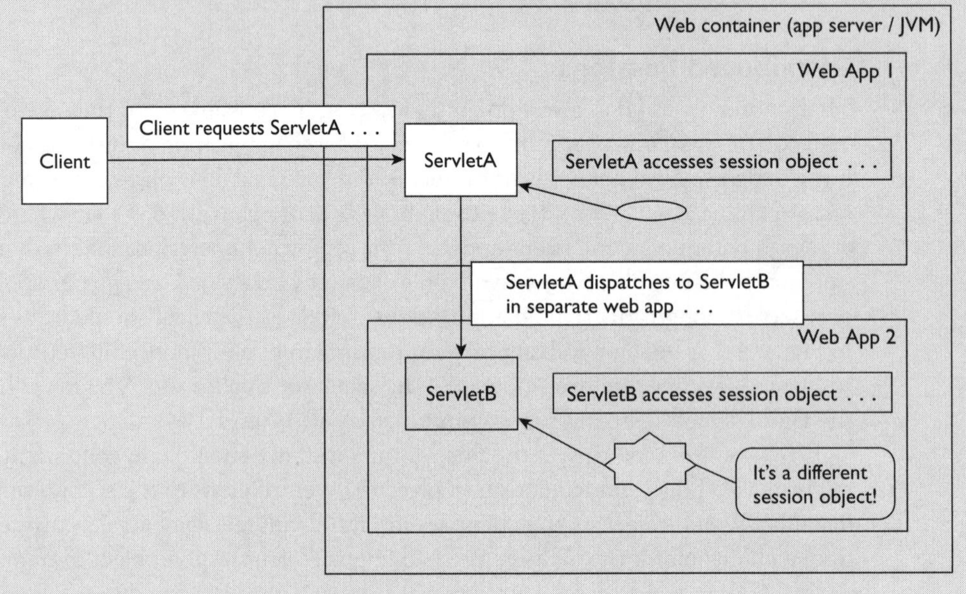

Session Death

So how does a session die? There is no obvious trigger. As we well know, servlets work on a series of requests and responses. The protocol doesn't demand a continuous connection between the client making the request and the server providing the response. So how do you know when the client has made its last request, and take this as a cue to free up the session?

The answer is that you *don't* necessarily know. The HttpSession API provides an `invalidate()` method—so if your application has a "Log Off" button and the user clicks it, a LogOff servlet should summon the session and call the method. But what if this user, despite repeated and prolonged training followed up with heavy threats, just closes the browser window? The session is over because the client has gone. Even if the user reopens the browser and connects back to the same web application, the web container will interpret this as a new session. Yet the server is blissfully unaware that the *original* client (aka browser session) won't be making any more requests.

The solution is to have a time-out mechanism, and that's precisely what is built into the web container model. If a session has not been used for a prescribed amount of time, the web container invalidates the session itself. This is what's illustrated at (7) in Figure 4-1. For the clock to start ticking for a session's time-out, all requests using the session must have come to an end—that is, their servlets must have exited their `service()` method, and any enclosing filters exited their `doFilter()` method.

The time-out value is controlled in one of three ways.

Application Server Global Default Most application servers provide their own mechanism for imposing a global default on session length. The specifics of this don't matter for the exam, and they vary by server in any case.

Web Application Default You can set up a default value in the deployment descriptor. Here's an example of how to do this:

```
<web-app>
  <session-config>
    <session-timeout>60</session-timeout>
  </session-config>
</web-app>
```

The value in the `<session-timeout>` element is expressed as whole *minutes*. Any integer value is fine. A value of 0, or a negative value, denotes that the default for sessions created in the web application is to never expire. Note that

`<session-timeout>` is `<session-config>`'s only subelement, and `<session-config>` is a direct child of the root element `<web-app>`.

Individual Session Setting On obtaining a session, your servlet code can set the time-out value for that individual session only using the `HttpSession.setMaxInactiveInterval(int seconds)` API. Note that the unit of time is in *seconds*—contrasting with the deployment descriptor `<session-timeout>` element, which contains a value in minutes. Again, a negative value supplied as an argument causes the session to never expire. But by contrast with the deployment descriptor, a value of zero *doesn't* have the same effect. `setMaxInactiveInterval(0)` causes the session to expire immediately—which is rarely desirable!

Let's set the deployment descriptor and API characteristics side by side in a table, for you can pretty much count on seeing a question on this theme:

	`<session-timeout>` element in deployment descriptor	`HttpSession.setMaxInactiveInterval(int seconds)` API
Scope:	The default value for all sessions created in the web application.	The value for the session for which the method is called *only*.
Unit:	Minutes.	Seconds.
Zero value denotes:	Sessions should never expire.	Immediate expiration of session.
Negative value denotes:	Sessions should never expire.	Session should never expire.

Note that there is a corresponding `HttpSession.getMaxInactiveInterval()` method. This returns an int primitive representing the number of seconds permitted between client requests before the web container invalidates the related session. It doesn't matter which of the three time-out-setting approaches you use for this method to return a value. So—for example—you might use the deployment descriptor and set a 30-minute time-out: `<session-timeout>30</session-timeout>`. The `getMaxInactiveInterval()` method will then return a value of 1800—the equivalent in seconds.

A final word of warning: Don't try to prolong a session's life by artificial means—or, at least, don't hold me responsible for the consequences! How could you contrive such an infringement? Perhaps by attaching a session object as an attribute to your context, then trying to get it back when the session scope has passed. The results are likely to be unpredictable, or even catastrophic to your web application.

That's not to say that an application server might not preserve session objects. Just as for request objects, it is probably more efficient to maintain a pool of session objects instead of going through instantiation and garbage collection whenever a new session is required or jettisoned. The web container just has to provide the appearance of a new session object, stripped of attributes and returning "true" to `isNew()` requests. Whether this is a session object that has been newly constructed or has already been through many previous incarnations is something about which you should not have to know or care. As a web developer, confine yourself to the session APIs you have at your disposal.

Multithreading and Session Attributes

In most circumstances you can regard session objects and their associated attributes as thread safe. The following illustration shows how this looks for the client request threads to a web application.

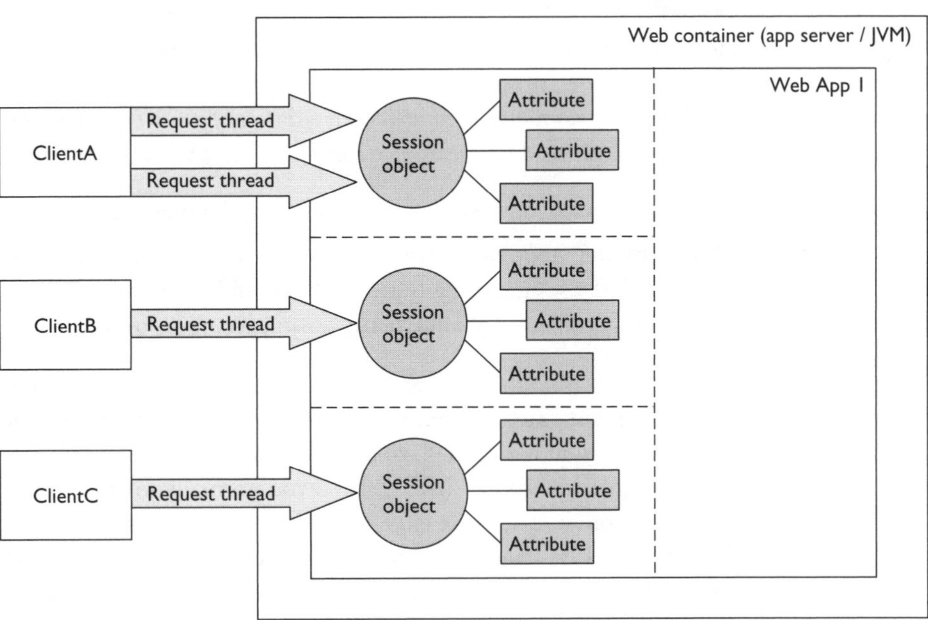

However, as far as the servlet specification goes—and therefore the exam as well—you can't rely on session attributes being thread safe. You see in the preceding illustration—for ClientA—two requests, which both access the same session object. Nothing strange about that: After all, that's the point of the session object—to provide continuity between requests. The issue is whether those two requests from the client could ever overlap. It's my experience that in normal web browser usage, you don't (and mainly, can't) overlap requests from the same main browser window. However, it is a theoretical possibility: See the "On the Job" feature (see page 242) to learn how it might happen. So you should design your web applications such that access to session attributes is synchronized. Or if you don't—perhaps for performance reasons—ensure that multithreaded access to your session attributes will not compromise the well-being of your web application.

Other Session APIs

We touched on `HttpSession.invalidate()` above. This invalidates the session and then removes any attributes associated with the session. Invalidation works by making (almost) all of the methods on HttpSession unworkable: If you try to use them, an IllegalStateException is thrown. This is even true on the `invalidate()` method itself: You can't use this method on an already invalid session! The three HttpSession methods that don't throw this exception are `get` and `setMaxInactiveInterval()`, and `getServletContext()`—quite why these are unlike the other methods is not clear to me—but I point it out in case some meaner-than-usual exam question tries to trip you up.

There are two methods that return a date and time (as a **long** primitive that you will most likely feed to the appropriate java.util.Date constructor):

- `getCreationTime()`—unsurprisingly, the time the session was created.
- `getLastAccessedTime()`—the last time the client sent a request associated with the session. Clearly, this API is useful to the web container itself in determining when to invalidate the session according to the time-out value.

This leaves `getServletContext()`, `getId()`, and a sprinkling of deprecated methods. `HttpSession.getServletContext()` returns the SessionContext to which the session is attached, so it can be used as an alternative to `ServletConfig.getServletContext()` (the method you normally invoke directly from a servlet). `HttpSession.getId()` we explore in the next section. You won't be tested on the deprecated APIs. That said, you might want to familiarize yourself with them if you are maintaining older code (supporting Servlet Spec 2.2 and before). Most have to do with a standardization of method names whereby session attributes used to be known as session values—for example, `get` and `putValue()` were used once upon a time instead of `get` and `setAttribute()`.

EXERCISE 4-1

Displaying the Session Life Cycle

In this exercise, you'll write a servlet that associates itself with a session and displays information about the session: how many times the session has been accessed, the session's age, and whether it's a new session.

Create the usual web application directory structure under a directory called ex0401, and proceed with the steps for the exercise. There's a solution in the CD in the file sourcecode/ch04/ex0401.war—check there if you get stuck.

Set Up the Deployment Descriptor

1. Declare a servlet named SessionDisplayer, with a suitable servlet mapping. If needed, refer to Chapter 2 to refresh yourself on `<servlet>` element setup.

Write the SessionDisplayer Servlet

2. Create a Java source file SessionDisplayer.java in /WEB-INF/classes or an appropriate package directory. Write the class declaration in the source file, extending HttpServlet.
3. Do the necessary preliminaries to obtain the reponse's PrintWriter, and set the content type to "text/html."
4. Check for a parameter called *getSession* (`request.getParameter("getSession")`). Most of the remaining steps should depend on the value of *getSession* being "true."
5. Get hold of the session from the request.
6. If this is a new session, display the fact. Also, if the session is new, set up a session attribute that records the number of accesses to the session, initialized to a value of 1.
7. Increment this session attribute on every subsequent access to the session.
8. Display the number of times this session has been accessed, retrieving the information from the session attribute.
9. Get the time the session was created. Display the session's age in minutes and seconds by obtaining the current time and by working out the difference between this and the session creation time.

Run the SessionDisplayer Servlet

10. Deploy and run the servlet, using a URL such as

```
http://localhost:8080/ex0401/SessionDisplayer?getSession=true
```

11. Try recalling the servlet with the above URL, sometimes changing the *getSession* parameter to a value of "false."

Optional Experiments

12. Add capabilities to the servlet to reset the maximum inactive interval and to immediately invalidate the session. These could be controlled by parameters into the session.
13. Try various session method calls immediately after the session is invalidated. Remind yourself which three methods can (strangely but legally) still be called even though the session is invalid.

CERTIFICATION OBJECTIVE

Session Management (Exam Objective 4.4)

Given a scenario, describe which session management mechanism the web container could employ, how cookies might be used to manage sessions, and how URL rewriting might be used to manage sessions, and write servlet code to perform URL rewriting.

So now you have a good grasp of session scope. To complete your understanding of the session life cycle, we need to look at the actual mechanisms used to keep a session up and running. So far we have talked about exchanging tracking information between the client (browser) and the web application. Now we'll see precisely what that tracking information might consist of, according to which type of session management mechanism is in force.

Session Management

There are two principal methods for session management "officially" recognized by the servlet API. One method is management by cookie exchange, and the other is management by rewriting URLs. In this section we'll explore in some detail what these mean.

That's not to say that these are the only approaches. Secure Sockets Layer (SSL), which ensures secure communications between browsers and web applications, has its own session data built into it. You can always manufacture your own mechanism: A typical technique involves holding session data in hidden fields on a web form. However, you don't need understanding of these other approaches for the web component exam.

Session Management: General Principles

Whatever session management approach you take, the end game is the same: to associate a group of requests. Each of these requests needs to carry a unique ID, which identifies the session to which it belongs. Indeed, once you have a handle to the session, you can display this ID using the `HttpSession.getId()` method. This returns a String whose contents will depend on the application server you use—you can usually expect it to be long!

The web application will allocate this unique ID on the first request from the client (at which point the client has no idea about its value). The ID must be passed back to the client so that the client can pass it back again with its next request. In this way, the web application will know to which session the request belongs. This implies that the client must need to store the unique ID somewhere—and that's where session management mechanisms come in.

Cookies

The preferred way for a web application to pass session IDs back to a client is via a cookie in the response. This is a small text file that the client stores somewhere. Storage can be on disk but is just as likely to in memory: This is the case with a "transient" cookie, which is useful for a short time only. You are no doubt well aware of cookies just from your general use of the Internet, for many web sites employ them. Cookies are used to support all kinds of session-like activity on the Web, regardless of whether the back-end technology is Java based.

In the case of J2EE web applications, the cookie returned has a standard name—JSESSIONID—all uppercase, just as written here. Even if you can't inspect the cookie at the browser end (because it's probably transient—in memory, and not available to view from the hard disk using a text editor), you can catch the cookie coming back from the browser using the `HttpServletRequest.getCookies()` method that we examined in Chapter 1. You can then prove to your own satisfaction that the value of the cookie matches the session ID you can view with `HttpSession.getId()`.

You probably know also that client browsers—mostly—have the ability to switch cookies off. Although most cookies are benign in nature, and designed to enhance a user's web experience, the malign few have given cookies a bad name. So for privacy reasons, a user may choose to reject cookies completely. For this reason, you might need to use the second (and second-best) standard session-tracking mechanism—URL rewriting.

URL Rewriting

We have already seen in earlier chapters how to pass information to a web application via the URL. This might take the form of path information (supplementary "directory" information appended to a servlet path) or parameters in a query string (name/value pairs after a question mark).

URL rewriting is an extension of this idea. A "pseudo-parameter" called *jsessionid* is placed in the URL between the servlet name (with path information, if present) and the query string. Here's an example—note that this would be one continuous line on your browser address line with no breaks:

```
http://localhost:8080/examp0401/SessionExample;jsessionid=
58112645388D9380808A726A27F92997?name=value&othername=othervalue
```

You see a semicolon after the servlet mapping name (`SessionExample`), then the *jsessionid* pseudo-parameter (`jsessionid=verylongstring`), followed by a question mark, which introduces the query string information.

This is fine, but it gives your web application a real problem. Every web page your application returns in the response is likely to have a number of hyperlinks within it of one sort or other—regular links, buttons, image links, or whatever. Each one of these links must contain `jsessionid=<correctLongString>` as part of the URL.

This is very hard to achieve, unless you have servlets dynamically generating those web pages. There is a method—`HttpServletResponse.encodeURL()`—which accepts a String (representing the URL link on the web page minus session information) and returns a String (the same URL link, but now with the session information embedded). This method is, in fact, clever enough to know that if some other session mechanism is in force—at least one it recognizes, such as cookies—then there is no need to bother embedding any session information. Under these circumstances, it returns the String representing the URL unchanged. Best practice dictates that every URL link you create in a servlet should be put through this method. Then, even if you are expecting your application to operate in a cookie-friendly environment, it will still survive when it unexpectedly finds itself in cookie-hostile territory.

As a postscript to this, there is another method, `HttpServletResponse.encodeRedirectURL()`, which operates in pretty much the same way as `encodeURL()`. You give it a URL String; it gives back a URL String, with *jsessionid* embedded where necessary. This resulting URL String should then be used to plug into the `HttpServletResponse.sendRedirect()` method. The output String will look no different from a similar call to `encodeURL()`; the reason for providing `encodeRedirectURL()` is that the logic for determining whether or not to embed session information may be different when considering normal URLs versus redirect URLs.

exam watch

Beware of the deprecated methods `encodeUrl()` and `encodeRedirectUrl()`. These have "Url" in mixed case and were deprecated in a Java standardization exercise that mandated capitals for the abbreviation URL wherever it appeared in method or other names. It would be a mean exam question that attempted to trip you up on this arcane point, but you have to remember that examiners are entitled to get their kicks in any way they can.

Request Methods

There are a couple of HttpServletRequest methods that identify which of the two standard session mechanisms are in use—cookies or URL rewriting. You might find it surprising that these methods belong to the request object—not to HttpSession. There's a minor advantage in that you can execute these methods without having to first access the session object via the request. Here are the two methods:

- `HttpServletRequest.isRequestedSessionIdFromCookie()`
- `HttpServletRequest.isRequestedSessionIdFromURL()` (and yes, there is a deprecated version of this method, where "URL" is in mixed case: "Url")

Never use a pithy name for a method when you can use a sentence instead! Both methods return a primitive **boolean**, set to **true** if the session mechanism specified is in force. There can be circumstances where both of these methods, called consecutively for the same request, both return **false**—even though a session is present. This will happen:

- for SSL sessions.
- for bespoke session mechanism logic (hidden form fields, for example).
- when the session is new! Because at this point, the session ID isn't coming from a URL or a cookie—but it has been generated by the web container.

EXERCISE 4-2

Displaying the Session Management Mechanism

This exercise builds on the SessionDisplayer servlet that you wrote in Exercise 4-1. You'll now add some capabilities to display what kind of mechanism is in use for supporting the session.

Create the usual web application directory structure under a directory called ex0402, and proceed with the steps for the exercise. There's a solution in the CD in the file sourcecode/ch04/ex0402.war—check there if you get stuck.

Set Up the Deployment Descriptor

1. Copy the web.xml deployment descriptor from Exercise 4-1. You'll recall that this declared the SessionDisplayer servlet.
2. Change each occurrence of SessionDisplayer (name of servlet, name of class, URL pattern for mapping) to SessionDisplayer2.

Update the SessionDisplayer2 Servlet

3. Copy the Java source file for SessionDisplayer.java from ex0401/WEB-INF/classes (or its appropriate package directory) to ex0402/WEB-INF/classes (or appropriate package directory), and rename it to SessionDisplayer2 (make sure the class declaration reflects this as well).
4. In the code—if you haven't done so already—put an <a href> link that recalls this same SessionDisplayer2 servlet. Encode the URL using the appropriate HttpServletResponse method.
5. In the web page, display some text that shows whether the session came from the JSESSIONID cookie or from the URL.
6. Optionally, use the `request.getCookies()` method to get hold of the JSESSIONID cookie, and display all the attributes of the cookie that you can on the web page.

Run the Updated SessionDisplayer2 Servlet

7. Deploy and run the servlet, using a URL such as

```
http://localhost:8080/ex0402/SessionDisplayer2?getSession=true
```

8. You're most likely to find that your browser uses cookies as the session mechanism. To test out the URL redirection method, try turning off cookies altogether in your browser — or target the domain where your web server (Tomcat) is running, usually localhost / 127.0.0.1, and turn off cookies for that. Ensure that you restart your browser before expecting URLs to be used instead of cookies.
9. The screen print below shows part of the output from the solution code, when the session information is delivered through the JSESSIONID cookie.

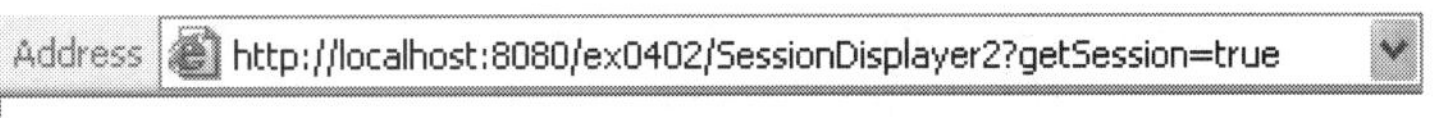

Session has been accessed **3** times

Session id is **413A326A6825E1E7D0B72AF6BCF58EA3**.

The session is old.

The session is 4 minutes and 3 seconds old.

Maximum inactive interval for session is **1800** seconds.

Session id comes from cookie JSESSIONID.

Cookie

JSESSIONID
Domain: null
Max Age: -1
Path: null
Value: 413A326A6825E1E7D0B72AF6BCF58EA3
Version: 0

CERTIFICATION OBJECTIVE

Request and Context Listeners (Exam Objective 3.4)

Describe the web container lifecycle event model for requests, sessions, and web applications; create and configure listener classes for each scope lifecycle; create and configure scope attribute listener classes; and, given a scenario, identify the proper attribute listener to use.

We're going to take a brief departure from sessions now and begin to explore the world of listeners. The certification objective actually pertains to the "web container model" and so is a leftover from Chapter 3. For veterans of the old Sun Certified Java Programmer (SCJP) exam—which included Swing user interface mechanisms on its syllabus—listeners will not be a new idea. The idea is simple and elegant: Something of interest happens in your framework, and the framework lets the interested parties know. The interested parties are called "listeners" in Java (and design pattern) parlance. And whereas the Swing framework has listeners for mouse movements and keyboard strokes, the J2EE web application model has a set of server-side events that you can listen for. These are what we're going to cover in the next two sections.

Listeners

We'll start in this section with the listeners that apply to request and context objects. There are two for each object, and their function is very similar. The following table shows the listeners, what objects they apply to, and the listener function.

Listener Interface Name	Applies to	Function
ServletRequestListener	Request objects	Responds to the life and death of each request.
ServletContextListener	The context object	Responds to the life and death of the context for a web application.
ServletRequestAttributeListener	Request objects	Responds to any change to the set of attributes attached to a request object.
ServletContextAttributeListener	The context object	Responds to any change to the set of attributes attached to the context object.

exam watch *There is no getting away from it—you have to memorize the names of all the listeners, together with their methods and their purpose: what events trigger calls to them and what object they affect. It's a lot to ask—and the SCWCD asks it.*

Listener Preparation

There are two things you need to do to set up a listener in a web application:

- Write a class that implements the appropriate listener interface.
- Register the class name in the web application deployment descriptor, web.xml.

Let's first deal with the deployment descriptor aspects, which are reasonably trivial. All you need to do is to place a `<listener>` element somewhere underneath the root element, and with this embed a `<listener-class>` element. The value held in the `<listener-class>` element is the fully qualified class name of a listener class. No need to specify which type of listener you're talking about: The web container just works this out through Java's reflection capabilities. This neatly covers the fact that the same class could, potentially, implement more than one kind of interface. Here's how some listener declarations might look in web.xml:

```
<listener>
  <listener-class>com.osborne.RequestTrackingListener</listener-class>
</listener>
<listener>
  <listener-class>com.osborne.SessionLoggingListener</listener-class>
</listener>
```

It could be that you have more than one listener class implementing the same interface. Moreover, you might care about the order in which the classes are called when a triggering event occurs. Simply list your listener declarations in the desired order in the deployment descriptor, and let the web container ensure the correct invocation sequence.

exam watch *Closedown of a web application triggers a call to the matching closedown events in session and context listeners. The order in which listeners are called is then in reverse order of deployment description declaration, with session listeners being processed before context listeners.*

Writing a listener class simply involves providing the requisite methods to satisfy the interface you are implementing. You can always write a "do-nothing" method if there are some events that don't interest your web application. It's worth remembering that listener classes must have a no-argument constructor. You can let the Java compiler supply one automatically if no other constructors are present. However, this approach is vulnerable if constructors with arguments are added later. (But it's not obvious why they would be—the web container is going to instantiate your listener only through the no-argument constructor. And there wouldn't be a good reason to instantiate a listener in your own web application code.)

The Request Listener

So now that we've explored the general features of listener classes, it's time to start looking in detail at each listener in turn. We'll start with ServletRequestListener. A class implementing this interface has two methods to implement: `requestInitialized()` and `requestDestroyed()`. The names of the methods pretty much describe the events that trigger the web container to call them. So `requestInitialized()` is called the moment that any request in the web container becomes newly available—in other words, at the beginning of any request's scope. This is at the beginning of a servlet's `service()` method—or earlier than that if a filter chain is involved (the request's scope begins at the first `doFilter()` method call of the chain). Conversely, `requestDestroyed()` is called for each request that comes to an end—either at the end of the servlet's `service()` method or at the end of the `doFilter()` method for the first filter in a chain. This is shown diagrammatically in Figure 4-2.

Each of these ServletRequestListener methods accepts a ServletRequestEvent as a parameter. This event object has two methods for access to useful objects:

- `getServletContext()` returns the ServletContext for a web application.
- `getServletRequest()` returns the ServletRequest object itself (cast this to HttpServletRequest if you need to).

You write code like the following in your ServletRequestListener class to preload an attribute into every request made to your web application:

```
public void requestInitialized(ServletRequestEvent requestEvent) {
  HttpServletRequest request = (HttpServletRequest)
                               requestEvent.getServletRequest();
  request.setAttribute("com.osborne.bookrecommendation",
                       "Core JSPs 2.0");
}
```

FIGURE 4-2 Two Requests Triggering Request Events

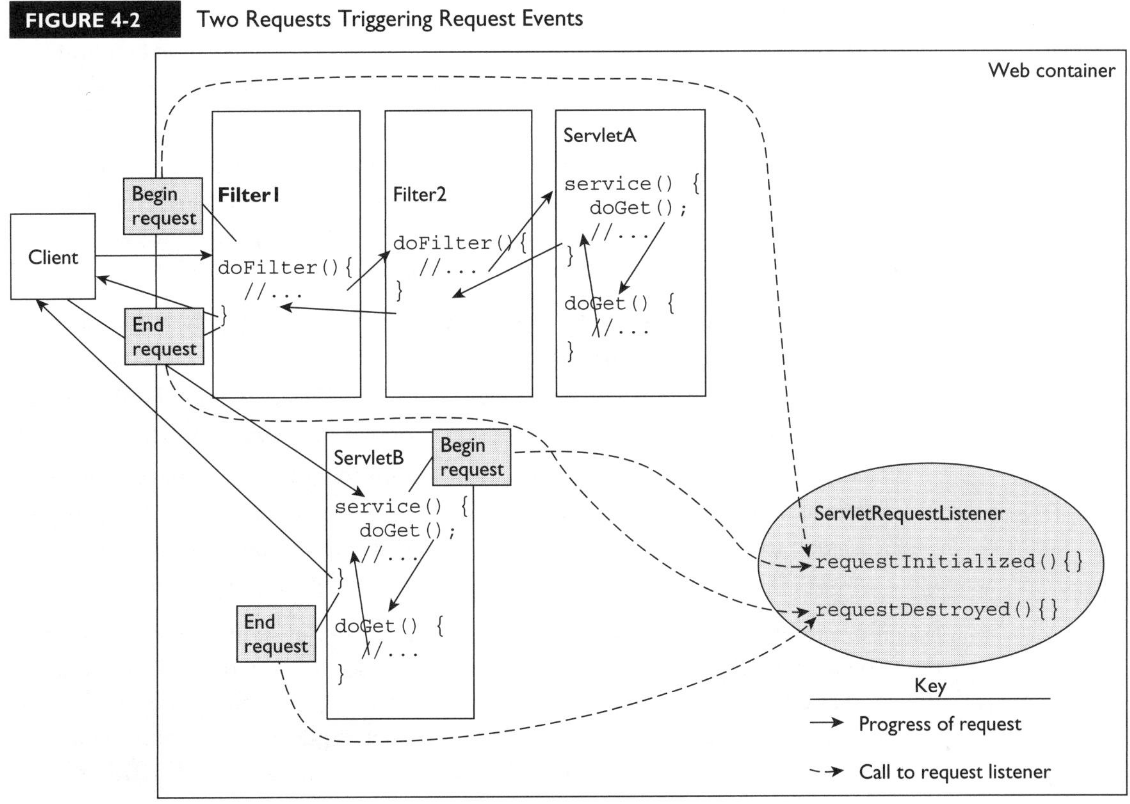

The Request Attribute Listener

So we've now dealt with our first listener—ServletRequestListener—which deals with the life cycle of each request object. What about the life cycle of the attributes attached to request objects? For these we have classes that implement the Servlet RequestAttributeListener interface. Here are the methods to implement:

- **`attributeAdded(ServletRequestAttributeEvent srae)`** is called whenever a new attribute is added to any request. In other words, *any* call (from *any* request object at *any* time) to **`ServletRequest.setAttribute()`** will trigger a call to this method—provided that the name of the attribute being added to the request is a not a name already in use as an attribute of that request.
- **`attributeRemoved(ServletRequestAttributeEvent srae)`** is called whenever an attribute is removed from a request (as a result of any call to **`ServletRequest.removeAttribute()`**).

- `attributeReplaced(ServletRequestAttributeEvent srae)` is called whenever an attribute is replaced (as a result of any call to `ServletRequest.setAttribute()` for an attribute name already in use on the request whose call this is).

Again, there are two useful methods on the event object passed as a parameter to these methods. The method `getName()` is straightforward: It returns the String holding the name of the attribute being added, removed, or replaced. `getValue()` is less clear-cut, for what's returned varies slightly in meaning:

- `attributeAdded()`, `getValue()` returns the Object that is the value parameter on the `setAttribute()` call.
- `attributeRemoved()`, `getValue()` returns the Object that has been removed as a value from the request as a result of a `removeAttribute()` call.
- `attributeReplaced()`, `getValue()` returns the *old* value of the attribute before a call to `setAttribute()` changed it. Why not the new value? Because—as we'll see in a moment—it's possible to get at the new value by alternative means. But there's no other way of trapping the old value at this point.

Because ServletRequestAttributeEvent inherits from ServletRequestEvent, you get the two handy methods we looked at in the previous section—which allow you to get the context object and the request object. Having the request object, you can always get to the current value of an attribute that's just been replaced. Here's some code that displays to the server console the old and new values for a replaced attribute:

```
public void attributeReplaced(ServletRequestAttributeEvent event) {
  String name = event.getName();
  Object oldValue = event.getValue();
  Object newValue = event.getServletRequest().getAttribute(name);
  System.out.println("Name of attribute: " + name);
  System.out.println("Old value of attribute: " + oldValue);
  System.out.println("New value of attribute: " + newValue);
}
```

The inheritance chain for ServletRequestAttributeEvent doesn't stop there—as you can see in the illustration on the following page.

The "grandparent" of ServletRequestEvent is java.util.EventObject. You might remember this from user interface programming, for it features in the hierarchy of Swing events also. This has one method—`getSource()`—which returns the object that is the source of the event. This—surprisingly perhaps—proves to be the ServletContext object: It represents the web application framework, which is, ultimately, the source of all events.

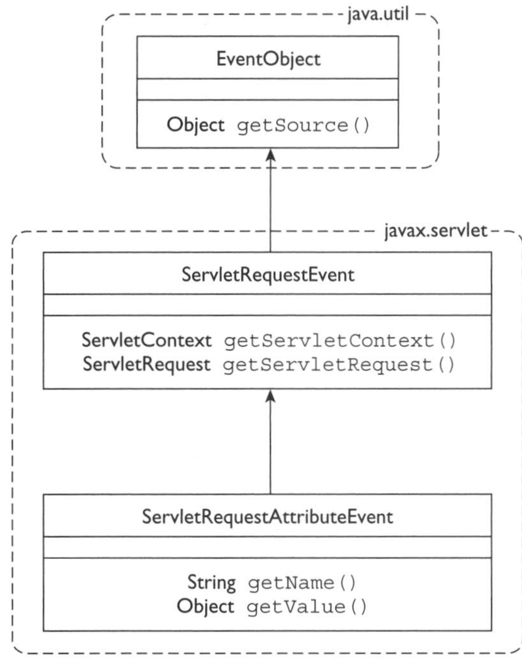

The Context Listener

Now that you've learned about ServletRequest Listeners, you'll find the ServletContextListener easy to learn, for it follows just the same pattern. Instead of `requestInitialized()` and `requestDestroyed()`, you have `contextInitialized()` and `contextDestroyed()` as the two methods to implement. And in life cycle terms, these are called at the beginning and end of scope—this time of the context, of course, rather than of the request. And as we learned previously, the context life cycle matches that of the web application: It's the first object made available on web application startup and the last to disappear at shutdown. So the `contextInitialized()` method gets called before any servlet's `init()` method or any filter's `doFilter()` method. And every filter and servlet `destroy()` method must have executed before the `contextDestroyed()` method is called.

Both the methods get passed a ServletContextEvent object, which just has the one method, `getServletContext()`, to get at the context object itself. So in `contextInitialized()`, you have a chance to attach context attributes before any servlet gets a crack of the whip.

The `contextInitialized()` method of a ServletContextListener is a great place to read in parameters from initialization files that are fundamental to the operation of your application. It's a better alternative than relying on the `init()` method in a servlet that loads on startup. Although you can configure your servlet to be the first one that loads in the application, that's vulnerable to later configuration changes. But you can guarantee that the `contextInitialized()` method will be the first piece of your code to run on startup of the web application.

The Context Attribute Listener

The ServletContextAttributeListener has the same trio of methods as the ServletRequestAttributeListener: namely `attributeAdded()`, `attributeRemoved()`, and `attributeReplaced()`. They have the same function as their request equivalents—except, of course, that they fire when things happen to context attributes:

- `attributeAdded(ServletContextAttributeEvent scae)` is called whenever a new attribute is added to the servlet context. In other words, any call (from any web application code that has access to the servlet context) to `ServletContext.setAttribute()` will trigger a call to this method— provided that the name of the attribute being added to the context is a not a name already in use as an attribute of the context.

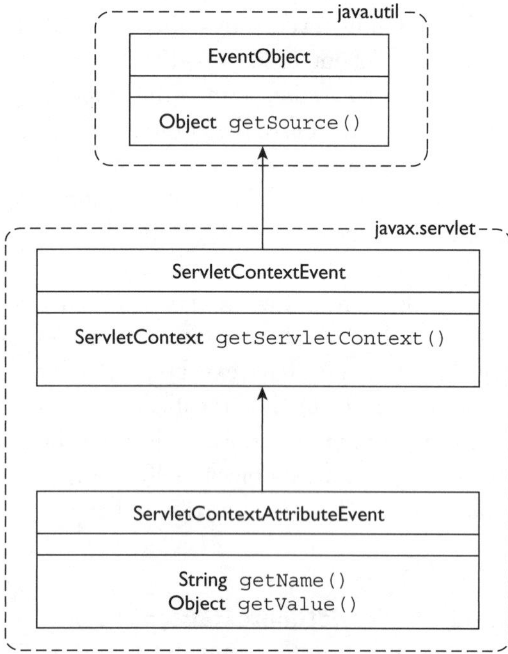

- `attributeRemoved(ServletContextAttributeEvent scae)` is called whenever an attribute is removed from the context (as a result of any call to `ServletContext.removeAttribute()`).
- `attributeReplaced(ServletContextAttributeEvent scae)` is called whenever an attribute is replaced (as a result of any call to `ServletContext.setAttribute()` for an attribute name already in use by the servlet context).

And lo—the ServletContextAttributeEvent received as a parameter by these methods has the same two methods as the equivalent ServletRequestAttributeEvent—namely `getName()` (to get the name of the attribute affected) and `getValue()` (to get the value of the attribute: added, removed, or—in the case of replacement—the *old* value of the attribute).

There's an inheritance hierarchy for this as well, back through ServletContextEvent and java.util.EventObject, as illustrated.

EXERCISE 4-3

Proving the Execution Order of Listeners

In this exercise you'll write code to explore context listeners. In particular, you will prove that the `contextInitialized()` method is called before any servlet is initialized. You'll also write code to trap changes to context attributes.

Create the usual web application directory structure under a directory called ex0403, and proceed with the steps for the exercise. There's a solution in the CD in the file sourcecode/ch04/ex0403.war—check there if you get stuck.

Set Up the Deployment Descriptor

1. Declare a servlet named SetContextAttributes, with a suitable servlet mapping. Ensure that it loads on startup of the web server. If needed, refer to Chapter 2 to refresh yourself on `<servlet>` element setup.
2. Declare two listeners, MyContextListener and MyContextAttributeListener.

Write the SetContextAttributes Servlet

3. Create a Java source file SetContextAttributes.java in /WEB-INF/classes or an appropriate package directory. Write the class declaration in the source file, extending HttpServlet.
4. Write an `init()` method, using `System.out.println()` to send a message to the console.
5. Write a `doGet()` method, which adds, replaces, and removes one or more context attributes. Optionally, output some text on the response so that you'll know when the servlet has been called successfully (to be useful, this might list all the context attributes).

Write MyContextListener

6. Create a Java source file MyContextListener.java in /WEB-INF/classes or an appropriate package directory. Write the class declaration in the source file, implementing javax.servlet.ServletContextListener.
7. Write a `contextInitialized()` method, which sends a message to the console and creates a context attribute.
8. Write a `contextDestroyed()` method, which sends a message to the console and removes the context attribute you added in the `contextInitialized()` method.

Write MyContextAttributeListener

9. Create a Java source file MyContextAttributeListener.java in /WEB-INF/classes or an appropriate package directory. Write the class declaration in the source file, implementing javax.servlet.ServletContextAttributeListener.
10. Write an `attributeAdded()` method, which displays the name and value of the added attribute on the server console.
11. Write an `attributeReplaced()` method, which displays the name, old value, and new value of the replaced attribute on the server console.

12. Write an `attributeRemoved()` method, which displays the name and value of the removed attribute on the server console.

Deploy and Run

13. Deploy the WAR file. Check the console messages you get on deployment: Do they match what you expected to get?
14. Call the SetContextAttributes servlet with a URL such as

    ```
    http://localhost:8080/ex0403/SetContextAttributes
    ```

15. Again, check the console messages—do the methods get called in My ContextAttributeListener as you would expect?
16. Undeploy the WAR file (for instructions on how to do this for Tomcat, see Appendix B). Yet again, check the console messages. Does the `contextDestroyed()` method in MyContextListener still have access to context attributes?
17. Here is sample browser output from the SetContextAttributes servlet:

Address http://localhost:8080/ex0403/SetContextAttributes

Context Attributes

Name: javax.servlet.context.tempdir, value: C:\Program Files\Apache Software Foundation\Tomcat 5.5 \work\Catalina\localhost\ex0403
Name: attribute1, value: changed first attribute value
Name: org.apache.catalina.resources, value: org.apache.naming.resources.ProxyDirContext@6b496d
Name: servletInitAttribute, value: This attribute value added in servlet init() method.
Name: contextInitAttribute, value: Made in the ServletContextListener
Name: org.apache.catalina.WELCOME_FILES, value: [Ljava.lang.String;@1a19458

CERTIFICATION OBJECTIVE

Session Listeners (Exam Objective 4.3)

Using session listeners, write code to respond to an event when an object is added to a session, and write code to respond to an event when a session object migrates from one VM to another.

We covered request and context listeners in the last section—both those for the requests and context themselves, and separate pairs of listeners for their attributes. Now we're going to meet the set of listeners available to session objects. Because the session has—potentially—a more exciting and diverse lifetime than requests or contexts, it may not surprise you to learn that the session has some additional listener interfaces that don't occur in other scopes.

Session-Related Listeners Declared in the Deployment Descriptor

Sessions have two listeners that are equivalent in every way to the lifetime and attribute listeners we've already met for context and request:

- HttpSessionListener, which is very like ServletContextListener and Servlet RequestListener
- HttpSessionAttributeListener, which is very like ServletContextAttribute Listener and ServletRequestAttributeListener

But there are also a couple of extra listeners related to sessions— or more correctly, session attribute value objects. In a typical web application, session attributes are more numerous and volatile than the attributes attached to request or context. Consequently, the value objects that might be attached to a named session attribute can implement a couple of interfaces of their own:

- HttpSessionBindingListener receives events when a value object is used as a session attribute.
- HttpSesssionActivationListener receives events when a value object is transported across JVMs. This happens when the object is an attribute of a session in a distributed environment.

So now we'll look in a little more detail at each of these listener interfaces in turn.

HttpSessionListener

Like every other listener we have looked at so far, a class implementing HttpSession Listener must be set up in the deployment descriptor. The rules are described in the "Listener Preparation" section of the chapter.

HttpSessionListener has two methods, like its request and context counterparts—and again these fire at the beginning and end of scope. There's a nasty little difference in the naming convention for these methods, though. The method `sessionDestroyed()` matches the pattern of `requestDestroyed()` and `context Destroyed()`, and it marks the end of a session. However, the beginning of a session is marked by a `sessionCreated()` event—which doesn't follow the pattern of `requestInitalized()` and `contextInitialized()`.

Let's look at the methods in more detail.

`sessionCreated(HttpSessionEvent event)` This method is called by the web container the moment after a request first calls the `getSession()` method—in other words, whenever a new session is provided. All the subsequent `HttpServletRequest.getSession()` calls will return the same existing session—which is, of course, not a cue for firing a call to this event. The `sessionCreated()` method receives an event, of type HttpSessionEvent. This has only the one method of its own, which is `getSession()`—to return the HttpSession object that has just been created.

`sessionDestroyed(HttpSessionEvent event)` This method is called by the web container at the moment a session is about to be invalidated—within the call to `HttpSession.invalidate()`, but before the session becomes invalid and unusable. Just as for `sessionCreated()`, an HttpSessionEvent object is passed as a parameter to the method, which gives access to the about-to-be-invalidated session through its `getSession()` method. Whether the call to `HttpSession.invalidate()` comes about as a result of your own explicit call, or the web container timing out a session, the effect is the same: The `sessionDestroyed()` method will fire.

exam Watch

The behavior of this method has changed since previous versions of the exam! It used to be that the call to `sessionDestroyed()` came after the session had been invalidated. This isn't the case anymore. The method is now called before the invalidation process begins—before any attributes are stripped from the session and their corresponding life cycle events are called.

HttpSessionAttributeListener

HttpSessionAttributeListener is just like ServletRequestAttributeListener. Here are the methods to implement:

- `attributeAdded(HttpSessionBindingEvent hsbe)` is called whenever a new attribute is added to any session. In other words, any call (from any session object at any time) to `HttpSession.setAttribute()` will trigger a call to this method—provided that the name of the attribute being added to the session is a not a name already in use as an attribute of that session.

- `attributeRemoved(HttpSessionBindingEvent srae)` is called whenever an attribute is removed from any session (as a result of any call to `HttpSession.removeAttribute()`).
- `attributeReplaced(HttpSessionBindingEvent srae)` is called whenever an attribute is replaced (as a result of any call to `HttpSession.setAttribute()` for an attribute name already in use on the session whose call this is).

Again, the event object passed as parameter—this time HttpSessionBindingEvent—serves as a conduit to the name and value of the attribute affected, through the `getName()` and `getValue()` methods—see the notes above on ServletContextAttributeEvent and ServletRequestAttributeEvent for a full explanation: The rules are the same. You might expect HttpSessionBindingEvent to inherit from HttpSessionEvent—following the pattern of ServletContextAttributeEvent inheriting from ServletContextEvent and ServletRequestAttributeEvent inheriting from ServletRequestEvent—and indeed it does. See the comparative inheritance hierarchies in Figure 4-3.

FIGURE 4-3

Comparative Inheritance Hierarchies for Event Classes

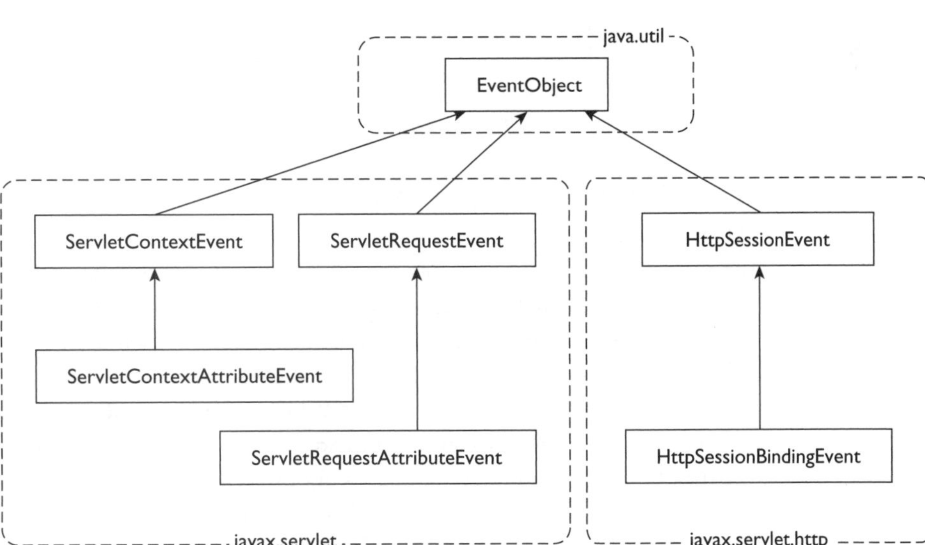

Most of the time, you can rely on listeners and events having matching names. So* HttpSession*Listener* *goes with* HttpSession*Event*, Servlet Request*Listener goes with* Servlet Request*Event, and* ServletContext Attribute*Listener goes with* Servlet ContextAttribute*Event. But there's a mismatch for HttpSessionAttributeListener. Its methods take an HttpSession*Binding *Event as a parameter. HttpSession* Attribute*Event does not exist—except in fallacious exam answers!

Session-Related Listeners Not Declared in the Deployment Descriptor

Now we move on to two other session-related listeners which are different in character to the listeners we have previously encountered, whether on session, request, or context. These listeners are:

- HttpSessionBindingListener
- HttpSessionActivationListener

Classes implementing these listener interfaces are *not* declared in the deployment descriptor. They become known to the web container through a different mechanism entirely. We learn about this and other aspects of session binding and activation listeners in the following sections.

HttpSessionBindingListener

HttpSessionBindingListener is the next listener interface we'll consider. It's very easy to misunderstand its function and confuse it with HttpSessionAttributeListener. You'll see that its methods even receive the same kinds of event, namely HttpSession BindingEvent (so this time, the name of the event does match the listener name). However, this listener is *not* declared in the deployment descriptor web.xml. Instead, it's implemented by an object you intend to use as the "value" parameter in a call to `HttpSession.setAttribute(String name, Object value)`. So whereas any HttpSessionAttributeListener classes are funnels for any update to any attribute on any session, an HttpSessionBindingListener class has methods that are called only on the individual object being used as a session attribute. Let's first find out what the methods are and next see an example of HttpSessionBindingListener:

- `valueBound(HttpSessionBindingEvent hsbe)` is called whenever the object implementing the interface is the value object passed to an `HttpSession .setAttribute()` call.
- `valueUnbound(HttpSessionBindingEvent hsbe)` is called whenever the object implementing the interface is removed from the session as a result of an `HttpSession.removeAttribute()` call.

Now let's look at the full code for a class that implements HttpSessionBinding Listener. It's called SessionAttrObject: It has one private instance variable (a String called *data*) and prints this to the console when the `valueBound()` or `valueUnbound()` methods are called:

```
public class SessionAttrObject implements HttpSessionBindingListener {
  private String data;
  public SessionAttrObject(String value) {
      data = value;
  }
  public String getData() {return data;}
  public String toString() {return data;}
  public void setData(String data) {
      this.data = data;
  }
  public void valueBound(HttpSessionBindingEvent event) {
    System.out.println("valueBound() call on object " + getData());
  }
  public void valueUnbound(HttpSessionBindingEvent event) {
      System.out.println("valueUnbound() call on object " + getData());
  }
}
```

Let's now consider some servlet code that adds, replaces, and removes session attributes—some of whose values are of type SessionAttrObject:

```
SessionAttrObject boundObject1 = new SessionAttrObject("Prometheus1");
SessionAttrObject boundObject2 = new SessionAttrObject("Prometheus2");
HttpSession session = request.getSession();
session.setAttribute("bound", boundObject1);
session.setAttribute("bound2", boundObject2);
session.setAttribute("nonBound", "Icarus");
session.setAttribute("bound", boundObject2);
session.setAttribute("bound", null);
session.removeAttribute("bound2");
session.removeAttribute("nonBound");
```

The output when we execute this code (on the console) looks something like this (line numbers don't appear—they're for reference in the text):

```
>B>B> valueBound() called for object Prometheus1
>B>B> valueBound() called for object Prometheus2
>B>B> valueBound() called for object Prometheus2
>U>U> valueUnbound() called for object Prometheus1
>U>U> valueUnbound() called for object Prometheus2
>U>U> valueUnbound() called for object Prometheus2
```

How does this work? Let's consider what happens in the lines of code:

- In lines 11 and 12, we create two local variables—*boundObject1* and *bound Object2*— of our new HttpSessionBindingListener-implementing class, Session AttrObject.
- At line 13, we obtain the session.
- At line 14, we set up a new attribute called *bound* and use *boundObject1* as the value for this. This triggers a call to the `valueBound()` method for *boundObject1* (first line of output).
- At line 15, we set up a new attribute called *bound2* and use *boundObject2* as the value for this. This triggers a call to the `valueBound()` method, this time for *boundObject2* (second line of output).
- At line 16, we set up another new attribute called *nonBound* and use a plain String literal as a value for this. There are no listener calls at this point; unsurprisingly, String doesn't implement HttpSessionBindingListener.
- At line 17, we change our first attribute. We replace the existing value (*bound Object1*) with a different value (*boundObject2*). This causes two lines of output. The `valueBound()` method is called for *boundObject2*— sensible enough, as it's being bound to another attribute (third line of output). And because *bound Object1* is displaced from this attribute, there's a call to valueUnbound for *boundObject1* (fourth line of output). So at this point, *boundObject1* isn't tied to any session attribute, but *boundObject2* is tied both to the *bound* and *bound2* attributes.
- At line 18, we remove session attribute *bound* by setting its associated value to **null**, which has the same effect as a `removeAttribute()` call. So *boundObject2* is no longer associated with attribute *bound*, and as a result its `valueUnbound()` method fires (fifth line of output).

- At line 19, we remove session attribute *bound2* with a straight (no chaser) call to `removeAttribute()`. Now *boundObject* is no longer associated with *bound2*, and its `valueUnbound()` method is called again (sixth and last line of output).
- At line 20, we remove the *nonBound* attribute with its plain String value; this has no effect in terms of calls on HttpSessionBindingListener-implementing classes.

exam watch

What happens if you have one or more objects implementing HttpSessionBindingListener, and have an HttpSessionAttributeListener defined in the deployment descriptor as well? Both have methods that are potentially called when session attributes are added, replaced, or removed—so which is called first? The answer is that the web container must call all appropriate HttpSessionBindingListener `valueBound()` and `valueUnbound()` methods first, and only then call HttpSessionAttributeListener methods `attributeAdded()`, `attributeReplaced()`, or `attributeRemoved()`.

exam watch

All listener classes (and that's request and context ones as well as session) have to be declared in the deployment descriptor, web.xml. All, that is, except two—which the session attribute "value object" implements, not a class that is part of the container. These interfaces are HttpSessionBindingListener and HttpSessionActivationListener.

HttpSessionActivationListener

HttpSessionActivationListener is the second example of an interface that is *not* declared in the deployment descriptor. Like HttpSessionBindingListener, which we just examined, it's an interface that objects are welcome to implement if they are going to be attributes of a session. This time, however, the event methods that might be called have nothing to do with the addition, replacement, or removal of the attributes themselves. The methods are called in distributed environments, at the point where a session is moved from one JVM to another. In the source JVM, all objects bound to the session need to be serialized, and—of course—deserialized in the JVM that is the destination for the moved session. Armed with this information, we can make sense of the methods:

- `sessionWillPassivate(HttpSessionEvent hse)` is called on each implementing object bound to the session just prior to the serialization of the session (and all its attributes). In Star Trek terms, this is the point just before the characters in the transporter go fuzzy and dematerialize.
- `sessionDidActivate(HttpSessionEvent hse)` is called on each implementing object bound to the session just after deserialization of the session (and all its attributes). To press the Star Trek analogy further than it should boldly go, this is the point where the characters have lost their fuzziness and materialize on the planet's surface.

exam watch ***HttpSessionActivation Listener is yet another of those interfaces whose methods don't have a matching parameter name. HttpSessionActivation Listener methods take an HttpSession Event object as a parameter—and there's no such thing as an HttpSessionActivation Event.***

We've met HttpSessionEvent as a parameter before—it's used as the parameter for methods on the HttpSessionListener interface. So you'll no doubt recall that it has the one method—`getSession()`—which returns a handle to an HttpSession. In this case, it's the one that is either about to start or has finished migration.

There is a logical condition that any object implementing this interface must fulfill if the web container is to call the `sessionWillPassivate()` or `sessionDidActivate()` method. The object must be bound to the session as one of its current attributes. It's no good if the object has never been the subject of an `HttpSession.setAttribute()` call; equally, if it was once bound to a session but has now been removed, the HttpSessionActivationListener methods will never get called.

EXERCISE 4-4

Session Listeners and Order of Execution

In this exercise you'll write code to explore some of the session listeners. As in Exercise 4-3, where you explored the order of execution of different methods in listeners, you'll look in some detail at the more involved rules for session listeners. You'll start with code you've already seen in the "HttpSessionBindingListener" section.

Create the usual web application directory structure under a directory called ex0404, and proceed with the steps for the exercise. There's a solution in the CD in the file sourcecode/ch04/ex0404.war—check there if you get stuck.

Set Up the Deployment Descriptor

1. Declare a servlet named SetSessionAttributes, with a suitable servlet mapping. Ensure that it loads on startup of the web server. If needed, refer to Chapter 2 to refresh yourself on `<servlet>` element setup.
2. Declare two listeners, MySessionListener and MySessionAttributeListener.

Write the SessionAttrObject Object

3. Create a Java source file SessionAttrObject.java in /WEB-INF/classes or an appropriate package directory. Write the class declaration in the source file: It's a plain object (doesn't extend anything), but it should implement Http SessionBindingListener.
4. You can steal the code for this object wholesale from the "HttpSession BindingListener" section (see page 269). This contains implementations of the `valueBound()` and `valueUnbound()` methods (as required for Http SessionBindingListener), as well as a few utility methods. The object is a simple wrapper for a String, with additional listener features.

Write the SetSessionAttributes Servlet

5. Create a Java source file SetSessionAttributes.java in /WEB-INF/classes or an appropriate package directory. Write the class declaration in the source file, extending HttpServlet.
6. Write a `doGet()` method, which adds, replaces, and removes one or more SessionAttrObject instances as attributes of the session. Again, you can crib this code from the "HttpSessionBindingListener" section, but don't remove all the session attributes (so you can see what happens when the session is later destroyed).
7. Write additional code in the `doGet()` method that will terminate the session according to some trigger—a request parameter, perhaps.

Write MySessionListener

8. Create a Java source file MySessionListener.java in /WEB-INF/classes or an appropriate package directory. Write the class declaration in the source file, implementing javax.servlet.http.HttpSessionListener.
9. Write a `sessionCreated()` method, which sends a message to the console and creates a session attribute.

10. Write a `sessionDestroyed()` method, which sends a message to the console and removes the session attribute created in the `sessionCreated()` method.

Write MySessionAttributeListener

11. Create a Java source file MySessionAttributeListener.java in /WEB-INF/classes or an appropriate package directory. Write the class declaration in the source file, implementing javax.servlet.http.HttpSessionAttributeListener.
12. Write an `attributeAdded()` method, which displays the name and value of the added attribute on the server console.
13. Write an `attributeReplaced()` method, which displays the name, old value, and new value of the replaced attribute on the server console.
14. Write an `attributeRemoved()` method, which displays the name and value of the removed attribute on the server console.

Deploy and Run

15. Deploy the WAR file, and call the SetSessionAttributes servlet. You are likely to use this URL:

    `http://localhost:8080/ex0404/SetSessionAttributes`
16. Check the console messages—in particular, the order of method calls for the HttpSessionBindingListener objects and the one HttpSessionAttribute Listener object. Do the methods get called in the order you expected?
17. Terminate the session, using whatever mechanism you put into the Set SessionAttributes servlet to do so (step 7). What further listener method calls do you get, and in what order?
18. The following screen shot shows the solution code console output after pointing a browser to the URL in step 15:

```
Session created method fired...
>Add>Add> attributeAdded() with name: sessionCreatedAttribute, value; Added in s
essionCreated() method
>B>B> valueBound() called for object Prometheus1
>Add>Add> attributeAdded() with name: bound, value; Prometheus1
>B>B> valueBound() called for object Prometheus2
>Add>Add> attributeAdded() with name: bound2, value; Prometheus2
>Add>Add> attributeAdded() with name: nonBound, value; Icarus
>B>B> valueBound() called for object Prometheus2
>U>U> valueUnbound() for object Prometheus1
>Rpl>Rpl> attributeReplaced() with name: bound, OLD value; Prometheus2, NEW valu
e: Prometheus2
>U>U> valueUnbound() for object Prometheus2
>Rmv>Rmv> attributeRemoved() with name: bound, value; Prometheus2
```

19. The following screen shot shows the solution code console output after invalidating the session, which is achieved with a URL of

```
http://localhost:8080/ex0404/SetSessionAttributes?invalidate=true
```

```
Session destroyed method fired...
>>>Session attribute name nonBound, value Icarus
>>>Session attribute name sessionCreatedAttribute, value Added in sessionCreated
() method
>>>Session attribute name bound2, value Prometheus2
>Rmv>Rmv> attributeRemoved() with name: sessionCreatedAttribute, value; Added in
 sessionCreated() method
>Rmv>Rmv> attributeRemoved() with name: nonBound, value; Icarus
>U>U> valueUnbound() for object Prometheus2
>Rmv>Rmv> attributeRemoved() with name: bound2, value; Prometheus2
```

CERTIFICATION SUMMARY

In this chapter you started by learning about the session life cycle. You saw that a session is something that belongs to the HTTP world (java.servlet.http package) and doesn't have an equivalent in the "naked" servlet environment. Hence, the interface defining session behavior is called "HttpSession." You learned that sessions are obtained from the request (`HttpServletRequest.getSession()`)—perhaps not too surprisingly, for the function of a session is to tie a number of requests together.

You learned that a session is created—quite simply—when a request from a particular client (browser session) first asks for a session. At this point, you learned that the session is "new" and stays that way while the client doesn't know about the session, or if it's told about the session and refuses to join it. You saw that you test for newness of a session with the `HttpSession.isNew()` method. You then got to grips with different ways in which you can get hold of the session, dependent on whether one is there already or not. You saw that a `getSession()` call with no parameters is equivalent to a `getSession(true)` call (single boolean parameter)—and that this will create a session if one does not exist already. You then learned that a `getSession(false)` call can be used if you want only to get hold of a session if one exists already—perhaps because creation of a session can be done only in a servlet validating a user ID and password, for example.

Having seen how sessions live, you learned how they die: either through your servlet code invalidating them explicitly (`HttpSession.invalidate()`) or through a time-out mechanism. You learned about three possible time-out mechanisms. The first is a global default provided by some web container-specific mechanism. The second is in a web application's deployment descriptor—setting a time in minutes in the deployment descriptor like this: `<session-config><session-timeout>30 </session-timeout></session-config>`. The third sets a particular session's time-out in code, using the `HttpSession.setMaxInactiveInterval(int seconds)` method. You learned that a session—once invalidated—is pretty much useless: Nearly all methods, if used, will throw an IllegalStateException.

You learned that you can attach attributes to a session in very much the same way as you can for request and context scopes. You saw the boundaries of session scope: that a session is confined to a particular web application and that a Request Dispatcher call across web applications will meet a new session. You learned that session information is not strictly thread safe, for two requests can come concurrently from the same client—and that although this is unusual, you might want to take suitable precautions.

You looked then at the tracking information for sessions, and how this is passed between client and server. You saw that there is support for two principal mechanisms: cookies and URL rewriting—although you appreciated that other mechanisms are possible (such as SSL and hidden form fields). You found that cookies are the default mechanism for session support, with URL rewriting a moderately poor second. You learned that the cookie used in session support is called JSESSIONID and that the name part of the name/value pair passed in URLs is jsessionid. The uppercase/lowercase difference is significant. With cookies, you saw that there is no particular action you need to take in your code to provide support—the web container does it for you. By contrast, you learned that URL rewriting requires every link you encode in your servlets to be run through one of two methods—`HttpServletResponse.encodeURL` (for regular links) or `HttpServletResponse .endcodeRedirectURL` (for redirect links). You also saw that HttpSession has methods to determine if the session requested is supported by cookies or by URL rewriting—from the long-named `isRequestedSessionIdFromCookie()` and `isRequestedSessionIdFromURL()` methods.

From there, you left sessions for a while to explore the world of request and context listeners, followed up by session listeners. You saw that listeners are classes that implement interfaces known to the web container framework, with methods called under particular circumstances. You saw that (with a couple of exceptions we'll mention again later) listener classes are declared in the deployment descriptor—each class having a separate `<listener>` element, with a class declared like this: `<listener><listener-class>com.osborne.ListenerClassName</listener-class></listener>`. You met listeners that cover beginning and end of scope:

ServletRequestListener, HttpSessionListener, and ServletContextListener—with corresponding initialized (or created) and destroyed methods, called as the scopes begin and end. You also met listeners covering attributes attached to each scope: ServletRequestAttributeListener, HttpSessionAttributeListener, and ServletContext AttributeListener. You saw the same trio of methods on each of these listeners—for the addition, replacement, and removal of attributes.

You also learned that listener methods invariably accept a listener event class as a parameter. Each one of these listener event classes has methods that yield information about appropriate scope-level objects—such as ServletRequestEvent (with `getServletRequest()` and `getServletContext()` methods), HttpSessionEvent (with a `getSession() method`), and ServletContextEvent (with a `getServlet Context()` method). You saw how the corresponding attribute listener events inherit from the scope-level event classes: ServletRequestAttributeEvent from Servlet RequestEvent, HttpSession*Binding*Event from HttpSessionEvent, and Servlet ContextAttributeEvent from ServletContextEvent. You saw how all these attribute/binding event classes have `getName()` and `getValue()` methods—to obtain the name or value of the attribute added, removed, or replaced. It's obvious what the value is in the case of addition and removal—you saw that it is less obvious in the case of replacement, where `getValue()` gets the *old* value (the value that has been replaced).

You learned that session scope has a couple of additional listeners that are not declared in the deployment descriptor. Both are interfaces designed to be implemented by classes to be used as the values of session attributes. These are HttpSessionBindingListener, whose `valueBound()` and `valueUnbound()` methods are called on the value object as it is added or removed from use as a session attribute. You learned that calls to `HttpSession.setAttribute()` and `HttpSession .removeAttribute()` are typical triggers for calls to the methods both on HttpSessionBindingListener and HttpSessionAttributeListener—and in that case, the HttpSessionBindingListener `valueBound/Unbound()` methods are called first. You also saw that `valueBound/Unbound()` accepts the HttpSessionBinding Event as a parameter—again like the `attributeAdded/Replaced/Removed()` methods of HttpSessionAttributeListener.

Finally, you met the HttpSessionActivationListener. You found that the web container uses classes of this type for distributed applications and will call methods in this class when sessions migrate from one JVM to another. You saw that it is like the HttpSessionBindingListener, in that classes implementing this interface are intended for use as session attributes. You learned that when a session is about to be serialized (prior to migration), the web container calls the `sessionWillPassivate()`

method on each object implementing this interface that is currently attached to the session as an attribute. And you saw that when the session is deserialized in a different JVM, the web container ensures that the `sessionDidActivate()` method is called on the same set of objects. You finally learned that these methods receive an HttpSessionEvent (giving access to the session—the same parameter as received by methods on HttpSessionListener methods).

TWO-MINUTE DRILL

Session Life Cycle

- ❑ A session is begun when servlet (or filter) code invokes the `HttpServletRequest.getSession()` method.
- ❑ A session object is of type HttpSession, in the javax.servlet package. Sessions exist only in the HTTP servlet model; there is no non-HTTP equivalent such as javax.servlet.Session.
- ❑ `getSession()` can be called without parameters or with a single **boolean** parameter.
- ❑ A call to `getSession()` is equivalent to the call to `getSession(true)`. Both these calls will create a session if none exists already.
- ❑ The call `getSession(false)` will not create a session, but it will return a session if one exists already.
- ❑ A newly created session is deemed to be "new." This can be tested with the `HttpSession.isNew()` method, which returns a **boolean**—**true** for new, **false** for old.
- ❑ There are two possible conditions for "newness": Either the client doesn't know about the session yet or the client has refused to join the session.
- ❑ A session is normally confined to one web application and one JVM. However, if a web application is marked `<distributable />` in the deployment descriptor, a session may be cloned into a second running copy of the same web application, in a separate JVM.
- ❑ A session cannot cross web applications (unlike a request). A request that gets a session inside of one application, then dispatches to a different web application (different context), and then gets hold of the session in the separate application will get hold of a separate session object.
- ❑ Session death can come about through an explicit call (in servlet code) to `HttpSession.invalidate()`.
- ❑ Session death is more likely to come about through a time-out mechanism. If there is no activity on a session for a predefined length of time, the web container invalidates the session. There are three time-out mechanisms.
- ❑ Time-out mechanism 1: Most J2EE containers establish a "global default" for time-out. How this is specified and achieved is container-specific.

- Time-out mechanism 2: A web application can specify a time-out period—in minutes—in the deployment descriptor, using a `<session-timeout>` element nested inside a `<session-config>` element.
- A negative or zero value for `<session-timeout>` denotes that the session should not ever expire.
- Time-out mechanism 3: Servlet (or filter) code can override the time-out period for any individual session by calling the `HttpSession.setMaxInactiveInterval(int seconds)` method.
- A negative (but *not zero*) value as a parameter to `setMaxInactiveInterval()` denotes that the session should not expire.
- Note the difference in units: minutes in the deployment descriptor (mechanism (2)) and seconds in the HttpSession method (mechanism (3)).
- Apart from three methods, all HttpSession methods fail with an IllegalStateException if any attempt is made to use them after the session has been invalidated.
- You can attach attributes to a session (in the same way as you can for a request or context).
- Session attributes are not—strictly speaking—thread safe. It is possible to have two client windows open making concurrent requests, both sharing the same session.

Session Management

- Sessions are maintained by passing tracking information between the client and the web application server. There is no alternative, for the connection between client and server is almost always broken after each HTTP request.
- When you obtain a session (using `HttpServletRequest.getSession()`), the web container manufactures a unique ID string for the session. This is passed as a token between the client and server.
- The servlet API recognizes two mechanisms for this token-passing session management—cookies and URL rewriting—but that is not to say that these are the only two.
- Other session mechanisms you might encounter include SSL (Secure Sockets Layer) and hidden form fields.

- ❑ With cookies, the unique ID generated by the web container is embedded as the value of a cookie whose name is JSESSIONID. This name is mandated by the servlet specification and must be spelled exactly as shown (all uppercase).
- ❑ Cookies are the preferred mechanism for J2EE web container session management. Where they can't be used (because the client doesn't support them or has switched off cookies because of privacy concerns), URL rewriting is used instead.
- ❑ With URL rewriting, every HTML link written by a servlet has the unique session ID embedded in the URL itself. The session information is in the form of a name/value pair: *jsessionid=1A2B3C4D* (etc.). The name is always *jsessionid*, spelled exactly as shown (all lowercase).
- ❑ URL rewriting looks very much like parameter passing in the query string, except that the *jsessionid=1A2B3C4D* part comes after a semicolon instead of the question mark denoting the query string. This example shows the session ID appearing before the query string: `http://localhost:8080/ex0402;jsessionid=1A2B3C4D?user=david`.
- ❑ As a servlet code developer, you put any URL for HTML links through the method `HttpServletResponse.encodeURL(String myURL)`. This returns your URL with *jsessionid* information inserted—but only when necessary (if cookies are used, there is no need).
- ❑ URLs that act as parameters for the `HttpServletResponse.sendRedirect()` method should use the `HttpServletResponse.encodeRedirectURL()` method to insert *jsessionid* information. The rules for when its appropriate to insert *jsessionid* may be different from those used in `HttpServletResponse.encodeURL(String myURL)`.
- ❑ The HttpServletRequest object can determine which standard session mechanism is in use through the methods `isRequestedSessionIdFromCookie()` and `isRequestedSessionIdFromURL()`. Both methods return a **boolean**.

Request and Context Listeners

- ❑ Listeners are part of the web container model. They work in much the same way as listeners in the Swing user interface environment. For both frameworks (web containers and Swing), the listener methods are called in response to relevant events (examples: for Swing, a mouse movement; for the web container, an attribute added).

- There are listeners pertinent to every scope.
- Nearly all listeners (with a couple of exceptions we cover in the session section) should be declared in the deployment descriptor.
- The `<listener>` element has the root element `<web-app>` for its parent. Within the `<listener>` element, you include a `<listener-class>` element—the value for this is the fully qualified class name of a class implementing one or more listener interfaces.
- You need one `<listener>` (with embedded `<listener-class>`) for each listener class you wish to declare in the deployment descriptor.
- Request scope possesses two sorts of listener: ServletRequestListener and ServletRequestAttributeListener. Both of these are interfaces in the javax .servlet package.
- ServletRequestListener listens for the life and death of each request. The corresponding methods called on these events are `requestInitialized()` and `requestDestroyed()`.
- The call to `requestInitalized()` comes at the point where a client request is about to reach its target servlet's `service()` method (or alternatively, where the client request is about to reach the first filter's `doFilter()` method, if the request is intercepted by a filter chain).
- The call to `requestDestroyed()` comes at the point where the request's target servlet `service()` method ends (or alternatively, where the first filter in a chain reaches the end of its `doFilter()` method, with the first filter in the chain being the last to finish executing).
- These methods receive a ServletRequestEvent object as a parameter. From this you can obtain the ServletRequest itself (with `getServletRequest()`) or obtain the web application context (with `getServletContext()`).
- The ServletRequestAttributeListener listens—as you might expect—for any update to the attributes attached to a request.
- A call to `ServletRequest.setAttribute()` with a new name causes a call to the `attributeAdded()` method on ServletRequestAttributeListener.
- A call to `ServletRequest.setAttribute()` with an existing name causes a call to the `attributeReplaced()` method on ServletRequestAttribute Listener.

- A call to `ServletRequest.removeAttribute()` (or `ServletRequest.setAttribute()`with a **null** value) with an existing name causes a call to the `attributeRemoved()` method on ServletRequestAttributeListener.
- Each of the `attributeAdded/Replaced/Removed()` methods receives a ServletRequestAttributeEvent object as a parameter.
- ServletRequestAttributeEvent inherits from ServletRequestEvent (giving access to methods to get at the request and the context). The class also adds two methods of its own: `getName()` and `getValue()` (which return the String name or Object value for the attribute in question).
- `getValue()` returns the *old* value of the attribute in the `attributeReplaced()` method.
- Context (web application) scope possesses two sorts of listener: ServletContextListener and ServletContextAttributeListener. Both of these are interfaces in the javax.servlet package.
- ServletContextListener listens for the life and death of each request. The corresponding methods called on these events are `contextInitialized()` and `contextDestroyed()`.
- The call to `contextInitalized()` comes at the point where a web application starts up, before any request has been processed by a filter's `init()` method or a servlet's `service()` method.
- The call to `contextDestroyed()` comes at the point where a web application is taken out of service. This could be because of the controlled close-down of the server or because the server allows the application to be taken out of service. Every filter and servlet `destroy()` method must execute before this method is called.
- These methods receive a ServletContextEvent object as a parameter. From this you can obtain the ServletContext itself (with `getServletContext()`).
- The ServletContextAttributeListener listens for any update to the attributes attached to a context.
- This listener works in just the same way as ServletRequestAttributeListener: Review the rules above for this and substitute "Context" for "Request" as appropriate.
- The parameter to the listener methods is a ServletContextAttributeEvent object; this inherits from ServletContextEvent (giving access to the `get`

`ServletContext()` method). Following the request pattern, this class adds two methods of its own: `getName()` and `getValue()` (which return the String name or Object value for the attribute in question).

Session Listeners

- There are four listeners related to sessions.
- HttpSessionListener: very like ServletContextListener and ServletRequest Listener.
- HttpSessionAttributeListener: very like ServletContextAttributeListener and ServletRequestAttributeListener.
- Also HttpSessionBindingListener and HttpSessionActivationListener, which have no counterpart in request and context scope.
- Classes implementing HttpSessionListener and HttpSessionAttributeListener should be set up in the deployment descriptor (like request and context scope listeners).
- Classes implementing HttpSessionBindingListener and HttpSession ActivationListener are intended for use by objects that are used as attribute values on a session, and are *not* declared in the deployment descriptor.
- HttpSessionListener has `sessionCreated()` and `sessionDestroyed()` methods, designed to be called at the beginning and end of a session's life.
- `sessionCreated()` is called when a request from a particular client first asks for a session.
- `sessionDestroyed()` is called when a session object is explicitly invalidated in servlet code (through the `HttpSession.invalidate()` method) or when the web container times the session out because there have been no requests for it for a predefined length of time.
- An HttpSessionEvent object is passed as a parameter to these two methods—this has a `getSession()` method to access the session.
- The HttpSession object is still accessible with all its attributes in the `sessionDestroyed()` method through the HttpSessionEvent object passed as a parameter. This is a change from past implementations of the servlet specification.
- HttpSessionAttributeListener works in the same way as ServletRequest AttributeListener and ServletContextAttributeListener. It has the same

three methods—`attributeAdded/Replaced/Removed()`—called in the same circumstances (but obviously for session attributes, not request or context).

- The parameter passed to these three methods is an HttpSessionBindingEvent object. Like ServletRequestAttributeEvent and ServletContextAttribute Event, this provides `getName()` and `getValue()` methods—which work in the same way.
- HttpSessionBindingEvent inherits from HttpSessionEvent, though which it has a `getSession()` method—to get at the session object whose attributes are affected.
- HttpSessionBindingListener is an interface defined by objects that are used as the values of attributes attached to a session.
- It has two methods: `valueBound()` and `valueUnbound()`.
- `valueBound()` is called when an object is attached as an attribute to a session.
- `valueUnbound()` is called when an object is removed as an attribute from a session.
- These methods on HttpSessionBindingListener are called before any methods on any HttpSessionAttributeListener (which are often triggered by the same events).
- These methods also receive an HttpSessionBindingEvent as a parameter—just as the HttpSessionAttributeListener methods do.
- The fourth and final listener interface for sessions is HttpSessionActivation Listener.
- This has two methods: `sessionWillPassivate()` and `sessionDid Activate()`.
- Both methods receive an HttpSessionEvent object as a parameter (discussed above—this type is a parameter for HttpSessionListener methods as well).
- `sessionWillPassivate()` is called just before a session is serialized to be cloned to another JVM.
- `sessionDidActivate()` is called just after a cloned session is deserialized in a target JVM.

SELF TEST

The following questions will help you measure your understanding of the material presented in this chapter. Read all the choices carefully because there might be more than one correct answer. The number of correct choices to make is stated in the question, as in the real SCWCD exam.

Session Life Cycle

1. (drag-and-drop question) A complete `doGet()` method for a servlet is listed next. Match the circumstances in which the servlet is called with the possible outputs (there are more possible outputs listed than are needed, and any of the possible outputs may be used more than once).

```
protected void doGet(HttpServletRequest request,
  HttpServletResponse response)
  throws ServletException, IOException {
  PrintWriter out = response.getWriter();
  response.setContentType("text/html");
  out.write("<HTML><HEAD>");
  out.write("<TITLE>Session Aspects</TITLE>");
  out.write("</HEAD><BODY>");
  HttpSession session = request.getSession();
  out.write("<BR />" + session.isNew());
  out.write("<BR />" + request.isRequestedSessionIdFromURL());
  out.write("<BR />" + request.isRequestedSessionIdFromCookie());
  out.write("</BODY></HTML>");
}
```

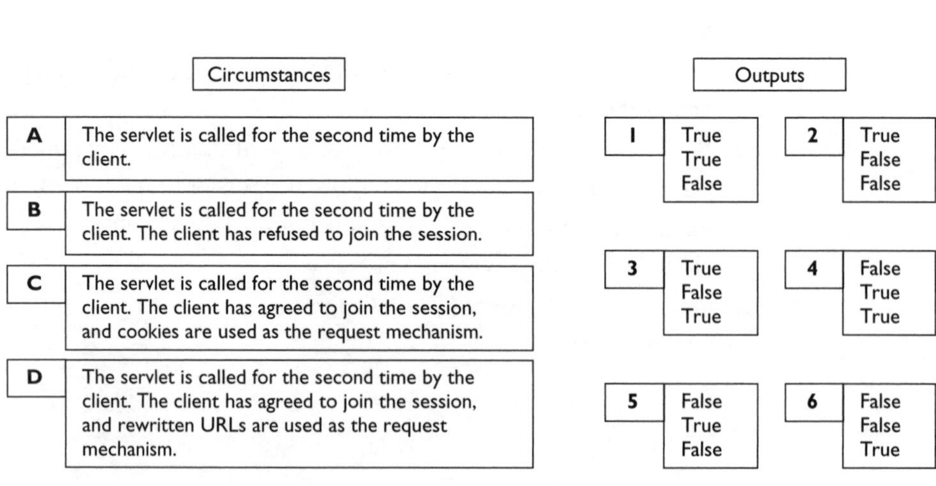

Circumstances
A The servlet is called for the second time by the client.
B The servlet is called for the second time by the client. The client has refused to join the session.
C The servlet is called for the second time by the client. The client has agreed to join the session, and cookies are used as the request mechanism.
D The servlet is called for the second time by the client. The client has agreed to join the session, and rewritten URLs are used as the request mechanism.
Outputs
1 True True False
2 True False False
3 True False True
4 False True True
5 False True False
6 False False True

2. What is the outcome of attempting to compile, deploy, and run the following servlet code? Line numbers are for reference only and should not be considered part of the code. (Choose one.)

```
10 import java.io.*;
11 import javax.servlet.*;
12 import javax.servlet.http.*;
13 public class Question2 extends HttpServlet {
14   protected void doGet(ServletRequest request,
15     ServletResponse response) throws ServletException, IOException {
16   HttpSession session = request.getSession(false);
17   session.invalidate();
18   session.setAttribute("illegal", "exception thrown"");
19 }
20 }
```

A. Won't compile

B. NullPointerException at line 16 on client's first call to servlet

C. IllegalStateException at line 18

D. Some other runtime exception

E. None of the above

3. Identify the two equivalent method calls in the list below. (Choose two.)

A. `HttpServletRequest.getSession()`

B. `ServletRequest.getSession()`

C. `ServletRequest.getSession(true)`

D. `HttpServletRequest.getSession(false)`

E. `ServletRequest.getSession(false)`

F. `HttpServletRequest.getSession(true)`

G. `HttpServletRequest.getSession("true")`

H. `ServletRequest.getSession("false")`

4. Identify true statements about sessions from the list below. (Choose two.)

A. Sessions can span web applications.

B. Sessions can be cloned across JVMs.

C. Sessions are destroyed only after a predefined period of inactivity.

D. Sessions can be set to never time out.

E. You can use the deployment descriptor to cause sessions to expire after a set number of requests.

5. Which of the following mechanisms will guarantee that every session in a web application will expire after 1 minute? You can assume that for each answer below, this is the only session time-out mechanism in force for the web application. (Choose two.)

   A. In the deployment descriptor:

   ```
   <session-config>
     <session-timeout>1</session-timeout>
   </session-config>
   ```

   B. In the deployment descriptor:

   ```
   <session-config>
   <session-timeout>60</session-timeout>
   </session-config>
   ```

   C. In the `doFilter()` method of a filter that has the following `<url-pattern>` mapping in the deployment descriptor: "/." *request* is an instance of HttpServletRequest, cast from the ServletRequest parameter passed to the method.

   ```
   HttpSession session = request.getSession();
   session.setMaxInactiveInterval(60);
   ```

   D. In the `doGet()` method of a servlet. *request* is an instance of HttpServletRequest, passed as a parameter to the method.

   ```
   HttpSession session = request.getSession();
   session.setMaxInactiveInterval(1);
   ```

   E. In the `init()` method of a servlet that loads on start up of the web application. *request* is an instance of HttpServletRequest, passed as a parameter to the method.

   ```
   HttpSession session = request.getSession();
   session.setMaxInactiveInterval(60);
   ```

Session Management

6. Identify the default mechanism for session management from the list below. (Choose one.)

   A. URL rewriting

   B. Hidden Form Fields

   C. Cookies

D. SSL

E. jsessionId request parameter

7. Identify correct statements about session management from the list below. (Choose two.)

   A. Session management is usually dependent on a hidden form field called *JSessionId*.

   B. The unique identifier for a session may be passed back and forward through a name/value pair in the URL. The name is *jsessionid*.

   C. If a cookie used for default session management, there is some flexibility with the name used for the cookie.

   D. The cookie used for default session management must be added to the response using the `HttpServletResponse.addCookie(Cookie theCookie)` method.

   E. The rules for rewriting URLs for links may be different from those for rewriting URLs for redirection.

8. (drag-and-drop question) In the following illustration, match the concealed parts of the code (lettered) with appropriate choices (numbered) on the right.

```
protected void doGet([        A        ]
 request, [        B        ] response) throws
 ServletException, IOException {

 PrintWriter out = response.getWriter();
 response.setContentType("text/html");
 out.write("<HTML><HEAD>");
 out.write("<TITLE>Session Aspects</TITLE>");
 out.write("</HEAD><BODY>");
 [   C   ]session = request.[     D     ];
 out.write("\n<P>Session id is <B>" +
  session.[ E ] + "</B>.</P>");
 if (request.isRequestedSessionIdFromCookie())
 {
   out.write("\n<P>Session id comes from
    cookie [   F   ].</P>");
 }
 if (request.[              G              ])
 {
   out.write("\n<P>Session id comes from
    URL element [   H   ].</P>");
 }
 String URL = response.encodeURL("Q8");
 out.write("\n<P><A HREF=" + URL
 + ">Link to summon this servlet again.</A>");
 out.write("</BODY></HTML>");
}
```

1	`HttpSession`
2	`Session`
3	`ServletRequest`
4	`HttpServletRequest`
5	`getSession()`
6	`HttpServletRespons`
7	`getHttpSession()`
8	`JSESSIONID`
9	`isRequestedSessionIdFromURL()`
10	`jsessionid`
11	`isRequestedSessionIdFromUrl()`
12	`ServletResponse`
13	`getSessionID()`
14	`getId()`

9. Given the following servlet code called with this URL—`http://127.0.0.1:8080/examp0402/Q9`—and also given that URL rewriting is the session mechanism in force, identify the likely output from the servlet from the choices below. (Choose one.)

```
PrintWriter out = response.getWriter();
response.setContentType("text/html");
out.write("<HTML><HEAD>");
out.write("<TITLE>Encoding URLs</TITLE>");
out.write("</HEAD><BODY>");
HttpSession session = request.getSession();
out.write("\n<P>Session id is <B>"
  + session.getId() + "</B>.</P>");
String URL1 = response.encodeURL("Q9");
String URL2 = response.encodeURL
  ("http://127.0.0.1:8080/examp0401/Q1");
out.write("\n<P>URL1: " + URL1 + "</P>");
out.write("\n<P>URL2: " + URL2 + "</P>");
out.write("</BODY></HTML>");
```

A. Output:

Session ID is **4EDF861942E3539B1F3C101B71636C1A**.

URL1: Q9;JSESSIONID=4EDF861942E3539B1F3C101B71636C1A

URL2: http://127.0.0.1:8080/examp0401/Q1

B. Output:

Session ID is **4EDF861942E3539B1F3C101B71636C1A**.

URL1: Q9

URL2: http://127.0.0.1:8080/examp0401/Q1? jsessionid=4EDF861942E3539B1F3C101B71636C1A

C. Output:

Session ID is **4EDF861942E3539B1F3C101B71636C1A**.

URL1: Q9;jsessionid=4EDF861942E3539B1F3C101B71636C1A

URL2: http://127.0.0.1:8080/examp0401/Q1

D. Output:

Session ID is **4EDF861942E3539B1F3C101B71636C1A**.

URL1: Q9;jsessionid=4EDF861942E3539B1F3C101B71636C1A

URL2: http://127.0.0.1:8080/examp0401/Q1;jsessionid=4EDF861942E3539B1F3C101B71636C1A

E. Output:

Session ID is **4EDF861942E3539B1F3C101B71636C1A**.

URL1: Q9?JSESSIONID=4EDF861942E3539B1F3C101B71636C1A

URL2: http://127.0.0.1:8080/examp0401/Q1

10. Which of the following statements contain accurate advice for web developers? (Choose two.)
    - A. Because the server determines the session mechanism, there is no need to rewrite URLs when cookies are switched on.
    - B. Rewrite every URL embedded in your servlets and JSP code with the `HttpServletResponse.encodeURL()` method.
    - C. Cookies are not necessarily supported by J2EE-compliant web containers, so always use URL rewriting as an additional precaution.
    - D. Because the client determines whether cookies are permitted or not, it's a good idea always to encode URLs as a fallback session mechanism.
    - E. Static pages in your web application can disrupt session management.

Request and Context Listeners

11. Identify actions that won't fix a potential problem in the following ServletRequestListener code. (Choose two.)

```
01 public void requestDestroyed(ServletRequestEvent reqEvent) {
02 HttpServletRequest request = (HttpServletRequest)
03   reqEvent.getServletRequest();
04 HttpSession session = request.getSession();
05 session.setAttribute("name","value");
06 }
```

- A. Ensure that an HttpSession is created in the `requestInitialized()` method of the same ServletRequestListener.
- B. Ensure that any servlet in your web application obtains a session.
- C. Substitute the code below for lines 04 and 05:

```
HttpSession session = request.getSession(false);
if (session != null) session.setAttribute("name", "value");
```

- D. Take no action, for the code will work in all circumstances.
- E. Place lines 04 and 05 inside a try/catch block.

12. What is the outcome of attempting to compile and run the servlet code below? (Choose one.)

```
import java.io.*;
import javax.servlet.*;
import javax.servlet.http.*;
public class Question12 extends HttpServlet {
  protected void doGet(HttpServletRequest request,
    HttpServletResponse response)
    throws ServletException, IOException {
    ServletContext context = getServletContext();
    context.addAttribute("mutable", "firstvalue");
    context.replaceAttribute("mutable", "secondvalue");
    context.removeAttribute("mutable");
    context.removeAttribute("mutable");
  }
}
```

A. There will be three method calls to any ServletContextAttributeListener classes registered to the web application.

B. An exception will be thrown on trying to remove the same attribute for a second time.

C. There will be four method calls to any ServletContextAttributeListener classes registered to the web application.

D. An exception will be thrown if the context cannot be obtained.

E. None of the above.

13. Identify true statements about listener interfaces and related classes from the list below. (Choose three.)

A. It is possible to add context attributes in the `contextDestroyed()` method.

B. During controlled closedown of a web application, the last listener whose methods are potentially called is the ServletContextListener.

C. You can access the current session from methods in classes implementing the Servlet RequestListener interface.

D. You can access the current session from methods in classes implementing the Servlet ContextAttributeListener interface.

E. The ServletContextAttributeEvent class extends java.util.EventObject.

F. It is unwise to change request attributes in the `attributeReplaced()` method of a class implementing the ServletRequestAttributeListener interface.

14. Identify the number and nature of the errors in the code below, which is taken from a class implementing the ServletRequestAttributeListener interface. (Choose one.)

```
public void attributeAdded(ServletRequestAttributeEvent event) {
  HttpServletRequest request = event.getServletRequest();
  Object o = event.getSource();
  System.out.println("Source of event is: "
    + o.getClass().getName());
  String name = event.getName();
  String value = event.getValue();
  System.out.println("In ServletRequestAttributeListener."
    + "attributeAdded() with name: "
    + name + ", value; " + value);
}
```

A. No compilation errors, no runtime errors

B. No compilation errors, one runtime error

C. One compilation error

D. Two compilation errors

E. Three compilation errors

15. If a request attribute has been replaced, which of the following techniques will not obtain the current (new) value of the attribute? (Choose two.)

A. Use the `ServletRequest.getAttribute()` method anywhere in servlet code following the replacement.

B. Use the `ServletRequestAttributeEvent.getValue()` method anywhere in the `attributeReplaced()` method of a class implementing ServletRequestAttributeListener.

C. Use the `ServletRequest.getAttribute()` method anywhere in filter code following the replacement.

D. Use the following code in a class implementing ServletRequestAttributeListener:

```
public void attributeReplaced(ServletRequestAttributeEvent event) {
  String name = event.getName();
  Object newValue = event.getServletRequest().getAttribute(name);
}
```

E. Use the `ServletRequestAttributeEvent.getValue()` method anywhere in the `attributeUpdated()` method of a class implementing ServletRequestAttributeListener.

Session Listeners

16. The code below is from a class implementing the HttpSessionListener interface (you can assume that the whole class compiles successfully). What will happen when the class is deployed in a web application and servlet code requests a session? (Choose one.)

```
public void sessionInitialized(HttpSessionEvent event) {
  System.out.println("Session Initialized...");
  HttpSession session = event.getSession();
  Boolean loginOK = (Boolean) session.getAttribute("login");
  if (loginOK == null || !loginOK.booleanValue()) {
      session.invalidate();
  }
}
```

A. A runtime exception.
B. Session will be invalidated dependent on the "login" attribute.
C. Session will always be invalidated.
D. Can't determine what will happen.

The code below shows code for the class MySessionAttribute (Listing A). An instance of this class is attached to an HttpSession (Listing B). From the list below, pick out the things that will happen when this session is migrated from a source JVM to a target JVM. (Choose four.)

```
LISTING A
import java.io.*;
import javax.servlet.http.*;
public class MySessionAttribute implements
  HttpSessionActivationListener, Serializable {
  private static String data;
  public String getData() { return data; }
  public void setData(String newData) {
      data = newData;
  }
  public void sessionWillPassivate(HttpSessionEvent arg0) {
      System.out.println(data);
  }
  public void sessionDidActivate(HttpSessionEvent arg0) {
      System.out.println(data);
  }
}
```

```
LISTING B
import java.io.*;
import javax.servlet.*;
import javax.servlet.http.*;
```

```
public class TestMySessionAttribute extends HttpServlet {
  protected void doGet(HttpServletRequest request,
  HttpServletResponse response) throws ServletException, IOException {
        HttpSession session = request.getSession();
        MySessionAttribute msa = new MySessionAttribute();
        msa.setData("My Data");
    }
}
```

A. `sessionWillPassivate()` method called in the source JVM
B. `sessionWillPassivate()` method called in the target JVM
C. `sessionDidActivate()` method called in the source JVM
D. `sessionDidActivate()` method called in the target JVM
E. "My data" written to the source JVM's web server console
F. "My data" not written to the source JVM's web server console
G. "My data" written to the target JVM's web server console
H. "My data" not written to the source JVM's web server console

18. (drag-and-drop question) Match the lettered missing pieces of code with choices from the numbered list. The choices may be used more than once.

```
import [    A    ].*;
public class SessionAttrListener implements
HttpSession[    B    ] {
public void
attributeAdded([    C    ] event)
{
    String name = [    D    ];
    String value = "" + [    E    ];
  }
public void
attributeRemoved([    F    ]
event) {
}
public void
attributeReplaced([    G    ]
event) {
  HttpSession session = event.[    H    ];
  String newValue = "" +
session.[    I    ](name);
  }
}
```

1	`event.getValue()`
2	`getAttribute`
3	`getValue`
4	`HttpSessionAttributeEvent`
5	`AttrListener`
6	`event.getName()`
7	`getSession()`
8	`javax.servlet.http`
9	`HttpSession`
10	`HttpSesssionBindingEvent`
11	`AttributeListener`
12	`javax.servlet`
13	`getSessionID()`
14	`Listener`
15	`getHttpSession()`

19. Pick out true statements from the list below. (Choose two.)

A. Classes implementing HttpSessionBindingListener must be declared in the deployment descriptor.

B. More than one session listener interface may take effect from the same deployment descriptor declaration.

C. HttpSessionAttributeEvent is a parameter for methods on more than one of the session listener interfaces.

D. A single class cannot implement both the interfaces ServletRequestAttributeListener and HttpSessionAttributeListener.

E. `sessionDidPassivate()` is one of the methods of the HttpSessionActivationListener interface.

F. An HttpSessionListener's `sessionDestroyed()` method will be called as a result of a client refusing to join a session.

20. A web application houses an HttpSessionAttributeListener and an object (SessionAttrObject) that implements HttpSessionBindingListener. Pick out the correct sequence of listener method calls that follows from executing l the servlet code below inside this web application. (Choose one.)

```
import java.io.*;
import javax.servlet.*;
import javax.servlet.http.*;
public class Question20 extends HttpServlet {
  protected void doGet(HttpServletRequest request,
    HttpServletResponse response) throws ServletException, IOException {
    HttpSession session = request.getSession();
    session.invalidate();
    HttpSession newSession = request.getSession();
    SessionAttrObject boundObject = new SessionAttrObject("value");
    newSession.setAttribute("name", boundObject);
    newSession.setAttribute("name", "value");
    newSession.setAttribute("name", null);
  }
}
```

A. `attributeAdded(), valueBound(), attributeRemoved(), valueUnbound(), attributeReplaced(), attributeRemoved()`

B. `valueBound(), attributeAdded(), valueUnbound(), attributeRemoved(), attributeReplaced(), attributeRemoved()`

C. `valueBound(), attributeAdded(), valueUnbound(), attributeReplaced(), attributeRemoved()`

D. `attributeAdded(), valueBound(), attributeReplaced(), valueUnbound(), attributeReplaced()`

E. `valueBound(), attributeAdded(), valueUnbound(), attributeRemoved(), valueBound(), attributeAdded(), valueUnbound(), attributeRemoved()`

F. None of the above.

LAB QUESTION

Let's use the skills you have learned in this chapter for a practical purpose—well, nearly practical! You're going to design a memory game. Someone setting up the game will use your application to type in ten words. These are presented back in the order in which they were entered.

The person playing the game signs on to a fresh browser session. She has an allotted number of seconds to remember the words and their order. She presses a button to begin the game. After she tries her best guess at the words, the application tells her how well she has done.

Some technical suggestions on achieving this: The words put in by the person setting up the game might be transferred from request parameters to session attributes—or a single session attribute whose value is a collection class, maintaining the order of the words entered. When the setup is done, transfer the session attribute(s) to context attribute(s). Make this happen as a consequence of invaliding the session, doing the transfer in an HttpSessionListener's `sessionDestroyed()` method. When playing the game, the request parameters (for the guesses) can again be transferred to session attributes. On conclusion of the game, compare the session attributes with the context attributes to come up with a mark.

Feel free to add as much needless complexity as you like. For example, you could pass each request parameter to a request attribute, listen for the removal of the request attribute, and transfer the word to a session attribute. This is just to explore the capacities of listener classes in preparation for the exam—in your real development life, keep it simple!

SELF TEST ANSWERS

Session Life Cycle

1. ☑ **A** matches to output **2**. The session is new, and because it's newly established by the web container, the `isRequestedSessionId*` methods both return false. **B** matches to output **2** also; if the session is refused by the client, it is still new—and the session ID can't come from a URL or cookie (it hasn't been returned by the client). **C** matches to output **6**; the session is not new (it's the second request). Because the ID has been returned with a cookie, the session is not from a URL and is from a cookie—so false, false, true. **D** matches to output **5**; the session is again not new (false output), and the session has come from a URL (true output) and not a cookie (false output).
   ☒ All other combinations are wrong, as shown by the reasoning for the correct answers.

2. ☑ **A** is the correct answer: The code will not compile. The parameters of the `doGet` method are defined as types ServletRequest and ServletResponse—not HttpServletRequest and HttpServletResponse. Hence, when at line 16 the code tries to get a session from the request, there's a compiler error saying that ServletRequest has no such method (all the session infrastructure is part of the javax.servlet.http package).
   ☒ **B** is incorrect but sounds plausible; however, even if the compiler error were corrected, the NullPointerException would occur at line 17 (when the code might try to use a null session reference). **C** is incorrect but would be true if the compiler error were corrected: An Illegal StateException would result from trying to use `setAttribute()` on an invalidated session. **D** is incorrect because we never get as far as any runtime exception. **E** is excluded because **A** fits the bill here.

3. ☑ **A** and **F** are the correct answers. A call to `HttpServletRequest.getSession()` with no parameters is equivalent to a call to `HttpServletRequest.getSession(true)`. Both calls will create a session if none exists already.
   ☒ **B**, **C**, **E**, and **H** are incorrect and can be dismissed straightaway, because the method for retrieving sessions is associated with HttpServletRequest, not ServletRequest. **D** is incorrect—a call to `HttpServletRequest.getSession(false)` is the odd one out—and under these circumstances, a session will not be created; the method obtains a session only if there is one already. **G** is incorrect because `HttpServletRequest.getSession()` does not accept a String parameter.

4. ☑ **B** and **D** are the correct answers. In distributed applications, session objects are cloned across JVMs. And sessions can be set to never time out, using `HttpSession.setMaxInactive`

`Interval()` with a negative parameter or using a zero or negative number as the value for the `<session-timeout>` element in the deployment descriptor.
☒ **A** is incorrect: Session objects are scoped to a single web application. **C** is incorrect because you can use code to explicitly invalidate a session as well as allowing its destruction after a predefined period of inactivity. **E** is incorrect: There is no deployment descriptor mechanism to specify that sessions will end after a set number of requests (you could, of course, write servlet code to achieve this end).

5. ☑ **A** and **C** are the correct answers. **A** is a correctly constructed part of the deployment descriptor file, and it correctly specifies a time-out of 1 minute. **C** is also correct. Because the filter has a mapping of "/," it will receive every request to the web application. The code correctly obtains the session from the request parameter and uses the right method—`setMaxInactive Interval`—using the correct number of seconds, 60.
☒ **B** is incorrect: The deployment descriptor is correctly constructed, but the value for `<session-timeout>` is specified in minutes (not seconds), and the value of 60 represents a whole hour. **D** is incorrect on two counts. Although the code is correct, the only sessions affected will be those invoking this servlet (nowhere are we told that it has a generic mapping). Also, a value of 1 passed to `setMaxInactiveInterval` represents just 1 second for time-out. **E** is incorrect because the `init()` method called on the startup of a web application does not receive an HttpServletRequest as a parameter. True, you could construct an overloaded `init()` method that did this—bizarre as this would be—but the answer would still be wrong, for only the sessions involved in calls to this servlet would be affected.

Session Management

6. ☑ **C** is the correct answer. Cookies are used by default for session management.
☒ **A** is incorrect: URL rewriting is a substitute mechanism when cookies are disallowed. **B** is incorrect: You can do your own session management with hidden form fields, but it's not a standard mechanism supported by J2EE web containers (let alone the default). **D** is incorrect: SSL does have its own session management features, but it is used only for secure transactions. **E** is a complete red herring: jsessionId looks like something used in URL rewriting (yet it is in the wrong case), but is not strictly speaking a request parameter and is in any case only part of the mechanism.

7. ☑ **B** and **E** are the correct answers. *jsessionid* is the unique identifier for the session ID passed in URL rewriting—and it must be all lowercase, as shown. It's also true that you should use different methods to rewrite URLs for links versus URLs for redirection (`HttpServletResponse .encodeURL()` vs. `HttpServletResponse.encodeRedirectURL()`).

☒ **A** is incorrect: You could write a mechanism as described, but it would not be the usual way of managing sessions. **C** is incorrect: The cookie used for default session management must be called JSESSIONID (exactly that, all capitals). **D** is incorrect: If you are using the default session management mechanism, the web container adds the JSESSIONID cookie automatically to the response—you don't need to explicitly code for it.

8. ☑ **A** matches to **4**, and **B** matches to **6**: HttpServletRequest and HttpServletResponse are the appropriate parameter types for the `doGet()` method. **C** matches to **1**: It's an HttpSession type the code needs. **D** matches to **5**: the request method that obtains an HttpSession is `getSession()` (not any variant). **E** matches to **14**: The simple HttpSession method `getId()` returns the unique session identifier. **F** matches to **8**: JSESSIONID in capitals is the name of the cookie for session management. **G** matches to **9**: `isRequestedSessionIdFromURL()` is the correctly named method (not "Url" in mixed case). **H** matches to **10**: *jsessionid* is the URL element that names the unique session ID when URL rewriting is used for session management.
☒ All other matches are red herrings, based on the correct choices above.

9. ☑ **C** is correct. The session ID is encoded in URL1 (with correct syntax), but the session ID is not encoded in URL2. Because URL2 is clearly located in a different context from URL1, then it's not appropriate for the `encodeURL()` logic to attach the session ID. Sessions do not cross contexts (i.e., they don't span different web applications).
☒ **A** is incorrect because JSESSIONID is the name reserved for session management cookies; it should be jsessionid in URL rewriting, all lowercase. **B** is incorrect because the wrong URL has been rewritten (URL2 instead of URL1)—and also, *jsessionid* should be separated from the main part of the URL with a semicolon, not (as here) a question mark, which denotes the beginning of the query string. **D** is incorrect: Although syntactically OK, the session number is attached to URL2 (and the correct answer explains why this is wrong). Finally, **E** is incorrect because JSESSIONID is in capitals, and again a question mark is used where a semicolon should be.

10. ☑ **D** and **E** are the correct answers. **D** correctly states that it's the client that determines whether cookies are allowed or not: Because you may not have control over all the clients using your web application, it's always a good idea to rewrite URLs as a fallback. **E** is also correct: Static pages won't disrupt cookie management during sessions, but they will disrupt a URL-rewriting approach (static pages can't possibly contain a just-generated session ID in their links).
☒ **A** is incorrect: Although there isn't, strictly speaking, a need to rewrite URLs if cookies are used for session management, it's not true to say that this is determined by the server—it's the client's choice to accept or reject cookies. **B** is incorrect because there is a separate method (`HttpServletResponse.encodeRedirectURL()`) for URLs rewritten for redirection. **C** is in-

correct: Cookies are the default session support mechanism, and they must always be supported by J2EE-compliant web containers.

Request and Context Listeners

11. ☑ **B** and **D** are the correct answers, for neither suggestion will fix the potential problem. The issue is that by the time the `requestDestroyed()` method has been reached, the response has been committed. At this point, it's illegal to attempt to create a new session (an IllegalState Exception is thrown)—but still OK to get hold of a session that exists. The method call at line 04—`request.getSession()`—will obtain a session if it already exists (no problem), but will also attempt to create a session if none exists already (which is the problem). Hence, **D** is an incorrect suggestion, for there will be a problem with the code in some circumstances. **B** might go a long way to solving the problem (ensuring that all servlets in your application obtain a session). But if the request is for some other type of resource (a static HTML page, for example), the request listener will still kick in, so the solution doesn't cover all circumstances.
    ☒ **A** is a correct suggestion, hence an incorrect answer. By creating a session in the corresponding `requestInitialized()` method, there will definitely be a session to obtain in the `requestDestroyed()` method. **C** will also fix the problem (hence is an incorrect answer) by explicitly passing **false** to the `getSession()` method: A session will be returned only if one exists already. The potential NullPointerException on `session.setAttribute()` is avoided by testing the session reference returned. **E** will also work, by trapping the potential IllegalState Exception.

12. ☑ **E** is the correct answer. In fact, there will be two compilation errors: The context methods `addAttribute()` and `replaceAttribute()` do not exist. You use the method `setAttribute()` for adding and replacing attributes.
    ☒ **A** is incorrect, for the code never runs (though if the compilation errors were corrected, this would be a true statement). **B** is incorrect—apart from the code not running, it's perfectly OK to remove the same attribute name as many times as you like. **C** is incorrect—were the code to be corrected and run, even, the second `removeAttribute()` call would not cause a method call to a listener (as the attribute has already gone). **D** is incorrect: It's inconceivable that you wouldn't get a context, anyway.

13. ☑ **A**, **C**, and **F** are the correct answers. **A** is counterintuitive, but you can indeed add context attributes (or replace or remove them) in the `ServletContextListener.contextDestroyed()` method—however pointless this may seem. **C** is correct—you have access to the current session via the current request, which is available from the event object passed as a parameter to ServletRequestListener interface methods. **F** is also correct—if you change a

request attribute in the `ServletRequestAttributeListener.attributeReplaced()` method, this will itself cause a call to that same method again—so you have the potential for a perpetual loop (or, more accurately, a StackOverflowError).

☒ **B** is incorrect: The last listener methods potentially called are those in those classes implementing ServletContextAttributeListener. The web container removes attributes from the context after the `ServletContextListener.contextDestroyed()` method has completed, which may cause calls to `ServletContextAttributeListener.attributeRemoved()`. **D** is incorrect: You can access the context only in a context listener (not the request or session). **E** is incorrect: ServletContextAttributeEvent extends ServletContextEvent—which in turn extends java.util.EventObject.

14. ☑ **D** is the correct answer: There are two compilation errors. Both have to do with casting. In line 02, the `getServletRequest()` method returns a ServletRequest object. In an HTTP environment (i.e., most of the time!), this is safe to cast to an HttpServletRequest—which is what's required here. In line 07, the `getValue()` method returns an Object, not a String. If you know the attribute value is a String, then it's safe to cast to String here.

    ☒ **A**, **B**, **C**, and **E** are incorrect because of the reasoning in the correct answer.

15. ☑ **B** and **E** are the correct answers, for neither approach will get the new value. **E** is an invented method (`attributeUpdated()`)—you can define such a method in a listener class, but the web container framework won't call it! **B** is a good approach—but use it for getting the *old* value of the attribute, not the new one.

    ☒ **A** is incorrect; it's a perfectly standard way to get hold of the current attribute value. **C** is incorrect for the same reason. **D** is incorrect; although it's a more convoluted way, you will get hold of the new value that has just been added.

Session Listeners

16. ☑ **D** is the correct answer: You can't determine from this code what will happen. The nasty trick here is that the method shown—`sessionInitalized()`—is not one defined in the HttpSessionListener interface. Sure, you can define such a method in a class implementing the interface, but the method is never called by the web container. The method that IS called on the creation of a session is the `sessionCreated()` method.

    ☒ **A** is incorrect because the code never gets to run—at least not automatically on creation of a session. Also, there is nothing in the code likely to cause an exception. **B** and **C** are incorrect for the same reason—though had the method actually been the `sessionCreated()` method, C would have been the correct answer. Because the `sessionCreated()` method is called as soon as a session is first accessed, there can't have been an opportunity to add any session attributes. This means that there won't be a session attribute named "login," and so the Boolean local variable called "loginOK" will be *null*. According to the logic, this will cause the session to invalidate itself.

17. ☑ **A**, **D**, **E**, and **H** are the correct answers. When the session is about to migrate from the source JVM, any session attribute objects implementing the HttpSessionActivationListener get a call to their `sessionWillPassivate()` method; hence, **A** is correct. When the session has materialized in the target JVM, the migrated session attribute objects have their `sessionDid Activate()` method called (answer **D**). As to why "My data" is written to the source JVM's console (**E**) but not the target JVM's console (**H**), that's because the data is a class variable. Only instance variables are serialized, and so reconstituted in the target JVM. Note that the code in MySessionAttribute employs the dubious practice of returning static data using instance methods.
    ☒ **B**, **C**, **F**, and **G** are incorrect because of the reasoning you see in the correct answer.

18. ☑ **A** matches to **8**; all the types declared come from the javax.servlet.http package. **B** matches to **11**; given the other information, this can only be an HttpSessionAttributeListener. **C** matches to **10**, as does **F** and **G**: An HttpSessionBindingEvent is passed as parameter to each of the three methods. **D** matches to **6**, and **E** matches to **1**: obvious method names for getting hold of the attribute name and value. **H** matches to **7**: another obvious method name for getting hold of the session. **I** matches to **2** (for the new value, simply get hold of the current attribute from the session).
    ☒ The remaining answers are eliminated because of the correct answers above. Look out for "faux" method names (such as answer **15**: `getHttpSession()`).

19. ☑ **B** and **F** are the correct answers. **B** is correct because there is no problem with a single class implementing more than one sort of session listener interface—and that single class will only require a single `<listener>` declaration in the deployment descriptor. **F** is correct because a client's refusal to join a session effectively "orphans" the session: The session will then time out according to the usual criteria, at which point `sessionDestroyed()` will be called. However, beware of any suggestions that the client's refusal to join immediately invalidates the session, for that is not necessarily true.
    ☒ **A** is incorrect because it's not appropriate to declare classes implementing HttpSession BindingListener in the deployment descriptor: Its methods will be called by virtue of having the class as a value object for a session attribute. **C** is incorrect because HttpSessionAttribute Event—while sounding like a logical enough name—is made up. HttpSessionBindingEvent is the type passed to the HttpSessionAttributeListener and HttpSessionBindingListener interface methods. **D** is incorrect: Although ServletRequestAttributeListener and HttpSessionAttribute

Listener have the same trio of methods (`attributeAdded/Replaced/Removed()`), these accept different types as parameters. So a single class can have methods for both request and session just by overloading the methods. **E** is incorrect: The correct name is `sessionWillPassivate()`—which better reflects the exact timing of the method call (i.e., just before the session is serialized).

20. ☑ C is the correct answer. First, `valueBound()` is called. This is because you're adding an attribute whose value implements the HttpSessionBindingListener interface. This takes precedence over the `HttpSessionAttributeListener.attributeAdded()` call, which follows immediately afterward. You then change the attribute, replacing the HttpSessionBindingListener-implementing object; hence, the next call is `valueUnbound()`. Because you're replacing the value of the attribute, next comes an `attributeReplaced()` call. No more calls now to HttpSessionBindingListener methods, for you have added a plain String as the attribute value (and that doesn't implement that interface). However, by nullifying the attribute's value, you remove the attribute—hence the final call to `attributeRemoved()`.
   ☒ **A**, **B**, **D**, **E**, and **F** are incorrect, following the reasoning above.

LAB ANSWER

Deploy the WAR file from the CD called lab04.war, in the /sourcecode/chapter04 directory. This contains a sample solution. You can call the initial servlet to start the test setup and taking process with a URL such as http://localhost:8080/lab04/Reset.

5

Security

CERTIFICATION OBJECTIVES

- Security Mechanisms
- Deployment Descriptor Security Declarations
- Authentication Types

✓ Two-Minute Drill

Q&A Self Test

Up until now, we have considered the essential mechanics of servlet applications. In this chapter you will explore how you can attach a layer of security to the web applications that you have learned about so far.

This chapter will take you through the three security objectives for the SCWCD exam. The first section is devoted to the "simple" definition of terms. It's straightforward enough, but be warned that your grip on these terms needs to be firm enough to recognize when they apply to any given security requirement.

The second section returns to the deployment descriptor—with a vengeance. Most web application security can be defined without writing a line of code. Although we do touch on a few Java APIs, you are encouraged to do as much as possible "declaratively." And you'll find that there are any number of elements that concern resources, users, and roles, and yet more that cover security across a network.

The third section will look at how you can cater for "logging in" to a web application (the proper term for this as we'll shortly discover is "authentication"). You'll see how this is also achieved through deployment descriptor configuration, through yet more elements.

A rough count reveals that of the 18 or so top-level deployment descriptor elements you need to learn for the exam (that's the elements that are direct children of `<web-app>`), 3 of those are explicitly about security. So that's one-sixth. However, when you look at all the elements (including subelements), around 20 out of 60 are security related. That accounts for a third of your deployment descriptor knowledge for the SCWCD! All this and more are covered in this chapter.

CERTIFICATION OBJECTIVE

Security Mechanisms (Exam Objective 5.1)

Based on the servlet specification, compare and contrast the following security mechanisms: (a) authentication, (b) authorization, (c) data integrity, and (d) confidentiality.

We start off with definitions of four terms. These aren't here for background: The exam explicitly tests this knowledge. The definitions used all come from the servlet specification, so what you're learning is J2EE's take on security. That said, the explanations that the servlet specification provides for security terms are more or less standard in any security environment.

Security Mechanisms

There are four terms you need to know. "Authentication" is the first: This is the process of identifying some party to a web application. The term "party" is deliberately vague, for authentication can occur not only between human users and web applications, but also between other systems and web applications.

Once authentication has taken place, "authorization" comes into play. Authorization rules determine what an identified party is allowed to do within a web application—which resources can be accessed and what can be done with those resources. Authentication and authorization go hand in hand. For one thing, you can't have authorization without authentication happening first. For another, it's rare to find a system that goes to the trouble of authenticating someone without employing some kind of authorization rule as well—even if it's all or nothing (authenticated users can use anything in the web application; unauthenticated users can't). In fact, as we'll discover, the base mechanics of web application security invite you to authenticate only if you attempt to access a resource protected by authorization rules.

It's an obvious point to make, but security is really necessary only because of a network. Accepted, if you have a stand-alone PC, you might want to have password protection in place. But who has a stand-alone PC these days? And in the context of J2EE and web applications, we are always considering a network. And a network provides an open invitation to malcontents and evildoers: What is a network packet for if not to have its contents spilled open and perhaps repackaged in some twisted form? This is where the other two security concepts come in. There's "data integrity," which is the business of proving that what you sent to or from a web application has not been tampered with on the way. And in addition, you're likely to want "confidentiality" (or "data privacy")—mechanisms to encrypt your network traffic so that no code-cracking approach can reveal the plain contents.

Security Definitions in Detail

So now let's consider these four security mechanisms in a bit more detail, including the definitions as found in the servlet specification. These may seem a bit formal, but they're precise—and very often, this wording is directly quoted in exam questions.

Authentication As we've said, authentication is the process of proving you are who (or what) you claim to be. The servlet specification puts it this way: "The means by which communicating entities prove to one another that they are acting on behalf of specific identities that are authorized for access." In the web application sense, "communicating entities" typically indicates a client web browser on one end of the telephone and a J2EE web container on the other.

What does the spec mean, though, when it talks about "acting on behalf of specific identities"? It's most obvious from the client-to-server perspective. The server (web application) wants to know that you (the browser user) are a paid-up and registered member of the exclusive club the web application serves. In technical terms, the server is simply interacting with a piece of software described as a Mozilla-compatible browser, but clearly, it wants some means of knowing that behind that browser is a "specific identity," perhaps a human being called David Bridgewater. Let's not neglect the other direction, though. If I'm using a web application to check on my personal bank accounts, I need the server to prove to me at every step of the way (with every request/response) that it is acting on behalf of my bank.

Various means exist for trading authentication details. At the simplest and most insecure end, authentication involves a user providing a user ID and a password, sent unencrypted over the network. This is absolutely fine for the server to establish trust in the client, as long as some provision is made to protect the network between them (maybe through a virtually private network, or through an internal network unconnected with the wider world). More secure approaches might go for encrypting the authentication information, or even the entire request and response. The most secure means of authentication is through digital certificates—which contain rather more information than a mere user ID and password, and which can be used to establish trust in either direction: for the server in the client, or the client in the server.

In the final section of this chapter, we'll see how web applications ask the web container for authentication support. This is through the `<login-config>` element in the deployment descriptor, and we'll learn that this element makes provision for everything from basic user/password authentication to full-blown digital certificates.

Authorization Our simple definition of authorization stated that it's the mechanism controlling what you are allowed to do in a system. Again, the servlet specification is a little more formal and precise—it uses the term "access control for resources" to spell out what authorization does, and it defines this term as "The means by which interactions with resources are limited to collections of users or programs for the purpose of enforcing integrity, confidentiality, or availability constraints."

When talking about "interactions with resources," we are mostly concerned with HTTP requests and responses to specific URLs (the "R" in this stands for "resource"). The process of authentication tells us what user (or program—i.e., system) is attempting to interact with our protected resource. But what does the definition mean by "collections of users or programs"? What this acknowledges is that you have within your J2EE web server some means or other of associating those users and systems with particular roles. The J2EE specification doesn't say how this is to be achieved—it's server specific. For once, it's not something that's defined in the web application's deployment descriptor. Using Tomcat as an example, we find within it a configuration file called tomcat-users.xml. This contains a list of roles, followed by a list of users together with a comma-separated list of the roles to which they belong. Here's the file from my very simple configuration:

```
<?xml version='1.0' encoding='utf-8'?>
<tomcat-users>
  <role rolename="tomcat"/>
  <role rolename="role1"/>
  <role rolename="lowlife"/>
  <role rolename="manager"/>
  <user username="tomcat" password="tomcat" roles="tomcat"/>
  <user username="role1" password="tomcat" roles="role1"/>
  <user username="both" password="tomcat" roles="tomcat,role1"/>
  <user username="david" password="tomcat" roles="lowlife,manager"/>
</tomcat-users>
```

You can see that the last user listed, "david," has a password of "tomcat" and belongs to both the "lowlife" and "manager" roles.

Other servers offer more sophisticated user registries, but whatever one you use, the important thing—in J2EE terms—is the association of someone or something you can authenticate with a given role. When you come to protecting resources in your web application, you say nothing about individual users in the deployment descriptor: What you do is associate a URL with a particular role. Only users within that role can use that URL. There are a few more nuances that we'll visit when we look at the `<security-constraint>` deployment descriptor security declaration, but here we have the essence of how to enforce "availability constraints" as talked about in our servlet specification definition of access control to resources above.

The only aspect of the definition we haven't covered is the enforcing of integrity and confidentiality constraints—but that has less to do with authorization and everything to do with the next two security terms: data integrity and data privacy.

Data Integrity The servlet specification is straightforward: "The means used to prove that information has not been modified by a third party while in transit." The means themselves may be complex—and invariably involve some kind of encryption. If a client encrypts its request in a way that only the server will understand (and vice versa), that's a guarantee that no modification has occurred. If there was some kind of tampering, the request could not be de-encrypted: One byte out of place will ruin the whole.

You could rightly point out that encryption is an over-the-top method to prove the integrity of data. A client could, for example, use a "checksum" algorithm to compute a unique number dependent on the request contents. The server could verify integrity by running the same checksum algorithm over the request on arrival. The problem is that anyone snooping on the request could easily work out the algorithm and, having tampered with the request body, recalculate an appropriate checksum to fool the server. So encryption is invariably used, blurring the line between data integrity and data privacy (our next security term).

Before we move on, know that the deployment descriptor is again used when requesting data integrity for a particular resource: Look out for the line `<transport-guarantee>INTEGRAL</transport-guarantee>` in web.xml. We'll see how this fits into the wider scheme when we look at the deployment descriptor in more detail.

Confidentiality (Data Privacy) The servlet specification defines this last term as "The means used to ensure that information is made available only to users who are authorized to access it." The means is always encryption—translating your plain text into indecipherable code. This usually involves the use of a pair of matching keys, termed private and public. The public key (for a server or client) can be issued to any interested party. The private key is held absolutely privately: client's private key by the client and server's private key by the server. It's impossible to deduce what the private key is from the public key (or vice versa). You can encrypt plain text with (say) the public key, but then you'll need the matching private key to decrypt the enciphered message.

Let's consider the case of sending data that must remain confidential from the server to the client: Figure 5-1 shows this scenario. In (1) the client asks the server for a secure resource. So the server responds (2) by sending its public key. This can be used to encrypt messages in such a way that only the server will understand—only its private key can decode the messages. So the client takes advantage of this in (3) to send its own public key to the server, but encrypted in such a way that only the server can make use of it. Because it's a public key, the client doesn't have to encrypt it, but it gives an added layer of security: Why give your public key to anyone except those who want to make legitimate use of it? Then the server can encrypt the secure resource using the *client's* public key (4) and transmit it to the client. Now the resource can pass through the insecure medium of the Internet in the comfortable knowledge that nobody can de-encrypt it—except the intended client, using its private key.

FIGURE 5-1

Encryption

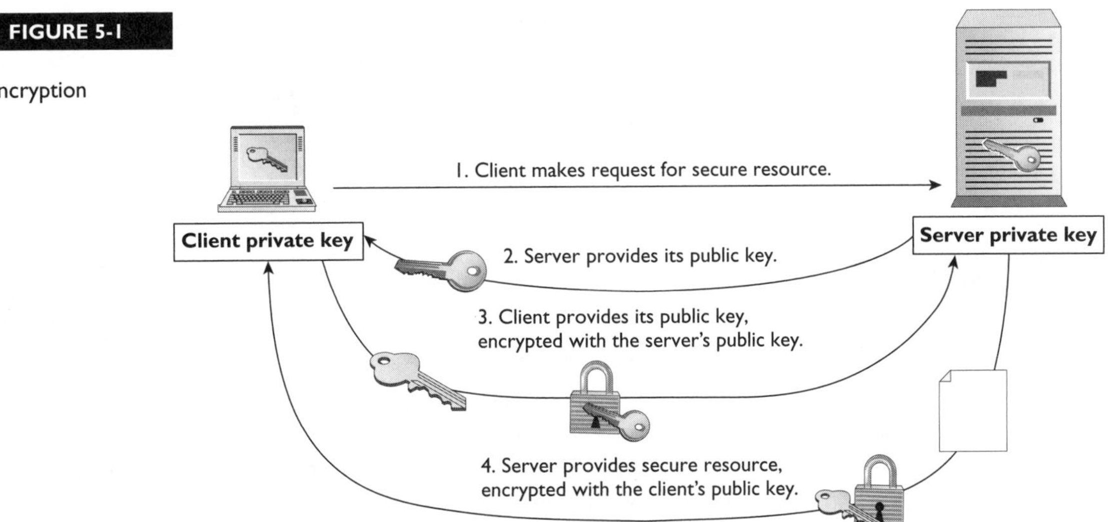
1. Client makes request for secure resource.
Client private key
Server private key
2. Server provides its public key.
3. Client provides its public key, encrypted with the server's public key.
4. Server provides secure resource, encrypted with the client's public key.

This is a somewhat simplified picture of the full set of likely security interactions between the client and server. For one thing, private/public (asymmetric) key encryption takes a great deal of computing power. What usually happens is that asymmetric encryption is used as a secure means for exchanging symmetric keys (same one encodes and decrypts); then the symmetric keys are used for communication beyond this point. Why? Symmetric key encryption is that much faster—and still just as secure, provided you can be absolutely sure nobody other than the intended parties has hold of the symmetric key. And because new symmetric keys can be manufactured for each request/response pairing as necessary . . . well, you get the picture that security is an involved business. I am content to be a humble web component developer, not a security programmer. And for purposes of the SCWCD, we have gone as deep as we need to into encryption mechanisms!

Note that you might want to encode a message with your own private key instead of someone else's public key. That may not make sense at first: Surely, anyone with your public key can read the message. And the whole point of a public key is that it's—well—public? The point is that you're encrypting for a different purpose. As long as those who have your public key are sure it's your public key and no one else's, then they can be sure that a message you encoded with your private key comes from you. So that's how encryption solves the integrity issue.

And just as for data integrity, confidentiality in a web application is ensured by the deployment descriptor element `<transport-guarantee>`, this time with a value of CONFIDENTIAL. The actual medium used by web containers is very often SSL—secure sockets layer (you know when you're using SSL because the URL your browser points to begins "https"—the secure version of HTTP). SSL is a private/public key technology for communicating privately over the Internet that was originally developed by the Netscape Communications Corporation and is now incorporated in practically every web device under the sun.

EXERCISE 5-1

Security Mechanisms You Have Encountered

Because we haven't looked at any specific web application technology yet, this exercise is one of recollection. Note down all the application security mechanisms you have met in the past (at least, those that you can remember). For each one, identify which parts had to do with each of the four "big ideas": authentication, authorization, data integrity, and confidentiality.

For the authorization part, sketch out the structure of the steps involved: How exactly were authorized users, groups, or principals tied to specific resources? From this, imagine how web applications might solve the authorization problem. The combined exercise of memory (or imagination!) will prepare you well for the specifics that we encounter in the next two sections.

You can look at my take on the above exercise by deploying the web application ex0501.war, found in the CD in /sourcecode/ch05. Point to the following URL:

```
http://localhost:8080/ex0501/security.html
```

CERTIFICATION OBJECTIVE

Deployment Descriptor Security Declarations (Exam Objective 5.2)

In the deployment descriptor, declare a security constraint, a Web resource, the transport guarantee, the login configuration, and a security role.

Most applications that I worked with in the past have their own security structure described in program code. J2EE web applications make a valiant attempt to separate out the security layer. The idea is that application developers can hand over their work to deployers, who can then construct a security mechanism without touching the program code. In business terms, the deployer has to know what each resource in the web application does but can remain thankfully oblivious of program code details.

The mechanism is "declarative": In other words, you declare the security you want in the deployment descriptor instead of enshrining it in code. Declarative mechanisms bring everything to the surface and keep management simpler. That said, it's not altogether simple—there are three top-level deployment descriptor elements that we explore in this section. The first is `<security-constraint>`, the most complex of the three—it defines what resource we're securing, what roles can access the resource, and how the resource is to be transmitted across the network. The second is `<login-config>`, which defines what authentication mechanism is to be used. The third (and easiest) is `<security-role>`, which simply catalogues any security roles in use by the web application. We'll look at these in turn in the headings that follow.

exam watch

You should not be asked about the order of the three top-level security elements, for order at this level doesn't matter—as we have previously noted. However, the traditional order (that used to be enforced) is <security-constraint>, <login-config>, then <security-role>. I would advise you to stick to this for compatibility with servers enforcing the old servlet level 2.3 DTD. However, do note that order of the subelements within the three top-level elements does still matter in servlet level 2.4 and that you could well be quizzed on this.

The `<security-constraint>` Element

The `<security-constraint>` element has three parts to it, each represented by a subelement:

- Web resource collection (`<web-resource-collection>`) defines the resource to be protected and also the HTTP methods by which it can be accessed (GET, POST, PUT, DELETE, etc.).
- Authorization constraint (`<auth-constraint>`) determines which roles are allowed access to the resource.

- User data constraint (<user-data-constraint>) decides what protection (if any) is required when transporting the resource over the network.

We're going to look at each of the three parts in detail. Figure 5-2 maps out where these fall and what subelements each contains.

Web Resource Collections

The one thing a security constraint must contain is one (or more) web resource collections. Figure 5-2 shows you that a <web-resource-collection> consists of a name, some optional description lines, one or more URL patterns, and an optional list of HTTP methods. Let's look at each of these in turn.

<web-resource-name> This is just a logical name for the web resource collection. You have to include it, but it has no technical significance—it's just a memory aid to help you understand why you have grouped what are potentially many URL patterns together.

<description> Any number of description lines contained by <description> tags can follow—including none at all. This is no different from the many other appearances we have seen for the <description> element. A pop quiz question (don't worry, I don't see this one appearing in an exam, but it will encourage you

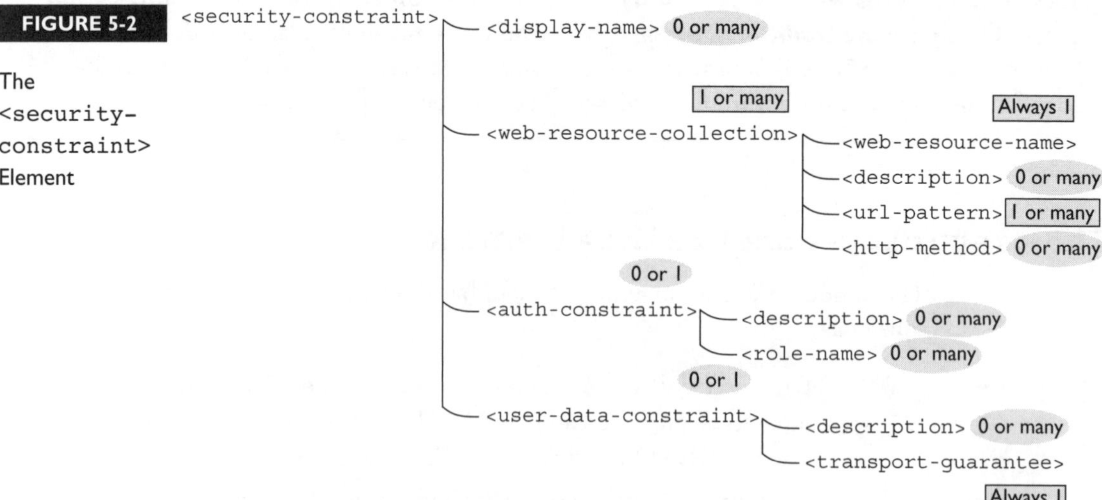

FIGURE 5-2 The <security-constraint> Element

to look at the deployment descriptor). Where else have you encountered the description element?

<url-pattern> This is a URL pattern just like the ones you have seen in `<servlet-mapping>` and `<filter-mapping>`: The same rules apply—see the section on URL pattern strategies for a refresher on these (see Chapter 2). You can define a URL pattern for any resource in your web application. You're not restricted to matching URL patterns with those for servlets (though you may well want to do that)—you can also reference static HTML or JSP pages in the directly available web content for your application.

There must be at least one `<url-pattern>` included for the web-resource-collection, and you're quite likely to include a whole list in a full-sized production application. These will then all be governed according to the same security rules defined elsewhere in the security constraint.

<http-method> Finally, you can include a list of HTTP methods. More often, you're likely to miss out this element, which means that any HTTP method (that's the "big seven" we discussed in Chapter 1 plus any other more obscure ones) executed against the resources defined by your URL patterns will be subject to the same rules. No matter if you POST or GET or DELETE or PUT, the same roles will be needed for access, and the same transport guarantees will apply.

However, you can specify individual methods as needed. For example, you might want to impose a blanket ban on the use of dangerous HTTP methods on resources in your web application. You could achieve that with the following `<security-constraint>` configuration:

```
<security-constraint>
  <web-resource-collection>
    <web-resource-name>All Resources</web-resource-name>
    <url-pattern>/</url-pattern>
    <http-method>DELETE</http-method>
    <http-method>PUT</http-method>
  </web-resource-collection>
  <auth-constraint />
</security-constraint>
```

The URL pattern here (/) encompasses all resources within the context for the current web application. The HTTP methods listed are DELETE (to remove a resource at the requested URL) and PUT (to place a resource at the requested URL, overwriting what's there). We'll meet `<auth-restraint />` next—suffice to say for now that this is the configuration setting you use to deny access to any request for these HTTP methods to this web resource collection.

If you use a browser that can generate DELETE methods (such as the one you used in the exercises in Chapter 1), and target a resource protected as above, you'll get an HTTP 403 error (access forbidden).

on the job

It's a really good idea to be as restrictive as possible. Limit any given resource to only the HTTP methods that are reasonable to execute on that resource. This usually means GET and HEAD, with POST thrown in only when required.

Authority Constraint

So second up in subelements of `<security-constraint>` is `<auth-constraint>`. If you refer back to Figure 5-2, you'll see that it's an optional element with the security constraint and contains two elements of its own—the ubiquitous `<description>` element and the crucial `<role-name>`. The purpose of an authority constraint is to list permitted roles: Any users within the roles can operate on the resources defined in the web resource collection.

The normal use of this element might look like this:

```
<auth-constraint>
  <role-name>employee</role-name>
  <role-name>supervisor</role-name>
</auth-constraint>
```

Anyone falling within the employee or supervisor roles—or both—will have access to the resource. Even more simply, the following definition:

```
<auth-constraint>
  <role-name>supervisor</role-name>
</auth-constraint>
```

restricts resource access to only those in the supervisor role.

The roles names that you choose must (according to the servlet specification) be listed in the `<security-role>` element, which we have yet to meet.

You'll recall that the mapping of specific users to these roles is not a job for the deployment descriptor. The server must provide some way of achieving the mapping, but the exact mechanism is server specific. We met the tomcat-users.xml file earlier on, which showed you one way in which the Tomcat server resolves this need.

There are three special cases to consider with regard to `<auth-constraint>`:

Absent from the Security Constraint What if there is no `<auth-constraint>` for your security constraint? That's fine—it simply means that the web resource collection is open to all, regardless of role or authentication. You may wonder what the point of this is—why go to the trouble of setting up a web resource collection if you're not going to ascribe it to any role? We'll discover one possible reason when we look at `<user-data-constraint>`.

Present with No Role Names The `<auth-constraint>` element might be present in the security constraint, but with no role names listed. It might manifest itself like this:

```
<auth-constraint></auth-constraint>
```

Or this:

```
<auth-constraint />
```

which is the XML shorthand for an opening and closing tag with no value, or this:

```
<auth-constraint>
  <description>Trust No-one!</description>
</auth-constraint>
```

The effect in every case is to deny access to the resource for any role whatsoever. We saw an example of this when we looked at the `<http-method>` element a little earlier and discovered a technique to deflect any DELETE or PUT methods executed against any resource in our web application.

When more than one security constraint is set up for the same web resource collection—which can happen—the effect of the no-value authority constraint is overriding. No matter if you set up a web resource collection open to the world—if the same URL patterns (for the same HTTP methods) are protected elsewhere with the no-value authority constraint, access will be denied.

Present with the Special Role Name of "*" You might want to use an `<auth-constraint>` element that uses the special role name of "*":

```
<auth-constraint>
  <role-name>*</role-name>
</auth-constraint>
```

This role name is a shorthand way to include all the roles defined within the web application. These are all the roles that appear in all the `<security-role>` elements (which we will be discussing very shortly).

exam watch

What HTTP response codes result from the authentication and authorization process? When a resource is requested to which access is always denied (because of the "no-value" authorization constraint), the web server rejects the request with a 403 (SC_FORBIDDEN) response code. Authentication (identification of the user) may not even have happened at this point: There's no need, for any user would be forbidden. If there are potential roles, then authentication must happen. If it hasn't happened already, the web server sends a 401 (SC_UNAUTHORIZED) response code, which causes the browser to supply authentication information in some form or other. If subsequent checking shows that the authenticated user is not a role entitled to the resource, the web server rejects the request with a 403 (SC_FORBIDDEN) response code.

User Data Constraints

In addition to — or as well as — authority constraints, you can impose user data constraints. These apply to the requests and responses that pass to and from the web container. Figure 5-2 shows you that when you include a `<user-data-constraint>`, you must have a `<transport-guarantee>` element within it. This has three valid values, as shown next.

NONE No constraints are applied to the traffic in and out of the container. The requests and responses can pass in plain text over the network. Setting the transport guarantee to this value is the same as leaving out `<user-data-constraint>` altogether.

INTEGRAL The web container must impose data integrity on requests and responses: That's the term we defined earlier as meaning that messages are not tampered with in transit. How it does this is up to the web container, but typically it will use SSL (secure sockets layer) as the communication medium.

CONFIDENTIAL The web container must ensure that communicated data remains private—no one must be able to understand the secret messages passed between the client and the web container. In theory, the CONFIDENTIAL guarantee is stronger than INTEGRAL: If you have confidentiality, integrity is implied. However, web containers again mostly achieve the guarantee by using SSL—and so may look no different from a transport guarantee of INTEGRAL.

Let's return to that question we posed earlier—what's the point of a web resource collection without an `<auth-constraint>`—such that any user (even an unathenticated user) can access the resource? Well, you might still protect your resource collection with a `<user-data-constraint>` but allow open access. Consider a web page for a user to register personal details. Anyone can access this page, but it's best to ensure that their details remain private when transmitted back to the web server. By specifying a CONFIDENTIAL transport guarantee without any authority constraint, you achieve this end.

INSIDE THE EXAM

Addition with Security Constraints

The exam might well test your knowledge on adding together security constraints for identically defined web resource collections. Suppose you have two security constraints declared as follows:

```
<security-constraint>
 <web-resource-collection>
    <web-resource-name>Employee Page</web-resource-name>
    <url-pattern>/EmployeeServlet</url-pattern>
    <http-method>PUT</http-method>
    <http-method>DELETE</http-method>
    <http-method>POST</http-method>
 </web-resource-collection>
 <auth-constraint>
   <description>Administrator Permissions</description>
   <role-name>administrator</role-name>
 </auth-constraint>
</security-constraint>
```

INSIDE THE EXAM (continued)

```
<security-constraint>
  <web-resource-collection>
    <web-resource-name>Employee Page</web-resource-name>
    <url-pattern>/EmployeeServlet</url-pattern>
    <http-method>GET</http-method>
    <http-method>POST</http-method>
  </web-resource-collection>
  <auth-constraint>
    <description>Any Authenticated Permissions</description>
    <role-name>*</role-name>
  </auth-constraint>
</security-constraint>
<!—Other details like login configuration omitted for brevity . . . →
<security-role>
  <role-name>administrator</role-name>
</security-role>
<security-role>
  <role-name>employee</role-name>
</security-role>
```

The same URL pattern is protected in both cases (/EmployeeServlet). There are two valid roles for users to be in when logging on to the application—administrator and employee. It's clear from the first security constraint that users in the administrator role can execute the HTTP PUT, DELETE, or POST methods on this URL. But from the second security role, we can see that a user in any valid role (administrator or employee) can GET or POST to the URL—both roles are part of the "*" (all roles defined) role name. So the second security constraint extends the range of things that an administrator can do: GET as well as PUT, DELETE, and POST from the first security constraint. An employee is covered only by the second security constraint and so can only GET or POST.

And don't forget that if `<auth-constraint />` appears against a URL pattern/HTTP method combination, this "addition of permissions" rule is irrelevant: The resource is blocked.

Enforcing security by HTTP method is fine, but it can be obscure to the hapless deployer charged with imposing security. At least when a deployer provides security for EJBs (Enterprise JavaBeans), he or she is likely to be confronted with method names that reflect a business process: **`transferFunds()`** ***might be an example. HTTP methods are—well—HTTP methods; they say nothing by themselves about a business process. Two design practices may help your deployer: (1) make it obvious what a resource does, and (2) keep the scope of any one resource narrow. For (1), this usually comes down to naming your resources well—if a deployer is faced with the name "TransferFundsServlet," it's pretty clear what the resource does—all that's left is to protect all HTTP methods (or at least GET and POST). Achieving (2) is trickier. After all, the TransferFundsServlet may be capable of transferring funds in one direction, from customer to branch accounts, and also in the other direction, from branch to customer. However, different security roles may well apply to the two different directions of fund transfer. Separate resources—a BranchToCustomer Servlet and a CustomerToBranchServlet—may make security easier to impose. (And if you're thinking this might lead to code duplication, you're right—but remember that the same underlying servlet class can be declared twice in the deployment descriptor, with different initialization parameters and with independent servlet mappings that can be protected separately.)***

The `<login-config>` Element

Now we move on to the next top-level deployment descriptor element governing security, which is `<login-config>`. This governs authentication: how you "log on" to the web application. We're going to see one way we can use `<login-config>` to control authentication here, just to get us going, but revisit it more fully in the next section, for authentication methods are an exam objective in their own right.

The simplest way to ensure that some kind of authentication occurs is to have `<login-config>` set up as follows:

```
<login-config>
  <auth-method>BASIC</auth-method>
</login-config>
```

This works as follows: When a browser (or other client) requests a secure resource from a web application for the first time, the web application doesn't return the resource straightaway (naturally enough!). Instead, the server requests authentication from the browser. Nearly all browsers are built to understand such a request, and they respond by popping up a dialog box that requests a user ID and password—the following illustration shows how this looks in Internet Explorer in Windows XP.

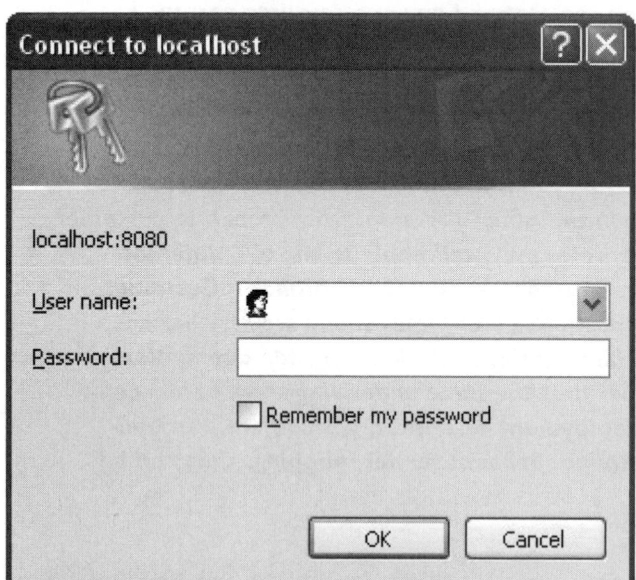

The user fills in the details and presses OK, and the server checks the user ID and password against whatever database or other registry it is set up to use. Assuming that it finds a match (and other valid criteria are met—such as the user being in the correct role), the server returns the resource to the user.

Whenever a Request Dispatcher is used to forward or include a resource—be it dynamic (servlet) or static (plain HTML)—the security model does not apply. It is applicable only to web resources requested by a client.

The <security-role> Element

As we've noted already, `<security-role>` is the simplest of the "big three" security-related deployment descriptor elements. We use it to catalogue all the security roles in use in an application. You can see in the following illustration that it has only one functional subelement, called `<role-name>`. (I'm not counting `<description>`, which is just for documentation purposes.)

```
<security-role> ─┬─ <description> 0 or many
                 └─ <role-name> Always 1
```

exam watch

The current specification says this about valid role names: They have to obey XML "name token" (NMTOKEN) rules. (Actually, this is a throwback to the old style of DTD validation for the deployment descriptor, but if the current specification still says it, who am I to argue?) This means that you should not have embedded spaces or punctuation in the name. Characters and numbers are fine (and you can even begin the role name with a number).

This might also be a good time to point out that the web container matches role names case sensitively when determining access to secured resources, so "rolename" is not the same as "RoleName."

You only include one role name per security role, but `<security-role>` can appear as many times as needs be in the deployment descriptor.

The idea is that any role names used anywhere in the deployment descriptor must appear here. This means any role names you use for authority constraints within a security constraint, and any for role links in the security role reference in the servlet element.

The servlet specification insists that role names "must" appear as a role name here. I find Tomcat's default behavior is to treat the absence of a security role in this list as a warning-type message on startup. However, for exam question purposes, you should go with the servlet specification version of the truth.

on the job

Programmatic security—that is, using APIs in your code to enforce authentication and authorization rules—is not officially covered by the exam. Why not? Perhaps to encourage J2EE application builders to place their trust in declarative security. However, programmatic security is more flexible, and there are often good reasons to use it. Http Servlet Request has three methods: `getRemoteUser()`, `isUserInRole()`, and `getUserPrincipal()`. `getRemoteUser()` returns a String containing

the name of the authenticated user. getUserPrincipal() is essentially a replacement for getRemoteUser(). Instead of returning a plain String, it returns a java.security.Principal object, partly because Java prefers to call authenticated parties "principals" rather than "users." Users tend to be human beings; principals might be human beings or other computer systems. However, ultimately the only useful thing you can do with a Principal object is to call getName() to return a String with the user's (sorry—principal's) name. The third method—isUserInRole(String roleName)—returns a boolean indicating if the user is in the role name passed as a parameter to the method. Note that you don't first have to discover the user's name to make use of this method. isUserInRole() will take account of the roles you have set up in security constraints in your deployment descriptor. However, it also takes account of some subelements in the <servlet> element. You might find declarations such as the following:

```
<servlet>
  <servlet-name>EmployeeDetails</servlet-name>
  <servlet-class>com.osborne.EmployeeDetails</servlet-class>
  <security-role-ref>
    <role-name>MGR</role-name>
    <role-link>manager</role-link>
  </security-role-ref>
</servlet>
```

Suppose that anyone can access the EmployeeDetails servlet but that certain sensitive details are viewable only by managers. So there's no need to associate the servlet with a security constraint, but we do have a reason to use programmatic security to limit some of the output. For this to work, in addition to the servlet's deployment declarations above, the role name "manager" should be defined as an allowed security role for the application—i.e., as a <role-name> in the <security-role> element. The servlet code has the option of using isUserInRole("manager") or isUserInRole("MGR") as a check on whether the authenticated user is a manager of not. The <role-name> of MGR in the <security-role-ref> is mapped on to the <role-link> of manager, which is a real security role defined in the deployment descriptor. What this facility allows for is taking servlets coded against one set of role names, then deploying them in an environment where a different set of role names is defined—without having to revisit the code.

EXERCISE 5-2

Securing a Servlet

In this exercise, we'll take a servlet and make it a secured resource. Just for good measure, we'll include some programmatic security inside the servlet so that some of the web page will display itself only if the user belongs to a specific role. Because we don't yet officially know how to turn on authentication, we'll see what happens when you try to access this servlet in an unauthenticated manner. This will be a frustrating experience, for the web page will not display properly until we introduce authentication in the next exercise.

The context directory for this exercise is ex0502, so set up your web application structure under a directory of this name.

Set Up the Deployment Descriptor

1. Define a servlet called CheckedServlet, with a suitable servlet mapping. I doubt you'll need to refer back to Chapter 2 now for this—you've done it many times!
2. However, by way of a departure, include a `<security-role-ref>` subelement within `<servlet>`, with a `<role-name>` of MGR and a `<role-link>` of manager.
3. Define a `<security-constraint>` element.
4. Define a `<web-resource-collection>` for the `<security-constraint>`. The `<web-resource-name>` must be included, but it's immaterial what text you choose. However, the `<url-pattern>` should match the `<url-pattern>` of the `<servlet-mapping>` for CheckedServlet—that's the resource we are trying to protect.
5. Define an `<auth-constraint>` for the `<security-constraint>`. Set the value of `<role-name>` to *.

Write CheckedServlet

6. Create a Java source file CheckedServlet.java in /WEB-INF/classes or in an appropriate package directory. Write the class declaration in the source file, extending HttpServlet.
7. Override the `doGet()` method in CheckedServlet.

8. Obtain the authenticated user name—you can use the `HttpServletRequest.getRemoteUser()` method or the more tortuous (but preferred) approach to `HttpServletRequest.getUserPrincipal()` to return a Principal object, on which you can execute the `getName()` method. Protect yourself from null values—when we run the servlet in this exercise, there won't be an authenticated user (that comes in the next exercise).
9. Write out some text to the response's writer, including the user name (even if it will be null at present).
10. Use the `HttpServletRequest.isUserInRole()` as the condition for writing some additional text to the web page. The role to check is MGR.

Run the Application

11. Once you're satisfied that the servlet is compiled, deploy the application, and run it with an appropriate URL, such as

```
http://localhost:8080/ex0502/CheckedServlet
```

12. You should get output much like that shown in the following illustration. Because there's been no attempt to authenticate a user, no user name can be displayed. Also, the extra text that appears by virtue of being an authenticated user in the MGR role fails to appear.

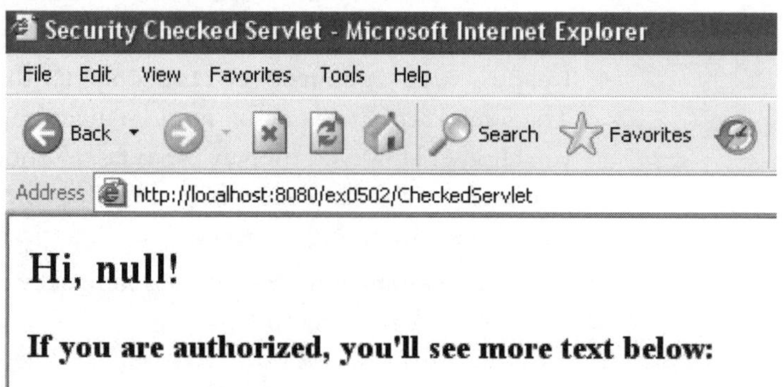

Revise the Application

13. Now revisit the deployment descriptor web.xml. Change the `<role-name>` of `<auth-constraint>` to say lowlife. Remake the WAR, and redeploy the application.

14. Note any startup messages your web container produces. Do you get an informational/warning message complaining about the absence of a `<security-role>` element for the lowlife role in your deployment descriptor? I do with Tomcat, though it doesn't stop the servlet from being deployed.
15. Try running the servlet with an appropriate URL, such as

```
http://localhost:8080/ex0502/CheckedServlet
```

16. Note the error that you get. Tomcat gives me an HTTP 403 error (shown in the following illustration), and tells me that the resource is not available to an unauthenticated user. We'll fix this in the next exercise.

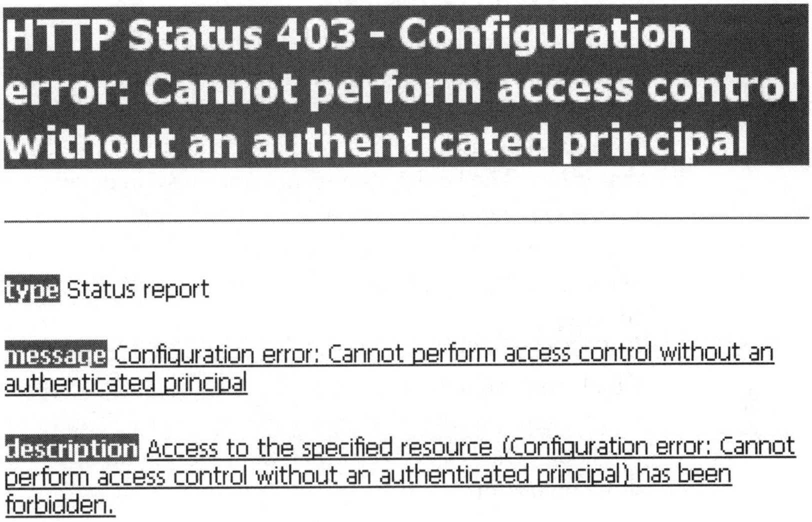

HTTP Status 403 - Configuration error: Cannot perform access control without an authenticated principal

---

type Status report

message Configuration error: Cannot perform access control without an authenticated principal

description Access to the specified resource (Configuration error: Cannot perform access control without an authenticated principal) has been forbidden.

CERTIFICATION OBJECTIVE

Authentication Types (Exam Objective 5.3)

Compare and contrast the authentication types (BASIC, DIGEST, FORM, and CLIENT-CERT); describe how the type works; and, given a scenario, select an appropriate type.

As I intimated earlier, there is more to be said about the `<login-config>` element, which we saw in the last section. We met the simplest authentication type it supports—BASIC—which we're going to find out is also the least secure. In fact, this element allows for four authentication types in all. We'll discuss all of these in this section—how to set up their configuration, how they work, and what their benefits and drawbacks are.

Authentication Types

The four authentication types are BASIC, FORM, DIGEST, and CLIENT-CERT. Let's do a quick survey of the types before exploring in detail. BASIC, as we've seen, forces the appearance of a dialog box in browsers inviting user and password details. Behind the scenes, we'll see that although these details aren't quite sent over the wire in plain text, they're not very secure either. FORM is more or less a cosmetically improved version of BASIC—you supply your own design of web page to solicit user and password details, instead of being stuck with the browser's dialog box. The behind-the-scenes transmission details are just the same. DIGEST imposes encryption rules on the password, improving this situation. CLIENT-CERT goes a step further—all security details are kept in an electronic document called a certificate. We'll see how this is the most secure arrangement but also the most work to set up.

Let's first of all have a look at the full layout of the `<login-config>` element, which controls authentication. You see in Figure 5-3 that this element has several subelements but that the only one common to all authentication types is `<auth-method>`, which describes which of the four authentication types is in force for the web application.

exam watch

In common with all the other top-level deployment descriptor elements (those directly under the root element, `<web-app>`), `<login-config>` is described in the schema as being able to appear "0 or many" times. The truth is that `<login-config>` should appear 0 or 1 time only: If present, it applies to the whole web application, so it only makes sense for it to appear once. So although it's legal (in XML terms) for `<login-config>` to appear more than once, the container is supposed to do additional validation to trap and reject such a faux pas. Indeed, this is true for all the top-level elements that end in -config, including `<session-config>` and `<jsp-config>`.

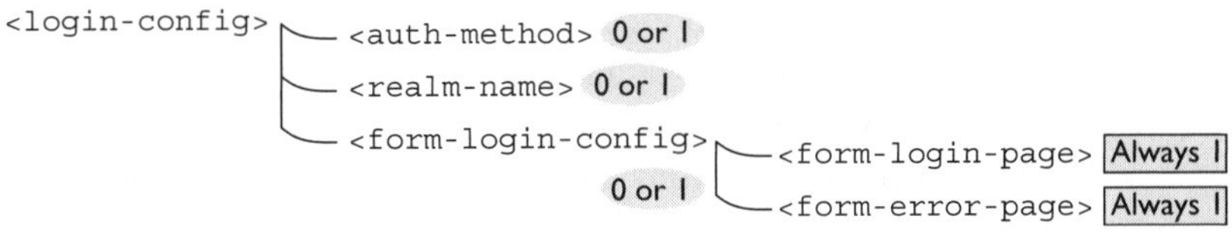

FIGURE 5-3

The <login-config> Element

BASIC Authentication

We saw BASIC authentication at work in the last section. There isn't that much left to say, except for a subelement we bypassed called `<realm-name>`. Here's the deployment descriptor for BASIC authentication, this time with the realm name included:

```
<login-config>
  <auth-method>BASIC</auth-method>
  <realm-name>MyUserRegistry</realm-name>
</login-config>
```

The realm is simply the registry used to store user account information. It could be that your server has more than one realm at its disposal and that a deployer will need to specify which one is meant here in web.xml. However, it's not mandatory—mostly, servers are concerned only with validating against one realm, so there is no need to specify. Another quirk of realms is that they are applicable only to BASIC and DIGEST forms of authentication.

When you press the OK button on the browser dialog and transmit your user ID and password over the Internet, there is a token attempt made to fool prying eyes. The password is not sent as plain text but is passed through a process called Base64 encoding. This turns the password into something that is no longer human-readable. But it's not the same as encryption: A hacker with any level of sophistication will have a Base64 decoder to turn the password back into plain text. (Base64 encoding and decoding tools are freely available on the Web—there's even one in the J2SDK, though it's pretty well hidden and lacks Javadoc.)

This doesn't make BASIC authentication useless, however. It's perfectly secure when you provide a transport guarantee to ensure encryption. That way, all parts of the request—including password details—are concealed from theft across the network.

DIGEST Authentication

DIGEST authentication improves a little on BASIC by using a secure algorithm to encrypt the password and other security details. When the browser tries to access a secure resource, the server generates a random value called a "nonce" and passes this to the browser. The nonce can be based on anything— often, a unique identifier for the server (such as an IP address) and a timestamp.

The browser uses this value and, together with other pieces of information—always the user ID and password, sometimes URI and HTTP method as well—applies the digest encryption algorithm (usually the very secure MD5 algorithm). This is a one-way process: The idea is to turn the seed information into junk, which can never be translated back into human-readable text. This junk is called the digest, and the client sends it to the server.

The server can't use the digest to decode security details. What it can do, though, is to generate its own digest—using the nonce value it provided and known user and password details—and compare this with the digest passed from the browser. If they match, the client is considered authenticated. The process is shown in Figure 5-4.

Because nonces are generated on the fly from transient information, each session (and sometimes each request) uses unique digests—the possibility of intercepting and using an existing digest to fool a server is practically nonexistent. So it's very secure. What it does rely on, though, is that the server and browser have identical expectations about the digest: which algorithm to use and which pieces of information to apply the algorithm to. And there's the rub—different browser vendors do different things in support of DIGEST authentication. You need to know (and test) the clients you expect your web application to support, and that may not be easy (or even possible) to predict. Hence, DIGEST lags behind other

FIGURE 5-4 Digest Authentication

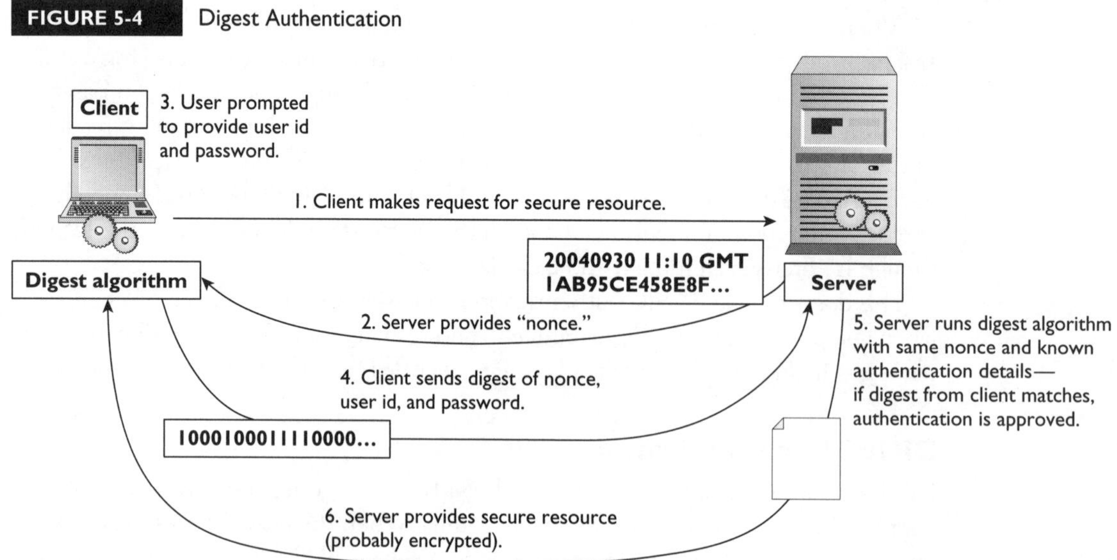

authentication types in terms of adoption, though it is much more widely supported than it used to be.

FORM Authentication

FORM authentication is primarily provided for aesthetic purposes. Why be at the mercy of an ugly browser dialog when you can provide your own nicely designed logging-in page? There are only a few rules you have to abide by when constructing such a page:

- The HTML form must use the POST method (GET is not acceptable).
- The form must have "j_security_check" as its action.
- The form must include an input-capable field for user called "j_username."
- The form must also include an input-capable field for password called "j_password."

Here's an example form that puts all the rules together (though in aesthetic terms, it's more minimalist than the authentication dialog box my browser provides):

```
<html>
<head><title>Login Form</title></head>
<body>
<form action="j_security_check" method="POST">
<br />Name: <input type="text" name="j_username" />
<br />Password: <input type="password" name="j_password" />
<br /><input type="submit" value="Log In" />
</form>
</body>
</html>
```

The above is a static HTML page, but dynamic JSP pages are just as valid.

Form-based authentication also demands that you provide an error page. There are no rules for the content of such a page. Once the pages are designed, you need to look at how to plug them into the deployment descriptor. This is a variant of `<login-config>` that fits the criteria:

```
<login-config>
  <auth-method>FORM</auth-method>
  <form-login-config>
    <form-login-page>/login.html</form-login-page>
    <form-error-page>/error.html</form-error-page>
  </form-login-config>
</login-config>
```

The <auth-method> is FORM, as you might expect. <realm-name> has gone: It's not used for form authentication. However, form authentication has an element that is unique to its type: <form-login-config>. This in turn has two subelements—<form-login-page> and <form-error-page>—whose values point to the location and name of these pages within the web context.

The mechanism of logging in works like this: The first secure resource you attempt to access in a web application will not be sent to you directly. Instead, the server caches the URL you are trying to reach and redirects you to the form login page. You supply a user ID and password; assuming that the server is happy with these credentials, you are then passed on to the URL you requested in the first place. However, if your login fails for any reason, the server redirects you to the error page you specified.

For login and error pages, the path you specify must begin with a forward slash ("/"). This denotes the root of the web context

Assuming successful login, access to subsequent secure resources will not require re-authentication. It's the web server's business to achieve this in any way it can—the servlet specification doesn't mandate an approach. Most of the time, this comes down to attaching some additional information to the JSESSIONID cookie. This implies that invalidating the session will log you out of the system, but this implication can't be guaranteed.

One of the frustrations of form-based authentication is that you can't go directly to the login form. You have to attempt to access an otherwise secured resource and let the server redirect you to the login page. Try putting the address for your login page directly in your browser address line—experience the error that you get (usually something along the lines of "cannot perform j_security_check directly"). So if you want to design an unsecured home page with a login field for registered users in the top right-hand corner, then form-based authentication is not for you.

Also in common with BASIC authentication, there is no intrinsic protection for security information. You don't even get the Base64 encoding of the password. But again, as for BASIC authentication, you can get around that by using a virtually private network, or a secure protocol such as SSL for your transport guarantee.

CLIENT-CERT Authentication

The fourth and final method to discuss is CLIENT-CERT, which uses digital certificates to achieve authentication. This is the most secure form of authentication, but it also requires the most understanding and the most setup.

When we talked about data privacy earlier in the chapter, we introduced the idea of public and private keys for encryption. Digital certificates build on this idea by providing a home and an identity for a public key. Anyone can create a certificate, using specialized (but publicly available) software such as "keytool," which is shipped with the J2SDK. By passing the right parameters, keytool (or the equivalent) generates a private key and a matching public key, usually stored in some fully encrypted form on the creating computer's hard drive.

From this "keystore" you can extract a certificate file that is fully technically valid. But if anybody can mint one of these things, what trust can be placed in it? The usual procedure is to pass on your "self-signed" certificate details to a properly established certificate authority. The VeriSign Corporation (http://www.verisign.com) is well known, as is Thawte Consulting (http://www.thawte.com). These companies verify your identity (with different grades of background checking possible, reflecting different levels of cost and trustworthiness) and "rubber-stamp" your certificate—or, more correctly, produce a new certificate based on the details you supplied, vouched for by them. The most important action they take is to use their own private keys to digitally sign your certificate. Practically all browsers and web servers are in possession of these company's public keys. This gives them the means to check a digital signature (from VeriSign, Thawte, or whomever) on your certificate, verifying that your certificate is at least vouched for by a trusted third party. Here's what you can expect to find in an X.509 certificate (X.509 is the most popular standard):

- Version of the X.509 standard (v1, v2, or v3).
- A serial number unique to the certificate authority (VeriSign, Thawte) issuing the certificate. (The certificate authorities can use these numbers to maintain a "blacklist" of revoked certificates.)
- The signature algorithm used to digitally sign the certificate.
- Validity period: when the certificate will start and expire.
- The subject: in other words, you, the requester of the certificate. This is held as a "distinguished name"—nothing to do with your social standing, but more about uniqueness. A distinguished name has several components, including a common name (an individual—"David Bridgewater"), organizational unit (department), organization name (company), locality name (often, city), state name (or province), and country (two-character ISO code).
- Issuer name: the name of the certificate authority, again held as a distinguished name.

- A digital signature, encoded with the certificate authority's private key. This will be a digest of information within the certificate—which also means that tampering with the certificate (not just the digest itself) will render it immediately invalid.
- Last but very much not least: the subject's (your) public key.

Once you have your certificate, you can install it into your browser. Every browser is different, but most have a relatively simple mechanism for installation. Then, when you access a web application that demands client certification, your browser can supply a client certificate. If this is on the approved list of the server's allowed certificates, the transaction can continue.

From general use of the Internet, you're probably fairly used to this process working in reverse—where the server provides a certificate to your browser. Depending on your browser's security settings, you generally see a dialog box asking whether or not you want to trust the certificate the server is offering you (we hope signed by Thawte, VeriSign, or whomever). If you accept, the transaction can continue, and the server's public key can be used to encrypt communications between you. So certificates provide the foundation for secure transport as well as dealing with the issue of identify.

There's nothing stopping a web server vendor from supporting its own style of authentication and permitting new values (other than BASIC, FORM, DIGEST, and CLIENT-CERT) for the `<auth-method>` element. Of course, a web application subscribing to a vendor-specific authentication mechanism will almost certainly not transfer cleanly to a different vendor's web container.

EXERCISE 5-3

Setting Up FORM Authentication

In this exercise you'll set up authentication for the servlet you built in the previous exercise. You'll use a custom web page for the login, so the `<auth-method>` will be FORM.

The context directory for this exercise is ex0503, so set up your web application structure under a directory of this name.

Set Up the Deployment Descriptor

1. Copy the deployment descriptor web.xml from the previous exercise (ex0502) into the WEB-INF directory for this exercise (under ex0503). You'll still be using CheckedServlet, declared in the deployment descriptor. When you copy it forward to this web application (in a few steps' time), you may choose to change the package structure (as the solution code does). In that case, don't forget to change the package name in the `<servlet-class>` element here in web.xml.
2. Define a `<login-config>` element.
3. Within `<login-config>`, define an `<auth-method>` element with the value FORM.
4. Still with `<login-config>`, define a `<form-login-config>` element, using the appropriate subelements to set up a login page called "login.html" and an error page called "error.html." Predictability may be boring, but your support staff will love you for it!

Define Error and Login Pages

5. Create a web page called "error.html." Put any text you like into this page, just so that you will recognize it as the error page.
6. Create a web page called "login.html." Include a form with a method of POST and an action of j_security_check. Within the form, include a text field (named j_username) for the login name, and a password field (named j_password) for the password. See Chapter 1 if you need a refresher on constructing form fields. Don't forget a submit button in the form.

Copy CheckedServlet

7. Copy CheckedServlet from the previous exercise (it should be somewhere under ex0502/WEB-INF/classes), and paste it into the current web application's directory structure. If you follow the pattern of the solution code, you'll copy the source and change the package structure to reflect this exercise. If you do that, don't forget to change the package statement in the source code, or you won't be able to compile the servlet!

Run the Application

8. Deploy the application—it should start up without error or warning messages.
9. Try running the servlet with an appropriate URL, such as

```
http://localhost:8080/ex0503/CheckedServlet
```

10. You should be redirected to the login page. Log in with an invalid user ID and/or password. Make sure that you get the error page. If you don't get the expected result (at any point), close down all browser windows and restart the browser—in case the browser is caching users and passwords for the duration of the session.
11. Now add a user into your server's user directory, for the lowlife role. For Tomcat, this means editing the tomcat-users.xml file in the <TOMCAT-INSTALL-LOCATION>/conf directory. You can see my additions (for user "david") to this file in bold:

```
<?xml version='1.0' encoding='utf-8'?>
<tomcat-users>
  <role rolename="tomcat"/>
  <role rolename="role1"/>
  <role rolename="lowlife"/>
  <user username="tomcat" password="tomcat" roles="tomcat"/>
  <user username="both" password="tomcat" roles="tomcat,role1"/>
  <user username="role1" password="tomcat" roles="role1"/>
  <user username="david" password="tomcat" roles="lowlife"/>
</tomcat-users>
```

12. Restart the server. Re-access the servlet, and log on using your user ID and password. At this point, the servlet should display properly—everything except the text protected by the `isUserInRole()` method. Unlike our run of the servlet in the previous exercise, you should also see your authenticated user name displayed in the text. Refresh your memory of the source code if all this seems strange and unfamiliar.
13. To make the protected text visible, give your user the role of manager as well as lowlife. My tomcat-users.xml user entry now looks like this:

```
<user username="david" password="tomcat" roles="lowlife,manager" />
```

14. Restart the server (with Tomcat, this will in fact automatically add in the role of manager into the roles list in tomcat-users.xml).
15. Access the servlet again. Now all text should display. The solution page is shown in the following illustration.

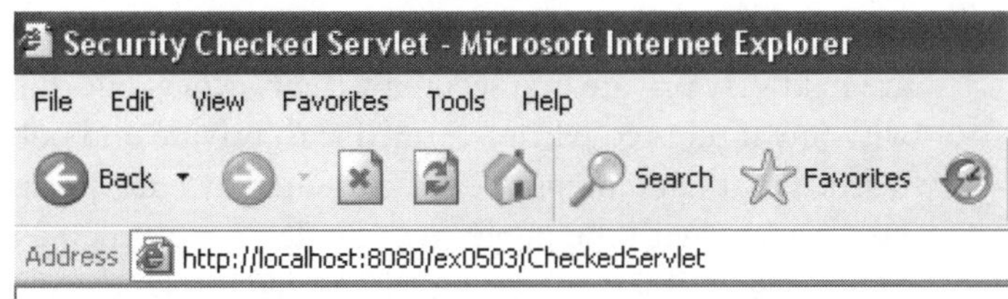

CERTIFICATION SUMMARY

In this chapter you explored the world of web application security. First of all, you met some fundamental security terms as defined by the servlet specification:

- Authentication: proving you are who (or what) you claim to be
- Authorization: ensuring that an authenticated party gains access only to the resources he or she is entitled to
- Data Integrity: ensuring that any messages passed through a network have not been tampered with in transit
- Confidentiality (data privacy): ensuring that the information in a message is available only to users authorized to see that information

You learned that there were several methods for supplying authentication, ranging from the simple (user IDs and passwords) to the sophisticated (digital certificates). You saw that authorization—in web application terms—first of all involves identifying resources as identified by their URLs and the HTTP methods used to access them. Second, you saw that these can be associated with logical roles.

Third, you learned that each web server has its own method for associating those logical roles with specific users in a registry of users. You learned that encryption is a key component for both data integrity and confidentiality, and that at the root of encryption lie matching pairs of public and private encryption keys (often known as asymmetric keys). You learned that one of the matching pair can encrypt a message, but then only the other half can do the de-encryption. You saw that private keys are held very private and secure by their owners but that public keys can be shared with any interested parties. Armed with private and public key knowledge, you learned that data integrity can be ensured by encrypting a message with a private key. Anyone with the public key can de-encrypt such a message—provided no tampering has taken place, for that would render the message useless. You further learned that confidentiality can be ensured by using keys in the other direction. Using someone's public key to encrypt the message, you can rest assured that only that someone can read the message—as only that person will have a private key.

We then moved on to look at web applications in more detail—and in particular, the role played by deployment descriptor definitions. You learned that the preferred way of providing web application security is through "declarative" means—in other words, putting information inside the deployment descriptor instead of in code. You had a glimpse of programmatic security, using such methods as `HttpServletRequest.getRemoteUser()` and `HttpServletRequest.isUserInRole(String roleName)`—but quickly dismissed those because they are not core SCWCD syllabus items!

Back in the deployment descriptor, you met three top-level elements controlling security: `<security-constraint>`, `<login-config>`, and `<security-role>`. You saw that a `<security-constraint>` consists of the subelements `<web-resource-collection>`, `<auth-constraint>`, and `<user-data-constraint>`. You learned that the web resource collection defines the actual resources to protect, that the authority constraint associates the resources with logical roles (the authorization element), and that the user data constraint can provide guarantees of data integrity and probably, in addition, confidentiality.

You went on to learn that the `<web-resource-collection>` element has several subelements: a mandatory `<web-resource-name>`, some optional `<description>` lines, at least one `<url-pattern>`, and some optional `<http-method>`s. You heard that the web resource name has no technical significance and is simply there to help administrators. You learned that the `<url-pattern>` element behaves in just the same way as it does within servlet and filter mappings, with the same four possibilities for values: exact path (/exactmatch), path prefix (longest match first) (/partial/*), extension matching (*.jsp), and default (/). You saw that you can protect this URL pattern for specific HTTP methods, but leaving out the <http-method> element implies that every HTTP method used on this URL will be subject to the same authority and user data constraints.

From there, you looked at <auth-constraint>, which simply consists of an optional number of <role-name>s. You learned that leaving out any role names and supplying a "no value" authority constraint is equivalent to saying that no user in any role can access the resource. You saw that this is an overriding setting: Even if other security constraints give permissions to the same resource, this "no-value" authority setting takes precedence and blocks access. You also met the special <role-name> with a value of asterisk (*), and learned that this is a shorthand way of saying that all role names defined in the <security-role> element are allowed access to the resource. You learned that when you have separate web resource collections but with the same URL pattern/HTTP methods, protected by separate sets of authority constraints, that the authority constraints should be considered "added together."

After that, you examined <user-data-constraint> and found that this has one subelement—<transport-guarantee>—which dictates how communication between client and server should be handled. You learned that <transport-guarantee> has three possible values—NONE (which is equivalent to using no user data constraint at all; there are no guarantees made about client/server communication), INTEGRAL (which promises data integrity between client and server), and CONFIDENTIAL (which promises confidentiality, i.e., data privacy, in addition to data integrity). You also saw that web servers generally use SSL (secure sockets layer) as the network transport layer to deal with encrypted messages passed in INTEGRAL and CONFIDENTIAL communication.

Before looking at the next top-level deployment descriptor element, <login-config>, in any detail, you were introduced to <security-role>. You learned that there can be as many <security-role> elements in the deployment descriptor as required, each containing a single <role-name> element. You saw that the function of this is simply to list all the valid logical authorization roles known to the web application. You also learned that the web container is supposed to validate the use of role names elsewhere in the deployment descriptor (in authority constraints, and as the <role-link> in <servlet> elements) by reference to this list of security roles. You incidentally learned that a valid role name value can contain characters and numbers—even begin with a number—but should not contain embedded white space or punctuation.

In the third and final section of the chapter, you learned in more detail about authentication types and saw how these are controlled by the <login-config> element. You learned that the first and most crucial subelement of <login-config>

is called <auth-method> (authentication method) and that this has four valid values: BASIC, DIGEST, FORM, and CLIENT-CERT—and vendor-specific values are possible.

You learned about BASIC authentication and saw that this works by the server issuing a standard response to a browser requesting a secure resource. You saw that this will prompt any standard browser to launch a dialog box, requesting a user ID and password. You learned that this dialog box can display a piece of text called a realm name and that this text can be set using the <realm-name> subelement of <login-config>. Although no server-side validation is performed on the realm name text, you saw that it should in some way describe the server-side registry that is used to validate user authentication credentials. You learned that by itself, BASIC authentication provides practically no security for authentication details—that this is limited to encoding the password with an easily-reversed Base64 algorithm.

Then you met DIGEST authentication. You saw how this is a more secure method as far as the transmission of authentication details go. You saw that this security is provided by a one-way encryption process (the digest algorithm) and that the resulting "digest" will reveal nothing. You learned that the principle of authentication using digests goes like this: Both the client and server use the same digest algorithm on the same input data, which includes user and password details. You saw that the server can compare both digests, and if they match, the client is deemed to be authenticated. To prevent anyone sending an old digest to the server (pretending to be the real client), you saw that the digests are never repeated, because part of the input data is a semirandom "nonce" value generated by the server. You learned in passing that a realm name (<realm-name>) can be associated with DIGEST authentication, which then appears in the browser's dialog box requesting user name and password—and that BASIC and DIGEST are the only forms of authentication for which realm names are used.

You then moved on to perusing FORM authentication and were introduced to the idea that this represents little more than a cosmetic improvement over browser dialog boxes. You learned that this method of authentication demands its own subelement within <login-config>, called <form-login-config>. You saw that this comprises two subelements, <form-login-page> and <form-error-page>. You learned that the value of <form-login-page> points to the location of a custom login page for the input of user ID and password, and that the <form-error-page> defines the location of a custom error page. You were warned that these values hold a path to a filename and must begin with a forward slash ("/") to denote the root of the web context. You learned the mechanism of FORM authentication: that when a user accesses a secure resource in a web application for the first time, he or she is redirected to the custom login page. If the user provides a bona fide user ID and password, the server redirects the user to the secure resource, and subsequent access to secure resources in the same web application should not require re-authentication. You also learned that on failure to authenticate through the custom login page, the server redirects the user to the custom error page. You learned that the custom error page doesn't obey any particular rules, but that there are some formalities for the custom login page: It must contain an HTML <FORM> whose method is POST; the action of the form must be called j_security_check (exactly that, all lowercase and complete with underscores); and that there must be two input fields on the form, one named j_username and the other j_password (no prizes for guessing their purpose). You learned that FORM authentication is no more secure than BASIC, for authentication details are passed in plain text in the request body.

You had seen by now that the three authentication methods—BASIC, DIGEST, and FORM—are generally supplemented with SSL encryption when used anywhere but over a very secure network. You finally met CLIENT-CERT authentication and saw that certificates are always transmitted over a secure network using SSL (so a transport guarantee of CONFIDENTIAL is firmly implied, even though the servlet specification doesn't say you have to have one). You learned that a client certificate contains a public key and attaches identification details to the public key. You saw that the identification details can be underwritten by a third-party certification authority, who can digitally sign your certificate—meaning that anyone using your certificate is assured that you are who you say you are, at least in the eyes of the certification authority. You learned that you supply your client certificate in place of a user ID and password to a server that secures resources—and that the server checks this certificate against a known list of certificates.

TWO-MINUTE DRILL

Security Mechanisms

- There are four security mechanisms detailed by the servlet specification: authentication, authorization (access to controlled resources), data integrity, and confidentiality (data privacy).
- Authentication is the process of proving you are who (or what) you claim to be.
- The servlet specification has much to say on client-to-server authentication: clients (human beings or other systems) proving their identity to our web applications.
- The servlet specification has little to say about server-to-client authentication (do I trust this web application?); however, it is still an aspect you should be aware of.
- Authentication can be achieved through basic means (user IDs and passwords) versus complex means (digital certificates). The trade-off is usually simplicity versus security.
- Authorization is the process of ensuring that an authenticated party gains access only to the resources it is entitled to.
- In servlet spec terms, this process means identifying resources by their URLs (and the HTTP methods used to access them), and associating these with logical roles.
- It's the web server's job to supply some means or other for relating these logical roles to specific users or groups of users. There's no standard way to achieve this—it is server specific. Indeed, a web server may have more than one way of approaching this, for the registries (databases) of users with which it has to interact may be quite diverse.
- Data integrity is the process of ensuring that any messages passed through a network have not been tampered with in transit.
- Data integrity very often involves encrypting the contents of a message. Integrity comes about because any tampering with an encrypted message will render the message impossible to decrypt.
- Confidentiality (data privacy) goes one step further than data integrity, by promising that the information in a message is available only to users authorized to see that information.

- ❑ Again, encryption is the key to confidentiality. The encryption used by any particular web server may be stronger than the encryption used to ensure integrity, though very often the same algorithms are used for integrity and confidentiality.
- ❑ The encryption process usually involves public and private keys (sometimes called asymmetric—they're a matched pair, but not identical).
- ❑ Private keys are kept strictly private, whether client-side or server-side.
- ❑ Public keys are broadcast to interested parties.
- ❑ If a server uses a client's public key to encrypt a message, only the client's private key can decode it.

Deployment Descriptor Security Declarations

- ❑ Inside the root element `<web-app>`, there are three top-level elements devoted to security: `<security-constraint>`, `<login-config>`, and `<security-role>`.
- ❑ `<security-constraint>` is the biggest and most complex of these three.
- ❑ Its purpose is to associate resources (and HTTP methods executed on those resources) with logical roles for authorization, and also with guarantees on resource security in transit over a network.
- ❑ `<security-constraint>` has three main subelements—`<web-resource-collection>`, `<auth-constraint>`, and `<user-data-constraint>`.
- ❑ The first of these main subelements, `<web-resource-collection>`, defines the resources to be secured.
    - ❑ The first element inside `<web-resource-collection>` must be `<web-resource-name>`, whose value is a logical name to describe the group of resources protected.
    - ❑ Next, `<web-resource-collection>` defines the URL patterns to protect using one or more `<url-pattern>` subelements.
    - ❑ The value of a URL pattern is a path to a resource (or resources) within the web application.
    - ❑ Valid values for URL patterns are the same as for servlet mappings and filter mappings: exact path (/exactmatch), path prefix (longest match first) (/partial/*), extension matching (*.jsp), and default servlet (/). As for servlet mappings, web resource collection URL patterns types are processed in that order.

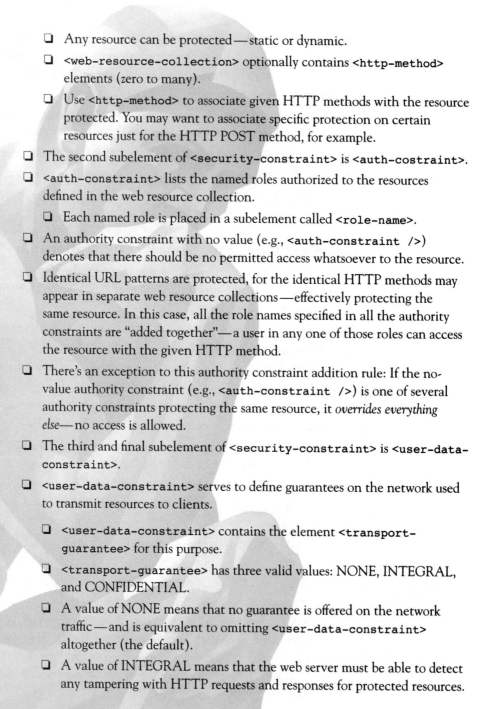

- Any resource can be protected—static or dynamic.
- `<web-resource-collection>` optionally contains `<http-method>` elements (zero to many).
- Use `<http-method>` to associate given HTTP methods with the resource protected. You may want to associate specific protection on certain resources just for the HTTP POST method, for example.

- The second subelement of `<security-constraint>` is `<auth-costraint>`.
- `<auth-constraint>` lists the named roles authorized to the resources defined in the web resource collection.
  - Each named role is placed in a subelement called `<role-name>`.
- An authority constraint with no value (e.g., `<auth-constraint />`) denotes that there should be no permitted access whatsoever to the resource.
- Identical URL patterns are protected, for the identical HTTP methods may appear in separate web resource collections—effectively protecting the same resource. In this case, all the role names specified in all the authority constraints are "added together"—a user in any one of those roles can access the resource with the given HTTP method.
- There's an exception to this authority constraint addition rule: If the no-value authority constraint (e.g., `<auth-constraint />`) is one of several authority constraints protecting the same resource, it *overrides everything else*—no access is allowed.
- The third and final subelement of `<security-constraint>` is `<user-data-constraint>`.
- `<user-data-constraint>` serves to define guarantees on the network used to transmit resources to clients.
  - `<user-data-constraint>` contains the element `<transport-guarantee>` for this purpose.
  - `<transport-guarantee>` has three valid values: NONE, INTEGRAL, and CONFIDENTIAL.
  - A value of NONE means that no guarantee is offered on the network traffic—and is equivalent to omitting `<user-data-constraint>` altogether (the default).
  - A value of INTEGRAL means that the web server must be able to detect any tampering with HTTP requests and responses for protected resources.

- A value of CONFIDENTIAL means that the web server must ensure the content of HTTP requests and responses so that protected resources remain secret to all but authorized parties.
- It is common practice for a web server to employ SSL (secure sockets layer) as the network transport layer to fulfill INTEGRAL and CONFIDENTIAL guarantees.

- Neither `<auth-constraint>` nor `<user-data-constraint>` is a mandatory element of `<security-constraint>`. Either or both may be used to protect resources. It makes little sense to go to the trouble of defining a `<web-resource-collection>`, then to omit both these elements, but it is legal to do so.
- After `<security-constraint>`, the next security-related deployment descriptor element is `<login-config>`. This determines how users (or other systems) authenticate themselves to a web application.
- The last security-related deployment descriptor element is `<security-role>`.
- Each `<security-role>` element (there can be as many as you like) must contain one `<role-name>` element.
- The value of `<role-name>` is a logical role name against which resources are authorized.
- Role names listed here may be used in the `<role-name>` element in `<auth-constraint>` and in `<security-constraint>`, and in the `<role-link>` element in `<security-role-ref>` in `<servlet>`.
- A logical role name must not contain embedded spaces or punctuation.

Authentication Types

- Authentication types are set up in the `<login-config>` deployment descriptor element.
- The subelement `<auth-method>` names the authentication scheme. There are four standard values: BASIC, DIGEST, FORM, and CLIENT-CERT.
- It's possible to name a vendor-specific authentication scheme not covered by the four standard values above (but then your web application will be tied to that vendor's application server).
- The simplest `<auth-method>` of BASIC will trigger a browser to show a standard dialog when accessing a secure resource for the first time in your

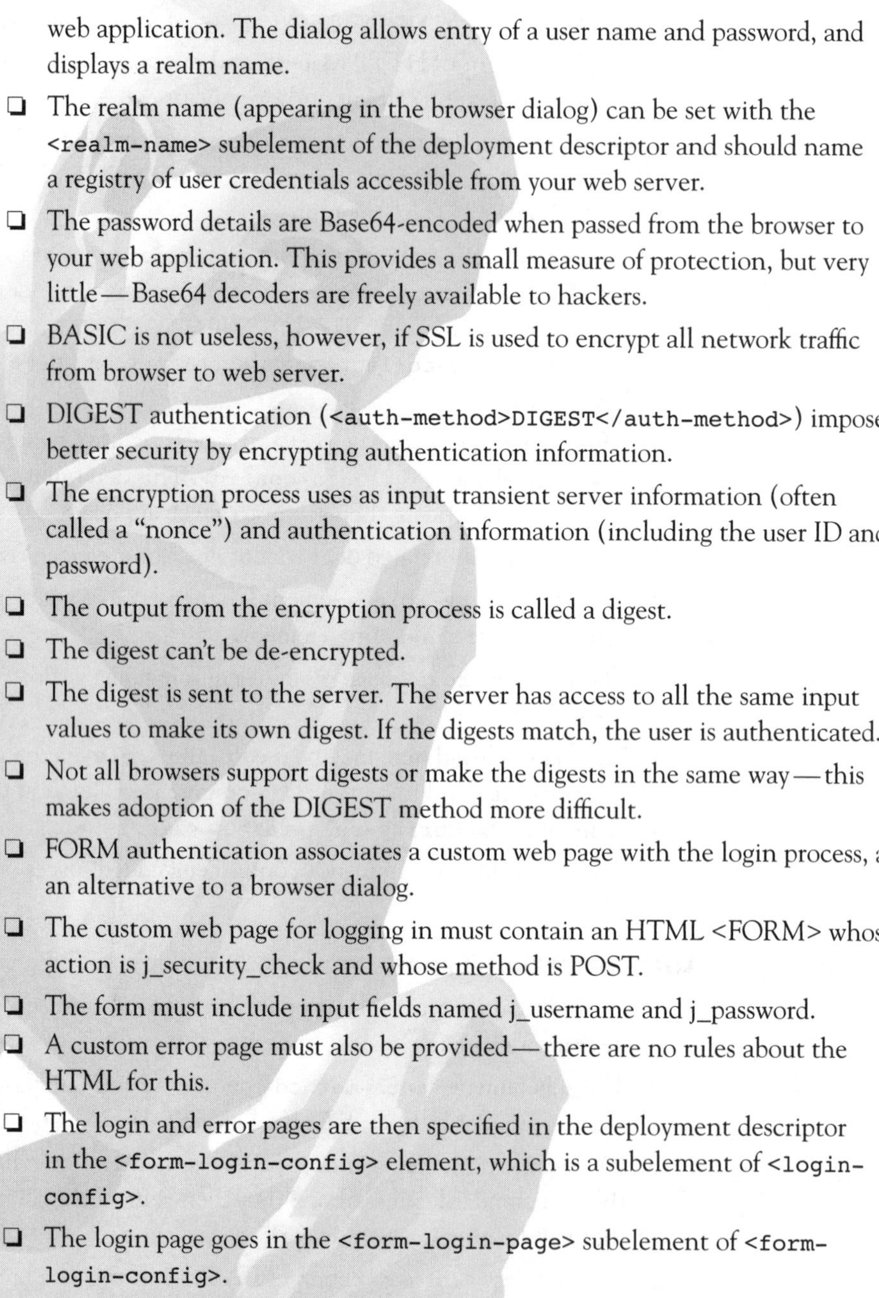

web application. The dialog allows entry of a user name and password, and displays a realm name.

- The realm name (appearing in the browser dialog) can be set with the `<realm-name>` subelement of the deployment descriptor and should name a registry of user credentials accessible from your web server.
- The password details are Base64-encoded when passed from the browser to your web application. This provides a small measure of protection, but very little—Base64 decoders are freely available to hackers.
- BASIC is not useless, however, if SSL is used to encrypt all network traffic from browser to web server.
- DIGEST authentication (`<auth-method>DIGEST</auth-method>`) imposes better security by encrypting authentication information.
- The encryption process uses as input transient server information (often called a "nonce") and authentication information (including the user ID and password).
- The output from the encryption process is called a digest.
- The digest can't be de-encrypted.
- The digest is sent to the server. The server has access to all the same input values to make its own digest. If the digests match, the user is authenticated.
- Not all browsers support digests or make the digests in the same way—this makes adoption of the DIGEST method more difficult.
- FORM authentication associates a custom web page with the login process, as an alternative to a browser dialog.
- The custom web page for logging in must contain an HTML <FORM> whose action is j_security_check and whose method is POST.
- The form must include input fields named j_username and j_password.
- A custom error page must also be provided—there are no rules about the HTML for this.
- The login and error pages are then specified in the deployment descriptor in the `<form-login-config>` element, which is a subelement of `<login-config>`.
- The login page goes in the `<form-login-page>` subelement of `<form-login-config>`.

- The error page is specified in the `<form-error-page>` subelement of `<form-login-config>`.
- The values for these elements *must* begin with a forward slash, which denotes the root of the web context.
- `<form-login-config>` is — obviously — only relevant when the `<auth-method>` is FORM.
- The first secured resource you request in a web application will cause you to be redirected to the login page.
- If there is an error logging in, you are redirected to the error page.
- Log-in information (user, password) is not protected in any way across the network with FORM authentication. As for BASIC authentication, you need to also use a secure protocol such as SSL if greater protection is needed.
- CLIENT-CERT is the fourth and final authentication method. It is the most secure but also the trickiest to set up.
- This method relies on asymmetric keys — that is, a pair of keys, one public (available to anyone) and one private (kept secure on the key owner's hardware). Anything encrypted with the public key can be decrypted with the private key — and vice versa.
- The client (and would-be digital certificate owner) first generates a private and public key. The client sends the public key — and other information — to a third-party certificate authority. The certificate authority binds this information and the client public key into a certificate.
- The certificate authority adds a digital signature encrypted with its private key, which makes a digest of information already in the certificate.
- This process serves two purposes: (1) to prove the certificate is vouched for by the certificate authority (only its public keys can be used to read the signature) and (2) to prevent tampering with any aspect of the certificate.
- The certificate is returned to the client, who installs it in his or her browser (or other client device).
- When the server requests authentication from the client browser, the browser supplies the certificate. If the certificate is on the server's approved list of certificates, authentication takes place.

SELF TEST

The following questions will help you measure your understanding of the material presented in this chapter. Read all the choices carefully because there might be more than one correct answer. The number of correct choices to make is stated in the question, as in the real SCWCD exam.

Security Mechanisms

1. Which security mechanism proves that data has not been tampered with during its transit through the network? (Choose one.)

   A. Data validation

   B. Data integrity

   C. Authentication

   D. Packet sniffing

   E. Data privacy

   F. Authorization

2. Which security mechanism limits access to the availability of resources to permitted groups of users or programs? (Choose one.)

   A. Authentication

   B. Authorization

   C. Data integrity

   D. Confidentiality

   E. Checksum validation

   F. MD5 encryption

3. Which of the following deployment descriptor elements play some part in the authentication process? (Choose three.)

   A. `<login-config>`

   B. `<transport-guarantee>`

   C. `<role-name>`

   D. `<auth-method>`

   E. `<form-error-page>`

   F. `<security-role-ref>`

4. In a custom security environment, for which security mechanisms would a filter be incapable of playing any useful part? (Choose one.)

   A. Authentication

   B. Authorization

   C. Data integrity

   D. Confidentiality

   E. All of the above

   F. None of the above

5. Review the following scenario; then identify which security mechanisms would be important to fulfill the requirement. (Choose two.)

   An online magazine company wishes to protect part of its web site content, to make that part available only to users who pay a monthly subscription. The company wants to keep client, network, and server processing overheads down: Theft of content is unlikely to be an issue, as is abuse of user IDs and passwords through network snooping.

   A. Authorization

   B. Authentication

   C. Indication

   D. Client certification

   E. Data integrity

   F. Confidentiality

Deployment Descriptor Security Declarations

6. Identify which choices in the list below show immediate subelements for `<security-constraint>` in the correct order. (Choose two.)

   A. `<security-role-ref>,<auth-method>,<transport-guarantee>`

   B. `<web-resource-name>,<auth-constraint>`

   C. `<web-resource-collection>,<auth-constraint>,<user-data-constraint>`

   D. `<auth-method>,<web-resource-name>`

   E. `<web-resource-collection>,<auth-constraint>`

   F. `<auth-constraint>,<web-resource-name>`

   G. `<web-resource-collection>,<transport-guarantee>,<auth-method>`

7. Identify valid configurations for the <transport-guarantee> element in the deployment descriptor. (Choose four.)

   A. <transport-guarantee>CONFIDENTIAL</transport-guarantee>

   B. <transport-guarantee>ENCRPYTED</transport-guarantee>

   C. <transport-guarantee>FAILSAFE</transport-guarantee>

   D. <transport-guarantee>ENCIPHERED</transport-guarantee>

   E. Absent altogether from the deployment descriptor

   F. <transport-guarantee />

   G. <transport-guarantee>NONE</transport-guarantee>

   H. <transport-guarantee>INTEGRAL</transport-guarantee>

8. Given the following incomplete extract from a deployment descriptor, what are possible ways of accessing the protected resource named TheCheckedServlet? (Choose three.)

```
<security-constraint>
    <web-resource-collection>
      <web-resource-name>TheCheckedServlet</web-resource-name>
      <url-pattern>/CheckedServlet</url-pattern>
    </web-resource-collection>
    <auth-constraint />
</security-constraint>
<security-constraint>
    <web-resource-collection>
      <web-resource-name>TheCheckedServlet</web-resource-name>
      <url-pattern>/CheckedServlet</url-pattern>
      <http-method>GET</http-method>
    </web-resource-collection>
    <auth-constraint>
      <role-name>bigwig</role-name>
    </auth-constraint>
</security-constraint>
```

   A. Via another URL pattern (if one is set up elsewhere within the deployment descriptor).

   B. Any authenticated user can access the resource.

   C. Any user (authenticated or not) can access the resource.

   D. Via `RequestDispatcher.include()`.

   E. Via `RequestDispatcher.forward()`.

   F. Via the URL pattern /CheckedServlet, provided the user is authenticated and has bigwig as a valid role.

9. Which of the following might a web server consider important in ensuring a transport guarantee of CONFIDENTIAL? (Choose four.)

A. Base64 encoding

B. Server-side digital certificates

C. Symmetric keys

D. Asymmetric (public/private keys)

E. SSL

F. Client-side digital certificates

10. (drag-and-drop question) The following illustration shows the declaration of a security constraint in a deployment descriptor. Match the lettered blanks in the declaration with numbered choices from the list on the right.

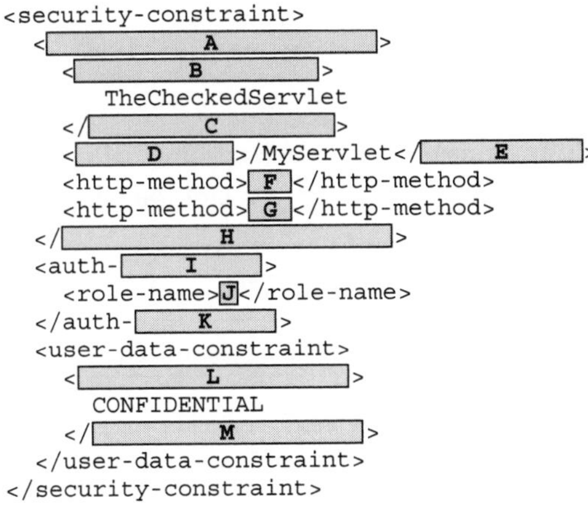

1	collection
2	check
3	url-collection
4	transport-guarantee
5	resource-collection
6	?
7	method
8	web-resource-name
9	POST
10	transport-constraint
11	web-resource-collection
12	url-pattern
13	constraint
14	*
15	GET

Authentication Types

11. The following web page is defined as the custom form login page for authentication. Assuming that you have attempted to access a protected resource and been redirected to this web page, what is the result of filling in the user name and password fields and pressing SUBMIT? (Choose one.)

```
<html>
<head><title>Login Form</title></head>
<body>
<form action="jsecuritycheck" method="POST">
<br />Name: <input type="text" name="jusername" />
<br />Password: <input type="password" name="jpassword" />
<br /><input type="submit" value="Log In" />
</form>
</body>
</html>
```

A. You will not be redirected to this page in the first place.
B. HTTP 401 or 403 error (forbidden/not authorized).
C. HTTP 404 error (page not found).
D. HTTP 500 error (server error).
E. The page is redisplayed.

12. (drag-and-drop question) The following illustration shows the declaration of a login configuration in a deployment descriptor. Match the lettered blanks in the declaration with numbered choices from the list on the right.

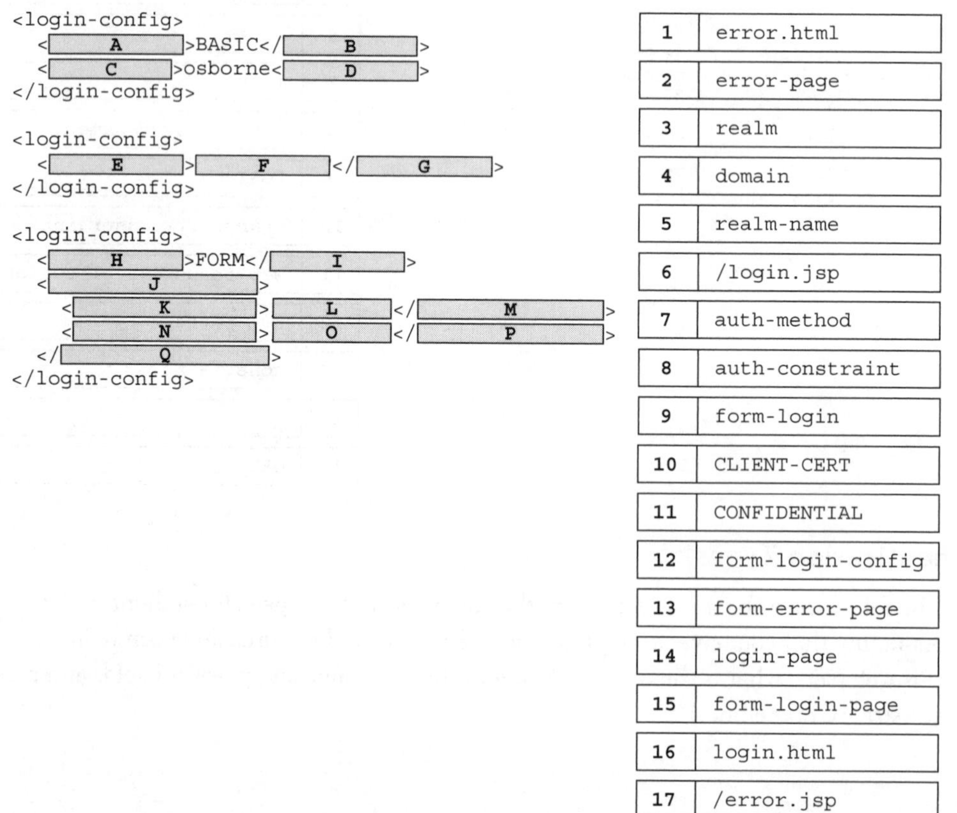

13. What is the result of the following login configuration? (Choose one.)

```
<login-config>
  <auth-method>FORM</auth-method>
  <form-login-config>
    <form-login-page>login.html</form-login-page>
    <form-error-page>error.html</form-error-page>
  </form-login-config>
</login-config>
```

A. Application fails to start.

B. Application starts with warning errors.

C. Application runs, but access to a protected resource results in an HTTP 404 error.

D. Application runs and presents login form on a user's first access to a protected resource.

14. Which of the following subelements might you expect to find in the `<login-config>` for BASIC authorization? (Choose two.)

A. `<auth-constraint>`

B. `<form-login-config>`

C. `<role-name>`

D. `<form-login-page>`

E. `<realm>`

F. `<auth-method>`

G. `<realm-name>`

15. Which of the following subelements would you not expect to find in the `<login-config>` for CLIENT-CERT authorization? (Choose four.)

A. `<auth-constraint>`

B. `<role-name>`

C. `<form-login-page>`

D. `<auth-method>`

E. `<realm-name>`

LAB QUESTION

In this lab, you're going to attempt to set up secure transport over SSL using a server-side certificate. Exactly how you do this is somewhat dependent on your environment. Because I'm working with the Tomcat server running under Windows XP, my instructions are biased toward that environment. However, even if you're using another server and operating system, it shouldn't be too hard to discover your local equivalents for what I describe below.

First, we need a certificate, and we'll use Java's J2SDK facilities for creating one. Here are the (Windows XP) blow-by-blow instructions for this:

- Get to a command prompt. You'll need access to the keytool command (in <your J2SDK installation directory>\bin).
- Enter the following command:

```
keytool -genkey -alias webcert -keyalg RSA
```

- Follow the on-screen prompts—the questions are straightforward! Take careful note of the password you create—you'll need it later.
- By default (on a Windows machine), the key information you have just generated is stored in your home directory—for me, that's C:\Documents and Settings\David. Look for a file there called .keystore.
- In the absence of involving (and paying for) the services of a VeriSign or Thawte, you are going to self-certify your key information. Do this by entering the command

```
keytool -selfcert -alias webcert
```

- You'll be prompted for the password you created earlier.

That's your certificate, created and safely stored in a Java-style keystore.

Next, you need your server to recognize the certificate you have just set up. For Tomcat, that means pointing a configuration item called a "connector" toward your keystore file. Find Tomcat's main configuration file—server.xml—in <Tomcat Installation Directory>/conf. Because you are going to make changes to this file—and restore the original configuration later—*make a copy of server.xml.*

I'm running the 5.5 version of Tomcat, which meant I had to find the lines referring to the secure connector shown below. By default, this connector configuration is commented out (with <!-- --> tags), so I uncommented the element and added the lines in bold:

```
<!--Define a SSL Coyote HTTP/1.1 Connector on port 8443-->
<Connector port="8443"
  maxThreads="150" minSpareThreads="25" maxSpareThreads="75"
```

```
enableLookups="false" disableUploadTimeout="true"
acceptCount="100" debug="0" scheme="https" secure="true"
clientAuth="false" sslProtocol="TLS"
keystoreFile="C:\Documents and Settings\David\.keystore"
keypass="passwordyouchose">
```

Note that the value for the keypass attribute is the password you supplied when making the keystore, so substitute the right value in the XML above. I'm hoping the steps for you are very similar—they're slightly different for earlier versions of Tomcat (but then why are you using an earlier version?)—and clearly, on a different server you'll need to find your own salvation!

All that remains is to implement a web application with a resource that's protected by a CONFIDENTIAL transport guarantee. Install this on your server, point your browser to the protected resource, and see what happens.

SELF TEST ANSWERS

Security Mechanisms

1. ☑ **B** is the correct answer. The process of ensuring that data has not been tampered with in transit through a network is described as proving the integrity of the data.
☒ **A** is incorrect: Data validation is not a term generally applied to security (it's more usually applied to checking the input data on a form, for example). **C** is incorrect: Authentication is the process of proving you are who you claim to be. **D** is incorrect: Packet sniffing is a technique for monitoring TCP/IP network traffic, used for good or evil—so is not in itself any kind of security mechanism. **E** is incorrect—just because data has not been tampered with in transit does not mean it's remained private. Finally, **F** is incorrect: Authorization is the process of determining what resources an authenticated user can use.

2. ☑ **B** is the correct answer. Authorization is the security mechanism that limits the availability of resources to permitted groups.
☒ **A** is incorrect, even though authentication (identifying who you are) is a prerequisite for authorization. **C** and **D** are incorrect: The integrity and confidentiality of network traffic have no bearing on resources to which you may or may not be authorized. **E** and **F** are incorrect—checksum validation is a (weak) technique for proving integrity, whereas MD5 encryption is a (strong) technique to assist in encryption (often of passwords), but neither has to do with authorization.

3. ☑ **A**, **D**, and **E** are the correct answers. The deployment descriptor element that has to do with authentication is `<login-config>`, and `<auth-method>` and `<form-error-page>` are subelements (or sub-sub-elements) of `<login-config>`.
☒ **B** is incorrect, for `<transport-guarantee>` has to do with specifying data integrity and confidentiality. **C** is incorrect: `<role-name>` turns up in several places in the deployment descriptor. But regardless of position, its role (no pun intended) is always in authorization. **F** is incorrect: `<security-role-ref>` can be found as a subelement of `<servlet>`, and has to do with programmatic authorization (not authentication).

4. ☑ **F** is the correct answer. Filters can potentially play a part in all four aspects of security; hence, they are not excluded from any aspect listed, and "none of the above" is the correct answer. Filters can intercept user and password data on requests, and perform look-ups on appropriate user directories, and hence perform authentication. Because filters are tied to resources by URL pattern, and can in any case look at the requested URL, they can further make a determination about whether a user is authorized to a resource. Furthermore, filters can perform any check you want on incoming data to prove its integrity and perform any amount of encryption and de-encryption in a chain of confidentiality. Of course, to do any or

all of this yourself in filter code might involve ignoring what your web container provides for free, but the point remains that a filter can be used for almost any security purpose when a web container mechanism is insufficient. And to go further than that—it could well be that your web container (under the covers) is already making use of filters to provide the standard J2EE security requirements described in this chapter.

☒ **A**, **B**, **C**, **D**, and **E** are incorrect according to the reasoning in the correct answer.

5. ☑ **A** and **B**. **A** (authentication) is necessary to identify subscribed users. **B** (authorization) is necessary to tie in the protected content with subscribing users.

   ☒ **C** is incorrect and is simply a red herring word: "indication" is not a security mechanism. **D** is incorrect—although client certification is a form of authentication (which will be required in some form), it's the least likely to be used in this circumstance—certificates imply heavy use of encryption, which will add to processing overheads on client and server (and this is contrary to the company's requirements). **E** and **F** are incorrect, for while they are bona fide security mechanisms, the requirements make it clear that absolute data integrity and privacy are not crucial.

Deployment Descriptor Security Declarations

6. ☑ **C** and **E** are the correct answers. **C** gives the full set of the three top-level elements; **E** has only the first two (you don't have to have a `<user-data-constraint>`—the default of NONE for `<transport-guarantee>` is implied when this element is missing).

   ☒ **A** is incorrect, for it mixes in security elements from wholly different parts of the deployment descriptor and has `<transport-guarantee>` as an immediate child of `<security-constraint>` when it is a grandchild. **B** is close, but still incorrect—`<web-resource-name>` is a subelement of `<web-resource-collection>`, which would be correct. **D** is incorrect: again, because of `<web-resource-name>`, and `<auth-method>`, which has strayed over from `<login-config>`! **F** is incorrect for similar reasons; **G** is incorrect: Only the first element is correct, and the other two are repeats of errors in earlier choices.

7. ☑ **A**, **E**, **G**, and **H** are correct. The valid values for `<transport-guarantee>` are CONFIDENTIAL, INTEGRAL, and NONE. In addition, having the element absent altogether is just fine (provided the parent element, `<user-data-constraint>`, is absent also)—and will be interpreted as equivalent to the element being present with a value of NONE.

   ☒ **B**, **C**, and **D** are incorrect—all have bogus values. **F** is incorrect: To have the element present with no value at all is illegal, and—even if not caught on application startup—may cause unpredictable results.

8. ☑ **A**, **D**, and **E** are the correct answers. **D** and **E** are correct because authority constraints are applicable only for direct client requests. Internal web application servlet code that forwards or includes a resource (even with the same URL pattern) entirely bypasses authority checking. Of course, you can protect the method calls to forward and include with your own programmatic authority checking if you wish. **A** is correct because it's not the actual resource you are protecting—rather, it's a URL pattern to a resource. Authority checking on another URL pattern is completely independent.
☒ **B** and **C** are both incorrect and show a misunderstanding of a "blank" `<auth-constraint />` element. The significance is that the URL pattern is denied to any user in any role—and because as the `<http-method>` element is missing, this applies to any HTTP method used to access the resource. **F** is incorrect: Although additional `<security-constraint>` elements for the same URL pattern are generally compounded together, the effect of the "blank" `<auth-constraint />` element is to override any other specification.

9. ☑ **B**, **C**, **D**, and **E** are the correct answers. **B** is correct—to establish SSL between client and server, the server has to supply the client with its public key—and the best way of doing that is typically through supplying a digital certificate. **D** is correct because asymmetric (public/private) keys are part and parcel of encryption. **C** is also correct—symmetric keys (usually of 128 bits) are usually used for secure communication once asymmetric keys have been used to pass the symmetric keys confidentially! Symmetric key encryption is faster than asymmetric encryption, hence the attraction of this approach. **E** is correct because SSL (secure sockets layer) is the usual network transport layer used for encrypted traffic.
☒ **A** is incorrect—the one thing in the list that won't do anything toward confidentiality is Base64 encoding, which is a highly insecure (but better than nothing) approach to obfuscating the password when BASIC authentication is used. **F** is also incorrect—client-side digital certificates may well contribute to confidentiality, but their use has more to do with highly secure authentication of clients. They are not essential for ensuring transport guarantees.

10. ☑ The correct pairings are **A**, **11**; **B**, **8**; **C**, **8**; **D**, **12**; **E**, **12**; **F**, **9**; **G**, **15** (or **F**, **15**; **G**, **9**); **H**, **11**; **I**, **7**; **J**, **14**; **K**, **7**; **L**, **4**; and **M**, **4**. Either you know your `<security-constraint>` elements or you don't!
☒ Beware of almost correct but plausible choices such as `<transport-constraint>` instead of `<transport-guarantee>`.

Authentication Types

11. ☑ **E** is the correct answer. The key to the question is noticing that the form HTML has something close to the right values for the form action, user name, and password fields—but

not close enough. The proper attribute values have underscores: j_security_check, j_username, j_password. So the form submits to the server. Instead of (as you might expect) an HTTP 404 error (because the resource jsecuritycheck doesn't exist), the server sees that no authorization data has been provided, so it simply redirects to the log-in page again.

☒ **A** is incorrect— only a deployment descriptor error would prevent forwarding to the page, not the HTML of the page itself. **B** is incorrect because you haven't had a chance to access anything with incorrect authentication information—you're still in the process of gathering that information. **C** is incorrect for reasons explained in the correct answer. And finally, **D** is incorrect: The server doesn't get to run a resource that is likely to terminate in an error.

12. ☑ The correct pairings are **A, 7**; **B, 7**; **C, 5**; **D, 5**; **E, 7**; **F, 10**; **G, 7**; **H, 7**; **I, 7**; **J, 12**; **K, 15**; **L, 6**; **M, 15**; **N, 13**; **O, 16**; **P, 13**; and **Q, 12**. Again, there's no real wiggle room here—you just have to know what permutations of `<login-config>` make sense.

    ☒ No other combinations for `<login-config>` make sense from the choices that are available.

13. ☑ **A** is the correct answer—the application fails to start, for the application loading process ends (or should end) in a deployment descriptor parsing error. The values for `<form-login-page>` and `<form-error-page>` *must* begin with a forward slash ("/").

    ☒ **B**, **C**, and **D** are incorrect because of the reasoning in the correct answer.

14. ☑ **F** and **G** are the correct answers. **F** is correct because you must have an `<auth-method>` element set to a value of basic. **G** is correct because you might (optionally) expect to find a `<realm-name>` specified for BASIC (or DIGEST) authentication.

    ☒ **A** is incorrect because an `<auth-constraint>`—while being a valid element name—is part of `<security-constraint>`, not `<login-config>`. **B** and **D** are incorrect because they are valid `<login-config>` elements, but are only appropriate for FORM authentication. **C** is incorrect because the role-name element—while appearing in several places in the deployment descriptor—has no "role" in login configuration. Finally, **E** is incorrect—the element is `<realm-name>`, not `<realm>`.

15. ☑ **A**, **B**, **C**, and **E** are the correct answers. **A** and **B** belong to other elements entirely. **C** and **E** do belong to `<login-config>` but are appropriate to other forms of authentication, not CLIENT-CERT.

    ☒ **D** is incorrect, for `<auth-method>` is the one and only subelement of `<login-config>` that should appear when client certification is used for authentication (with the appropriate value of CLIENT-CERT, of course).

LAB ANSWER

There is a WAR file from the CD called lab05.war, in the /sourcecode/chapter05 directory. This contains a sample web application, with a servlet called ConfidentialServlet appropriately protected in the deployment descriptor. Call the servlet using a URL such as

```
http://localhost:8080/lab05/ConfidentialServlet
```

You should find that you're prompted to accept a certificate in your browser (suitably dubious, given that you signed it yourself—but at least you know where it came from!). Then you gain access to the servlet, but you should notice the address line in your browser will subtly change to something like

```
https://localhost:8443/lab05/ConfidentialServlet
```

In other words, you have been redirected to the secure port, and https gives you the clue that SSL is being used for the transport layer. The solution page is shown in the following illustration:

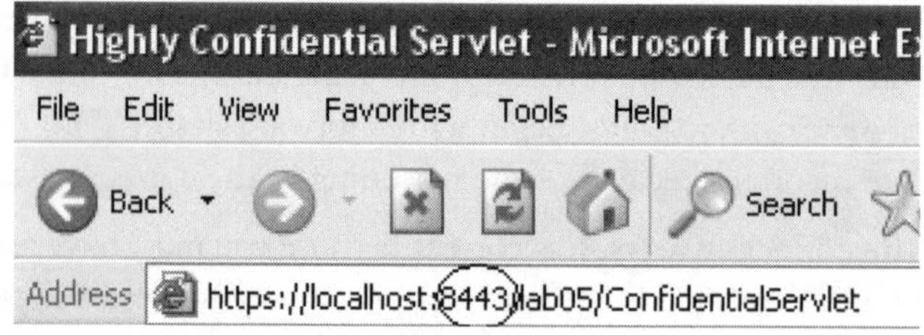

This all assumes that you managed to create your certificate and configure your server correctly—and there, I'm afraid, I can't give you more help than I did in the lab instructions.

Don't forget to restore Tomcat to its original state without security. Stop Tomcat. Take server.xml in the conf directory and rename this to server.xml.secure. Take the copy you made of server.xml, and replace this in the conf directory (if you renamed the copy, make sure you rename it back to server.xml). Restart Tomcat.

6

JavaServer Pages

CERTIFICATION OBJECTIVES

- JSP Life Cycle
- JSP Elements
- JSP Directives
- JSP Implicit Objects
- ✓ Two-Minute Drill
- Q&A Self Test

In the previous chapters, you completed a thorough exploration of servlets. In most of the remaining chapters, we will explore a technology that turns servlets on their head: JavaServer Pages, also known as JSP technology, JSP pages, and sometimes simply JSPs. In the pure servlet model, servlet writing is at the front of the development process. JavaServer Pages, by contrast, place servlet creation at the back end of development. Servlets still play a crucial part, but they are, in fact, generated and compiled from JavaServer Page sources.

This is such an important subject that you'll find a big emphasis placed on it in the exam—you're likely to encounter JSP technology in almost half the questions. If you're already familiar with JavaServer Pages at version 1.2, you'll know that they already contain an abundance of neat features. The current exam tests you on version 2.0, which roughly doubles what you need to know about JSPs. If that's the bad news, then the good news is that the enhancements built into version 2.0 make JSP technology an ever more practical and flexible choice for web application development, so the skills you're learning should be both useful and marketable.

CERTIFICATION OBJECTIVE

JSP Life Cycle (Exam Objective 6.4)

Describe the purpose and event sequence of the JSP page life cycle: (1) JSP page translation, (2) JSP page compilation, (3) load class, (4) create instance, (5) call the jspInit method, (6) call the _jspService method, and (7) call the jspDestroy method.

So is JSP technology "better" than servlets? Should you now forget what you learned in the first five chapters (except for passing the exam, of course!) and hone your JSP skills instead? I prefer to view servlets and JavaServer pages as complementary. You might find that a typical web application consists 90 percent of JavaServer pages to encapsulate individual pages or "screens," with 10 percent servlets to control interaction between pages and business components.

The best way to understand when each approach is appropriate to use is to dive into the detail. We'll start with the above exam objective concerning page life cycle: not actually the first in Sun's list, but the one I view as fundamental to getting a handle on JSP technology.

JSP Translation and Execution

So why turn the servlet pattern on its head? Through the exercises, you have written numerous servlets that produce HTML, generally by peppering a liberal sprinkling of `out.write()` statements throughout the `doGet()` or `doPost()` method. By contrast, JavaServer Page technology allows you to write snippets of Java code between HTML statements. Here's an example page that displays the current date and time (note that the line numbers are not part of the source—imagine that you're looking in a text editor that displays line numbers):

```
01 <%@ page language="java" %>
02 <%@ page import="java.util.*" %>
03 <html><head><title>Simple JSP Example</title></head>
04 <body>
05 <h1>Simple JSP Example</h1>
06 <%= new Date() %>
07 </body>
08 </html>
```

Let's just look at the overall "mix" of the lines. Lines 01, 02, and 06 are a bit peculiar, so we'll ignore them for now. However, the remaining five lines are straight HTML. Clearly, this approach confers a huge advantage. You'll find that JavaServer Page source can consist primarily—even wholly—of HTML syntax. So the process of page design is much more natural than writing HTML within a Java servlet source file. And although the majority of JSP pages are designed to produce HTML, you'll see in later chapters how much work has been done to allow JSP pages to create XML output.

JSP pages were intended to be a boon for project management—the web designer could concentrate on the page design (without requiring Java knowledge), and the Java programmer could later insert the dynamic Java elements within the page design. Certainly this approach can work, although it throws up a change control issue, for there will be occasions when both the page designer and the Java programmer want to make changes to the same page at the same time. You'll see through the following chapters that there is more and more emphasis in JSP technology on taking Java out of the page and replacing it with other elements (Expression Language, custom tags) that can—at least in theory—put the dynamic side of page construction in the hands of the nonprogrammer.

The JSP Translation Phase

As it stands, our JSP example above (displaying the date and time) doesn't look much like something that could one day become a Java object. How might this happen? You deploy a JSP page into a JSP container (servlet containers such as Tomcat are invariably JSP containers as well). The JSP container has mechanisms that "translate" the page into something we do recognize as Java code: namely, a servlet. The process is shown in Figure 6-1.

The translation occurs only when necessary, at some point before a JSP page has to serve its first request. Translation doesn't have to happen again—unless the JSP source code is updated and the page redeployed. A JSP container has discretion regarding when the translation occurs. It can occur on demand: as late as the first time a user requests a JSP page. At the other extreme, JSP pages can be translated on installation into a JSP container (a process often referred to as JSP precompilation). Any point in between is possible (though less usual)—for example, when a web application is loaded, a JSP container might choose to translate any new or changed JSP pages.

FIGURE 6-1

The JavaServer Page Translation Phase

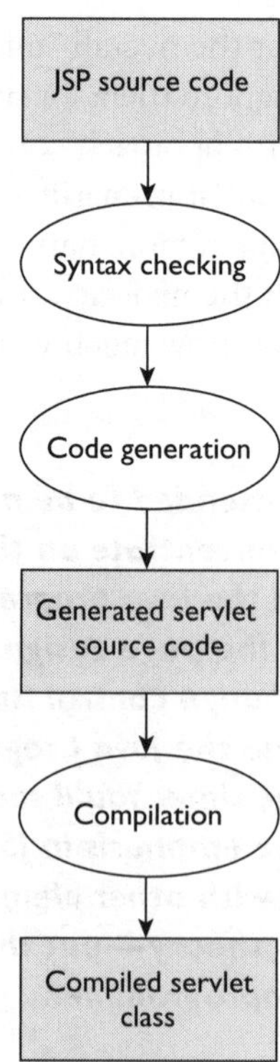

Figure 6-1 shows that there are two outputs within the translation phase. The first is an interim output: a Java source file for a servlet. The second is the compiled class file from the servlet source. The class file is retained for future use, and most JSP containers give you an option whereby you can retain the servlet source for debugging purposes (the default is generally to discard the source within the translation phase). The servlet created isn't just any old servlet—it has some special characteristics. In particular,

- The servlet (or one of its superclasses) must implement the javax.servlet.jsp .HttpJspPage interface, or . . .
- For the tiny minority of non-HTTP, specialist JSP containers, the servlet (or one of its superclasses) must implement the javax.servlet.jsp.JspPage interface.

How does this work? Well, you get an individual servlet based on your Java source—naturally, every JavaServer Page is different. And remember it's the container that provides this, through very clever code generators. Because it's a servlet, the code is likely to inherit from GenericServlet, which incorporates lots of useful servlet behavior. But because JSP servlets have to obey some special rules, a vendor will typically have a specialized JSP base servlet—perhaps extending HttpServlet or GenericServlet, and extended by all generated JSP servlets. In Tomcat, this is called org.apache.jasper.runtime.HttpJspBase. The inheritance tree for the Tomcat-generated servlet from JSP source is shown in Figure 6-2. Although it's "vendor-specific," showing it is instructive. You can see Tomcat makes as much use as possible of existing classes and interfaces in the standard javax.servlet and javax.servlet.http packages.

exam watch

Note that the HttpJspPage interface extends JspPage, so generated JSP servlets (or their superclasses) always implement the defined methods within JspPage.

What did I mean when I mentioned non-HTTP JSP containers? HTTP is by far the main protocol, but the JSP spec is flexible enough to accommodate any request/response protocol you wish to implement. The JspPage interface API documentation says that you have to implement a `_jspService()` method, but it doesn't include the method definition in the interface code. In this way, you are free (as a JSP container designer) to define whatever types you like for the request and response parameters. For the majority of us JSP developers, though, we'll be more than happy that our conventional HTTP containers implement the HttpJspPage interface—which contains the following signature for the `_jspService()` method:

```
public void _jspService(HttpServletRequest request,
            HttpServletResponse response);
```

FIGURE 6-2

Class Hierarchy for Generated Servlet from JSP Source (Tomcat)

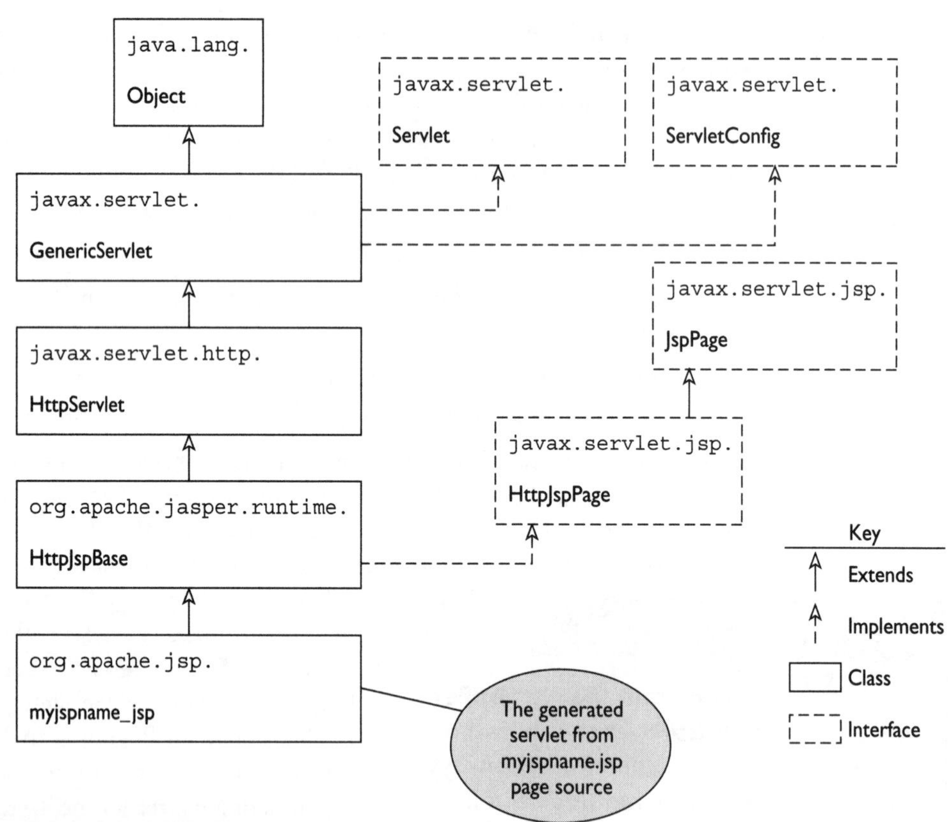

exam watch

You'll see that the exam objective we're covering talks about translation followed by JSP page compilation as two separate stages. My understanding of the JSP spec tells me that translation includes servlet source compilation (as well as syntax checking and servlet source generation). You're unlikely to encounter a question in which this distinction matters—just be aware that "translation" is slightly ambivalent, even within documentation originating from Sun.

As for the exact form the code in your generated servlet takes, that's vendor-specific. The exercise at the end of this section tells you where you might find the Tomcat container's source code.

A final note about translation: If a page fails to translate, an HTTP request for the page should give rise to a 500 (server error) communicated back in the HTTP response.

FIGURE 6-3

The JavaServer Page Request Phase

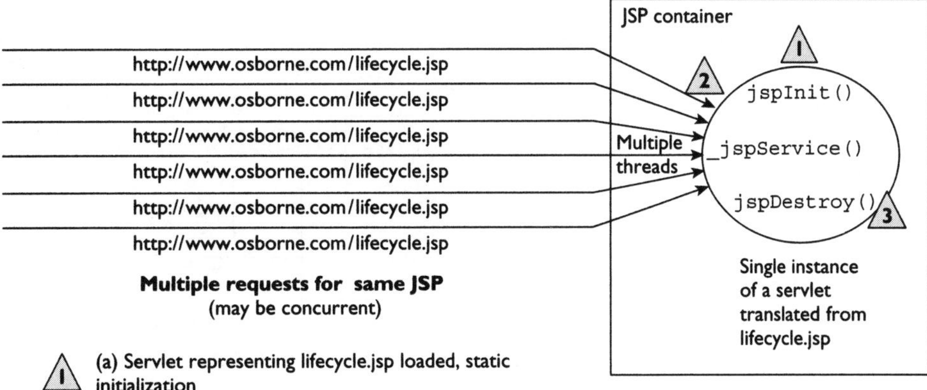

1 (a) Servlet representing lifecycle.jsp loaded, static initialization

(b) Instance of representing servlet created

(c) `jspInit()` called

Rules: must happen in order (a), (b), (c) (though these don't have to happen in quick succession)

Must happen before 2

2 Requests to lifecycle.jsp processed by calling the `_jspService()` method on the corresponding servlet. May occur in multiple concurrent threads.

3 Servlet representing lifecycle.jsp taken out of service:

- `jspDestroy()` called
- instance of servlet garbage collected

The JSP Request/Execution Phase

The request (or execution) phase of a JSP page is remarkably similar to the servlet life cycle. You can remind yourself of this by looking at Figure 1-9 in Chapter 1—then comparing this with Figure 6-3. Of course, because JSP pages are—ultimately—servlets, the request life cycle of a JSP page is controlled from within a servlet's life cycle, and we'll need to discuss how the two relate.

Just as for any other servlet, the JSP page's servlet class is loaded, and an instance of it is created. Generally speaking, there will only be one instance corresponding with a JSP. One of the delights of JSP pages is that they don't have to be registered at all. Just place them in the accessible area of a web application directory structure, as shown in the following illustration.

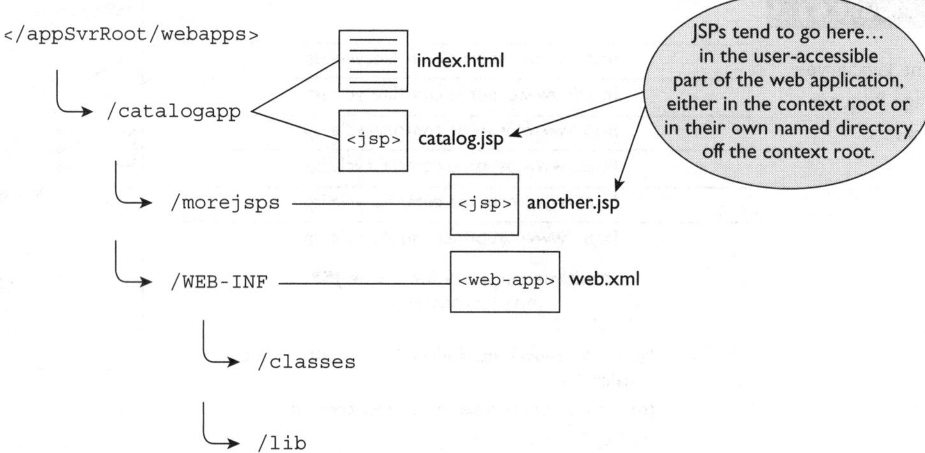

And, provided they have a file extension (usually .jsp) recognized by your application server, no further work needs to be done. However, you can register a JSP page in the same way as a servlet. You even use the `<servlet>` element, with one vital difference—where the `<servlet-class>` would appear, you substitute `<jsp-file>` instead. Here's part of web.xml file that registers the same JSP twice over, under separate names and with separate mappings:

```
<servlet>
  <servlet-name>JspName1</servlet-name>
  <jsp-file>/instanceCheck.jsp</jsp-file>
</servlet>
<servlet-mapping>
  <servlet-name>JspName1</servlet-name>
  <url-pattern>/jspName1</url-pattern>
</servlet-mapping>
<servlet>
  <servlet-name>JspName2</servlet-name>
  <jsp-file>/instanceCheck.jsp</jsp-file>
</servlet>
<servlet-mapping>
  <servlet-name>JspName2</servlet-name>
  <url-pattern>/jspName2</url-pattern>
</servlet-mapping>
```

So I have a JSP page called "instanceCheck.jsp" installed directly in the root of my web application. Suppose that I install this under Tomcat using a context directory called examp0601. I have three valid URLs for accessing this JSP. This is the normal way, which ignores any registration details—just use the name of the JSP itself:

```
http://localhost:8080/examp0601/instanceCheck.jsp
```

Alternatively, I can use the servlet mapping corresponding to my first registered name for the JSP page, JSPName1:

```
http://localhost:8080/examp0601/jspName1
```

Or, of course, I can use the second mapping:

```
http://localhost:8080/examp0601/jspName2
```

The point to note is that just like servlets (and after all, a JSP page is—ultimately—a servlet), each of these three methods of access establishes three separate instances of the servlet class within the web container. Multiple instances will occur like this only when the JSP page is registered in more than one way. The following illustration shows how this might look inside the JSP container's JVM.

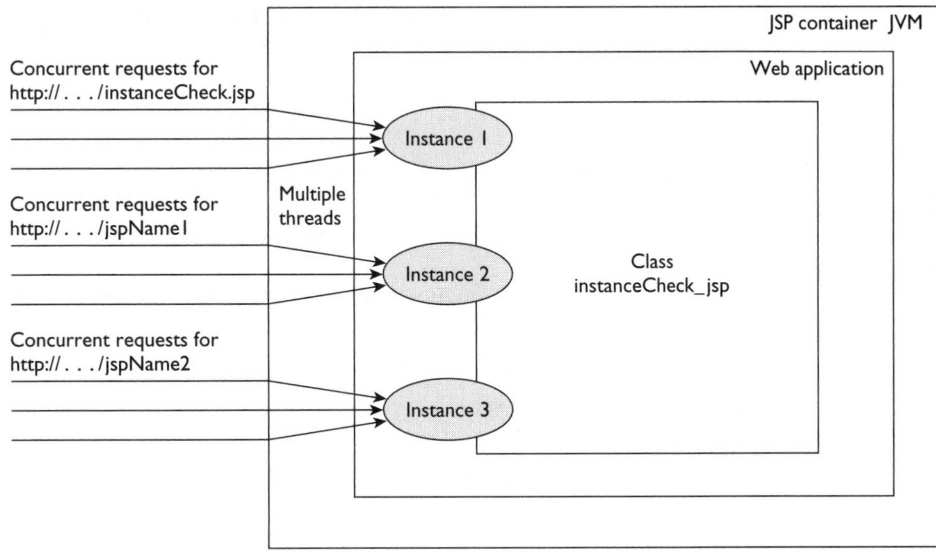

It's worth noting that you can exploit all the other `<servlet>` elements in web .xml for your JSP page. Most usefully, you can set up initialization parameters exactly as you would for a normal servlet.

If you want to suppress direct access to a JSP (so that users have to go through a registered name and a servlet mapping), locate the JSP page under WEB-INF.

Having established how instances of a JSP's servlet get created, let's return to the life cycle diagram in Figure 6-3. At 1 in the figure, we see that three things happen (very often in succession, but not always). The servlet class is loaded, and any static initialization occurs. Then an instance of the servlet comes into being through normal construction processes. After this, the servlet's `init(ServletConfig config)` method is called by the servlet container (as per normal servlet life cycle rules)—which *must* call the `jspInit()` method. So `jspInit()` becomes a JSP page's equivalent of `init(ServletConfig config)`—it gets called once when the JSP page's servlet instance is created, and never again for that instance. So you are welcome to use this method for any one-off setup processes required for the JSP page.

Then at 2 in Figure 6-3, we see multiple requests being made to the JSP. Under the covers, this calls the generated servlet's `service(request, response)` method, which in turn is obliged to call the method `_jspService()`, passing on the request and response parameters. `_jspService()` constitutes the bulk of your generated JSP servlet. For one thing, all that HTML text in our original JSP source—lines such as

```
<html><head><title>Simple JSP Example</title></head>
```

has to be turned into servlet code equivalent—for example,

```
out.write("<html><head><title>Simple JSP Example</title></head>");
```

The same applies to the dynamic elements of the JSP source as well. So

```
<% = new Date() %>
```

might become

```
out.write(new Date());
```

in the `_jspService()` method.

Multiple threads may access `_jspService()` at the same time, so all the comments about thread safety and the servlet's `service()` method are just as applicable to the `_jspService()` method.

Ultimately, a JSP container will decide to discard your generated servlet instance—the circumstances are the same as for servlets. It could be to save resources, because the web application or entire server is being closed down, or for arbitrary reasons of its own. At this point, the servlet's `destroy()` method is called (nothing new here)—which, because it's a JSP page servlet, *must* call the `jspDestroy()` method. So `jspDestroy()` is called before the instance of the JSP servlet is nullified and garbage collected, giving you the opportunity to reclaim resources in a controlled fashion. The container guarantees that `jspService()` will have completed for all requesting threads on the instance before `jspDestroy()` is called—unless this is overridden by a server-specific timeout.

exam watch

If you want to harness `jspInit()` and `jspDestroy()` for your own setup and tear-down processes, you can—by overriding either or both in a JSP declaration, which we explore a little later in this chapter. What if you decided to override the servlet equivalents, `init(ServletConfig config)` and `destroy()`? Well, the JSP spec says you can't and mustn't do this. Most JSP container providers prevent this happening by making all Servlet interface methods final in the base JSP servlet that they provide—your generated JSP servlet that inherits from this can't possibly override them.

And while on the subject of overriding, you can't override `_jspService()` either. This method represents your page source in Java code form—it's up to the clever container's page generators to worry about the implementation and generation of this method for each individual JSP. It makes no sense for you to override it within the JSP page itself.

EXERCISE 6-1

JSP Life Cycle

This exercise has you write a JSP that documents its own life cycle. We'll also get the JSP to indicate which class your JSP servlet inherits from. You'll meet a couple of concepts documented fully later in the chapter, but don't worry: The steps in the exercise give you enough explanation to follow through without reading ahead.

If you haven't removed any server security settings from the previous chapter, do so now in case they interfere with this and subsequent exercises. The instructions (for Tomcat) can be found with the lab solution at the end of Chapter 5.

For this exercise, create the usual web application directory structure under a directory called ex0601, and proceed with the steps. There's a solution in the CD in the file sourcecode/ch06/ex0601.war—check there if you get stuck.

Create the JSP

1. Create an empty file directly in your newly created context directory, ex0601. Call it lifecycle.jsp.
2. Within lifecycle.jsp, include simple HTML for a complete web page, such as shown below:

```
<html>
<head>
<title>JavaServer Page Lifecycle</title>
</head>
<body bgcolor="#FFFFFF">
<h1>To illustrate JavaServer Page lifecycle</h1>
</body>
</html>
```

3. Now you'll add some Java code. This must be earmarked as a JSP declaration—we learn what that is later in the chapter. Beneath the HTML, type the syntax for opening a JSP declaration:

```
<%!
```

Then leave some blank lines (this is where you will type Java code, as described in the next steps). Close the declaration after the blank lines with the closing syntax:

```
%>
```

4. As described in the chapter already, your JSP page will be turned into a servlet that extends some base class provided by your application server (and we've been using Tomcat). This base class will implement the interface HttpJspBase, which in turn extends interface JspBase. This means that the

methods `jspInit()` and `jspDestroy()` are available to override. Write the `jspDestroy()` method between the <%! and %> exactly as if it were your Java source editor, and type the Java in just as you would any other method in a normal .java file. Make this method do something to indicate it has fired—`System.out.println("This method is jspDestroy()")` will do fine.

5. Immediately after `jspDestroy()` and before the closing %> marker, write a `jspInit()` method. This should also indicate (through a `System.out.println`) which method has been called. However, also include some code to show the type name of the class generated (a hint if you're not familiar with Java's reflection facilities: `this.getClass().getName()`). Also include some code that shows at least the immediate superclass of this class (another hint: The Class class has a `getSuperClass()` method). Again, make this output visible through `System.out.println()`.
6. Now we'll introduce more Java code, this time as "scriptlet" code. Again, you won't have to wait long for an explanation—the following section of this chapter will furnish you with one. Like declarations, scriptlet code must go between two markers: this time <% at the beginning and (as for declarations) %> at the end. Put in these markers at the end of your lifecycle.jsp file, leaving some blank lines between them.
7. Scriptlet code doesn't include any kind of method declaration, for the resulting generated code is incorporated directly into the `_jspService()` method. Type in code between the <% and %> markers that gives some indication that it is the `_jspService()` method which is being executed. Again, a simple `System.out.println()` statement will suffice.
8. Ensure that you save the file lifecycle.jsp before exiting your text editor.

Deploy and Run the JSP

9. Create and deploy a WAR file that contains lifecycle.jsp to your web server, and start the web server.
10. Use your browser to request lifecycle.jsp using a suitable URL, such as

```
http://localhost:8080/ex0601/lifecycle.jsp
```

11. Refresh your browser a few times to re-request the JSP page. Take a look at your server console window. Here's some (edited) output from the solution code:

```
org.apache.jsp.lifecycle_jsp.jspInit(lifecycle_jsp.java:27)
Class org.apache.jsp.lifecycle_jsp
subclass of org.apache.jasper.runtime.HttpJspBase
  which implements interfaces: interface javax.servlet.jsp.HttpJspPage
subclass of javax.servlet.http.HttpServlet
  which implements interfaces: interface java.io.Serializable
subclass of javax.servlet.GenericServlet
  which implements interfaces: interface javax.servlet.Servlet, javax.servlet.
ServletConfig, java.io.Serializable
subclass of java.lang.Object
org.apache.jsp.lifecycle_jsp._jspService(lifecycle_jsp.java:108)
org.apache.jsp.lifecycle_jsp._jspService(lifecycle_jsp.java:108)
```

12. Your `jspInit()` code should show you the inheritance hierarchy of your servlet, as the solution code does above (the solution code also throws in a bit extra, by showing the interfaces implemented by each class in the hierarchy). You can see from the solution code output above that the generated servlet for the JSP page is called lifecycle_jsp. Its immediate parent is org.apache .jasper.runtime.HttpJspBase — supplied with Tomcat to act as a base class for all generated JSP servlets. Note that this implements the HttpJspPage interface (as per the rules for servlets of this kind). The hierarchy looks more familiar after that. HttpJspBase inherits from HttpServlet, which — as you'll remember from the earlier chapters — inherits from Generic Servlet.
13. You should also see a line of output for each time you refreshed your browser window, to indicate that the `_jspService()` method executed.
14. Causing the `jspDestroy()` method to execute is a little more difficult. You could close your application server altogether, but then you lose your console window! You can probably track down the file containing the log from console output (if your server is configured to save all console output). An alternative — at least in Tomcat — is to remove the context for this exercise but keep the server running. I achieve this by issuing a command to the Tomcat manager application, which should be running by default. The URL to issue the command looks like this, and you enter it as a regular address in your browser:

    ```
    http://localhost:8080/manager/stop?path=/ex0601
    ```

    You may well be prompted to sign on, for the manager application is secured by default. You need to choose a user in the manager role. The list of users (as discussed in Chapter 5) is in the <TOMCAT_INSTALLATION

_DIRECTORY>/conf/tomcat-users.xml. If there isn't a user already present with the manager role ascribed, add a `<user>` entry under an existing `<user>` entry, looking like this:

```
<user username="manager" password="tomcat" roles="manager"/>
```

Restart the Tomcat server, and reissue the stop command. Now sign on as user "manager" with password "tomcat," and you should get this message in your browser:

```
OK—Stopped application at context path /ex0601
```

Check the console. You should see some indication that the `jspDestroy()` method has fired. In the solution code output it looks like this:

```
org.apache.jsp.lifecycle_jsp.jspDestroy(lifecycle_jsp.java:54)
```

Check the Translation Output

15. If you're using Tomcat, the generated servlet Java source and compiled class will, by default, be kept in the following directory:

```
<Tomcat Installation Directory>/work/Catalina/localhost/<context-directory>/
org/apache/jsp
```

16. You are looking for a file called lifecycle_jsp.java. (Tomcat appears to name the generated servlet source file according to the name of the JSP source file, with a _jsp suffix added. The extension becomes .java to denote that this is a Java source file.)
17. Browse lifecycle_jsp.java with a text editor. Find the `jspInit()`, `jspDestroy()`, and `_jspService()` methods. Note how all the `jspInit()` and `jspDestroy()` code comes from what you typed into the JSP page source. Now look at `_jspService()`. You'll see that the code you supplied in the JSP page source is a relatively small percentage of the whole. There's lots of code dedicated to setting up "implicit" objects (we'll come across these at the end of this chapter) and plenty of code that simply writes out the template HTML text to an output stream—just as would happen if you were writing a servlet by hand. Here's an extract:

```
out.write("\n");
out.write("<html>\n");
out.write("<head>\n");
out.write("<title>JavaServer Page Lifecycle</title>\n");
out.write("</head>\n");
out.write("<body bgcolor=\"#FFFFFF\">\n");
out.write("<h1>To illustrate JavaServer Page lifecycle</h1>\n");
out.write("</body>\n");
out.write("</html>\n");
```

18. That's the end of the exercise—you've now seen the JSP life cycle in action and seen firsthand how closely tied it is to the servlet life cycle.

CERTIFICATION OBJECTIVE

JSP Elements (Exam Objective 6.1)

Identify, describe, or write the JSP code for the following elements: (a) template text, (b) scripting elements (comments, directives, declarations, scriptlets, and expressions), (c) standard and custom actions, and (d) expression language elements.

The exam objective above covers almost everything that can legally appear in a JSP page. When JSP technology was first released, it contained only template text and scripting elements—(a) and (b) in the objective in the section head above. This section will focus on these aspects, for they are the most fundamental. Standard and custom actions—(c)—came later, and will have a separate section (and exam objective) of their own in Chapter 7, as will expression language—(d)—which is a powerful but quite recent addition to the JSP repertoire.

Template text is easy to explain: It's any HTML or XML (or indeed any type of content at all) that you care to include in your JSP page. Template text is sent unchanged to response output. This is not so with scripting elements: There are several different sorts, and the JSP container works hard to turn these dynamic elements into something else—usually a coherent string of HTML or XML. Together with the template text, this completes the page response.

These are the topics we investigate in this chapter. In your own work environment, you may find such "traditional" scripting elements deemphasized in favor of custom tags and expression language. This is even reflected in the exam, which concentrates more on the newer aspects of JSP syntax. However, you must gain a sound knowledge of the older features. The exam still has plenty to say about them (often in combination with the newer JSP features), and you will doubtless be called upon to read, understand, and maintain JSP pages that rely heavily on traditional scripting elements. And although you're encouraged to use the newer features, they are not in any sense deprecated—there are times when these elements are the best or only approach to solving a problem.

Anatomy of a JSP Page

Before diving into the detail, take a look at Figure 6-4, which breaks down the composition of a JSP page into all its possible constituents.

You can see in Figure 6-4 show a JSP page divides into template text and elements. Elements fall into three types: directive, scripting, and action. There are two forms of scripting (EL or "traditional") and two forms of action element (standard or custom). The lightly shaded areas correspond to the topics covered in this chapter.

FIGURE 6-4

Anatomy of a JSP Page

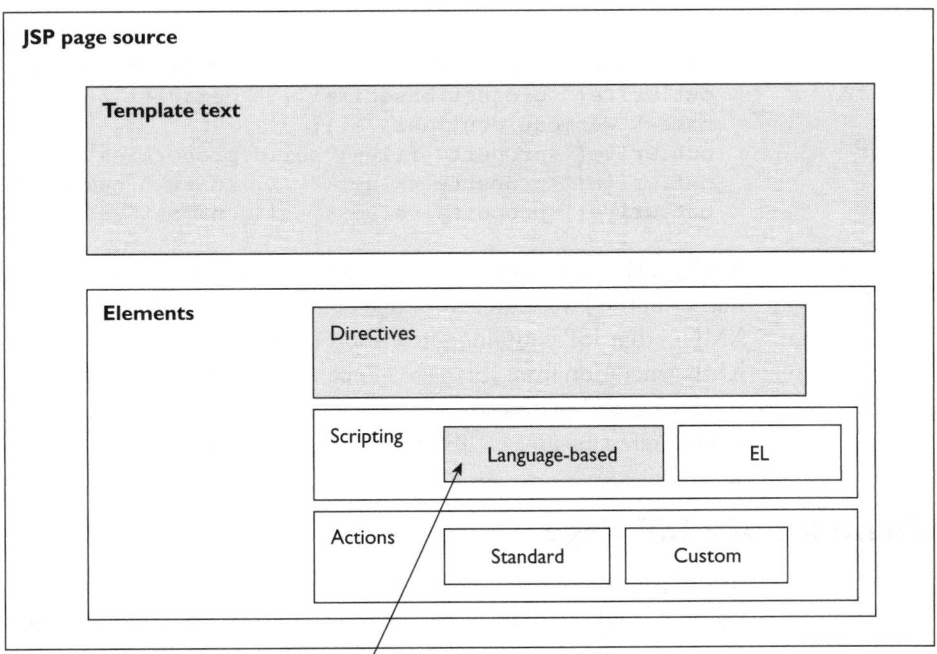

Template Data

A JSP source page generally starts life as a regular piece of static HTML or XML. As the JSP specification puts it, JSP technology supports the "natural manipulation" of text and XML—you can write it as it would appear in a normal document. And this constitutes the template data in a JSP page—anything that's static: source that the JSP container doesn't have to translate into anything else beyond String parameters to simplistic "out.write()" servlet source code statements.

We saw how this worked at the end of the exercise in the previous section. Here's a further example, this time for XML. This is the opening of some JSP page source, containing only XML template text:

```
<project name="webmodulebuilder" default="deploy" basedir=".">

  <!-- set global properties for this build -->
  <property file="build.properties" />
  <property name="dist" value="../../dist" />
  <property name="web" value="../" />
```

This manifests itself in the generated servlet I'm looking at (from Tomcat) like this:

```
out.write("<?xml version=\"1.0\" encoding=\"UTF-8\"?>\n");
out.write("<project basedir=\".\" default=\"deploy\"
name=\"webmodulebuilder\">");
out.write("<property file=\"build.properties\"/>");
out.write("<property value=\"../../dist\" name=\"dist\"/>");
out.write("<property value=\"../\" name=\"web\"/>");
```

So the XML is more or less unchanged—apart from the addition of lots of backslashes in the Java source to escape double quotes. You'll find—particularly with XML—that JSP containers give short shrift to ill-formed documents. We revisit XML generation from JSP page source in Chapter 7.

Having dealt with the constant template aspects, let's turn our attention to the more interesting areas of JSP page source: page elements.

Elements of a JSP Page

In JSP page source, if it's not template text, it must be an element. An element is simply something that can't stand as it is—it needs to be translated. An element is always recognizable through a standard set of characters to mark its beginning and end. Many elements use XML-style opening and closing tags for this purpose. Other elements use different conventions—here's a scriptlet element:

```
<% System.out.println("A scriptlet"); %>
```

However, the principle is the same— opening characters (`<%`) and closing characters (`%>`).

There are three types of element possible in a JSP page:

1. **Directive elements.** You most often use these to communicate global information to your page, which is independent of any particular request. For example, you might use an appropriate directive for importing classes you need: These will translate to Java source import statement in the generated servlets. We explore directive elements in the next section of this chapter.
2. **Action elements.** These use XML-style tags for the inclusion of dynamic data. You get many as "standard" with JSP containers, but can still build your own "custom" actions. We start exploring actions at the beginning of Chapter 7.
3. **Scripting elements.** There are two kinds. There is a newer, preferred syntax called Expression Language, or EL. We meet this in Chapter 7. Then there is the Java language-based approach. Either way, the purpose is to incorporate dynamic information or execute presentation logic. We explore the "traditional" Java language approach in this section of the chapter.

So let's look at the language-based scripting elements in more detail—all are retained in JSP 2.0, despite the wealth of alternatives. There are four in all:

1. expressions, which exploit Java code to place some output directly in the JSP page. We've met an example already: `<%= new Date() %>`.
2. scriptlets, for more extended pieces of Java code, as long as it's legal Java code that works in the context of the `_jspService()` method. The code doesn't necessarily contribute anything to the page output—for example, you might write a scriptlet like this—`<% System.out.println("in the jspService() method"); %>`—just to log some information to the server console, as we did in the last exercise.
3. declarations, for any piece of Java code that needs to exist in the generated servlet but outside the `_jspService()` method. Declarations usually consist of whole methods, more rarely of instance and class data members (and why

would you use them? A JSP becomes a servlet with its related thread-safety issues—you should be using session or context attributes instead!). Here's a short declaration example: `<%! public void jspInit() { // Do nothing } %>`.

4. comments, to denote any lines you want to be completely ignored by the JSP page translation process. They'll appear in the JSP page source but nowhere else. Example: `<%-- Author: David Bridgewater --%>`.

You can see that all four of these scripting elements have similar syntax—all contain angle brackets, percent signs, and some additional characters as well. Whichever kind you're using, there is a rule that the beginning and end markers (such as `<%` and `%>` for a scriptlet) must appear in the same physical source file. Beyond that, anything goes (well, most things): White space, carriage returns, and tabs are all permissible, just as in normal source code.

With that preliminary survey complete, let's look a little more closely at the niceties of each of these four scripting elements.

Expressions

As we noted before, expressions use the result of evaluating a piece of Java code directly in the page output. You might understand this better if you see how an expression is dealt with in the generated servlet. Let's take the example we've used all along: including a call to the no-argument constructor of the java.util.Date object in the JSP source. The Date object produced by the constructor call represents the current date and time. Here's how it looks when used in the JSP page source:

```
<%= new java.util.Date() %>
```

When this is generated into servlet code, the resulting Java statement will probably look like this:

```
out.print(new java.util.Date());
```

`out` is an instance of a javax.servlet.jsp.JspWriter, and it is associated with the response for the generated servlet. And you can see what happens: The contents of your JSP expression are used directly as the parameter to the `print()` method. You'll see from the API documentation that this is an overloaded method. In this case, we're invoking the version that accepts an object. The object is turned into a String through a call to the `String.valueOf(Object)` method, which ultimately uses the `toString()` method on the object to return a String value. In the case of the

Date object, it will be the current date and time formatted according to the default locale on the server running your JSP container. So the onus on you as the JSP page developer is to ensure that whatever expression you use (and it can be as complex as you like), the result is a String object.

exam watch

JspWriter's `print()` methods are overloaded to accept primitives, so you won't run into difficulties including expressions that evaluate (for example) to an int. However, you must at all costs avoid void! If the expression you use is a method with no return value, your JSP page will fail the translation stage.

An expression must begin with <%= and conclude with %>. Whatever Java you place inside the expression, remember not to terminate it with a semicolon! The Java used will be employed as parameter code inside a method call (which is itself inside the `_jspService()` method).

Scriptlets

Scriptlets allow you to include an extended series of Java statements inside the `_jspService()` method that are executed on every request to the page. This time, the Java statements are incorporated "as is," so you must terminate each with a semicolon, unlike expressions. A scriptlet begins with a <% and ends with a %>. Here's an example JSP page, which incorporates four scriptlets and two expressions:

```
<html><head><title>The Planets</title></head><body>
<% /* Scriptlet 1 */
  String[] planets = {"Mercury", "Venus", "Earth", "Mars", "Jupiter", "Saturn",
"Uranus", "Neptune", "Pluto"};
%>
<table>
  <tr><th><b>The Planets - in order by distance from the Sun</b>  </th></tr>
<% for (int i = 0; i < planets.length; i++) { /* Scriptlet 2 */
  if (i == 3) { // fourth rock from the sun %>
      <tr><td><font color="red"><%=(planets[i] + ", the red planet").toUpper
Case()%></font></td></tr>
<%  } else { /* Scriptlet 3 */ %>
      <tr><td><%= planets[i] %></td></tr>
<%  } /* Scriptlet 4 */
  } %>
</table></body></html>
```

The Planets — in order by distance from the Sun
Mercury
Venus
Earth
MARS, THE RED PLANET
Jupiter
Saturn
Uranus
Neptune
Pluto

The output from this JSP page is shown in the illustration on the left. You should see that Mars (the fourth planet in the array) shows up in capital letters with some extra description and in a slightly different shade of gray to represent the red writing! Better still, use the electronic version of the book to copy the JSP source into a .jsp file, and deploy it on your server.

Let's analyze what the page source is doing. Scriptlet 1 sets up a String array, containing a list of planets. Some HTML follows, setting up a table with a heading row. Scriptlet 2 begins a loop to iterate through the planet names in the array and a condition to do something different for Mars, while Scriptlet 4—consisting of only two closing braces—ends the condition and the loop. Scriptlet 3 provides the default behavior for all the planets that aren't Mars. Interspersed among the second and third scriptlet we find two pieces of HTML containing expressions— one for normal planets and the other for Mars.

You see here two principal reasons for using scriptlets:

1. To set up data for display (first scriptlet)
2. To control the logic of what is displayed (second, third, and fourth scriptlets)

The template text (such as `<tr><td><font color="red">`) is incorporated as `out.write()` statements in the `_jspService()` method, and expressions (such as `<%= planets[i] %>`) as `out.print()` statements—we've discussed both already. To complete the picture, you must remember that template text, expressions, *and* scriptlets are all translated and generated into `_jspService()` *in order of their appearance in the JSP page source*. The power lies in mixing the three together. So you can dictate—for example—that a particular piece of template text and an expression lie within the body of a "for" loop.

There are some consequences following from this. For one thing, scriptlets don't have to comprise complete blocks of code. In the example, we saw a "for" loop begun in the second scriptlet and ended in the fourth. Indeed, it's mostly undesirable to have scriptlets self-contained, for you can't include expressions and template text within one scriptlet: Within the `<%` and `%>` scriptlet boundaries, you can insert only valid Java source code.

Another consequence: You can declare a local variable in one scriptlet and use that in another scriptlet or expression—as long as that happens at some later point in the code. So in the example, the first scriptlet declares the local variable *planets* of type String array, then uses this at two points in later expressions. You can imagine (or try out!) what occurs if you move the first scriptlet declaring the String array to the end of the Java page source. Of course, scoping rules apply: If you have a complex nesting structure with your braces, you have to be careful not to create visibility problems for your local variables. The moral is this: Keep it simple!

Before leaving the topic of scriptlets: Note in the example page source that I have been annoyingly inconsistent in my use of the `<%` and `%>` markers. Sometimes these appear in a line to themselves and sometimes on the same line as some Java source code. I have, of course, done this deliberately to make the point—it doesn't matter. The generated servlet code may have a few extra page breaks thrown in to correspond with extra carriage returns, but syntactically it just doesn't matter. However, I would advise choosing or adopting a consistent style to avoid annoying your coworkers.

exam watch

Any Java code can be placed within scriptlets. Most scriptlet-based questions in the exam are as much a test on Java behavior as they are on JSP syntax. So don't forget all that hard-won SCJP knowledge just yet!

on the job

Of course, because you can use the full power of Java within the JSP page source, the temptation is to do so. There are very real objections to doing this—though I have to say, less real than they used to be. JSP page source was traditionally impossible to debug until the JSP page was deployed and turned into a servlet. Then you would have to find the servlet and debug that—not generally easy, and sometimes impossible if the page translation process didn't result in a legal piece of Java source in the first place. JSP page source editors—again traditionally—had no capability to spot any Java syntax errors you made in your script. However, that position has changed. Page source editors—even free, open source ones (I use a product called Lomboz plugged into the Eclipse IDE)—give instant feedback on compilation problems before you get anywhere near deploying your page. Some commercial editors (IBM Rational Application Developer, for example) even allow real-time debugging of the Java page source: You can place breakpoints in the Java page source and "step through" the page as if it were real Java code.

But with all of that, I would still maintain that if you are writing complex Java code in your JSP page source, there is probably a better place for that code—in a custom tag or even a servlet. Expression Language and JSTL

(coming soon to your JSP page source!—see chapters 7 and 8) can usually provide a more maintainable way of dynamically determining page contents than can Java code. But the choice is still yours—and especially for "quick and dirty" pages to achieve small localized tasks quickly, I can rarely resist the temptation and ease of writing Java source directly into the JSP page.

Declarations

What if you want to place code in the generated servlet outside of the `_jspService()` method? Use a declaration. How do you spot a declaration? It begins with a `<%!` marker. The end marker is still `%>` (the same as it is for expressions and scriptlets).

You can place in your declaration any code that can legally appear in a servlet source file: instance methods, static methods, static initialization code, static or instance data members, inner classes—this covers just about everything. You can also use declarations to override some methods that appear further up in the JSP servlet hierarchy—namely `jspInit()` and `jspDestroy()`.

We'll look at an example that analyzes a sentence typed into a simple form, then works out the average length of the words used. Here is the JSP page source:

```
<%
String userInput = (String) request.getParameter("sentence");
if (userInput == null) {
  userInput = "Antidisestablishmentarianism rules OK";
}
%>
<html>
<head><title>Sentence Analyzer</title></head>
<body>
<p>Type in a sample sentence to analyze:</p>
<form method="GET" action="sentenceAnalyzer.jsp">
<input size="80" name="sentence" type="text" value="<%= userInput %>" />
<br />
<input type="submit" />
</form>
<p>Average length of word is <%=avgWordLength(userInput)%>.</p>
</body>
</html>
<%!
private double avgWordLength(String sentence) {
  java.util.StringTokenizer st = new java.util.StringTokenizer(sentence, " ");
  double wordCount = st.countTokens();
  int totalChars = 0;
```

```
  while (st.hasMoreTokens()) {
    totalChars += st.nextToken().length();
  }
  return totalChars / wordCount;
}
%>
```

The output from this JSP page is shown in the following illustration.

Type in a sample sentence to analyze:

Antidisestablishmentarianism rules OK

Submit Query

Average length of word is 11.666666666666666.

You've seen several elements in this page already. The page starts with a scriptlet. This sets up a local variable called *userInput*, whose value is derived from a request parameter called *sentence*. If this parameter is missing (as happens when you first load the page), then local variable *userInput* is loaded with a default value. Some HTML follows, notably a small form with one text field and a button. The text field has a name of *sentence*, providing the request parameter of that name to the JSP. The text field's value is loaded from the local variable *userInput*, which the page user can then overtype as needed.

Beneath the form is an expression. This calls a method, `avgWordLength()`, and passes the method the *userInput* local variable as a parameter. Where is the method defined? Here we come finally to our declaration: at the bottom of the JSP page source. The following shows the beginning of the declaration and the method signature:

```
<%!
private double avgWordLength(String sentence)
```

There's nothing special about the method itself—you have no doubt written dozens like it. The logic parses the sentence, works out the word and character count, and returns a `double` to represent the average number of characters used per word. Because the method call was in an expression, this value is displayed on the web page.

exam watch

Declaration code has no access to implicit objects; you have to pass these as parameters to the methods you declare. You can feel legitimately ignorant about implicit variables—they haven't yet been introduced—although there is one not very artfully concealed (`request`) at the beginning of the previous code example. Revisit this exam watch when you get to the end of the chapter!

Although I have put the declared method at the end of the example, there's no particular significance to this. All declarations are gathered up by the translation process, and they are placed consecutively in the generated servlet source code.

Comments

You can include two types of comment in your JSP source code. One of these has the following syntax: `<%--` to start the comment and `--%>` to end it. The advantage of this method is that the JSP translation process completely ignores the lines between the comment markers. This is useful as a device during development for temporarily commenting out code, as well as being useful for including comments that should never be reproduced in the web page output. One thing you can't do is to nest one comment of this type within another: As soon as the translation phase reaches the first end marker (`--%>`), which goes with the inner comment, translation recommences, as shown in the following illustration.

```
<%-- <% for (int i = 0; i < 10; i++) {
<%--      if(i==3) System.out.println("i is 3!"); --%>
          System.out.println("i squared is " + i * i);
        } --%>
```

In the code example in the illustration, the grayed-out text is ignored in translation. Translation begins again with the `System.out.println()` statement. Does this cause a compilation error? Actually, no—the translation process sees no marker denoting the beginning of a scriptlet, so it treats the ungrayed Java source as template text—i.e., text that should be directly output in the web page.

However, beware of using this style of commenting within a scriptlet or declaration: It's not allowed. *Only valid Java syntax is allowed within a scriptlet or declaration*—and it doesn't include this style of comment. Of course, you can still use Java's own commenting mechanisms: `//` for single-line comments, `/* ... */` for extended comments, and `/** ... */` for JavaDoc comments. (How or why you would extract JavaDoc comments from a piece of JSP page source or its generated servlet is a different question.)

exam watch

For the four scripting elements we've talked about—expressions, scriptlets, declarations, and comments—none will nest inside each other or inside themselves. You can't have an expression inside a scriptlet, or a scriptlet inside a declaration, or a scriptlet in a scriptlet—or any other combination.

If you want comments sent within the web page output, you can use regular HTML comment syntax: Open the comment with `<!--` and close with `-->`. Of course, this text is not visible in the displayed web page of most browsers, but it is available if you take your browser's option to view the HTML source code. Why would you do this at all? It can be a useful technique to incorporate debugging or support information. An HTML comment is treated exactly like other HTML template text. So it's perfectly acceptable to include JSP scriptlets, expressions, expression language, or any other legal JavaServer Page syntax within the comment—and it will be processed at translation time.

exam watch

Here's a summary table that shows the different forms of scripting elements and key facts for each—many exam questions revolve around a grasp of these!

Element Type	Starts with	Ends with	Semicolons on End of Java Source Statements?	Code Generated into the `jspService()` Method?
Expression	`<%=`	`%>`	No	Yes
Scriptlet	`<%`	`%>`	Yes	Yes
Declaration	`<%!`	`%>`	Yes	No
Comment	`<%--`	`--%>`	Not applicable	Not generated at all

EXERCISE 6-2

JSP Elements

Putting this all together, you're now going to write a JSP page that uses scripting elements to work out and display a table that converts a distance in miles to a distance in kilometers. You'll display the results in an HTML table, so the result will look something like that shown in the illustration on the left.

Miles	Kilometers
1	1.6
2	3.2
3	4.8
5	8
10	16
15	24
20	32
50	80
100	160
200	320
500	800

Create the usual web application directory structure under a directory called ex0602, and proceed with the steps for the exercise. There's a solution in the CD in the file sourcecode/ch06/ex0602.war—check there if you get stuck.

Create the JSP Page Source

1. Create an empty file directly in your newly created context directory, ex0602. Call it milesToKilometers.jsp.
2. At the top of the page source, write a JSP declaration that includes one method with the following signature:

```
private String convert(int miles)
```

In the method, take the miles value passed as a parameter, and multiply this by a constant 1.6 to obtain a value in kilometers. From the resulting numeric kilometers value, produce a suitably formatted String with a sensible number of decimal places (java.text.DecimalFormat may help you here). You don't have to do the formatting—if you prefer, pass back the double value instead.

3. After this declaration, write a scriptlet that declares a local variable: a primitive **int** array. Load the array with approximately a dozen values to represent values in miles to convert (e.g., 1, 2, 3, 5, 10, 15, 20, . . .).
4. Now write the HTML to display the output. Within the body of the page, declare a table with two heading columns: the first for the miles amount, the second for the converted kilometers amount.
5. Within the table, write a scriptlet to loop through all the elements in the **int** array declared in step 3.

6. Break the scriptlet into two scriptlets—the first for the loop logic and the second for the closing brace.
7. Between these two scriptlets, include HTML to create a table row and two cells. Within the first cell, include an expression to show the miles value—taken straight from an occurrence in your **int** array, this occurrence being the value of your loop counter. Within the second cell, include another expression that calls the `convert()` method and passes in the miles value.

Deploy and Run the JSP

8. Create a WAR file that contains milesToKilometers.jsp, and deploy this to your web server. Start the web server if it is not started already.
9. Use your browser to request milesToKilometers.jsp using a suitable URL, such as

```
http://localhost:8080/ex0602/milesToKilometers.jsp
```

CERTIFICATION OBJECTIVE

JSP Directives (Exam Objective 6.2)

Write JSP code that uses the directives: (a) "page" (with attributes "import," "session," "contentType," and "isELIgnore"), (b) "include," and (c) "taglib."

In the first half of this chapter, you have already delved deeply into the mechanics of JavaServer Pages. The second half of the chapter goes further and shows some features that can make your JSP development tasks more convenient.

This section concentrates on directives, which—like scripting elements—are pieces of JSP tag-like syntax. Like an XML or HTML tag, directives have attributes that dictate their meaning and effect. In almost all cases, the effects produced by directives can't be replicated using expressions, scriptlets, or declarations.

We'll consider the three directives mentioned in the above exam objective in this section: `page`, `include`, and `taglib`.

Directives

The page Directive

You can include a `page` directive anywhere in your JSP page source: beginning, middle, or end. Here's an example of how one looks:

```
<%@ page import="java.util.*" %>
```

The effect that this particular directive achieves is to introduce an **`import`** statement into the source of the generated servlet. We'll discuss the import of *import* very shortly, but for now let's just examine how the directive is made up:

- An opening marker: `<%@`
- The word "`page`," which denotes that this is a *page* directive (as opposed to any other kind—*include* or *taglib*, for example)
- The word "`import`," which is one of the valid attributes for the `page` directive
- An equal sign after the attribute name
- The value of the attribute itself, normally in double quotes
- A closing marker—just like the one for scripting elements: `%>`

exam watch

Don't be thrown by weird but legal variants for directive syntax. You don't need white space after the opening marker or before the closing marker:

```
<%@page import="java.util.*"%>
```

You can also put extra white space before or after the equal sign for the attribute:

```
<%@ page import = "java.util.*"%>
```

Single quotes are as acceptable as double quotes for attribute values:

```
<%@ page import='java.util.*' %>
```

You're not confined to having only one valid attribute for a directive. For example, there's a (mostly redundant) attribute for the *page* directive called *language*, to denote what kind of scripting language your JSP uses. The only normally valid value is Java, unsurprisingly. You could include this attribute alongside an *import* attribute if you wanted to:

```
<%@ page import="java.util.*" language="Java" %>
```

However, it is common practice to keep one attribute per directive line:

```
<%@ page import="java.util.*" %>
<%@ page language="Java" %>
```

So now that we've seen the syntax for the *page* directive, let's explore some of the valid attributes.

import You use the `import` attribute to create import statements in the generated servlet source produced by the JSP container's translation phase. When we were looking at declarations in the previous section of this chapter, we looked at an example piece of code that used the java.util.StringTokenizer class. Because we hadn't examined the import mechanism for JSP pages at that point, we were forced into some cumbersome source code:

```
<%!
private double avgWordLength(String sentence) {
  java.util.StringTokenizer st = new java.util.StringTokenizer(sentence, " ");
  //... rest of method omitted
```

By including a *page* directive such as the following anywhere in the JSP page source,

```
<%@ page import="java.util.StringTokenizer" %>
```

you can rewrite the source code in a more succinct and normal fashion:

```
<%!
private double avgWordLength(String sentence) {
  StringTokenizer st = new StringTokenizer(sentence, " ");
  //... rest of method omitted
```

If you hunt down the generated servlet source code, you will doubtless find a perfectly normal Java **import** statement:

```
import java.util.StringTokenizer;
```

There are some packages you get for free within the JSP, so it's redundant to import them (although it doesn't matter if you do). There's java.lang, of course: All the classes in that are available to any piece of Java source, generated servlet or otherwise. Then there are these:

- javax.servlet
- javax.servlet.http
- javax.servlet.jsp

If you look closely at the generated servlet source, you'll see that the boilerplate code (i.e., anything you didn't provide in the way of scriptlets, etc.) uses classes that appear in these three packages.

You can't include classes from the default package. Every class name used in a JSP must be qualified (since the advent of the JSP 2.0 specification).

The value for the `import` attribute can be any of the following:

- A fully qualified class name
- A generic package name (e.g., java.util.*)
- A comma-separated list of either of the above (you can mix and match as needed)

This is the only attribute of the *page* directive that can be specified more than once—either across separate *page* directives that contain *import* once or even (silly as it is) using the *import* attribute more than once in the same *page* directive.

`session` The *session* attribute of the *page* directive is used to determine whether an HttpSession object is available within your JSP page source (if available, it's provided through an implicit variable called—surprise, surprise—*session*, which we explore in the next section of this chapter). If you leave this directive out altogether, the session is available—or you can explicitly say

```
<%@ page session="true" %>
```

This will have the equivalent effect of writing the following servlet code:

```
HttpSession session = request.getSession();
```

Truth to tell, the mechanism for getting hold of the session is usually a little more convoluted in generated JSP servlet source. The reason for using this directive is to eliminate the time spent on creating or obtaining an HttpSession object, in which case you write the directive as follows:

```
<%@ page session="false" %>
```

If your JSP page genuinely doesn't need access to the session (though most will), there's a small performance gain to be made.

Valid values for the session attribute are "true" or "false"—like **boolean** literals in plain Java source. Unlike **boolean** literals, however, these values are case insensitive (so "TRUE" and "FaLsE" are also valid values).

`contentType` In the "Responses" section of Chapter 1, we encountered the `ServletResponse.getContentType(String type)` method. Now you're about to learn the JSP way of achieving the equivalent of this method. By way of reminder, the *type* parameter into this method is a String that specifies the MIME type of the response to be sent back.

Here is the solution code from the ImageLoader servlet in Exercise 1-4, reworked as a JSP. The old servlet and the new JSP simply take an existing .gif from the web application and write this to the response's output stream. Before doing so, both servlet and JSP set the appropriate MIME type for the response, namely "image/gif."

```
<%@ page contentType="image/gif" %>
<%@ page import="java.io.*" %>
<% /* response.setContentType("image/gif"); */
String path = getServletContext().getRealPath("tomcat.gif");
File imageFile = new File(path);
long length = imageFile.length();
response.setContentLength((int) length);
OutputStream os = response.getOutputStream();
BufferedInputStream bis =
  new BufferedInputStream(new FileInputStream(imageFile));
int info;
while ((info = bis.read()) > -1) {
  os.write(info);
}
os.flush(); %>
```

The development of this page source was very simple. I took the code directly from the `doGet()` method of the servlet and pasted this as a scriptlet into the JSP page source. I added a *page* directive to import the java.io package. I also added the *page* directive to set the content type to illustrate what we're talking about here. However, this is a case where scriptlet code works just as well as the *page* directive—the commented-out line of scriptlet code

```
/* response.setContentType ("image/gif"); */
```

is the equivalent of the `page` directive

```
<%@ page contentType="image/gif" %>
```

That's almost true, anyway. You could remove the content-type **page** directive and comment the line of source code back in. What you will then observe in the generated servlet source—near the beginning of the `_jspService()` method—are the following lines of Java:

```
response.setContentType("text/html");
// A few other lines of boiler-plate code, omitted...
response.setContentType("image/gif");
```

The second occurrence of `response.setContentType()` comes about because of your commented-in scriptlet code. The first occurrence comes about because even if you omit the **page** directive for attribute contentType, the JSP container is bound to set a default MIME-type of "text/html." Because no content has been committed, this doesn't matter—the setting of "image/gif" comes later, so it takes precedence—but the moral is that you should use the **page** directive to do a proper job of content-type setting.

isELIgnored The "EL" in this attribute name stands for "Expression Language." This is something we look at properly in Chapter 7. However, there's no harm in giving you a small foretaste here. As you have noted a few times now, the scripting elements we have discussed so far—while not being deprecated—have fallen out of favor. There are better options available, and Expression Language is one of those options. Suppose you wanted to manipulate a request attribute that is set up as follows:

```
<% request.setAttribute("squareIt", new Integer(7)); %>
```

To display the square of this number, you could use a scriptlet/expression combination like this later in the JSP page source:

```
<% int i = ((Integer)
request.getAttribute("squareIt")).intValue(); %> <%= i * i %>
```

Using Expression Language, you could achieve the same result like this:

```
${squareIt * squareIt}
```

Whichever approach you use (or prefer), the result is the same: 49 is output on the page.

At the moment, we'll ignore the "magic" that makes EL work. The important thing to note is that the JSP translation phase has a new piece of syntax to cope with: the ${ to begin the EL expression, and the matching } to end it. In the past, these symbols would have been rendered as template text in your JSP page source. It could be that this is still the effect you want—in other words, you want `${squareIt * squareIt}` to appear as just that string of characters instead of the number 49. After all, if `${` appears in pre-JSP 2.0 source (i.e., JSP 1.2 or before), it's unlikely to be intended as EL.

So you can switch off EL evaluation and have the text be treated as template text. There are several ways to do this (a topic we revisit in Chapter 7), but we're only interested in one of those here. If in your JSP page source you have the directive:

```
<%@ page isELIgnored="true" %>
```

then any EL expressions remain unevaluated, and they appear as template text.

The other valid value is "false." You might think this is the default—in other words, this is what you get if you leave out the directive. However, the situation isn't quite that simple. Suppose that you stick an (old) JSP 1.2 application into a JSP 2.0 container. Chances are that the following is true:

- Your web.xml file is at version 2.3.
- You don't want to be bothered including the `isELIgnored` attribute separately in all your JSP page sources.

To deal with this, the JSP 2.0 sets a default of `isELIgnored="true"` so that any occurrences of ${ in your old application will be correctly treated as template text. Only if the deployment descriptor web.xml is at the up-to-date version level of 2.4 is the default of `isELIgnored` set to "false," for an up-to-date web.xml implies an application that is EL-aware.

Besides this directive, there are other ways to control EL-awareness—we'll complete the picture in Chapter 7.

There are several other attributes of the page directive that are not on the exam syllabus as such. Following is a list with brief definitions so that you're not thrown when you encounter these attributes in real life.

language	<%@ page language="Java" %> Denotes the scripting language. "Java" is the only value supported by all J2EE-compliant containers. Your container might support something different and specialized, but your page won't in all likelihood be portable to other containers then.
extends	<%@ page extends="com.osborne.webcert.MyBaseJSPServlet" %> If you want to override the base servlet that your container provides when generating servlets, you can—and substitute your own through this directive. Do so at your own peril; your container may not like you for it.
buffer, autoFlush	<%@ page buffer="none" autoFlush="true" %> You can use these attributes to control whether or not you have a buffer (you can specify a size in kilobytes), and how this buffer is flushed. The example above causes the response to be flushed as soon as it is generated.
isThreadSafe	<%@ page isThreadSafe="true" %> Causes the generated JSP servlet to implement the deprecated SingleThreadModel interface: not recommended. The default is, of course, false.
info	<%@ page info="My Clever Hacks Page" %> Use this attribute to publish information about your JSP page, accessible through the `getServletInfo()` method.
errorPage, isErrorPage	<%@ page errorPage="errorPage.jsp" %> <%@ page isErrorPage="true" %> Use errorPage to set a URL pointing to another JSP within the same web application. Should an exception occur, your users will be forwarded to this other JSP. The page you forward to must have "isErrorPage" set to true, and is the only sort of page to have access to the implicit variable exception.

The `include` Directive

We're done with the *page* directive; now let's look at the *include* directive. The good news is that there isn't much to this directive: the directive name itself (include) and one mandatory attribute (file). The purpose of *include* is to merge the contents of one JSP source file into another (the one doing the including). This happens at the point where the including JSP page source goes through *translation*. It's not a dynamic operation happening at run time!

A piece of terminology: A JSP source file and the pages it includes through the `include` directive are collectively referred to as a "translation unit." The file type you include doesn't have to be JSP page source, nor does it have to have a .jsp extension. Once included, the file contents must make sense to the JSP translation process, but this gives scope to include entire HTML or XML documents, or document fragments.

The value you can attach to the file attribute is a filename together with its path. The path is relative—either beginning with a forward slash: "/" or not. A path beginning with a forward slash starts at the servlet context directory. Paths without the initial forward slash are determined relative to the location of the page doing the including, and they cannot stray beyond the current context. This obeys the same rules as the `ServletRequest.getRequestDispatcher(String path)` method, which you met in Chapter 3.

Here's an example without the initial forward slash:

```
<%@ include file="stubs/header.html" %>
```

Suppose that this directive is found in a JSP located in directory ex0603/jsps .ex0603 is the context directory. The JSP translator will expect to find the following file and path:

```
ex0603/jsps/stubs/header.html
```

To include the same file relative to the context root, the *include* directive would look like this:

```
<%@ include file="/jsps/stubs/header.html" %>
```

on the job

Don't spread complex logic across different included files—or any logic at all, if you can help it. Doing so can land you in real trouble. Especially consider the prospect of changing the logic in the included page—but translation not picking this up. These days, most containers will reperform translation if either the including or included file is updated. However, this is not mandated by the JSP specification, even though it states a preference for that behavior. Imagine debugging a problem where you think an updated file has been re-included into a top-level JSP page. Imagine then your frustration when half a day later you discover that the page is in fact executing the old logic, based on the old version of the file. Problems of this sort can be utterly baffling: Plan to avoid them!

At the beginning of Chapter 7, you'll come across a different mechanism for inclusion: the `<jsp:include>` standard action. The key difference between this and the `include` directive is that `<jsp:include>` executes afresh with every new request to the including JavaServer Page. Don't forget that the `include` directive discussed here happens at *translation* time. You are almost certain to get an exam question that relies on your knowledge of the difference between these two—but we'll save that piece of cruelty for Chapter 7!

The `taglib` Directive

The *taglib* directive makes custom actions available in the JSP page by referencing a tag library. We don't meet tag libraries until Chapter 8 and custom actions not until Chapter 9, so this may not make much sense at this point. We'll just briefly touch on the syntax of the directive at this point—you'll get plenty of practice with it later. There are two mandatory attributes, *prefix* and *uri*. Every custom action you include in your JSP page must use a prefix specified in one of the *taglib* directives in the page. *uri* gives an indication where the tag library file (which defines the custom actions) can be found. The exact retrieval mechanism will be explained later. So here's an example of the directive:

```
<%@ taglib prefix="mytags" uri="http://www.osborne.com/taglibs/mytags" %>
```

EXERCISE 6-3

JSP Directives

This exercise demonstrates a moderately useful application for the *include* directive: providing a standard header and footer for your HTML JSP pages. Along the way, we'll practice with a couple of the *page* directive attributes and do a little bit of preparatory work for the next section of the book, which talks about implicit variables.

Create the usual web application directory structure under a directory called ex0603, and proceed with the steps for the exercise. There's a solution in the CD in the file sourcecode/ch06/ex0603.war—check there if you get stuck.

Create JSP Page Source for a Standard Header

1. Create an empty file directly in your newly created context directory, ex0603, called header.jsp.
2. In this file, include HTML tags for the start of the document, the start and end of the head section, and the beginning of the body section.

3. Include an HTML title tag within the head section to display some text saying "Exercise 6-3 on " and follow this with an expression showing the date and time. If you use java.util.Date to assist you with this, then you will want a *page* directive to import this class.

Create JSP Page Source for a Standard Footer

4. Create an empty file in ex0603 called footer.jsp.
5. In this file, put in the end of body and end of document HTML tags.
6. Before the end of body, put in a copyright notice. Derive the text for the copyright notice from a context-wide initialization parameter. If you need a refresher on how to set one of these up in web.xml, check out the beginning of Chapter 3. A programming hint for accessing the initialization parameter in your JSP: You'll need to make use of the *application* implicit variable inside an expression scripting element. *application* is an instance variable referencing the ServletContext object for this web application, so it has access to the `getInitParameter()` method.

Create JSP Page Source for a Setup Page

7. Create an empty file in ex0603 called setup.jsp.
8. Use a *page* directive to import the java.util package.
9. In a scriptlet, create a list of things (the solution code uses a TreeMap containing a short list of countries and capitals). Set the object representing the list of things as an attribute of the ServletContext (use the *application* implicit object).

Create the JSP Page Source for a Master Page

10. Create an empty file in ex0603 called master.jsp.
11. Use a *page* directive to import the java.util.package.
12. Use two *include* directives to include header.jsp, followed by setup.jsp.
13. Use a combination of scriptlets and expressions to do the following:
    - retrieve the list you stored in an application attribute in setup.jsp (again, you'll want the *application* implicit variable).
    - display each item (or set of items) in the list as a table row.
14. Conclude the page by including footer.jsp.

Deploy and Run the Master Page

15. Create a WAR file that contains the full directory structure for the exercise context. You've created four JSP files and have amended the deployment descriptor web.xml, so all these resources must be present in the WAR file. Start the web server if it has not started already.
16. Use your browser to request master.jsp using a suitable URL, such as

```
http://localhost:8080/ex0603/master.jsp
```

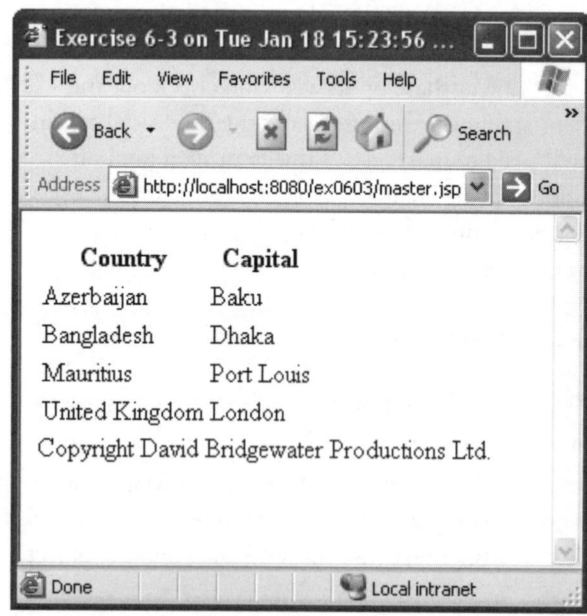

17. The solution code output is shown in the illustration on the left—yours may look a little different.

CERTIFICATION OBJECTIVE

JSP Implicit Objects (Exam Objective 6.5)

Given a design goal, write JSP code using the appropriate implicit objects: (a) request, (b) response, (c) out, (d) session, (e) config, (f) application, (g) page, (h) pageContext, and (i) exception.

To finish this chapter, we're going to look at another convenience provided by JSP technology: implicit objects. A couple of these have been introduced by stealth already in examples and exercises in the chapter so far. There are nine you need to know in all.

However, the good news is that with only two exceptions, these implicit objects are variables *that reference classes you have learned about already*. So your learning burden is lighter than you might otherwise presume when presented with the raw exam objective.

JSP Implicit Objects

The best way to get a handle (no pun intended) on implicit objects is to take a look at the source for any generated servlet. You can use any JSP page source as the basis for the generated code, even one that does nothing—it's the boilerplate code at the beginning of the `_jspService()` method that is of interest. Here's how that code looks for the version of Tomcat used in preparation of this book:

```
public void _jspService(HttpServletRequest request,
  HttpServletResponse response)
  throws java.io.IOException, ServletException {
JspFactory _jspxFactory = null;
PageContext pageContext = null;
HttpSession session = null;
ServletContext application = null;
ServletConfig config = null;
JspWriter out = null;
Object page = this;
JspWriter _jspx_out = null;
PageContext _jspx_page_context = null;
try {
  _jspxFactory = JspFactory.getDefaultFactory();
  response.setContentType("text/html");
  pageContext = _jspxFactory.getPageContext(this,
    request, response, null, true, 8192, true);
  _jspx_page_context = pageContext;
  application = pageContext.getServletContext();
  config = pageContext.getServletConfig();
  session = pageContext.getSession();
  out = pageContext.getOut();
  //... etc. rest of jspService() method
```

So there's nothing very taxing about implicit objects—they are just local variables declared at the outset of the `_jspService()` method. Because they have standardized names, they are available for use within your expressions and scriptlets. By the end of this method opening, we have seen eight out of the nine implicit objects. (The ninth—*exception*—is the exception: We'll see how this implicit object gets declared and initialized later.)

Two are parameters to the `_jspService()` method. In an HTTP context (i.e., most of the time), these represent HttpServletRequest and HttpServletResponse objects. Most of the remainder consists of variables with class or interface types known to us already, in familiar packages. The following table lists all nine, with their types:

Implicit Object Name	Type
request	javax.servlet.http.HttpServletRequest interface (rarely—javax.servlet.ServletRequest)
response	javax.servlet.http.HttpServletRequest interface (rarely—javax.servlet.ServletResponse)
application	javax.servlet.ServletContext interface
config	javax.servlet.ServletConfig interface
session	javax.servlet.http.HttpSession interface
out	javax.servlet.jsp.JspWriter abstract class
pageContext	javax.servlet.jsp.PageContext abstract class
page	java.lang.Object class
exception	java.lang.Throwable class

The only really new concepts are contained in the *out* and *pageContext* implicit objects, whose types live in a package we haven't had cause yet to examine: `javax.servlet.jsp`. *out* is the equivalent of the PrintWriter you get from the response in normal servlets. It's not a PrintWriter, but rather another kind of Writer: javax.servlet.jsp JspWriter. *pageContext* is entirely new: a master controlling object for JSP pages. You can see from the tail end of the `_jspService()` source extract above that this object plays a vital role in initializing several of the other implicit objects.

Hoping that this overview convinces you that there isn't much new to take on board, let's look at each implicit object in a little more detail.

request and response

Because you don't control the `_jspService()` method declaration, you need a guarantee that the request and response parameters passed in will always be called by a consistent name. The most obvious names have been guaranteed for you: *request* and *response*. So wherever your scriptlet or expression code appears, you can make reference to the methods on request and response. So, for example, the expression

```
<%= request.getMethod() %>
```

would display the HTTP method (generally GET or POST) used by the request for the JSP. The following scriptlet code, using the *response* implicit object, would return an HTTP 500 error from a JSP page:

```
<% response.sendError
  HttpServletResponse.SC_INTERNAL_SERVER_ERROR); %>
```

You can't dictate exactly what class the request and response objects are going to be, but you will know that 99.99% of the time that class will implement the javax.servlet.http.HttpServletRequest or javax.servlet.http.HttpServletResponse interface as appropriate. The remaining 0.01% will be taken up with JSP containers that don't implement the HTTP protocol. The *request* and *response* implicit variables are still guaranteed to be there, provided the container is JSP-spec compliant. However, the guarantee is that the objects they represent will implement the javax.servlet.ServletRequest or javax.servlet.ServletResponse interfaces (so a subset of their HTTP equivalents).

application

The *application* implicit variable is an object implementing the `javax.servlet.ServletContext` interface. With it, you can save yourself the bother of defining your own context variable using scriptlet code like this:

```
<% ServletContext context = this.getServletContext(); %>
```

You can use *application* to do all the things we saw in the servlet code from Chapter 3. The following expression could be used to display the name of your web application (as defined in the `<display>` element of the deployment descriptor, web.xml):

```
<%= application.getServletContextName() %>
```

session

The *session* implicit variable is an object implementing the `javax.servlet.http.HttpSession` interface. As we saw with `application`, it's a labor-saving device. You can still get hold of the session with a scriptlet line such as

```
<% HttpSession mySession = request.getSession(); %>
```

but there is no need to, because it's provided already. As we discussed in the previous section of the chapter, you can make the *session* implicit object *un*available using the following directive:

```
<%@ page session="false" %>
```

But by default (or with an explicit *page* directive where the *session* attribute is set to "true"), it will be present in the `_jspService()` method.

As for straight servlets, the most common use of the *session* object is to store and retrieve attributes. You can also control the session status using the same methods as before. So a scriptlet like this:

```
<% session.invalidate(); %>
```

will invalidate your session, as you would expect.

exam watch

There is one other circumstance in which you don't get a session implicit object. That is in the shady hinterland of JSP containers that don't operate with the HTTP protocol. session is an HTTP-protocol specific concept.

page

This is a reference to the JSP page object itself—in other words, the generated servlet. You can see from the generated servlet source that began this section on implicit objects that it's even set from the Java implicit variable **this.**

Somewhat surprisingly, the type of the variable is java.lang.Object. So in itself it is pretty useless—you can call Object methods only on `page`—nothing servlet-specific! You could safely downcast the reference within the Tomcat container like this:

```
<%!
public String getServletInfo() {
  return "My Downcast Page :-(";
}
```

```
%>
<% HttpServlet servlet = (HttpServlet) page; %>
<%= servlet.getServletInfo() %>
```

It might not be safe to cast *page* to an HttpServlet reference variable in all JSP container environments: There's always non-HTTP JSP containers to consider. Even though nearly every servlet in the world derives from GenericServlet (even non-HTTP ones), you couldn't safely cast to this either—as a JSP container author, you could still write a set of JSP-implementing servlet classes from scratch. Consequently, *java.lang.Object* is the only safe choice for the page reference variable!

Not that this causes any practical difficulty. You could equally well substitute the following for the last two lines of the above mini-JSP:

```
<%= this.getServletInfo() %>
```

Or, of course, just:

```
<%= getServletInfo() %>
```

In summary, *page* is not—as most JSP books end up by telling you—terribly useful to page authors.

config

While on the subject of not very useful implicit objects, let's consider *config* next. You may never have to use it. The only practical reason for using the *config* object, which implements javax.servlet.ServletConfig, is to get hold of initialization parameters associated with the JSP page. If there are any, they will be in the deployment descriptor, as `<init-param>` elements associated with the `<servlet>` element for this JSP page.

However, in a JSP, you are already inside an instance of a servlet—which is very likely to implement the ServletConfig interface. So under most circumstances you can use the method `getInitParameter()` directly in a scriptlet. If you are feeling ultracautious, use `config.getInitParameter()` instead.

pageContext

Now to the *pageContext* implicit object. This will be your JSP container's implementation of the javax.servlet.jsp.PageContext abstract class, which in turn inherits from the java.servlet.jsp.JspContext class. The PageContext class is only really exciting to developers who implement JSP containers, not so much page authors. For example, *pageContext* provides a mechanism for handling exceptions on a page, and forwarding to another page. The workings of this mechanism can be seen in the generated servlet code, but as a page author and exam taker, you need only to know how to take advantage of the mechanism (more on this when we examine the `exception` implicit object).

The `pageContext` object knows about all the other implicit objects, and it has methods to get hold of them. Again, as a page author, you don't usually bother with these, for the implicit variable names are available for use directly. However, you can see several of these methods in action—`getServletContext()`, `getServletConfig()`, `getSession()`, and `getOut()`—in the generated servlet source that begins this section.

Most usefully, `pageContext` provides a new scope for attributes: unsurprisingly called page scope. You've encountered three sorts of attributes already, here listed from most local to most global:

- Request attributes
- Session attributes
- Context attributes

Page scope attributes are more local still—confined as they are to the JSP page. You'll already have realized that *request, session*, and *application* implicit objects have the requisite attribute methods that go with their types (`HttpServletRequest`, `HttpSession`, and `ServletContext`). The *pageContext* implicit object goes further. As you would expect, it has methods to access attributes in its own page scope. However, *pageContext* also gives access to attributes in any scope, using slightly modified versions of the `get`, `set`, and `removeAttribute()` methods. Table 6-1 summarizes the operation of those methods.

exam watch

Get clear in your mind which methods belong to which class. The `pageContext` object inherits from PageContext, which inherits from JspContext. The attribute methods actually reside in JspContext. And while you're checking out the API documentation for these two classes (javax.servlet.jsp package), do take a look at the exceptions that can be thrown by `pageContext` attribute methods—don't take for granted that they are exactly the same as attribute methods you have met before.

TABLE 6-1 Some of the `pageContext` Attribute Methods

Method Signature	Explanation

Object getAttribute (String name, int scope)	This is like the other `getAttribute()` methods you have encountered—you supply a named attribute, and get back an object in return. The difference is the addition of a second parameter, scope. The allowed scopes are defined as **public**, **final**, **static** constants on the PageContext class:
	`PageContext.PAGE_SCOPE`
	`PageContext.REQUEST_SCOPE`
	`PageContext.SESSION_SCOPE`
	`PageContext.APPLICATION_SCOPE`
	The method will search only the scope supplied as a parameter. If the named attribute isn't found, **null** is returned (there's no other penalty, such as an exception).

void setAttribute (String name, Object value, int scope)	Again like other `setAttribute()` methods, in that you pass in a String name and an Object value. Other things in common: ■ If you pass in a null Object for the value, this has the same effect as calling the equivalent `removeAttribute()` method. ■ Attribute names are unique, so if a name already exists (*in a given scope, of course*), a later value will overwrite the earlier value. The only difference is that you must pass the scope as well, which uses the same set of PageContext constants as before.
void removeAttribute (String name, int scope)	Removes the named attribute in the given scope. Has no effect if no attribute of this name exists in the given scope.
Object findAttribute (String name)	This is the most interesting method. You merely pass in an attribute name, and the method works through the scopes in order: page, request, session, and application. The first attribute found is returned; consequently, an attribute in a more local scope (such as page) will "shield" one of the same name in a less local scope (such as session), so you can use this method only to get the most local attribute value when names are duplicated across scopes. For this among other reasons, I try to keep my attribute names unique across scopes unless there is a very good reason to do otherwise. If no attribute of the supplied name is found in any scope, null is returned—as is the case for `getAttribute()`.
get, set, remove Attribute() without the scope parameter . . .	`get`, `set`, and `removeAttribute()` are overloaded methods. The signatures *without* the scope parameter specifically target *page* scope and nowhere else.

out

The *out* implicit variable represents a writer associated with the response for your JSP page. You would automatically think this is the same as the PrintWriter you can get directly from the response object, but you would be wrong. Instead, out is a javax.servlet.jsp.JspWriter. The main thing that JspWriter gives you is buffering: The content in your page (template text, expressions, whatever) isn't—at least by default—committed to the response straightaway. What advantages does this confer? As we learned earlier, there are things you can't do once output has been committed, such as setting response headers. So to absolve you from having to take exceptional care—having to set all your response headers before even the tiniest fragment of template text appears in your JSP page—the JspWriter is buffered.

You can control the buffering through page directives, but that's a bit beyond the scope of the exam. For amusement and instruction, though, let's consider what happens if you try to mix and match use of the out implicit object and the regular PrintWriter from the response. Here's a complete piece of JSP page source (use the electronic version of the book to copy and paste into a file editor and deploy the JSP):

```
<%@ page import="java.io.PrintWriter" %>
<html><head><title>Wacky Alphabet</title></head>
<body><h4>Why you shouldn't mix your Writers</h4>
<p>JspWriter buffer size: <%= out.getBufferSize() %></p>
<% PrintWriter direct = response.getWriter();
char[] alphabet = {'a','b','c','d','e','f','g','h',
'i','j','k','l','m','n','o','p','q','r','s','t','u',
'v','w','x','y','z'};
for (int i = 0; i < alphabet.length; i++) { %>
 <% out.print(alphabet[i]); %>
<%i++;%>
 <% direct.print(alphabet[i]);
}// end loop%>
</body></html>
```

Here are the main things the JSP does:

- Uses the *out* implicit variable to display the buffer size—just to prove that there is a buffer involved.
- Gets hold of the response's PrintWriter into a local variable called *direct*.
- Puts the letters of the alphabet into a char array called *alphabet*.
- Loops around the array, printing all the letters of the alphabet with spaces in between, alternately using the implicit object *out* followed by the forbidden PrintWriter *direct*.

The page compiles and runs just fine, but the output is surprising, as shown in the following illustration.

bdfhjlnprtvxz

Why you shouldn't mix your Writers

JspWriter buffer size: 8192

a c e g i k m o q s u w y

As you can see, every other letter (the ones written using the forbidden PrintWriter) has appeared at the very beginning of the web page! This is because PrintWriter is unbuffered, so the response output is sent to the page directly. The buffered JspWriter output is appended to the end once the page is complete.

The other thing to be aware of is that every time you use an expression, or template text, the generated servlet uses the heavily overloaded `out.print()` method—so even though you may make no explicit use of *out*, chances are that it's still the most often used of all the implicit objects.

exception

The final implicit object to consider is *exception*, whose type is java.lang .Throwable—the parent of the Exception class hierarchy in Java. This is present only in the generated servlet for a JSP page designated as an error page, meaning that it contains the following directive:

```
<%@ page isErrorPage="true" %>
```

Furthermore, you never call such a page directly. Instead, you include another directive in all those JSP pages that might give rise to an error. This is in the form:

```
<%@ page errorPage="/jsps/myErrorPage.jsp" %>
```

The value for the errorPage attribute is the name of a JSP page where *isErrorPage* is set to true, and can give a path to that page. The path can begin with a forward slash, in which case it is relative to the context root.

This gives you more control over the presentation of errors to the user. You can make as much or as little use of the *exception* implicit object as you wish. The following error page uses the *exception* object to print the main error message in a visible way, and again to print the stack trace. However, the stack trace is confined to an HTML comment. In this way, the error may appear not so scary for an application user, but support staff can still view the HTML source of the output for details.

```
<%@ page isErrorPage="true" %>
<%@ page import="java.io.*" %>
<html><head><title>Error Page</title></head>
<body><h1>You're here because an error occurred</h1>
<p>The main error message is: <%= exception.getMessage() %></p>
<p>To see the error message detail, view the source of this web page.</p>
<!--<% exception.printStackTrace(new PrintWriter(out)); %>--!>
</body></html>
```

EXERCISE 6-4

JSP Implicit Objects

In this exercise, we'll use Java reflection techniques to investigate all the implicit objects and display information about them on a web page. You'll write a Java class called Reflector to do most of the hard work, and separately a JSP page called implicitObjects.jsp to display the results.

Create the usual web application directory structure under a directory called ex0604, and proceed with the steps for the exercise. There's a solution in the CD in the file sourcecode/ch06/ex0604.war—check there if you get stuck. For this exercise, there's also a halfway-house cheat. If you're not comfortable writing Java reflection code (and you won't be asked about that in the exam!), you could take the webcert .ch06.ex0604.Reflector class ready-made from the solution package—this leaves you free to concentrate on writing the JSP (which is more germane to your aspirations to be a web component developer).

Create the Reflector Class

1. Create a source file called Reflector.java, under your WEB-INF/src directory in an appropriate package directory. It must be in some named package, for the JSP that is going to use it can't use classes in the default package. You can choose any package name you like, or use the solution package name, which is webcert.ch06.ex0604.

2. Define three private instance variables in the class:
   - a String called *className*
   - a Set called *interfaces*
   - a Set called *methods*

   Write "getter" methods for each of these three variables (no need for "setters").
3. Define a constructor for Reflector.java that accepts an Object as a parameter.
4. Within the constructor (or using linked methods from the constructor), write code that will
   - Extract the Class object from the Object passed in (using the `Object .getClass()` method).
   - From the Class object, extract the name (`Class.getName()`) and store this in the *className* instance variable.
   - From the Class object, extract the interfaces implemented by the class, and add the names of each of these to the *interfaces* instance variable. (There's a `Class.getInterfaces()` method that returns an array of classes.)
   - From the Class, extract the methods implemented by the class, and add the names of each of these to the *methods* instance variable. (There's a `Class.getMethods()` method that returns an array of methods.)
5. Compile Reflector.java just as you would compile servlet code (so that Reflector.class ends up under the WEB-INF/classes directory—see Appendix B if you need refreshing on this).

Create the implicitObjects.jsp JSP Page Source

6. Create an empty file called implicitObjects.jsp directly in the context directory ex0604.
7. Use a *page* directive to import your Reflector class and the java.util package.
8. Next, include a scriptlet that defines a String array initialized with the names of the eight implicit objects (all except *exception*, which we're not going to bother with). In the same scriptlet, define an Object array initialized with the eight implicit objects—make sure that these appear in the same order as the names in the String array.

9. Define the appropriate elements to begin your HTML document. Then include a table with four headings: Implicit Object Name, Class Name, Interfaces Implemented, and Methods Available.
10. Write the beginning of a **for** loop to iterate around the eight implicit objects in the Object array. At the beginning of the loop, instantiate a Reflector object, passing the implicit object from the Object array into its constructor. Now you have a Reflector object loaded with the information you want to display. Close this scriptlet.
11. Within the **for** loop you will write out the rows of your table, each containing four cells.
12. In the first `<td>` cell, use an expression to display the name of the implicit object. This is taken from the String array you established earlier, using the loop counter for the appropriate occurrence.
13. In the second cell, use an expression to display the name of the class implemented by the implicit object. Use the `getClassName()` method from your Reflector object.
14. In the third cell, use a combination of a scriptlet and an expression to display the names of all the interfaces implemented by the implicit object. You'll want to use the `getInterfaces()` method from your Reflector object. This returns a Set, from which you can derive an Iterator—structure the loop around this.
15. In the fourth cell, use a similar technique to display the names of all the methods implemented by the implicit object. This time, use `getMethods()` on Reflector, and again derive an Iterator from the Set returned.
16. Finally, don't forget a separate scriptlet to close off the **for** loop with a terminating curly brace.
17. Round off the table with `</table>` and any other closing HTML document tags as appropriate

Deploy and Run the JSP Page

18. Create a WAR file that contains the contents of ex0604.
19. Start the web server, if it is not started already.
20. Use your browser to request implicitObjects.jsp using a suitable URL, such as

```
http://localhost:8080/ex0604/implicitObjects.jsp
```

21. A truncated extract from the solution code output is shown in the following illustration, for the `request` implicit object. You can see how the implementing class is Tomcat-proprietary: something called CoyoteRequestFacade! However, it's J2EE-standard in that the one interface this class implemented is javax.servlet.http.HttpServletRequest. The methods implemented are legion (I cut the list short)—all the methods from superclasses (including Object) can be found in the list. There are plenty of refinements you could make to this code—showing all the superclasses, the interfaces they implement, and so on.

Implicit Object Name	Class Name	Interfaces Implemented	Methods Available
request	org.apache.coyote.tomcat5.CoyoteRequestFacade	javax.servlet.http.HttpServletRequest	clear equals getAttribute getAttributeNames getAuthType getCharacterEncoding getClass getContentLength getContentType getContextPath getCookies getDateHeader getHeader getHeaderNames

CERTIFICATION SUMMARY

This chapter gave you a lot of basic grounding in JSP technology. In the four major sections of the chapter, you first learned about the life cycle of JSP pages within a JSP container, then about scripting elements, then page directives you can use to influence mainly global aspects of your page, and finally the nine implicit objects available to you in JSP source code.

You first saw how JSP pages turn servlets on their head. You learned that instead of putting HTML inside Java code (the servlet pattern), you place Java code (and other bits of syntax) inside an otherwise normal HTML page. You also saw that JSP technology is not limited to HTML: XML is viable to include in a JSP page. You learned that a JSP container (usually just another facet of the servlet container you use, as with Tomcat) takes JSP page source and turns this into a working program—in fact, a generated and compiled servlet. This puts the HTML (or XML) back inside Java code. You learned that this phase is called "translation" of a JSP page and that it incorporates the code generation and compilation. You experienced translation firsthand in the exercise and saw that it usually occurs on first request to a JSP (or on request to a JSP that has changed), but can in fact happen at any time a JSP container chooses before the first request is received.

You saw that generated servlets implement the interface JspPage or, much more likely, its subinterface, HttpJspPage. You learned that this involves providing three methods:

- `jspInit()`
- `jspService()`—with request and response parameters
- `jspDestroy()`

You learned that the JspPage interface keeps the request and response parameters nonspecific, whereas the HttpJspPage interface narrows these down to HttpServlet Request and HttpServletResponse. You saw that this means that the `_jspService()` method ends up looking very much like the signature of a servlet's `service()` method—and it came as no surprise to you that the generated servlet's service method does indeed call `_jspService()`. You learned that the parallels between servlet life cycle and JSP life cycle go further: `init(ServletConfig config)` calls `jspInit()`, `service()` calls `_jspService()`, and `destroy()` calls `jspDestroy()`.

Having explored the JSP page life cycle, you went to look at the composition of JSP page source. You learned that the source subdivides into template text and elements. Of elements, there are three kinds: directive, scripting, and action. Of actions, you confined your knowledge to the fact that they divide into standard or custom types. You learned that there is a recent innovation in scripting called Expression Language, but that the traditional language-based scripting you explored in this chapter is still retained in JSP 2.0. You met the four traditional scripting elements:

- expressions (for displaying data)
- scriptlets (for logic embedded in the request method, `_jspService()`)
- declarations (for separate code outside of `_jspService()`)
- comments (for the translation phase to ignore)

You saw that expressions are demarcated with `<%=` at the beginning, and `%>` at the end. You learned that any Java expression can be inserted in the middle of this, provided that it evaluates to any primitive or object. You learned that an expression, although being Java source, cannot terminate in a semicolon, for expressions are actually incorporated inside existing statements in the generated Java source (usually `out.print(your expression goes here);` statements). You also learned that expressions are inserted into the `_jspService()` method and so are potentially executed on every request to a page.

You saw that scriptlets can be long or short, and contain complete Java statements—as many as required. You learned that <% denotes the beginning of a scriptlet and %> the end. You saw that scriptlets can be used for several purposes, but typical ones include local data setup, presentation logic (e.g., dynamically generating HTML table rows), and, more occasionally, direct output to the page using the implicit object `out`. You also learned that scriptlet code, like expression code, is incorporated directly into the `_jspService()` method at the point of insertion into the JSP page source.

You then explored declarations and found that the Java code in them goes into the generated servlet but *outside* the `_jspService()` method. You discovered that you can include all sorts of things in declarations—instance and class variables, for example—but that their best use is for defining complete methods. You learned that you can use declarations to override the life cycle methods `jspInit()` and `jspDestroy()`. You found that a declaration begins with `<%!` characters and ends the same as expressions and scriptlets—with `%>`.

Finally, in scripting elements, you looked at comments. You learned about two styles—the first beginning with `<%--` and ending with `--%>`. You saw that the translation phase completely ignores everything between these two markers and that anything can go within such a comment—except `<%` (in other words, you can't nest comments of this style). You also learned that you can use HTML/XML-style comments (`<%--` commented out words `--%>`) and that anything within such a comment (expresson, scriplet, declaration) is translated normally. You saw that the advantage of this style is for sending back comment text in the response.

In the next section, you learned about directives. You saw that they have a style that is similar to scripting elements (`<%@` opening characters and `%>` closing characters) but play no direct role in producing response output. You met the three sorts of directive: *page*, *include*, and *taglib*. You saw that every directive has one or more attributes, consisting of name/value pairs—very much like HTML or XML tags. You found that *page* is the most complex directive, having a dozen or so possible attributes (of which you only need know four in detail for the exam). You used the *import* attribute to have import statements in your generated servlet code. You learned that the *session* attribute can be used to make the `session` implicit object unavailable in a page (`<%@ page session="false" %>`). You saw that the *contentType* attribute determines the MIME type of the response sent back. And you learned that the *isELIgnored* attribute can be used to stop translation evaluating Expression Language.

You then met the *include* directive and saw that it is far simpler—having only one mandatory attribute, file. You learned that you can use *include* to incorporate entire files within your JSP page source—crucially, at *translation* time. You then saw the third and final directive—*taglib*. You learned that this is used to allow the page access to custom actions defined in a tag library, whose location is hinted at in the *uri* attribute. You also learned that custom actions used within the page use the value for the prefix attribute specified in the *taglib* directive.

In the final section of this chapter, you explored implicit objects. You saw that these are nothing more or less than local variables defined at the beginning of the `_jspService()` method and that since the names of these variables are standardized, you can rely on them in your expressions and scriptlets. You were able to greet many of these as old friends from the servlet chapters: *request* (almost always an HttpServletRequest object), *response* (almost always HttpServletResponse), *application* (invariably ServletContext), *session* (HttpSession), and *config* (ServletConfig). You also learned that *out* is nothing more than a writer, albeit a buffered JspWriter—not the PrintWriter directly available from the response. You saw that *exception* is just a Throwable object, available only in `page` designated for error handling (having a *page* directive where the attribute *isErrorPage* is set to true). This left only *page* and *pageContext*. You saw that `page` represents the generated servlet (so as a page author, you don't really need it). You found that *pageContext* supplies a very localized set of attribute functions for `page` scope but can also be used to access the attributes in request, session, or application scope. You learned that `pageContext` performs other vital functions that are generally of more use to JSP container designers than to page authors.

TWO-MINUTE DRILL

JSP Life Cycle

- Servlets are typically Java programs containing HTML elements. JavaServer Pages are HTML or XML documents containing Java elements.
- JavaServer Page source is "translated" into a servlet class file, thanks to the JSP container (part of a J2EE application server such as Tomcat).
- If a page fails to translate, an HTTP 500 error is given back to the requester.
- HTTP is not the only protocol: It is possible (but rare) to have JSP containers that implement other request/response protocols.
- Every servlet generated in this way must contain a `_jspService()` method, which receives two parameters: a request object and a response object.
- In a typical HTTP implementation, the two parameters are of types HttpServletRequest and HttpServletResponse.
- Every generated servlet must contain a `jspInit()` and `jspDestroy()` method (or inherit these through one of its superclasses).
- Every generated servlet must implement (itself or in superclasses) at least the JspPage interface.
- Most implement HttpJspPage (whose super-interface is JspPage).
- A JSP container can translate a page at any time but often does so at the point when a page is first requested.
- Once requested, a JSP page enters the request or execution phase.
- Class loading and initialization of static information occur, as for any other Java class.
- An instance of the JSP page servlet is made.
- `jspInit()` is called once, before any requests for an instance of the JSP page are serviced.
- `_jspService()` is called for every request made to the page.
- Concurrent container threads can call the same `_jspService()` method on the same JSP page instance at the same time.
- `jspDestroy()` is called once after all requests to the JSP page have completed—no further requests are admitted once `jspDestroy()` has been called.

- There is usually only one instance of a JSP page servlet.
- A JSP page can be explicitly registered in the `<servlet>` element of a deployment descriptor, but it doesn't have to be.
- The same JSP page can be registered more than once, under a different `<servlet-name>`.
- A different instance of the same JSP page servlet is created for each separate `<servlet-name>`.
- You must not override servlet life cycle methods (`init(ServletConfig config)`, `service()`, `destroy()`) in your JSP pages.

JSP Elements

- A JSP page is composed of template text and elements.
- Template text is any content in a JSP page that is not a scripting element, standard or custom action, or expression language syntax.
- Template text normally comprises HTML or XML, but there are no constraints on the type of content.
- Template text doesn't require "translation," beyond the insertion of some escape characters when necessary.
- There are three sorts of elements: directive, scripting, and action.
- There are two sorts of action: custom and standard.
- There are two families of scripting element: "traditional" and "modern" (Expression Language).
- There are four sorts of "traditional" scripting element: expressions, scriptlets, declarations, and comments.
- An expression displays output in the response and looks like this:

  ```
  <%= expression %>
  ```
- A scriptlet is generally for more extended Java logic and looks like this:

  ```
  <% scriptlet statement 1; scriptlet statement 2; %>
  ```
- A declaration is typically used to include complete methods in the generated servlet and looks like this:

  ```
  <%! methodSignature() { method content } %>
  ```
- A comment is for any area translation should ignore and looks like this:

  ```
  <%-- Anything at all goes here --%>
  ```

- ❑ Expressions can contain any valid Java code that returns something, primitive or object (i.e., not **void**).
- ❑ Expression code is incorporated in `out.print()` statements in the `_jspService()` method.
- ❑ Expression code must not end in a semicolon (expression code forms part of a statement).
- ❑ Scriptlets can contain most valid Java code.
- ❑ Scriptlet code is generated into the `_jspService()` method, at the point of insertion into JSP page source, so don't use scriptlets to define whole methods.
- ❑ Scriptlet code can contain multiple statements, a single statement, or even a single curly brace ({ or }—block delimiter).
- ❑ Local variables declared in one scriptlet can be accessed in another later in the page source.
- ❑ Declarations are for Java syntax that appears in the generated servlet source outside of the `_jspService()` method.
- ❑ Declarations can be used to override the life cycle methods `jspInit()` and `jspDestroy()`.
- ❑ Comments of the `<%-- lines commented out --%>` variety must not be nested.
- ❑ Use the `<!-- comment lines -->` HTML/XML style of commenting for a comment that is returned in the response.

JSP Directives

- ❑ Directives have similar syntax to scripting elements: opening characters `<%@` and closing characters `%>`.
- ❑ Within these delimiters, directives consist of a name and attributes.
- ❑ Attributes consist of *name*="*value*" (or *name*='*value*') pairs, as in HTML or XML.
- ❑ There are three sorts of directive: *page*, *include*, and *taglib*.
- ❑ The *page* directive has several possible attributes.
- ❑ There can be many *page* directives within a piece of JSP page source.
- ❑ Each *page* directive can have one or several attributes.
- ❑ The *import* attribute produces import statements in the generated servlet code. Example: `<%@ page import="java.util.*, java .io.PrintWriter" %>`.

- The *session* attribute can be used to make the *session* implicit object unavailable. Example: `<%@ page session='false' %>`.
- The *contentType* attribute specifies the MIME type of the response. Example: `<%@ page contentType="image/gif" %>`.
- The *isELIgnored* attribute determines if expression language should be interpreted, or just treated as template text. Example: `<%@ page isELIgnored="true" %>`.
- There are several other `page` attributes that aren't on the exam objectives.
- The *include* directive is used to incorporate files into JSP page source at translation time.
- Files included do not have to be JSP page source (with a .jsp extension)—anything that will translate is permitted.
- A JSP page and its included files are referred to as a translation unit.
- The *include* directive has one mandatory attribute—file.
- The *file* attribute gives an absolute or relative path to the file to be included. Example: `<%@ include file="stubs/header.html" %>`.
- The *taglib* directive makes custom actions from a tag library available in a JSP page.
- The *taglib* directive has two mandatory attributes—*prefix* and *uri*.
- The *uri* attribute indicates how the container should find the tab library.
- The *prefix* attribute is used to preface all tags from the tab library used within the JSP page. Example:

```
<%@ taglib prefix="mytags" uri="http://www.osborne.com/taglibs/mytags" %>
```

JSP Implicit Objects

- There are nine implicit objects: *request*, *response*, *application*, *session*, *config*, *page*, *pageContext*, *out*, and *exception*.
- Implicit objects are just local variables with standard names in the `_jspService()` method.
- *request* and *response* are passed as parameters into `_jspService()`.
- For HTTP containers, *request* must implement the HttpServletRequest interface.
- Otherwise, *request* must implement ServletRequest.

- For HTTP containers, *response* must implement the HttpServletResponse interface.
- Otherwise, *request* must implement ServletResponse.
- *application* is the web application's context object (of ServletContext type).
- *session* is a web application session object (of HttpSession type).
- *config* is the ServletConfig object associated with the generated servlet, so it can be used to access initialization parameters for the servlet/JSP page.
- *out* is a JspWriter, used within JSP pages to write to the response instead of the standard PrintWriter from the response.
- *out* is—by default—buffered.
- *exception* is available only in designated error pages, which have the directive `<%@ page isErrorPage="true" %>`
- Error pages are not called directly. Another JSP with this kind of directive is required:
  `<%@ page errorPage="myErrorPage.jsp" %>`
- if the page containing this directive throws an exception, the JSP container forwards to the named error page.
- In the named error page, *exception* (a Throwable object) can be used to execute methods (such as `printStackTrace()`, `getMessage()`) on the exception.
- *page* is synonymous with *this:* the generated servlet itself.
- *pageContext* provides "page scope" attributes for the JSP page.
- *pageContext* has methods that can set, get, and remove attributes in any of the four scopes: page, request, session, or application.
- The `set`, `get`, and `remove` methods of *pageContext* are overloaded—some signatures accept an **int** parameter to represent scope.
- Valid values for the scope parameter are defined as constants in the Page Context class: PAGE_SCOPE, REQUEST_SCOPE, SESSION_SCOPE, and APPLICATION_SCOPE.

SELF TEST

The following questions will help you measure your understanding of the material presented in this chapter. Read all the choices carefully because there might be more than one correct answer. The number of correct choices to make is stated in the question, as in the real SCWCD exam.

JSP Life Cycle

1. What will be the most likely outcome of attempting to access the following JSP for the second time? (Choose one.)

```
<%@ page language="java" %>
<%@ page import="java.util.*" %>
<html><head><title>Chapter 6 Question 1</title></head>
<body>
<h1>Chapter 6 Question 1</h1>
<%!
public void jspInit() {
  System.out.println("First half of jspInit()");
%>
<%> new Date() %>
<%!
  System.out.println("Second half of jspInit()");
}
%>
</body></html>
```

A. Translation error (HTTP response code of 500)

B. Page not found error (HTTP response code of 404)

C. Web page returned showing a heading and the current date; two lines of output written to the server log

D. Web page returned showing "First half of jspInit()," "Second half of jspInit()," a heading, and the current date

E. Web page returned showing a heading and the current date

2. What is output to the web page on the second access to the same instance of the following JSP? (Choose one.)

```
<%@ page language="java" %>
<html>
```

```
<head><title>Chapter 6 Question 2</title></head>
<body>
<h1>Chapter 6 Question 2</h1>
<%! int x = 0; %>
<%!
public void jspInit() {
  System.out.println(x++);
}
%>
<%= x++ %>
<% System.out.println(x); %>
<% jspInit(); %>
</body></html>
```

A. 0

B. 1

C. 2

D. 3

E. 4

F. Page does not translate.

G. Page translates, but there is another runtime error.

3. For what reason does the following JSP fail to translate and compile? (Choose one.)

```
<%@ page language="java" %>
<html>
<head><title>Chapter 6 Question 3</title></head>
<body>
<h1>Chapter 6 Question 3</h1>
<%! int x; %>
<%!
public void jspDestroy() {
  System.out.println("self-destructing");
} %>
<%!
public void jspInit() {
  System.out.println(<%= x %>);
}
%>
</body></html>
```

A. Expression embedded in declaration.

B. Data member *x* not initialized before use.

C. Local variable *x* not initialized before use.

D. Placement of `jspDestroy()` method before `jspInit()` method.

E. The page actually compiles and translates without any problem.

F. None of the above.

4. Which of the following are true statements about the JavaServer Page life cycle? (Choose two.)

   A. The `_jspService()` method is called from the generated servlet's `service()` method.

   B. `jspInit()` is only ever called on the first request to a JSP instance.

   C. `jspDestroy()` is only ever called on the last request to a JSP instance.

   D. All servlet methods are accessible from the `jspInit()` method.

   E. You cannot override or provide a no-parameter `init()` method in a JSP page.

5. What is the consequence of attempting to access the following JSP page? (Choose two.)

```
<%@ page language="java" %>
<html>
<head><title>Chapter 6 Question 5</title></head>
<body>
<h1>Chapter 6 Question 5</h1>
<%!public void _jspService(HttpServletRequest request,
  HttpServletResponse response) {
  out.write("A");
} %>
<% out.write("B"); %>
</body>
</html>
```

   A. Cannot resolve symbol compilation error.

   B. "A" is output to the response.

   C. "B" is output to the response.

   D. "A" is output to the response before "B."

E. Duplicate method compilation error.

F. "B" is output to the response before "A."

JSP Elements

6. What is the result of attempting to access the following JSP page? (Choose one.)

```
<html>
<head><title>Chapter 6 Question 6</title></head>
<body>
<h1>Chapter 6 Question 6</h1>
<%! public String methodA() {
        return methodB();
    }
%>
<%! public String methodB() {
        return methodC();
    }
%>
<% public String methodC() {
        return "Question 6 Text";
    }
%>
<h2><%= methodA() %></h2>
</body>
</html>
```

A. "Question 6 Text" is output to the resulting web page.

B. A translation error occurs.

C. A runtime error occurs.

D. The text between the `<h1></h1>` HTML tags appears, followed by a Java stack trace.

E. The web page is blank.

7. (drag-and-drop question) The following illustration shows a complete JSP page source. Match the lettered values, which conceal parts of the source, with numbers from the list on the right, which indicate possible completions for the source.

```
<html>
<head><title>Chapter 6 Question 7</title></head>
<body>
<h1>Chapter 6 Question 7</h1>
<form action="Question7.jsp">
Type distance abbreviation here:
<input type="text" name="abbrev" />
Request made at: [A] Date d = new Date();
java.text.DateFormat fmt =
java.text.DateFormat.getDateInstance(DateFormat.S
HORT);
String s = fmt.format(d);[ B ]s%>
<input type="submit" [C]
</form>
<%=
fullTextOfUnits(request.getParameter("[ D ]")[E])
%>
[F] page import="java.text.*,java.util.*" %>
[G] public String fullTextOfUnits(String key) {
      if ("km".toLowerCase().equals(key)) {
        return "kilometers";
      }
      if ("m".toLowerCase().equals(key)) {
        return "miles";
      }
      return "";
    }
%>
</body>
</html>
```

1	<%
2	<%=
3	%>
4	<%@
5	<%#
6	<%--
7	--%>
8	#%>
9	;
10	' ' (a single blank space)
11	/>
12	%><%=
13	<%!
14	;%>
15	abbrev

8. What true statements can you make about the following JSP page source? The line numbers are for reference only and should not be considered part of the source. (Choose two.)

```
01 <%@ page import="java.io.*" %>
02 <html>
03 <head><title>Chapter 6 Question 8</title></head>
04 <body>
05 <%
06 PrintWriter out = response.getWriter();
07 out.write("P");
08 %>
09 <% out.write("Q"); %>
10 </body>
11 </html>
```

A. In line 09, the scriptlet markers should not be on the same line as the Java source statement.

B. In JSP technology, it's a bad idea to get hold of the PrintWriter directly from the response.

C. "P" will be written to the response, followed by "Q."

D. "Q" will be written to the response, followed by "P."

E. Only "Q" will be written to the response.

F. The page has a compilation error because of a directive syntax error.

G. The page has a compilation error because the *import* in the directive syntax is for the wrong Java package.

H. The page has a compilation error for other reasons.

9. Which of the following are false statements to make about JSP scripting elements? (Choose three.)

A. It is illegal to embed a `<%--` style comment inside another comment.

B. It is illegal to embed an expression inside a scriptlet.

C. It is legal to embed an expression inside a declaration.

D. It is legal to embed an expression inside a directive.

E. It is legal to include a declaration at any point in the JSP page source, provided that it appears outside of other elements.

F. It is legal to embed a scriptlet inside an expression inside a `<%--` style comment.

10. What is the result of attempting to access the following JSP page source? (Choose one.)

```
<% <%-- for (int i = 0; i < 10; i++) {
<%-- if(i==3) System.out.println("i is 3!"); --%>
    System.out.println("i squared is " + i * i);
} %> --%>
```

A. Doesn't translate because the page source is incomplete.

B. Doesn't compile because nesting comments in this way is illegal.

C. The JSP page would compile if the terminating curly brace were removed.

D. The JSP page would compile if one of the percent (%) signs were removed.

E. Runs as is and produces output (possibly not the output intended).

JSP Directives

11. Which of the following constitute valid ways of importing Java classes into JSP page source? (Choose two.)

A.

```
<%! import java.util.*; %>
```

B.

```
<%@ import java.util.* %>
```

C.

```
<%@ page import="java.util.StringTokenizator" %>
```

D.

```
<%@ page import='java.util.*, java.io.PrintStream'
import="java.text.*" %>
```

E.

```
<%@page import = " java.util.* "%>
```

12. What is the outcome of accessing the first JSP page, includer12.jsp, shown below? (Choose one.)

```
<%-- file includer12.jsp begins here --%>
<% for (int i = 0; i < 10; i ++) { %>
<%@ include file="included12.jsp" %>
<% } %>
<%-- End of file includer12.jsp --%>

<%-- Beginning of file included12.jsp --%>
<html>
<head><title>Chapter 6 Question 12</title></head>
<body>
<h1>Chapter 6 Question 12</h1>
For the <%=i%>th time<br />
</body>
</html>
<%-- End of file included12.jsp --%>
```

A. An ill-formed HTML page will be the output.

B. The call will fail because variable *i* is not declared in included.jsp.

C. Translation will fail because elements denoting the beginning and end of an HTML document must be in the including JSP document, not the included.

D. "For the 10th time" appears in the output.

E. Translation fails for other reasons.

13. What statements are true about the following two JSP page sources, given the intention of always requesting includer13.jsp? (Choose two.)

```
<%-- file includer13.jsp begins here --%>
<%@ page import="java.util.*" contentType="text/html" session="true"%>
<html>
<head><title>Chapter 6 Question 13</title></head>
<body>
<h1>Chapter 6 Question 13</h1>
<%ArrayList al = new ArrayList();
al.add("Jack Russell");
al.add("Labrador");
al.add("Great Dane");%>
<%@ include file="included13.jsp" %>
</body>
</html>
<%-- file includer13.jsp ends here --%>

<%-- file included13.jsp begins here --%>
<%@ page import="java.util.*" contentType="text/html" %>
<table>
  <%for (int i = 0; i < al.size(); i++) {%>
  <tr><td><%= al.get(i) %></td></tr>
  <%}%>
</table>
<%-- file included13.jsp ends here --%>
```

A. Translation will fail because the *import* attribute of the *page* directive is repeated across the page sources.

B. Translation will fail because the *contentType* attribute of the *page* directive is repeated across the page sources.

C. Removing the *Session* attribute from includer13.jsp will make no difference to the generated servlet code.

D. The local variable *al* in included13.jsp will not be recognized.

E. The *import*, *contentType*, and *session* attributes should appear in separate *page* directives.

F. The order of the *import* and *contentType* attributes in both JSP page sources is immaterial.

14. Which of the following are invalid directives? (Choose three.)

   A. <%@page isELignored = "false" %>
   B. <%@ page session="true' %>
   C. <%@ page contentType="image/music/text" %>
   D. <%@include uri="header.jsp" %>
   E. <%@ taglib prefix="mytags" uri="http://www.osborne.com/taglibs/mytags" %>

15. Given the beginning of the JSP page source below, which set of lines should be used to complete the JSP page source in order to print out all the song lyrics? (Choose one.)

```
<%! static String[] suedeShoes = new String[4];
static { suedeShoes[0] = "One for the Money,";
suedeShoes[1] = "Two for the Show,";
suedeShoes[2] = "Three to Get Ready,";
suedeShoes[3] = "And Go, Cat, Go!";} %>
<% pageContext.setAttribute("line1", suedeShoes[0]);
request.setAttribute("line2", suedeShoes[1]);
session.setAttribute("line3", suedeShoes[2]);
config.getServletContext().setAttribute("line4", suedeShoes[3]);
%>
```

   A.

```
<%@ page contentType="text/plain"
info="Blue Suede Shoes" session="false" %>
<%for (int i = 0; i < suedeShoes.length; i++) {
  String songLine =
  (String) pageContext.findAttribute("line" + (i + 1));%>
  <%= songLine %>
<%}%>
```

   B.

```
<%@ page contentType="text/plain"
info="Blue Suede Shoes" session="true" %>
<%for (int i = 0; i < suedeShoes.length; i++) {
  String songLine =
  (String) pageContext.findAttribute("line" + (i + 1));%>
  <%= songLine %>
<%}%>
```

   C.

```
<%@ page contentType="text/plain"
info="Blue Suede Shoes" session="true" %>
```

```
<%for (int i = 1; i < suedeShoes.length; i++) {
  String songLine =
  (String) pageContext.findAttribute("line" + i);%>
  <%= songLine %>
<%}%>
```

D.

```
<%@ page contentType="text/plain"
info="Blue Suede Shoes" session="true" %>
<%for (int i = 0; i < suedeShoes.length; i++) {
  String songLine =
  (String) pageContext.getAttribute("line" + (i + 1));%>
  <%= songLine %>
<%}%>
```

E.

```
<%@ page contentType="text/plain"
info="Blue Suede Shoes" session="true" %>
<%for (int i = 0; i < suedeShoes.length; i++) {
  String songLine =
  (String) pageContext.getAttribute("line" + (i + 1));%>
  <%= songLine; %>
<%}%>
```

JSP Implicit Objects

16. Which of the following techniques is likely to return an initialization parameter for a JSP page? (Choose two.)

 A. <%= request.getParameter("myParm") %>

 B. <% String s = getInitParameter("myParm"); %>

 C. <% = application.getInitParameter("myParm") %>

 D. <%= config.getInitParameter("myParm"); %>

 E. <%= getParameter("myParm") %>

 F. <% Object o = config.getParameter("myParm"); %>

 G. <% String s = config.getAttribute("myParm"); %>

 H. <% String s = getAttribute("myParm"); %>

17. (drag-and-drop question) The following illustration shows a complete JSP page source. The desired output on the web page is 0 0 1 2 3. Match the lettered values, which conceal parts of the source, with numbers from the list on the right. The numbered fragments indicate possible completions for the source that will achieve the desired output. The numbered fragments may be used more than once, and not all of them are needed.

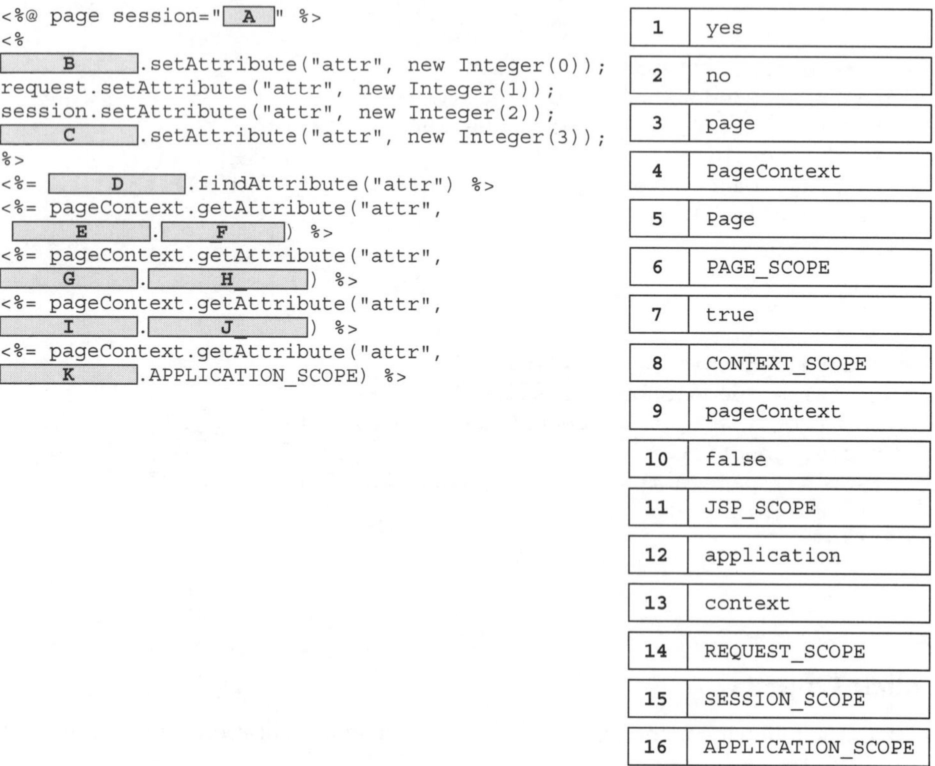

<%@ page session="[A]" %>
<%
[B].setAttribute("attr", new Integer(0));
request.setAttribute("attr", new Integer(1));
session.setAttribute("attr", new Integer(2));
[C].setAttribute("attr", new Integer(3));
%>
<%= [D].findAttribute("attr") %>
<%= pageContext.getAttribute("attr",
[E].[F]) %>
<%= pageContext.getAttribute("attr",
[G].[H]) %>
<%= pageContext.getAttribute("attr",
[I].[J]) %>
<%= pageContext.getAttribute("attr",
[K].APPLICATION_SCOPE) %>
1 yes
2 no
3 page
4 PageContext
5 Page
6 PAGE_SCOPE
7 true
8 CONTEXT_SCOPE
9 pageContext
10 false
11 JSP_SCOPE
12 application
13 context
14 REQUEST_SCOPE
15 SESSION_SCOPE
16 APPLICATION_SCOPE

18. What is the result of requesting errorProvoker.jsp for the first time? Assume that neither of the JSP pages below has yet been translated. (Choose one.)

```
<%-- Beginning of errorProvoker.jsp page source --%>
<%@ page errorPage="/errorDisplayer.jsp" %>
<% request.setAttribute("divisor", new Integer(0)); %>
<html>
<head>
<% int i = ((Integer) request.getAttribute("divisor")).intValue(); %>
<title>Page Which Terminates In Error</title>
```

```
</head><body>
<%= 1.0 / i %>
</body></html>
<%-- End of errorProvoker.jsp page source --%>
<%-- Beginning of errorDisplayer.jsp page source --%>
<%@ page isErrorPage="true" %>
<%@ page import="java.io.*" %>
<html><head><title>Divide by Zero Error</title></head>
<body><h1>Don't divide by zero!</h1>
<pre><% exception.printStackTrace(new PrintWriter(out)); %></pre>
</body></html>
<%-- End of errorDisplayer.jsp page source --%>
```

A. errorProvoker.jsp will not translate and compile because of faults in the page source.

B. errorDisplayer.jsp will not translate and compile because of faults in the page source.

C. errorDisplayer.jsp will not be translated.

D. A stack trace will be displayed in the requesting browser.

E. The browser's title bar will display "Divide by Zero Error."

F. errorProvoker.jsp displays output.

19. Which of the following are false statements about implicit objects and scope? (Choose four.)

A. *out* is of type java.io.PrintWriter.

B. *config* can be used to return context initialization parameters.

C. `PageContext.findAttribute()` can't be used to return a session scope attribute if an attribute of the same name exists in page scope.

D. *page* is of type java.lang.Object.

E. *application* can't be used to access other web application resources.

F. It is illegal to have attributes of the same name existing in more than one scope.

20. What is the result of attempting to access attributeFinder.jsp below, typing text into the input field, and pressing the submit button? (Choose one.)

```
<%-- Beginning of attributeFinder.jsp page source --%>
<%@ include file="fieldSetter.jsp" %>
<html><head><title>Echo Input</title></head>
<body><h5>Type in the field below and press the button to echo
input...</h5>
<form>
<input type="text" name="<%= session.getAttribute("echoFieldName")%>" />
<input type="submit" />
```

```
</form>
<h3>Echoed Text: <%= request.getAttribute("echoInput") %></h3>
</body></html>
<%-- End of attributeFinder.jsp page source --%>
<%-- Beginning of fieldSetter.jsp page source --%>
<% session.setAttribute("echoFieldName", "echoInput"); %>
<%-- End of fieldSetter.jsp page source --%>
```

A. Can't be accessed: translation error in attributeFinder.jsp.

B. Can't be accessed: translation error in fieldSetter.jsp.

C. Can't be accessed: translation errors in both attributeFinder.jsp and fieldSetter.jsp.

D. **null** is displayed for the echoed text.

E. Echoed text is displayed as intended.

LAB QUESTION

This lab encourages you to use techniques from across this chapter, plus one or two from previous chapters. You're going to write a simple JSP version of the game tic-tac-toe (or as we know it in England, noughts and crosses).

This can be accomplished in a single JSP file. For the playing "grid," construct a table with three rows, each with three cells. Place an input text field in each of the nine cells, to receive input of "X" or "O." Include a button beneath the table that submits the enclosing form. The action associated with the form should be the same JSP file again. However, because you have made a server request, you will have to recall the state of play and reload the table cells with the appropriate value—"X," "O," or nothing at all, if nothing has been marked in the cell.

There are plenty of refinements you can make to the above specifications. The solution code prevents a cell from being "input capable" once an "X" or "O" has been placed within it and the confirm button pressed. You might like to have a go at that and introduce bells and whistles absent from the solution: validating that "X" and "O" are placed alternately, perhaps, or spotting a winning line and presenting an appropriate message.

SELF TEST ANSWERS

JSP Life Cycle

1. ☑ **E**. A web page is returned showing a heading and the current date.
☒ **A** is incorrect. It certainly looks strange splitting a declared method (`jspInit()`) in two halves (it's pretty pointless, and I don't recommend it as good style!), but as declarations are imported contiguously into the generated servlet, the page translates just fine. **B** is wrong—had there been a translation error, a 500 error should result in any case, not a page not found 404 error. **C** could be right under unusual circumstances, but for the most part, if this is the *second* access to this JSP, and so the same instance is used again, then `jspInit()` won't be executed (as for the same instance, it would have fired on the *first* access to the JSP, writing two lines to the server log). **D** is definitely wrong: The suggestion here is that the `System.out.println` output goes to the returned response, whereas it goes to the server log.

2. ☑ **D**. 3 is output to the web page. The sequence of events is this: On or before the first access to the JSP, the page is instantiated. The initialize event fires, so the JSP container calls `jspInit()`. The declared instance variable **int** *x* is incremented from 0 to 1 within the method. Then the web page takes this current value of *x* for display through the expression `<%= x++ %>`; only afterward is *x* incremented again from 1 to 2. `jspInit()` is called again in the last scriptlet in the JSP. This causes *x* to be incremented from 2 to 3. On the second request to the web page, the JSP container doesn't call `jspInit()` again: It happens only once per life cycle. So the first thing that happens is that the expression `<%= x++ %>` is evaluated—for a current value of 3, which is then displayed in the web page. Any subsequent increments to *x* don't matter for the purposes of the question.
☒ **A**, **B**, **C**, and **E** are incorrect because of the reasoning in the correct answer. **F** and **G** are incorrect because the page is correct syntactically, and translates and runs just fine. The manual call to `jspInit()` may have given you pause for thought, but outside of the fact that this is a method called automatically by the JSP container, it can be treated just as any other regular method. It's not usual, it's not good style, and I hope you'll encounter this kind of obscure coding only in exam questions, but the important thing is to recognize it as legal!

3. ☑ **A**. An expression belongs in the middle of the `_jspService()` method of the JSP's generated servlet. So it makes no sense to locate an expression inside of another declared method in the JSP, whether `jspInit()` or any other.
☒ **B** and **C** are incorrect. You need to recognize for one thing that `<%! int x; %>` causes the variable *x* to be declared as a data member, not a local variable. Because data members are always initialized to a value (in this case 0 for the primitive type **int**), there is no initialization problem. **D** is incorrect because the placement of the life cycle methods `jspInit()` and

`jspDestroy()` within the JSP doesn't matter. You can put them in any order, and the result will be the same. **E** is incorrect because there is a fault with the page, and **F** is ruled out because there is a correct explanation for the fault.

4. ☑ **A** and **D**. **A** is true because `_jspService()` does originate from a servlet's `service()` method. **D** is also true: All servlet methods are accessible at this point. For a couple of them (`destroy()`, `service()`), it would make no sense to use them at this point, but they are accessible.
☒ **B** is probably correct nearly all of the time but can't be taken for granted: A JSP servlet could be instantiated and the `jspInit()` method called before any request reaches the JSP container. The specification leaves room for the container vendor to do what seems best—as long as the call to `jspInit()` has occurred before the first request. **C** is incorrect: You can't determine (from within the server) when the last request to a JSP will occur. **E** is also incorrect, because (surprisingly) you can override or supply an `init()` method. It's likely that your JSP's implementing servlet will inherit an `init()` method with no parameters from GenericServlet. However, this method is *not* defined in the Servlet interface—rather, there's one that receives a parameter: `init(ServletConfig config)`. This one you can't override in JSPs, and that's true for all the methods defined in the Servlet and ServletConfig interfaces (indeed, most vendors supply a parent JSP servlet—from which your generated servlets inherit—which has the Servlet and ServletConfig methods marked as **final**).

5. ☑ **A** and **E**. Two compilation errors occur. Because the servlet generated from JSP source already contains a `_jspService()` method, any attempt to include one (with the same parameters) will fail with a duplicate method error (can't have two methods with the same names and same parameters in the same piece of Java source). Furthermore, the implicit variable *out* (for the JspWriter) isn't implicitly available within any method of your own that you define in a declaration—which gives rise to the "cannot resolve symbol" error.
☒ **B**, **C**, **D**, and **F** are incorrect; because the JSP as it stands makes no sense and won't compile, you certainly won't get any kind of output to the response.

JSP Elements

6. ☑ **B** is correct. There is a translation error because `methodC()` is inside a scriptlet element, whereas it should be inside a declaration. Consequently, `methodC()`'s source is generated directly into the middle of the `jspService()` method, so compilation (part of the translation process) fails.
☒ **A** is incorrect because there will be no output to the browser apart from an HTTP 500 error—this rules out **E** as well. **C** is incorrect because there is no compiled code to run. **D** is

incorrect because only the HTTP 500 error is visible in the browser. This may indeed include a Java stack trace—but this is from the translation phase classes, not from the generated servlet, which is the only code that could produce the HTML heading 1 output.

7. ☑ **A** maps to 1: It's the beginning of a scriptlet. **B** maps to 12, for it denotes the end of the scriptlet and the beginning of an expression. **C** maps to 11, for this denotes the end of tag for an HTML element with no body. **D** maps to 15: *abbrev* is the name of the parameter passed on the input text field. **E** maps to 10—only a single white space will do here! (It's an expression—this was an attempt to fool you into picking the semicolon. Expressions don't terminate with a semicolon.) **F** maps to 4, for it's the beginning of a directive (admittedly placed in a stupid position in the middle of the source, but it's still legal and works). **G** maps to 13, for it marks the beginning of a declaration for the `fullTextOfUnits()` method.
   ☒ There are no other correct permutations, to the best of my knowledge.

8. ☑ **B** and **H** are the correct answers, for both are true statements about the Java page source. **B** is correct because it is a bad idea to use the response's PrintWriter directly. You should instead use the JspWriter associated with the *out* implicit variable. The effects of buffering can jumble the output if *out* and the response's PrintWriter are mixed. **H** is correct: The page in fact fails to compile because a duplicate local variable is defined. *out* is automatically provided in generated JSP source—but this is also the name chosen in this case for the local variable associated with the PrintWriter at source line 06.
   ☒ **A** is incorrect, for scriptlet markers can share a line with Java source statements entirely as needed. **C**, **D**, and **E** are incorrect because the page doesn't compile, so there is no response. I find if I correct the compilation problem, I do get the output described in answer **C** (P followed by Q—as you might expect. If you have time, though, correct the question source and try swapping the two scriptlets around—observe what happens). **F** and **G** are incorrect answers because the directive is the correct syntax and java.io is the correct package for the PrintWriter class (which is the only unqualified class name in the source).

9. ☑ **A**, **C**, and **D** are the correct answers, for they are all false statements. **A** is correct because you can legally embed one `<%--` comment inside another—it's just not a sensible thing to do, for the translator will think the outer comment has ended as soon as it encounters the inner comment end marker. Doing this may lead to compilation errors, but is not in itself a cause for a translation failure. **C** and **D** are correct because you can never embed an expression inside a declaration or a directive (so **C** and **D** are false statements).
   ☒ **B** is incorrect because it is a true statement: Expressions can't be embedded inside scriptlets. Although both scriptlets and expressions are generated to the `_jspService()` method, it would almost never lead to legal Java to include one inside the other; hence, the translator won't allow it. **E** is incorrect because it's also a true statement—you can include declarations

anywhere in the JSP page source (they don't have to appear at the beginning or end). And **F** is also true (and so an incorrect answer)—it's legal to embed illegal syntax (a scriptlet inside an expression) or anything else inside a `<%--` style comment; the translator simply ignores anything inside the comment.

10. ☑ **D** is the correct answer. If the percent sign associated with opening of the scriptlet were removed, the JSP page would compile. The angle bracket would be treated as template text—the opening of an HTML tag. The translator would ignore everything from the first comment sign to the first comment end sign. The rest of the page (from "System.out.println" onward) would be interpreted as template text. The browser rendering the dubious output (unbalanced angle brackets in the HTML) might have problems, but the JSP page would compile.
☒ **A** is incorrect: JSP page sources can have no characters in them at all and still be "complete" as far as the translation process is concerned. This is part of their convenience. So don't feel that this fragment is an incomplete page. **B** is incorrect—as discussed in the previous question, you can have nested comments as far as the compiler is concerned; it's just not a sensible thing to do. **C** is incorrect because even if you did remove the curly brace—thus making the scriptlet almost legal Java—compilation would still fail because the declaration for variable *i* is still commented out. And for all the reasons discussed so far, **E** must be incorrect: The page won't run and produce output if left unaltered.

JSP Directives

11. ☑ **D** and **E** are the correct answers. Although **D** looks strange, because it includes two import attributes in the same directive and uses a different style of quote for each set of attribute values, this translates, compiles, and works. Again, **E** looks strange because of the surfeit of white space in places and absence in others—but again, it works fine.
☒ **A** is incorrect: You might think it is reasonable to include an import statement in a declaration element, but it simply fails to translate. **B** is incorrect: *import* is not a directive in its own right (it's an attribute of the *page* directive). Finally, **C** is incorrect because although the JSP syntax is legal, the class java.util.StringTokenizator does not exist—consequently, compilation will give rise to an unresolved import error (and yes, it is fair to test such knowledge in a web application exam!).

12. ☑ **A** is the correct answer. An ill-formed HTML document will be the output—including ten beginning of document `<html>` and end of document `</html>` tags. Everything else about the inclusion process works. On most browsers (which aren't too fussy about well-formed HTML), the page will display.

☒ B is incorrect—the *include* directive causes the source of included12.jsp to meld into includer12.jsp. Together they form a single "translation unit"; it is as if there is only one JSP to translate. So the declaration of variable *i* in includer12.jsp makes *i* available to the source of included12.jsp. **C** is incorrect—however incorrect the template HTML, the translation process won't mind (you might design a JSP container to do additional checks, but the JSP spec doesn't mandate this, and the exam questions are according to the JSP spec). **D** is incorrect: The loop is zero-based, so "For the 9th time" is the highest value in the output. And because translation doesn't fail, **E** must also be incorrect.

13. ☑ **C** and **F** are the correct answers. **C** is correct because the *session* attribute for the page directive is set to "true"—which is the default—so removal would have no impact. **F** is correct because it's OK for more than one attribute to appear in the same *page* directive, and the order of attributes won't cause an error.
☒ **A** is incorrect because it's always fine to repeat the *import* attribute over the same *page* directive or over several *page* directives. The translator will even forgive you importing the same package or class twice. **B** is incorrect because while it isn't wise to repeat the *contentType* attribute more than once in the same translation unit, as long as the values are the same wherever it appears, then no error will occur. **D** is incorrect: *al* would not be recognized if included13.jsp was translated directly, but we're told in the question that the intention is to call (and translate) includer13.jsp, which declares the variable. **E** is incorrect because there is no issue with having a *page* directive with several attributes. Stylistically, you may want to spread different attributes over different directives—but the exam is a syntax test, not a style test!

14. ☑ **A**, **B**, and **D** are the correct answers, for all illustrate invalid directives. **A** is mistaken in the case for an attribute name, which should be isELIgnored (the second "I" must be a capital letter). **B** mixes double quotes and single quotes to hold an attribute value. Although different attribute values—even in the same directive—can differ in quote style, a single value must stick to the same style. **D** is wrong (and so a correct answer) because *uri* is an attribute of the *taglib* directive, not the *include* directive (which has one mandatory attribute of *file*).
☒ **C** is an incorrect answer because it is a valid directive. Even though the MIME-type ("image/music/text") is rubbish, this won't throw any JSP translation or runtime error. The receiving browser might have a hard time coping with the response, though! **E** is an incorrect answer, for it perfectly expresses a tag library directive.

15. ☑ **B** is the correct answer. This sets up the session variable, finds the attributes for the song lines in the right scope, and prints out all the lines.
☒ **A** is incorrect because the *session* attribute for the page directive has a value of false, yet the implicit variable *session* is accessed. The page will not compile in this state. **C** is incorrect

because the logic for finding the attributes is slightly flawed. The loop has been adjusted so the counter starts at 1 instead of 0 (making it simpler to compose the attribute names) but will now only loop through the first three lines. **D** is wrong because the `getAttribute` method for the *pageContext* implicit variable will find attributes only in page scope. So the logic will only find one of the lines. **E** is wrong for the same reason as **D**, and also because the expression to print out the song line terminates incorrectly in a semicolon (so the page will not compile successfully).

JSP Implicit Objects

16. ☑ **B** and **D** are the correct answers. **D** is correct because the *config* implicit object (which must be available in your JSP page) has a `getInitParameter()` method that accepts a String for the parameter name and returns a String representing the parameter object. **B** is correct because you are in the middle of servlet code, and the servlet you inherit from almost certainly implements the `ServletConfig.getInitParameter()` method.

    ☒ **A** is incorrect because the parameters you retrieve from requests are tied to the request, usually from fields on an HTML form—so have nothing to do with servlet (JSP) initialization parameters. **C** is incorrect because while *application* does have a `getInitParameter()` method, the parameter values returned are for the ServletContext (i.e., the web application as a whole). **E** is incorrect because there is no `getParameter()` method available in the generated servlet. **F** is incorrect because *config*'s method for returning servlet parameters is `getInitParameter()`, not `getParameter`. **G** and **H** are incorrect because there are no attribute methods associated with ServletConfig or servlets directly—and besides, attributes are not parameters.

17. ☑ **A** maps to **7** (because session scope is used, it must be "true" that the *session* implicit object is available). **B** maps to **9** (the Integer 0 must be in page scope because the later expression containing the method `findAttribute()` will then find a value of 0 to print at the right time). **C** maps to **12** (*application* matches APPLICATION_SCOPE in the last line of the page source, for printing out the number 3). **D** maps to **9** again (only *pageContext* has a `findAttribute()` method). **E**, **G**, **I**, and **K** all map to **4** (the class PageContext—required for the final, static constants used as the second parameter in each occurrence of the `getAttribute()` method). **F** maps to **6** (must be PAGE_SCOPE—no other scope will do), **H** maps to **14** (must be REQUEST_SCOPE), and **J** maps to **15** (must be SESSION_SCOPE).

    ☒ No other combinations will work to produce the correct output.

18. ☑ **C** and **F** are the correct answers. **C** is correct because errorDisplayer.jsp will not be translated, for no error occurs to transfer processing from errorProvoker.jsp. **F** is correct because errorProvoker.jsp does display output: the word "Infinity." The key to answering the question is the knowledge that division involving a double (and 1.0 is a double constant) does not result in an ArithmeticException, as integer division does.

☒ A is incorrect, for the page source for errorProvoker.jsp is absolutely fine, as is that for errorDisplayer.jsp , so B is incorrect as well. You might have thought the scriptlet

```
<% exception.printStackTrace(new PrintWriter(out));>
```

strange—but this use of the `out` implicit variable is perfectly acceptable (I'm indebted to Phil Hanna's book—*JSP 2.0: The Complete Reference*, McGraw-Hill/Osborne—for pointing out this handy technique for printing a stack trace to the web page). **D** is incorrect, for no error occurs—so no stack trace. **E** is incorrect—the title "Divide by Zero Error" would occur only if processing was diverted to errorDisplayer.jsp.

19. ☑ **A**, **B**, **E**, and **F** are the correct answers, for all of these are false statements. **A** is false (and so a correct answer) because `out` is a `javax.servlet.jsp.JspWriter`, not a `java.io.PrintWriter`. **B** is false (so a correct answer) because `config` can be used to return initialization parameters for an individual JSP, but not for the entire context (for which you would use the `application` implicit object). **E** is false (so a correct answer) because `application` is just a `ServletContext` object—and this provides the `getContext()` method for accessing different contexts outside of the current web application. **F** is false (so a correct answer) because it is absolutely possible to have attributes of the same name in different scopes (as you would have understood from Question 17 if nowhere else!).
☒ **C** and **D** are incorrect, for both are true statements. **C** is true (so an incorrect answer) because `findAttribute()` will indeed look to the innermost scope (`page`) first for attributes, and will look no further once it has found an attribute for the sought name. **D** is true (so an incorrect answer), for `page` is surprisingly defined as an `Object` reference—not a `Servlet`, or `GenericServlet` or `HttpJspPage`. It is likely that you can *cast* the `page` reference to something more useful, such as one of those listed, but you probably wouldn't bother, for you have `this` to use as a more useful alternative.

20. ☑ **D** is the correct answer. The constant **null** is invariably displayed as the echoed text. Everything translates fine—there is nothing syntactically incorrect in the page sources. However, in attributeFinder.jsp, the developer should have used `request.getParameter("echoInput")` instead of `request.getAttribute("echoInput")`. Field values from HTML forms are made available as parameters, not attributes.
☒ **A**, **B**, and **C** are incorrect because no translation errors occur. You may have thought that using an expression for an HTML form field is illegal—but no, it's fine, even with the peculiar logic here, with the name set in an included JSP page source. **E** is incorrect because you have to make the adjustment described in the correct answer to get the input echoing properly.

LAB ANSWER

Deploy the WAR file from the CD called lab06.war, in the /sourcecode/chapter06 directory. This contains a sample solution. You can call the JSP using a URL such as

```
http://localhost:8080/lab06/tictactoe.jsp
```

This is a very basic version of the game—you may find it hard to stop yourself from improving the code!

7

JSP Standard Actions, XML, and EL

CERTIFICATION OBJECTIVES

- JSP Standard Actions
- Dispatching Mechanisms
- JSPs in XML
- Expression Language
- ✓ Two-Minute Drill
- Q&A Self Test

In the last chapter you covered the fundamentals of JavaServer Pages and did a lot of work with the "traditional" scripting elements. In this chapter you start by learning about standard actions. These are interesting in that they have been available for a long while and—like "traditional" scripting—were common topics in the previous version of the exam. Yet they also foreshadow the more recent innovations in JSP technology, which continues to push in an XML direction.

You'll also explore in the first half of the chapter how standard actions play a role in dispatching mechanisms: forwarding to and including other resources (you'll remember that you have come across one inclusion mechanism already—the `<%@ include %>` directive—and this chapter rounds out that topic).

In the second half of the chapter, you are introduced to two topics that are recent additions to JSP technology, and so also to the latest syllabus of the web component developer exam:

- JSP documents, which are JSPs written entirely in well-formed XML
- Expression Language, the "modern" alternative to language-based scripting

You've seen Figure 7-1 before, which shows the makeup of a JSP page—it's been slightly modified to indicate the topics you covered previously and which JSP elements are explained in this chapter.

CERTIFICATION OBJECTIVE

JSP Standard Actions (Exam Objective 8.1)

Given a design goal, create a code snippet using the following standard actions: jsp:useBean (with attributes: "id," "scope," "type," and "class"), jsp:getProperty, and jsp:setProperty (with all attribute combinations).

Standard actions are used for the same purpose as Java language-based scripting: Most if not all the goals that you can achieve with standard actions are achievable with other scripting elements. But in contrast to the techniques we've used so far, they are written using entirely conventional XML syntax.

FIGURE 7-1

Anatomy of a JSP Page Revisited

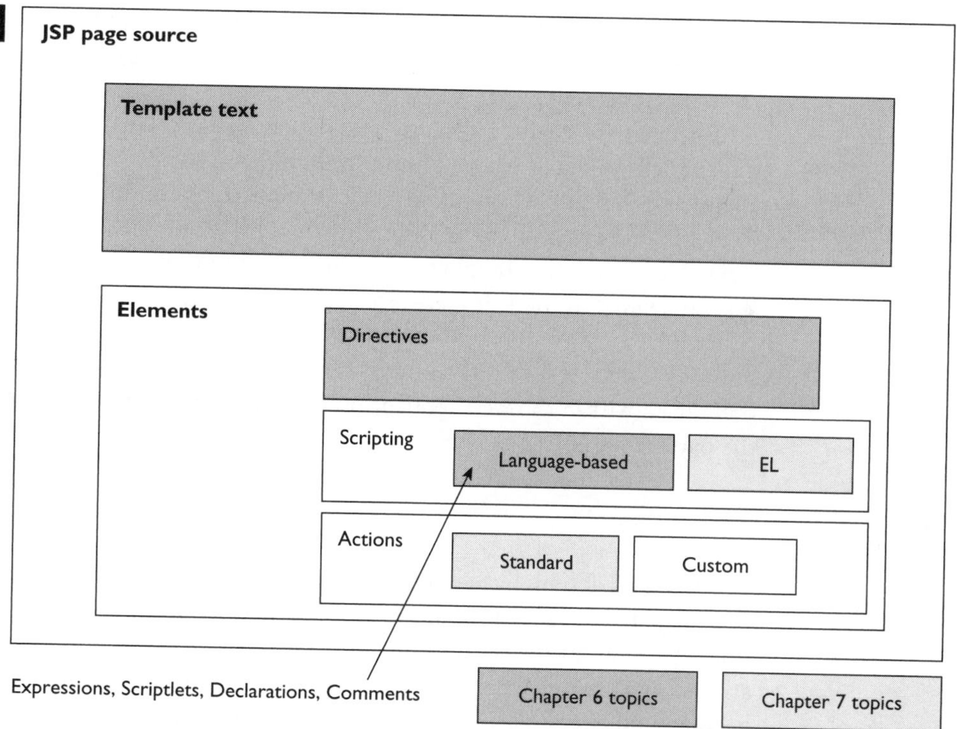

So why use them? The answer is that they get the job done more elegantly. They often provide an alternative to inserting screeds of Java logic into your neatly designed presentation page. Standard actions are also—arguably—tools that can be used by the nonprogrammer to introduce dynamic behavior that would otherwise entail Java language knowledge. (Actually—given the range of standard and custom actions available, combined with Expression Language and JSTL, which we cover later—you probably need a programmer mentality to embrace even the "non-Java-language" tools that are available in JSP page source these days.)

Seven standard actions are provided from JSP 1.2 onward: Three are considered here; three are in the next section, on dispatching; and one is out of scope for the exam (`<jsp:plugin>`). Although a few more have been added in JSP 2.0, they are not directly on the exam syllabus.

The trio of standard actions in this section (`<jsp:useBean>`, `<jsp:getProperty>`, `<jsp:setProperty>`) work together to incorporate information from existing Java objects into your JSP page. These existing Java objects must be written to rules within the JavaBean specification, so before we approach the standard actions themselves, we'll do some preliminary work exploring the least you need to know about beans.

Why are they *standard* actions? The reason is that you can have *custom* actions as well, which you build yourself using tag libraries, a subject that we fully explore in Chapters 8 and 9. Both standard and custom actions are similar in appearance: XML elements that encapsulate functionality on a JSP page. The difference is that you can rely on any J2EE-compliant JSP container to provide support for all the standard actions defined in the JSP spec. Not so custom actions, because they are—well—customized for your web applications. Not that you can't use custom actions across several projects, just that the onus is on you to deliver all the apparatus to make them work within the web application (you can't rely on the JSP container to have the parts required).

Beans

The standard actions we explore first are designed to instantiate Java objects, then write data to or read data from those objects. Java objects come in many shapes and sizes, so it's little wonder that standard actions can work only if those objects obey at least some minimal conventions. Enter the JavaBeans Specification, which has been around almost as long as Java itself. The idea of JavaBeans is that you can have Java components (typically classes) that can be interrogated by interested software, using the reflection techniques we have employed several times in the exercises up to now. "Interested software" includes the web container code that implements the standard actions we're about to discuss. By interrogating the methods available on a JavaBean, a standard action can obtain information about the properties that the bean supports—in other words, the data that it stores.

This process works in a remarkably simple way. All your bean has to do is to provide "getter" and "setter" methods. Here's a short class that defines information about a dog:

```
public class Dog {
  private String name;
  private float mass;
  private boolean insured;
  private char sex;
  private String barkVolume;
  public String getName() { return name; }
  public void setName(String name) { this.name = name; }
  public float getWeight() { return mass; }
```

```
    public void setWeight(float weight) { mass = weight }
    public boolean isInsured() { return insured; }
    public void setInsured(boolean insured) {
        this.insured = insured;
    }
    public char getSex() { return sex; }
    public void setSex(char sex) { this.sex = sex; }
    public String getBarkVolume() {
        return barkVolume;
    }
    public void setBarkVolume(String barkVolume) {
        this.barkVolume = barkVolume;
    }
}
```

You can see that the Dog class contains five pieces of information pertaining to the dog. The first is the data member *name*. Because *name* is private, the class provides a public `setName()` method to update the dog's name within a dog instance and, of course, a `getName()` method to read the data. Note how the method names use the instance variable name but capitalize the initial letter: `setName()`. In this way, the standard Java naming conventions for instance variables and method names remain unbroken. This is such a standard convention in Java that you're probably wondering why I've wasted a precious paragraph on the topic.

However, there are a couple of twists if you've never encountered beans before. Tools that use beans (which include JSP standard actions) care only about the methods on the bean. From `setName()` and `getName()`, a bean-literate tool understands that there is a property on any dog "bean" called *name* (i.e., what you would expect the instance variable to be called after allowing for the capitalization difference). But let's look at the next pair of methods—`setWeight()` and `getWeight()`. From this, we infer there is a property called *weight*. And this is correct—even though the instance variable connected to these methods is called something quite different: *mass*, in this case. How we represent the data in the bean (and we may not bother at all) doesn't matter.

The only other convention to mention is that for primitive **boolean** properties, such as *insured* in our dog bean, you have the option (as a bean developer) to supply a method called `isInsured()` instead of (or as well as) `getInsured()` for reading the property value.

Another thing about a bean is that you—as a developer—don't normally have control over creation of your beans. You don't write code like this:

```
Dog d = new Dog();
```

Instead, you leave the instantiation to the bean tool you are using— in our case, standard actions. Consequently, your bean must have a no-argument constructor—either one you provide or the default one the compiler provides in the absence of others. This is the only kind of constructor that your bean tool can assume as universal across all the beans it has to deal with.

on the job

If you carry on down the J2EE road beyond the SCWCD, you'll go on to learn about Enterprise JavaBeans (EJBs). These do quite often have getter and setter methods, but beyond that, the resemblance to the "normal" JavaBeans we have just discussed comes to an end. EJBs are a completely different ball game—they require a specialized container, much as servlets and JSPs do. So don't try to connect your `<jsp:useBean>` standard action to an EJB, because you are doomed to fail!

Standard Actions

After what may seem like a digression, we can return to the core syllabus matter of standard actions. Let's first look at the general syntax of actions, whether standard or custom. As we've said, they adhere to strict XML syntax. Here's a generalized picture:

```
<prefix:tagname firstAttribute="value" secondAttribute="value"> ...
</prefix:tagname>
```

Each standard action element consists of a start tag, `<prefix:tagname>`, and an end tag of the same name (with a forward slash inserted after the first angle bracket), `</prefix:tagname>`. The start tag may contain named attributes, separated from their corresponding value by equal signs. The value is typically surrounded by double quotes or by single quotes (which is sometimes convenient). After so much exposure to the deployment descriptor, web.xml, and HTML web pages, this syntax must feel refreshingly familiar.

But just in case you didn't know, the area between the start and end tag (represented by the ellipsis [. . .] above) is termed the body of the element. A standard action may have a body, but it often has no body at all. This can be represented in one of two ways:

1. By having start and end tag touching, thus: `<prefix:tagname attr="value"></prefix:tagname>`
2. By omitting the end tag but using a special /> terminator for the start tag, thus: `<prefix:tagname attr="value" />`

It makes no difference which of the above forms you use; the JSP container will interpret both identically. So with that in mind, let's look at the three standard actions for the exam objective:

- `<jsp:useBean>`
- `<jsp:setProperty>`
- `<jsp:getProperty>`

You can see three tag names here: `useBean`, `setProperty`, and `getProperty`. You can also see a common prefix—`jsp`—separated from the tag name by a colon. Indeed, the prefix for all standard actions is `jsp`. When you come to write your own custom actions later, you'll have to supply a prefix—it may come as no surprise to learn that `jsp` is reserved, even if your page eschews all standard actions in favor of your own custom ones.

<jsp:useBean>

The `<jsp:useBean>` standard action declares a JavaBean instance and associates this with a variable name. The instance is then available for use elsewhere in your JSP page: either in Expression Language (highest grades), other standard actions (still good practice), or in Java language scripting (frowned upon—but still legal! You'll see plenty of to-ing and fro-ing between standard actions and scriptlets and expressions in this chapter—all in the name of education, of course).

In general, you'll use `<jsp:useBean>` to set up your bean and two more standard actions to write and read properties on your bean. These standard actions are called `<jsp:setProperty>` and `<jsp:getProperty>`—which makes pretty good sense in light of our bean discussion a little earlier.

So how exactly do you use `<jsp:useBean>` to do this? The answer is to get to work with its attributes. The simplest approach is this:

```
<jsp:useBean id="theDog" class="animals.Dog" />
```

For this to work, several things have to be true:

- The class attribute must specify the fully qualified name of a class (the import attribute of the page directive will be no help to you, unfortunately).
- `animals.Dog` must obey JavaBean conventions.

- `animals.Dog` must be visible somewhere in the web application—mostly this means it will exist as a class in WEB-INF/classes or within a JAR file in WEB-INF/lib.
- An *id* with a value of *theDog* must not have been used in `<jsp:useBean>` already; in other words, all *ids* for beans on a page must be unique.

Inserting this in your JSP page source will result in some quite complex code in your generated servlet's `_jspService()` method. Ultimately, the code will create an instance of the bean `animals.Dog`. How will the code reference the object? In two ways:

1. As a local variable in the method, whose name comes from value of the *id* attribute (so *theDog* becomes a local variable).
2. As an attribute in some scope or other—page, request, session, or application. In this case, *theDog* is the name of the attribute.

On this second point: Because we didn't specify the scope anywhere in our example, where did `theDog` go? The answer is into page scope. The following cumbersome combination of directive and scriptlet code—following on from the `<jsp:useBean>` standard action declaring *theDog* JavaBean above—will get hold of our bean object into the local variable *myDog*:

```
<%@ page import="animals.Dog" %>
<% Dog myDog=(Dog)
pageContext.getAttribute("theDog"); %>
```

I'm not suggesting that you should ever do this—this code is only here to unravel the mystery of bean location.

If we want our bean to be a little more permanent than page duration, we need to use another attribute of `<jsp:useBean>`: namely, *scope*. To put *theDog* into session scope, it really is this simple:

```
<jsp:useBean id="theDog" class="animals.Dog" scope="session" />
```

The valid values for *scope* are page, request, session, and application—exactly as expected. So now we can access *theDog* across a series of requests from the same user. What if the *theDog* already exists in session scope when the standard action above is encountered? That's OK—`<jsp:useBean>` recycles the existing bean; it doesn't create a new one.

We haven't explored all the ramifications of `<jsp:useBean>` just yet, in particular a fourth attribute named *type*. But before we do that, we should look at the two standard actions inevitably used in conjunction with `<jsp:useBean>`, which are of course `<jsp:setProperty>` and `<jsp:getProperty>`.

on the job

There is an attribute of `<jsp:useBean>` called beanName, off scope for the exam. The main functionality this offers (over and above the class and type attributes) is the possibility of using a serialized bean from your file system. To learn more, take a careful look at section 5.1 of the JSP specification, and the J2SDK API for the `instantiate()` method on the java.beans.Beans class.

<jsp:setProperty>

The purpose of `<jsp:setProperty>` is to set the values of one or more properties on a bean previously declared with `<jsp:useBean>`. The most obvious way to use it is as follows:

```
<jsp:setProperty name="theDog" property="weight" value="6.4" />
```

The first thing to watch is the attribute *name*. This is the name of the bean itself. The value for this attribute has to be the same as a previous value for a `<jsp:useBean>` *id* attribute. It's a pity that the attributes don't match—it's another thing you have to remember for the exam: *id* on `<jsp:useBean>` = *name* on `<jsp:setProperty>` (and `<jsp:getProperty>` as well, when we get to it).

exam watch

Actually, the truth is that you can use `<jsp:setProperty>` and `<jsp:getProperty>` without a previous `<jsp:useBean>`. All `<jsp:setProperty>` and `<jsp:getProperty>` do is to use `PageContext.findAttribute()`—so if an attribute of the right name exists—set up, perhaps, in a previous servlet—these standard actions will find it. However, it's good practice to include `<jsp:useBean>` before these actions in the same JSP page. After all, it won't replace beans of the same name that you have set up by other means, and it will create beans of the right name that don't exist already. Furthermore, if your `<jsp:setProperty>` and `<jsp:getProperty>` standard actions try to access an attribute that doesn't exist, they are liable to die a horrible death with HTTP 500 errors returned to the requester.

The *property* attribute specifies a property on the bean. Because the property here is "weight," then the underlying code will assume the existence of a `getWeight()` method on the *theDog* bean. The *value* attribute supplies the data for the property—or in code terms, the parameter that is passed into the getter method. In our example, `getWeight()` expects a float parameter, yet the value for the value attribute looks very like a String constant: `value="6.4."` Yet we don't have to worry—it's the responsibility of the JSP container to handle the type conversions involved.

The *value* attribute has another feature not shared by any other attributes in `<jsp:useBean>`, `<jsp:setProperty>`, or `<jsp:getProperty>`. Instead of supplying a literal value, you can substitute an expression. Here are two examples:

```
<% float w = 6.4f; %>
<jsp:setProperty name="theDog" property="weight" value="<%=w%>" />
```

Another:

```
<% String dftWeight = config.getInitParameter("defaultDogWeight"); %>
<jsp:setProperty name="theDog" property="weight" value="<%= dftWeight %>" />
```

All these are viable ways to "soft-code" the value of *value*, so as to set a property in your application. The first sets up a float variable called *w* in a scriptlet, and uses this directly in an expression embedded into the following standard action. Note how the double quotes are retained to demarcate the beginning and end of the value, and the expression plugs between them: `value="<%=w%>."` The second example uses a scriptlet to obtain an initial parameter called defaultDogWeight associated with the JSP, and plugs this into the *value* expression. Later, you'll see that you're not stuck with Java language expressions to supply values. Expression Language also fits the bill, and we'll revisit standard actions with Expression Language before the end of this chapter.

You'll very often want to use request parameters (say from an HTML form) to set properties. You could follow on from the examples above and write code like this:

```
<jsp:setProperty name="theDog" property="weight"
value="<%= request.getParameter("dogWeight") %>" />
```

The expression plugged into the value attribute this time uses the *request* implicit object to retrieve the parameter "dogWeight." In fact, this is such a common thing to want to do that `<jsp:setProperty>` provides some convenient syntax to avoid ungainly code like this. This is how it looks:

```
<jsp:setProperty name="theDog" property="weight" param="dogWeight" />
```

This is shorthand for saying take the request parameter called "dogWeight," and use the value for this to set the property called "weight" on the bean called "theDog." Very neat, and it can get neater still. It could well be that name of a request parameter (from your HTML form) matches the corresponding property name. In that case, you can omit the param attribute altogether:

```
<jsp:setProperty name="theDog" property="weight" />
```

This time, the underlying code will look for a parameter (from the ServletRequest or HttpServletRequest) called "weight" and use this to set the property value for "weight" on "theDog." This shorthand goes further still. If you have a number of request parameters that match the names of several properties on your target bean, you can simply write

```
<jsp:setProperty name="theDog" property="*" />
```

Now *any* property whose name matches a request parameter name will have its value preloaded from that request parameter.

exam watch

The param and value attributes are mutually exclusive. After all, it doesn't make sense to have both on the same `<jsp:setProperty>`. Either you use the convenience of param to set a property from a request parameter or you take a more explicit approach with the value attribute. Note that you can also omit both the param and value attributes: This is equivalent to supplying param with the same value as the property attribute.

`<jsp:getProperty>`

That leaves `<jsp:getProperty>`. This is the easiest of the three standard actions we've used. You use it to output the value of a bean's property to the response (for display on a web page, inclusion in an XML document—whatever). There are two attributes to supply: *name* (the name of the bean) and *property* (the name of the property). They're both mandatory (as are the identical attributes on `setProperty`, by the way). So to get hold of our dog's weight property, you simply write the following:

```
<jsp:getProperty name="theDog" property="weight" />
```

Like `<jsp:setProperty>`, *theDog* bean has to be there—preferably declared with `<jsp:useBean>` earlier in the page.

INSIDE THE EXAM

Before leaving these three standard actions, let's put them together in a bigger example. This is here to reinforce some of the points made earlier, but also to illustrate some of the subtler aspects of `<jsp:useBean>` that you need to know for the exam. We'll be working with the Dog JavaBean that started this chapter, in a slightly modified form.

Let's suppose that you're writing a system to register animals at your local veterinary clinic. The clinic copes with all kinds of animals: dogs, cats, parakeets, and rattlesnakes. But whatever the animal, there are some details that will be common. Others may be animal-specific. We'll look at a portion of the system: that deals both with some general animal characteristics and also ones that are dog-specific. Here's an illustrative screen flow:

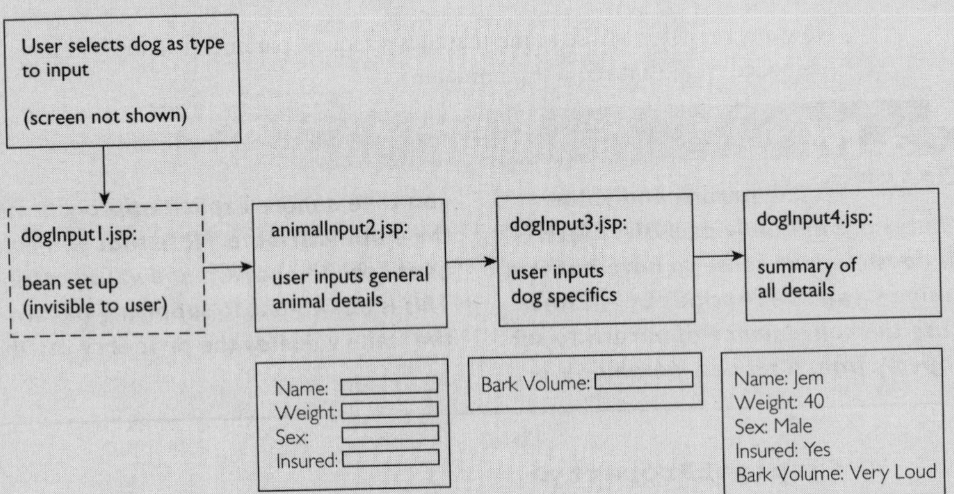

First of all, the vet's receptionist selects the type of animal to be registered—in our case, dog. In the background, a Dog JavaBean is set up with some defaults (this happens in dogInput1.jsp). The receptionist is presented with a screen to fill in some details about the animal in general (animalInput2.jsp), followed by a screen for specific dog details (dogInput3.jsp). On pressing ENTER, the receptionist finally sees a summary screen of all the dog details that have been saved to the database (dogInput4.jsp). (You'll have to imagine the database in the example code that follows—the intention here is just to show the JSP aspects.) You can run this code (and look at the full source) from the WAR file /sourcecode/ch07/examp0701.war. Start at the following URL:

INSIDE THE EXAM (continued)

```
http://localhost:8080/examp0701/dogInput1.jsp
```

The point about this design is that the general animal details screen—animal Input2.jsp—will work regardless of animal type, for there is nothing dog-specific within it. Yet it makes use of a Dog JavaBean set up with `<jsp:useBean>`. How can this be? We'll solve this mystery in a page or two, as we step carefully through the code. Let's first take a look at dogInput1.jsp:

```
<jsp:useBean id="currentAnimal"scope="session"
class="webcert.ch07.examp0701.Dog">
 <jsp:setProperty name="currentAnimal" property="name" value="Fido" />
 <jsp:setProperty name="currentAnimal" property="weight" value="6.5" />
 <jsp:setProperty name="currentAnimal" property="sex" value="F" />
 <jsp:setProperty name="currentAnimal" property="insured" value="false" />
 <jsp:setProperty name="currentAnimal" property="barkVolume" value="Loud" />
</jsp:useBean>
<%session.setAttribute("animalSort", "dog");
  RequestDispatcher rd =
  application.getRequestDispatcher
  ("/animalInput2.jsp");
  rd.forward(request, response); %>
```

Recall at this point that the receptionist has made a choice of animal type. First of all, a Dog bean called "`currentAnimal`" is set up in session scope. Nothing unusual there, but notice that the `<jsp:useBean>` tag is not "self-closing" as we've seen before—like this:

```
<jsp:useBean id="currentAnimal" scope="session"
class="webcert.ch07.examp0701.Dog" />
```

In this case, there is an end tag a few lines further on: `</jsp:useBean>`. So this tag has a body—in this case, filled with five `<jsp:setProperty>` standard actions. The presence of a body signifies that some logic will execute:

- If the currentAnimal bean doesn't exist, it will be created, and the `<jsp:setProperty>` tags will execute to set up some default values.
- If the currentAnimal bean exists already, it will be *left alone*, and the `<jsp:setProperty>` tags will not execute, so any property values already set will remain unchanged.

INSIDE THE EXAM (continued)

Not that it does, but if our screen flow came back through dogInput1.jsp, currentAnimal would stay unaffected.

The scriptlet at the end of dogInput1.jsp does two things: First, it sets up a session attribute called `animalSort` with a value of "dog," to indicate to future screens that it's a dog we're dealing with (not a cat or a hamster). Secondly, it uses standard Request Dispatcher code to forward to the next screen in sequence—animalInput2.jsp (you'll see how to replace this code with a standard action a bit later in the chapter). So notice that all you ever do in dogInput1.jsp is "pass through"—the response isn't returned to the user.

The code for animalInput2.jsp is shown below. Notice that there isn't anything dog-specific anywhere in the source code:

```
<html><head><title>General Animal Information</title></head>
<body>
<h2>Fill in general animal information here, regardless of what sort of
animal...</h2>
<jsp:useBean id="currentAnimal" scope="session" type="webcert.ch07
.examp0701.Animal" />
<p>Overtype the defaults in the form below...</p>
<form action="<%= session.getAttribute("animalSort")%>Input3.jsp">
<br />Name: <input type="text" name="name" value="<jsp:getProperty
name="currentAnimal" property="name" />" />
<br />Weight: <input type="text" name="weight" value="<jsp:getProperty
name="currentAnimal" property="weight" />" />
<br />Sex: <input type="text" name="Sex" value="<jsp:getProperty
name="currentAnimal" property="sex" />" />
<br />Insured: <input type="text" name="insured" value="<jsp:getProperty
name="currentAnimal" property="insured" />" />
<br /><input type="submit" value="Continue..." />
</form></body></html>
```

After the template text at the beginning, inviting you to fill in general animal information, you find the `<jsp:useBean>` standard action, requesting the same bean called currentAnimal in session scope. But instead of the class attribute, we find another attribute called type instead:

```
type="webcert.ch07.examp0701.Animal"
```

It's the same bean that we get hold of, which is a Dog object. However, if we look in the generated servlet code, any reference to this bean will be of Animal type. This can only work under the following circumstances:

INSIDE THE EXAM (continued)

- Dog is a subclass of Animal.
- Or Dog implements an interface called Animal.

In other words, the type you choose must be compatible with the actual class of the object. Let's suppose that Dog implements an Animal interface and that its class declaration now looks like this:

```
public class Dog implements Animal
```

And the Animal interface declares all the methods about general animal characteristics:

```
public interface Animal {
    public abstract String getName();
    public abstract void setName(String name);
    public abstract float getWeight();
    public abstract void setWeight(float weight);
    public abstract boolean isInsured();
    public abstract void setInsured(boolean insured);
    public abstract char getSex();
    public abstract void setSex(char sex);
}
```

Dog implements all these methods as we've already seen, plus a couple that are dog-specific—to set and get the barkVolume property.

Using type in `<jsp:useBean>` without the `class` attribute relies on the fact that the bean has already been created. You can simultaneously create a bean object and type it to something else for use in the current JSP page by using both attributes at the same time, like this:

```
<jsp:useBean id="currentAnimal"
scope="session" class="Webcert.ch07.examp0701.Dog"
type=""webcert.ch07.examp0701.Animal" />
```

The form in animalInput2.jsp uses `<jsp:getProperty>` standard actions to display the default values already set up on the Dog bean, which can be overtyped in the form. Of course, *barkVolume* is missing from the list. The only other point to note is that—to keep

INSIDE THE EXAM (continued)

animalInput2.jsp generic—the `<form>` *action* attribute uses an expression to complete the name of the next JSP in sequence. The start of the name comes from the session attribute animalSort, which you'll recall was set up as "dog" way back at the beginning. So the user will navigate to dogInput3.jsp, but you can see that a different initial choice of animal might have led to catInput3.jsp or budgerigar3.jsp.

In dogInput3.jsp, not a great deal happens that we haven't seen already. Here's the code:

```
<html><head><title>Specific Dog Information</title></head>
<body>
<h2>Fill in specific dog information here...</h2>
<jsp:useBean id="currentAnimal" scope="session" class="webcert.ch07
.examp0701.Dog" />
<jsp:setProperty name="currentAnimal" property="*" />
<p>Overtype the defaults in the form below...</p>
<form action="dogInput4.jsp">
<br />Bark Volume:<input type="text" name="barkvolume"
value="<jsp:getProperty
name="currentAnimal" property="barkVolume" />" />
<br /><input type="submit" value="Continue..." />
</form></body></html>
```

The receptionist uses this screen to type in vital dog-specific properties—we have only the one, *barkVolume*. There's a vital line here:

```
<jsp:setProperty name="currentAnimal" property="*" />
```

This line has nothing to do with the setup of the current page, in fact. Its purpose is to take the request parameters typed in to the previous animalInput2.jsp, and save these to properties on the bean. Without this, the original default values would stick and the receptionist's overtyping would be in vain. This time, clicking the submit button navigates to the last page in sequence, dogInput4.jsp:

```
<html><head><title>Your Completed Dog</title></head>
<body>
<h2>The animal database has been updated with these DOG details:</h2>
<jsp:useBean id="currentAnimal"
scope="session"
type="webcert.ch07.examp0701.Dog" />
```

INSIDE THE EXAM (continued)

```
<jsp:setProperty name="currentAnimal" property="*" />
<br />Name: <jsp:getProperty name="currentAnimal" property="name" />
<br />Weight: <jsp:getProperty name="currentAnimal" property="weight" />
<br />Sex: <jsp:getProperty name="currentAnimal" property="sex" />
<br />Insured: <jsp:
getProperty name="currentAnimal" property="insured" />
<br />Bark Volume: <jsp:
getProperty name="currentAnimal" property="barkVolume" />
</body></html>
```

All this page does is to display all the bean properties, whether dog-specific or general. In a real system, the receptionist might scan the details and confirm the database update. Notice one thing here: The `<jsp:useBean>` standard action uses the *type* attribute but actually names the class Dog instead of the interface Animal: `type="webcert.ch07.examp0701.Dog."` Only a Dog will do if we want to get hold of the *barkVolume* property, not present on Animal. And indeed, the code could just as well have used the class attribute:

```
<jsp:useBean id="currentAnimal" scope="session"
class="webcert.ch07.examp0701.Dog" />
```

The point this makes is that the value for the *type* attribute can be the same as the *class*—there's no compulsion to make it different (although it normally makes sense to do so).

EXERCISE 7-1

JSP Standard Actions

In this exercise you're going to put together two web application pages: an HTML page with a form whose action takes you to a JSP page. The HTML page will invite you to put in details about a music CD. On clicking a Continue button, you're taken to a summary form (the JSP) that confirms the details you entered.

Not the world's most exciting application—but the first in this book in which the JSP component is *completely free of Java code*! The only building blocks required are HTML and the standard actions you have just learned. That's not to say you won't write any Java, though—as you still need a JavaBean on which the standard actions can operate.

Create the usual web application directory structure under a directory called ex0701, and proceed with the steps for the exercise. There's a solution in the CD in the file sourcecode/ch07/ex0701.war—check there if you get stuck.

Create the HTML Page

1. Create an empty file directly in your newly created context directory, ex0701. Call it musicCDform.html.
2. Provide a form with four text fields for title, artist, year of release, and favorite track. Give names to the input fields as follows: title, artist, year, and track.
3. Don't forget a submit button. Make the action of the form "musicCDsummary.jsp."

Create the MusicCD JavaBean

4. Create a package directory in ex0701/WEB-INF/src, and within it create a Java source file called MusicCD.java.
5. Include four private instance variables as follows:
   - `String title`
   - `String artist`
   - `int yearOfRelease`
   - `String favoriteTrack`
6. Provide a no-argument do-nothing constructor (you could leave this out and let the compiler provide it) and getters and setters for the instance variables. Make sure these are public and that they exactly follow the bean convention (e.g., `getTitle()`).
7. Compile the source into ex0701/WEB-INF/classes/<package directory>.

Create the JSP Page Source

8. Create an empty file in ex0701, called musicCDsummary.jsp.
9. Use the `<jsp:useBean>` standard action to create a MusicCD bean in page scope.
10. Set the properties of the bean from the request parameters passed in from the HTML form. In two cases, the request parameter names match the bean property names (for title and artist). So use `<jsp:setProperty>` with the "*" setting for the property attribute to take advantage of this.

11. The other two request parameters have different names from their corresponding bean properties: Request parameter "year" must map on to bean property "yearOfRelease," whereas "track" needs to map on to "favoriteTrack." So use two invocations of the `<jsp:setProperty>` standard action to achieve this mapping (you'll need to set the `property` *and* `param` attributes).
12. Finally, display the four properties on the page, using four separate occurrences of `<jsp:getProperty>`.

Deploy and Run the Application

13. Create a WAR file that contains the contents of ex0701, and deploy this to your web server. Start the web server if it has not started already.
14. Use your browser to request musicCDform.html, with a URL such as

    ```
    http://localhost:8080/ex0701/musicCDform.html
    ```

15. Enter some details (note that the year field must be numeric), click the button to submit the form, and check that the output is correct on musicCDsummary.jsp. The following illustration shows the screen flow for the solution.

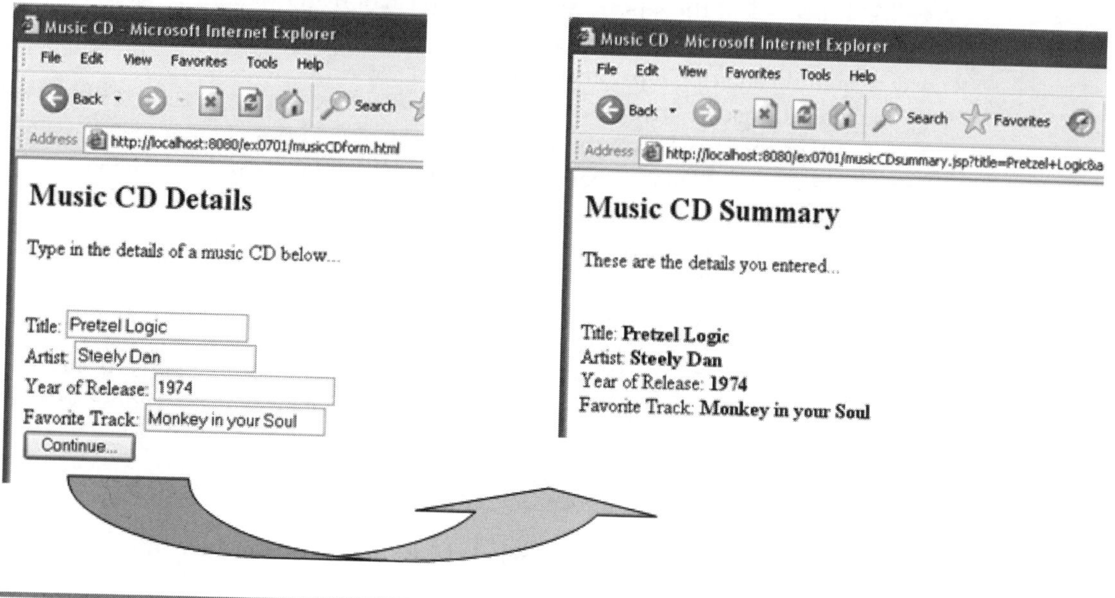

CERTIFICATION OBJECTIVE

Dispatching Mechanisms (Exam Objectives 6.7 and 8.2)

Given a specific design goal for including a JSP segment in another page, write the JSP code that uses the most appropriate inclusion mechanism (the include directive or the jsp:include standard action).

Given a design goal, create a code snippet using the following standard actions: jsp:include, jsp:forward, and jsp:param.

In this section of the chapter, we're going to explore three more standard actions. These give you the equivalent of the `forward` and `include` RequestDispatcher mechanisms, which we explored in Chapter 3 in servlet code. The two main standard actions are called `<jsp:include>` and `<jsp:forward>`, which serve to include content into a JSP or forward on to another resource altogether (JSP, servlet, or any resource that can be described with a URL). We'll see how these are a bit easier to set up than the coding equivalent, and also how there are one or two differences between the standard actions and a naked RequestDispatcher.

We'll also look at the `<jsp:param>` standard action and see how this can be embedded into either of `<jsp:include>` and `<jsp:forward>`. It provides an easy way to graft on additional parameters to the request.

You'll recall that we encountered the include directive (`<%@ include file="..." %>`) in the last chapter. So we devote some time in this chapter to understanding the differences between this directive and the `<jsp:include>` standard action. That way we can tick off both the exam objectives above for the price of one section in the book.

Including

The standard action `<jsp:include>` can be used to include the response from another file within your JSP page output. You specify the file whose response should be included with the page attribute, like this:

```
<jsp:include page="pageToInclude.jsp" />
```

The file whose response should be included has to reside somewhere in your web application but doesn't have to be present until the page is actually requested.

on the Job

You might use `<jsp:include>` to include files that don't exist at the point where you deploy your including pages. This could be for a number of reasons: Perhaps the included files are produced as output from other systems and are uploaded to your web application directory structure only at scheduled intervals. This doesn't stop you from precompiling your including JSPs when you deploy them, however. There's no check on the existence of the page specified in `<jsp:include>` during the translation phase. Obviously, you'll get a run-time error if you let your users access JSPs that try to include a page that doesn't exist—it's then up to you to introduce controls that prevent access to the including JSP until the files needed for inclusion are actually present in your web application directory structure.

The value for the *page* attribute is a URL pointing to a resource within the current web application (you can't go outside the web application with `<jsp:include>`). The URL used follows rules similar to those we've seen many times elsewhere:

- If the page URL begins with a slash, this is interpreted as starting from the context directory for the web application.
- If the page URL doesn't begin with a forward slash, this is interpreted as relative to the directory containing the including page.

Any kind of file can be the target of the page attribute. It's typical to target other JSP pages but by no means mandatory—you can include any file of any MIME type (though bear in mind that if this isn't compatible with the MIME type for the rest of the response, you may well run into run-time issues).

A delightful feature of `<jsp:include>` is that it runs at request time. This may not sound like much, but what it means is that the value for the *page* attribute can be an expression embedded within the standard action. So code like this is perfectly legitimate:

```
<jsp:include page='<%= request.getParameter("thePage") %>' />
```

You can see from this that I can nominate the page whose response should be included from a parameter value passed in my request. This gives you a great deal of flexibility.

The `<jsp:include>` standard action has a second (optional) attribute, *flush*. This can have the values "true" or "false," and if you leave off the attribute, the default is "false." To understand this, recall that JSP page output is buffered as a rule—not immediately committed to the response. If you set the value to "true,"

```
<jsp:include page="aPageToInclude.html" flush="true" />
```

this has the effect of flushing the buffer in the including page (i.e., committing the response so far) before anything is done about including the target page.

Even if you set the *flush* attribute to "false," and both the including and included page have unfilled, unflushed buffers, there are still restrictions on included pages. Included pages can't do anything to the response header—in just the same way that servlets can't if anything has been written to the response. The assumption is that somewhere along the chain to the included page, some part of the response has been written (and don't forget that you may well have a long chain: through several filters and servlets before you get to the including, and then the included, JSP pages). So code like the following:

```
<% response.addCookie(myCookie); %>
```

Or:

```
<% response.setHeader("Date", utcFormatDate); %>
```

is simply ignored in the *included* JSP page. This is no different from the world of servlet code: A servlet that has been included from another servlet by a RequestDispatcher object is treated in the same way.

`<jsp:include>` vs. `<%@ include %>`

It's very hard to talk about `<jsp:include>` without comparing it with the include directive, so let's not put that off anymore. After all, it's an exam objective in its own right!

When I introduced `<jsp:include>`, you may have noticed the pedantic phrase "include the response from another file" several times. Why didn't I just say "include the file"? Because that's not quite true—not in the sense we mean, for example, when we talk about the include directive (`<%@ include file="..." %>`). Let's say I have a JSP page a.jsp that includes b.jsp with the standard action. Neither has been translated yet. Figure 7-2 shows what happens when I request a.jsp for the first time.

You can see from Figure 7-2 that the two JSPs a.jsp and b.jsp remain independent and that b.jsp provides a service to a.jsp. a.jsp requests a response from b.jsp and incorporates this in its own output. The situation is fundamentally different with the `include` directive. Figure 7-3 shows what happens when a.jsp includes b.jsp with the `include` directive.

FIGURE 7-2

a.jsp Using `<jsp:include>` to Include b.jsp

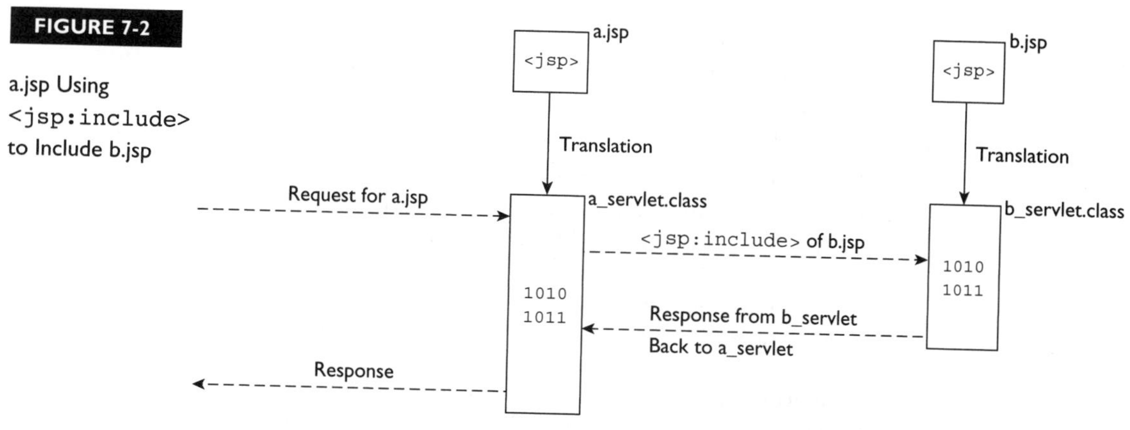

FIGURE 7-3

a.jsp Using `<%@ include %>` to Include b.jsp

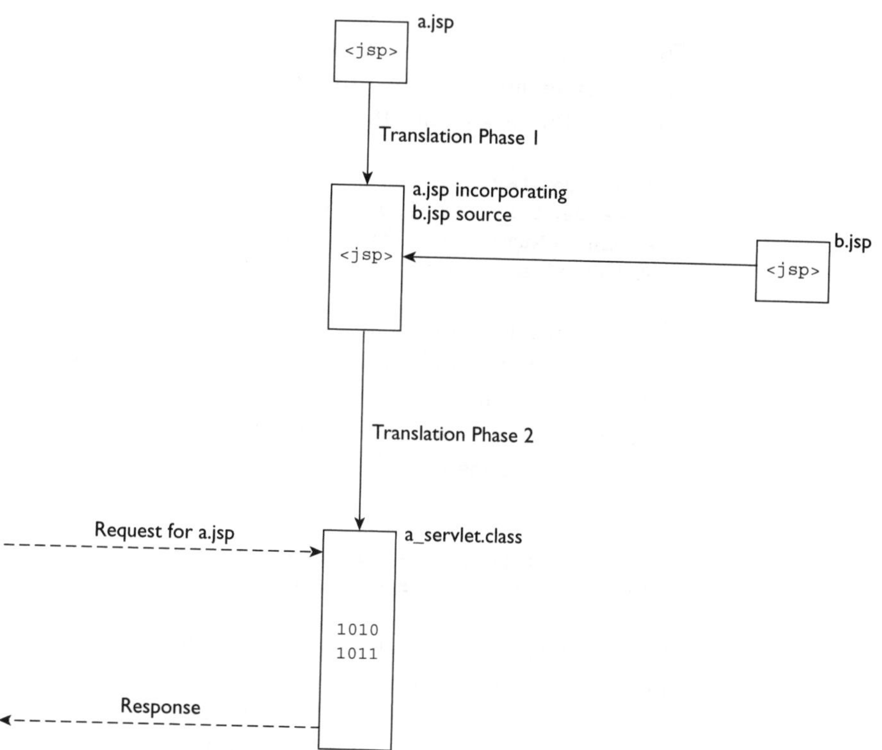

Figure 7-3 shows how the lines of b.jsp are first incorporated into a.jsp. It's as if a.jsp is a composite of its own page source and b.jsp's as well. Only after this has happened does the translation to generated servlet occur. This has some interesting consequences. Let's look at an example—and please, please note that this is to illustrate a point: Don't write your JSPs this way! Suppose that you declare a local variable in one JSP (we'll call it declaration.jsp), then use that local variable in another JSP (display.jsp) that includes declaration.jsp. Here's the code for each:

```
<!-- declaration.jsp -->
<% int aNumber = (int) (Math.random() * 100); %>
```

So in declaration.jsp, we have a local variable called *aNumber* that is initialized to a random value between 0 and 99. Here's display.jsp, which uses an expression to show the random number on the page output:

```
<!-- display.jsp -->
<%@ include file="declaration.jsp" %>
Think of a number: <%= aNumber %>
```

This works absolutely fine (despite coming with a massive design health warning!). The `include` directive causes the amalgamation of the JSPs—the result is a composite JSP looking like this:

```
<!-- display.jsp -->
<!-- declaration.jsp -->
<% int aNumber = (int) (Math.random() * 100); %>
Think of a number: <%= aNumber %>
```

This is the whole "translation unit." If neither JSP page has been accessed, and our container translates and compiles only when a JSP is requested, then a request to display.jsp will result in only one generated servlet for your web application that represents the composite page source. So what happens if we change display.jsp to use a `<jsp:include>` standard action?

```
<!-- display.jsp -->
<jsp:include page="declaration.jsp" />
Think of a number: <%= aNumber %>
```

Result: misery. The functionality of `<jsp:include>` isn't invoked until post-translation, and display.jsp won't get past translation. If you try to request it, you're likely to get an HTTP 500 error accompanied by a stack trace that informs you that the local variable *aNumber* is used but not declared. So if you're using

TABLE 7-1

Comparing and Contrasting the Two JSP Inclusion Mechanisms

`<jsp:include>` Standard Action	`<%@ include %>` Directive
Attributes: page (and flush)	Attribute: file
Page attribute accepts relative and absolute URLs.	File attribute accepts relative and absolute URLs.
Response from target page included at *request* time.	Target file included during *translation* phase.
Target page to include can be *soft-coded* as an expression.	Target file must be a *hard-coded* literal value.
Can execute *conditionally* in the middle of page logic.	Will be processed *unconditionally*—can't be embedded in page logic.
Target page doesn't have to exist until request time.	Target file must exist at translation time.
Always includes the latest version of the target page.	Does not necessarily include the latest version of the target file: depends on your container (not mandated by the JSP specification).

`<jsp:include>`, each of your JSPs must be able to "stand alone"—at least in translation terms.

With `<jsp:include>`, you are always guaranteed to get the latest versions of responses from included files because the included files are still accessed at run time. They have to be there to complete the picture. This isn't necessarily the case for files that are included through the `include` directive. After all, once a file has been incorporated through the `include` directive, the resulting composite servlet is whole and complete. This leads to an interesting question: If a file included by the `include` directive is updated, will the JSP container spot the fact and re-do the file inclusion when the JSP doing the including is next accessed? The answer is that the JSP specification recommends that this should happen, but doesn't say that it has to be this way.

In conclusion, take a look at Table 7-1, which summarizes the differences between the two approaches. Do some experiments so you're comfortable with the difference—it's a favorite topic on the exam!

Forwarding

After `<jsp:include>`, `<jsp:forward>` is moderately straightforward. As the name implies, the purpose of this standard action is to forward processing to another resource within the web application. There is only one mandatory attribute, which (as with `<jsp:include>`) is `page="URL."` Consider the following example—a complete page source called doThis.jsp:

```
<!-- doThis.jsp -->
<p>You won't see this in the response</p>
<jsp:forward page="doThisInstead.jsp" />
<p>You won't see this either</p>
<% /* Will the following line of code be executed? */
session.setAttribute("doThis", "isDone"); %>
```

The effect of accessing doThis.jsp is to transfer responsibility for the output to doThisInstead.jsp. The template text before the `<jsp:forward>` action is effectively ignored, for anything that doThis.jsp writes to the output buffer is cleared. What happens after the `<jsp:forward>`, though? Were this a hand-coded servlet, the code following a `RequestDispatcher.forward()` method would still be executed (if we wanted it to be). But this isn't a hand-coded servlet: The corresponding servlet code is generated by the JSP container, as we well know. And to respect the fact that the JSP specification says that a "`<jsp:forward>` effectively terminates the current page," the reference implementation—Tomcat—returns from the `_jspService()` method. Consequently, the last line of page source in doThis.jsp—which sets an attribute in session scope—will not be executed, even though it has nothing to do with writing output to the response.

There's no *flush* attribute as there is for `<jsp:include>`—instead, certain things have to be true about the state of the response for the `<jsp:forward>` to be processed successfully. It all comes down to the thorny question of whether any part of the response has already been committed—in other words, written back to the client. Responses are considered uncommitted when anything written to them already is still in the memory buffer and the buffer has never been flushed. So a `<jsp:forward>` won't work if

- There is no buffer (in a JSP, this can be achieved with a `page` directive, setting the `buffer` attribute to "`none`"), and even one character has been written to the response.
- The buffer has been explicitly flushed (`response.flushBuffer()`).
- The buffer has been automatically flushed on filling up (in a JSP, this will happen by default—see the `page` directive attribute *autoFlush* for more information).

If you try to do any of the above, you'll get an IllegalStateException.

Parameters

Whether you are including or forwarding, you can add in additional parameters to the request. For this, you use the `<jsp:param>` standard action and include it in the body of a `<jsp:include>` or `<jsp:forward>`. This is the only reason for including a body in these two standard actions, which as you have probably noticed have been expressed as self-closing tags without any body up until now.

There are three important things to take account of when you add parameters into a request using the `<jsp:param>` standard action:

1. They only last for the duration of the `include` or `forward`. Once you're back in the including or forwarding JSP page, the parameters disappear.
2. They don't replace existing parameters of the same name—they merely augment the list of values. (Recall that parameters—unlike attributes—can have multiple values for the same name.)
3. When they do augment the list of values, their values come at the front of the list.

To illustrate these points, suppose that you make the following HTTP request to forwarder.jsp:

```
http://localhost:8080/examp0702/forwarder.jsp?animaltypes=dog
```

forwarder.jsp does nothing other than forward the request with a supplementary value for the animaltypes request parameter, so

```
<jsp:forward page="animalHouse.jsp">
  <jsp:param name="animaltypes" value="cat" />
</jsp:forward>
```

Now, if the forwarded-to JSP page, animalHouse.jsp, has code like the following:

```
<% String[] a = request.getParameterValues("animalTypes");
for (int i = 0; i < a.length; i++) {
    out.write(a[i] + ";");
}
%>
```

then the output will be

```
cat;dog;
```

exam watch

The value for <jsp:param>'s value attribute can come from a run-time expression—for example: value="<%=calcValue%>." That's not the case for the name attribute, which must be a literal in the page source.

You can see from this that the original parameter value (dog) is not lost but that the value added with <jsp:param> (cat) has taken precedence, and now comes first in the list.

Meanwhile, once you return to forwarder.jsp, you will find the request parameter animalTypes has reverted to having only the one value, dog.

All the points described above hold just as true for <jsp:param> standard actions embedded in the body of a <jsp:include> standard action.

EXERCISE 7-2

Dynamic Inclusion

This exercise shows you how to include a JSP dynamically from a request parameter. The idea is to have a small application that chooses and displays a poem at random. Each poem is kept in a separate static HTML page of its own. There are two JSP pages involved. One, "poemOfTheDay.jsp," receives the name of one of these static web pages as a request parameter and includes this into its body. The other JSP page, "choosePoemOfTheDay.jsp," chooses one of the available filenames at random and forwards it to "poemOfTheDay.jsp," setting up the chosen filename within the body of the <jsp:forward> standard action.

Create the usual web application directory structure under a directory called ex0702, and proceed with the steps for the exercise. There's a solution in the CD in the file sourcecode/ch07/ex0702.war—check there if you get stuck.

Write Poems

1. Create a number of HTML pages directly in ex0702 (three is a good number, but make as many as you like). Call these poem1.html, poem2.html, and so on.
2. In each page, include the title (between <h1> tags) and the text of any poem you like (between <pre> tags). You can write your own original poems as a diversion from exam cramming, but I'd recommend doing what I did:

copying and pasting a few of your favorites from the Web. Of course, if poems don't appeal, you can use any text you like—as long as you can tell your HTML pages apart.

Create the Including JSP Page Source

3. Create a file called poemOfTheDay.jsp in ex0702.
4. Put in template text for a skeleton web page—`<html>`, `<head>`, `<title>`, and `<body>` tags (and the corresponding end tags).
5. In the body, place a `<jsp:include>` standard action. Use an expression as the value for the page, taken from a request parameter called *poem*.

Create the Forwarding JSP Page Source

6. Create a file called choosePoemOfTheDay.jsp in ex0702.
7. Have a scriptlet at the beginning of the file that sets up a String array, and initialize this with the filenames of each of your poem HTML pages. (If you want more of a challenge, use `ServletContext.getRealPath()` and recover the names of any filenames beginning with the characters "poem" in the context directory. From this, load a String array or collection class: harder certainly!)
8. In the same scriptlet, set up a local variable to hold the name of one of the files. Use `Math.random()` as the basis for picking a name randomly from the String array (or collection class).
9. Set up a `<jsp:forward>` standard action following the scriptlet, to forward to the poemOfTheDay.jsp page. Ensure that this standard action has a body (and so has both a beginning and end tag; it should not be a self-closing tag).
10. In the body of the <jsp:forward> standard action, place a `<jsp:param>` action. Name the parameter poem, and set the value of the parameter using an expression—this should use the local variable set up in step 8.

Deploy and Run the Application

11. Create a WAR file that contains the contents of ex0702, and deploy this to your web server. Start the web server if it has not started already.

12. Use your browser to request musicCDform.html, with a URL such as

```
http://localhost:8080/ex0702/choosePoemOfTheDay.jsp
```

13. With luck, one of your poems will be displayed in the browser. Press the refresh button a few times to check that other poems are selected randomly (another extra challenge is to consider how you might prevent the same poem from being selected twice in succession). Here's some sample output from the solution code.

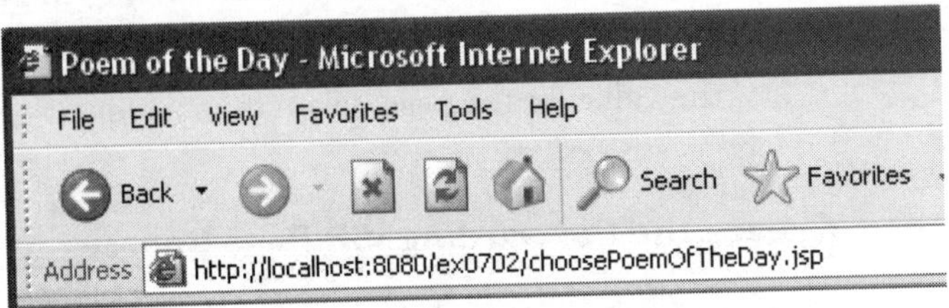

Sonnet - Thomas Wyatt

```
My galley chargèd with forgetfulness
Through sharp seas in winter nights doth pass
'Twene rock and rock; and eke mine enemy, alas,
That is my lord, steereth with cruelness.
And every oar a thought in readiness
As though that death were light in such a case;
An endless wind doth tear the sail apace
Of forcèd sighs and trusty fearfulness.
A rain of tears, a cloud of dark disdain
Hath done the wearied cords great hindrance,
Wreathèd with error and eke with ignorance.
The stars be hid that led me to this pain,
Drownèd is reason that should me comfort,
And I remain despairing of the port.
```

CERTIFICATION OBJECTIVE

JSPs in XML (Exam Objective 6.3)

Write a JSP Document (XML-based document) that uses the correct syntax.

This innocently short objective encompasses a large number of things you need to know. What is a JSP document? Well, it's JSP page source that's written in XML. Quite often (but not by any means always), you use a JSP document to produce XML as well.

XML is a big and scary topic in its own right. Fortunately, only a basic knowledge is required for the SCWCD exam. So if you're relatively new to XML, don't worry. In any case, you've already handled plenty of XML in the course of this book. The standard actions you covered in the previous section of this chapter are XML. And whereas HTML isn't necessarily XML, all the examples and exercises in this book have been using an XML-compliant version called XHTML. So although there's no room to turn this part of the chapter into a full-blown XML tutorial, I'll be taking a "least you need to know" approach. Fortunately, full-blown XML tutorials litter the Web, as do excellent books on the topic.

JSP documents also have more facets than can be covered in just one section of one chapter. You'll meet the basics in this section, and from this point in the book onward, most of the JSP examples and exercises (and quite a few of the questions) will use XML syntax.

XML for JSPs

Why are JSPs moving to XML-style page source at all? After all, they have a perfectly viable syntax all their own. Likely reasons include (but are not limited to) the following list:

- It makes a lot of sense if you are in the business of producing XML anyway. You've already encountered the idea that template text in a JSP page isn't limited to HTML, and XML is the most usual alternative. If you have an XML file you want to produce, it can immediately become the template text for a piece of JSP Page Source—all that remains is to mark it up with some more XML for the dynamic parts.
- You can check that your page source is valid in XML terms, using proper XML validators (and that's something your JSP container does during the translation phase for JSP documents).

- If you use XML-authoring tools (such as XML Spy), then those same tools can handle the production and validation of your JSP page source as well as other XML files you write.
- Arguably, XML-style source is easier to write and read than a mishmash of template text and Java language. So XML might mark a step along the way toward production of JSP page source by nonprogrammers.
- You certainly get the impression from the JSP specification that Sun would like page authors to move in an XML direction—that in itself might be a good reason to make the switch. While support for the `<% .. %>` way of doing things is bound to last for a long while, you might find yourself excluded from newer, trendier tool developments if you stick doggedly to the old-style syntax.

Given that you're persuaded that XML-style JSPs are a good thing, let's make a few top-level statements about XML itself. I won't assume any previous knowledge, though the chances are you've heard this before.

- XML is a tag language. Its structure is often compared to HTML: Both contain opening and closing tags. But while HTML is narrowly focused on marking up text, XML is much more general purpose. XML can be used for marking up text (as in XHTML), but it has a pretty much infinite set of other possible uses.
- You can define your own tags in XML, calling them whatever you like. You just have to make sure that for every opening tag of a particular name, you have a balancing closing tag:

```
<painting>
  <artist>Leonardo da Vinci</artist>
  <title>Mona Lisa</title>
  <location museum="Louvres"></location>
</painting>
```

- There may be some data content between the opening and closing tags ("Mona Lisa" for the `<title>` tag above), or simply other tags (`<painting>`), and sometimes nothing at all (`<location>`). The area between the opening and closing tags is referred to as the "body."
- Tag names can have a prefix, separated from the main name by a colon. We met that in standard actions, such as `<jsp:useBean>`. The prefix ties the tag to a "namespace," which you can think of as a signpost with information about the tag.

- Tags can have attributes. Again, we've seen this in standard actions. Attributes are included in the opening tag, and they form name/value pairs, in the form *name="value"* (or with single quotes—*name='value'*). You'll recall `<jsp:getProperty>`:

```
<jsp:getProperty name="beanName" property="beanProperty" />
```

- The `<jsp:getProperty>` example shows us another common XML feature. Sometimes it doesn't make a lot of sense to have a closing tag, because there's no appropriate data content to insert in the tag body. Under those circumstances, an opening tag can be "self-closing" by including a slash before the final angle bracket: />.
- Tags must be properly nested. Here is a rogue version of the painting example—you can see that the closing tag `</artist>` comes within the body of the `<title>` tag, which just won't do:

```
<painting>
  <artist>Leonardo da Vinci<title></artist>Mona Lisa</title>
  <location museum="Louvres"></location>
</painting>
```

- There must be one root tag at the top of the document. For the deployment descriptor, web.xml, the root tag (as we've seen throughout) is `<web-app>`.

Of course, there's a lot more to XML than that, but these simple rules will get you most of the way there. All we need to consider now is how XML exactly applies in JSP documents.

XML-Friendly Syntax

When we talk about a JSP document, we mean a JSP page source that obeys all the rules of XML. However, the pseudo-tag-like structure of some JSP syntax will wreak havoc with any XML validator. Certain bits of syntax have to go—especially arbitrary angle brackets. Any XML parsing code sees an angle bracket as the beginning or end of a tag, so it won't know what to make of `<%`, `<%!`, `<%@`, `<%=`, `<%--`, `--%>`, and `%>`. All of these have to be replaced. So the JSP specification provides an XML equivalent for all of the above. In the main, these look like standard actions, behave like standard actions, and are standard actions. They extend the set of those we have already looked at, such as `<jsp:include>`. There are only one or two syntax differences implemented

TABLE 7-2

XML Equivalents for JSP Syntax

Scripting Elements	Original JSP Syntax	XML Syntax
Scriplets	<% ... %>	<jsp:scriptlet>... </jsp:scriptlet>
Expressions	<%= ... %>	<jsp:expression>... </jsp:expression>
Declarations	<%! ... %>	<jsp:declaration>... </jsp:declaration>
Directives		
page	<%@ page attr="value" %>	<jsp:directive.page attr="value" />
include	<%@ include file="abc.txt" %>	<jsp:directive.include file="abc.txt" />
taglib	<%@ taglib prefix= "abc" uri="..." %>	xmlns:abc="..."
Comments		
Exclude from translation (and output)	<%-- ... --%>	<!-- ... -->
Include HTML comment in HTML output	<!-- ... -->	<!-- ... -->

without the use of standard actions, however. Table 7-2 lists the different kinds of JSP syntax and shows the original syntax alongside its XML-friendly equivalent.

Scripting Elements

Note that this change to XML syntax doesn't—in itself—mean abandoning Java code in your JSP pages. All we're doing at the moment is making the XML well-formed, and for the most part, any old Java code can be dumped into the body of an XML element. Let's look at a few short examples.

Here's a scriptlet in the old style of syntax:

```
<% String s;
  s = request.getParameter("user"); %>
```

Here it is again as the body of a standard action:

```
<jsp:scriptlet>String s;
        s = request.getParameter("user"); </jsp:scriptlet>
```

There's nothing remotely difficult here—just a straight swap of opening markers (`<jsp:scriptlet> for <%`) and closing markers (`</jsp:scriptlet> for %>`). The contents of the scriptlet remain as before: valid Java syntax (with a slight modification we'll soon see). You can't embed any other sort of tag within the body of the `<jsp:scriptlet>` tag.

Declarations are no different. Again, here's a declaration before:

```
<%! public void jspInit() {
      System.out.println("My JSP is initialized");
    } %>
```

And the same declaration after:

```
<jsp:declaration> public void jspInit() {
                   System.out.println("My JSP is initialized");
                 } </jsp:declaration>
```

Note that the inclusion of indentation and white space is entirely my own choice, just as it is in normal Java source code. It will come as no surprise that a converted expression follows a similar pattern. Here's one before:

```
<%= session.getAttribute("user") %>
```

And one after XML-ification:

```
<jsp:expression>session.getAttribute("user")</jsp:expression>
```

Again, the choice of white space is mine. This is equally valid:

```
<jsp:expression> session.getAttribute("user") </jsp:expression>
```

As is this:

```
<jsp:expression>
  session.getAttribute("user")
</jsp:expression>
```

However, there are some things within the Java language itself that are anathema to XML validators. Take the following source code, showing the beginning of a **for** loop in a scriptlet:

```
<jsp:scriptlet>for (int i = 0; i < 10; i++) { </jsp:scriptlet>
```

The "less than" sign (<) looks like the beginning of an opening or closing tag, and an XML validator will assuredly treat it as such. However, it's difficult to write Java code without using < anywhere!

You have two options to deal with this. The first is to escape the source code, using what's referred to in XML as an "entity"—beginning with an ampersand (`&`) and ending in a semicolon (`;`). If you've written any amount of HTML, you'll recognize this device. The offensive < sign is replaced with the entity `<`. It doesn't make your Java code very readable, but it'll get through the XML validation process—and your JSP container will turn it back into valid code for your generated servlet. Here's how it looks in our example:

```
<jsp:scriptlet>for (int i = 0; i &lt; 10; i++) { </jsp:scriptlet>
```

You should treat the > sign in the same way, replacing it with `>` when it comes up in your code.

The second option is to mark up the offensive part as XML character data. This is part of an XML file that the XML validator treats as off-limits—it lets the characters stand just as they are. The syntax for this is more intrusive than entities, even though our < sign stays intact. Here's how this second solution might look:

```
<jsp:scriptlet>for (int i = 20; i <![CDATA[<]]> 30; i ++) {</jsp:scriptlet>
```

In this case, it's pretty hard to find the < sign in the middle buried in the middle of the syntax. A variation on this approach is to demarcate the whole body of the scriptlet as character data:

```
<jsp:scriptlet><![CDATA[for (int i = 10; i < 20; i ++) { ]]></jsp:scriptlet>
```

This at least keeps the Java code more integral, and an entire longer scriptlet or declaration consisting of multiple statements can be "wrappered" in this way.

Directives

Directives are dealt with in much the same way as scripting elements, by substituting standard actions.

There's a JSP directive for page directives called `<jsp:page.directive ... />`, which is a substitute for `<%@ page ... %>`. The syntax represented by the ellipsis (. . .) is identical in both cases. So

```
<%@ page import="java.util.*, a.b.MyClass" %>
```

becomes

```
<jsp:directive.page import="java.util.*, a.b.MyClass" />
```

Because the attributes (such as `import`) within the original directive follow XML syntax, they can be transferred directly into the XML tag. Note that the XML tag closes itself—there's no requirement for a directive to have a body. Other than that, the functionality is no different from the JSP syntax original.

The `include` directive follows exactly the same pattern, and it works identically in its XML form. So

```
<%@ include file="myFile.html" %>
```

becomes

```
<jsp:directive.include file="myFile.html" />
```

The one directive that doesn't follow this norm is the `taglib` directive for referencing tag libraries. This uses a namespace instead of a standard action to define a tag library in use in the JSP document. We'll soon learn more about namespaces, and a lot more about tag libraries in Chapter 8, where we revisit the `taglib` directive in both its guises: JSP and XML syntax.

Comments

Finally from Table 7-2, what happens about comments? You'll recall that JSP syntax allows for two styles—one that removes source text from the translation phase entirely (`<%-- not translated --%>`) and the other that causes an HTML-style comment to be buried in the output (`<!-- The user won't see this in a normal browser, but will when viewing source. -->`).

The first style of comment is XML-unfriendly, so it can't be used in a JSP document. The second (HTML-style) comment is, in fact, an XML-style comment. So it's fine to carry on using the second style, except that it acts slightly differently. It's like this:

```
<!-- In a JSP document, this style of comment will NOT be included
in the generated output; it's ignored by translation. -->
```

This begs the question: What if I am generating HTML-output from my JSP document and want to include an HTML-style comment? Because these are hijacked by XML, they'll never appear! Escape conventions come to our rescue. If you hide the < and > signs with their entity equivalents, you'll get your HTML comment:

```
&lt;!-- This comment will appear in the HTML output. --&gt;
```

exam watch

There is a standard action called `<jsp:text>` that exists solely to dig you out of trouble when writing JSPs in XML syntax. More or less all the content you put into an XML document (aside from white space) must exist in the body of a tag. Of course, you're always in the body of a tag in that there's a root tag that encloses everything. However, some tags (normally including the root tag) don't allow any content in their bodies—only other tags. If you have some content that needs to be placed in the "no-man's land" of a bodiless tag, then wrap it up with `<jsp:text> ... </jsp:text>`.

Namespaces

The conversions to JSP document syntax that we've seen are easy enough, mostly involving the substitution of XML standard actions for their traditional counterparts. However, whereas standard JSP syntax takes for granted that standard actions are simply available in your JSP page source, XML syntax demands more than that. If your tags use a prefix—as all standard actions do—that prefix must be associated with something that XML terms a "namespace."

Any opening tag within XML can define a namespace. Here's a very short JSP document example that includes a directive to specify the MIME type of the output:

```
<html>
<head><title>Namespaces</title></head>
<jsp:directive.page xmlns:jsp="http://java.sun.com/JSP/Page"
contentType="text/html" />
<body><h1>Namespace Demonstration</h1></body>
</html>
```

You can see that the `<jsp:directive.page>` element now contains an additional attribute:

```
xmlns:jsp="http://java.sun.com/JSP/Page"
```

The `xmlns` stands for XML namespace (unsurprisingly) and—after the colon—uses a name/value pair. The name (`jsp`) is the prefix you use for any elements belonging to this namespace—such as `<jsp:directive.page>`. The value is—more often than not—a URL, though it can be any text at all. Sometimes, the URLs actually correspond to pages on the Internet. Mostly—and http://java.sun.com/JSP/Page is a case in point—they don't. There's no technical need for the resource at the end of the URL to exist; a URL is often used because it has a good chance of being unique. So when you see the namespace http://java.sun.com/JSP/Page, you can safely assume that this is uniquely associated with a set of elements that have to do with JavaServer Page standard actions.

In our example above, the namespace is associated only with `<jsp:directive.page>`. This is because namespaces apply only to the element in which they are defined, plus any elements contained within that element. Because `<jsp:directive.page>` can't contain other elements, the namespace applies only to that element. So it's much more usual to place your namespace declarations farther up the XML document's containment ladder—usually, in fact, right in the root element. Here is the same example again with the namespace transferred to `<html>`, the root element for XHTML documents:

```
<html xmlns:jsp="http://java.sun.com/JSP/Page" >
<head><title>Namespaces</title></head>
<jsp:directive.page contentType="text/html" />
<body><h1>Namespace Demonstration</h1></body>
</html>
```

Now any standard action can be used anywhere in the document without repeating the namespace, for it's available throughout—the prefix `jsp:` is sufficient.

XML and the JSP Container

What tells the JSP container that it's dealing with a JSP document, as opposed to a page in normal JSP syntax? You might think that a page written in bona fide XML is a JSP document and will be treated as such, but actually, it isn't. The page will continue to work, but the JSP container is likely to treat it as a standard syntax page. You can include as much or as little of the XML syntax in a normal JSP page as you like—this is to encourage you to migrate your JSP pages to XML syntax at a pace to suit. Take this example:

```
<% String s = "Mixed syntax"; %>
<jsp:expression>s</jsp:expression>
```

This is perfectly viable JSP page syntax, though it has the makings of a maintenance nightmare—why use two syntaxes when you can stick to one?

There are three approaches that identify a page as a JSP document:

1. Ensure that your web application deployment descriptor web.xml is at version level 2.4 and that the file with your JSP page source has the extension `.jspx`.
2. Ensure that your web application deployment descriptor web.xml is at version level 2.4, and include some appropriate settings in deployment descriptor's `<jsp-config>` element (we'll see what these are in a moment).
3. Enclose your page source with the root element `<jsp:root>`. This element is backward-compatible with previous versions of the JSP container, so it doesn't rely on a particular version level for web.xml.

Method 1 is certainly the most straightforward. Assuming that your deployment descriptor is at version level 2.4 (and why wouldn't it be?), you should suffix your JSP documents with .jspx instead of .jsp. Method 2 is still straightforward. You just need to know how to configure the relevant element in web.xml. Here's an example configuration:

```
<jsp-config>
  <jsp-property-group>
  <url-pattern>/jspx/*</url-pattern>
  <is-xml>true</is-xml>
  </jsp-property-group>
</jsp-config>
```

This says that any for any file accessed with a URL ending in /jspx /anythingatall.any within the web application, treat this as a JSP document. The `<is-xml>` element takes two valid values: true (treat these as JSP documents with XML syntax) or false (treat these documents as JSP pages with standard syntax). The `<url-pattern>` element works in just the same way we saw within the `<servlet-mapping>` element way back in Chapter 2.

exam watch

Notice that the element `<jsp-property-group>` nests inside `<jsp-config>` and that the elements which do the work (such as `<url-pattern>` and `<is-xml>`) nest inside `<jsp-property-group>`.

This leaves method 3, which is to make `<jsp:root>` your document's root element, not forgetting to include the namespace in the opening tag:

```
<jsp:root xmlns:jsp="http://java.sun.com/JSP/Page">
```

This approach can have advantages if you need to remain compatible with older containers, or older applications in newer containers—this is how JSP documents were identified in the past, at JSP specification level 1.2. An older-style web.xml won't matter. Even if your application and container are bang up-to-date, `<jsp:root>` can be handy if your source files can't have the `.jspx` extension for some reason, and if their URL patterns are too diverse to warrant defining inside the `<jsp-config>` element.

on the Job

We know now that a JSP document is written in XML. What dictates what it outputs? Well, by default, a JSP document wants to produce XML. This is regardless of the MIME type that you set with `<jsp:directive.page contentType="..." />`. If you do nothing, an XML header statement appears at the very beginning of the page output, looking like this: `<?xml version="1.0" encoding="UTF-8"?>`. If what you're producing is not XML, you really ought to suppress this. There are a couple of approaches:

- ***Use `<jsp:root>` as your root element. This suppresses the XML header statement by default (if you're using `<jsp:root>` for some other reason, there are ways to retain the XML header statement if you actually need it).***
- ***Include a `<jsp:output>` element as follows: `<jsp:output omit-xml-declaration="true" />`.***

There is quite a bit more to `<jsp:output>` than this one attribute—to find out more, take a look at JSP Specification section 5-16.

EXERCISE 7-3

JSP Syntax to XML Syntax

This exercise differs a little from most of its predecessors, for you deliberately start with the solution code. Your mission is to take a moderately complex JSP page, written in JSP syntax, and convert this to XML syntax. The page works in combination with a servlet and a JavaBean. The servlet receives the name of a comma-separated values file and parses the contents of this, placing the results in the JavaBean. The JSP page uses the JavaBean to display the results in an HTML table.

Any comma-separated values (.csv) file will do. There is one provided called Timesheet.csv, but you can supply one of your own. The expectation is that the first row of the file contains header information—here's the first row of Timesheet.csv:

```
Date,Start Time,End Time,Duration,Description,Code
```

And each subsequent row contains data corresponding to the heading fields. Here's an example data row from Timesheet.csv:

```
Mon-30-Jun,09:00,11:00,2:00,Certification article,ARTICLE4
```

Having checked you can run the application, you'll take the regular JSP version of the file and duplicate that *in situ* to a new file that will be a JSP document. You'll work through this document, making alterations to remove source that works only in JSP syntax terms. On the way, you'll try accessing the document, and observe the syntax errors you get. The result will be a genuine JSP document that works as the solution code does.

So this time, start by finding the solution file from the CD (which is sourcecode /ch07/ex0703.war), and then follow the instructions below.

Deploy and Test the Application

1. Deploy ex0703.war on your server—start the server if it's not started already.
2. Use your browser to run the application, using a URL such as

   ```
   http://localhost:8080/ex0703/CSVReader/Timesheet.csv
   ```

   CSVReader is the mapping for a servlet in the ex0703 context. The servlet uses the path information that appears after the servlet mapping in the URL—in this case, Timesheet.csv. The servlet looks for the named file in the context directory. So if you are using your own CSV file, place this in the context directory (e.g. ex0703) on your server, and change the name in the URL from "Timesheet.csv" to the name of your file. Make sure to respect upper and lower case.
3. Make sure that you get output like that shown in the following illustration.

CSV File Presented As HTML Table

JSP Syntax Version

There are 25 rows of data, and 6 columns.

	Date	Start Time	End Time	Duration	Description	Code
Row 1	Mon-30-Jun	09:00	11:00	2:00	Certification article	ARTICLE4
Row 2	Mon-30-Jun	12:00	15:00	3:00	Question Software	QUEST
Row 3	Tue-01-Jul	10:50	11:20	0:30	Question Software	QUEST
Row 4	Tue-01-Jul	11:20	11:30	0:10	Timesheet	ADMIN
Row 5	Tue-01-Jul	11:50	13:45	1:55	Question Software	QUEST
Row 6	Tue-01-Jul	13:55	14:00	0:05	Showing F my timesheet	ADMIN
Row 7	Tue-01-Jul	14:00	14:07	0:07	Inputting questions	WEBSITE
Row 8	Tue-01-Jul	14:07	14:10	0:03	Helping F with timesheet	ADMIN
Row 9	Tue-01-Jul	14:10	14:28	0:18	Inputting questions	WEBSITE
Row 10	Tue-01-Jul	14:28	14:30	0:02	Helping F with timesheet	ADMIN
Row 11	Tue-01-Jul	15:45	16:00	0:15	Inputting questions	WEBSITE

4. Now use a text editor to change the deployment descriptor web.xml directly in the server directory—which for me is

```
<Tomcat installation directory>/webapps/ex0703/WEB-INF/web.xml
```

5. You'll see that the servlet CSVReader has an initialization parameter, which is the name of the JSP page to forward to. Change the extension on the name of the file to .jspx, which points to the JSP Document solution file. The whole line looks like this:

```
<param-value>/csvRenderer.jspx</param-value>
```

6. Save and close web.xml. Restart your server. Use your browser to access the servlet, using exactly the same URL as in step 2. The output should look identical, as shown in the following illustration—just the heading has changed to indicate that the output came from a JSP document.

CSV File Presented As HTML Table

JSP Document (XML) Version

There are 25 rows of data, and 6 columns.

	Date	Start Time	End Time	Duration	Description	Code
Row 1	Mon-30-Jun	09:00	11:00	2:00	Certification article	ARTICLE4

Create Your Own JSP Document

7. Now find the original JSP syntax file in the context directory, the one called csvRenderer.jsp (i.e., *not* the version with the .jspx extension). Copy this into the same directory, and call it csvRenderer2.jspx (*with* a .jspx extension—very important!). This is going to be the file you'll work on—you'll change all the JSP syntax within it to JSP document XML syntax, stage by stage.
8. Edit web.xml again as you did in step 5—change the name of the parameter value to that of your copied file, csvRenderer2.jspx:

```
<param-value>/csvRenderer2.jspx</param-value>
```

9. Stop and start your web server again. Again, invoke the application with the same URL as in step 2. This time, the application should fail—the target JSP, csvRenderer2.jspx, won't translate until its syntax is corrected. You may well get an error in your browser like the one shown in the following illustration, which complains that "The prefix 'jsp' for element 'jsp:useBean' is not bound." Don't worry if you see something different; the point is that we need to fix the errors.

HTTP Status 500 -

---

type Exception report

message

description The server encountered an internal error () that prevented it from fulfilling this request.

exception

```
org.apache.jasper.JasperException: /csvRenderer2.jspx(2,76) The prefix "jsp" for element "jsp:useBean" is not bound.
	org.apache.jasper.compiler.DefaultErrorHandler.jspError(DefaultErrorHandler.java:39)
	org.apache.jasper.compiler.ErrorDispatcher.dispatch(ErrorDispatcher.java:407)
```

10. Now open csvRenderer2.jspx with a text editor. Change the `<h2>` heading on line 5 to read

```
<h2><b>My</b> JSP Document Version</h2>
```

11. The JSP page source uses standard actions. When these appear in JSP documents, a namespace must be supplied to say where the XML elements for the standard actions are defined. You can supply this by altering the `<html>` tag exactly as shown below:

```
<html xmlns:jsp="http://java.sun.com/JSP/Page" >
```

    Save the file, but leave your text editor open ready to make more changes.

12. Refresh your browser for the same URL. The application should still fail, but this time the error should be deferred to later in the page source. The next error I get is located at the second character on the third line of page source: "The content of elements must consist of well-formed data or markup" (the location is given in the stack trace).
13. The issue is the `page` directive doing the import, with its `<%` syntax. Change this to use XML `page` directive syntax:

```
<jsp:directive.page import="java.util.*" />
```

14. Save the file, and again refresh your browser—note the next error. For me, this is on line 14, and it says that "the entity 'nbsp' was referenced, but not declared." This is a pure XML problem. In HTML, ` ` denotes a nonbreaking space. This style of denoting a special character (beginning with an ampersand and ending in a semicolon) is fine for XML; a character denoted this way is called an entity. However, it needs to be defined to the XML file in order to be respected. We're not going to do this, but instead cheat. There's a "get out of jail free" card to counter any dodgy text in an XML file, which is to describe the text as "character data." This uses some involved syntax. Replace ` ` with exactly what is written below:

```
<![CDATA[ ]]>
```

15. Save the file, and refresh the browser. My latest error is now on line 15—again complaining about the lack of well-formed character data or markup. As you've probably guessed, it's the scriptlet syntax. Go through the

code, replacing every occurrence of <% with <jsp:scriptlet>, and every corresponding %> with </jsp:scriptlet>.

16. Save and refresh. I get the same error, now transferred to line 16. This time, it's an expression causing the grief. Replace every occurrence of <%= with <jsp:expression>, and every *corresponding* %> with </jsp:expression>.
17. Save and refresh. There's still a problem! Look at the **for** loop in the first scriptlet—the condition test contains the "<" sign. This is—of course—good Java but lousy XML. To the XML parser, it looks like the beginning of a tag that never ends. Change the "<" sign to escape characters <. Repeat the exercise for the later **for** loop (around line 24), which also contains a "<" sign.
18. With luck, when you now save and refresh, the page will work correctly.
19. In a future exercise, we'll take the XML JSP document source from this exercise and improve on it so that most of the language scripting is removed.

CERTIFICATION OBJECTIVE

Expression Language (Exam Objectives 7.1, 7.2, and 7.3)

Given a scenario, write EL code that accesses the following implicit variables including pageScope, requestScope, sessionScope, and applicationScope, param and paramValues, header and headerValues, cookie, initParam and pageContext.

Given a scenario, write EL code that uses the following operators: property access (the . operator), collection access (the [] operator).

Given a scenario, write EL code that uses the following operators: arithmetic operators, relational operators, and logical operators.

Expression Language (EL) is all about the EL-imination of Java syntax from your pages. Here's how the JSP specification eloquently states the goal of EL: "The EL can be used to easily access data from the JSP pages. The EL simplifies writing *script-less* JSP pages that do not use Java scriptlets or Java expressions and thus have a more controlled interaction with the rest of the Web Application" (JavaServer Pages 2.0 Specification, page xix).

As the name implies, Expression Language provides an alternative to the expression aspect of Java language scripting—`<jsp:expression>...</jsp:expression>` or `<%...%>`. EL by itself is not a replacement for scriptlets. For that, you'll need to wait for the JSP Standard Tag Language (JSTL) in Chapter 8.

The goal of EL is simplicity. Although EL sacrifices some of the sophistication possible in a Java language expression, it is easier to use: The syntax is succinct and robust. Apart (obviously) from the syntax, EL is different from Java in other ways. Some rules are the same, and some are different. Because EL is a new and popular addition to JSP technology, you can be sure that many questions in the exam will test you on these rules.

exam watch

The exam creators have a nasty habit of mixing up EL and scriptlet syntax within the same question. This book organizes its content by exam objective, but don't expect the questions (here or in the real exam) to take a purist approach! After all, they reflect real life—and you may well have to deal with scriptlets and EL in the space of a few consecutive lines of JSP source.

Expression Language Overview

Expression Language began life as part of the JSP Standard Tag Library (JSTL), which we meet in Chapter 8. EL is now incorporated as part of the JSP 2.0 specification and is entirely independent of JSTL. However, it's only with JSTL that it fully comes into its own. EL can supply only the equivalent of the "right-hand side of the equal sign" in a typical computing statement. For example, EL lacks any looping constructs. And although there are conditional operators in EL, you can't take any action on them: There's not even an "if . . . then . . ." mechanism. JSTL supplies the missing pieces, so you will still find EL used most often in conjunction with JSTL.

That's not to say that you can't use EL independently. And especially when your goal is the SCWCD, there's plenty to learn about it. So in this section we'll concentrate exactly on that—EL capabilities. Some of the time we'll use EL in conjunction with Java language scripting elements, such as scriptlets. There's nothing technically wrong with that, but it's not considered best practice—after all, EL is meant to encourage Java-free JavaServer Pages! However, until we do learn about JSTL, scriptlets remain the easiest way to create expressions with data to display.

on the job

Expression Language can be enabled or disabled in three different ways. We encountered one of these ways in Chapter 6, when we looked at the page directive settings. The page directive attribute* isELEnabled *can turn on EL for a single page—or not.

There are a couple of alternative ways of controlling EL enablement that aren't explicit exam objectives. One is with the* `<jsp-property-group>` *element, which has a subelement* `<el-enabled>`*. We met* `<jsp-property-group>` *in the context of identifying JSP documents (subelement of* `<jsp-config>`*).

Finally, EL is enabled at an application level by having a deployment descriptor at servlet level 2.4. A previous deployment descriptor level indicates that EL should be switched off.

Expression Language Basics

As we saw briefly in Chapter 6, an expression begins with `${` and ends with `}`. The part between the curly braces must be a valid EL expression. The string in the JavaServer Page source code is subject to translation, like anything else in the page. Translation checks syntax validity but won't (for reasons that we'll come to) check that the variables you use actually exist (remember that translation incorporates compilation). At run time, the string representing the expression is sent to a method called `resolveVariable()`, in an object supplied by your JSP container provider of type VariableResolver. This returns an object, which is sent to the JSP output stream—typically via an `out.print()` statement in your generated servlet source. Mostly, the expression will resolve one way or another. Even if your variables don't exist, sensible defaults are provided, which mostly prevent the expression ending in a run-time error.

EL is equally valid in standard JSP syntax or JSP document (XML) syntax. So the following are equivalent. First a JSP in normal syntax:

```
<html>
<head><title>As a normal JSP</title></head>
<body>
<% request.setAttribute("whichever", "EL in either syntax"); %>
<p>${whichever}</p>
</body></html>
```

And now the same as a JSP document:

```
<html xmlns:jsp="http://java.sun.com/JSP/Page">
<head><title>As a JSP document</title></head>
<jsp:output omit-xml-declaration="true" />
```

TABLE 7-3 The Five Kinds of EL Literal

Type	Example	Comments
Boolean	`${true}`	Valid values are true and false—just like Java Boolean literals.
Integer	`${18782}`	Underpinned by a java.lang.Long value. Don't append "l" or "L" to the literal value as would happen for a Java long literal.
floating point	`${1.618034}` or `${2.998e+9}`	Underpinned by a java.lang.Double value.
Strings	`${"Galleon"}` or `${'Coracle'}`	Characters surrounded by double or single quotes.
Null	`${null}`	Equivalent to the Java **null** literal. Doesn't output anything.

```
<jsp:directive.page contentType="text/html" />
<body>
<jsp:scriptlet>
  request.setAttribute("whichever", "EL in either syntax");
</jsp:scriptlet>
<p>${whichever}</p>
</body></html>
```

In both cases, the EL syntax `${whichever}` picks up and displays the value of the whichever attribute set up in the scriplet: "EL in either syntax."

However, you do have to keep Java code (such as scriptlets) free of EL (after all, EL is not valid *Java* syntax). So the following will not work:

```
<% request.setAttribute( "anAttribute", ${aValueFromEL} );
```

EL Literals

EL has a smaller range of literals than Java. The ones it does use are similar. Table 7-3 shows the different values. Because you don't declare variables or assign to variables in EL, there are no explicit keywords for types; nonetheless, there are five that are defined.

EL Operators

Operators in EL come in four categories:

- arithmetic
- relational

- logical
- empty

EL operators (like EL literals) offer a subset of what's available in the Java language, and again you have to beware of some differences in behavior between EL and Java.

Arithmetic Operators

There are five arithmetic operators—for addition (+), subtraction (−), multiplication (*), division (/), and modulo (%). As you can see, the operator symbols are identical to Java. However, there are alternative forms for the division and modulo operators—`div` and `mod`, respectively. Let's consider each of the operators in turn.

Addition Addition is expressed like this: `${a + b}`. Addition works much as you would expect. If *a* represents an Integer object of value 2, and *b* an Integer object of value 3, then the result is 5. The inputs don't have to be numeric objects—string values for *a* and *b* of "2" and "3" would work as well. If either of attributes *a* and *b* doesn't exist, and is null, that's not a problem—they are treated as zero values. A zero-length string—""—is likewise treated as zero. As in much of EL, there's quite a bit of work behind the scenes to ensure that a result is obtained somehow, as long as the inputs to the calculation are remotely sensible. However, the following calculation won't work: `${"Not a Number" + 3.0}`. You will get a javax.servlet.jsp.el.ELException, complaining that "Not a Number" cannot be converted to a java.lang.Double value. This example also goes to show that the addition operator in EL—unlike Java—is not overloaded to handle string concatenation. There's no operator overloading or string concatenation in EL.

Subtraction Subtraction is expressed as you would expect: `${a - b}`. The same comments made about the addition operator apply to subtraction as well.

Multiplication Multiplication is expressed `${a * b}`. No surprises there.

Division Division is expressed `${a / b}` or `${a div b}`. Even if the inputs are both integers, double division is performed—not whole-number division ignoring the remainder. There is no direct EL equivalent for Java's integer division behavior. Being as EL division is always double division, it behaves like Java floating decimal division, so divide by zero is not an error but results in an answer of "Infinity." EL also shares an irritating feature of double division on binary-oriented computers, and the result may be imprecise. This isn't unique to EL; it's equally true of floating-point division in regular Java syntax, and indeed of many other programming languages on most computing platforms. For example, it might surprise you to learn that `${9.21 / 3}` doesn't give the neat result of 3.07, but rather 3.0700000000000003.

Modulo Modulo is expressed `${a % b} or ${a mod b}`. This time, integers are respected as integers, but a double for either input causes the calculation to be worked as a double. Again, the caveat about imprecise double arithmetic applies (try, for example, `${9.1 mod 3}`).

exam watch

Just as Java arithmetic has "promotion" rules for the inputs to a calculation, so does EL. In Java language, for example, in the calculation 9.0 + 3, "3"—an integer literal—is promoted to a double before the calculation takes place, and the result is a double. This is because the other operand (9.0) is a double literal. This is the ceiling for Java arithmetic—after all, there's nowhere to go beyond a double in Java primitive terms. In EL, promotion applies on a grander scale—there isn't a double (or java.lang.Double) ceiling. In some cases, the operands might be of type java.math.BigInteger or java.math.BigDecimal. There's only an outside chance you will have to face questions involving the promotional rules with BigInteger and BigDecimal, but you might want to check out the arithmetic promotion (or "coercion") rules laid out in the JSP 2.0 Specification, section 2.3.5.

Relational Operators

EL has a full complement of relational operators, which have conventional and alternate forms, as shown in Table 7-4. Alternative forms exist to make writing JSP documents that much easier. You'll remember from earlier in the chapter that the

TABLE 7-4 EL Relational Operators

Greater than	>	gt
Less than	<	lt
Equals	==	eq
Greater than or equals	>=	ge
Less than or equals	<=	le
Not equals	!=	ne

< and > signs are bad news for well-formed XML, except when used to mark the beginning and end of tags. To avoid having to use escape sequences such as >= every time you want to express "greater than or equals" in an expression, use *ge* instead. It's a good habit to get into, for the alternative form works just as well in conventional syntax and is much more readable in JSP document syntax.

The result of a relational operation is boolean *true* or *false*. So the following not very useful expression will cause "true" to be written to output: `${9 ge 3}`. You are not restricted to numeric inputs. Most usefully, you can do lexical string comparison, so `${"zebra" eq "antelope"}` will return "false." Under the covers, the String `equals()` method is invoked rather than a straight comparison of objects. In general, EL relational evaluation will invoke useful comparison methods on objects (such as `equals()` and `compareTo()`) when they are appropriate and available.

Logical Operators

EL has a more limited set of logical operators than the Java language. As for relational operators, there is a symbolic and alternative form. These are both shown in Table 7-5. These operators allow you to join conditional tests together to return a composite boolean result. For example, `${9 > 3 && "z" gt "a"}` would return true. Like Java, EL will evaluate only the left-hand side of an expression involving `&&` and `||`, if that is sufficient to intuit the overall result:

- If the left-hand side of an expression involving && is false, the whole expression must be false.
- If the left-hand side of an expression involving || is true, the whole expression must be true.

In either case, the right-hand side remains unevaluated. For all the examples we've seen, this doesn't matter. However, it might matter more to you after you see EL functions in Chapter 8.

TABLE 7-5 EL Logical Operators

	Symbolic	Alternative
Logical "and"	&&	and
Logical "or"	||	or
Logical "not"	!	not

The *empty* Operator

EL's *empty* operator can be invoked like this: `${empty obj}`. This expression will evaluate to *true* if `obj` represents something **null**—as would happen if the `obj` attribute didn't exist. However, the *empty* operator generalizes the concept of emptiness beyond a crude **null** test. There are other circumstances where `${empty obj}` results in **true**, which is any of the following:

- `obj` is an empty string ("").
- `obj` is an empty array.
- `obj` is an empty Map or an empty Collection (which covers every collection class in the java.util package—all of them inherit Map or Collection somewhere along the line).

Under any other circumstance, `${empty obj}` will return **false**.

exam watch

For all the operators—arithmetic, relational, logical—the precedence rules work in the same way as for the equivalent operators in the Java language. Parentheses can (and should) be used to clarify potential misinterpretations of code. However, you should have some awareness of precedence for the exam. Expressed crudely, the order is as follows:

not, empty;
multiplication, division, modulo;
addition, subtraction;
relational;
and, or.

For more precision, refer to the JSP Specification, section 2.3.10.

EL Property Access

Having dealt with the basics of EL—syntax, literals, operators—we can move on to some of its more exciting aspects. As you would have suspected from the preceding discussion, EL can access objects. Mostly, EL is used to access attributes that have been set up in some scope: page, request, session, or application. In this respect, EL is like the standard action `<jsp:getProperty>`, although its syntax works rather differently—and that's what we need to explore next.

The . and [] Operators

Any attribute in any scope can be displayed with EL. The scope doesn't even need to be specified. Suppose that there is an attribute called "title," holding a String object with some text; then `${title}` is all that is required to display that text. What happens, though, if the attribute isn't as simple as a String? What if you are holding a complex object as an attribute? For such an object to be useful to EL, it has to be a JavaBean—at least in the sense of having "getter" methods. Let's suppose that the object in question is the Dog JavaBean we met at the beginning of the chapter. This had five methods: `getName()` (returning a String), `getWeight()` (returning a float), `isInsured()` (boolean), `getSex()` (char), and `getBarkVolume` (another String). According to bean law, this exposes five properties derived from the "getter" method names: name, weight, insured, sex, and barkVolume. The properties share the type of their corresponding "getter" method.

Now let's suppose that a Dog object exists as a session attribute, with a name of "currentDog." To display a property of the dog, you use the attribute name and the property name. The simplest approach is to separate the two with a dot. So

```
${currentDog.name}
```

would display the name of the dog, and

```
${currentDog.insured}
```

would display "true" or "false" according to whether the dog was insured or not. Type conversion from boolean to String is managed somewhere before the result reaches page output, as is true for all other primitive types or objects returned by an expression.

This is the best way to use EL for property access. However, there is an alternative syntax, although it's really better kept for a different purpose we'll come to in a moment. These variants will also display the dog's name:

- `${currentDog["name"]}`
- `${currentDog['name']}`

You're not limited to one level, either. Let's suppose our Dog class had an additional method, `getFather()`, which returned another Dog object—representing the father of the current dog. This would expose another property on the current dog, called "father." The father dog—being a Dog object—has all the same properties as the current dog. So if you now wanted to display the name of the current dog's father, you could do so this way:

```
${currentDog.father.name}
```

The alternative syntax would look like this:

- `${currentDog["father"]["name"]}`
- `${currentDog['father']['name']}`

You can even mix and match double quotes and single quotes, as long as you are consistent within any particular pair of square brackets, so although it's inconsistent, `${currentDog['father']["name"]}` would also work. In essence, anything that EL can interpret as a String can go between the square brackets.

Arrays, Lists, and Maps

EL capabilities go further. Suppose that I have an array defined as a page attribute through the following scriptlet:

```
<% String[] dayArray = {"Mon", "Tue", "Wed", "Thu", "Fri", "Sat", "Sun"};
pageContext.setAttribute("days", dayArray); %>
```

An expression later in the JSP page source can access the days of the week using syntax that is practically identical to array syntax. For example, `${days[0]}` will send "Mon" to page output, while `${days[6]}` will send "Sun." Within the expression's curly braces is the name of the attribute (days) followed by square brackets. Within the square brackets you can place any integer—either a literal or some attribute that can be sensibly converted to an integer. So if you wrote this code farther down the page, it would output "Wed Thu":

```
<% pageContext.setAttribute("two", new Integer(2));
pageContext.setAttribute("three", "3"); %>
${days[two]}
${days[three]}
```

The first page attribute, called "two," is set to an Integer with a value of 2. So `${days[two]}` gets the third value in the array—"Wed." You can see, though, from the second attribute, that you don't have to stick with explicit numeric types as with java.lang.Integer. The second page attribute, called "three," still works when loaded with a String. Provided that a method like `Integer.parseInt()` can extract an **int** value from the String, everything will work.

exam watch

If you write an expression such as `${days[7]}`, you might expect an ArrayIndexOutOfBoundsException or an ELException arising from this as an underlying cause. Not so. EL silently suppresses this problem—you just get blank output. Even if you use an attribute name that doesn't exist—`${days[notAnAttributeName]}`—nothing goes wrong; you just get blank output. However, let's consider what happens if the attribute supplied is a valid attribute but can't be converted to an integer value. Given this page attribute, `<% pageContext.setAttribute("four", "the_Word_Four"); %>` the expression ${days[four]} would end in a run-time error (ELException).

Having worked through Arrays, you'll be delighted to know that Lists work in the same way. Any collection class that implements java.util.List can have its members accessed with identical syntax. Under the covers, the `List.get(int index)` method is executed.

Finally, there is the case of classes that implement java.util.Map. You'll recall from the SCJP (if nowhere else) that Maps hold a collection of key-value pairs. Each key must be unique, and is normally a String value (but can be any Object). Let's consider a variation on the days of the week example, which uses a Map:

```
<jsp:directive.page import="java.util.*" />
<% Map longDays = new HashMap();
longDays.put("MON", "Monday");
longDays.put("TUE", "Tuesday");
longDays.put("WED", "Wednesday");
longDays.put("THU", "Thursday");
longDays.put("FRI", "Friday");
longDays.put("SAT", "Saturday");
longDays.put("SUN", "Sunday");
pageContext.setAttribute("longDays", longDays);
pageContext.setAttribute("wed", "WED");
%>
<br /> ${longDays[wed]}
<br /> ${longDays["THU"]}
<br /> ${longDays.FRI}
```

The output from this code is

```
Wednesday
Thursday
Friday
```

What happens is this: The code loads a HashMap object with the full names of the seven days of the week, keyed by abbreviated capital codes ("MON," "TUE," etc.). The HashMap is loaded into a page attribute called longDays. Another page attribute is set up, called "wed" and with a value of "WED"—which matches one of the keys in the HashMap. In general terms, expressions accessing a Map work on this principle: `${nameOfMap[keyValue]}`. From the two expressions in the code, you can see that it doesn't matter if the key value is a literal ("`THU`") or derived from an attribute (`wed`).

What about the third expression, though: `${longDays.FRI}`? That appears to use the JavaBean syntax we used earlier—even though there is obviously no "`getFRI()`" method to fall back on within the Map. Yet it still works. If you use a Map's key value as if it were a property name on a bean, you will still find the corresponding value.

EL Implicit Objects

To add to EL's versatility still further, it has its own set of implicit objects. It's similar to the idea of implicit objects that you can use in general JSP page source, but it's important—especially for the exam!—that you learn the distinctions between the two sets. The full list is shown in Table 7-6. Note that all the EL implicit objects, with the exception of *pageContext*, are of type java.util.Map, so they obey the Map rules we just explored.

Let's briefly explore these implicit objects in turn.

pageScope, requestScope, sessionScope, and applicationScope These implicit objects are used to access attributes in a given scope. Of course, you can just name an attribute in expression language without any qualification, like this: `${myAttribute}`. Under the covers, `PageContext.find("myAttribute")` is used to search all scopes through page, request, session, and application, stopping when it finds an attribute of the right name. But if you want to target only a session scope attribute, then `${sessionScope.myAttribute}` will do the trick. All the alternative Map syntaxes will work as well—`${applicationScope ["myAttribute"]}` to find the attribute in application scope, for example.

param, paramValues These are used to recover parameter values—singly or in bulk. Let's suppose that your HTTP header request contains the following query string: `?myParm=firstValue&myParm=secondValue`. Let's also suppose this is a GET request, so there are no additional parameter values for `myParm` hidden in a POSTed request body. The result of `${param.myParm}` is "firstValue." The result of `${paramValues.myParm[1]}` is "secondValue." To put it another way, the implicit

TABLE 7-6 EL Implicit Objects

Variable Name	Description	Closest JSP Scripting "Equivalent"
pageContext	Represents the JSP `PageContext` object	Accessing properties of the `pageContext` implicit object
pageScope	A Map of page scope attributes	`pageContext.getAttribute()`
requestScope	A Map of request scope attributes	`request.getAttribute()`
sessionScope	A Map of session scope attributes	`session.getAttribute()`
applicationScope	A Map of application scope attributes	`application.getAttribute()`
param	A Map of ServletRequest parameter names and first values	`request.getParameter()`
paramValues	A Map of ServletRequest parameter names and all values	`request.getParameterValues()`
header	A Map of HttpServletRequest header names and first values	`request.getHeader()`
headerValues	A Map of HttpServletRequest header names and all values	`request.getHeaders()`
cookie	A map of HttpServletRequest cookie names and cookie objects	`request.getCookies()` and iterating through the returned Cookie array for a cookie of a given name
initParam	A Map of Servlet**Context** parameter names and values	`config.getServletContext() .getInitParameter()`

object param can be used solely to access the first value of a parameter (so in this example, it is impossible to use param to retrieve "secondValue"). However, using array syntax as shown, you can use the implicit object paramValues to access any of the available values for a given parameter.

header, headerValues These are used in a very similar way to param and paramValues, but they are targeted to recover request headers. The request header "Accept" is a good one to experiment with. This specifies the MIME types that a client is willing to receive back in the response, and it often consists of multiple values. The syntax is identical as for param and paramValues, so `${header.accept}` returns the first value of the accept header, and `${headerValues.accept[2]}` returns the third value. ("Accept" is one of the headers set up by the browser you met in Chapter 1, Exercise 1. Try pointing this browser to your own JSP, which contains the EL header and headerValues syntax described here.)

initParam This is used to access ServletContext initialization parameters, whose values are available across the entire web application. Don't be fooled into thinking that Servlet initialization parameters are returned! The syntax is exactly as for param, so `${initParam.myParm}` is used to return the value of an initialization parameter named "myParm."

cookie This is used to access a named Cookie in the HttpRequestHeader. A good example is the session cookie. Here are some variant approaches, all of which will display the value of the cookie:

```
${cookie.JSESSIONID.value}
${cookie["JSESSIONID"].value}
${cookie["JSESSIONID"]["value"]}
```

on the job

The implicit objects* cookie, header, *and* headerValues *are available only in JSP containers supporting the HTTP protocol, which, of course, most will do. These implicit objects relate to HTTP-only concepts.

exam watch

An implicit object name always takes precedence. Suppose that I set up a page attribute called "header"; then `${header}` would still refer to the implicit object header, not my page attribute (or attribute in any other scope, come to that).

pageContext This can be used to access properties of the PageContext object associated with the JSP page. Properties, as always, mean anything available from a "get" method that has no parameters. So request, session, and servletContext (not application!) are all available as properties by virtue of `getRequest()`, `getSession()`, and `getServletContext()` methods. If these objects have properties of their own, they can be used in expressions. So `${pageContext.request.method}`, for example, will display the HTTP method (GET, POST, etc.) associated with the request.

EXERCISE 7-4

An EL Calculator

In this exercise, you'll write a single JSP document that acts as a simple calculator. You'll be able to type in two figures, select an operation (add, subtract, multiply, divide, modulo), and display the result. You'll use EL both to perform the calculations and to display the result.

There's a double purpose to this exercise. Writing the calculator will help your fluency with EL. *Using* the calculator will help you see how EL handles calculations. Try all kinds of inputs, with and without decimal points—some of the results may surprise you! You'll be much better prepared for anything the exam can throw at you in terms of EL arithmetic.

Create the usual web application directory structure under a directory called ex0704, and proceed with the steps for the exercise. There's a solution in the CD in the file sourcecode/ch07/ex0704.war—check there if you get stuck.

Create the JSP Document

1. Create a file called calculator.jspx directly in context directory ex0704.
2. Include a `<jsp:output>` element to omit the XML declaration that otherwise gets inserted into page output for JSP documents.
3. Include a `<jsp:directive.page>` element to set the content type to "text/html."
4. Write HTML elements to make a valid HTML document—`<html>`, `<head>`, `<body>`, etc. Make sure `<html>` is the root element in your document.
5. Include a namespace reference in the opening `<html>` tag to qualify the `jsp:` elements (`xmlns:jsp="http://java.sun.com/JSP/Page"`).
6. Place an HTML form in the document. This should have an input text field named `arg1`, a select field named `operation`, an input field named `arg2`, and a submit button. Give the select field five options to match the five arithmetic operations: add, subtract, multiply, divide, and modulo.
7. Beneath the form, place some template text saying "Did you miss out one of the numbers?" Next to this, write an EL expression that will output "true" if either of the input parameters `arg1` or `arg2` is empty.
8. Beneath this text, you're going to place a mixture of template text, scriptlets, and expressions that restate the calculation and show the result. For example, "Result: 1 plus 2 = 3." This is easier said than done; some hints follow.
9. "Result:" is just template text, and the value of the first input to the calculation (`arg1`) can be derived in EL using the *param* implicit object.
10. To display the operation (add, subtract, multiply, etc.), you could again use the param implicit object with the `operation` parameter. Alternatively, use a `<jsp:scriptlet>` to obtain the request parameter value for `operation`, and condition your text accordingly. (This is what the solution code does—the

option values are abbreviations such as "Add," "Sub," and "Mlt." There is logic to test the value and display a suitable word or phrase instead, such as "plus," "minus," and "multiplied by.")

11. The value of the second input to the calculation (`arg2`) can be derived in EL by using the param implicit object again. The equal sign (=) is template text.
12. For the calculation itself, you'll need to write five EL expressions involving the `arg1` and `arg2` parameters. You'll need a scriptlet (or rather, a series of scriptlets using `if...` and `else if {...}` to test the `operation` parameter such that only one of the EL expressions is executed).

Deploy and Run the Application

13. Create a WAR file that contains the contents of ex0704, and deploy this to your web server. Start the web server if it has not started already.
14. Use your browser to request calculator.jspx, with a URL such as

```
http://localhost:8080/ex0704/calculator.jspx
```

15. Test it out with all five arithmetic operations, using a mixture of integers and doubles (i.e., anything with a decimal point) as inputs.
16. The following illustration shows the solution page in action.

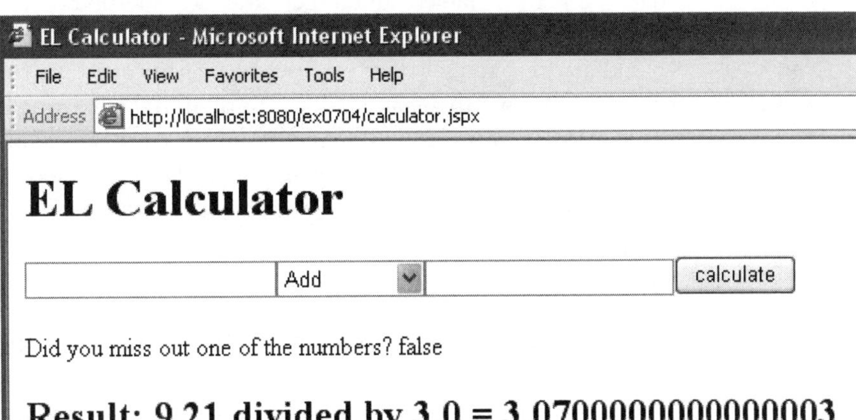

CERTIFICATION SUMMARY

In this chapter you began by learning about standard actions. You saw that these observe strict XML element syntax, comprising opening tags, closing tags, and attributes. The first three standard actions you encountered were `<jsp:useBean>`, `<jsp:setProperty>`, and `<jsp:getProperty>`. You found that `<jsp:useBean>` can be used to make an object available in a page, either by obtaining an object from an existing attribute or by creating a new object and attaching it to an attribute. You also saw that the object targeted by `<jsp:useBean>` must adhere to JavaBean standards—at least in having a no-argument constructor, and (for it to be at all useful) having "get" and "set" methods. You found that `<jsp:useBean>` has an *id* attribute, whose value is shared with the name for the page, request, session, or application scope attribute it is bound to. You learned that the *class* attribute specifies the actual class of the object created, but that a *type* attribute can be used to specify a different type of reference variable (implemented interface or superclass) for the bean object. You saw that a *scope* attribute can be used to associate the object with any one of the four different scopes (`scope="page|request|session|application"`).

You then learned that `<jsp:setProperty>` can be used to set the value for one of the properties on the bean object declared with `<jsp:useBean>`. You saw that a property is named after a "get" and "set" method on the bean, such that `getLoan()` exposes a property called "loan" and that `setBankBalance()` exposes "bankBalance." You saw that you use the *property* attribute to name one of the properties and use the *name* attribute to tie in to an existing bean (as named in the *id* attribute of `<jsp:useBean>`). You learned that the value can be set using the *value* attribute (where the value of the *value* attribute can be a literal or a run-time expression), or by using the *param* attribute (associating the value with a request parameter). You then saw that `<jsp:getProperty>` can be used—like an expression—to send the value of a property to page output. You saw that this also has attributes of *name* (the name of the bean: matching the *id* value on `<jsp:useBean>`) and *property* (the name of the property whose value to display).

In the next section of the chapter, you met three more standard actions—`<jsp:forward>`, `<jsp:include>`, and `<jsp:param>`. You learned that `<jsp:forward>` and `<jsp:include>` do much the same job as the `forward()` and `include()` methods on a RequestDispatcher object. You saw that `<jsp:forward>` and `<jsp:include>` each have a *page* attribute, and this is used to specify a page within the web application using an absolute or relative URL (beginning with a slash or not).

You learned that `<jsp:include>` also has a *flush* attribute to control whether or not existing response output should be sent to a client before including a file, but that `<jsp:forward>` doesn't—because if output has been written to the client already, it's illegal to forward to another resource. You learned the differences between the `<jsp:include>` standard action and the `<%@ include file="..."> page` directive. You saw that the `include` standard action doesn't include a target file until request time; hence, the value for the file can be a run-time expression. You learned that, by contrast, the `include` directive incorporates the contents of a file at translation time.

You moved on to `<jsp:param>`, and saw how this can be used to graft on parameters available to the forwarded-to or included resource. You also learned that these parameters are no longer available on return to the forwarding or including resource.

The next main topic covered was that of JSP documents. You learned that JSP documents are JSP page source written in well-formed XML and by default are used to produce XML as output. You learned the basics of well-formed XML documents: how each one must have a root element, how opening tags must match to closing tags, and how every element must nest inside another without overlapping (aside from the root element). You saw that JSP traditional scripting element syntax has to be replaced with equivalent XML elements—so `<jsp:scriptlet>... </jsp:scriptlet>` for `<%...%>`, `<jsp:expression>...</jsp:expression>` for `<%=...%>`, and `<jsp:declaration>...</jsp:declaration>` for `<%!...%>`. You found that the Java language contents of scriptlets, expressions, and declarations can remain unaltered—except that some symbols (in particular < and >) need character sequences called entities to keep the XML syntax well-formed (so `<` for < and `>` for >).

You also saw that directive syntax changes as well, so `<jsp:directive .page .../>` for `<%@ page ...%>` and `<jsp:directive.include .../>` for `<%@ include ...%>`. However, you found that the attributes for `page` and `include` directives remain unaltered between the two styles. You learned that comment syntax changes subtly, so `<!-- ... -->` becomes the equivalent of `<%-- ... --%>` for commenting out lines in page source.

You learned that there are three different ways for the JSP container to recognize JSP documents. Two of the methods rely on a web.xml file at servlet specification level 2.4: (1) having a .jspx extension on the file, and (2) setting the `<is-xml>` element to "true" in the deployment descriptor for a given `<url-pattern>`—this within `<jsp-property-group>` in element `<jsp-config>`. The third method, you saw, works whatever level of deployment descriptor you have, and that is to use `<jsp:root>` as the root element in your document.

In the final section of the chapter, you learned about Expression Language, abbreviated EL. You saw how EL is a Java-language free equivalent for expressions. You saw that EL has access to any attribute in any scope and that the simplest way to display an attribute value in your page output is like this: `${attributeName}`. You learned that if that attribute is a bean, you can access properties on the bean using dot syntax (`${attributeName.propertyName}`) or square bracket syntax (`${attributeName["propertyName"]}`). You saw how the square bracket syntax is useful for accessing Array or List elements, by providing an integer in the square brackets. You also learned that an attribute that is a java.util.Map can have its key values treated like bean properties, using the dot or square bracket syntax.

You saw that you have a range of five literals available to you in EL—integers, floating point numbers, booleans (true or false, like Java), strings (enclosed with single or double quotes), and a **null** literal. You were introduced to the five arithmetic operators in EL: +, −, *, / or div, and % or mod, and a range of relational and logical operators. You saw that there are character equivalents for relational operators so that you can more easily write XML-friendly syntax. You also met EL's *empty* operator and found that this qualifies empty strings and empty arrays and collections as returning **true** for an empty test as well as, of course, a **null** value.

Finally, you met the range of EL's implicit objects. You found that you can access attributes in a particular scope using *pageScope*, *requestScope*, *sessionScope*, or *applicationScope*. You saw that you can use *param* or *paramValues* to access request parameters, and *header* or *headerValues* to access request headers. You learned that *initParam* is used to access ServletContext parameters and that *cookie* is used to access a named cookie on a request.

✓ TWO-MINUTE DRILL

JSP Standard Actions

- ❑ Standard actions follow XML syntax, with opening and closing tags.
- ❑ The opening tag of a standard action almost always has attributes, which are *name*="*value*" pairs.
- ❑ The `<jsp:useBean>` standard action makes an attribute available in a JSP page.
- ❑ This example creates an attribute in page scope: `<jsp:useBean id="bankAccount" class="a.b.BankAccountBean" />`.
- ❑ The *id* attribute identifies the name of the attribute.
- ❑ The *class* attribute identifies the fully qualified name of the object attached to the attribute.
- ❑ The class used in this standard action should obey JavaBean rules—so it should have a no-argument constructor, and getter and setter methods.
- ❑ If such a class has methods called `getLoan()` and `setLoan()`, it is deemed to have a property called loan, which can be read or updated.
- ❑ Properties can be updated using the `<jsp:setProperty>` standard action.
- ❑ Properties can be read (sent to page output) using the `<jsp:getProperty>` standard action, which is like an expression.
- ❑ One possible syntax for `<jsp:setProperty>` is `<jsp:setProperty name="bankAccount" property="loan" value="5000" />`. This effectively calls `setLoan()` on the object attaching to the `bankAccount` page scope attribute, passing in a parameter of 5000.
- ❑ One possible syntax for `<jsp:getProperty>` is `<jsp:getProperty name="bankAccount" property="loan" />`. This effectively calls `getLoan()` on the object attaching to the `bankAccount` page scope attribute, and sends the result to page output.
- ❑ Both `<jsp:setProperty>` and `<jsp:getProperty>` have mandatory `name` and `property` attributes.
- ❑ The `name` attribute in both cases must (or should) tie back to the *id* attribute in a `<jsp:useBean>` standard action in the same page.
- ❑ The `value` attribute on `<jsp:setProperty>` can be set with literals, or with a run-time expression (EL or Java language syntax).

- Another possible syntax for `<jsp:setProperty>` is `<jsp:setProperty name="bankAccount" property="loan" param="loanField" />`. This effectively calls `setLoan()` on the object attaching to the `bankAccount` page scope attribute, passing in the value for the request parameter `loanField` as a parameter.
- `<jsp:setProperty name="bankAccount" property="*" />` has the effect of calling set methods on all the properties of the `bankAccount` bean whose names match the names of request parameters.
- `<jsp:useBean>` has an optional attribute called *scope*, with valid values of "page", "request", "session", or "application". The bean is created or retrieved from the given scope (the default—if *scope* is absent—is "`page`").
- `<jsp:useBean>` has another optional attribute called *type*. This must be a superclass of, or interface implemented by, the *class* attribute value.
- The *type* attribute enables the use of a different type of reference variable from the underlying class of the object that holds the attribute value.

Dispatching Mechanisms

- The `<jsp:include>` standard action acts very much like the `RequestDispatcher.include()` method.
- The `<jsp:forward>` standard action is likewise like the `RequestDispatcher.forward()` method.
- Both `<jsp:forward>` and `<jsp:include>` have one mandatory attribute: `page`.
- Example `forward:<jsp:forward page="/anotherPage.jsp" />`.
- The *page* attribute references the file to include or forward to.
- The value for the *page* attribute can begin with a forward slash. The JSP container then treats the web application context directory as the root.
- No forward slash for the *page* attribute denotes a relative URL. The JSP container looks for the forwarded-to or included file relative to the location of the forwarding or including page.
- A `<jsp:forward>` is illegal (IllegalStateException) if any of the response has already been sent to the client.
- `<jsp:include>` also has an optional attribute, *flush*. This determines whether any existing page output should be sent to the client before including the file.

- ❑ `<jsp:param>` can be included in the body of `<jsp:forward>` or `<jsp:include>`.
- ❑ `<jsp:param>` has *name* and *value* attributes: `<jsp:param name="parmName" value="parmValue" />`.
- ❑ `<jsp:param>` adds in request parameters that are available to the forwarded-to or included resource but disappear on return to the forwarding or including pages.
- ❑ In the case of more than one value being present for a given parameter name, `<jsp:param>` request parameter values are loaded at the front.

JSPs in XML

- ❑ JSP documents are JSP source files written entirely in XML syntax.
- ❑ JSP documents typically have a .jspx extension.
- ❑ JSP documents can also be identified by setting `<is-xml>true</is-xml>` in the deployment descriptor for a given `<url-pattern>`. Both these elements are subelements of `<jsp-property-group>`, which is a subelement of `<jsp-config>`.
- ❑ Otherwise, a JSP document must use `<jsp:root>` as its root element.
- ❑ XML syntax demands a single root element in a file (as `<web-app>` is for the deployment descriptor).
- ❑ XML syntax demands that each element is properly nested. It is illegal for the closing tag from one element to come between the opening and closing tag of another element.
- ❑ JSP document syntax provides replacements for all the <%-type scripting element syntax.
- ❑ `<jsp:scriptlet>...</jsp:scriptlet>` replaces `<%...%>`.
- ❑ `<jsp:expression>...</jsp:expression>` replaces `<%=...%>`.
- ❑ `<jsp:declaration>...</jsp:declaration>` replaces `<%!...%>`.
- ❑ Otherwise, Java language syntax remains unchanged, but XML-unfriendly characters (such as < and >) need to be replaced with entities (such as `<` and `>`).
- ❑ `<jsp:directive.page .../>` replaces `<%@ page ...%>`.
- ❑ `<jsp:directive.include .../>` replaces `<%@ include ...%>`.
- ❑ `<!-- ... pp>` replaces `<%-- ... --%>`.

Expression Language

- Expression Language (EL) replaces Java-language syntax expressions.
- The base syntax is `${expression}`.
- The result from an EL expression is sent to page output.
- Any attribute in any scope can be accessed in an expression.
- An EL expression *cannot* access local variables in `_jspService()` directly.
- There are five literal types in EL: boolean, integer, floating decimal, string, and **null**.
- An EL boolean has values of true and false, like Java.
- An EL integer is any number without a decimal point, while floating decimals have a decimal point.
- An EL string is denoted by double or single quotes around the literal ("myString" or 'myString').
- There are five arithmetic operators in EL: +, −, *, / (or div), and % (or mod).
- There are six relational operators in EL: < (or lt), > (or gt), <= (or le), >= (or ge), != (or ne), and == (eq).
- There are three logical operators in EL: && (or and), | | (or or), and ! (or not).
- There is also an *empty* operator in EL, which returns true for null, empty strings, empty arrays, and empty collections.
- EL can access properties on beans with the dot operator.
- `${bankAccount.balance}` returns a property called balance for an attribute bean in some scope called bankAccount.
- EL can access items in arrays or java.util.List objects with square bracket syntax.
- `${daysOfWeek[6]}` accesses the seventh element in an array or java.util.List object associated with an attribute called daysOfWeek.
- Dot or square bracket syntax can be used to return keyed items in a java.util .Map object.
- Assuming that "capital" is the name of an attribute holding a java.util.Map, `${capital.Poland}` or `${capital["Poland"]}` would return the value associated with the key "Poland."
- EL has 11 implicit objects: *pageContext*, *pageScope*, *requestScope*, *sessionScope*, *applicationScope*, *initParam*, *param*, *paramValues*, *header*, *headerValues*, and *cookie*.

- *pageContext* can be used to access properties associated with the page's PageContext object.
- For example, `${pageContext.request.header}` returns the HTTP method associated with the request.
- *pageScope*, *requestScope*, *sessionScope*, and *applicationScope* can be used to access an attribute in a specific scope.
- So whereas `${myAttr}` will search through page, request, session, and application scopes for an attribute called myAttr, `${sessionScope.myAttr}` confines the search to session scope.
- *initParam* returns ServletContext parameter values.
- *param* returns the first value associated with a named ServletRequest parameter; *paramValues* returns all values.
- *header* returns the first value associated with a named HttpServletRequest header; *headerValues* returns all values.
- *cookie* returns a named cookie associated with HttpServletRequest.

SELF TEST

The following questions will help you measure your understanding of the material presented in this chapter. Read all the choices carefully because there might be more than one correct answer. Choose all the correct answers for each question.

JSP Standard Actions

1. (drag-and-drop question) The following illustration shows a complete JSP page source. Match the lettered values, which conceal parts of the source, with numbers from the list on the right, which indicate possible completions for the source.

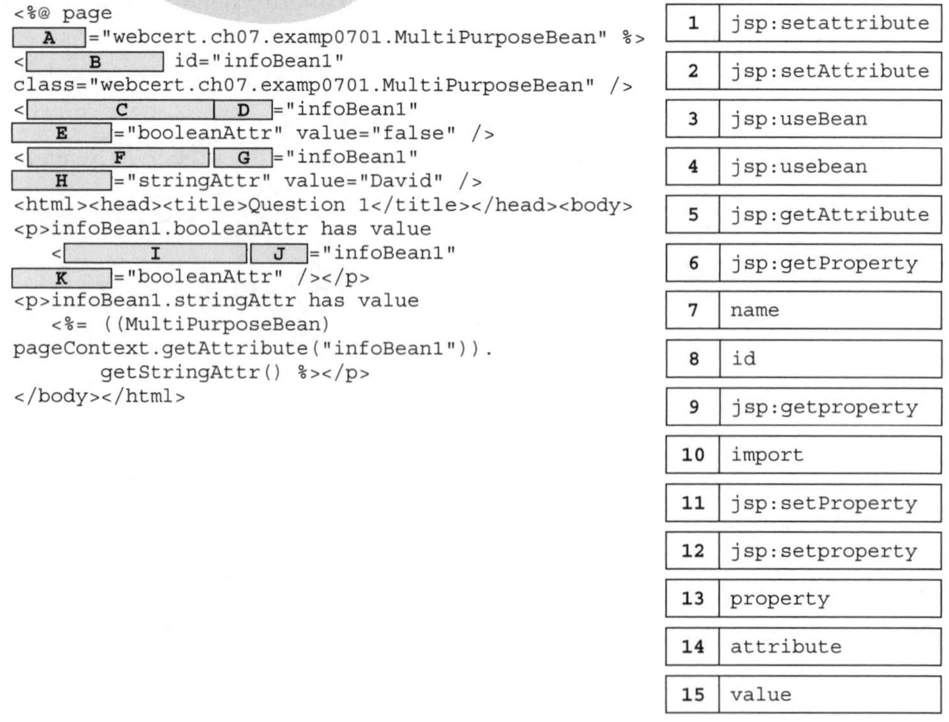

<%@ page
A ="webcert.ch07.examp0701.MultiPurposeBean" %>
< B id="infoBean1"
class="webcert.ch07.examp0701.MultiPurposeBean" />
< C D ="infoBean1"
E ="booleanAttr" value="false" />
< F G ="infoBean1"
H ="stringAttr" value="David" />
<html><head><title>Question 1</title></head><body>
<p>infoBean1.booleanAttr has value
< I J ="infoBean1"
K ="booleanAttr" /></p>
<p>infoBean1.stringAttr has value
<%= ((MultiPurposeBean)
pageContext.getAttribute("infoBean1")).
getStringAttr() %></p>
</body></html>
1 jsp:setattribute
2 jsp:setAttribute
3 jsp:useBean
4 jsp:usebean
5 jsp:getAttribute
6 jsp:getProperty
7 name
8 id
9 jsp:getproperty
10 import
11 jsp:setProperty
12 jsp:setproperty
13 property
14 attribute
15 value

2. Which of the following are potentially legal lines of JSP source? (Choose two.)

A.

```
<jsp:useBean id="beanName1" class="a.b.MyBean" type="a.b.MyInterface" />
```

B.

```
<% String className = "a.b.MyBean"; %>
<jsp:useBean id="beanName2" class="<%=className%>" />
```

C.

```
<% String beanName = "beanName3"; %>
<jsp:useBean id="<%=beanName3%>" class="a.b.MyBean" />
```

D.

```
<% String myValue = "myValue"; %>
<jsp:setProperty name="beanName1" property="soleProp" value="<%=myValue%>" />
```

E.

```
<% String propName = "soleProp"; %>
<jsp:getProperty name="beanName1" property="<%=propName%>" />
```

3. Which of the following are false statements about `<jsp:useBean>` standard action attributes? (Choose three.)

   A. If present, the *class* attribute must match the object type of your bean.

   B. If the *type* attribute is used, the *class* attribute must be present.

   C. The reference variable used for a bean doesn't always have the same type as the bean object it refers to.

   D. If both are used, *class* and *type* attributes must have different values.

   E. If both are used, *class* and *type* attributes must have the same value.

   F. If both are used, *class* and *type* attributes can have the same value.

4. Given a NameBean with a "name" property and an AddressBean with an "address" property, what happens when the following JSP is requested with the following URL? (Choose one.)

   Calling URL:

```
http://localhost:8080/examp0701/Question4.jsp?name=David%20Bridgewater&address=
Leeds%20UK
```

   JSP page source:

```
<jsp:useBean id="name" class="webcert.ch07.examp0701.NameBean" />
<jsp:useBean id="address" class="webcert.ch07.examp0701.AddressBean" />
<jsp:setProperty name="name" property="name" />
<jsp:setProperty name="address" param="*" />
<jsp:getProperty name="name" property="name" />
<jsp:getProperty name="address" property="address" />
```

A. A translation time error occurs.

B. A request time error occurs.

C. "null null" is displayed.

D. "David Bridgewater null" is displayed.

E. "null Leeds UK" is displayed.

F. "David Bridgewater Leeds UK" is displayed.

5. Which of the following techniques would correctly put a bean into application scope? (You can assume that any necessary page directives are present and correct elsewhere in the JSP page.) (Choose four.)

A.

```
<jsp:useBean id="app1" class="webcert.ch07.examp0701.AddressBean"
scope="application" />
```

B.

```
<% AddressBean ab2 = new AddressBean();
application.setAttribute("app2", ab2); %>
```

C.

```
<% AddressBean ab3 = new AddressBean();
pageContext.setAttribute("app3", ab3, PageContext.APPLICATION_SCOPE); %>
```

D.

```
<% AddressBean ab4 = new AddressBean();
ServletContext context = getServletContext();
context.setAttribute("app4", ab4); %>
```

E.

```
<% AddressBean ab5 = new AddressBean();
pageContext.setAttribute("app5", ab5); %>
```

F.

```
<jsp:useBean name="app6" class="webcert.ch07.examp0701.AddressBean"
scope="application" />
```

Dispatching Mechanisms

6. Consider the source for the following two JSP pages, a.jsp and b.jsp. What is the outcome of requesting each in turn? You can assume that "c.jsp" is available in the same web application directory as a.jsp and b.jsp. (Choose two.)

Source for a.jsp:

```
<%@page buffer="none" autoFlush="true"%>
<jsp:forward page="c.jsp"/>
```

Source for b.jsp:

```
<%@page buffer="none" autoFlush="true"%><jsp:forward page="c.jsp"/>
```

A. Neither JSP page translates.

B. a.jsp translates; b.jsp does not.

C. b.jsp translates; a.jsp does not.

D. Both JSP pages translate.

E. Neither JSP page runs successfully.

F. a.jsp runs successfully; b.jsp does not.

G. b.jsp runs successfully, a.jsp does not.

H. Both a.jsp and b.jsp run successfully.

7. What is the outcome of making the HTTP GET request shown to params.jsp (source follows)? (Choose one.)

The HTTP request is in this form:

```
http://localhost:8080/examp0702/params.jsp?X=1&Y=2&Z=3
```

Source of params.jsp:

```
<jsp:include page="included.jsp">
  <jsp:param name="X" value="4" />
  <jsp:param name="X" value="5" />
  <jsp:param name="Y" value="6" />
</jsp:include>
${param.X}
<%=request.getParameter("Y")%>
```

Source of included.jsp:

```
${param.X}
${param.Y}
<% String[] x = request.getParameterValues("X");
for (int i = 0; i < x.length; i++) {
  out.write(x[i]);
}
%>
```

A. 1 2 45 4 6

B. 1 2 145 4 6

C. 4 6 451 4 6

D. 1 2 145 1 2

E. 4 6 451 1 2

F. 4 6 45 1 2

G. None of the above

8. Which of the following are helpful statements about the `include` standard action and the `include` directive? (Choose three.)

   A. The `include` directive is useful for the inclusion of pages that change frequently.

   B. The `include` standard action is useful when soft-coding the page to include.

   C. Given the same page to include, the `include` directive may be more efficient than the `include` standard action at request time.

   D. The body of the `include` standard action can influence existing request parameters.

   E. Given the same page to include, the `include` directive may be more efficient than the include standard action at translation time.

   F. An `include` directive can be processed or not according to JSTL, EL, or scriptlet page logic.

9. What will be the result of requesting the JSP page represented by the following source? Assume that "forwardedTo.jsp" is an empty file. (Choose one.)

```
<%@ page import="java.util.*,java.text.*" %>
<%! private String returnTimeStamp(PageContext pageContext) {
  DateFormat df = DateFormat.getDateTimeInstance();
  String s = df.format(new Date());
  pageContext.setAttribute("timestamp", s);
  return s;
} %>
<jsp:forward page="forwardedTo.jsp" />
<%=returnTimeStamp(pageContext)%>
<%System.out.println(pageContext.getAttribute("timestamp"));%>
```

   A. Translation error.

   B. Run-time error.

   C. A formatted date appears in the page output.

   D. A formatted date appears in the server console.

E. A formatted date appears both in the page output and in the server console.

F. None of the above.

10. What is the outcome of making the HTTP GET request shown to params.jsp (source follows)? (Choose one.)

The HTTP request is in this form:

```
http://localhost:8080/examp0702/params.jsp?X=1&Y=2&Z=3
```

Source of params.jsp:

```
<jsp:forward page="included.jsp">
  <jsp:param name="X" value="4" />
  <jsp:param name="X" value="5" />
  <jsp:param name="Y" value="6" />
<jsp:forward/>
${param.X}
<%=request.getParameter("Y")%>
```

Source of included.jsp:

```
${param.X}
${param.Y}
<% String[] x = request.getParameterValues("X");
for (int i = 0; i < x.length; i++) {
   out.write(x[i]);
}
%>
```

A. 1 2 145

B. 4 6 451

C. 1 2 145 1 2

D. 4 6 451 1 2

E. 4 6 451 4 6

F. None of the above

JSPs in XML

11. What is the outcome of accessing the following page, defined as a JSP document in a web application? The line numbers are for reference only and should not be considered part of the JSP page source. (Choose one.)

```
01 <html xmlns:jsp="http://java.sun.com/JSP/Page">
02 <jsp:directive.page contentType="text/html" />
03 <jsp:declaration>
04   public int squared(int value) {
05     return value * value;
06   }
07 </jsp:declaration>
08 <jsp:scriptlet>
09   int value = Integer.parseInt
10   (request.getParameter("number"));
11   int squared = squared(value);
12   out.write(value + " squared is " + squared);
13   if (squared < 100) {
14     out.write("; try a bigger number.");
15   }
16 </jsp:scriptlet>
17 </html>
```

A. Translation error at line 1

B. Translation error at line 2

C. Translation error at line 4

D. Translation error at line 12

E. Translation error at line 13

F. Run-time error

G. No errors, with page displaying successfully

12. Which of the following JSP documents will produce output? You can assume that a.b.StringBean exists and has a valid property called "string." (Choose two.)

A.

```
<jsp:useBean id="string" class="a.b.StringBean">
<jsp:setProperty name="string" property="string" value="Question12" />
  <jsp:getProperty name="string" property="string" />
</jsp:useBean>
```

B.

```
<jsp:useBean xmlns:jsp="http://java.sun.com/JSP/Page"
id="string" class="a.b.StringBean">
  <jsp:setProperty name="string" property="string" value="Question12" />
  <jsp:getProperty name="string" property="string" />
</jsp:useBean>
```

C.

```
<jsp:useBean xmlns:jsp="http://java.sun.com/JSP/Page"
id="string" class="a.b.StringBean">
  <jsp:setProperty name="string" property="string" value="Question12" />
  <data><jsp:getProperty name="string" property="string" /></data>
</jsp:useBean>
```

D.

```
<jsp:useBean xmlns:jsp="http://java.sun.com/JSP/Page"
id="string" class="a.b.StringBean">
  <jsp:setProperty name="string" property="string" value="Question12" />
</jsp:useBean>
<data><jsp:getProperty name="string" property="string" /></data>
```

E.

```
<jsp:root xmlns:jsp="http://java.sun.com/JSP/Page" version="2.0">
<jsp:useBean id="string" class="a.b.StringBean">
  <jsp:setProperty name="string" property="string" value="Question12" />
</jsp:useBean>
<data><jsp:getProperty name="string" property="string" /></data>
</jsp:root>
```

13. Which of the following techniques will cause JSP page source to be treated as a JSP document by the JSP container? (Choose two.)

    A. Setting the `<is-xml>` subelement of `<jsp-config>` to a value of true
    B. Using a .jspx extension with a version 2.4 deployment descriptor
    C. Using a .xml extension with a version 2.4 deployment descriptor
    D. Using `<jsp:root>` as the root element of your source
    E. Using a deployment descriptor at level 2.4
    F. Writing your page source in XML syntax

14. Of the five JSP page source extracts below, there are two pairs. Each member of the pair gives rise to identical output. Which is the odd one out? (Choose one.)

    A.

```
<% int i, j, k;
  i = 1; j = 2; k = 3; %>
<%= i + j / k %>
```

B.

```
<jsp:scriptlet>int i, j, k;
  i = 1; j = 2; k = 3;</jsp:scriptlet>
<jsp:expression>(i + j) / k</jsp:expression>
```

C.

```
<% int i, j, k;
  i = 1; j = 2; k = 3; %>
<%= (i + j) / k + ".0" %>
```

D.

```
<% pageContext.setAttribute("i", new Integer(1));
pageContext.setAttribute("j", new Integer(2));
pageContext.setAttribute("k", new Integer(3));
%>${pageScope.i + pageScope.j / pageScope.k}
```

E.

```
<% pageContext.setAttribute("i", new Integer(1));
pageContext.setAttribute("j", new Integer(2));
pageContext.setAttribute("k", new Integer(3));
%>${(pageScope.i + pageScope.j) / pageScope.k}
```

15. Which of the following tags will successfully complete the following JSP page extract, at the points marked `<jsp:???>` and `</jsp:???>` ? (Choose one.)

```
<html xmlns:jsp="http://java.sun.com/JSP/Page" >
<jsp:directive.page contentType="text/html" />
<head><title>Question 15</title></head>
<jsp:???><![CDATA[<img src="]]></jsp:???>
<jsp:expression>session.getAttribute("theImage")</jsp:expression>
<jsp:???><![CDATA[" />]]></jsp:???>
</html>
```

A. `<jsp:param>` and `</jsp:param>`

B. `<jsp:element>` and `</jsp:element>`

C. `<jsp:img>` and `</jsp:img>`

D. `<jsp:output>` and `</jsp:output>`

E. `<jsp:text>` and `</jsp:text>`

Expression Language

16. What is the consequence of accessing the following JSP page with the URL shown? (Choose one.)

URL for accessing Question16.jsp:

```
http://localhost:8080/examp0704/Question16.jsp?A=1&A=2
```

JSP page source:

```
<!-- Source for Question16.jsp -->
<p>Parameter A has values
<% for (int j = 0; j < request.getParameterValues("A").length; j++) { %>
${paramValues.A[j]},
<% } %> </p>
```

A. Translation error

B. Run-time error

C. Output of: "Parameter A has values 1,2,"

D. Output of: "Parameter A has values 1, ,"

E. Output of: "Parameter A has values 0,0,"

F. Output of: "Parameter A has values , ,"

17. Which of the following are implicit variables in EL? (Choose two.)

A. `session`

B. `param`

C. `paramValues`

D. `initParams`

E. `request`

F. `page`

G. `contextScope`

18. Which of the following EL expressions will return a `<servlet-name>` associated with the JSP executing the expression? (Choose one.)

A.

```
${pageContext.config.getServletName}
```

B.

```
${pageContext.config.servletName}
```

C.

```
${pageContext.servletConfig.servletName}
```

D.

```
${pageContext.servletConfig.getServletName}
```

E.

```
${pageContext.getServletConfig().getServletName()}
```

19. What expression is required at the point marked ??? in the following JSP page to output the number 46? (Choose two.)

```
<html xmlns:jsp="http://java.sun.com/JSP/Page" >
<head><title>Question 19</title></head>
<jsp:output omit-xml-declaration="true" />
<jsp:directive.page contentType="text/html" />
<body>
<jsp:scriptlet>
  request.setAttribute("a", new Integer(2));
  session.setAttribute("b", new Integer(3));
  application.setAttribute("c", new Integer(4));
  request.setAttribute("d", new Integer(5));
</jsp:scriptlet>
???
</body></html>
```

A.

```
${pageContext.c * pageContext.d * pageContext.a
+ pageContext.a * pageContext.b}
```

B.

```
${applicationScope.c * requestScope.d * requestScope.a
+ requestScope.a * sessionScope.b}
```

C.

```
${(applicationScope.c * requestScope.d * requestScope.a)
+ (requestScope.a * sessionScope.b)}
```

D.

```
${(pageContext.c * pageContext.d * pageContext.a)
+ (pageContext.a * pageContext.b)}
```

E.

```
${(application.c * request.d * request.a)
+ (request.a * session.b)}
```

F.

```
${application.c * request.d * request.a
+ request.a * session.b}
```

20. (drag-and-drop question) The following illustration shows a complete JSP page source. Match the lettered values, which conceal parts of the source, with numbers from the list on the right, which indicate possible completions for the source.

```
<html [    A    ]="http://java.sun.com/JSP/Page" >
<head><title>Question 20: Drag and
Drop</title></head>
<jsp:output omit-xml-declaration="true" />
<jsp:[      B      ] contentType="text/html" />
<body>
<jsp:[     C     ]>
  private Integer generateLuckyNumber() {
    Double d = new Double (Math.random() * 100);
    Integer i = new Integer (d.intValue());
    return i;
  }
</jsp:[     D     ]>
<jsp:[    E    ]>pageContext.setAttribute("luckyNo",
generateLuckyNumber());
</jsp:[    F    ]>
<p>Your session cookie has the name
${[  G  ].JSESSIONID.name} (which should come as no
surprise)<br />
and the value ${[  H  ].JSESSIONID.value} (which is
harder to predict).</p>
<br />
<p>Your lucky number for the day is
${[    I    ][[    J    ]]}</p>
</body></html>
```

1	declaration
2	Declaration
3	scriptlet
4	cookies
5	page.directive
6	directive.page
7	Scriptlet
8	Cookie
9	xmlns:jsp
10	xlmns;jsp
11	cookie
12	luckyNo
13	"luckyNo"
14	expression
15	Expression
16	pageContext
17	pageScope
18	page

LAB QUESTION

For this question, you're going to take the solution code from a previous exercise and apply many of the techniques you learned in this chapter. The previous exercise to use is Exercise 6-3 (from Chapter 6), packaged on the CD in /sourcecode/chapter06/ex0603.war. Establish a new context directory called lab07, and unpackage the WAR file into this.

The solution code from Exercise 6-3 displays a short list of countries and capitals. There are four JSPs involved in the solution: master.jsp, which includes header.jsp, setup.jsp, and footer.jsp. Your mission is to turn master.jsp and setup.jsp into JSP documents (i.e., in XML syntax), so rename these to master .jspx and setup.jspx. When including files into master.jspx,

- Include header.jsp and footer.jsp via an `include` directive.
- Include setup.jspx via an `include` standard action.

Other than this, use expression language and standard actions wherever possible. You'll need to revisit header.jsp and setup.jsp so that when these are incorporated into master.jspx, they don't damage the XML syntax. You'll quickly discover any problems as you deploy the JSPs and attempt to access master.jspx.

SELF TEST ANSWERS

JSP Standard Actions

1. ☑ **A** matches with **10** (must be an `import` attribute for the page directive); **B** matches with **3** (only a `<jsp:useBean>` has *id* and *class* attributes); **C** and **F** match with **11** (has to be `<jsp:setProperty>` because of the *value* attribute); **D**, **G**, and **J** match with **7** (must be the *name* attribute in all cases); **E**, **H**, and **K** match with **13** (must be the *property* attribute in all cases); **I** matches with **6** (must be `<jsp:getProperty>` to display the property, which is the clear intention of the code here).
   ☒ No other combinations will work.

2. ☑ **A** and **D**. **A** is correct; it's normal `<jsp:useBean>` syntax. Of course, a.b.MyBean must implement a.b.MyInterface for the action to translate. **D** is also correct. It's a valid `<jsp:setProperty>` element. There's one slightly unusual aspect: The value attribute's value setting comes from a run-time expression. But this is one of the few cases when it's legal to embed a run-time expression inside an action attribute.
   ☒ **B** and **C** are incorrect because you can't use a run-time expression for either the *class* attribute or *id* attribute values of `<jsp:useBean>`. Both must be known at translation time (these values are, effectively, hard-coded in the generated servlet). Because there is compile-time checking done on class existence and validity, the *class* attribute could never be soft-coded. **E** is incorrect for similar reasons: The property name of a `<jsp:getProperty>` element must be known when the servlet is translated, for the generated servlet must select the right method to turn the property into a String for display.

3. ☑ **B**, **D**, and **E** are correct answers, for all are false statements. **B** is a false statement (so a correct answer) because *type* can be used without *class*—in which case, your bean must exist already, or you will get a run-time error. **D** and **E** are false statements (and so correct answers) because it's neither true that *class* and *type* must be different nor that they must be the same.
   ☒ **A** is a true statement (so an incorrect answer), for the *class* attribute does indeed define the object type of the bean. **C** is a true statement (so an incorrect answer) as the type of the reference variable used for the bean can be different from the object type of the bean itself (if *class* and *type* are set differently). **F** is a true statement (so an incorrect answer)—it's pretty pointless setting the *class* and *type* attributes to the same value, but it's still legal. You might as well omit the *type* attribute under these circumstances, though.

4. ☑ **A** is the correct answer: A translation-time error occurs. The second `<jsp:setProperty>` element should have the attribute setting of *property*="*" for the page to translate and compile; *param*="*" is incorrect syntax.

☒ B is incorrect because the incorrect syntax of the standard action prevents translation. C, D, E, and F are incorrect because there is no output (**F** would be the correct answer if the syntax error were corrected).

5. ☑ **A**, **B**, **C**, and **D** are correct. **A** is the `<jsp:useBean>` standard action used exactly as it should be to create a bean in application scope. **B** sets up a bean in a scriptlet and uses the *application* implicit object to set the bean up as an attribute. **C** also uses a scriptlet but uses the three-parameter version of `pageContext.setAttribute` to provide the name, the bean, and the scope of the attribute. **D** again uses a scriptlet—there's more manual work this time, getting hold of the servlet context with the `getServletContext()` method instead of using the *application* implicit object—but the net result is still as intended.
☒ **E** is incorrect because using the two-parameter version of `PageContext.setAttribute()` results in a bean being placed in page scope, not application scope. **F** is incorrect because *name* is used instead of *id* (*name* is a valid attribute of `<jsp:getProperty>` and `<jsp:setProperty>` but not of `<jsp:useBean>`).

Dispatching Mechanisms

6. ☑ **D** and **G**. Both pages translate successfully (so answer **D** is correct). However, b.jsp runs successfully (forwarding to c.jsp, whose output is displayed), whereas a.jsp terminates with an IllegalStateException when run (hence answer **G** is also correct). Why should this be? The only material difference between the sources for a.jsp and b.jsp is the carriage return separating the page directive from the `<jsp:forward>` standard action. This is present in a.jsp, but not in b.jsp. To understand why this should make a difference, you need to note that the page directive effectively does away with the normal output buffer (by setting ***buffer***=*"none"* and ***autoFlush***=*"true"*). This means that any output at all – *even an innocent carriage return in the template text* – is instantly committed to the response output. Once anything has been committed to the response output, a forward call is illegal.
☒ **A**, **B**, **C**, **E**, **F**, and **H** are incorrect, according to the reasoning in the correct answer.

7. ☑ **E** is correct. Consider first of all that parameter Z is not displayed in either JSP, so it is a red herring. On arrival at params.jsp, the request has parameter X with a value of 1, and Y with a value of 2. Now X is supplemented with two additional values. These are placed in order of their appearance in `<jsp:param>` standard actions, but at the "front" of the parameter's value list. So X's values are 4, 5, and 1—in that order. Y is supplemented with one additional value, making its values 6 and 2—again, in that order. Because the first instruction is to include the page included.jsp, we must go there first. The *param* EL implicit object is used to display

the value of X. *param* retrieves the first available value, so we have our first output, 4. This technique is repeated for Y, so the next output is 6. Now a scriptlet is used to iterate through all of the values of parameter X. The method `request.getParameterValues()` will respect the correct order, so the next output is 451 (the three values of X in succession). Now we return back to params.jsp. Any parameter values added within the body of the `<jsp:include>` action are lost. So X has only a single value of 1, and Y a single value of 2. These are displayed—first 1 (from X with the same EL technique we saw before), then 2 (from Y, retrieved with a Java language expression using the `ServletRequest.getParameter()` method).
☒ **A**, **B**, **C**, **D**, **F**, and **G** are incorrect, according to the reasoning in the correct answer.

8. ☑ **B**, **C**, and **D** are the correct answers. **B** is correct: You can supply an expression for the value of the page attribute of the include standard action, and thereby soft-code your choice of page. **C** is correct, though it's not absolutely clear-cut (hence "*may* be more efficient"). The `include` directive probably involves harder work at translation time. But unlike the standard action, everything that's needed is then there in the same servlet. The `<jsp:include>` standard action will involve a request-time trip to the included file, translating this if not translated already, and returning the response for inclusion in the including servlet. **D** is correct: By including a `<jsp:param>` standard action in the body of a `<jsp:include>`, you can augment the values of existing request parameters.
☒ **A** is incorrect—it's the `<jsp:include>` standard action that is best for including pages that change frequently, not the `include` directive. You're guaranteed with the `<jsp:include>` standard action that the latest version of the included page will be processed; the `include` directive doesn't have the same guarantee in the JSP spec. Even if your JSP container provides that guarantee, there will be more to translate (both including and included pages have to be amalgamated and translated with the `include` directive; whereas only the included page has to be revamped when using the `<jsp:include>` standard action). **E** is incorrect. It's not obvious whether the include directive or the `<jsp:include>` standard action will win out at translation time. Let's say page P includes page Q. With the `include` directive, Q must be merged into P, and then there is one big servlet to translate and compile. With the `<jsp:include>` standard action, P and Q stay separate and are translated and compiled into two separate servlets. Who can say which will be processed more quickly? So I deem this to be an unhelpful statement. **F** is out and out incorrect—an `include` directive can't be influenced by page logic (unlike a `<jsp:include>` standard action). It will be processed at translation time come what may (unless it's commented out!).

9. ☑ **F** is the correct answer. A blank page is output, and nothing is output to the server console. The crucial thing to recognize is that a `<jsp:forward>` standard action effectively causes the rest of the page logic to be bypassed (do not pass go; do not collect $200/£200 . . .).

☒ A is incorrect—there's nothing to cause a page error (including forwarding to a .jsp file containing nothing at all—that's still legal). **B** is incorrect—there's nothing to cause a run-time error either. **C** is incorrect and shows a misunderstanding of forwarding: The use of forward negates any page output from the forwarding JSP. **D** is incorrect, though you could be forgiven for thinking otherwise, for a regular servlet behaves differently. The `System.out.println()` statement is an innocent bystander that has nothing to do with JSP page output, after all. However, it is bypassed as explained in the correct answer. **E** is incorrect for a combination of the reasons given for **C** and **D**.

10. ☑ **F** is the correct answer. In fact, this page will not translate because of the malformed end tag for the forward standard action: It should be `</jsp:forward>`. This question uses a number of evil psychological techniques that are not unknown on the real exam. First, it looks almost identical to a previous question (question 7), so you tend to assume the same kind of approach will pay off—and waste time trying to work out what the code is actually doing. Secondly, there is a decoy red herring. Because the forwarded-to page is called included.jsp, a casual glance makes you think this is a question about including. Then you spot this obvious mistake and think "Aha! This is really a question about forwarding!"—when really it's a syntax question all along. If there's a moral (and I'm not sure there is), then I suppose it's to be on the alert for syntax errors first and foremost. You have to become the translation phase!

    ☒ **A**, **B**, **C**, **D**, and **E** are all incorrect because the syntax error mentioned prevents translation, so there's no output at all. For what it's worth, if the syntax error were corrected, **B** would be the correct answer.

JSPs in XML

11. ☑ **E** is the correct answer. There will be a translation error at line 13. The "<" sign is illegal XML syntax within the `<jsp:scriptlet>` tag (or indeed, in any tag), for to the parser it looks like another tag beginning before the present one has ended. You have to "escape" the sign in some way—for example, by writing `<`.

    ☒ **A** is incorrect because the `<html>` tag is correctly formed, including the XML namespace component (remember—this can appear in any tag you want). **B** is incorrect because the page directive is correctly formed, with a legal MIME value. **C** is incorrect because a Java method signature within a `<jsp:declaration>` is normal practice. **D** is incorrect because access to implicit variables like `out` is still perfectly OK, and there's nothing wrong with the Java syntax (and nothing to offend XML syntax). **F** and **G** are incorrect—since there is a translation error, the page won't produce a run-time error, let alone display successfully.

12. ☑ **C** and **E** are the correct answers. Both produce output: **C** produces valid XML output with an XML declaration, and **E** produces valid non-XML output without an XML declaration.

☒ **A** is incorrect because when using XML syntax, you have to supply a namespace for any tags that you use (unlike JSP Syntax, where standard actions are found even without a `taglib` directive). **B** is incorrect because although output is produced, it's identified as XML output (has an XML declaration)—but doesn't constitute valid XML (because the output, "Question12," isn't surrounded by any tags. That's solved by the inclusion of the <data> tag in correct answer **C**. **D** doesn't work because it's invalid JSP source in XML terms: There are two top-level tags. You can have only one top-level tag in an XML document, including JSP page source—so the page doesn't translate (that's a problem solved by the `<jsp:root>` element in correct answer **E**).

13. ☑ **B** and **D**. **B** is correct—provided that web.xml is at version 2.4, a file with a .jspx extension will be recognized as a JSP document. **D** is also correct—`<jsp:root>` at the root element of your source constitutes a JSP document, even at prior levels of web.xml.
☒ **A** is incorrect, though very nearly correct: `<is-xml>` is a correct element, but it's a subelement of `<jsp-property-group>`, which is in turn a subelement of `<jsp-config>`. **C** is incorrect—although you can use XML files directly as JSP page source, an .xml suffix is insufficient to identify them as XML JSP page source to the container. **E** is incorrect—just using a level 2.4 deployment descriptor won't do anything by itself toward interpretation of your JSP page sources as JSP documents. And finally, **F** is incorrect—you can write a syntactically correct JSP page in XML syntax and still have it treated as JSP syntax (rather than as a JSP document). The mere presence of XML in the source is not enough.

14. ☑ **D** is the correct answer. This is not an easy question! The output is 1.6666666666666665 from this piece of code, and none of the other JSP fragments give that result. Owing to precedence rules, the division in the expression (2/3) is done first. EL division is double-based (not integer-based), hence the imprecise double answer. This is added to 1, to give the answer shown.
☒ **A**, **B**, **C**, and **E** are incorrect answers, for all pair up: **A** and **B** produce identical output, and so do **C** and **E**. **A** and **B** both output 1, for different reasons. In **A**, precedence dictates that the division is done first. This is Java language division, so the result of 2/3 is 0. Adding this to 1 therefore gives 1. The parentheses force a different calculation in **B**: (1 + 2)/3. The result of this is also 1. **C** and **E** both output 1.0. **C** does the same calculation—(1 + 2)/3. This is then concatenated with ".0" to give an end result of 1.0. In **E** the EL expression performs effectively the same calculation, derived from the Integer page attributes: (1 + 2)/3. However, for division, EL arithmetic coerces the operands to Doubles. The result is a Double literal (in Java terms), expressed with a .0 on the end even though this isn't required.

15. ☑ **E** is the correct answer. The HTML `<img>` element is broken up to accommodate the expression that soft-codes the images to display. The broken pieces are incorrect XML, so they have to be treated as character data and accordingly have to be wrapped up in XML's

intimidating CDATA syntax. However, that leaves the two pieces of character data unenclosed by tags, making the JSP page source illegal XML. Under these circumstances, you use the `<jsp:text>` element, which satisfies this requirement and does nothing else. A bland but useful tag.
☒ **A** is incorrect—`<jsp:param>` is a standard action for enclosing in `<jsp:forward>` and `<jsp:include>`. **B** is incorrect—there is a tag called `<jsp:element>`, but it's for soft-coding XML elements to include in the output, and won't do here. **C** is incorrect, for `<jsp:img>` is made up. Finally, **D** is incorrect—`<jsp:output>` is a tag that exists, but for adjusting the output type of the document produced by the JSP, so it has no role to play in solving the problem posed here.

Expression Language

16. ☑ **F** is the correct answer. The local counter variable, *j*, is not visible inside the code that evaluates the expression. The expression evaluation code will try to find an attribute called "j" using `PageContext.findAttribute("j")`. Because *j* won't be there, the expression returns nothing at all, so only the template text appears.
☒ **A**, **B**, **C**, **D**, and **E** are incorrect according to the reasoning for the correct answer.

17. ☑ **B** and **C** are the correct answers—*param* is used to get hold of the first value for a named request parameter, and *paramValues* to get hold of all the values for a named request parameter.
☒ **A**, **E**, and **F** are incorrect—although *page*, *request*, and *session* are implicit variables in Java language scriptlets and expressions, they don't work directly inside expressions. Instead, use `pageContext.page`, `pageContext.request`, and `pageContext.session`. **D** is incorrect, but not by much: use *initParam* (no "s") to get hold of a named context initialization parameter. And **G** is incorrect—there's an *applicationScope* implicit variable, but not a *contextScope*.

18. ☑ **C** is the correct answer. The implicit variable *pageContext* represents a PageContext object. This has a `getServletConfig()` method to return the ServletConfig object associated with the PageContext. ServletConfig, in turn, has a `getServletName()` method to return the servlet name. To turn this into EL syntax, you take each method name and strip off the "get" and the terminating parentheses. What you're left with is a bean property name—as long as you turn the first capital letter now into lowercase. Put the dot operators between each, and you get `${pageContext.servletconfig.servletName}`, which works.
☒ **A** is incorrect—there is no config property for PageContext (it's `servletConfig`), and a method name (`getServletName`) even without the parentheses won't work. **B** is incorrect, though closer: `config` just has to change to `servletConfig`. **D** has one of the faults of **A**, whereas **E** is wrong altogether because it uses Java language syntax. By using correct method names, though, **E** does furnish a clue toward the correct property names when using EL syntax.

19. ☑ **B** and **C** are the correct answers. The implicit variables ending in "scope" are the ones to go for when trying to retrieve attributes. In this example, it doesn't matter if the parentheses are used to group the arguments in the expression (as in **C**)—precedence takes care of the result (as in **B**).
☒ **A**, **D**, **E**, and **F** are incorrect. **A** and **D** are incorrect because although *pageContext* is an EL implicit variable, you can't use it like this to access attributes in any scope. **E** and **F** are incorrect because they use implicit variable names that are legal in Java language scripting, but not in EL.

20. ☑ **A** matches with **9** (the `xmlns:jsp` announces a namespace declaration); **B** matches with **6** (the correct answer is `directive.page`—not `page.directive`!); **C** and **D** match with **1** (must be the beginning and end of a `<jsp:declaration>`, for the content is an entire Java method); **E** and **F** match with **3** (beginning and end of a `<jsp:scriptlet>`); **G** and **H** match with **11** (`cookie` is the implicit variable name; there are some misleading alternatives); **I** matches with **17** (`pageScope` is clearly where the "luckyNo" attribute is stored); and **J** matches with **13** ("luckyNo"—needs to be a String to return the named attribute value with square bracket syntax—dot syntax would probably be better here, as in `${pageScope.luckyNo}`).
☒ No other combinations will work.

LAB ANSWER

Deploy the WAR file from the CD called lab07.war, in the /sourcecode/chapter07 directory. This contains a sample solution. Once the WAR file is deployed, you can call the top-level JSP document, master.jspx, using a URL such as

```
http://localhost:8080/lab07/master.jspx
```

The resulting solution should look as it did in Exercise 6-3, and is shown in the following illustration.

8

JSP Tag Libraries

CERTIFICATION OBJECTIVES

- Tag Libraries
- JSTL
- EL Functions
- The "Classic" Custom Tag Event Model
- ✓ Two-Minute Drill
- Q&A Self Test

In the previous two JSP chapters, you got to use the low-level facilities in the technology. In this and the next chapter, you'll meet some higher-level tools and techniques, and finally get to reduce Java language syntax in your JSP page source to little or none.

First, we'll look at how to use tag libraries. You'll learn how to use tags that are not delivered with the JSP container but that you either create yourself or obtain from elsewhere. You'll revisit the deployment descriptor to see the role it plays in supporting your own and third-party tag libraries.

In this chapter you'll also learn all about a "custom" tag library now provided as "standard"—if that's not too much of a contradiction: This is the Java Standard Tag Language core library. This supplies the missing logic elements you need in order to use EL without Java language syntax.

After that, we move back to Expression Language. You'll see how EL itself is underpinned by tag technology, and you'll learn how to write your own functions that can be accessed with EL syntax on a JSP page. You'll also see how these EL functions use definitions in tag libraries.

Finally in the chapter, you'll get to write your own custom tags—a step beyond making use of an existing tag library. This is one of the most challenging of the exam objectives but also one of the most rewarding: You'll see how to harness the full power of Java while keeping your JSP pages syntactically simple and elegant.

CERTIFICATION OBJECTIVE

Tag Libraries (Exam Objectives 9.1, 9.2, and 6.6)

For a custom tag library or a library of Tag Files, create the "taglib" directive for a JSP page.

Given a design goal, create the custom tag structure in a JSP page to support that goal.

Configure the deployment descriptor to declare one or more tag libraries, deactivate the evaluation language, and deactivate the scripting language.

The three exam objectives here take us some little way into the world of custom tags. In this section of the chapter, you'll get to use some existing custom tags within JSP page source. Later exam objectives and sections address how to write a custom tag from scratch.

You'll also begin to appreciate the benefits of tags. The JSP pages we look at here are scriptless and so are much more maintainable. Java code maintenance is pushed back to where it belongs—into standard Java classes.

The Custom Tag Development Process

There are four essential steps to writing a custom tag for use in your JavaServer Pages:

1. Writing a Java class called a tag handler
2. Defining the tag within a tag library definition (TLD) file
3. Providing details of where to find the TLD file in the deployment descriptor, web.xml
4. Referencing the TLD file in your JSP page source and using the tags from it

You can see from this process that there are four "artifacts" involved with a custom tag: a Java class file, a TLD file, web.xml, and the JSP page itself. The relationship among these four is shown in Figure 8-1.

We're actually going to concentrate on steps 2, 3, and 4 in this section of the chapter—not the writing of a custom tag, but merely using one. Writing the tag handler code (step 1) comes in the last part of this chapter. As an example, we'll take a simple tag that solves (or at least masks) one of the annoyances of Expression Language arithmetic with double values.

Hunting the Tag

To illustrate the process of how the JSP container finds the tag, we'll use a custom tag for rounding a figure to an arbitrary number of decimal places. The process is shown in overview in Figure 8-1.

You'll recall from Chapter 7 that double arithmetic on most computers, contrary to most people's expectations, is not an exact science. Small errors creep in because of the nature of binary storage of double primitives. So the expression ${9.21 / 3} displays 3.0700000000000003 instead of the exact result you might expect—3.07. The solution—at least for display purposes—is to round the resulting figure to a convenient number of decimal places. However, EL doesn't have any kind of syntax to handle formatting. Instead, we'll pass the responsibility for this on to a custom tag.

FIGURE 8-1 Tag Building Blocks

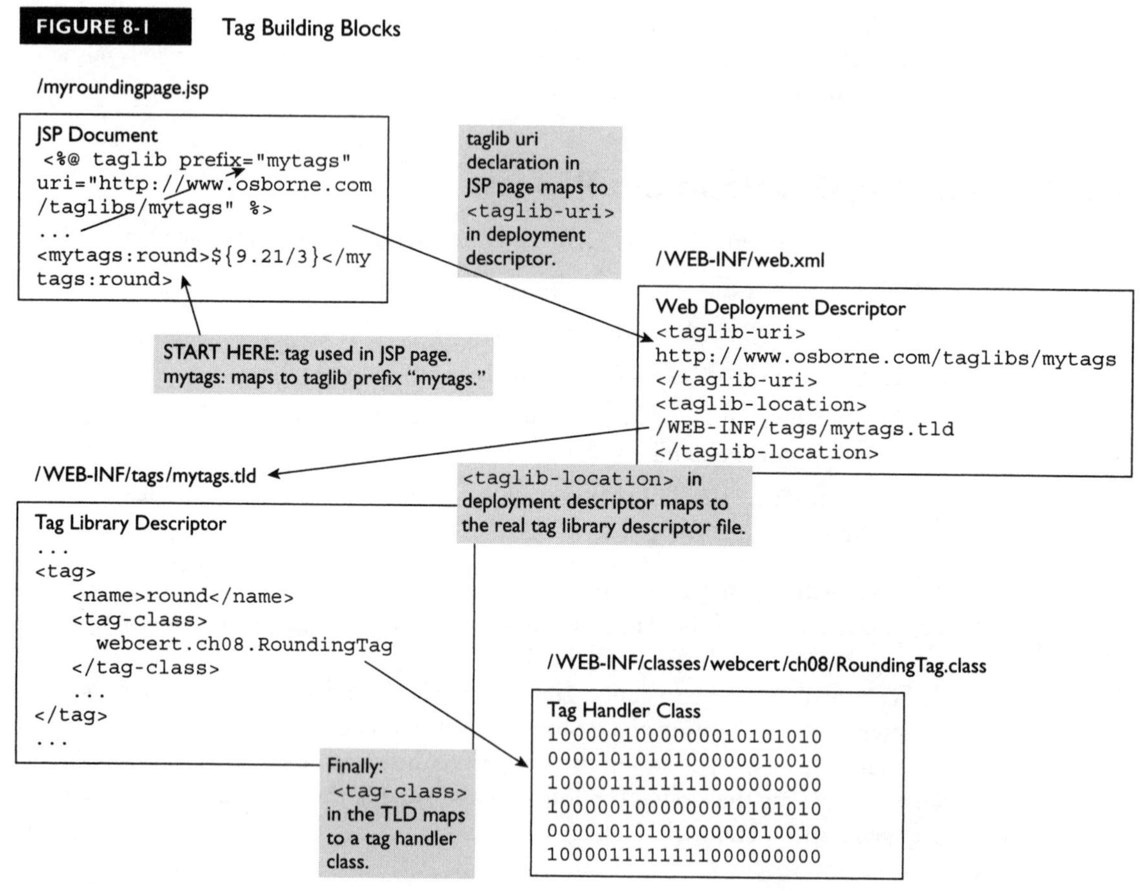

Here's a complete JSP page in traditional syntax that uses a rounding tag:

```
01 <html>
02   <%@ taglib prefix="mytags" uri="http://www.osborne.com/taglibs/mytags" %>
03   <head><title>Rounding Example: JSP syntax</title></head><body>
04   <h1>Round EL Calculation To 2 Decimal Places</h1>
05   <p>EL calculation without rounding:${9.21 / 3}</p>
06   <p>EL calculation with rounding:
07      <mytags:round decimalPlaces="2">${9.21 / 3}</mytags:round></p>
08 </body></html>
```

You can see the tag on line 7. It looks just like a JSP standard action. The element is called `mytags:round`, and it consists of an opening and closing tag, with a body.

The body contains the EL expression we've just been discussing—`${9.21 / 3}`.The opening tag contains an attribute named **`decimalPlaces`**, set to a value of 2. The functionality is what you might expect—the result of the expression is rounded to two decimal places. This is displayed on the page instead of the "raw" result of the EL calculation.

What are the actual steps involved at run time to produce this result? Behind the scenes, the JSP container interacts with the real Java class associated with the tag, which happens to be called RoundingTag. Here's a high-level sequence of events:

1. The JSP container calculates the EL expression.
2. The JSP container locates an instance of RoundingTag.
3. The JSP container passes information to Rounding Tag—the value of the attribute (2 for decimalPlaces) and the result of the EL calculation.
4. RoundingTag does the necessary math to convert the result to two decimal places.
5. RoundingTag clears out the original EL calculation result from the JSP's output buffer and substitutes the rounded result instead.
6. The JSP container carries on outputting the rest of the page.

At this stage, we're only interested in how the JSP container locates RoundingTag. The process is reasonably straightforward. First of all, as used on the page, the tag has a name and a prefix:

exam watch ***You have complete freedom of choice as to what prefix to use, within legal XML naming conventions. However, all the prefixes used in all the `taglib` directives on a given JSP page (and any of its statically included files) must be unique.***

```
07 <mytags:round ...
```

The prefix (`mytags`) must match the value of a prefix attribute in a `taglib` directive in the JSP page source, which it does:

```
02 <%@ taglib prefix="mytags"
...
```

The `taglib` directive has another attribute, `uri`:

```
02 <%@ taglib prefix="mytags"
uri="http://www.osborne.com/taglibs/mytags" %>
```

The URI doesn't point anywhere! Well, it might—but that's purely incidental to the tag library resolution going on here. The URI should match an entry in the deployment descriptor web.xml, which looks like this:

```
<web-app>
  <jsp-config>
    <taglib>
      <taglib-uri>http://www.osborne.com/taglibs/mytags</taglib-uri>
      <taglib-location>/WEB-INF/tags/mytags.tld</taglib-location>
    </taglib>
  </jsp-config>
</web-app>
```

You've met `<jsp-config>` already—as you can see, it sits under the root element `<web-app>`. One of its subelements is `<taglib>`. `<taglib>` has two subelements of its own. The first—`<taglib-uri>`—has a body value that exactly matches the `uri` quoted in the `taglib` directive. The second subelement, `<taglib-location>`, gives the actual location in the web application where the taglib library descriptor (TLD file) is located. The usual rules apply on the path cited in `<taglib-location>`:

- If the path begins with a slash, it's a path beginning at the context root.
- If the path doesn't begin with a slash, it's a relative path—relative to this file, web.xml—so in other words, always relative to where web.xml is located, which is in the /WEB-INF directory.

INSIDE THE EXAM

One thing that has changed quite a bit since the Servlets 2.3/JSPs 1.2 (and so the last version of the exam) is the section of the deployment descriptor devoted to controlling matters that are tag-library related. It used to be very simple: There was an element under `<web-app>` called `<taglib>`, which had `<taglib-uri>` and `<taglib-location>` subelements. All these elements are retained at level 2.4 of the servlet specification, but they are now housed in a new element called `<jsp-config>`, which comes under the root element `<web-app>`. `<jsp-config>` isn't just about tag libraries, though—it controls many aspects of JSP behavior, some of which we have seen already. The following diagram shows the complete layout of the `<jsp-config>` element.

INSIDE THE EXAM (continued)

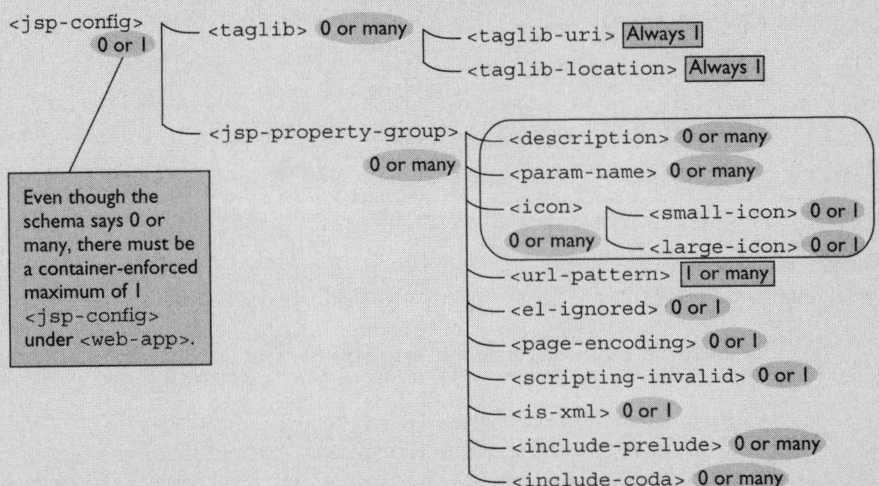

There are several elements whose meaning you don't have to know for the exam—these are grayed out in the illustration. Of the remainder,

- **<taglib>** and its subelements are described elsewhere in this chapter.
- **<is-xml>** is described in the JSP document section of Chapter 7.

These leaves two elements (**<el-ignored>** and **<scripting-invalid>**) that control expression language and Java as a scripting language. Here's an example **<jsp-config>** setting that does both:

```
<jsp-config>
  <jsp-property-group>
    <url-pattern>/*</url-pattern>
    <el-ignored>true</el-ignored>
    <scripting-invalid>true</scripting-invalid>
  </jsp-property-group>
</jsp-config>
```

The **<url-pattern>** element works exactly as the same-named element for servlet declarations. So /* here indicates that all resources in the web application are affected by the settings shown. For other possible URL patterns, see Chapter 2, in

INSIDE THE EXAM (continued)

the "Deployment Descriptor Elements" section.

- <el-ignored> when set to true causes expression language to be unevaluated—so treated as template text. The default (if this element is omitted from <jsp-property-group>) is false.
- <scripting-invalid> when set to true causes a translation time error if JSP scriptlets, expressions, or declarations are used. The default (if this element is omitted) is false.

The only piece of the puzzle left is the TLD file itself, which looks like this:

```
<taglib xmlns="http://java.sun.com/xml/ns/j2ee"
  xmlns:xsi="http://www.w3.org/2001/XMLSchema-instance"
  xsi:schemaLocation="http://java.sun.com/xml/ns/j2ee/web-
jsptaglibrary_2_0.xsd"
  version="2.0">
  <tlib-version>1.0</tlib-version>
  <short-name>My Tag Library</short-name>
  <tag>
    <name>round</name>
    <tag-class>webcert.ch08.examp0801.RoundingTag</tag-class>
    <body-content>scriptless</body-content>
    <attribute>
      <name>decimalPlaces</name>
      <required>false</required>
      <rtexprvalue>true</rtexprvalue>
    </attribute>
  </tag>
</taglib>
```

A few things to point out about this TLD file:

- The root element is <taglib>.
- The first mandatory element under the root is <tlib-version>. This denotes the tag library version number. That's a version number you impose for your own versions of the tag library (it doesn't represent—for example—the JSP version

you are using). So you're not tied to 1.0—when you revise the tag definitions, you might reset this to 1.1, or whatever.

- The next mandatory element is `<short-name>`—every tag library must have one.
- Anything else is optional—though you would expect something to be defined in the file! In this case, there is a single tag defined, which has its own `<tag>` element containing various subelements:
  - `<name>`—this is the name for the tag as used on the JSP page (on line 07—`<mytags:`**`round`**` decimalPlaces="2">`).
  - `<tag-class>`—the fully qualified name of the class implementing the tag functionality—in this case, webcert.ch08.exam0801.RoundingTag. For the tag to run, the class file must be available in one of the usual locations—directly in its package directory under WEB-INF/classes or inside a .jar file in WEB-INF/lib.
  - `<body-content>` dictates what can go in the body of the tag. There are four valid values:
    - `empty`—the body of the tag must be empty (so `<pfx:mytag />` or `<pfx:mytag></pfx:mytag>`).
    - `tagdependent`—the body of the tag contains something that isn't regular JSP source. The tag handler code works out what to do with it. A typical use is to put an SQL statement in the body so that the tag handler takes the statement, runs it, and (perhaps) returns the resulting data to the body of the tag in place of the original SQL statement.
    - `scriptless`—the body of the tag does contain regular JSP source, but nothing involving scripting language. So Java language syntax is forbidden—whether in scriptlets or expressions. EL, though, is absolutely fine in a body specified as scriptless—and will be evaluated.
    - `JSP`—the body of the tag contains any kind of regular JSP source. This is the most permissive value (and, as we'll learn later, not allowed for some kinds of tag handlers, the so-called "simple" kind). Java language syntax is just fine.
  - A tag may have any number of attributes, from zero to many. These are represented by `<attribute>` elements nested within the `<tag>` element. There's one attribute in our example, to represent the number of decimal places. The `<attribute>` element has a number of subelements:

- `<name>`—for the name of the attribute (`decimalPlaces` in the example).
- `<required>`—true if the attribute is mandatory, false otherwise.
- `<rtexprvalue>` (short for "run-time expression value")—true if you can use EL or an expression (`<%= ... %>` or `<jsp:expression>`) to provide the attribute's value at run time, false if the attribute's value must be a literal.

So finally, within the `<tag-class>` element of the `<tag>` element in the `<taglib>` root element of the tag library descriptor file, we find the actual Java that does the work—RoundingTag.class. We'll explore what goes on in that class in the last section of this chapter, and meanwhile just be grateful to have followed the trail from a tag reference in the JSP page to a real piece of code. Look back to Figure 8-1 for a "route map" that summarizes the entire trail.

on the job

Whatever happened to the `<jsp-version>` element, a mandatory element in JSP version 1.2 TLD files, and used to specify JSP version 1.2? The answer is that it has been replaced within the root element, `taglib`, which must now always contain the attribute/value pair `version="2.0"` to reference JSP specification level 2.0.

Other Ways to the TLD

The best way to set up mappings from your JSP pages to the TLDs lodged in your web application is through the web.xml entries we have described. This makes the tag library mapping explicit and obvious to anyone reading the deployment descriptor. However, there are alternatives where nothing is needed in the deployment descriptor—so-called "implicit" mapping entries for tag libraries.

First, you can place files with a .tld extension directly in the /WEB-INF directory or one of its subdirectories. Alternatively, you can package .tld files in a JAR file that is placed in /WEB-INF/lib. The .tld files within the JAR file must have a path that begins /META-INF (such that if you were to unpack the JAR file, the .tld would be located directly in the /META-INF directory or one of its subdirectories).

Apart from this restriction on location, the .tld files must contain the optional `<uri>` element, which must match the `uri` of the `taglib` directive or (if using JSP documents) the namespace value. Figure 8-1 showed the (superior) explicit technique. Figure 8-2 summarizes both the implicit mapping techniques for finding tag library descriptors.

FIGURE 8-2 Routes to Tag Library Descriptors

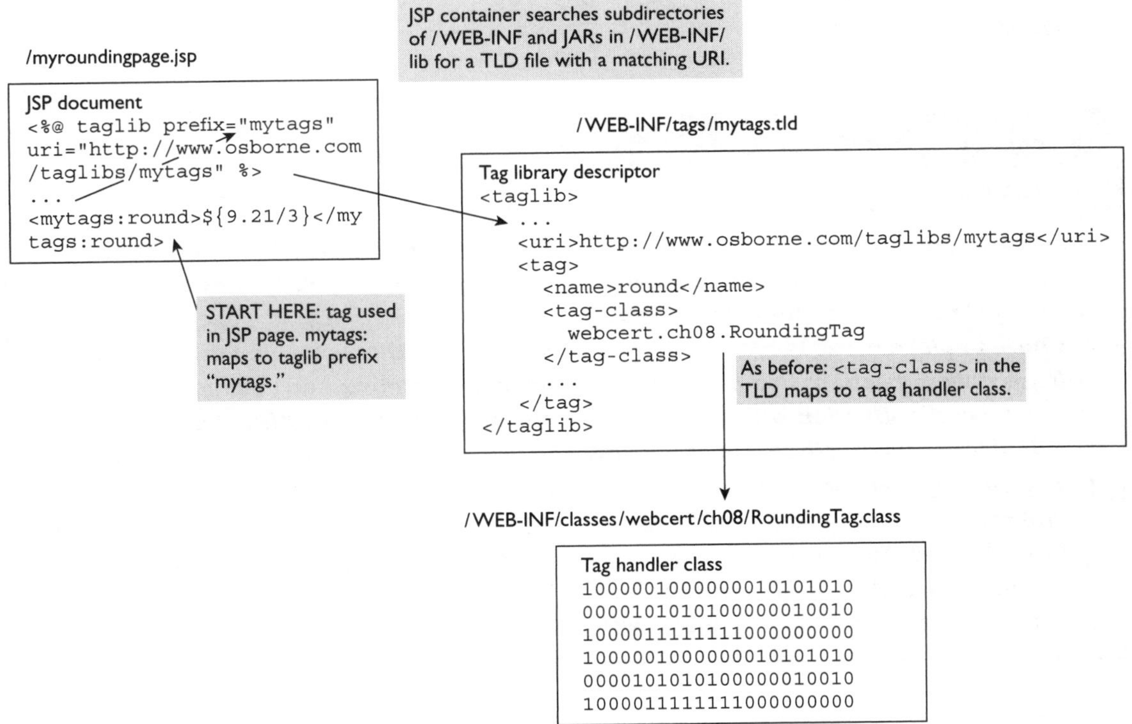

Tag Library Descriptors in JSP Documents

You might recall, though, that the tag directive doesn't have a direct equivalent in JSP document syntax—you have to use namespaces instead. Here's the same JSP page source for the rounding example converted to XML syntax in a JSP document:

```
<html xmlns:mytags="http://www.osborne.com/taglibs/mytags"
      xmlns:jsp="http://java.sun.com/JSP/Page">
  <jsp:output omit-xml-declaration="true" />
  <jsp:directive.page contentType="text/html" />
  <head><title>Rounding Example</title></head>
  <body>
    <h1>Round EL Calculation To 2 Decimal Places</h1>
```

```
08      <p>EL calculation without rounding:${9.21 / 3}</p>
09      <p>EL calculation with rounding:
10        <mytags:round decimalPlaces="2">${9.21 / 3}</mytags:round></p>
11   </body>
12 </html>
```

exam Watch

The tags you make look identical to JSP standard actions. This is no accident, for JSP standard actions derive from tag libraries. Given that, why do you not have to place a `taglib` directive when you use standard actions in a page? Well, it's a bit like the situation with writing standard Java source. When you use a class from java.lang, you don't have to include an import statement in your source; you get that for free. Such is the case with standard actions; the tag library is just understood to be there and available, with a `jsp:` prefix. Therefore, you can't use the `jsp:` prefix yourself for your `taglib` directives, even if you are not using any standard actions in your page. However, don't forget that when you use JSP document syntax, `taglib` directives disappear in favor of XML namespace definitions, as you've seen. In that case, even standard actions must be explicitly referenced with a namespace—in exactly the same way as your own custom tag libraries.

The essential part is on line 01: Instead of the tag library directive, you find a namespace (xmlns). The prefix `mytags` comes after `xmlns`:, and the URI `http://www.osborne.com/taglibs/mytags` is the value for the namespace. This approach is, in fact, exactly the same one taken for declaring a namespace for JSP custom actions on line 02. The actual way you use the custom tag—shown on line 10—hasn't changed at all from the regular JSP (nondocument) source that began this chapter.

exam Watch

There are certain "reserved prefixes" that you can't use for your own custom tag library declarations, whether as directives or namespaces: jsp, jspx, java, javax, servlet, sun, and sunw. They are case sensitive, so watch out for questions that feature prefixes that are not all lowercase, such as Sun or JAVA: These are in fact legal!

EXERCISE 8-1

Tag Libraries

In this exercise you will finish off an incomplete JSP document and deployment descriptor by providing the details required to find and use a tag in an existing tag library—as per the main exam objective for this section. First, you'll install the solution code and make sure that the existing solution runs successfully. The theme is taxation—you enter a gross income figure and some other details required by the taxation office, and get back (through the custom tag) a net income figure. For those of you who hate filing tax returns (I guess I'm speaking to most readers here), grit your teeth and focus on the exam objective!

Install and Run the Solution Code

1. The solution file is in the CD as sourcecode/ch08/ex0801.war. Install this WAR file into Tomcat (or your web application server) in the normal way.
2. Run the code using a URL such as

```
http://localhost:8080/ex0801/income.html
```

3. You should see a page like the one illustrated here:

4. Enter a gross income figure (e.g., 10000), a tax allowance (the amount of the gross income that remains untaxed, e.g., 4500), and a percentage tax rate (e.g., 40). Then press the "Calculate Net Income" button.
5. You should see a page (produced by a JSP document) like the one shown here:

6. This page uses a custom tag to calculate the net income according to the formula: net income = tax allowance + ((gross income – tax allowance) * (100 – tax rate) / 100). If the figures supplied in the HTML form don't make sense or are missing, you should see a message on the page saying "Bad Input Figures." The logic is performed in a Java class called the tag handler—we explain tag handlers later in the chapter, but feel free to look at the source now in /WEB-INF/src/webcert/ch08/ex0801/TaxationTag.java.
7. Check the HTML code for the file /income.html. You're not going to change this in any way—just look to see how this sets up three parameters in a form and submits the result to the JSP document called /taxation.jspx.
8. Open the tag library descriptor file, /WEB-INF/tags/mytags.tld. You can see here that four attributes are defined for the tag.

Prepare Files for Your Own Solution

9. Once you're satisfied that the solution works, stop your server. You're going to edit some files in place where they are deployed on your server.
10. There are "unfinished" versions of the deployment descriptor and the JSP document. Perform the following renames so that the unfinished versions end up having the "real" names:
    - Rename /WEB-INF/web.xml to /WEB-INF/webSolution.xml.
    - Rename /taxation.jspx to /taxationSolution.jspx.

- Rename /WEB-INF/webUnfinished.xml to /WEB-INF/web.xml.
- Rename /taxationUnfinished.jspx to /taxation.jspx.

Complete the Deployment Descriptor

11. Open up web.xml, the deployment descriptor. Edit this to provide a reference to a tag library (if you need to, refer to earlier in the chapter to remind yourself how the XML elements are nested). The tag library location (as you saw in step 8) is /WEB-INF/tags/mytags.tld. Save and close the deployment descriptor.

Complete the JSP Document

12. Open up taxation.jspx. You'll see two clearly marked places where you need to intervene. Put in the namespace details for the tag library, together with an appropriate prefix. Then put in the call to the netincome tag. Three of the attributes—grossIncome, allowance, and taxRate—should be set with EL values from run-time parameters. Remember that the HTML form passes in these parameters, whose names are gross, allowance, and rate respectively. Hard-code the value for the fourth—currency—attribute. Any three-character ISO code for currency will be recognized (e.g., GBP, USD, EUR) provided that the relevant locale is recognized by your system. Save and close the JSP document.

Run and Test Your Solution

13. Restart your server, and access income.html as before (step 2). Of course, because of the renaming, when you click the submit button now, your solution page will be invoked.
14. If you don't get the desired result, compare your solution with the original solution (now held in files /WEB-INF/webSolution.xml and /taxation Solution.jspx).

CERTIFICATION OBJECTIVE

JSTL (Exam Objective 9.3)

Given a design goal, use an appropriate JSP Standard Tag Library (JSTL v1.1) tag from the "core" tag library.

We are finally ready to meet the JSP Standard Tag Library. This adds a host of facilities that are otherwise only available through Java language scripting. These facilities are entirely available through JSP tag technology—the same technology we have been exploring in this chapter. So what makes the JSTL special?

It's more the underlying philosophy. When custom tags became available, everybody started building tag libraries. Frameworks of tag libraries became available to simplify the application construction—mostly open source and free. You could guarantee that each of these frameworks would have some custom tag or other devoted to common tasks. Take the example of iterating through each item in a loop. One framework might have a tag called "iterate," while another might have one called "loop."

One such framework came out of the Jakarta Apache taglib project, which attempted to define a common standard and implementation for a universally useful set of tag libraries. These contain functionality that is common to practically every JSP development: from basic control flow (iteration, conditions) to XML parsing to database access. Such was the popularity of these libraries that their tag definitions have been officially adopted as part of the JavaServer Page specification by Sun as the JavaServer Page Standard Tag Library—or JSTL.

You'll need an implementation. JSP containers (such as Tomcat) don't necessarily come with one already supplied. Fortunately, it's easy and free to acquire an implementation, which is also easy to install into most containers.

JSTL

The JSTL comprises five tag libraries:

- **core**: custom actions that do the programming "grunt work"—such as conditions and loops—and also fundamental JSP tasks such as setting attributes, writing output, and redirecting to other pages and resources
- **xml**: custom actions that alleviate much of the work in reading and writing XML files
- **sql**: custom actions dedicated to database manipulation
- **fmt**: custom actions for formatting dates and numbers, and for internationalization of text
- **function**: a set of standardized EL functions.

For the exam, you are required to know only about the core library. This is fortunate, for there are sixteen or so custom actions in the core library alone, and these form a mini tag language in their own right. Of course, you're likely to want to explore the other three libraries because they are liable to prove useful on your projects—but that's the last on them from this chapter. (Phil Hanna surveys all four libraries in his book *JSP 2.0* [McGraw-Hill Osborne].)

You can download the specification for JSTL from the Sun web site—a very useful resource that goes beyond its brief as a specification, and is almost a developer manual. What you don't get from Sun is an implementation of the tags themselves, and this is *essential for the rest of the work in this book*! Do take the following steps—either right now or just before you undertake the next exercise:

1. To get hold of the standard reference implementation, visit:

   `http://jakarta.apache.org/taglibs/binarydist.html.`

2. Ensure that you download JSTL 1.1, which goes with JSP version 2.0—this is the appropriate level for the exam.
3. Extract the downloaded JSTL zip or tar file anywhere you like.
4. Make the crucial files from the extracted distribution available to your server installation. For Tomcat, I take the following step: Copy standard.jar and jstl.jar to `<TOMCAT INSTALLATION>/common/lib`.
5. After a server restart, the JSTL features should be available to you.

on the job

There is a previous and still supported standard for JSTL, which is 1.0. This goes with JSP level 1.2. Quite a few of the details—including, for example, the URIs to access the standard tag libraries—are different in the earlier implementation. Note that this book talks only about the 1.1 version of JSTL, which goes with JSP level 2.0. The exam doesn't cover the earlier version at all.

To make use of the core tag library in your own JSP pages, you must include a `taglib` directive (or namespace reference) containing the right URI:

```
http://java.sun.com/jsp/jstl/core
```

You can choose whichever prefix you like to use with these tags, although popular convention suggests the use of "c." So a complete `taglib` directive to include the core JSTL library might look like this:

```
<%@ taglib prefix="c" uri="http://java.sun.com/jsp/jstl/core" %>
```

Groupings of Actions

In all, there are fourteen actions contained in the JSTL core library. The JSTL specification splits these up into four groups: General Purpose actions, Conditional actions, Iterator actions, and URL-Related actions. I keep these same headings in the explanations that follow. This table briefly summarizes the actions in each group.

Group	Actions	Purpose

General Purpose	`<c:out>`
	`<c:set>`
	`<c:remove>`
	`<c:catch>`
		Manipulating attributes, controlling output to the JSPWriter, catching exceptions

Conditional	`<c:if>`
	`<c:choose>`
	`<c:when>`
	`<c:otherwise>`
		Control flow (branching)

Iteration	`<c:forEach>` `<c:forTokens>`	Control flow (looping)

URL-Related	`<c:import>`
	`<c:url>`
	`<c:redirect>`
	`<c:param>`
		Use of other resources

General Purpose Actions

There are four "general purpose" actions in the core library. These are for setting (and removing) attribute values in any scope, writing output, and catching exceptions.

<c:out> This action is used for writing expressions and template text to page output. You may well ask why you might need such a tag—after all, can't you include expressions and template text directly in your JSP page source? The answer is that you can, and for most purposes this tag is "surplus." However, `<c:out>` has a couple of neat, specialized features.

The first is the provision of a default value if the main value expression evaluates to **null**. Here's how it looks:

```
<c:out value=${user.name} default="User name not recognized" />
```

If the name property of the user attribute has a value, that value is displayed. If the name property evaluates to **null**, then the text "User name not recognized" will be displayed instead. As an alternative, the default value can be placed in the body of `<c:out>`. The result is the same, and with rejigged syntax, here's the alternative form for the previous example:

```
<c:out value=${user.name}>User name not recognized</c:out>
```

The second feature is the ability to escape XML-unfriendly characters, such as < and >. Entities are substituted instead, such as `<` and `>`. Whatever characters go to output—whether in the value or the default value—they are escaped in this way. This feature is enabled by default but can be invoked explicitly:

```
<c:out value=${xmlUnfriendlyAttribute} escapeXml="true" />
```

Or switched off:

```
<c:out value=${xmlUnfriendlyAttribute} escapeXml="false" />
```

The following table shows the list of characters that are converted through the XML-escaping facility.

Character	Converted To
<	<
>	>
&	&
'	'
"	"

on the job

It can be limiting to have the value you want to display with `<c:out>` constrained to an attribute. It's fine for simple expressions (`<c:out value=${user.name} />`) but no use if you want the value to contain, say, other tags. Under those circumstances, you can use the body of `<c:out>` to set up

a default value, using tags or anything else you want. Then force the default value to display by placing a constant of* null *for the value. Here's an example:

```
<c:out value="${null}" escapeXml="true">
  <jsp:include page="xmlUnfriendly.jsp" />
</c:out>
```

Since the value attribute contains the null literal expressed in EL, the default value (contained in the body) is processed. In the body is a* <jsp:include> *standard action to include a JSP file. Because* escapeXml *is set to "true," the page will be incorporated, and any XML-unfriendly characters implied in the included file's name will be turned into entities.

<c:set> This is used for setting attributes in any scope. This tag is a convenient and lightweight alternative to the standard action combination of <jsp:useBean> and <jsp:getProperty>. Here's an example:

```
01 <c:set value="9.21" var="numerator" />
02 <c:set value="3" var="denominator" />
03 <c:set value="${numerator/denominator}" var="calculationResult" />
04 ${calculationResult}
```

The var attribute is used to name a variable, and the value attribute sets a value for that variable. The variable becomes an attribute in page scope by default. So in the example, at line 01 a page attribute called numerator is set with a literal floating point decimal value of 9.21, and on line 02 another called denominator with a literal integer value of 3. On line 03, <c:set> is used to set another variable called calculationResult. This time, an EL expression is used to set the value instead of a literal:

```
value="${numerator/denominator}"
```

Finally, an expression is used to display the value of the calculationResult page attribute—just to show that something really happened. If you try out the code, you should find that the output is 3.0700000000000003.

As an alternative to using the value attribute, you can place the value in the body of the tag. Here's an alternative to line 03 in the example:

```
<c:set var="calculationResult">${numerator/denominator}</c:set>
```

If you want to set up attributes in different scopes, `<c:set>` has a `scope` attribute for the purpose—taking the expected values of page, request, session, and application. Here is how `calculationResult` can be put into session scope:

```
<c:set var="calculationResult"
scope="session">${numerator/denominator}</c:set>
```

You are not restricted to using attributes in some scope. Any available object can be the object of a `<c:set>` action, provided that the object can be construed as a Java Bean. An alternative syntax is used. As an example, consider that HttpSession has a maxInactiveInterval property—by virtue of having `set` and `getMaxInactiveInterval()` methods. You can set this property using the following `<c:set>` syntax:

```
<c:set value="28" target="${pageContext.session}"
      property="maxInactiveInterval" />
```

The `target` attribute specifies the bean under consideration—here, session is available in EL through the implicit variable `pageContext`. The `property` attribute specifies the name of the property, maxInactiveInterval. The `value` attribute (which we've seen before) specifies the value for the property—in this case, 28 (seconds). As before, the body of `<c:set>` can be used to specify the value, instead of using the `value` attribute:

```
<c:set target="${pageContext.session}"
      property="maxInactiveInterval">28</c:set>
```

exam watch

It's very important to note which tag attributes are allowed to take expressions (and so be evaluated dynamically), and which are not. There are tables at the end of each of the four groupings of actions (general purpose, conditional, iterator, URL-related) that summarize all the attributes for all the core tags and show which ones allow expressions.

<c:remove> This is the inverse of `<c:set>`, and it can be used to remove a scoped attribute. The action has only two attributes—`var` to name the variable, and the optional `scope` to specify the scope. As always, `page` is the default when `scope` is not specified. So to remove a variable, a statement such as

```
<c:remove var="calculationResult" />
```

may be all that's required, or one such as

```
<c:remove var="calculationResult" scope="session" />
```

when it is necessary to specify the scope.

<c:catch> This action allows you to catch an error in your page, without it propagating to (for example) an error page defined in web.xml.

At first sight, it appears like a catch block in Java, but it's more like a try/catch rolled into one, where the catch does nothing: All errors are suppressed. If you look at the generated servlet code after inserting a `<c:catch>` action, you'll see that the exception caught is a java.lang. Throwable—right at the top of the hierarchy. So you should use `<c:catch>` only for minor elements of your JSP page whose successful execution really doesn't matter.

The `<c:catch>` action relates only to anything that goes on in its body. So it suppresses a Java language ArithmeticException in the following example:

```
<c:catch>
  <jsp:scriptlet>int zero = 0; out.write(3/zero);</jsp:scriptlet>
</c:catch>
```

You can specify a named, page-scope attribute to represent the exception, and access this after the `<c:catch>` block. You use the `var` attribute to do this (there is no scope attribute; the exception dies with the page). So, adapting the example above,

```
<c:catch var="numException">
  <jsp:scriptlet>int zero = 0; out.write(3/zero);</jsp:scriptlet>
</c:catch>
<p>If there was an exception, the message is: ${numException.message}</p>
```

Attribute Name	Run-time Expression Allowed?	Mandatory?	Default Value	Type
<c:out>				
value	Yes	Yes	None	Object
escapeXml	Yes	No	True	boolean
default	Yes	No	Empty String	Object
<c:set>				
value	Yes	No	None	Object
var	No	No	None	String
scope	No	No	Page	String
target	Yes	No	None	Object
property	Yes	No	None	String
<c:remove>				
var	No	Yes	None	String
scope	No	No	Page	String
<c:catch>				
var	No	No	None	String

Conditional Actions

JSTL is provided with conditional actions, which give you the branching aspects of a programming language. As always, the moral is to keep the logic simple! These actions are designed to ease complexity, not to let you replicate full-blown Java syntax in JSTL.

First, we'll consider the `<c:if>` action, which tests a condition and executes its body when this condition is true. Then we'll consider the trio of actions `<c:choose>`, `<c:when>`, and `<c:otherwise>`, which work in consort in a way not dissimilar from the Java language switch statement.

<c:if> This action evaluates its body content if a condition is true. The condition is expressed in EL as the value for the test attribute. The following example shows how the syntax works:

```
<c:if test="${user.loyaltyPoints gt 1000}">
  <p>Welcome to one of our best customers!</p>
</c:if>
```

The `<c:if>` action doesn't have to have a body, which at first may seem pointless. However, you can store the result of the test in a scoped variable, thanks to the `var` and `scope` attributes. There is some point to this if you want to use the result of a test later, without repeating the test. This may make even more sense in the context of EL functions that we examine later in this chapter but that we'll introduce very briefly here. An EL function is a Java method, called with EL syntax. Let's look at an example:

```
<c:if test="${mytags:checkRole(user, 'Manager')}"
var="userInManagerRole" scope="session" />
```

The test uses an EL function called checkRole, which receives two parameters—a user name and a role name, one an attribute called "user," the other a String literal "Manager." The checkRole function returns a **boolean** result. If the function returns **true**, the intent is that the user is allowed to see or do things within the application that are off-limits to users who are not within the "Manager" role. The act of checking the role might be quite expensive—perhaps involving a secure network call to another machine hosting a user-role registry. But the result is held in a session attribute called "userInManagerRole," whose value is a java.lang.Boolean. So anywhere else within this session, the application can conditionally check this variable instead of reperforming the function. The following test makes use of this variable, and returns sensitive information only if `userInManagerRole` evaluates to true.

```
<c:if test="${userInManagerRole}">Salary field: $1,234,567</c:if>
```

<c:choose> In combination with `<c:when>` and `<c:otherwise>`, this action works something like a Java **switch** statement. However, these three tags behave a little differently and more flexibly than the Java equivalent.

The structure is this: The `<c:choose>` action is just a container for two possible other actions—`<c:when>` and `<c:otherwise>`. Between the opening and closing tags for `<c:choose>`, you can include only white space (any amount) or these two actions. The rules on including `<c:when>` and `<c:otherwise>` are as follows:

- `<c:when>`: there *must* be at least one occurrence.
- `<c:otherwise>`: optional—but if included, there cannot be *more than* one occurrence.

As we'll see, `<c:when>` executes a test—like `<c:if>`. Within the body of the `<c:choose>` each `<c:when>` test is performed in strict order of appearance. If a test is **false**, the body of `<c:when>` is ignored—again, just like `<c:if>`. If a test is **true**, the body of that `<c:when>` action is executed. *Anything* that follows within the `<c:choose>` action—either `<c:when>` actions or the `<c:otherwise>` action—will be ignored once a true test has triggered (and this is where the similarity to the Java switch action ends in that you use **break** statements to prevent execution of the statements within other cases or the **default** block). If *none* of the `<c:when>` tests evaluate to true, then and only then will the body of `<c:otherwise>` be executed.

<c:when> This has only a single, mandatory attribute: `test`. The test expression must evaluate to a boolean **true** for the body to be executed. The test expression won't break if the result evaluates to non-boolean; instead, the expression will be treated as equivalent to a boolean **false**.

<c:otherwise> This has no attributes. The body will be executed only when the preceding `<c:when>` actions within the enclosing `<c:choose>` all evaluate to **false**. Note that `<c:otherwise>` must be the last action in the `<c:choose>` group, coming after the final `<c:when>` action.

Here's a complete example that shows the trio of actions together:

```
<c:choose>
  <c:when test="${userInDeveloperRole}">
    Welcome, fellow developer.
  </c:when>
  <c:when test="${userInManagerRole}">
    You are a manager! I'll take the next bit slowly for you.
  </c:when>
  <c:otherwise>
    Hmm—I'm not sure what you are. Should I be talking to you?
  </c:otherwise>
</c:choose>
```

The example assumes the preexistence of a couple of attributes, `userInDeveloper Role` and `userInManagerRole`. Actually, it doesn't matter if these attributes don't exist, but the test they appear in will be treated as evaluating to **false**. Should the first `<c:when>` test prove true (because the attribute `userInDeveloperRole` has the value true), then the "welcome" text will display. If not, the next `<c:when>` test will be performed. If `userInManagerRole` has a value of true, the associated text for that is displayed. If that test evaluates to false, then the catchall text within the body of the `<c:otherwise>` action will be displayed. If a user is both a developer and a manager, note that only the text in the first `<c:when>` will be displayed: Processing resumes at the end of the `<c:choose>` block after a positive test.

Attribute Name	Run-time Expression Allowed?	Mandatory?	Default Value	Type
<c:if>				
test	Yes	Yes	None	boolean
var	No	No	None	String
scope	No	No	Page	String
<c:choose>				
No attributes. Body may contain only one or more `<c:when>` actions, and zero or one `<c:otherwise>` action at the end of the block.				
<c:when>				
test	Yes	Yes	None	boolean
<c:otherwise>				
No attributes				

Iterator Actions

There are only two iterator actions—and less is better when it comes to exam preparation! They are also very similar: The `<c:forEach>` action is a general-purpose construct for looping, and `<c:forTokens>` has nearly the same syntax, but is specialized for splitting up Strings in the same way as the Java StringTokenizer class. There is bad news, however: These actions have an impressive number of attributes and, consequently, a few variant syntaxes. A few examples should set us right on these.

<c:forEach> This has two main uses: to iterate over a collection of objects (like a Java language "while" loop working with an Iterator or Enumeration), or to iterate a fixed number of times (like a Java language standard "for" loop). EL helpfully provides some ready-made implicit variables that are collections of objects—for example, `${headerValues}`, which represents the collection of values for request headers. Here is a `<c:forEach>` loop that displays these values in an HTML table:

```
<table border="1">
<c:forEach var="hdr" items="${headerValues}">
  <tr><td>${hdr.key}</td><td>${hdr.value[0]}</td></tr>
</c:forEach>
</table>
```

The value for the **items** attribute must contain the collection object to loop around—in this case, a java.util.Map object (**${headerValues}**—see Chapter 7 for a full explanation of this EL implicit object). On each circuit of the loop, an object from this collection is placed in the variable represented by the value for the var attribute: **hdr**. Each object in a Map is a Map.Entry object, with **getKey()** and **getValue()** methods, exposing the two bean-like properties key and value. So the EL syntax **${hdr.key}** has the effect of getting the request header's key value and writing this to the current JspWriter. Map.Entry's **getValue()** method returns an Object—but here some inside knowledge is necessary. We know (from the EL specification) that each Map.Entry value object in the **headerValues** Map is a String array. EL allows the use of Java-language such as array syntax (**${hdr.value[0]}**) to obtain—in this case—the first available value for the named request header.

The **<c:forEach>** action allows many different types for the **items** attribute. These are listed in the following table, together with the corresponding type for the **var** attribute exposed.

Type for items Attribute	Corresponding Type for var Attribute
java.lang.Array (of some type of Object)	The declared type for the Array
java.lang.Array (of primitives)	The wrapper type (Integer, Double, etc.) corresponding with the declared primitive type (**int**, **double**, etc.) for the array
java.util.Collection, java.util .Iterator, java.util.Enumeration	Whatever type of Object is returned from the underlying Collection, Iterator or Enumeration (and remember there is nothing that forces all the Objects in a collection to be of the same type, beyond all being Objects)
java.lang.String	java.lang.String (the String in items is split up into a separate Strings for each comma encountered—like the tokens in StringTokenizer)

You don't have to use **<c:forEach>** with a collection of items. Alternatively, it can be used to perform a set number of iterations—much like a Java **for** loop. This is what happens in the following example:

```
<table border="1">
  <c:set var="num" value="1" />
  <c:forEach begin="1" end="128" step="2">
    <c:set var="num" value="${num + num}" />
    <tr><td>${num}</td></tr>
  </c:forEach>
</table>
```

The JSTL tag `<c:set>` is used to set a variable called *num* with a value of 1. Then the `<c:forEach>` loop begins. The loop is set up to begin at 1 and end at 128, in steps of 2—as indicated by the **`begin`**, **`end`**, and **`step`** attribute values. So the loop counter will initially have a value of 1, then 3, then 5, and so on up to 127. On the next iteration, the counter will have a value of 129, which is greater than the end value, so the loop ends. Within the loop, another `<c:set>` action is used to set the *num* variable to double its present value, and display this within a table cell.

exam watch

The possibilities of `<c:forEach>` go further than space in this book allows to give a complete account. You can combine use of a collection (expressed in the `items` attribute) with the `begin`, `end`, and `step` attributes to pick out particular objects within the collection. You can also define a `varStatus` attribute that exposes information about each iteration—most usefully, a number representing the current round. For complete exam readiness, check the documentation in the JSTL 1.1. specification document.

<c:forTokens> `<c:forTokens>` is a specialized version of the `<c:forEach>` action, designed to perform String tokenization much like the StringTokenizer class does in straight Java language syntax. In fact, `<c:forEach>` will also do String Tokenization when the items attribute is set to a String but it is restricted to observing commas as delimiters only. There's no way to make `<c:forEach>` break up a String on encountering tabs or white space. This is where `<c:forTokens>` comes in. It has mostly identical parameters but differs in two important respects:

- The `items` attribute will accept only a String as a value (not Maps, Collections, etc.).
- An additional attribute, **`delims`**, is used to specify the delimiter to recognize when breaking up the String into tokens.

The following example expands on the first <c:forEach> example we saw a few moments ago.

```
<table border="1">
<c:forEach var="hdr" items="${headerValues}">
  <tr><td>${hdr.key}</td><td>${hdr.value[0]}</td></tr>
  <c:if test="${hdr.key eq 'Accept'}">
    <c:set value="${hdr.value[0]}" var="acceptValues" />
  </c:if>
</c:forEach>
</table>
<table border="1"><tr><th><b>Accept values</b></th></tr>
<c:forTokens items="${acceptValues}" delims="," var="value">
  <tr><td>${value}</td></tr>
</c:forTokens>
</table>
```

The first part of the code is unchanged—a <c:forEach> action is used to iterate through request header values supplied by the EL implicit variable `${headerValues}`. Most request headers have single values, but this is rarely true of the header `Accept`, which lists a range of file (MIME) types that the requesting client will accept back in the HTTP response. The `Accept` header could be represented as multiple request headers, each with an individual value (the request header mechanism allows for this). But more usually, the file types are returned as a comma-delimited list. This is where the <c:forTokens> action comes in handy.

In a change from the original code, a <c:if> action is used to spot when the Accept header is under consideration, and save its values using <c:set> to an EL variable called *acceptValues*:

```
<c:if test="${hdr.key eq ' Accept'}">
  <c:set value="${hdr.value[0]}" var="acceptValues" />
</c:if>
```

This *acceptValues* variable becomes the input to the <c:forTokens> action, as the value for the `items` attribute. Each value within *acceptValues* is recognized as separate from the next because comma is set as the value for the `delims` attribute. The `var` attribute is used to produce the *value* EL variable to display in a table cell on each iteration of the loop:

```
<c:forTokens items="${acceptValues}" delims="," var="value">
  <tr><td>${value}</td></tr>
</c:forTokens>
```

When I run this code in my browser, the result looks like this:

Accept values
image/gif
image/x-xbitmap
image/jpeg
image/pjpeg
application/vnd.ms-excel
application/vnd.ms-powerpoint
application/msword
application/x-shockwave-flash
/

Attribute Name	Run-time Expression Allowed?	Mandatory?	Default Value	Type
`<c:forEach>`				
`var`	No	No	None	String
`items`	Yes	No	None	Object
`varStatus`	No	No	None	String
`begin`	Yes	No	None	int
`end`	Yes	No	None	int
`step`	Yes	No	None	int
`<c:forTokens>`				
`Var`	No	No	None	String
`items`	Yes	Yes	None	String
`delims`	Yes	Yes	None	String
`varStatus`	No	No	None	String
`begin`	Yes	No	None	int
`End`	Yes	No	None	int
`Step`	Yes	No	None	int

URL-Related Actions

The final group of actions we need to consider in the JSTL core library is URL related. You can use these actions to import resources from a given URL, re-encode URLs, redirect to URLs, as well as pass additional request parameters where necessary.

<c:import> This is a souped-up version of `<jsp:include>`. It performs request-time inclusion of other resources. But whereas `<jsp:include>` is restricted to resources within the same web application, `<c:import>` can be used for resources in other contexts on the same server, or even to other servers entirely. Furthermore, the result of the import doesn't have to be sent directly to page output. Instead, you can store the result for later use. Some examples follow. First is the simple case, importing a resource from the same application, and placing that in page output:

```
<c:import url="trailer.jsp" />
```

You can see that the only attribute you need to set up is *url*, which takes a relative or absolute URL value. When the URL is relative, it can have a forward slash or not. The usual rules apply: Minus a forward slash, the URL is relative to the file doing the importing. With a forward slash, the URL is interpreted as starting from the context root of the current web application.

If you want to go outside of the current context, the syntax is this:

```
<c:import url="/rounding.jspx" context="/examp0801" />
```

The *context* attribute specifies the context root for the resource named in the *url* attribute. The context must reside (or at least be known to) the same container that houses the context for the file doing the importing. The important thing to remember is that for this syntax, both the *url* and *context* values must begin with a forward slash.

Absolute URLs can be used too. Here's a slightly longer example that introduces two new concepts—importing from an external resource using an absolute URL and storing the result in a variable:

```
<c:import url="http://c2.com/index.html" var="importedPage" scope="page" />
<jsp:scriptlet>String fiftyChars = ((String)
  pageContext.getAttribute("importedPage")).substring(0,50);
  pageContext.setAttribute("fiftyChars", fiftyChars);
</jsp:scriptlet>
<pre>${fiftyChars}</pre>
```

To specify an external URL, you simply include the protocol and server name in the value for the *url* attribute. By using the *var* and *scope* attributes, the specified URL is imported into a page-scoped attribute called *importedPage*. Next, a scriptlet takes the first fifty characters of the *importedPage* attribute value, setting this in an attribute called *fiftyChars*. Beyond the scriptlet, an HTML `<pre>` tag surrounds some EL that displays the *fiftyChars* attribute.

An alternative to *var* is the *varReader* attribute. With this, you have the opportunity to import a page into a Reader object. In Exercise 8-2, we'll use this feature to build a mini-filter on the imported data. You can only make use of the reader within the body of the `<c:import>` tag—beyond that, it's unavailable. The code to set up a reader for use might look like this:

```
<c:import url="http://c2.com/index.html" varReader="myReader">
<!-- Make use of myReader in the body of the import action -->
...scriptlet goes here...
</c:import>
```

<c:url> This works out a URL string for inclusion in page output. By default, the URL generated through this action is sent directly to page output—which is rarely useful. More usually, you make use of the *var* attribute to store the URL for later use—perhaps in an EL expression for the *href* parameter value for an HTML link, as shown here:

```
<c:url value="/rounding.jspx" context="/examp0801" var="myLink" />
<a href="${myLink}">Link to another page in another context</a>
```

The syntax has a lot in common with `<c:import>`. The *value* attribute replaces the *url* attribute. In the example, a different context (/examp0801) is specified with the *context* attribute, so the URL in the *value* attribute is interpreted beginning at the root of that context. The *var* attribute stores the generated URL in the named attribute (*myLink*) as a String. As usual, this attribute defaults to the page context—but by using the *scope* attribute (not shown), you can place the attribute holding the URL in any scope you like.

You may well think that it would be more straightforward to put the link in directly: Why bother with `<c:url>`? So the anchor link above would simply read

```
<a href="/rounding.jspx">Link to another page in another context</a>
```

For a start, this wouldn't get to the other context. The value for *href* would need to be an absolute URL (such as `http://myserver.com/examp0801/rounding`

`.jspx`) or a contorted relative URL (such as `../examp0801/rounding.jspx`—the .. to go "up one level" to escape the current context). Moreover, `<c:url>` is an improvement because it seamlessly rewrites URLs whenever necessary to include the session ID (recall the discussion in Chapter 4 about how you need to rewrite URLs when cookies are banned on the client to maintain session identity).

<c:redirect> This causes the client to redirect to a specified URL. This action uses the `HttpServletResponse.sendRedirect()` method under the covers (we talked about that in Chapter 2). There's one compulsory attribute (*url*) and one optional one (*context*). The URL can be a complete URL, including the protocol and host name and port number:

```
<c:redirect url="http://localhost:8080/examp0801/rounding.jspx" />
```

At the other extreme, *url* can have a value that doesn't begin with a forward slash. Then it is interpreted relative to the directory in which the page doing the redirection is located:

```
<c:redirect url="iteration.jspx" />
```

You can begin the *url* value with a forward slash, in which case it is interpreted as starting at the context root:

```
<c:redirect url="/iteration.jspx" />
```

There's also an option to supply another context on the same server, by using the context attribute. Suppose you point your browser to a JSP using the following URL:

```
http://localhost:8080/examp0802/redirecting.jsp
```

You can see from the URL that the context root is `examp0802`. Within the page, `redirecting.jsp`, `<c:redirect>` is used like this:

```
<c:redirect url="/rounding.jspx" context="/examp0801" />
```

In this case, the value for *url* must begin with a forward slash—because it begins from the context specified. In other words, `<c:redirect>` composes a URL like this to cause your browser to repoint to the specified page:

```
http://localhost:8080/examp0801/rounding.jspx
```

One final point: Like the `<c:url>` action, `<c:redirect>` has the capacity to rewrite URLs to include the session ID—when it needs to.

<c:param> Used to attach parameters to any of the previous three URL actions `<c:import>`, `<c:url>`, or `<c:redirect>`. The following example expands the original `<c:url>` example to add some parameters:

```
<c:url value="/rounding.jspx" context="/examp0801" var="myLink">
  <c:param name="firstName" value="David" />
  <c:param name="secondName">Bridgewater</c:param>
</c:url>
<a href="${myLink}">Link to another page in another context</a>
```

Attribute Name	Run-time Expression Allowed?	Mandatory?	Default Value	Type
`<c:import>`				
`url`	Yes	Yes	None	String
`context`	Yes	No	None	String
`var`	No	No	None	String
`scope`	No	No	Page	String
`charEncoding`	Yes	No	ISO-8859-1	String
`varReader`	No	No	None	String
`<c:url>`				
`value`	Yes	No	None	String
`context`	Yes	No	None	String
`var`	No	No	None	String
`scope`	No	No	Page	String

EXERCISE 8-2

JSTL

In this exercise you'll build a mini-search engine. It won't quite be on the scale of Google or Yahoo, but it will make use of a wide range of the JSTL actions you've learned about in this section of the chapter. You'll need to have Internet access to make this exercise work properly.

For this exercise, go back to creating the usual web application directory structure this time under a directory called ex0802, and proceed with the steps for the exercise. There's a solution in the CD in the file sourcecode/ch08/ex0802.war. This is a moderately difficult exercise, so don't feel any shame in deploying and looking at the solution code.

A big health warning is required at this point: *For this example to work, and for most of the subsequent examples in the book, you have to have installed an implementation of JSTL*. The steps for doing this are described at the beginning of the JSTL section in this chapter.

Create a File of URLs

1. Create a file directly in the web application root ex0802 called urls.txt. Type in a set of genuine URLs, each separated by a carriage return—for example,

```
http://c2.com/index.html
http://www.ibm.com
http://www.microsoft.com
http://www.osborne.com
http://java.sun.com
```

Create a JSP Document for Entry of a Search Word (search.jspx)

2. Create a file directly in the web application root ex0802 called search.jspx.
3. The page will be an HTML document. In the root `<html>` element, include namespaces for standard actions (`http://java.sun.com/JSP/Page`) and the JSTL core library (`http://java.sun.com/jsp/jstl/core`).
4. Include the following standard actions to ensure you get standard HTML output:

```
<jsp:output omit-xml-declaration="true" />
<jsp:directive.page contentType="text/html" />
```

5. In the body of the HTML page, include a heading saying "The following URLs will be searched:". Use the core JSTL `import` action to import urls.txt (the file you created in step 1) into a variable called *searchUrls*.
6. After this, use the core JSTL `forTokens` action to split up the imported content of the urls.txt file. The *items* attribute will be the *searchUrls* variable you created in step 5 (use EL to represent this). Each line in the original file is a separate URL, so the delimiter (*delims* attribute) should be the carriage return for your platform (on the Windows platform I'm using, that's carriage return and line feed, so `

`). Retrieve each line into a variable called *currentURL*. Display each URL found in a separate row of an HTML table. Don't forget to close the `forTokens` action with an appropriate end tag.
7. Under this table, introduce a conventional HTML form. The action of the form should be "searchResults.jspx." Have a text field in the form named "searchWord" and a submit button. This is where the user will type a search word for matching against text in the list of URLs. Optionally, express the action of the form as an EL variable—and preload this by using the core JSTL `url` action.

Create a JSP Document to Perform the Search and Display the Results

8. Create a file directly in the web application root ex0802 called search.jspx.
9. Repeat steps 3 and 4 for this file, to reference the right namespaces and ensure HTML output.
10. Use the JSTL actions `import` and `forTokens` exactly as you did in the search.jspx file, to iterate through the URLs in the urls.txt file. All the remaining steps for this document should be inserted within the `for Tokens` loop.
11. Use the `import` action again, but this time to import the current URL (`${currentURL}`) into a variable called *currentFile*.
12. Insert the following scriptlet (code supplied here!), which scours the current file for the search word passed in as a parameter, and sets up an attribute called *isFound* to indicate whether the word has been found in the

file or not. To save typing, you can copy in the following lines of code from the electronic version of the book (or the solution code):

```
<jsp:scriptlet>
  // Get hold of the search word, and the file-as-String
  String searchWord = request.getParameter("searchWord").toLowerCase();
  String file =
    ((String) pageContext.getAttribute("currentFile")).toLowerCase();
  // Is the search word in the file?
  int foundAt = file.indexOf(searchWord);
  if (foundAt >= 0) {
    // Yes, it's found
    pageContext.setAttribute("isFound", new Boolean(true));
    // Find a position in the file a little bit before the search word
    int startAt = 0;
    if (foundAt > 50) {
      startAt = foundAt–50;
    } else {
      startAt = 0;
    }
    pageContext.setAttribute("startAt", new Integer(startAt));
  } else {
    // No, the search word isn't found in the file
    pageContext.setAttribute("isFound", new Boolean(false));
  }
</jsp:scriptlet>
```

13. Use the JSTL `if` action to test the *isFound* attribute set up by the previous scriptlet. All the remaining steps take place within the `if` action (the closing tag for `</c:if>` comes immediately before the closing tag for `</c:forTokens>`). This next part of the JSP document should be accessed only if *isFound* is true.
14. Use the JSTL `import` action to import the same file again, but this time into a Reader variable.
15. Insert the following scriptlet, which returns 200 characters of the file surrounding the search word. The idea is to present a small part of the content to the user of this application to place the search word in some kind of context—this is placed in an attribute called *firstBitOfFile* so that it can easily be accessed using EL later in the code. As an aside—note how

this scriptlet is surrounded in XML CDATA syntax. Why should this be? (Answer at the end of the exercise!)

```
<jsp:scriptlet><![CDATA[
  // Now you have the file as a Reader - skip to where you
  // want to start at, a little before the found search word.
  Reader r = (Reader) pageContext.getAttribute("currentReader");
  long skipAmount = ((Integer)
pageContext.getAttribute("startAt")).longValue();
  r.skip(skipAmount);
  int i;
  char c;
  int counter = 200;
  StringBuffer sb = new StringBuffer();
  try {
    // Just read a couple of hundred characters
      while ((i = r.read()) > -1 &&--counter > 0 ) {
      c = (char) i;
        if (c == '<') {
        sb.append("&lt;");
      } else if (c == '>') {
        sb.append("&gt;");
  } else {
    sb.append(c);
  }
    }
} catch (IOException e) {
    e.printStackTrace();
}
  pageContext.setAttribute("firstBitOfFile", sb.toString());
]]></jsp:scriptlet>
```

16. Using EL variables, display the current URL (preferably as a hyperlink) and the first bit of the file within table cells in an HTML table row.

Run and Test Your Code

17. Create a WAR file that contains the contents of ex0802, and deploy this to your web server. Start the web server if it has not started already.
18. Use your browser to request search.jspx, with a URL such as

    ```
    http://localhost:8080/ex0802/search.jspx
    ```

19. Make sure that the URLs to be searched are displayed. Your page should look something like this:

20. Enter a search word, and click the submit button. The resulting page (searchResults.jspx) should look something like this:

Results of your Search

http://c2.com/index.html	<P>We are proud to host and edit the Portland Pattern Repository which is an online journal for patterns about programs and the de facto home of the extreme programming discipline. </P> <UL>
http://www.microsoft.com	a></li><li><a href="http://g.msn.com/mh_mshp/811">Patterns & Practices</a></li></ul></div><div class="s" id="dS6"><a href="http://g.msn.com/mh_mshp/938"><img src="/h/en-us/r/company_info.gif" alt="co

There were 2 files which matched your search

21. Remember the question earlier: Why is the scriptlet code surrounded in XML CDATA (character data) syntax? The answer is that you are writing XML documents, which have to contain legal XML. Because the code in the second Java scriptlet contains characters that are XML-hostile (such as "<" in the `if` statement), it has to be demarcated as character data that XML parsers will effectively ignore.

CERTIFICATION OBJECTIVE

EL Functions (Exam Objective 7.4)

Given a scenario, write EL code that uses a function; write code for an EL function; and configure the EL function in a tag library descriptor.

EL functions can be used almost as an alternative to custom tags. Many things that you can accomplish with a custom tag can be achieved with an EL function instead. The payback is in simplicity—the development process is easier, and the use of the function within the JSP page is as easy as using a custom tag.

EL Functions

We'll take the rounding tag that we met at the beginning of this chapter and recast it as an EL function. The process of developing and using an EL function very closely parallels the same process for custom tags. There are four very similar stages:

1. Writing a Java class containing the method underpinning the EL function
2. Defining the function within a tag library definition (TLD) file
3. Providing details of where to find the TLD file in the deployment descriptor, web.xml
4. Referencing the TLD file in your JSP page source and using the EL functions from it

We'll look at these steps in turn in the headings that follow.

Writing Methods for EL Functions

Any class will do as a repository for EL functions. The only requirement of a *method* that acts as an EL function is that it should be declared (1) public and (2) static. This means that any existing public static method in any class—either of your own, or as part of your Java environment—is already a candidate for EL function-hood. Most of the functions in java.lang.Math, for example, can be made available as EL functions without having to write a line of code—you simply follow steps 2 to 4 within the EL function-making process.

Here is the logic of the rounding tag we met in the first part of this chapter, rendered in a public static method for use as an EL function:

```
package webcert.ch08.examp0803;
public class Rounding {
  public static double round(double figure, int decimalPlaces) {
    /* Do the rounding */
    long factor = (long) Math.pow(10, decimalPlaces);
    // Shift decimal point to right...
    figure *= factor;
    // Do the rounding...
    long interimResult = Math.round(figure);
    /* Shift decimal point to left (cast of numerator to double
    * because you don't want
    * integer division to occur, and then promote to double) */
    double output = ((double) interimResult) / factor;
    return output;
  }
}
```

As you can see, there is nothing special about this class that makes it specific to the world of tags and JavaServer pages. You can use any prebuilt class—including those supplied with the Java environment.

exam watch

You might have thought that returning nothing (void) from an EL function is illegal. However, there's nothing wrong with it—provided you state that void is returned from the function signature in the TLD:

```
<function-signature>void voidFunction(int)</function-signature>
```

Why might you want to do this? You might need to call a function that causes some effect in your application (sets up some attributes, perhaps) but shouldn't or mustn't return anything to the JSP page.

The class that implements an EL function has two usual locations—as a straight class file in WEB-INF/classes, or wrapped up in a JAR in WEB-INF/lib.

Defining the Function within the TLD File

Having written (or chosen) the class and method for your EL function, the next step is to define it—in a TLD file. You use the `function` element to do so. The definition for our rounding function might look like this:

```
<function>
  <description>Rounds figure to given number of decimal places</description>
  <name>round</name>
  <function-class>webcert.ch08.examp0803.Rounding</function-class>
  <function-signature>double round(double, int)</function-signature>
</function>
```

The subelements of `<function>` are as follows:

<description> This is an optional description for the function.

<name> This is the name of the function as it will be used within EL expressions. This doesn't have to match the Java method name—it can be any logical name.

<function-class> This is the fully qualified name of the Java class containing the implementation of the function.

<function-signature> This is the signature of the function, almost as it would appear in regular Java syntax. The similarities and differences are these:

- Qualifiers are omitted (after all, the method must be public and static, so these keywords would be redundant).
- A return type must be supplied (or **void**)—just like Java. If the function returns an object type (rather than a primitive), the fully qualified name of the class must be given. This applies even to classes in java.lang (java.lang.String, not just String).

- The method name follows, and this has to match the method name in the Java class. Just as in Java, a pair of parentheses follows the method name—to enclose the parameters.
- Parameters must be listed in order, following the order within the Java method. However, only the types are provided—the parameters don't have an accompanying name in the TLD signature. Primitives are listed as in Java, and—as for the return type—objects must have their fully qualified name.

Finding the TLD

Now we're at the point where we need to put the TLD file somewhere where pages in the web application can find it. This process is absolutely no different from locating a TLD for custom tags, as we explored at the beginning of the chapter. Refer back to that for an account of what to do.

You don't need a separate TLD for EL functions, different from a TLD that contains custom tags. You can mix EL functions and custom tags (and, as we'll see later, other elements as well) in the same TLD. The only rule is on names: Each must be unique across all functions, custom tags, and other top-level elements within the TLD.

Declaring the TLD and Using the EL Function

We're finally ready to use the EL function within a JSP page! This means two things:

1. Declaring the TLD with the page
2. Using the rounding function

Your options for declaring the TLD file have already been covered at the beginning of this chapter: You can either use the `taglib` directive (for JSP syntax) or reference the taglib in a namespace (JSP document XML syntax).

However, using the function is different. You use EL rather than tag syntax. Our call to the `round` function is shown here in its simplest form, plugging in constants for the parameters to the function:

```
${mytags:round(9.21 / 3, 2)}
```

As is customary for EL, the whole statement is surrounded by `${...}`. Within the curly braces, first comes the function name—declared just like a tag name: `mytags:round`. Immediately following the function name are parentheses to contain the parameters—just as in Java language method calls. With the parentheses, each parameter is separated by a comma from the next. So the first parameter—the figure to round—is a constant calculation (`9.21 / 3`), and the second parameter—the number of decimals to display—is a constant 2.

Here's another example of the use of the `round` function, in a more realistic setting. Parameters to functions can be run-time expressions. Take a look at the following example:

```
<c:set var="unrounded" value="${param.num/param.denom}" />
${mytags:round(unrounded, 2)}
```

First of all, the JSTL action `<c:set>` is used to load an attribute called *unrounded* with the value from an EL calculation. The EL calculation performs a division based on two request parameters: one called *num* and the other called *denom*. Then the *unrounded* variable is plugged in to the EL `round` function—as the first parameter.

EXERCISE 8-3

EL Functions

In this exercise we'll rewrite the Taxation Tag you met in Exercise 8-1 as an EL function. You'll reuse some of the pieces of that exercise but also add some new components. The functionality is identical—you enter some details about income, tax allowance, and tax rate on a web page; click on a submit button; and then see a JSP document that presents a calculated net income figure. Refer to Exercise 8-1 for screen shots of how the finished application should look.

Copy Files from Exercise 8-1

1. First, create a context directory called ex0803 with the usual web application subdirectories.

2. From Exercise 8-1, copy the files income.html and taxation.jspx from the context directory ex0801, and paste them directly into your new context directory ex0803. You'll leave income.html exactly as it is and make only one small change to taxation.jspx later in the exercise.
3. Also from Exercise 8-1, copy the deployment descriptor web.xml from ex0801/WEB-INF to ex0803/WEB-INF.

Create the EL Function Code

4. In /ex0803/WEB-INF/src, create a package directory called webcert/ch08/ex0803, and in that create a file called Taxation.java (belonging to package webcert.ch08.ex0803).
5. Include a method in this class called `calcNetIncome`, with the following signature:

```
public static String calcNetIncome(double gross,
double rate, double allow, String currency)
```

6. This method accepts four parameters, as shown, and should return a formatted net income figure (complete with correct currency symbol). You can write the code to do this yourself, though— of course—it has no direct bearing on the SCWCD exam. You may prefer to cheat and use the following code:

```
double taxToPay = ((gross–allow) * rate / 100);
double net = (gross–taxToPay);
NumberFormat nf = NumberFormat.getInstance();
Currency c = Currency.getInstance(currency);
nf.setCurrency(c);
nf.setMinimumFractionDigits(c.getDefaultFractionDigits());
nf.setMaximumFractionDigits(c.getDefaultFractionDigits());
return c.getSymbol() + nf.format(net);
```

7. Compile the code to directory /ex0803/WEB-INF/classes/webcert/ch08/ex0803.

Declare the Function in a TLD File

8. You have now to link the static method in the class you have just written to a function definition in a tag library descriptor file.

9. Create an empty file called mytags.tld in directory /ex0803/WEB-INF/tags.
10. Edit the file, and provide an enclosing `<taglib>` element. Make sure that you include any necessary attributes in the taglib opening tag, and also add mandatory subelements (for the tag library version and short name). Refer to Chapter 7 for details on "heading level" information on tag library descriptors. If you need to, use the tag library descriptor from Exercise 8-1 as a template for this one (it's also called mytags.tld, and is located in /ex0801/WEB-INF/tags).
11. Include a function element in the TLD, referring to the preceding material in this chapter to remind yourself how the syntax of the function element works.
    - The description can be anything you like.
    - The name should be `netincome`.
    - The function class should tie in to the Taxation class you wrote, webcert.ch08.ex0803.Taxation.
    - The function signature should match the `calcNetIncome` function. Remember that parameter types don't need names and that all nonprimitive parameters and return types (even those from java.lang) need to have a fully qualified name.
12. Save and close the TLD file.

Adjust the JSP Document

13. In the JSP document you copied from Exercise 8-1 (taxation.jspx), you already had a reference to the TLD document mytags.tld, with a prefix of mytags.
14. So you have only one thing to change. Currently, the document uses the tag declaration `<mytags:netincome>` to display the calculated net income. Remove this, prior to doing the following steps to replace it with an EL function call.
15. Place the function call to `mytags:netincome` in EL syntax.
16. Remembering that you navigate to this document from an HTML page containing a form, add four parameters as follows:

- The first should be from a request parameter called `gross`.
- The second should be from a request parameter called `rate`.
- The third should be from a request parameter called `allowance`.
- Hard-code the fourth (the currency code) as "GBP."

17. Hint: Remember that EL has an implicit variable for obtaining parameter values.

Run and Test the Application

18. Create a .war file from your ex0803 context directory, and deploy this to your server.
19. Test your application with a URL such as

```
http://localhost:8080/ex0803/income.html
```

20. If you need to, refer to Exercise 8-1 to see how the pages in the application should look.

CERTIFICATION OBJECTIVE

The "Classic" Custom Tag Event Model (Exam Objective 10.1)

Describe the semantics of the "Classic" custom tag event model when each event method (doStartTag, doAfterBody, and doEndTag) is executed, and explain what the return value for each event method means; and write a tag handler class.

We have looked at a number of JSP technologies now that rely on tag technology—standard actions, Expression Language, and JSTL actions. Formerly—without EL and JSTL—you would always have to write your own custom tags (or acquire some from a third party) to avoid Java scripting. But although EL and JSTL are very flexible, there will come a time when the best solution to keeping your page Java-free is a custom tag. Hence, custom tags are still alive and well on the exam syllabus, and although they represent the most complex end of JSP technology, they are satisfying to write and powerful in scope.

In this section we'll tackle tags head-on by looking at the so-called "classic" custom tag event model. This is technology that has been around for a long time, featured in the older version of the SCWCD exam and still in the current one. In the next chapter, you'll meet newer technologies that make it possible to retain most or all of the power of classic tags, but with easier development approaches. But to appreciate these properly, you need to work through some classic tags first!

Tags for All Seasons

In actual fact, the classic custom tag event life cycle isn't a single life cycle. There are three possibilities you can choose from, based on three interfaces, all in the javax.servlet.jsp.tagext package: Tag, IterationTag, and BodyTag. Each of these extends the other, adding new possibilities into the basic life cycle:

- Tag is the simplest of the three.
- IterationTag extends Tag, adding (no surprises!) some looping capabilities.
- BodyTag extends IterationTag, adding further method calls to manipulate the body content of the tag (instead of just blindly appending more output to the page, as the other types do).

You can build your own custom tags by implementing any one of these three interfaces. More usually, you extend classes provided in javax.servlet.jsp.tagext that already implement these interfaces, and provide some useful base functionality. Figure 8-3 is a class diagram that shows the relationship among these classes and the interfaces already mentioned.

FIGURE 8.3

Tag Interfaces and Classes in javax.servlet.jsp.tagext

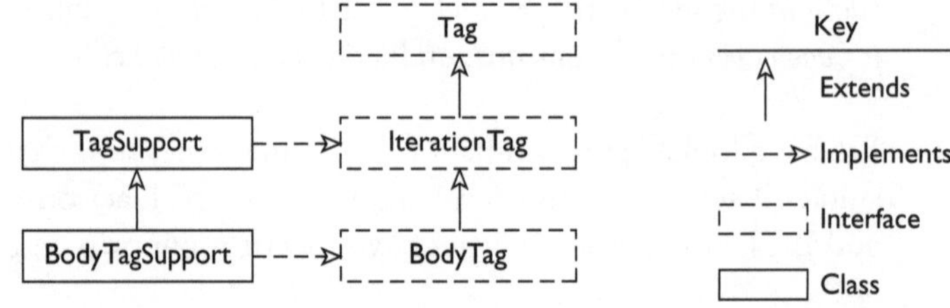

You can see from Figure 8-3 that there isn't a class that just implements the Tag interface. Your choices are TagSupport (implementing IterationTag as well as Tag) and BodyTagSupport (implementing everything possible).

Tag

If all you want to do is make the tag do something—you're not interested in the body at all—then the Tag interface is for you. Let's consider the case where you have so little interest in the body that you elect to leave it empty. The tag is there just to substitute some text or other into your page output. Perhaps you would like to insert the current date and time. You could use an expression such as this:

```
<%= new Date() %>
```

Here's how you might approach a tag replacement for this. First of all, you might write a class that implements the Tag interface. Here's the source for this:

```
import java.io.IOException;
import java.util.Date;
import javax.servlet.jsp.JspException;
import javax.servlet.jsp.JspWriter;
import javax.servlet.jsp.PageContext;
import javax.servlet.jsp.tagext.Tag;
public class DateStampTag1 implements Tag {
  private PageContext pageContext;
  private Tag parent;
  public void setPageContext(PageContext pageContext) {
    this.pageContext = pageContext;
  }
  public void setParent(Tag parent) {
    this.parent = parent;
  }
  public Tag getParent() {
    return parent;
  }
  public int doStartTag() throws JspException {
    dateStamp();
    return Tag.EVAL_BODY_INCLUDE;
  }
  public int doEndTag() throws JspException {
    return Tag.EVAL_PAGE;
  }
```

```
    protected void dateStamp() throws JspException {
      JspWriter out = pageContext.getOut();
      try {
        out.write("<i>" + new Date() + "</i>");
      } catch (IOException e) {
        throw new JspException(e);
      }
    }
    public void release() {
    }
}
```

This is more or less as simple as classic tag source gets. Let's examine the methods in turn. In the source, they appear roughly in "tag life cycle" order. The life cycle is illustrated in Figure 8-4.

FIGURE 8-4

Custom Tag Life Cycle (1): The Tag Interface

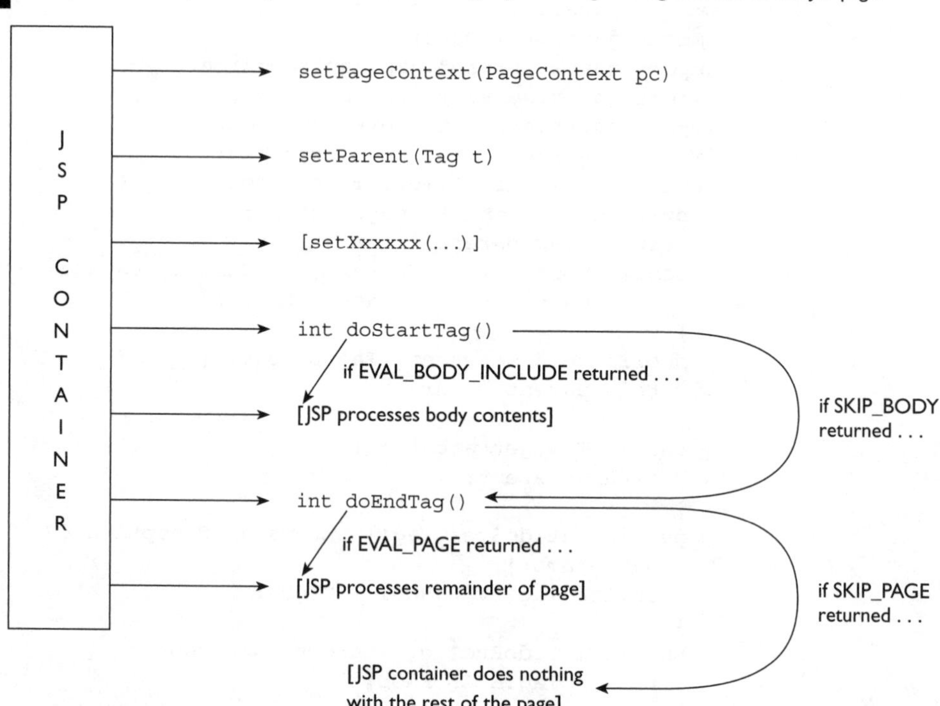

- First of all, the JSP container makes an instance of the DateStampTag1 class. The class must have a no-argument constructor—either explicitly defined or (as here) provided by the compiler in the absence of other constructors.
- Next, the JSP container calls `setPageContext(PageContext pc)`. This gives the tag an opportunity to save a reference to the page context of the JSP page that contains the tag, and this is exactly what happens here. DateStampTag1 has been defined with a javax.servlet.jsp.PageContext instance variable. The page context so provided lets the remaining code in the tag handler class do all the things that might otherwise be done using the *pageContext* implicit variable in a scriptlet.
- After this, the JSP container calls `setParent(Tag parent)`. Again, the idea is to save a reference for later use—this time to the tag that immediately encloses this tag. Although DateStampTag1 makes no use of its parent tag, it has to provide the method to properly implement the Tag interface. So DateStampTag1 does the right thing, by defining an instance variable of type Tag, and saving the parameter passed into this method for later use.
- Again to satisfy the Tag interface, the `getParent()` method (returning the parent Tag—or **null**) must be defined. This isn't called by the container, but it can be used by a later method within the tag handler class.
- Now the JSP container calls any other set methods on DateStampTag1 that relate to attributes for the tag. As it happens, there aren't any; we'll introduce an attribute in the next version of the tag handler coming up soon (imaginatively called DateStampTag2).
- Next the JSP container calls `doStartTag()`. You can think of this as corresponding to the point where the JSP container processes the appearance of datestamp's opening tag within the JSP page source. In this case, `doStartTag()` calls its own internal method—`dateStamp()`—to do the work of writing the date to page output. After doing this, `doStartTag()` must return an **int** value—this is a return code to tell the JSP container what to do next. Valid values are defined as **public final static int** data members within the Tag interface. There are two possibilities:
  - Tag.EVAL_BODY_INCLUDE—any JSP page source between the opening and closing tags for this action should now be processed.
  - Tag.SKIP_BODY—the exact opposite: Any JSP page source between the opening and closing tags for this action should be ignored. The JSP container proceeds directly to the `doEndTag()` method for this action.

- Dealing with the `dateStamp()` method: This is the only method in the DateStampTag1 class that is not an implementation of a Tag interface method. It does the specific work associated with this tag: namely, getting hold of the JspWriter from the *pageContext* variable and writing a new date and time to it. This is equivalent to using the implicit variable *out* in a scriptlet, but with the benefit that this tag handler class is completely separate from JSP page source.
- Next, the JSP container calls `doEndTag()`. In this version of DateStampTag1, this does nothing functional. However, the method is still obliged to send back a return code to the container. Again, there are two options:
  - Tag.EVAL_PAGE tells the JSP container to process the rest of the page after the closing tag.
  - Tag.SKIP_PAGE effectively tells the JSP container to abort the rest of the page following the closing tag.
- Finally, the JSP container calls `release()`. However, this won't happen every time the tag appears in a JSP page. The instance of the tag is potentially reused over and over again. If the container decides to take a particular instance of a tag out of service, then `release()` is called, which you can use to clean up any expensive resources associated with the tag.

exam watch

Instances of tag handler classes are reused—at least, potentially. So you don't necessarily get a new instance with every use of a particular tag on your JSP page, or even across JSP pages. That means that you can't rely on the constructor to do initialization that must take place for each specific use; it's far better to use `setPageContext()` for that, which will get executed for every tag appearance. Apart from the no-argument constructor and `release()`, all other Tag life cycle methods are executed for each appearance of the tag on the page, as shown in Figures 8-4, 8-5, and 8-6.

The difficult work—writing the tag handler class—is now done. However, there are additional things to do before we can use the datestamp tag within a page. For one thing, we must define the tag within a TLD file. We've seen how functions are defined already in a TLD file, and tags are—if anything—easier. Here's how the tag element looks (to save space, some mandatory taglib attributes are omitted, as are the top-level elements that go with tag libraries):

```
<taglib ...taglib attributes...>
<... elements omitted ...>
<tag>
  <name>dateStamp1</name>
  <tag-class>webcert.ch08.examp0804.DateStampTag1</tag-class>
  <body-content>empty</body-content>
</tag>
</taglib>
```

Each tag must have a `<tag>` element defined. The tag must have at least the three subelements shown:

- `<name>`: a unique name within the tag library. This name must remain unique not only within other tags but also within any EL functions or tag files defined in the tag library as well.
- `<tag-class>`: like `<function-class>` for EL function descriptors, or `<servlet-class>` for servlets—the fully qualified name of the tag handler class (but omitting the file extension ".class").
- `<body-content>`: the sort of content permitted in the body of the tag—between the opening and closing tags. There are four valid values: empty, scriptless, tagdependent, and JSP. In this case, dateStamp1 is defined as empty, so there can't be any body. The tag can appear in the page either as `<prefix:dateStamp1></prefix:dateStamp1>`, or—more usually—using the "self-closing" form `<prefix:dateStamp1 />`.

We covered the correct locations for the TLD file in the first section of this chapter.

So that leaves actually using the tag within the JSP page. The procedure is the same as for EL functions. Here is a complete JSP document that uses the dateStamp1 tag:

```
<html xmlns:mytags="http://www.osborne.com/taglibs/mytags"
      xmlns:jsp="http://java.sun.com/JSP/Page">
<jsp:output omit-xml-declaration="true" />
<jsp:directive.page contentType="text/html" />
<head><title>Date Stamp Example</title></head>
  <body>
    <h1>Date Stamp Example</h1>
    <p>Date Stamp 1: <mytags:dateStamp1 /></p>
  </body>
</html>
```

If you run this page, the output is as shown in the following illustration. As you can see, all you have to do to make the date stamp appear is to locate the tag within the template text at the right point. The JSP page container will run the code and substitute the output from the tag handler code into the page output at the right place.

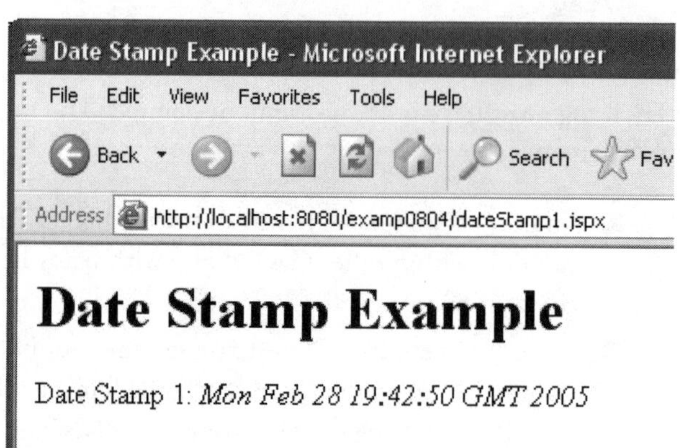

Just because a tag that only implements the Tag interface doesn't have a way of manipulating the body is not to say that such a tag *can't* have a body. Let's now look at a modified version of the date stamp tag, which allows a body and demonstrates the use of an attribute associated with the tag. In this version, the tag logic has changed in one important respect. Dependent on the setting of an attribute called *beforeBody*, the location of the date stamp will change in respect of the body. We'll first look at how this works in action, then revisit the code in the tag handler. Here's the JSP page using the modified tag, dateStamp2:

```
<html xmlns:mytags="http://www.osborne.com/taglibs/mytags"
      xmlns:jsp="http://java.sun.com/JSP/Page"
      xmlns:c="http://java.sun.com/jsp/jstl/core" >
  <jsp:output omit-xml-declaration="true" />
  <jsp:directive.page contentType="text/html" />
  <head><title>Date Stamp 2 Example</title></head>
  <body>
    <h1>Date Stamp 2 Example</h1>
    <h3>Example 1</h3>
    <p><mytags:dateStamp2 beforeBody="false">
      <b>Date after tag body: </b>
```

```
      </mytags:dateStamp2></p>
      <h3>Example 2</h3>
      <c:set var="trueVariable" value="true" />
      <p><mytags:dateStamp2 beforeBody="${trueVariable}">
        <b> – date before tag body through runtime expression.</b>
      </mytags:dateStamp2></p>
      <h3>Example 3</h3>
      <p><mytags:dateStamp2>
        <b>Date after tag body by default: </b>
      </mytags:dateStamp2></p>
    </body>
  </html>
```

This is what the output looks like when you access the document.

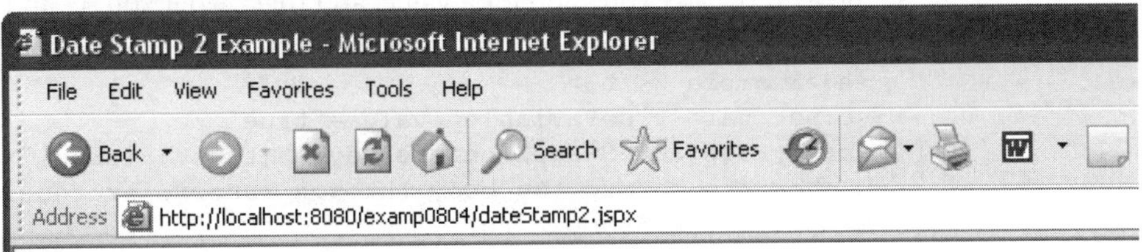

You can see that the dateStamp2 tag has one optional attribute, called *beforeBody*. When this is set to true, the date stamp appears before the body; and when set to false, after the body. Example 1 is the first of three uses of dateStamp2 in the JSP page source:

```
<h3>Example 1</h3>
<p><mytags:dateStamp2 beforeBody="false">
  <b>Date after tag body: </b>
</mytags:dateStamp2></p>
```

In this case, the attribute *beforeBody* is set from the constant value "false" in the opening tag. Unlike the previous tag examples, dateStamp2 has a body (the text "Date after tag body:" between the HTML bold face tags).

If the *beforeBody* attribute accepted only constant values, there would be very little point to having it. After all, you could just decide to place the bodiless version of the date stamp custom action (dateStamp1) either before or after some template text. However, there might be occasions when you want the placement decision made according to some logic in your JSP page. Consequently, the *beforeBody* attribute is set up to allow an expression for a value, and that's what you see in Example 2:

```
<h3>Example 2</h3>
<c:set var="trueVariable" value="true" />
<p><mytags:dateStamp2 beforeBody="${trueVariable}">
  <b>—date before tag body through runtime expression.</b>
</mytags:dateStamp2></p>
```

The `set` action from the JSTL core library is used to set a variable called *trueVariable* to a value of "true." Now in the dateStamp2 action's opening tag, the `beforeBody` attribute is set from an EL expression that pulls back the value from `trueVariable`. Because `beforeBody` is set to "true," the date stamp appears in front of the "—date before tag body . . ." template text. Though the example is trivial, it serves to make the point that run-time expressions can be fed into custom tag attribute values.

Finally, in Example 3, we see that the dateStamp2 custom action allows you to leave out the *beforeBody* attribute altogether:

```
<h3>Example 3</h3>
<p><mytags:dateStamp2>
  <b>Date after tag body by default: </b>
</mytags:dateStamp2></p>
```

In that case, the attribute still retains a default value, set by the tag handler code we'll see in a few moments. Because the default value of *beforeBody* is "false," the outcome is to place the date stamp after the "Date after tag body . . ." template text.

Here's the tag definition in the tag library (TLD file). The opening and closing tags used for tag library setup are omitted for brevity.

```
<...>
<tag>
  <name>dateStamp2</name>
  <tag-class>webcert.ch08.examp0804.DateStampTag2</tag-class>
  <body-content>JSP</body-content>
  <attribute>
    <name>beforeBody</name>
    <required>false</required>
    <rtexprvalue>true</rtexprvalue>
  </attribute>
</tag>
<...>
```

Again we see the unique `<name>` for the tag—dateStamp2. The tag handler class is referenced in the `<tag-class>` element, as we've seen before. The `<body-content>` element is set to JSP, which means that anything permitted in JSP page source can be placed between the opening and closing dateStamp2 tags. This includes template text, scriptlets, expressions, standard actions, and custom actions—in fact, any element you want. While "empty" is the most restrictive, "JSP" is the most permissive setting for `<body-content>`.

Next we come to a set of elements not discussed previously, enclosed by the `<attribute>` element. You can have as many enclosing `<attribute>` elements as you want in a `<tag>`, from zero to many. `<attribute>`—like `<tag>`—has no data of its own, but contains three mandatory subelements:

- `<name>`—a unique name for the attribute. The unique rule applies only to all the attributes *within* a single tag (different tags can have attributes of the same name, as you've already seen with the JSTL core library. For example, *var* is an attribute name that appears in many tags—such as `c:set` and `c:import`).
- `<required>`—if set to "true," the attribute must appear in the opening tag. If "false," the attribute's presence is optional. This implies that the tag handler class supplies a default value or doesn't otherwise need any value for the attribute to evaluate the action.
- `<rtexprvalue>`—if set to "true," a run-time (EL) expression value is permitted for the attribute's value setting. You are not forced to use a run-time expression; a constant value is still perfectly valid. If set to "false," run-time expressions are disallowed for the attribute value—a translation error results if you try to do so.

Finally, here's the revised code for the tag handler class. The changed lines of code are shown in boldface.

```
import java.io.IOException;
import java.util.Date;
import javax.servlet.jsp.JspException;
import javax.servlet.jsp.JspWriter;
import javax.servlet.jsp.PageContext;
import javax.servlet.jsp.tagext.Tag;
public class DateStampTag2 implements Tag {
  private PageContext pageContext;
  private Tag parent;
  private boolean beforeBody;
  public void setPageContext(PageContext pageContext) {
       this.pageContext = pageContext;
  }
  public void setParent(Tag parent) {
       this.parent = parent;
  }
  public Tag getParent() {
       return parent;
  }
  public boolean isBeforeBody() {
        return beforeBody;
  }
  public void setBeforeBody(boolean beforeBody) {
        this.beforeBody = beforeBody;
  }
  public int doStartTag() throws JspException {
        if (isBeforeBody()) {
             dateStamp();
        }
        return Tag.EVAL_BODY_INCLUDE;
  }
  public int doEndTag() throws JspException {
        if (!isBeforeBody()) {
              dateStamp();
        }
        return Tag.EVAL_PAGE;
  }
  protected void dateStamp() throws JspException {
        JspWriter out = pageContext.getOut();
        try {
              out.write("<i>" + new Date() + "</i>");
        } catch (IOException e) {
              throw new JspException(e);
        }
```

```
    }
    public void release() {
    }
}
```

In support of the attribute is a bean-style property, represented by the private instance variable *beforeBody*. The crucial aspect of attribute setup in the tag handler code is the presence of a setter method—in this case, `setBeforeBody()`—whose name matches the attribute name apart from the "set" portion, and the initial capital ("**B**eforeBody" instead of "**b**eforeBody"). The JSP container can infer from the attribute name what set method to call, passing in the value set within the page source.

As it happens, a "getter" is provided in this example, but that's not crucial to the tag life cycle (the JSP container will never call the "getter"). Because we're using a **boolean** for the attribute here, the getter is called "`isBeforeBody()`" ("`getBeforeBody()`" is still permissible—it's just that **booleans** more usually have "is"-style getter methods).

The `doStartTag()` logic has changed slightly. Remember this is executed when the JSP container encounters the opening dateStamp2 tag—before the body has been encountered. If the outcome of calling the `isBeforeBody()` method is true, then the date stamp is included at this point by calling the `dateStamp()` method (unchanged from before). Regardless of whether the date stamp is included at this point, the `doStartTag()` method returns the value Tag.EVAL_BODY_INCLUDE, indicating that the body should be evaluated in all circumstances.

The `doEndTag()` logic does a similar test. When the JSP container calls this method, the body of the tag has already been output. Now if the "`isBeforeBody()`" test evaluates to false, the `dateStamp()` method is called, placing the date stamp after the body. The return value from this method remains unchanged from before: Tag.EVAL_PAGE indicates that the JSP container should carry on and evaluate the rest of the page following on after this custom action.

IterationTag Interface and TagSupport Class

We've seen a simple case. Now we'll step up the complexity and consider a tag that repeats itself. This will also give an opportunity to look at how tags can interact when nested together. The example we'll take is the idea of a JSP page that shuffles and deals a pack of cards. We'll have a tag to manage the pack (called `cardDealer`) and a tag within it that "receives" cards from the pile (called, simply, `card`). The tag is structured so that it deals out all fifty-two cards from the pack.

Let's see an example of the tags in action as a preliminary to considering the code. Here's the JSP page source:

```
<html xmlns:mytags="http://www.osborne.com/taglibs/mytags"
    xmlns:jsp="http://java.sun.com/JSP/Page">
  <jsp:output omit-xml-declaration="true" />
  <jsp:directive.page contentType="text/html" />
  <head><title>Card Game</title></head>
  <body>
    <h1>Bridge Hand</h1>
    <table border="1">
      <tr>
        <th>Player 1</th>
        <th>Player 2</th>
        <th>Player 3</th>
        <th>Player 4</th>
      </tr>
      <mytags:cardDealer>
      <tr>
        <td><mytags:card /></td>
        <td><mytags:card /></td>
        <td><mytags:card /></td>
        <td><mytags:card /></td>
      </tr>
      </mytags:cardDealer>
    </table>
  </body>
</html>
```

Most of the page is template text, setting up a table with headings for each of four players. The `cardDealer` custom action surrounds the data row of the table. Within each data row are four cells, one under each player heading. The `card` custom action has the effect of taking a card off the shuffled pack and displaying the value of the card. After each player "takes" a card, processing reaches the end tag for the `cardDealer` custom action. If there are more cards to deal, the JSP container processes the whole body of the tag (the table row) again, and so on until all the cards are used up. The following illustration below shows a sample hand.

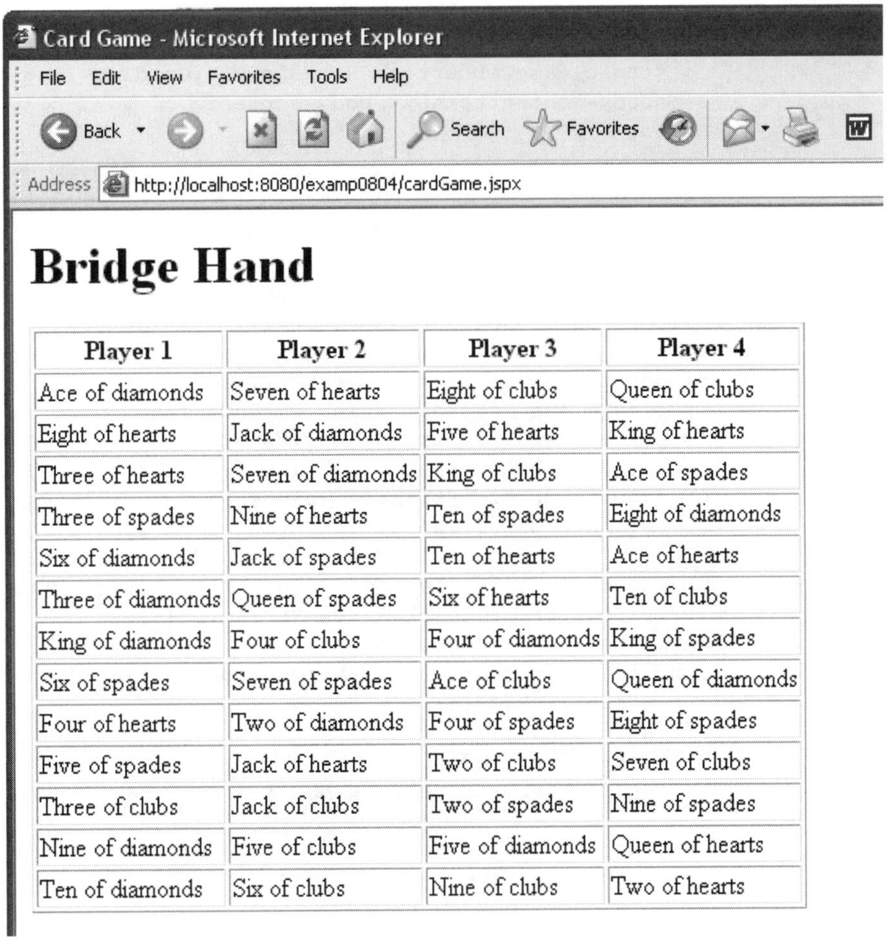

Card Game - Microsoft Internet Explorer

File Edit View Favorites Tools Help

Back Search Favorites

Address http://localhost:8080/examp0804/cardGame.jspx

Bridge Hand

Player 1	Player 2	Player 3	Player 4
Ace of diamonds	Seven of hearts	Eight of clubs	Queen of clubs
Eight of hearts	Jack of diamonds	Five of hearts	King of hearts
Three of hearts	Seven of diamonds	King of clubs	Ace of spades
Three of spades	Nine of hearts	Ten of spades	Eight of diamonds
Six of diamonds	Jack of spades	Ten of hearts	Ace of hearts
Three of diamonds	Queen of spades	Six of hearts	Ten of clubs
King of diamonds	Four of clubs	Four of diamonds	King of spades
Six of spades	Seven of spades	Ace of clubs	Queen of diamonds
Four of hearts	Two of diamonds	Four of spades	Eight of spades
Five of spades	Jack of hearts	Two of clubs	Seven of clubs
Three of clubs	Jack of clubs	Two of spades	Nine of spades
Nine of diamonds	Five of clubs	Five of diamonds	Queen of hearts
Ten of diamonds	Six of clubs	Nine of clubs	Two of hearts

The TLD descriptions for the two custom actions are pretty simple. Neither has any attributes. The notable difference is that `cardDealer` can contain any sort of body content, whereas `card` must be free of any body content.

```
<tag>
  <name>cardDealer</name>
  <tag-class>webcert.ch08.examp0804.CardDealingTag</tag-class>
  <body-content>JSP</body-content>
</tag>
```

```
<tag>
  <name>card</name>
  <tag-class>webcert.ch08.examp0804.CardTag</tag-class>
  <body-content>empty</body-content>
</tag>
```

Let's consider the tag handler code, first of the CardDealingTag class, which supplies the logic for the `cardDealer` custom action:

```
import javax.servlet.jsp.JspException;
import javax.servlet.jsp.tagext.IterationTag;
import javax.servlet.jsp.tagext.Tag;
import javax.servlet.jsp.tagext.TagSupport;
public class CardDealingTag extends TagSupport {
  private static String[] suits =
    { "spades", "hearts", "clubs", "diamonds" };
  private static String[] values =
    { "Ace of", "Two of", "Three of", "Four of",
      "Five of", "Six of", "Seven of", "Eight of",
      "Nine of", "Ten of", "Jack of", "Queen of", "King of" };
private String[] pack = new String[52];
private int currentCard;
public int doStartTag() throws JspException {
  initializePack();
  shufflePack();
  currentCard = 0;
  return Tag.EVAL_BODY_INCLUDE;
}
public int doAfterBody() throws JspException {
  if (currentCard >= pack.length) {
    return Tag.SKIP_BODY;
  } else {
    return IterationTag.EVAL_BODY_AGAIN;
  }
}
public String dealCard() {
  String card = pack[currentCard];
  currentCard++;
  return card;
}
protected void initializePack() {
  for (int i = 0; i < 4; i++) {
    for (int j = 0; j < 13; j++) {
      int cardIndex = (i * 13) + j;
```

```
    pack[cardIndex] = values[j] + " " + suits[i];
  }
    }
  }
  protected void shufflePack() {
    int packSize = pack.length;
      for (int i = 0; i < packSize; i++) {
        int random = (int) (Math.random() * packSize);
        // Swap two cards in the pack
        String card1 = pack[i];
        String card2 = pack[random];
        pack[i] = card2;
        pack[random] = card1;
      }
    }
  }
```

The first big difference about this tag handler class from the previous date stamp example is that it doesn't directly implement the Tag interface. Instead, it extends an existing class called javax.servlet.jsp.tagext.TagSupport. You can see from the class diagram (Figure 8-3) that TagSupport implements the IterationTag interface. Because IterationTag extends Tag, you get all the Tag methods as well, supplemented by those unique to IterationTag (there is only one!). However, there is a profound change to the life cycle with IterationTag, as you can see by looking at Figure 8-5 (compare this to the Tag life cycle in Figure 8-4).

exam watch ***Although there are two instance variables declared in the CardDealerTag class, neither of these is an attribute of the tag (which has no attributes at all). They are merely there to support the internal workings of the tag. Even if these instance variables had getter and setter methods, they still wouldn't be attributes. For an attribute to be available on the tag, it must be declared in an `<attribute>` element in the tag library descriptor.***

TagSupport—as it must—provides a default implementation of all the Tag and IterationTag methods, and supplements these with a few useful methods of its own that don't derive from any interface. So when writing your own tag that extends TagSupport, you are likely to have less work to do than if implementing IterationTag from scratch. You confine yourself to overriding only those methods where the default TagSupport behavior is insufficient. So, for example, `doEndTag()` is missing from our CardDealingTag code. The default TagSupport implementation—which is simply to return

FIGURE 8-5 Custom Tag Life Cycle (2): The IterationTag Interface

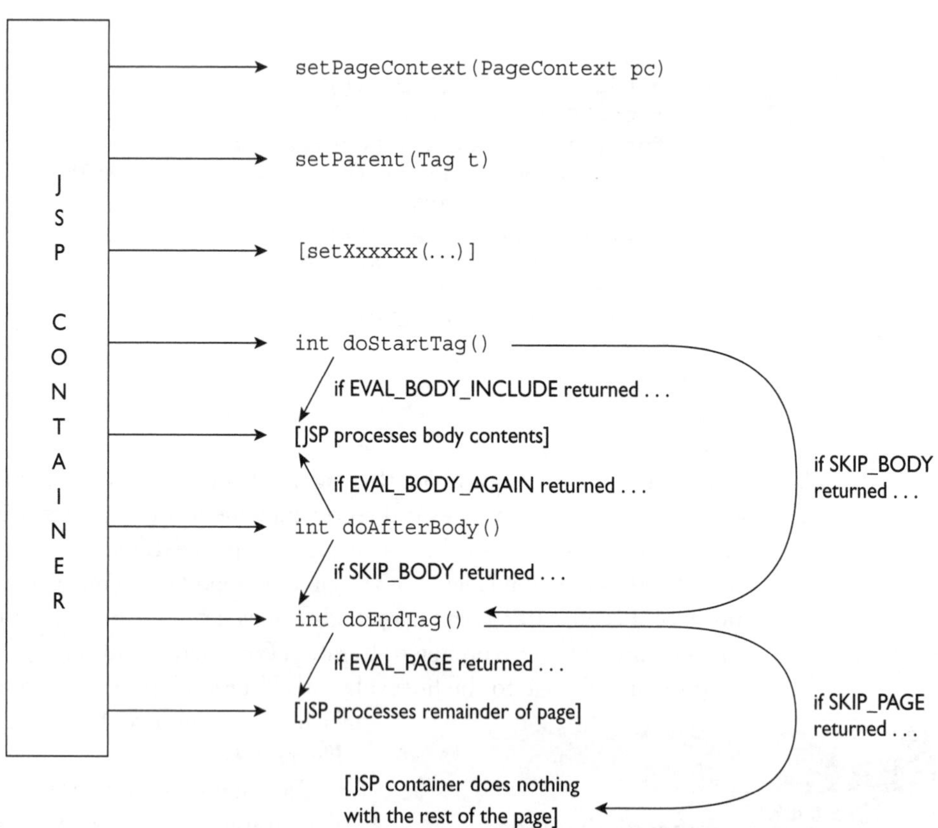

the value Tag.EVAL_PAGE—is just what we want here. There's no special processing to be done when the closing tag is encountered in the page.

At the beginning of the class are two static String arrays. These provide the base data (suits and card values) for the next String array, called *pack*, which is a private instance variable in the class. After some initialization work, the pack holds 52 String values representing the 52 playing cards, in a random sequence. Next comes a private instance variable, of type **int**, called *currentCard*. This is used later as an index to the *pack* array, and it dictates the next "card" to "deal" from the pack.

Next we get the `doStartTag()` method, which is overridden from TagSupport. Remember that this will be invoked whenever the JSP container encounters the opening cardDealer tag in any JSP page. The method calls the `initializePack()` and `shufflePack()` methods in the class, which serve to load up the pack String array with randomized card values. Their logic isn't explained in detail here, for it is straightforward and not central to the discussion of the tag life cycle (you can take the methods on trust!). The calls to these methods could have been placed in a no-argument constructor, but recall that tag instances get recycled—you don't get a dedicated instance for each access to the tag in your application. However, you can guarantee a `doStartTag()` call for every access to the tag, which guarantees a newly shuffled deck of cards every time. The `doStartTag()` method ends by returning Tag .EVAL_BODY_INCLUDE, which is necessary to ensure that the body is processed.

Following `doStartTag()` is a call to `doAfterBody()`. This is the one new method introduced by the IterationTag interface. The JSP container calls this method after evaluating the body but before `doEndTag()` (see Figure 8-5). The logic in the method demonstrates the two possible outcomes. If there are more cards to deal, then the method returns the **int** value Tag.SKIP_BODY (which, you'll remember, is also a valid return value from `doStartTag()`). This means that the JSP container won't process any further occurrences of the body, but proceed directly to the `doEndTag()` method. If, however, there are more cards available, then the method returns a new constant defined in the IterationTag interface: Iteration Tag.EVAL_BODY_AGAIN. As the name of this constant implies, the JSP container will evaluate the body of the tag again, and then once again invoke the `doAfterBody()` method. So you can see that there is no way out of this tag handler until Tag.SKIP_BODY is returned! You can also see that the body is evaluated at least once, for the logic tests present in `doAfterBody()` occur for the first time only after the body has been processed for the first time.

on the job

Should threading worry you? What if more than one person is trying to access the cardDealing.jspx file at the same time? Could there be other invocations of the same `cardDealer` tag instance that are trying to draw cards from the same pack? The answer is no. The JSP container must guarantee that any given instance of a tag handler class is dedicated to one thread at one given moment. How this is achieved is up to the JSP container designer—but you as a developer need not (in fact, should not) worry about synchronizing method calls within your tag handler classes.

So much for the life cycle methods of IterationTag. However, there is one "business" method left to explain, and that's `dealCard()`. It's an important method, for it retrieves a card from the pack—it's only by calling this method that the pack is reduced and the loop implied by the logic in `doAfterBody()` can be broken. However, there is no code inside of the CardDealingTag class that calls this method, so where is it called from? The answer lies in the code of the tag handler class for the card tag—the CardTag class:

```
import java.io.IOException;
import javax.servlet.jsp.JspException;
import javax.servlet.jsp.JspWriter;
import javax.servlet.jsp.PageContext;
import javax.servlet.jsp.tagext.Tag;
public class CardTag implements Tag {
  private PageContext pageContext;
  private Tag parent;
  private static int instanceNo;
  public CardTag() {
        instanceNo++;
  }
  public void setPageContext(PageContext pageContext) {
        this.pageContext = pageContext;
  }
  public void setParent(Tag parent) {
        this.parent = parent;
  }
  public Tag getParent() {
        return parent;
  }
  public int doStartTag() {
        return Tag.SKIP_BODY;
  }
  public int doEndTag() throws JspException {
        CardDealingTag dealer = (CardDealingTag) getParent();
        String card = dealer.dealCard();
        JspWriter out = pageContext.getOut();
        try {
              out.write(card);
              //out.write(card + "<br />" + instanceNo);
        } catch (IOException e) {
              throw new JspException(e);
        }
        return Tag.EVAL_PAGE;
  }
  public void release() {
      System.out.println("Releasing CardTag instance number: " + instanceNo);
  }
}
```

The CardTag tag handler is mostly simpler than the CardDealer tag handler. It implements the Tag interface rather than IterationTag, and has no body, as you can see from the tag library descriptor declaration:

```
<tag>
  <name>card</name>
  <tag-class>webcert.ch08.examp0804.CardTag</tag-class>
  <body-content>empty</body-content>
</tag>
```

This is reinforced by the `doStartTag()` method, which simply skips the body. All the action occurs in the `doEndTag()` method, whose purpose is to obtain the latest card from the pack and send the name of the card to page output. Its mechanism for doing this is simple enough.

`getParent()` works well when the tag in question is nested directly inside of its intended parent. But what if some other tag gets between the intended parent and child elements, by accident or design? Consider the following change to the JSP document that used the `cardDealer` and `card tags:`

```
<mytags:cardDealer>
<tr>
 <td><mytags:card /></td>
 <td><mytags:embolden><mytags:card /></mytags:embolden></td>
 <td><mytags:card /></td>
 <td><mytags:card /></td>
</tr>
</mytags:cardDealer>
```

You can see a new tag here, called "embolden," which surrounds the `card` tag for the second player (in the second column of the table). The tag's purpose is very simple: It introduces HTML boldface beginning and end tags to surround any body content (of course, it would be much easier just to write `<b><mytags:card /></b>;` bear with this as a teaching example!). For brevity, its tag handler code isn't shown here, but the class name is EmboldenTag. Now when the tag handler code for the card tag reaches the first line of code in its `doEndTag()` method:

```
CardDealingTag dealer = (CardDealingTag) getParent();
```

The actual tag handler instance returned by the `getParent()` method will be of type EmboldenTag—not the expected CardDealingTag instance as required. The page will fall down in a messy heap at run time with a ClassCastException.

There is a solution to this, provided by a static method on the TagSupport class, called `findAncestorByClass()`, which accepts two parameters: the first an instance of the tag whose ancestor is sought, and the second the class type of the ancestor tag. Here's the rewritten code for the `doEndTag()` method in `card`'s tag handler:

```
Class parentClass;
try {
  parentClass = Class.forName("webcert.ch08.examp0804.CardDealingTag");
} catch (ClassNotFoundException e1) {
  throw new JspException(e1);
}
CardDealingTag dealer = (CardDealingTag)
  TagSupport.findAncestorWithClass(this, parentClass);
// Code is unchanged from this point onwards...
String card = dealer.dealCard();
// etc.
```

First of all, the code makes an instance of Class type, using the static `Class.forName()` method. The instance required here is the CardDealingTag. Then in place of `getParent()`, `TagSupport.findAncestorWithClass()` is called, passing in "this" (the current instance of the CardTag tag handler), and the class instance we have just made. The method searches through the hierarchy of tags until it finds a parent, or grandparent, or great-great-grandparent (and so on) of the required class, CardDealingTag. The first (closest) relative is returned. The class match doesn't have to be exact: A subclass is acceptable (the API documentation states that the method will return "the nearest ancestor that implements the interface or is an instance of the class specified"). Under the covers, the code makes use of the `getParent()` method for each tag examined in the hierarchy, hence the importance of providing a functional `getParent()` method even if you never think your tag will need it.

on the job

This card-dealing example is not what I would regard as "production ready" code. If you forgot to include the `card` tag inside the `cardDealer` tag, you would produce an endless loop, which is not at all obvious just by looking at the tag declarations in the JavaServer Page source. There are mechanisms you can use—out of scope of the exam—to ensure that validation is performed at translation time. You might write a TagExtraInfo class to associate with a tag definition, and use it to perform complex validation on the tag's

attributes. However, to solve the validation problem posed here (checking the proper nesting of related tags), you would need to write a class extending javax.servlet.jsp.tagext.TagLibraryValidator. There are methods on this class called by the JSP container at translation time. In particular, the `validate()` method passes in an XML representation of the entire JSP page to be validated, giving you the opportunity to perform cross-tag checking and—if necessary—halting the translation process with an appropriate error message.

Other Methods on the TagSupport Class

TagSupport provides some other convenience methods that you should know about for the exam.

- `public void setId(String id)` and `public String getId()`—these methods assume that you will set up an attribute called `id` for your tag, intended to uniquely identify the tag on the page. It's up to you whether you do or not—but if you do, then the JSP container will invoke the `setId()` method in the normal way.
- `public void setValue(String name, Object o)`, `public Object getValue(String name)`, `public void removeValue(String name)`, and `public Enumeration getValues()`—these methods are underpinned by an instance variable Hashtable within the TagSupport class, just like the set of methods used to support attributes in different scopes (`request`, `session`, etc.). The idea is that you can associate named values with the tag instance and get them back according to their name (a unique String key). Note that the `getValues()` method returns not an Enumeration of values but of keys (you can use each key in turn with the `getValue()` method to return the underlying object).

exam watch

Note that the `setValue (String name, Object o)` method in TagSupport is not a substitute for you providing individually crafted "setter" methods for each attribute you want to expose on your tag. The JSP container will not call the `setValue()` method; it's there for your own internal use in the tag handler code.

The IterationTag life cycle is, to a large extent, superseded by JSTL's iteration capabilities. You can probably imagine how the card-dealing example could be rewritten using `<c:forEach>`. However, I still like to use the IterationTag life cycle when I have complex business functionality to incorporate. Encapsulation is usually more readily achieved inside tag handler code than when using naked JSTL within JSP page source.

BodyTag Interface and BodyTagSupport Class

So to the third and last manifestation of the custom tag life cycle: the BodyTag interface (see Figure 8-6). Because IterationTag expands the base life cycle, BodyTag expands the iteration life cycle. The additional capability that a BodyTag has over its predecessors is the ability to manipulate the content of its body (the part that lies between the opening and closing tags).

This statement might seem initially confusing. Surely, the types of tag we have encountered have this capacity already? All tags, regardless of type, can dictate the type of body content allowed through the `<body-content>` element in the tag library descriptor—even, as we have seen, to the extent of banning body content altogether (when `<body-content>` is set to "empty"). And an IterationTag can cause its body to be evaluated as many times as it chooses.

However, all we have really seen so far is the ability of tags to append (or prefix) to body content. None of the tags have actually taken what is in the body already and done something with it—perhaps changing the body out of all recognition or obliterating the body altogether. This is where the BodyTag interface comes in. Underpinning the BodyTag interface is a BodyContent object. This is a type of JspWriter, with an important distinction: The contents are buffered so that no part of the body has yet been committed to page output. This is what gives BodyTags their ability to take any liberties they wish with body content.

Let's first of all take a look at the BodyTag life cycle, shown in Figure 8-6. You can see two new life cycle methods over and above those provided by Tag and IterationTag.

- `setBodyContent()` gives you the opportunity to save the BodyContent object that will hold the buffered body contents. This method is called after `doStartTag()`, but before the next method, `doInitBody()`.
- `doInitBody()` is called before the JSP container enters and evaluates this tag's body for the first time. It is called only once per access to the tag, however many

FIGURE 8-6 Custom Tag Life Cycle (3): The BodyTag Interface

JSP container processing one occurrence of a tag implementing the BodyTag Interface in one JSP page:

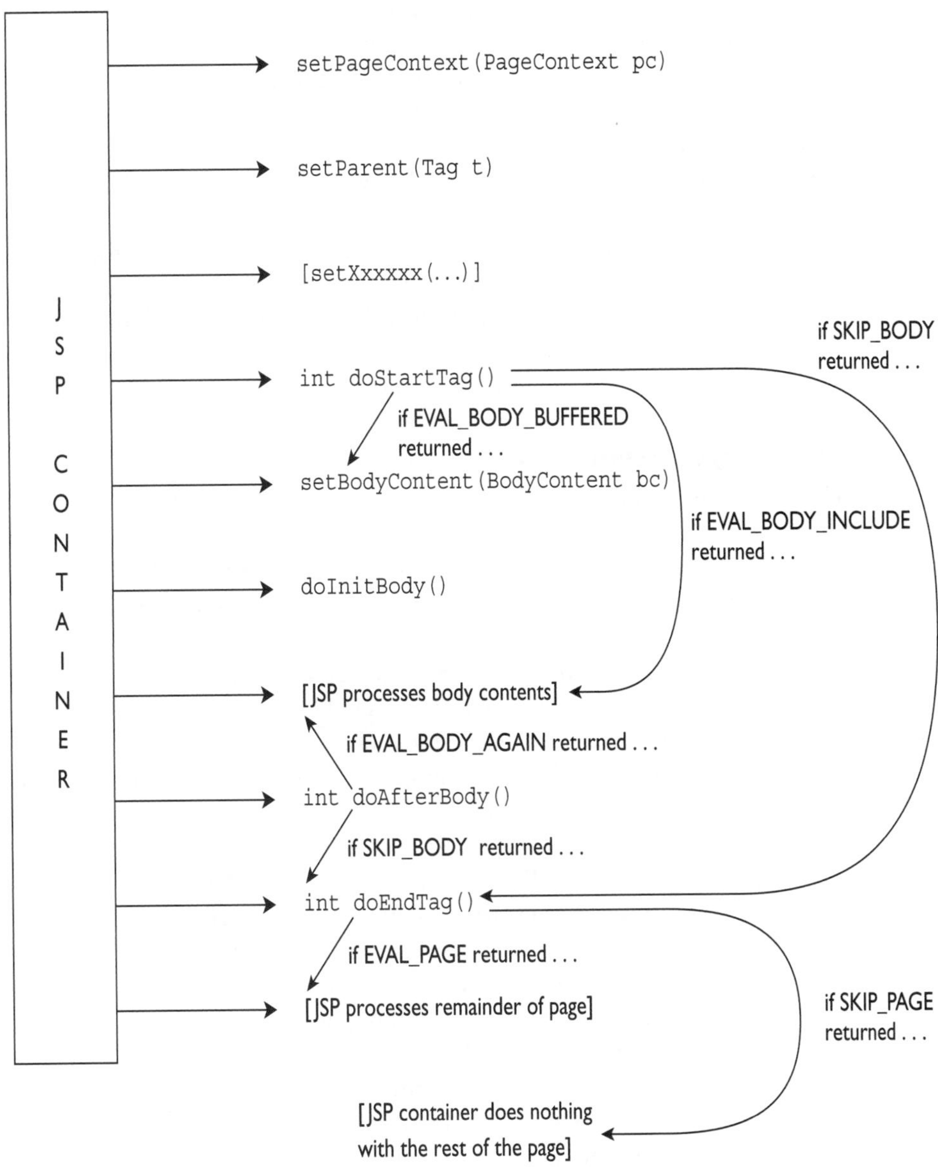

times you choose to iterate through the body. Remember that at this point, the BodyContent object—though available—is empty: The body hasn't been evaluated at all yet.

One additional field is provided in the interface: BodyTag.EVAL_BODY _BUFFERED. This gives a new, third return code option from `doStartTag()`. Now, as well as being able to skip the body altogether (Tag.SKIP_BODY) or evaluating the body as normal (Tag.EVAL_BODY_INCLUDE), you can choose BodyTag.EVAL_BODY_BUFFERED, which has the effect of making the BodyContent object available. (Unless you set this return code, then the `setBodyContent()` method is not called.)

Beyond `doInitBody()`, the life cycle is exactly the same—with the important exception that `doAfterBody()` still has access to the BodyContent object. Understanding the methods on this object is the real key to effectively learning Body Tag-style tags.

The BodyContent Object

The BodyContent object effectively traps the output from any evaluations of the body that occur within the tag. As noted, the BodyContent is a JspWriter, so you can (in your tag handler code) write additional content to the BodyContent object before, between, and after evaluations of the tag body that arrive in the Body Content object as well.

Although the BodyContent object is a writer, there is no real underpinning stream; everything that accumulates there is held in a string buffer. One consequence of this is that you can write as much as you like to BodyContent, but nothing arrives in the page output, which can be baffling and confusing unless you know what is going on. What you are meant to do, usually when you are finished doing all you need to evaluate in the tag (most likely at the end of `doEndTag()`), is redirect the output to some other writer. BodyContent has a method exactly for this purpose: `writeOut(Writer w)`. The entire contents of the BodyContent object are appended to the Writer of your choice. But which Writer should you choose? Again, BodyContent comes to the rescue with the method `getEnclosingWriter()`, which passes back a JspWriter object. This is quite likely to be the JspWriter that is associated with the JSP page as a whole. However, if you consider that your tag might be nested within another tag implementing the BodyTag interface, the enclosing writer could be another BodyContent object itself. Really, though, this doesn't matter; almost invariably, the right thing to do is to pass the output to the enclosing writer, for whatever logic is controlling the enclosing writer should have a chance to influence what happens to the output produced in your inner tag. So a typical invocation you will see at the end of your tag logic goes like this:

```
BodyContent bc = getBodyContent();
bc.writeOut(bc.getEnclosingWriter());
```

You might choose a different approach entirely, which is to use the capabilities of BodyContent to read what's been initially placed in the body of the tag, but never to write directly to BodyContent at all. You can always write whatever you like to the enclosing writer and silently drop the original content of the tag. This is especially useful when you set the content of your tag in the tag library to `<body-content>tagdependent</body-content>`. This means that the JSP container will make no effort at all to translate the body contents of your tag: It's up to the tag logic to do that. A very typical example of this use is when the body of the tag contains some completely non-Java dynamic content—such as an SQL statement to read a database. Suppose you have a JSP page with such a tag setup:

```
<mytags:sqlExecute>SELECT * FROM PRODUCT WHERE NAME LIKE
%1</mytags:sqlExecute>
```

Obviously, the user never wants to see "SELECT * FROM PRODUCT . . ."; he or she is far more likely to prefer to see a nicely formatted set of rows in an HTML table, showing details about a selection of products from the appropriate database table. Let's sketch out how you might approach writing a BodyTag to perform this translation:

- Ensure that you pass back EVAL_BODY_BUFFERED from the `doStartTag()` method (if you're extending BodyTagSupport, no need even to override the method—this is the default return code).
- Trap the BodyContent object in a private instance variable in your implementation of the `setBodyContent()` method (again—this work is done already if you're extending BodyTagSupport).
- Override `doAfterBody()`, calling the `getString()` method on the Body Content object—return this to a local String variable. This variable will contain the SQL string as an outcome of evaluating the body.
- Still in `doAfterBody()`, establish a data source connection to your database, and execute the SQL string. From the ResultSet returned, format the output as desired (in an HTML table, XML, or whatever). Write this to page output using the Jsp Writer returned by the BodyContent object's `getEnclosingWriter()` method.

- Still in `doAfterBody()`, release your data source connection, and return SKIP_BODY to prevent any further evaluations (no need for iteration here).

Before you develop database access tags along the lines of the pseudo-code drafted here, check out the capabilities of the JSTL SQL tag library.

EXERCISE 8-4

The "Classic" Custom Tag Event Model

In this exercise, you'll write a custom tag that will take a pair of numbers, and use this to generate a Fibonacci-like sequence of numbers. This works by taking the initial pair of numbers and adding them together, to produce a third. The second and third are then added together to produce a fourth, then the third and fourth to produce a fifth, and so on. If the pair of numbers you start with is 1 and 1, the output is the original Fibonacci sequence 1, 1, 2, 3, 5, 8, 13, 21, 34, and so on. Here we see the output from the tag in the solution code, using 1 and 1 as the first and second numbers in the sequence:

Fibonacci Sequence

1
1
2
3
5
8
13
21
34
55
10 rows of Fibonacci-like sequence generated

For this exercise, create the usual web application directory structure under a directory called ex0804, and proceed with the steps for the exercise. There's a solution in the CD in the file sourcecode/ch08/ex0804.war.

Create an HTML Form (fibonacci.html)

1. Create a file directly in the web application root ex0804 called fibonacci.html.
2. Create an HTML form that allows you to type values into three input fields named seed1, seed2, and rowLimit. seed1 is for the first number in the sequence, seed2 is for the second number, and rowLimit determines how many numbers in the sequence will be generated and displayed.
3. For the action on the HTML form, specify Fibonacci.jspx.

Create a JSP Document (fibonacci.jspx)

4. Create a file directly in the web application root ex0804 called fibonacci.jspx.
5. Declare a URI for a tag library as a namespace attribute (xmlns) of the root `<html>` tag.
6. Include the namespace for standard actions (xmlns:jsp="http://java.sun.com/JSP/Page") and the following boilerplate code, which ensures HTML (rather than XML) output:

```
<jsp:output omit-xml-declaration="true" />
<jsp:directive.page contentType="text/html" />
```

7. In the body of the HTML, include a call to a tag called fibonacci. Provide an attribute called `rowLimit`, whose value is set using the EL variable representing the `rowLimit` request parameter passed from the fibonacci.html web page.
8. In the body of the tag (i.e., between the opening and closing tags), include two EL variables separated by a comma. The first should return the seed1 request parameter and the second the seed2 request parameter.

Write a Tag Handler Class (Fibonacci.java)

9. In an appropriate package directory under WEB-INF/src, create a Java source file called webcert.ch08.ex0804.FibonnacciTag.java. Make sure that the class declaration extends BodyTagSupport.

10. In the source file, define an instance variable called *rowLimit* of type **int**, together with `getRowLimit()` and `setRowLimit()` methods—this will handle the *rowLimit* attribute on the tag.
11. Define an instance variable called *currentRowNum* of type **int**—to keep count of how many iterations the tag has performed. Initialize the value of this to 1 in an overriding `doInitBody()` method.
12. Define instance variables (all of type **int**) to hold the current sequence number, the previous sequence number, and the previous to previous sequence number (the solution code calls these *currentValue*, *backOneValue*, and *backTwoValue*, respectively).
13. In an overriding `doAfterBody()` method, have logic that is performed only when the current row number (*currentRowNum*) is equal to 1. This should set up an HTML table heading, and print two table rows and cells containing the first two numbers in the sequence. These can be obtained by parsing the two comma-separated numbers in the tag body—available in the BodyContent object (available to you because this tag extends BodyTagSupport). Don't forget to store these two numbers in their appropriate instance variables (*backOneValue* and *backTwoValue*).
14. Next in `doAfterBody()`, have logic that detects when the number of rows requested in *rowLimit* has been exceeded. If this condition is true, return immediately from the method with a Tag.SKIP_BODY return code.
15. Next in *doAfterBody()*, calculate the current value of the sequence from the previous two values, and output this as a further table row. Shuffle the variable values (of *currentValue*, *backOneValue*, and *backTwoValue*) ready for the next iteration of the loop.
16. Finally in `doAfterBody()`, increment the current row number (*currentRow Num*), and return IterationTag.EVAL_BODY_AGAIN—you want to keep going filling up table rows until the limit has been reached.
17. In an overriding `doEndTag()` method, terminate the HTML table with an appropriate closing tag.

Set Up the TLD File

18. Create a TLD file called mytags.tld in a WEB-INF/tags directory.
19. Include a tag entry with a name of fibonacci, a tag class of webcert.ch08 .ex0804.FibonacciTag, and a body content of "*scriptless*." (Note on *scriptless*:

This is the fourth and final legal value for body content that you have met in this chapter. This disallows Java language scriptlets, expressions, declarations, and the like, but still allows EL evaluations to go ahead.)

20. Include a definition with the tag entry for an attribute named *rowLimit*. This is a required attribute and should allow run-time expressions.

Add a Tag Library Mapping in the Deployment Descriptor (web.xml)

21. In WEB-INF/web.xml, ensure there is an appropriate `<taglib>` element within a `<jsp-config>` element.
22. The `taglib` URI should match whatever you declared in fibonacci.jspx.
23. The `taglib` location should point to /WEB-INF/tags/mytags.tld.

Run and Test the Code

24. Create a WAR file from your development directory ex0804, and deploy this to your server. Run and test the code with an appropriate URL such as

```
http://localhost:8080/ex0804/Fibonacci.html
```

CERTIFICATION SUMMARY

In this chapter you started by learning how to use preexisting tags from a tag library—how to use them in a JSP page or document, how to reference the tag library in the JSP page or document, and how to use the deployment descriptor to let the JSP container track the path from the JSP page or document to the tag library descriptor file.

You saw that tags within the JSP page are used in exactly the same manner as JSP standard actions, using XML-like syntax, declared in the form

```
<prefix:tagname attribute="value">any body content goes
here</prefix:tagname>
```

You further learned that you can use a `taglib` directive to declare the tag library that holds the tag you are using, and that this takes the form

```
<%@ taglib prefix="prefix" uri="anyStringYouLike" %>
```

You also touched on the alternative form found in JSP documents, which use namespace declarations instead of taglib directives, in this form:

```
<anyElement xmlns:prefix="anyStringYouLikeToRepresentTheURI">
```

You went on to discover how to reference a tag library in the web deployment descriptor, web.xml. You saw that this can be done within the `<taglib>` subelement of `<jsp-config>`. You saw that `<taglib>` has two subelements, one called `<taglib-uri>`—whose value must match the URI you place in the `taglib` directive—and another called `<taglib-location>`—whose value holds an path to the tag library descriptor file (.tld) holding tag definitions.

You learned more about the `<jsp-config>` element and, in particular, saw how this can be used to switch off EL for a group of JSP files defined in a `<jsp-property-group>`, by setting the `<el-ignored>` element to "true." You also saw how Java language scripting can be switched off for a group of JSP files by setting the `<scripting-invalid>` element to "true."

You then examined a tag library descriptor file in detail, seeing how to set up certain mandatory heading elements, such as `<tlib-version>` and `<short-name>`. You then learned about the elements used to define a tag, such as `<name>` (the name used in the JSP file after the prefix to target this tag), `<tag-class>` (to point to the actual Java tag handler class that does the work), and `<body-content>` (to define the permitted content between the opening and closing tags, with valid values ranging from empty through tagdependent, scriptless, and JSP). You also learned that a `<tag>` element might contain `<attribute>` elements, each with a trio of attributes: `<name>` (to specify the attribute name), `<required>` (true or false: whether mandatory or not), and `<rtexprvalue>` (true or false: whether a run-time expression, such as a Java language expression or piece of EL, can be used to set the attribute value).

In the next part of the chapter, you learned about the Java Standard Tag Libraries—in particular, the core library. You met fourteen custom tag actions you can use in your own JSP pages or documents, split across four groups: general purpose, conditional, iteration, and URL-related.

In the general purpose group, you saw that `<c:out>` can be used to output a value to the current JSPWriter, including the ability to escape XML-unfriendly characters. You used `<c:set>` to set values of attributes in the scope of your choice and `<c:remove>` to remove them again. Finally in this group, you learned how `<c:catch>` can be used to suppress minor errors within your JSP page.

In the conditional group, you saw how `<c:if>` can be used to perform a test, and so conditionally include pieces of JSP page source. You also saw how the result of the test can be saved to an attribute accessible through EL at a later time. You also learned how the `<c:choose>` action can be used to choose one true condition from many, defined in `<c:when>` subactions, with the possibility of including a single default action in a `<c:otherwise>` subaction.

In the iteration group, you saw that `<c:forEach>` can be used to work through all the objects in any kind of Collection or Map. You also saw that `<c:forEach>` has an alternative syntax, which allows iteration through a numeric sequence by steps—much like a Java "for" loop. You then met `<c:forTokens>` and found that most of its syntax is identical to `<c:forEach>` but that it specializes in breaking up Strings into separate Strings (much like Java's StringTokenizer class).

In the last JSTL core library group, URL-related actions, you learned about the `<c:import>` action and how this can be used in lieu of `<jsp:include>`. You saw how this action can be used to import local resources from the same web application, or resources in different web applications on the same server, or even external resources from other servers. You learned that the target of the import can be the JSPWriter directly or an interim reader (for more efficient processing of large imports). You also learned about `<c:url>`, for manufacturing URL strings (with session information automatically encoded when necessary), and `<c:redirect>`, to instruct clients to redirect to other resources. You finally met `<c:param>`, which can be used to provide additional request parameters to accompany any of the previous three URL-related actions.

Then you examined EL functions. You learned that any public static method in any class can be exposed as an EL function. You saw that making this happen requires a `<function>` element entry in the tag library descriptor—including the name of the function in the `<name>` element, the fully qualified name of the Java class containing the supporting method in the `<function-class>` element, and a stylized version of the method signature in the `<function-signature>` element. You learned the differences between `<function-signature>` and method signature: Keywords are omitted, parameters are expressed without parameter names (only types), and any Java objects returned or passed as parameters are always written with a fully qualified name. You finally learned that EL function-calling syntax looks like a mixture between tags and Java method calls: `${prefix:myfunction(param1, param2)}`.

In the last part of the chapter, you learned about custom tags. You saw that the custom tag life cycle grows in complexity, dependent on whether you implement the Tag, IterationTag or BodyTag interface. You learned that the package containing these interfaces (javax.servlet.jsp.tagext) also contains two classes that save you work by providing default implementations: TagSupport (implementing IterationTag and Tag) and BodyTagSupport (implementing BodyTag).

You saw that in all cases, methods are called by the JSP container to provide a tag handling class with a PageContext object and (if relevant) the object representing the enclosing tag, and that this is followed by JSP container calls to set attribute values. You saw that—still, in all cases—`doStartTag()` is the next method called by the JSP container. You saw that a return code (Tag.SKIP_BODY) from `doStartTag()` might cause the JSP container to skip the body altogether and proceed directly to calling the `doEndTag()` method. You saw that `doEndTag()` can abort the rest of the page (by providing a return code of Tag.SKIP_PAGE) or allow it to be processed (Tag.EVAL_PAGE).

You then learned about the divergent parts of the life cycle. In IterationTag, you saw how an additional method—`doAfterBody()`—can cause the body to be processed again (with a return code of IterationTag.EVAL_BODY_AGAIN) or proceed to the `doEndTag()` method (Tag.SKIP_BODY). You saw that BodyTag adds to this by allowing `doStartTag()` an additional return code—BodyTag.EVAL_BODY_BUFFERED. You learned that when this is set, your tag is provided with a BodyContent object—representing the buffered contents of the body—and that by using this, you can manipulate the body contents before they are written out to the enclosing JSPWriter.

TWO-MINUTE DRILL

Tag Libraries

- Tags are used in a JSP page using the syntax `<prefix:tagname attribute="value">`any body content goes here`</prefix:tagname>`.
- The prefix used must match the value of the prefix attribute in the `taglib` directive.
- A `taglib` directive has the following syntax: `<%@ taglib prefix="prefix" uri="anyStringYouLike" %>`.
- For JSP documents, `taglib` directives are disallowed.
- JSP documents use XML namespace syntax as an alternative to the `taglib` directive.
- Namespace syntax can be attached to any element (but usually the root element), like this: `<anyElement xmlns:prefix="anyStringYouLikeToRepresentTheURI">`.
- The URI declared in the `taglib` directive (or namespace value) should match the value of a `<taglib-uri>` element in the deployment descriptor.
- The `<taglib-uri>` element is paired with a `<taglib-location>` element, which points to the location within the web application where the tag library descriptor file is located.
- `<taglib-uri>` and `<taglib-location>` are both subelements of `<taglib>`, which is a subelement of `<jsp-config>`, which is a subelement of the root element `<web-app>`.
- Apart from `<taglib>`, `<jsp-config>` can have one other type of subelement: `<jsp-property-group>`.
- Within `<jsp-property-group>`, you can define a group of JSP files with the `<url-pattern>` element.
- Also within `<jsp-property-group>`, EL can be turned off for the defined group of JSP files by setting the `<el-ignored>` element to a value of "true."
- Again within `<jsp-property-group>`, scripting can be turned off for the defined group of JSP files by setting the `<scripting-invalid>` element to a value of "true."
- A tag library descriptor file (TLD) has a root element of `<taglib>`.

- A TLD must have elements `<tlib-version>` and `<short-name>` defined.
- A TLD can have any number of `<tag>` elements.
- The `<name>` subelement of `<tag>` defines the (unique) name of the tag, as it is called in the JSP page.
- The `<tag-class>` subelement of `<tag>` defines the fully qualified name of the Java tag handler class.
- The `<body-content>` subelement of `<tag>` defines what is allowed to appear between the opening and closing tags:
  - empty: The tag mustn't have a body.
  - tagdependent: The tag can have a body, but the contents (scriptlets, EL, etc.) are completely ignored and treated like template text.
  - scriptless: The tag body can contain EL or template text, but no Java language scripting constructs (expressions, scriptlets, declarations)—if these are present, a translation error results.
  - JSP: The tag body can contain anything: Java language scripting, EL, or template text.
- Another subelement of `<tag>` is `<attribute>`: This can appear zero, one, or many times.
- The `<attribute>` element is used to define attributes on a tag and has three subelements:
  - `<name>`—a name for the attribute (unique within the tag)
  - `<required>`—true or false—whether the attribute must be present or is optional.
  - `<rtexprvalue>`—true or false—whether the attribute value can be provided by an expression (Java language or EL).

JSTL

- There are five JavaServer Page Standard Tag Libraries (JSTL): core, relational database access (SQL), Formatting with Internationalization, XML Processing, and EL standard functions. The exam focuses only on the core library.
- The actions (tags) within the libraries represent a standard way of performing frequently required functionality within web applications.

- ❑ The following tag directive is used for access to core library actions in your pages:

```
<%@ taglib prefix="c" uri="http://java.sun.com/jsp/jstl/core" %>
```

- ❑ The "c" value for `prefix` is usual, but optional.
- ❑ The value for `uri` must be just as shown above.
- ❑ There are fourteen core library actions, divided into four groups: general purpose, conditional, iteration, and URL-related.
- ❑ There are four actions in the general purpose group: `<c:out>`, `<c:set>`, `<c:remove>`, and `<c:catch>`.
- ❑ `<c:out>` is for directing output to the JSPWriter. Its attributes are *value* (the output), *default* (the output if *value* is **null**), and *escapeXml* (for converting XML-unfriendly characters).
- ❑ `<c:set>` is for setting attributes in any scope. Its main attributes are*value* (contents of attribute), *var* (name of attribute), and *scope* (scope of attribute).
- ❑ `<c:set>` also has *target* and *property* attributes for setting properties on beans.
- ❑ `<c:remove>` is for removing attributes in any scope. It has only the attributes *var* (name of attribute to remove) and *scope* (scope of attribute).
- ❑ `<c:catch>` catches Throwable objects thrown from the statements it contains. It has only the one optional attribute, *var*, to store the Throwable object for later use.
- ❑ The conditional group in the JSTL library has four actions: `<c:if>`, `<c:choose>`, `<c:when>`, and `<c:otherwise>`.
- ❑ `<c:if>` is used to conditionally execute some JSP statements if a test proves true. Its attributes are *test* (expression for the test), *var* (optional attribute variable to hold the result of the test), and *scope* (scope of the optional attribute).
- ❑ `<c:choose>` is used to contain mutually exclusive tests, held in `<c:when>` actions.
- ❑ `<c:choose>` can only contain `<c:when>` and `<c:otherwise>` actions (and white space).
- ❑ `<c:when>` has only one attribute: *test*.
- ❑ Only the statements bounded by the first `<c:when>...</c:when>` action whose test is true will be executed.

- One `<c:otherwise>` can be included after any `<c:when>` actions.
- The statements within `<c:otherwise>` are executed only if all the preceding `<c:when>` tests prove false.
- There are two actions in the iterator group of the JSTL core library: `<c:forEach>` and `<c:forTokens>`.
- `<c:forEach>` is used to iterate through a series of items in a collection, or simply to loop for a set number of times.
- `items` can hold Arrays, Strings, and most collection types in java.util: Collections, Maps, Iterators, and Enumerations.
- When iterating through collections, `<c:forEach>` uses the attributes *items* (for the collection object) and *var* (to represent each item in the collection on each circuit of the loop).
- When looping a set number of times, `<c:forEach>` uses the attributes *begin* (the number to begin at), *end* (the number to end at), and *step* (the amount to step by when working through from the begin number to the end number).
- In either case, a special variable called *varStatus* can be used to obtain properties about the current iteration.
- All the above attributes can be combined in a hybrid syntax—for example, to step through every second item in a collection.
- `<c:forTokens>` works similarly to `<c:forEach>`—but is specialized for breaking up (tokenizing) Strings.
- It has the same six attributes as `<c:forEach>`, and an additional seventh of its own.
- The *items* attribute will accept only a String as input.
- The additional seventh parameter is *delims*, which holds the characters used to denote where to break up the String.
- There are four actions in the URL-related group of the JSTL core library: `<c:import>`, `<c:url>`, `<c:redirect>`, and `<c:param>`.
- `<c:import>` is used to include a URL resource within the current page at run time.
- `<c:import>` has six attributes. The main one is *url* (the expression representing the URL resource to import).
- The *context* attribute can be used to specify a different context housed in the same application server.

- The *var* and *scope* attributes can be used to place the contents of the URL resource in a scoped attribute (as a String).
- Alternatively, *varReader* can be used to keep the contents of the URL resource in a Reader object.
- `<c:url>` is used to compose URL strings (for use as links in documents, for example).
- `<c:url>` has four attributes: *value* (expression for the URL string), *context* (optional alternative context on the same web application server), *var* (optional String attribute to hold the result of the URL String expression), and *scope* (scope for *var*, if used).
- `<c:redirect>` is used to instruct the web client to point to an alternative resource.
- `<c:redirect>` has two attributes: *url* (the URL for the client to point to) and *context* (optional alternative context if the URL is in a different web application on the same server).
- `<c:param>` can be nested within `<c:url>`, `<c:import>`, or `<c:redirect>`.
- `<c:param>` is used to attach additional parameters to the requests made or implied by the other URL-related actions.
- `<c:param>` has two attributes: *name* (the name of the request parameter) and *value* (the value of the request parameter).

EL Functions

- Any **public static** method in any Java class can be exposed as an EL function.
- EL functions are defined in `<function>` elements in a tag library descriptor (TLD).
- Within the `<function>` element, an EL function must have three subelements defined: `<name>`, `<function-class>`, and `<function-signature>`.
- `<name>` is a unique name for the function.
- `<name>` must be unique not only within functions in the TLD but also within other elements that might be defined in the TLD, such as custom tags and tag files.
- `<function-class>` gives the fully qualified name of the Java class containing the method backing the EL function.

- <function-signature> reflects the signature of the method backing the EL function.
- <function-signature> must always use fully qualified names for Java classes returned or passed in to the function (even String must be expressed as java.lang.String).
- Parameter names are omitted from the function signature (only types are defined).
- The method name in the function signature must match the method name in the Java class.
- Qualifiers (such as **public** and **static**) are omitted in the function signature. So the Java method with signature . . .

```
public static String getDefinition(String word, int timeForSearch)
```

- . . . would yield the following <function-signature>:

```
<function-signature>java.lang.String getDefinition(java.lang.String,
int)</function-signature>
```

- This function might be called in the JSP page with the following EL syntax:

```
${myfunctions:getDefinition(wordHeldInAttribute, 30)}
```

The "Classic" Custom Tag Event Model

- Custom tags are supported by Java classes called tag handler classes.
- A tag handler class must implement one of the Tag, IterationTag, or BodyTag interfaces in the javax.servlet.jsp.tagext package.
- Each of these interfaces extends the next, so IterationTag augments the life cycle of Tag, and BodyTag augments the life cycle of IterationTag.
- Two classes implement default functionality for tags: TagSupport and BodyTagSupport.
- TagSupport implements IterationTag (and therefore Tag as well).
- BodyTagSupport implements BodyTag.
- When the JSP container meets an occurrence of a tag in the page, it makes calls to known methods on an instance of the tag handler class.
- The method calls and other events that can occur whatever the type of tag are shown here in order:

- ❑ `setPageContext()`—to give the tag access to the PageContext object
- ❑ `setParent()`—to give the tag instance access to the enclosing tag instance
- ❑ `setXXX()`—to set any attribute values on the tag
- ❑ `doStartTag()`
- ❑ The processing of the tag body
- ❑ `doEndTag()`
- ❑ The processing of the remainder of the page

- ❑ `If doStartTag()` returns Tag.SKIP_BODY, the JSP container ignores anything between the opening and closing tags.
- ❑ `If doEndTag()` returns Tag.SKIP_PAGE, the JSP container aborts evaluation of the rest of the JSP page after the closing tag.
- ❑ `doStartTag()` can return Tag.EVAL_BODY, and `doEndTag()` can return Tag.EVAL_PAGE, which tell the JSP container to process the tag body and rest of page, respectively.
- ❑ IterationTag introduces a `doAfterBody()` method, called after the body is processed for the first time.
- ❑ If `doAfterBody()` returns IterationTag.EVAL_BODY_AGAIN, the JSP container processes the body again and then calls `doAfteBody()` again.
- ❑ `doAfterBody()` must return Tag.SKIP_BODY to break this loop.
- ❑ BodyTag introduces the concept of buffering the tag body (before it is committed to the JSPWriter) into a BodyContent object.
- ❑ For a BodyTag, the JSP container calls the methods `setBodyContent()` and `doInitBody()` immediately after the call to `doStartTag()`.
- ❑ However, for these calls to happen, `doStartTag()` must return BodyTag .EVAL_BODY_BUFFERED.
- ❑ The BodyContent object is a type of JSPWriter and can be used to manipulate the contents of the body before it is sent to page output.
- ❑ Alternatively, the body content can be discarded entirely.
- ❑ Important methods of BodyContent include `getEnclosingWriter()` and `writeOut(Writer out)`.

SELF TEST

The following questions will help you measure your understanding of the material presented in this chapter. Read all the choices carefully because there might be more than one correct answer. The number of correct choices to make is stated in the question, as in the real SCWCD exam.

Tag Libraries

1. Given a tag declared as shown in the following tag library descriptor extract, what are valid uses of the tag in a JSP page? You can assume that the tag library is correctly declared in the JSP page with a prefix of "mytags." (Choose three.)

```
<tag>
<name>book</name>
<tag-class>webcert.ch08.examp0801.BookTag</tag-class>
<body-content>tagdependent</body-content>
<attribute>
  <name>isbn</name>
  <required>true</required>
  <rtexprvalue>true</rtexprvalue>
  </attribute>
</tag>
```

A.

```
<mytags:book />
```

B.

```
<mytags:book isbn="<%= isbn %>">
```

C.

```
<mytags:book isbn="${isbn}" />
```

D.

```
<mytags:book isbn="1861979258" />
```

E.

```
<mytags:book isbn="${isbn}">Some default text if book not found</mytags:
book>
```

2. Which of the following XML fragments, if placed below the root element in the deployment descriptor, will deactivate the scripting language for all files in the web application with a .jsp extension? (Choose one.)

A.

```
<jsp-config>
  <jsp-property-group>
    <url-pattern>*.jsp</url-pattern>
    <scripting-invalid>true</scripting-invalid>
  </jsp-property-group>
</jsp-config>
```

B.

```
<jsp-config>
  <url-pattern>*.jsp</url-pattern>
  <scriptless>true</scriptless>
</jsp-config>
```

C.

```
<jsp-config>
  <url-pattern>/*.jsp</url-pattern>
  <el-ignored>true</el-ignored>
</jsp-config>
```

D.

```
<jsp-config>
  <jsp-property-group>
    <uri-pattern>*.jsp</uri-pattern>
    <script-invalid>true</script-invalid>
  </jsp-property-group>
</jsp-config>
```

E.

```
<jsp-config>
  <jsp-property-group>
    <url-pattern>*.jsp</url-pattern>
    <el-ignored>true</el-ignored>
  </jsp-property-group>
</jsp-config>
```

3. (drag-and-drop question) In the following illustration, match the correct numbered tag library descriptor element names to the letters masking the element names in the tag library descriptor source.

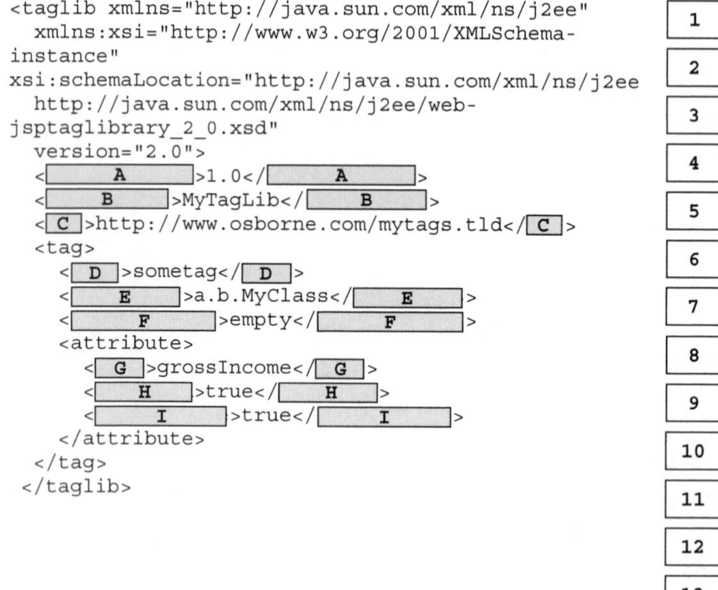

```
<taglib xmlns="http://java.sun.com/xml/ns/j2ee"
  xmlns:xsi="http://www.w3.org/2001/XMLSchema-
instance"
xsi:schemaLocation="http://java.sun.com/xml/ns/j2ee
  http://java.sun.com/xml/ns/j2ee/web-
jsptaglibrary_2_0.xsd"
  version="2.0">
  <[ A ]>1.0</[ A ]>
  <[ B ]>MyTagLib</[ B ]>
  <[ C ]>http://www.osborne.com/mytags.tld</[ C ]>
  <tag>
    <[ D ]>sometag</[ D ]>
    <[ E ]>a.b.MyClass</[ E ]>
    <[ F ]>empty</[ F ]>
    <attribute>
      <[ G ]>grossIncome</[ G ]>
      <[ H ]>true</[ H ]>
      <[ I ]>true</[ I ]>
    </attribute>
  </tag>
</taglib>
```

1	version
2	name
3	expression
4	runtime-expression
5	tlib-version
6	tag-class
7	class
8	name
9	short-name
10	uri
11	url-pattern
12	body
13	body-content
14	required
15	mandatory
16	rtexprvalue

4. Which of the following deployment descriptors will successfully and legally deactivate Expression Language for an entire web application? (Choose two)

A.

```
<?xml version="1.0" ?>
<!DOCTYPE web-app PUBLIC "-//Sun Microsystems, Inc.//DTD Web Application
2.3//EN"
"http://java.sun.com/dtd/web-app_2_3.dtd">
<web-app>
</web-app>
```

B.

```
<?xml version="1.0" ?>
<web-app version="2.4" xmlns="http://java.sun.com/xml/ns/j2ee"
xmlns:xsi="http://www.w3.org/2001/XMLSchema-instance"
xsi:schemaLocation="http://java.sun.com/xml/ns/j2ee
http://java.sun.com/xml/ns/j2ee/web-app_2_4.xsd">
</web-app>
```

C.

```
<?xml version="1.0" ?>
<!DOCTYPE web-app PUBLIC "-//Sun Microsystems, Inc.//DTD Web Application
2.3//EN"
"http://java.sun.com/dtd/web-app_2_3.dtd">
<web-app>
  <jsp-config>
    <jsp-property-group>
      <url-pattern>*.*</url-pattern>
      <el-ignored>true</el-ignored>
    </jsp-property-group>
  </jsp-config>
</web-app>
```

D.

```
<?xml version="1.0" ?>
<web-app version="2.4" xmlns="http://java.sun.com/xml/ns/j2ee"
xmlns:xsi="http://www.w3.org/2001/XMLSchema-instance"
xsi:schemaLocation="http://java.sun.com/xml/ns/j2ee
http://java.sun.com/xml/ns/j2ee/web-app_2_4.xsd">
  <jsp-config>
    <jsp-property-group>
      <url-pattern>/*</url-pattern>
      <el-ignored>true</el-ignored>
    </jsp-property-group>
  </jsp-config>
</web-app>
```

E.

```
<?xml version="1.0" ?>
<web-app version="2.4" xmlns="http://java.sun.com/xml/ns/j2ee"
xmlns:xsi="http://www.w3.org/2001/XMLSchema-instance"
xsi:schemaLocation="http://java.sun.com/xml/ns/j2ee
http://java.sun.com/xml/ns/j2ee/web-app_2_4.xsd">
```

```
<jsp-config>
    <jsp-property-group>
      <url-pattern>*.*</url-pattern>
      <el-invalid>true</el-invalid>
    </jsp-property-group>
  </jsp-config>
</web-app>
```

5. From the following use of the tag `<mytags:convert>`, what statements must be true about its setup and use? You can assume that the tag translates and executes correctly. (Choose three.)

```
<mytags:convert currency="${param.cur}"><%= amount %></mytags:convert>
```

A. The `taglib` declaration has a prefix of "mytags."

B. In the TLD, the tag's body content element has a value of JSP.

C. In the TLD, the tag's name element has the value of currency.

D. In the TLD, the tag's currency attribute has the required element set to true.

E. In the TLD, the tag's currency attribute has the rtexprvalue element set to true.

F. In the TLD, the tag's mandatory element is set to true.

JSTL

6. Which of the following characters are not converted by the `<c:out>` action when the attribute *escapeXml* is set to false? (Choose one.)

A. {

B. <

C. ;

D. @

E. All of the above

F. None of the above

7. Which of the following are invalid uses of the `<c:set>` action? (Choose three.)

A.

```
<c:set scope="page">value</c:set>
```

B.

```
<c:set value="value" var="${myVar}" />
```

C.

```
<c:set var="myVar" scope="${scope}">value</c:set>
```

D.

```
<c:set target="${myTarget}" property="myProp">propValue</c:set>
```

E.

```
<c:set value="${myVal}" target="myTarget" property="${myProp}" />
```

8. (drag-and-drop question) In the following illustration, match the numbered JSTL tag names, attribute names, and attribute values with the corresponding lettered points in the JSP document source shown. Your choices should lead to the output illustrated beneath the JSP document source.

```
<html xmlns:mytags="http://www.osborne.com/taglibs/mytags"
      xmlns:jsp="http://java.sun.com/JSP/Page"
      xmlns:c="http://java.sun.com/jsp/jstl/core" >
  <jsp:output omit-xml-declaration="true" />
  <jsp:directive.page contentType="text/html" />
  <head><title>JSTL Iterator Tags
Example</title></head>
  <body>
  <h1>Chapter 08 Question 08</h1>
  <h1>JSTL Drag and Drop</h1>
     <table border="1">
     <[A] [B]="num" [C]="1" />
     <[D]begin="1" end="7" [E]="[F]"
[G]="counter">
         <c:set var="num" [H]="${[I]}" />
<tr><td>${counter.count}</td><td>${num}</td></tr>
     </c:forEach>
     </table>
  </[J]>
</html>
```

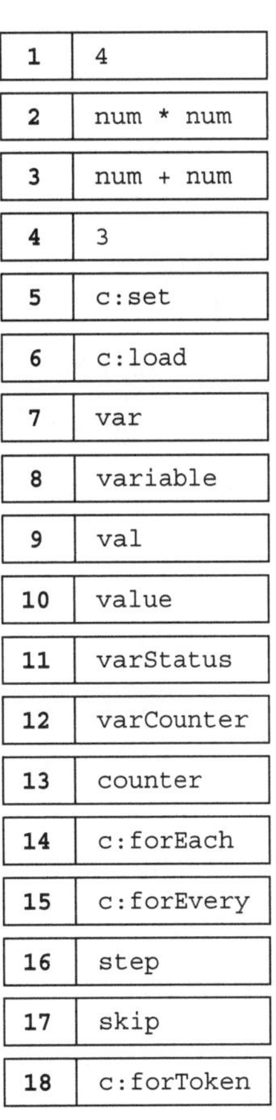

1	4
2	num * num
3	num + num
4	3
5	c:set
6	c:load
7	var
8	variable
9	val
10	value
11	varStatus
12	varCounter
13	counter
14	c:forEach
15	c:forEvery
16	step
17	skip
18	c:forToken

Chapter 08 Question 08

JSTL Drag and Drop

1	2
2	4
3	8

9. What is the result of attempting to access the following JSP page source? You can assume that the file countries.txt exists in the location specified. (Choose one.)

```
<html xmlns:mytags="http://www.osborne.com/taglibs/mytags"
      xmlns:jsp="http://java.sun.com/JSP/Page"
      xmlns:c="http://java.sun.com/jsp/jstl/core" >
  <jsp:output omit-xml-declaration="true" />
  <jsp:directive.page contentType="text/html" />
  <jsp:directive.page import="java.io.*" />
  <head><title>Question 9</title></head>
  <body>
    <c:import url="/countries.txt" varReader="myReader" />
    <jsp:scriptlet>
      Reader r = (Reader) pageContext.getAttribute("myReader");
      out.write(r.read());
    </jsp:scriptlet>
  </body>
</html>
```

A. The first character of the file countries.txt is sent to page output.

B. IOException occurs at run time.

C. NullPointerException occurs at run time.

D. Some other exception occurs at run time.

E. Translation error generating the source.

F. Translation error compiling the source.

10. What is the minimum number of attributes that must be specified in the `<c:forEach>` action? (Choose one.)

A. 1—*items*

B. 1—*collection*

C. 2—*var* and *items*

D. 2—*begin* and *end*

E. 3—*begin*, *end*, and *step*

F. 3—*var*, *collection*, and *varStatus*

EL Functions

11. Which of the following characteristics must a Java class have if it contains one or more EL functions? (Choose three.)

A. Instance variables matching the function attribute names

B. A no-argument constructor

C. A method that is **public**

D. A method that is **static**

E. A main method (signature: public static void main(String[] args))

F. A method that returns a nonvoid result

12. Which of the following represents a correct function declaration in the tag library descriptor? (Choose one.)

A.

```
<el-function>
  <description>Taxation Function</description>
  <name>netincome</name>
  <el-function-class>webcert.ch08.ex0803.Taxation</el-function-class>
  <el-function-signature>java.lang.String calcNetIncome(double, double,
      double, java.lang.String)</el-function-signature>
</el-function>
```

B.

```
<function>
  <description>Taxation Function</description>
  <name>netincome</name>
  <function-class>webcert.ch08.ex0803.Taxation.class</function-class>
  <function-signature>java.lang.String calcNetIncome(double, double,
      double, java.lang.String)</function-signature>
</function>
```

C.

```
<el-function>
  <description>Taxation Function</description>
  <name>netincome</name>
  <el-function-class>webcert.ch08.ex0803.Taxation</el-function-class>
  <el-function-signature>String calcNetIncome(double, double,
      double, String)</el-function-signature>
</el-function>
```

D.

```
<function>
  <description>Taxation Function</description>
```

```
    <name>netincome</name>
    <function-class>webcert.ch08.ex0803.Taxation</function-class>
    <function-signature>public static java.lang.String
      calcNetIncome(double grs, double allow, double rate,
      java.lang.String cur)
    </function-signature>
  </function>
```

E.

```
  <el-function>
    <description>Taxation Function</description>
    <name>netincome</name>
    <el-function-class>webcert.ch08.ex0803.Taxation</el-function-class>
    <el-function-method>public static String calcNetIncome(double, double,
        double, String)</el-function-method>
  </el-function>
```

13. What is the result of attempting to access the following JSP? You can assume that the EL functions are legally defined, that the EL function **mytags:divide** divides the first parameter by the second parameter, and that the EL function **mytags:round** rounds the result from the first parameter to the number of decimal places expressed by the second parameter. (Choose one.)

```
<html>
  <%@ taglib prefix="mytags" uri="http://www.osborne.com/taglibs/mytags" %>
  <head><title>Question 13</title></head>
  <body>
    <p>${mytags:round(${mytags:divide(arg1, arg2)}, 2)}</p>
  </body>
</html>
```

A. Translation error (in code generation).

B. Translation error (in code compilation).

C. Run-time error.

D. Zero, for arg1 and arg2 are not set to any value.

E. The expected result from the division, rounded to two decimal places.

14. Where in JSP page source can EL functions be used? (Choose two.)

A. In the body of a tag where body-content is set to scriptless

B. In the body of a tag where body-content is set to JSP

C. In the body of a tag where body-content is set to tagdependent

D. Within a JSP scriptlet

E. Within a JSP expression

F. Within a JSP declaration

15. Consider these pairings of Java method signatures and EL function method signatures for a TLD file. Which pairings go together and will work? (Choose two.)

A.

```
Java:
public String getNameForId(String id)
TLD:
public String getNameForId(String id)
```

B.

```
Java:
public static String getNameForId(int id)
TLD:
java.lang.String getNameForId(int)
```

C.

```
Java:
public static java.lang.String getNameForId(java.lang.String id)
TLD:
java.lang.String getNameForId(java.lang.String)
```

D.

```
Java:
static String getNameForId(String id)
TLD:
static java.lang.String getNameForId(java.lang.String id)
```

E.

```
Java:
public static String getNameForId(String id)
TLD:
public static java.lang.String getNameForId(java.lang.String)
```

The "Classic" Custom Tag Event Model

16. What is output from the following JSP document? (Choose one.)

```
JSP document:
<html xmlns:mytags="http://www.osborne.com/taglibs/mytags"
      xmlns:jsp="http://java.sun.com/JSP/Page"
      xmlns:c="http://java.sun.com/jsp/jstl/core" >
  <jsp:output omit-xml-declaration="true" />
  <jsp:directive.page contentType="text/html" />
  <head><title>Chapter 8 Question 16</title></head>
  <body>
    <c:set var="counter" value="0" />
  <p><mytags:question16>${counter}</mytags:question16></p>
  </body>
</html>
```

```
Tag Handler Code for question16 custom action:
import java.io.IOException;
import javax.servlet.jsp.JspException;
import javax.servlet.jsp.tagext.BodyTagSupport;
import javax.servlet.jsp.tagext.*;
public class Question16 extends BodyTagSupport {
  public int doAfterBody() throws JspException {
    int i = Integer.parseInt("" + pageContext.getAttribute("counter"));
    if (i > 5) {
      return Tag.SKIP_BODY;
    } else {
      pageContext.setAttribute("counter", "" + ++i);
  return IterationTag.EVAL_BODY_AGAIN;
    }
  }
}
```

A. 0123456

B. 01234

C. 12345

D. 23456

E. 123456

F. A blank page

17. Which of the following are valid statements relating to the `<body-content>` element in the tag library descriptor? (Choose two.)

    A. A closing tag may never be used for a custom action whose `<body-content>` element is set to "empty."

    B. A `<body-content>` setting of scripting-allowed permits JSP scriptlets in the body of the custom action.

    C. A `<body-content>` setting of jsp-document permits the use of JSP document syntax in the body of the custom action.

    D. To permit JSP expressions but not EL, `<body-content>` should be set to JSP.

    E. To permit EL but not JSP expressions, `<body-content>` should be set to scriptless.

    F. JSP expressions are legal in the body of a custom action whose `<body-content>` is set to tagdependent, but they will not be translated.

18. What is the result of accessing the following JSP document? (Choose one.)

JSP document:

```
<html xmlns:mytags="http://www.osborne.com/taglibs/mytags"
    xmlns:jsp="http://java.sun.com/JSP/Page"
    xmlns:c="http://java.sun.com/jsp/jstl/core" >
  <jsp:output omit-xml-declaration="true" />
  <jsp:directive.page contentType="text/html" />
  <jsp:directive.page import="java.io.Writer" />
  <head><title>Chapter 8 Question 18</title></head>
  <body>
    <jsp:scriptlet>Writer myOut = pageContext.getOut();</jsp:scriptlet>
  <p><mytags:question18>
      <jsp:scriptlet>myOut.write("Body");</jsp:scriptlet>
    </mytags:question18></p>
  </body>
</html>
```

Tag handler code for question18 custom action:

```
import java.io.IOException;
import javax.servlet.jsp.JspException;
import javax.servlet.jsp.tagext.*;
public class Question18 extends BodyTagSupport {
  public int doAfterBody() throws JspException {
    try {
      bodyContent.write("Legs");
      bodyContent.writeOut(bodyContent.getEnclosingWriter());
```

```
    } catch (IOException e) {
      throw new JspException(e);
    }
    return Tag.EVAL_PAGE;
  }
  public void doInitBody() throws JspException {
    try {
      bodyContent.write("Head");
    } catch (IOException e) {
      throw new JspException(e);
    }
  }
}
```

A. Translation error (source generation)

B. Translation error (source compilation)

C. Run-time error

D. Output of HeadBodyLegs

E. Output of BodyHeadLegs

F. Output of BodyHeadBodyLegs

19. Which TLD tag declarations would best fit this tag handler code? (Choose two.)

Tag handler code:

```
package webcert.ch08.examp0804;
import java.io.IOException;
import javax.servlet.jsp.JspException;
import javax.servlet.jsp.tagext.Tag;
import javax.servlet.jsp.tagext.TagSupport;
public class Question19 extends TagSupport {
  private int data;
  int getData() {
    return data;
  }
  void setData(int data) {
    this.data = data;
  }
  public int doEndTag() throws JspException {
    try {
      pageContext.getOut().write(id + ":" + data);
    } catch (IOException e) {
      throw new JspException(e);
```

```
    }
    return Tag.EVAL_PAGE;
  }
}
```

A.

```
<tag>
  <name>question19a</name>
  <tag-class>webcert.ch08.examp0804.Question19</tag-class>
  <body-content>empty</body-content>
  <attribute>
    <name>id</name>
    <required>false</required>
    <rtexprvalue>true</rtexprvalue>
  </attribute>
  <attribute>
    <name>data</name>
    <required>false</required>
    <rtexprvalue>true</rtexprvalue>
  </attribute>
</tag>
```

B.

```
<tag>
  <name>question19b</name>
  <tag-class>webcert.ch08.examp0804.Question19</tag-class>
  <body-content>empty</body-content>
  <attribute>
    <name>value</name>
    <required>false</required>
    <rtexprvalue>true</rtexprvalue>
  </attribute>
</tag>
```

C.

```
<tag>
  <name>question19c</name>
  <tag-class>webcert.ch08.examp0804.Question19</tag-class>
  <body-content>empty</body-content>
  <attribute>
    <name>data</name>
    <required>false</required>
```

```
      <rtexprvalue>true</rtexprvalue>
    </attribute>
  </tag>
```

D.

```
<tag>
  <name>question19d</name>
  <tag-class>webcert.ch08.examp0804.Question19</tag-class>
  <body-content>empty</body-content>
  <attribute>
    <name>id</name>
    <required>false</required>
    <rtexprvalue>true</rtexprvalue>
  </attribute>
</tag>
```

E.

```
<tag>
  <name>question19e</name>
  <tag-class>webcert.ch08.examp0804.Question19</tag-class>
  <body-content>empty</body-content>
</tag>
```

20. For the given interfaces, which of the following are valid sequences of method calls according to custom tag life cycle? (Choose three.)

   A. Tag: setParent, setPageContext, doStartTag
   B. Tag: setPageContext, setParent, doStartTag, doEndTag
   C. IterationTag: doStartTag, doInitBody, doAfterBody, doEndTag
   D. IterationTag: doStartTag, doAfterBody, doAfterBody, doAfterBody
   E. BodyTag: setBodyContent, doInitBody, doStartTag, doAfterBody
   F. BodyTag: doInitBody, setBodyContent, doStartTag, doEndTag
   G. BodyTag: doStartTag, setBodyContent, doInitBody, doAfterBody

LAB QUESTION

In this lab you are invited to write a custom tag that extends BodyTagSupport but overrides every tag life cycle method. Give the tag some attributes that will dictate the return codes from each of the life cycle methods. So, for example, suppose the tag has an attribute called *rcStartTag*, which accepts a value of 0, 1, or 2. Within the `doStartTag()` method for the tag handler, return Tag.SKIP_BODY if 0 is specified, Tag.EVAL_BODY_INCLUDE if 1 is specified, or BodyTag.EVAL_BODY_BUFFERED if 2 is specified for the *rcStartTag* attribute.

Write an HTML page that allows you to specify different values for each of the tag's attributes, and forward these to a JSP document that receives these values as parameters and uses EL to supply the values to an occurrence of your tag within the document. It doesn't really matter what the tag does, but try to get the page to reflect the tag life cycle methods called and the order in which they are called.

SELF TEST ANSWERS

Tag Libraries

1. ☑ **C**, **D**, and **E** are correct. **C** is correct because the attribute `isbn` can take a run-time expression and an EL expression is supplied using correct syntax. Also, the tag closes itself—although it's strange for a tagdependent tag to lack a body, it's not illegal. **D** is correct, this time supplying a constant for the required attribute `isbn`. **E** is correct—the opening tag has the same syntax as answer **C** (supplying an EL expression), but this time there is a body that is correctly rounded off by the end tag.
   ☒ **A** is incorrect because the attribute `isbn` is required, and it's missing in the syntax here. **B** is incorrect because the tag doesn't close itself, nor is there an end tag after a body. Though the tag may still work, the result could be catastrophic for any page source coming after, for this might be interpreted as the body of the tag.

2. ☑ **A** is the correct answer. **A** specifies the right sequence of elements—`<url-pattern>` and `<scripting-invalid>` nested inside `<jsp-property-group>` nested inside `<jsp-config>`. Furthermore, the URL pattern used (*.jsp) is correct—the leading slash is not required.
   ☒ **B** is incorrect: `<jsp-property-group>` is missing, and `<scriptless>` is an incorrect element name. **C** is incorrect because `<jsp-property-group>` is missing again, the value for `<url-pattern>` wrongly begins with a leading slash, and `<el-ignored>`—although a correct element name—controls expression language, not scripting. **D** is incorrect because `<uri-pattern>` and `<script-invalid>` are subtly wrong element names. **E** is incorrect—it's well formed with correct element names for ignoring expression language, but no good for suppressing scripting in all .jsp files.

3. ☑ **A** matches to **5** (tlib-version), **B** matches to **9** (short-name), **C** to **10** (uri), **D** to **8** (name), **E** to **6** (tag-class), **F** to **13** (body-content), **G** to **8** (name, again), **H** to **14** (required), and **I** to **16** (rtexprevalue).
   ☒ All other combinations are incorrect.

4. ☑ **A** and **D** are correct answers. **A** will work because web.xml is set to servlet version level 2.3, and, although empty of any detail, a JSP container will interpret that as meaning that EL should be ignored. **D** is correct, for although web.xml is at servlet version level 2.4, the necessary elements are included to turn off EL. Note the URL pattern to designate all files: /* (a single forward slash without the asterisk should also work, as this is the default mapping)

   ☒ **B** is incorrect, for the (empty) deployment descriptor is at servlet version level 2.4—at which EL is, by default, enabled. **C** is incorrect because the `<jsp-config>` element isn't recognized in a 2.3 deployment descriptor. Your web application won't even start if XML validation is performed against the DTD. **E** is incorrect on two counts: A pattern of *.* is illegal, and the element name is `<el-ignored>`, not `<el-invalid>`.

5. ☑ **A**, **B**, and **E** are correct. **A** is correct because the prefix "mytags" must match the `taglib` directive. **B** is correct because the body of the tag contains a Java language expression, and JSP is the only value that will permit this within the body content. **E** is correct because to support an EL expression as the value for the *currency* attribute, the attribute must have its *rtexprvalue* set to true.
   ☒ **C** is incorrect because the tag's `name` element is `convert`—it's the `name` attribute of one of its attributes, which is set to `currency`. **D** is incorrect because we can't infer anything just by looking at the tag use about whether the currency attribute is required or not; it might be fine to leave it out altogether. **F** is incorrect because tags don't have a mandatory element—that's made up.

JSTL

6. ☑ **E** is the correct answer. If *escapeXml* is set to false, then no characters are converted, so all of the listed characters are not converted.
   ☒ **A**, **B**, **C**, and **D** are incorrect because no character conversion takes place. If *escapeXml* were set to true, then the less than sign (<) would be converted to the entity <. **F** is incorrect because it implies that all the listed characters would be converted.

7. ☑ **A**, **B**, and **C** are the correct answers. **A** is incorrect because the syntax including the *scope* attribute demands that there is a *var* attribute—the name of the variable to set to a value. **B** is incorrect because although the *var* attribute is present, it can't accept a run-time EL expression. **C** is incorrect because the optional *scope* attribute can't accept a run-time EL expression either.
   ☒ **D** is valid syntax, so an incorrect answer. The *target* and *property* attributes are set correctly (*target* can accept EL expressions), and the value is in the body of the tag. **E** is also valid syntax, and so an incorrect answer. This time, *value*, *target*, and *property* are set as attributes, with the values for *value* and *property* coming from EL expressions, which is legal.

8. ☑ **A** matches to **5** (c:set), **B** matches to **7** (var), **C** to **10** (value), **D** to **14** (c:forEach), **E** to **16** (step), **F** to **4** (3), **G** to **11** (varStatus), **H** to **10** (value, again), **I** to **3** (num + num), and **J** to **14** (c:forEach, again).
   ☒ All other combinations are incorrect.

9. ☑ C is the correct answer. A NullPointerException occurs. This is because the Reader returned by the `<c:import>` action is available only within the body of the action. Because `<c:import>` has no body in the example code, the reader drifts out of scope immediately. When the scriptlet code accesses myReader, **null** is returned, and when the container attempts to invoke the `read()` method, a NullPointerException occurs.
   ☒ A is incorrect, for the file is never read. This would, however, be the correct answer if the scriptlet were properly enclosed inside the body of the `<c:import>` action. **B** is incorrect; the NullPointerException preempts the possibility of an IOException. **D** is incorrect; no other sorts of exception occur, and **E** and **F** are incorrect because the page source generates and compiles successfully.

10. ☑ A is the correct answer. It is possible to specify the *items* attribute on its own, in which case the loop will work through each item in the given collection.
   ☒ B is incorrect because there isn't a *collection* attribute. **C** is incorrect because although it is very common to specify the *var* attribute as well as the *items* attribute, you don't have to have each object in the collection available to you within the loop. **D** and **E** are incorrect—although they specify a correct combination of attributes, it is possible and legal to use less as shown in the correct answer. Finally, **F** is incorrect both because the number of attributes is too high, and because *collection* is a made-up attribute.

EL Functions

11. ☑ C, **D**, and **E** are the correct answers. All a Java class needs to support an EL function is a method that is declared as both public and static (hence, both **C** and **D** have to be true for the same function—but there is nothing in the answers that says that this can't be so). **E** is also true: Bizarre as it may seem, a class's main method can be exposed as an EL function, just because it is public and static. The facts that main returns nothing (**void**) and receives an array as a parameter are not barriers to EL function status.
   ☒ A and **B** are incorrect, because anything at instance level within the class (such as instance variables and constructors) is irrelevant for EL functions: It doesn't matter if these are present in the class or not. **F** is incorrect because it is allowable for an EL function not to return anything to the JSP page that uses it (provided the TLD states that the function signature has a return type of "void").

12. ☑ B is the correct answer, for it has the correct syntax for an EL function declaration in the TLD file.
   ☒ A is incorrect because three of the element names are prefixed with `el-`, which they should not be. **C** is incorrect for the same reason as **A**, and also because the String return type and

String parameter must both be expressed in fully qualified form: java.lang.String. **D** is incorrect because the function signature must not contain the **public** or **static** keywords, and the parameters must not be named— only the type is present in the function signature (unlike Java). **E** is wrong because it contains a combination of the errors in the other wrong answers, already explained.

13. ☑ **A** is the correct answer—there is a translation error in code generation. You cannot embed one EL function inside another, as depicted. The JSP code generator will choke on the second { (before encountering the terminating }).
☒ **B** and **C** are incorrect because the code is never generated to compile and run. **D** and **E** would occur only if the code did run. The reasoning in **D** is also incorrect: Just because `arg1` and `arg2` don't have values in the JSP you can see, that is not to say that these could not be attributes set in some previous code in request, session, or application scope.

14. ☑ **A** and **B** are correct. **A** is correct—where body-content is designated as scriptless, that only means that Java language constructs are disallowed: scriptlets, declarations, and Java language expressions. EL functions (and other EL constructs), though, can be used in a scriptless body. **B** is correct—if body content is defined as JSP, then any kind of legal JSP syntax (EL functions included) goes.
☒ **C** is incorrect—although you can place EL function syntax in the body of a tagdependent action, it will be treated simply as template text; the container will not attempt to invoke the function. **D**, **E**, and **F** are incorrect—scriptlets, expressions, and declarations can contain only legal Java syntax. EL syntax is clearly not Java syntax, so it will cause compilation failure.

15. ☑ **B** and **C** are the correct answers. **B** is correct in all respects: The Java method is declared as public and static, and the matching TLD function signature uses fully qualified types where necessary. **C** is also correct: Although it isn't necessary to declare the String class with its full package name in the Java method signature (java.lang is implicitly available in every class), there is nothing wrong with doing that. Crucially, the TLD function signature does use fully qualified types for both the parameter and the return type.
☒ **A** is incorrect for several reasons: The Java method is not static; the TLD must not use the public keyword; the TLD must fully qualify the String return type and parameter (as java .lang.String); and the TLD must not name the parameter as the Java method signature does (so `(java.lang.String)` instead of `(String id)`). **D** is incorrect for several reasons as well: The Java method must be public; the TLD must not use the static keyword; the TLD must not name the *id* parameter (only state its type). **E** is incorrect only because the TLD uses the public and static keywords (which it must omit; in this respect, it doesn't match the Java method signature).

The "Classic" Custom Tag Event Model

16. ☑ **F** is the correct answer. Because the tag handler inherits from BodyTagSupport, and does not override the `doStartTag()` method, the default `doStartTag()` method is invoked, which returns a value of EVAL_BODY_BUFFERED. So all the body content—through all the iterations—is written to the BodyContent object. However, the contents of the BodyContent object are never sent to its enclosing writer—so they are completely lost.
☒ **A**, **B**, **C**, **D**, and **E** are incorrect because there is no output. If the problem outlined in the correct answer were fixed, then answer **A** would be correct—the body would be evaluated seven times before exit from the implicit loop in `doAfterBody()`—giving an output of 0123456.

17. ☑ **E** and **F** are the correct answers. **E** is correct because a value of `scriptless` for `<body-content>` does allow EL to run, but bans any language scripting—so JSP expressions, declarations, and scriptlets result in a translation error. **F** is correct as a value of `tagdependent`, for `<body-content>` turns off the JSP container's translation process (and validation) for the body of a tag. It's up to the tag handler logic to do something with the body content; the JSP container won't translate JSP expressions as it normally would.
☒ **A**, **B**, **C**, and **D** are incorrect. **A** is incorrect because although a tag whose `<body-content>` is set to "empty" must not have a body, a closing tag can still be present, like this: `<mytags:dosomething></mytags:dosomething>`. **B** is incorrect because there is no such allowed value as scripting-allowed for `<body-content>`; use a value of JSP when JSP scriptlets are permitted in the custom action's body. **C** is incorrect because there is no such setting as jsp-document either—and indeed, no setting of `<body-content>` has any effect on permitting or denying JSP document syntax. **D** is incorrect because the settings of `<body-content>` are cumulative. JSP is more permissive than scriptless. A setting of scriptless allows EL; a setting of JSP allows EL and language scripting as well. There is no way to allow scriptlets but disallow EL.

18. ☑ **E** is the correct answer. The key point to note is that the tag handler extends BodyTagSupport. That means anything written to the BodyContent object is buffered. However, the scriptlet in the body of the tag uses the main JspWriter associated with the page. This is not buffered, so anything written to it is sent to page output straightaway, and *not* included in the body content for the tag. So the sequence of events is this: `doInitBody()` writes "Head" to BodyContent, which is buffered; the body is evaluated, so running the scriptlet that writes "Body" directly to page output; then `doAfterBody()` writes "Legs" to BodyContent, which is buffered; then `doAfterBody()` writes the current accumulated content of

BodyContent ("HeadLegs") to the enclosing writer—which is in this case the main JspWriter for the page.

☒ **A**, **B**, and **C** are incorrect, for there are no translation or run-time problems. **D** and **F** are incorrect because of the reasoning given in the correct answer.

19. ☑ **D** and **E** are the correct answers. The only attribute exposed by the tag handler is *id* (`setId` is inherited from TagSupport). So answer **D**, which declares the custom action with the *id* attribute, is a good choice. So is answer **E**, which declares no attributes; there is no compulsion to use an available setter method in tag handler code as a declared attribute in the tag library descriptor.

☒ **A** is incorrect because it exposes *data* as an attribute (as well as *id*, which is fine). Although there is a `setData()` method within the tag handler code, the method access is at package level, meaning that JSP container code cannot call the method. So it doesn't count from the point of view of attribute definition. **B** is incorrect because although there is a `setValue(String key, Object value)` method inherited from TagSupport, this style of signature is wrong for exposing an attribute called *value* (this method is designed for a different purpose altogether). **C** is incorrect for the same reason as answer **A**.

20. ☑ **B**, **D**, and **G** are correct. **B** is correct because it correctly places the setting of page context before parent. **D** is correct because you can have several successive calls to `doAfterBody()`in an IterationTag. **G** is correct because the setting of body content comes before `doInitBody()`, and both these methods are positioned correctly between `doStartTag()` and `doAfterBody()`.

☒ **A** is incorrect because the setting of parent comes after the setting of page context—not before. **C** is incorrect because IterationTags don't have a `doInitBody()` method—only Body Tags do. **E** is incorrect because of the bad positioning of `doStartTag()`. **F** is incorrect because of the bad positioning of `doStartTag()`, and the reversing of `doInitBody()` and `setBody Content()`.

LAB ANSWER

Deploy the WAR file from the CD called lab08.war, in the /sourcecode/chapter08 directory. This contains a sample solution. You can call the initial HTML page with a URL such as

```
http://localhost:8080/lab08/lifecycle.html
```

The resulting page looks something like the following illustration:

Tag Lifecycle Testing Framework

Enter the return code from doStartTag(): Tag.SKIP_BODY

Enter the body content for the tag: default body content

Enter the number of iterations:

When iterations is 0, doAfterBody() returns Tag.SKIP_BODY

When iterations is >=1, doAfterBody() returns IterationTag.EVAL_BODY_AGAIN

Enter the return code from doEndTag(): Tag.SKIP_PAGE

Invoke JSP document with lifecycle tag...

Example output after pressing the submit button looks like the following illstration.

setPageContext()

setParent()

setRcEndTag - value: 5

setIterations() - value: 0

setRcStartTag() - value: 0

doStartTag(); returning Tag.SKIP_BODY

doEndTag(): returning Tag.SKIP_PAGE

9

Custom Tags

CERTIFICATION OBJECTIVES

- Tags and Implicit Variables
- The "Simple" Custom Tag Event Model
- The Tag File Model
- Tag Hierarchies
- ✓ Two-Minute Drill
- Q&A Self Test

It has been a long haul, but you are almost through the many objectives for JavaServer Pages and tag technology.

This chapter begins by sweeping up loose ends on tag handling code—showing you how tag handler code can access implicit variables. JSPs have implicit variables within their syntax. In the Java for tag handler code, you have to work a little harder.

Then we move on to two bigger topics, which are new to this version of the exam (and to JSP 2.0). The first topic is the simple tag life cycle. This is something of a misnomer, for tags are never that simple, but after fighting your way through the life cycle of Tag, IterationTag and BodyTag, you will probably appreciate the reduced frills of the new approach. The second topic is tag files. These give you a means of writing simple tags without writing a line of Java—everything is encapsulated in a JavaServer Page-like structure called a tag file.

The chapter finishes by looking at hierarchies of tags. Whether or not they follow the classic or simple model, some tags need to look up to their parents and grandparents. You learn about two techniques for tag handlers to get hold of other tag instances in the hierarchy.

CERTIFICATION OBJECTIVE

Tags and Implicit Variables (Exam Objective 10.2)

Using the PageContext API, write tag handler code to access the JSP implicit variables and access web application attributes.

Whereas JSPs have their own implicit variables (such as *request*, *session*, and *application*), your tag handler classes don't. What they have instead is a PageContext object. This part of the chapter explores how you can use methods on this object to get hold of the implicit variable equivalents. It's hard to write a meaningful tag handler without reference to the supplied PageContext, so we have inevitably covered some of this ground already. This short chapter section will amplify the knowledge you have already gained.

The PageContext API

You have seen that in naked JSPs, you have access to a *pageContext* implicit object— of type javax.servlet.jsp.PageContext. Because this is an abstract class, you never meet an object of this type directly—your kindly JSP container provides an instance of a subclass that has implemented all the abstract methods it contains.

For the most part (in naked JSPs), you can avoid calling many of the methods on the *pageContext* implicit object—such as `getRequest()`, `getSession()`, and `getServletConfig()`. There's nothing stopping you from doing this, but you already have references to the objects returned by those methods. These take the shape of other implicit variables—such as *request*, *session*, and *application*.

In tag handler code, you don't have that luxury. The PageContext object is passed to you in the `setPageContext()` method. If your tag class inherits from TagSupport (or BodyTagSupport), `setPageContext()` saves the object to a protected instance variable so that you can access it directly in your code as *pageContext*—which conveniently matches the name of the *pageContext* implicit variable used directly inside JSP page source.

However, there is no equivalent mechanism for the remaining implicit variables. You could imagine the JSP container providing a call to a tag life cycle method called `setRequest(HttpServletRequest request)`, giving an opportunity to save the implicit request object, yet it doesn't. You have to do a little work yourself. But it's not hard. *pageContext* is a conduit to all the other implicit variables: You simply have to know the right method to call.

Accessing JSP Implicit Variables

Table 9-1 lists the nine JSP implicit variables, together with the PageContext method needed to obtain the equivalent instance objects.

exam watch ***Mostly, you can mentally convert the implicit variable name to the PageContext method name by prefixing "get" to the implicit variable. Just watch out for the two exceptions to this rule: config maps to getServletConfig, and application to getServletContext.***

TABLE 9-1

JSP Implicit Variables and Equivalent PageContext Methods

JSP Implicit Variable	PageContext Method Used to Obtain Equivalent Object
Request	`getRequest()`
Response	`getResponse()`
Out	`getOut()` (inherited from PageContext's parent class JspWriter)
Session	`getSession()`
Config	`getServletConfig()`
Application	`getServletContext()`
Page	`getPage()`
PageContext	(This *is* the PageContext object passed to your tag handler)
Exception	`getException()`

The following example shows tag handler code using PageContext to exercise methods on objects that are otherwise implicit to the JSP:

```
public int doStartTag() throws JspException {
  ServletRequest request = pageContext.getRequest();
  String var1 = request.getServerName() + ":"
    + request.getServerPort();
  ServletResponse response = pageContext.getResponse();
  String var2 = response.getCharacterEncoding() + ";"
    + response.getContentType();
  ServletConfig config = pageContext.getServletConfig();
  String var3 = config.getServletName();
  try {
    Writer out = pageContext.getOut();
    out.write(var1 + ";" + var2 + ";" + var3);
  } catch (IOException e) {
    e.printStackTrace();
  }
  return Tag.EVAL_BODY_INCLUDE;
}
```

You can deploy this code from the WAR file in the CD at /sourcecode/ch09/examp0901.war. Here is the URL to run it:

```
http://localhost:8080/examp0901/asTag.jsp
```

When I run this code, the output I see is this:

```
localhost:8080;ISO-8859-1;text/html;jsp
```

The output of localhost:8080 originates from the calls to `getServerName()` and `getServerPort()` on the ServletRequest object returned by `pageContext.getRequest()`. Likewise, ISO-8859-1 and text/html are derived from `getCharacterEncoding()` and `getContentType()` calls on the ServletResponse object returned by `pageContext.getResponse()`. The string jsp is the servlet name retrieved from the ServletConfig object.

All of these pieces of information are held in String variables and are concatenated together. `PageContext.getOut()` is used to return the JSP's associated Writer and send the output to the page.

If the above code were written within a JSP using implicit variables, it might look like this:

```
<p><%= request.getServerName() %>:<%= request.getServerPort() %>;
<%= response.getCharacterEncoding() %>;<%= response.getContentType() %>;
<%= config.getServletName() %></p>
```

This JSP is available in the same WAR file as you deployed above (examp0901.war), and the URL to run it is

```
http://localhost:8080/examp0901/asJSP.jsp
```

exam watch

The only implicit variable that isn't necessarily always available is exception. Recall that the exception implicit variable is available only in a JSP error page. The JSP container should be used to load your error page only indirectly—when another page specifies your error page and when that other page goes wrong. The exception produced by the other page is then available to your error page, as the implicit variable exception in the JSP source. If that JSP source has a custom tag within it, that custom tag can invoke pageContext `.getException()` and expect an Exception object back. Under other circumstances, the call will return null.

Accessing Attributes with PageContext

You already know how to access attributes with the PageContext object—take a look again at Chapter 6 if you need a reminder. All four scopes are available to you: page, request, session, and application.

All you haven't yet done is use PageContext inside of tag handler code to set or get attribute values. We'll consider a small example where a tag handler performs a simple mathematical function using attributes to handle the input and outputs to the JSP page. Here's the JSP page first of all:

```
01 <%@ taglib prefix="mytags" uri="http://www.osborne.com/taglibs/mytags" %>
02 <html><head><title>Squaring Function</title></head>
03 <body><p>The square of ${param.input}
04 <% pageContext.setAttribute("input", request.getParameter("input")); %>
05 <mytags:square />
06 is ${output}
07 </p></body></html>
```

This example is available from the same WAR file you deployed previously, examp0901.war. You can call this JSP with a URL such as

```
http://localhost:8080/examp0901/square.jsp?input=2
```

Then the output is

```
The square of 2 is 4
```

The tag handler code in `doStartTag()` that performs the calculation looks like this:

```
String input = (String) pageContext.getAttribute("input");
int i = Integer.parseInt(input);
i = i * i;
pageContext.setAttribute("output", new Integer(i));
return Tag.SKIP_BODY;
```

Let's follow through the logic of the request to the JSP:

- In the URL an input parameter called *input* is passed with a value of 2.
- The JSP displays the value of this input parameter using EL on line 03: `${param.input}`.
- In line 04 the JSP uses the *pageContext* implicit variable to set up an attribute called *input*. The value of this attribute is taken from the request parameter we

just saw displayed. Because no scope is specified within the `setAttribute()` method, scope will default to `page`.

- At line 05 of the JSP, we find the bodiless `<mytags:square>` tag inserted. There is no output from this, but the tag handler code is executed.
- Within the tag handler code, at line 01 the value of the page context attribute called `input` is recovered into a local String variable.
- At line 02 the value of the String input is coerced to an **int** value. (This code is not production-ready as you can see — there's no defensive coding for bad input!)
- At line 03 we have the calculation: The input is squared (and still held in the **int** local variable *i*).
- At line 04 the result of the calculation is stored in an Integer object. This is used as the value of an attribute called *output*, set up in page scope.
- At line 05 we return from `doStartTag()`, skipping the body.
- Now—back at line 06 in the JSP—we are ready to display the result of the calculation. EL has direct access to attributes by name, hence the simple statement `${output}`.

From this small example, you see combined several techniques that you have learned so far. In particular, you see how attributes can be used to communicate between a JSP and a tag handler.

EXERCISE 9-1

Tags and Implicit Variables

In this exercise you will set up a tag handling class with instance variables whose names match the implicit variables in a standard JSP. You already have an example—in TagSupport—in the protected instance variable *pageContext*. You might even find this class useful as the base class for tag handlers of your own.

For this exercise, create a web application directory structure under a directory called ex0901, and proceed with the steps for the exercise. There's a solution in the CD in the file sourcecode/ch09/ex0901.war.

Create the Tag Handler Class

1. Create a Java source code file in /WEB-INF/classes or an appropriate package directory within it called ImplicitsTag.java.
2. In the class declaration, extend (javax.servlet.jsp.tagext.)TagSupport.

3. Declare instance variables called *request*, *response*, *session*, *application*, *config*, *out*, *page*, and *exception*. These should match their appropriate (implicit variable) type.
4. Override the `setPageContext()` method. However, invoke `super.setPageContext()` so that TagSupport's default action (to save the page context in a protected variable called pageContext) is honored. In the following lines of code, invoke the appropriate methods on pageContext to initialize the instance variables you declared in the previous request. For example,

   ```
   request = pageContext.getRequest();
   ```

   to initialize the ServletRequest instance variable.
5. In `doStartTag()`, exercise any methods you like on any of your instance variables. Use this as an opportunity to revise long-unused javax.servlet APIs that you last tried in the early chapters.
6. Whichever methods you do choose, make sure to obtain some information from each available implicit attribute, and record this in a request attribute. So, for example, you might use the `request.getRemoteHost()` method to return String information to record in an attribute called `requestInfo`.
7. Conclude the `doStartTag()` method by skipping the body.
8. Save and compile ImplicitsTag.java.

Create a Tag File

9. Create a TLD file called mytags.tld in /WEB-INF/tags.
10. Include within it a definition for a tag named *implicits*. The tag class should tie in with the ImplicitsTag class you created previously. Remember that the tag has no body.

Create a JSP File

11. Create a JSP file called implicits.jsp directly in the context root directory ex0901.
12. Declare the tag file mytags.tld, with a prefix of mytags.
13. Include `<mytags:implicits />` somewhere in the JSP.
14. Somewhere after the tag, display the attributes you set up in the `doStartTag()` method of ImplicitsTag.java.

Create, Deploy, and Test a WAR File

15. Create a WAR file from your ex0901 context directory, and deploy this to the Tomcat server.
16. Test your application by invoking the JSP with a URL such as

```
http://localhost:8080/ex0901/implicits.jsp
```

17. The output will, of course, vary depending on the choices you made about information to retrieve to the displayed attributes. The solution code produces the following output:

Implicit Variables Tag

Display request attributes set up in implicits tag

pageClass	org.apache.jsp.implicits_jsp
pageInfo	A JSP housing a tag to access implicit variables
servletName	Implicits
serverInfo	Apache Tomcat/5.5.7
sessionAccess	Mon Apr 11 09:02:53 BST 2005
exception	null
outClass	org.apache.jasper.runtime.JspWriterImpl

CERTIFICATION OBJECTIVE

The "Simple" Custom Tag Event Model (Exam Objective 10.4)

Describe the semantics of the "Simple" custom tag event model when the event method (doTag) is executed; write a tag handler class; and explain the constraints on the JSP content within the tag.

In Chapter 8, you learned about the "classic" tag event model. Although this is highly flexible, it is complex to learn. This explains part of the motivation for the J2EE designers to produce a "simple" model for tag production. Instead of three life cycle choices based on the interfaces Tag, IterationTag, and BodyTag, you have only one. This is based on the javax.servlet.jsp.tagext.SimpleTag interface, and in this section, we'll see how to write a tag based on this interface and learn how the J2EE container makes use of it. You'll find that you can do almost all the things you are able to do in the classic model, but you "do it yourself" instead of relying on different API calls and method return codes.

Since SimpleTag is a new innovation with JSP 2.0, you can expect plenty of exam questions relating to it. Don't make the mistake of thinking that simple tags are simple—perhaps relative to classic tags they are, but they still demand study and practice!

The Simple Tag Model Life Cycle

The simple model for tags is shown in Figure 9-1. At first sight, it looks like the classic model. There is a method that provides some kind of content object. There is a method to set the parent tag, followed by methods to set attributes. Following this,

FIGURE 9-1 The Simple Model Tag Life Cycle

JSP container processing one occurrence of a tag implementing the SimpleTag Interface in one JSP page:

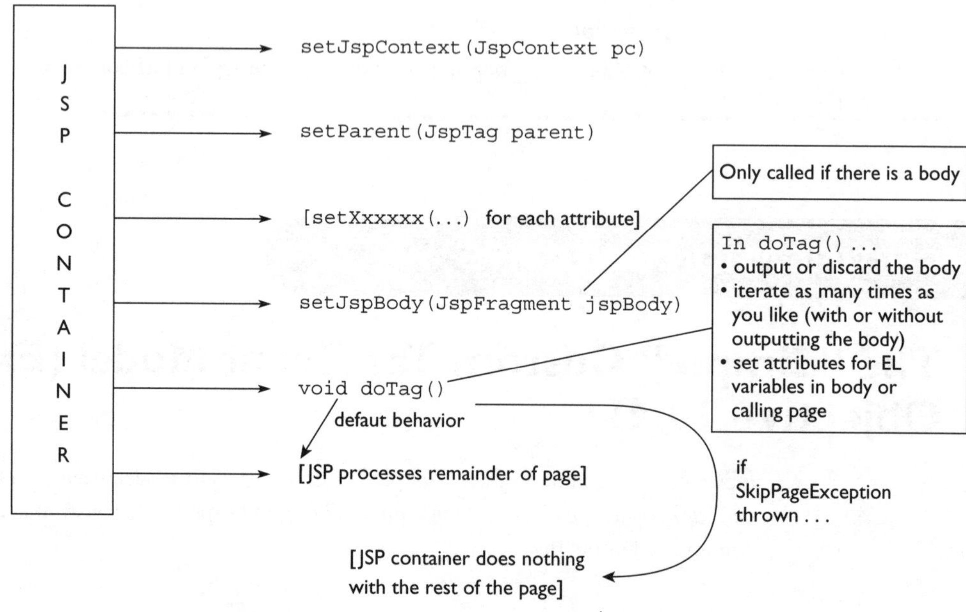

another method provides the body content of the tag to the tag handler. So far, so classic—though you might have already noticed some unfamiliar parameter types (such as JspContext, JspTag, and JspFragment—where you might have expected PageContext, Tag, and BodyContent).

Next comes the `doTag()` method, and this is where the big difference lies. This method replaces all of `doStartTag()`, `doAfterBody()`, and `doEndTag()`. All the processing that would have occurred in those methods moves to `doTag()`. Furthermore, `doTag()` returns nothing at all. With simple tags, you don't use return codes (such as Tag.SKIP_BODY or BodyTag.EVAL_BODY_BUFFERED) to influence the life cycle. The life cycle as it directly affects the tag output is controlled instead by your code inside `doTag()`.

Life Cycle Details

Any tag handler class you write needs to implement the javax.servlet.jsp.tagext .SimpleTag interface. Nearly all its methods are designed to have implementations that are called by the JSP container, as shown in Figure 9-1. Let's explore the complete life cycle in more detail. It begins within the thread running the servlet generated from your JSP page that uses an occurrence of the simple tag, and ends once that occurrence has been processed. The following table lists simple tag events in order.

Construction	When the JSP container meets an occurrence of a simple tag, it makes a new instance of the tag handler class. The container calls the zero-argument constructor, so the tag handler class must have one, either explicitly defined or implicitly put there by the Java compiler. Because (unlike classic model tags) you get a new instance for every use, you can safely initialize variables in your constructor or instance member declarations. There is no "pool" for simple tags.
`setJspContext (JspContext pc)`	Saves the JspContext object for later access to attributes in all scopes and the JspWriter currently associated with the page.
`setParent (JspTag tag)`	Saves the JspTag for later access to this action's immediate parent. This method is called only if the custom action has a custom action as a parent.
`set<AttributeName> (<Type> attributeValue)`	The JSP container calls any "set" methods for attribute names defined in the tag library descriptor (just as for classic tag handlers).
`setJspBody(JspFragment jspBody)`	The JSP container calls this method only if the custom action has a body. If so, save the JspFragment object for later use—you'll need it to process the body later (the JSP container doesn't do that for you automatically).

`doTag()`	Within this method, you can do whatever you like. You are most likely to want to do one or both of the following: 1. Process the body (more than once if required) 2. Write directly to page output
Variable Synchronization	This is an advanced topic that should not come up on the exam. In brief, you can specify the equivalent of output parameters from your simple tag handler. The variable synchronization process moves these into attributes accessible in your page after the end of your tag. Of course, you can achieve this effect quite easily manually by setting up your own attributes in the tag handler code—as happens with the tag examples in the book.
Garbage Collection	There is no `release()` method for simple tags. Once a tag instance has been used, it is thrown into touch. So any cleanup must happen in `doTag()` (or a method called from `doTag()`), for this is the last method called by the container before garbage collection. You could include a `finalize()` method, although there is never an absolute guarantee that `finalize()` will be called.

SimpleTagSupport

Just as TagSupport and BodyTagSupport exist to provide default implementations of the classic tag handler interfaces, so SimpleTag has one of its own. The name won't come as any surprise: SimpleTagSupport. Consequently, it is usually easiest to extend SimpleTagSupport for your own simple tag handler classes, instead of implementing the SimpleTag interface directly.

SimpleTagSupport provides some predictable support for each of SimpleTag's methods, plus some extra useful methods as explained below:

exam watch

A pedantic point, but one that might underpin a more picky examination question: All three set methods in the SimpleTagSupport class are implementations of SimpleTag interface methods. However, only one of the get methods—`getParent()`—derives from the interface. `getJspBody()` and `getJspContext()` are provided out of the kindness of SimpleTagSupport's designer's heart (or more likely because you need them to access otherwise private instance variables).

- `setJspContext(JspContext pc)`, `setParent(JspTag parent)`, and `setJspBody(JspFragment jspBody)` store the objects passed in by the container for later access in your code by corresponding get methods (`getJspContext()`, `getParent()`, `getJspBody()`).

- `doTag()` is a do-nothing implementation.
- `findAncestorWithClass(JspTag from, Class klass)` is an interesting static method that we look at in the final section of this chapter, on exploring tag hierarchies.

An Example: A Unicode Converter

Enough theory on the APIs—let's look at a working example. This lives on the CD in /sourcecode/examp0902.war—deploy this as you will. This example uses a simple tag handler to list a sequence of numbers in an HTML table, together with their corresponding Unicode character equivalents. If you use a range of numbers from 0 to 255, you will see the extended ASCII character set. You may find it more exciting to explore some of the upper ranges of Unicode. The supplied JSP that uses the simple tag sets a range of 1040 to 1100, which causes the web page to display Cyrillic characters as shown in Figure 9-2. Call it with a URL such as

```
http://localhost:8080/examp0902/unicodeDisplay.jspx
```

If you don't see Cyrillic characters (just boring boxes instead), the chances are that you don't have a Cyrillic font installed.

FIGURE 9-2

Unicode Character Converter—First Few Characters Shown

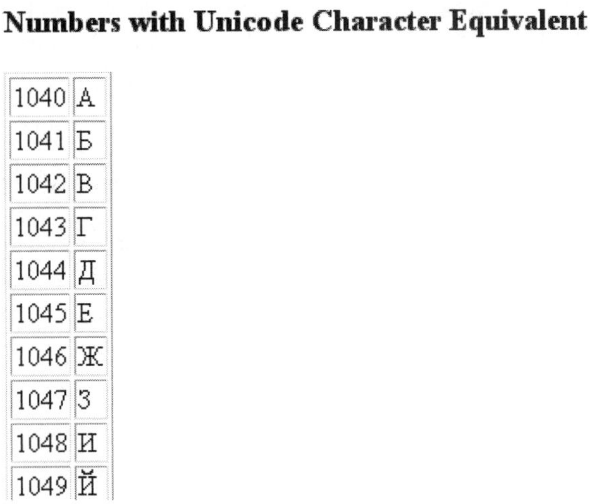

Numbers with Unicode Character Equivalent

1040	А
1041	Б
1042	В
1043	Г
1044	Д
1045	Е
1046	Ж
1047	З
1048	И
1049	Й

Here is a JSP document that uses the simple tag (called unicodeConverter). You can see nothing to differentiate it from a classic tag invocation—the mechanism is the same:

```
<html xmlns:jsp="http://java.sun.com/JSP/Page"
      xmlns:c="http://java.sun.com/jsp/jstl/core"
      xmlns:mytags="http://www.osborne.com/taglibs/mytags">
  <jsp:output omit-xml-declaration="true" />
  <jsp:directive.page contentType="text/html" />
  <head><title>Unicode Converter</title></head>
  <body>
    <h3>Numbers with Unicode Character Equivalent</h3>
    <table border="1">
      <mytags:unicodeConverter begin="1040" end="1116">
        <tr><td>${number}</td><td>${character}</td></tr>
      </mytags:unicodeConverter>
    </table>
  </body>
</html>
```

You can see in the body of the `unicodeConverter` action a table row with two table cells, their data supplied from two EL variables: `${number}` and `${character}`. You can infer from Figure 9-2 and the JSP document source above that the tag handler is preoccupied with two tasks: setting up these EL variables and adding as many rows as requested. The number of rows—and range of characters displayed—is determined by the *begin* and *end* attribute values for the action.

Before we see the tag handler code, we will peek at the TLD. There's not much to see here—again, there's nothing particular to indicate that this is a simple tag we are dealing with. The declaration looks just like a classic tag:

```
<tag>
  <description>Shows Unicode Character for Number</description>
  <name>unicodeConverter</name>
  <tag-class>webcert.ch09.examp0902.CharConvSimpleTag</tag-class>
  <body-content>scriptless</body-content>
  <attribute>
    <name>begin</name>
    <required>true</required>
    <rtexprvalue>true</rtexprvalue>
  </attribute>
  <attribute>
```

```
    <name>end</name>
    <required>true</required>
    <rtexprvalue>true</rtexprvalue>
  </attribute>
</tag>
```

It's true that the `<tag-class>` (CharConvSimpleTag) hints at the tag's simple origins, but that's merely a naming choice by this developer. The only constraint on simple tag file declaration within the tag library descriptor is that `<body-content>` is restricted to three (instead of four) allowed values: `empty`, `tagdependent`, and `scriptless`. The fourth value—`JSP`—may get through XML schema validation, but the JSP container will give you a translation error: Simple tags are not allowed the full range of JSP syntax. Java language syntax within scriptlets, declarations, or expressions is disallowed. After all, this is meant to be a *simple* tag.

So to the tag handler code. Here it is in its entirety:

```
package webcert.ch09.examp0902;
import java.io.IOException;
import javax.servlet.jsp.JspContext;
import javax.servlet.jsp.JspException;
import javax.servlet.jsp.tagext.JspFragment;
import javax.servlet.jsp.tagext.SimpleTagSupport;
  public class CharConvSimpleTag extends SimpleTagSupport {
  private int begin;
  private int end;
  public int getBegin() { return begin; }
  public void setBegin(int begin) { this.begin = begin; }
  public int getEnd() { return end; }
  public void setEnd(int end) { this.end = end; }
  public CharConvSimpleTag() { super(); }
  public void doTag() throws JspException, IOException {
    for (int thisChar = getBegin(); thisChar <= getEnd(); thisChar++) {
      JspContext ctx = getJspContext();
      ctx.setAttribute("number", new Integer(thisChar));
      ctx.setAttribute("character", new Character((char) thisChar));
      JspFragment fragment = getJspBody();
      fragment.invoke(null);
    }
  }
}
```

This class extends SimpleTagSupport, so most of the life cycle methods are inherited from there. Beyond that, over half of the class is taken up with import statements and attribute handling code (instance variables and getters and setters for the attributes *begin* and *end*). The interest is in the `doTag()` method, which does the following things:

- Defines a **for** loop, designed to start at the value specified in the begin attribute and finish at the end attribute value.
- Gets hold of the JspContext object, using the `getJspContext()` method inherited from SimpleTagSupport.
- Sets up an attribute on the JspContext object, called *number*. This reflects the numeric value of the loop counter held in variable *thisChar*.
- Sets up a second attribute on the JspContext object, called *character*. The value for the attribute is a Character wrapper object. This is constructed with a **char** value derived from downcasting the **int** counter variable *thisChar*. This supplies the Unicode character when *character* is later accessed in the JSP page as an EL variable (`${character}`).
- Next, the code gets the JspFragment defining the body of the custom action—in other words, the following line of JSP page source:

```
<tr><td>${number}</td><td>${character}</td></tr>
```

- Next, the code calls the `invoke()` method on the fragment. The effect of this is to process this piece of JSP page source. Template text (such as `<tr><td>`) is written directly to page output. Any EL expressions (such as `${number}`) are evaluated before being sent to page output. Which writer is used? The answer lies in the parameter passed into the invoke method. You can define your own Writer and divert the JspFragment output there. But by supplying **null** as the parameter value, you are writing to the JspWriter associated with the JspContext. In other words, `getJspBody().invoke(null)` is shorthand for `getJspBody().invoke(getJspContext().getOut())`.
- This marks the end of the loop—which goes around again and is repeated as many times as necessary before reaching the *end* attribute value. Each time, the body of the custom action is reevaluated afresh—with a new table row, number, and character.

INSIDE THE EXAM

Get clear in your mind the differences between the following:

- PageContext and JspContext
- BodyContent and JspFragment

PageContext and BodyContent belong to the classic tag model. JspContext and JspFragment are their equivalents (roughly speaking) in the simple tag model. There are many similarities, but there are significant differences as well. First, some points about javax.servlet.jsp.JspContext and javax.servlet.jsp.PageContext:

- Both PageContext and JspContext are classes, not interfaces.
- As a page author, you're never supposed to make a new one of either of these classes: You let the JSP container supply the instances.
- JspContext is the parent of PageContext (PageContext extends JspContext).
- JspContext contains all the methods to do with
  - Attribute access (e.g., `getAttribute()`, `setAttribute()`)
  - Writer access (`getOut()`)
  - Programmatic access to the EL evaluator (`getExpressionEvaluator()`, `getVariableResolver()`)—not something you are likely to encounter in the exam or encounter early in your simple tag development career.
- PageContext adds methods to do with
  - Accessing implicit objects in a servlet environment (e.g., `getRequest()`, `getResponse()`, `getServletContext()`).
  - Redirection (`forward()`, `include()`).

The idea behind JspContext was to abstract away all the parts that are not specific to the HTTP servlet environment. Of course, you are likely to be using JspContext in a HTTP servlet environment most, if not all, of the time. And indeed, many JspContext methods are designed to accept constants defined in the PageContext class, as in the following:

```
myJspContext.getAttribute("mySessionId", PageContext.SESSION_SCOPE)
```

However, at least you can be aware of the differences so you're not fooled by exam questions that include simple tag handler code of the following kind:

INSIDE THE EXAM (continued)

```
HttpServletRequest request = myJspContext.getRequest();
```

which, of course, won't compile.

So what about the differences between javax.servlet.jsp.tagext.BodyContent and javax.servlet.jsp.tagext.JspFragment? These are more pronounced:

- BodyContent inherits from javax.servlet .jsp.JspWriter, which is a java.io.Writer.
- JspFragment isn't a Writer of any sort; it inherits directly from java.lang.Object.
- BodyContent has some content in it already when your classic custom tag handler code gets hold of it. This is the result of the JSP container evaluating the body of the tag—processing any scriplets or EL contained therein.
- JspFragment is the opposite: Its content constitutes the body *before* any evaluation has taken place. In your simple tag handler code, you control when to do the evaluation—if at all—by calling the `invoke()` method on the JspFragment object.
- There is no concept of buffering with JspFragment, as there is with BodyContent. Nothing of the body is buffered because nothing has been output until you decide. You can *simulate* a buffer by all means: Have the `invoke()` method write to a StringWriter, and there you have evaluated content, very like a BodyContent object.

Terminating Early

Back in Figure 9-1, the simple tag life cycle diagram, you can see two routes out of the `doTag()` method: one the normal route, which results in the JSP container processing the rest of the page, the other bypassing evaluation of the rest of the page entirely.

Because `doTag()` has no return code associated with it, the mechanism for bypassing the rest of the page is through an exception. The exception to throw is javax.servlet.jsp.SkipPageException, a subclass of javax.servlet.jsp.Jsp Exception (which is in the *throws* clause of the `SimpleTag.doTag()` method signature).

EXERCISE 9-2

The "Simple" Custom Tag Event Model

This exercise is going to use a combination of an HTML file, JSP, and simple tag handler to display the contents of a given directory. For this exercise, create a web application directory structure under a directory called ex0902, and proceed with the steps for the exercise. There's a solution in the CD in the file sourcecode/ch09/ex0902.war.

Create the HTML File

1. Create an HTML file called fileBrowser.html directly in the context directory ex0902.
2. Include a form in the file that has a text input field, named *initDir*. The user will type into this field the name of the directory to browse. Don't forget to include a submit button in the form.
3. Make the action of the form a JSP document called fileBrowser.jspx.
4. Save and exit the file.

Create the JSP Document

5. Create a JSP document called fileBrowser.jspx directly in ex0902.
6. Include the following heading information, which ensures proper HTML output and declares standard actions, the core tag library, and your own tag library:

```
<html xmlns:jsp="http://java.sun.com/JSP/Page"
      xmlns:c="http://java.sun.com/jsp/jstl/core"
      xmlns:mytags="http://www.osborne.com/taglibs/mytags">
  <jsp:output omit-xml-declaration="true" />
  <jsp:directive.page contentType="text/html" />
```

7. Include an HTML table in the JSP document with three headings: "Name," "Size," and "Directory?"
8. After the headings, and before the main table row, include a tag declaration like this:

```
<mytags:fileBrowser initdir="${param.initdir}" size="true">
```

You can see that this is the opening tag of a tag named fileBrowser, with two attributes: *initdir* and *size*. The value for the *size* attribute is set to a constant of true. The value for *initdir* is supplied from the *initDir* request parameter set up in the HTML page (rendered through EL).

9. In the following table row, place `${file}` in the first table cell. This EL picks up an attribute set by the tag handler code we have yet to write.
10. In the next table cell, place `${size}`.
11. Place `${isDir}` in the next table cell.
12. After the table row, place the closing fileBrowser tag: `</mytags: FileBrowser>`.

Create the Tag Library Descriptor File

13. Create a TLD file called mytags.tld in /WEB-INF/tags.
14. Include within it a definition for a tag named fileBrowser. The tag class should be webcert.ch09.ch0902.FileBrowserSimpleTag (follow whatever package naming convention you are using). The body content should be scriptless.
15. Define two attributes for the tag: *initDir* and *size*. Both are required, and both should allow run-time expressions.
16. Save and exit the TLD file.

Enter a Tag Library Mapping in the Deployment Descriptor

17. In web.xml, ensure you have a tag library mapping. The URI is `http://www.osborne.com/taglibs/mytags`, and the tag library descriptor location is `/WEB-INF/tags/mytag.tld`.

Write the Simple Tag Handler Code

18. Create a Java source code file in /WEB-INF/classes or an appropriate package directory within it. Call the file FileBrowserSimpleTag.java.
19. In the class declaration, extend (javax.servlet.jsp.tagext.)SimpleTagSupport.
20. Provide instance variables and getters and setters for the two attributes *initDir* and *size*.
21. Override the `doTag()` method. Within the method, create a java.io.File object from the value given for *initDir*. Use the `listFiles()` method on the File object to obtain an array of Files.

22. Still in the `doTag()` method, obtain the JspContext as a local variable.
23. Start a **for** loop based on the contents of the File array. For each file found, use `setAttribute()` on the JspContext local variable to set three attributes. The first is called *file*, and the value is the name of the current file in the loop. The second is called *size*, and the value is the size of the current file in the loop (`length()` method on File). The third is *isDir*, and the value is a Boolean object created from the output of the `isDirectory()` method on the current file in the loop.
24. Still within the loop, get the JspFragment associated with the tag handler (`getJspBody()`). Call the `invoke()` method on the fragment, passing in a **null** value. This has the effect of processing the body of the tag in the JSP. The body contains references to the three attributes whose values you have set.

Create, Deploy, and Test a WAR File

25. Create a WAR file from your ex0902 context directory, and deploy this to the Tomcat server.
26. Test your application by invoking the JSP with a URL such as

```
http://localhost:8080/ex0902/
fileBrowser.html
```

27. Enter a valid directory (such as C:>), and click the submit button.
28. The output for the solution code (which includes one or two improvements not included in the exercise instructions) looks like the illustration to the left.

Show Files in Requested Directory

Directory: C:\Program Files

Name	Size	Directory?
Adobe	(Dir)	Yes
Ahead	(Dir)	Yes
Apache Software Foundation	(Dir)	Yes
C-Media 3D Audio	(Dir)	Yes
CLOX	(Dir)	Yes
Common Files	(Dir)	Yes
ComPlus Applications	(Dir)	Yes
CyberLink	(Dir)	Yes
Google	(Dir)	Yes
HighMAT CD Writing Wizard	(Dir)	Yes
IBM	(Dir)	Yes
IDM Computer Solutions	(Dir)	Yes

CERTIFICATION OBJECTIVE

The Tag File Model (Exam Objective 10.5)

Describe the semantics of the Tag File model; describe the web application structure for tag files; write a tag file; and explain the constraints on the JSP content in the body of the tag.

Now we come to a variant of the simple tags we have met and written so far: tag files. In appearance and behavior, tag files are like JavaServer Pages. They contain a mixture of template text and elements. They are translated into Java source code and then compiled. The result is a simple tag class—yet with no necessity to write a simple tag handler.

Tag files are also convenient to deploy. You don't write tag entries in a tag library descriptor. Tag files are self-contained, with their own deployment directives.

We'll rewrite the simple tags we created in the last section as tag files and make comparisons between the two approaches. And along the way, we'll tease apart the exam objectives for tag files.

Rewriting Simple Tags as Tag File

In the last section, you saw an example of a simple tag used to display a range of Unicode characters on a web page. We'll now look at a version of the tag when it is rewritten as a tag file—with some slight improvements. You may want to run the code, which is in the CD at /sourcecode/ch09/examp0903.war. Simply deploy the WAR file as you would any other solution code file. To run the code, point your browser to the following URL (adapt this to suit if you are not using standard Tomcat settings):

```
http://localhost:8080/examp0903/unicodeDisplay.jspx
```

This looks no different from the original version of the code (refer to Figure 9-2 to see how this looks in the browser). However, the underlying mechanism is different. In the remainder of this section, we'll revisit this example to explain how tag files work.

Where Does the JSP Container Find the Tag File?

To ensure that your web container will find your tag file, you have to ensure that it has an extension of .tag and that it is located in one of these places within your web application:

- /WEB-INF/tags
- A subdirectory of /WEB-INF/tags
- In a JAR file kept in /WEB-INF/lib. The directory of the tag file within the JAR file must be /META-INF/tags — or a subdirectory of /META-INF/tags.

Let us first consider the case of a tag file in /WEB-INF/tags. What happens at run time, when the tag file is first accessed? This is shown in Figure 9-3. Tag files bear the same relationship to tag handler classes as JSP pages do to servlets. Both are used as sources from which a class file is generated. For tag files, a SimpleTag class is created

FIGURE 9-3 Tag File Deployment and Run Time

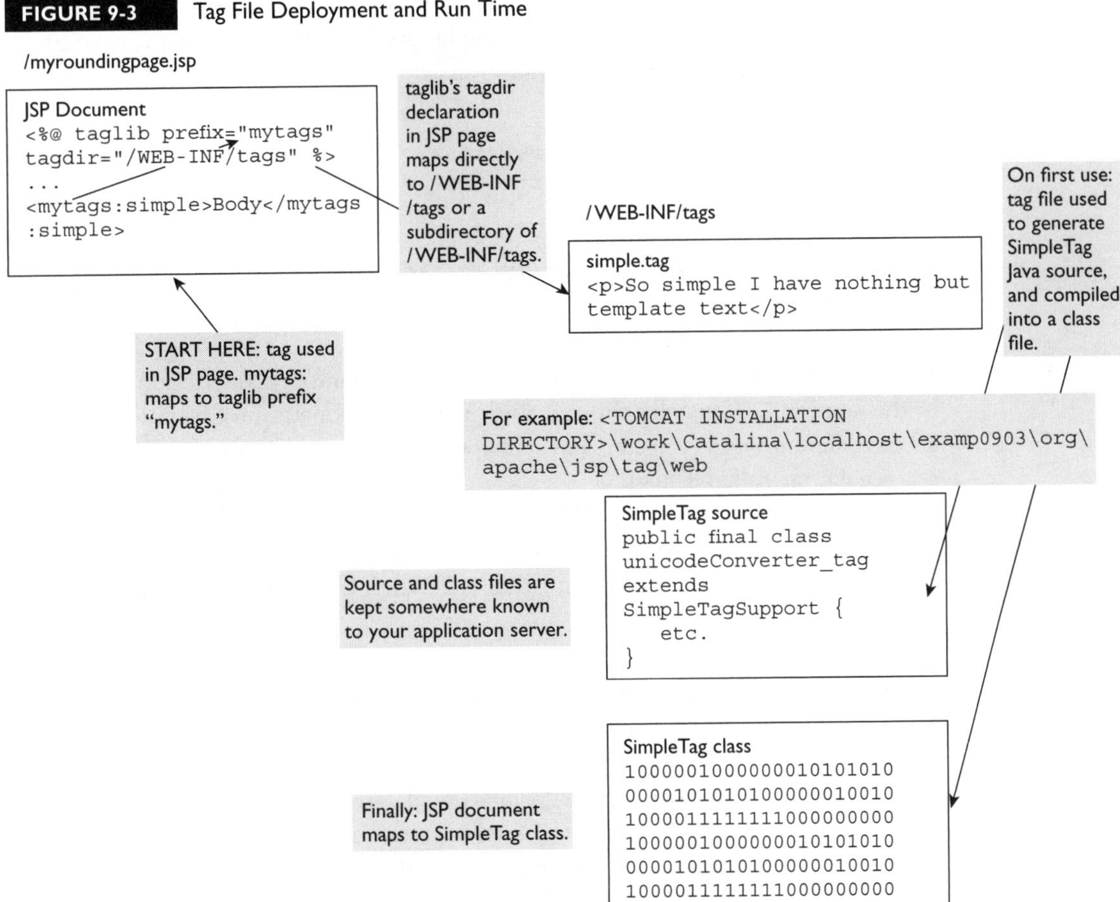

when the tag file is first used—in much the same way as the use of a JSP triggers generation and compilation of a servlet.

So your JSP page source invokes the tag, which maps to a tag file in a tag directory. If this is its first use, the container generates a Java source code file that implements SimpleTag (usually by extending SimpleTagSupport—JSP container writers like to keep their work to a minimum too!). This source is kept and compiled in a location known to the server—Figure 9-3 illustrates the current situation for Tomcat. Thereafter, the server keeps an internal mapping between invocations of the tag file and the actual compiled class.

Beyond that, everything works just as if this were a bona fide simple tag declared in a tag handler, and with a handcrafted tag handler. Life cycle methods and rules are exactly the same.

When a tag file sits inside a JAR file, there is one difference in the packaging: The tag file must have a declaration inside a tag library descriptor. Here is a very short TLD, containing a single tag file declaration:

```
<taglib>
  <tlib-version>1.0</tlib-version>
  <short-name>webcert</short-name>
  <tag-file>
      <name>mytag</name>
      <path>/META-INF/tags/mytag.tag</path>
  </tag-file>
</taglib>
```

You can mix tag file declarations with regular tag declarations and EL functions, all in the same TLD. Crucially, though, the `<name>` component must be unique across all the different types (you can't have a tag file called *mytag* existing in the same TLD as a regular tag called *mytag*).

For tag files kept directly in /WEB-INF/tags (or a subdirectory), there is no need for a tag library descriptor entry, although it is permitted: You could do this if (for some reason) you wanted a tag name that is different from the tag file name.

Tag File Source

Let's return to the Unicode characters example. What has changed from the last section, where this was a simple tag developed in Java source? The JSP document using the tag—unicodeDisplay.jspx—has hardly changed at all. However, there is a subtle difference in the namespace declaration. There's no need to have a namespace referencing a tag library. Instead, you must reference a tag *directory*—a directory that acts as a repository for tag files and must be declared in using JSPs. Here is the original declaration in unicodeDisplay.jspx:

```
<html xmlns:mytags="http://www.osborne.com/taglibs/mytags" ... >
```

Here it is again, the change highlighted:

```
<html xmlns:mytags="urn:jsptagdir:/WEB-INF/tags/" >
```

In the first case, the URL String "http://www.osborne.com/taglibs/mytags" doesn't point to anything—it just has to match the corresponding `<taglib-uri>` setting in the web deployment descriptor. In the second case, the URN (of type JSP tag directory) designates a real location within the web application: the directory /WEB-INF/tags.

exam watch

The truth is that you will still probably encounter more traditional JSPs than JSP documents as questions in the exam. So you need to know the traditional variant of the tag directive. This is the `<% taglib %>` directive—but with a change to one of its attributes. It retains `prefix`, but `tagdir` is substituted for `uri`. So the full declaration equivalent to `xmlns:mytags="urn:jsptagdir:/WEB-INF/tags/"` in a JSP document is `<% taglib prefix="mytags" tagdir="/WEB-INF/tags" %>`. You will often find questions that test whether `tagdir` and `uri` can coexist in the same `<% taglib %>` directive. They can't. `prefix` is always present, and you can have either `tagdir` or `uri`—not both.

Within the JSP document, the use of the tag hasn't changed very much, except that it no longer has a body with EL variables. All elements of the HTML table declaration have disappeared as well. Here's how it looks:

```
<html xmlns:jsp="http://java.sun.com/JSP/Page"
      xmlns:mytags="urn:jsptagdir:/WEB-INF/tags/">
  <jsp:output omit-xml-declaration="true" />
  <jsp:directive.page contentType="text/html" />
  <head><title>Unicode Converter–from Tag File</title></head>
  <body>
    <h3>Numbers with Unicode Character Equivalent–from Tag
File</h3>
    <mytags:unicodeConverter begin="1040" end="1116" />
  </body>
</html>
```

All the removed elements for presentation and data have migrated to the tag file, whose source we will see in a moment.

But before we consider that, how does the JSP find the tag? We've already said that no tag library descriptor is involved. So how is the name of the tag (`unicodeConverted`) derived? The mechanism is very simple. The tag directory (/WEB-INF/tags) referenced in the XML name space declaration contains the tag file. The tag file itself has the name `unicodeConverter.tag`. So the name before the file extension corresponds to the name as used in the JSP document. The extension must always be .tag.

So now we know how the JSP document finds it, let's look at the complete tag file—shown below, with line numbers:

```
01 <%@ taglib prefix="c" uri="http://java.sun.com/jsp/jstl/core" %>
02 <%@ taglib prefix="mytags" uri="http://www.osborne.com/taglibs/mytags" %>
03 <%@ attribute name="begin" %>
04 <%@ attribute name="end" %>
05 <table border="1">
06 <c:forEach begin="${begin}" end="${end}" step="1" varStatus="counter">
07   <tr>
08     <td>${counter.index}</td>
09     <td>${mytags:unicodeConverter(counter.index)}</td>
10   </tr>
11 </c:forEach>
12 </table>
```

Because there is no TLD entry to refer to, the tag file has to assume its own responsibility for providing some of the information. This explains lines 03 and 04 of the file, which declare attributes using the `<%@ attribute %>` directive. This may sound incestuous, but the `<%@ attribute %>` directive has attributes of its own. The only mandatory attribute is *name*, as used in the example here. This is entirely equivalent to a tag library descriptor file containing these elements:

```
<attribute>
  <name>begin</name>
</attribute>
```

`<% attribute %>` has other attributes, and, like *name*, all of them (*required*, *rtexprvalue*, *description*, *type*, and *fragment*) are equivalent to the TLD subelements of `<attribute>` we have already met.

As well as playing the declarative role formerly taken by the TLD, the tag file needs to find its own way of substituting the Java logic otherwise placed in the `doTag()` method of a genuine simple tag handler class. Actual Java logic is disallowed: A tag file chokes as soon as you try to introduce the smallest of Java language scriptlets. Instead, you use custom actions, and you are especially likely to choose actions from the JSTL. Hence, line 01 declares a reference to the JSTL core tag library.

Line 05 onward is a mixture of template text (HTML table elements), core library syntax, and EL. Line 06 introduces a `<c:forEach>` loop. The *begin* and *end* attributes in `<c:forEach>` have values supplied from the *begin* and *end* attributes defined in the tag—and represented in EL. The *step* attribute tells us we will be incrementing by 1 each time, and the *varStatus* attribute creates an EL variable called *counter* that we use in the table. This occurs at line 08: The *index* property of *counter* is displayed, which gives the current loop value. Remember that we're starting this loop at a number set in the JSP document: 1040. So the numbers we want to display are 1040, 1041, 1042, . . . (not 1, 2, 3, . . .).

What if there is logic that is beyond the bounds of what JSTL and EL can accomplish? Well, you can always access "real Java" by means of a (real) custom tag (not a tag file) used within the tag file. Or, as this example shows, through an EL function. At line 09, we want to display the Unicode character corresponding to the number displayed. Converting an integer to a character value is beyond simple EL; we need some Java to get the job done. Consequently, line 09 invokes a preprepared EL function called `unicodeConverter`, which accepts *counter.index* and returns an equivalent java.lang.Character wrapper object for display. (The code to achieve this is in CharConvFunction.java—not reproduced here, for it's not central to the explanation of tag files but present in the example code.) This, incidentally, explains why there is a tag library declaration at line 02: This references the tag library descriptor, which declares the EL function `unicodeConverter`.

Tag File Directives

There are two directives in the tag file example: `<%@ taglib %>`, which you have met many times before in JSPs, and `<%@ attribute %>`, which you are meeting for the first time and which only works in tag files. Let's consider—first of all—those attributes found in JSPs and how they are used in tag files:

- `<%@ page %>`—*only* suitable for JSP pages. Tag files have their own equivalent—`<%@ tag %>`.
- `<%@ taglib %>`, `<%@ include %>`—both work identically in tag files and in JSP pages.

There are three directives that are only for tag files:

- `<%@ tag %>`, which shares several attributes in common with `<%@ page %>` for JSPs (*language*, *import*, *pageEncoding*, *isELIgnored*)
- `<%@ attribute %>`, like the `<attribute>` subelement of `<tag>` in a TLD
- `<%@ variable %>`, like the `<variable>` subelement of `<tag>` in a TLD

`<%@ tag %>` sounds as though it should be crucial, but all its attributes are optional. For a full list (and for absolutely thorough exam preparation), check Table JSP.8-2 in the JSP 2.0 specification. Only one attribute is crucial to understand in terms of the exam objective that headed this chapter section, and that is *body-content*. The default value for the *body-content* attribute is `scriptless`. The only other allowed values are `empty` and `tagdependent`. Their meaning is identical to the equivalent values in the `<body-content>` element of a custom or simple tag declaration in a TLD. Because a tag file becomes a simple tag handler class (after generation and compilation), `JSP` is a strictly disallowed value.

So far, tag files have led us back to a more traditional JSP syntax. Although Java language is absent, the `<% ... %>` syntax predominates for all kinds of necessary declaration. What if you want your tag files to be written in pure XML, as JSP documents? That's fine; you can do that. There are custom actions equivalents, such as `<jsp:directive.tag ...>`. See the JSP 2.0 specification, especially sections 8.7 and 10.1.

EXERCISE 9-3

The Tag File Model

In this exercise you will rewrite the file browser from Exercise 9-2 as a slightly enhanced version of the original. You will also use a tag file to provide the core functionality instead of a tag handler class. The tag file makes use of a servlet, which houses some of the code that would otherwise be difficult or impossible to render as a combination of JSTL and EL within the tag file.

For this exercise, create a web application directory structure under a directory called ex0903, and proceed with the steps for the exercise. There's a solution in the CD in the file sourcecode/ch09/ex0903.war.

Copy the HTML File from Exercise 9-2

1. Copy the HTML file fileBrowser.html from context directory ex0902 to the current context directory for this exercise: ex0903.
2. Change the action in the form to target JSP page fileBrowser.jsp (instead of JSP document fileBrowser.jspx).

Create the JSP Page

3. Create a JSP page called fileBrowser.jsp directly in ex0903.
4. Include a `taglib` directive with a prefix of `mytags` and with the tag directory attribute set to "/WEB-INF/tags."
5. Most of the template text in the original JSP document from Exercise 9-2 is going to migrate to the tag file. Consequently, all you need to set up in the JSP page is (1) some template elements (`<html>`, `<body>`, etc.) to establish the page as proper HTML and (2) a call to the tag just as before:

```
<mytags:fileBrowser initDir="${param.initDir}" size="true" />
```

Set Up the Servlet and the Helper Class

6. The tag file we have yet to write is going to use a servlet, which in turn uses a helper class. You aren't going to write them yourself—they can be copied from the solution code WAR file.
7. Unzip the WAR file.
8. Copy /ex0903/WEB-INF/classes/webcert/ch09/ex0903/FileBrowserServlet .class to the equivalent directory located in your own directory structure for this exercise.
9. Do the same for /ex0903/WEB-INF/webcert/ch09/ex0903/FileFacade.class.
10. Also copy the deployment descriptor /ex0903/WEB-INF/web.xml. This sets up the servlet with a URL mapping of /FileBrowser.
11. Look at the source for FileBrowserServlet (in /ex0903/WEB-INF/src/ webcert/ch09/ex0903/FileBrowserServlet.java). Note how this obtains a value for the parameter *initDir*, representing the directory to start with. See how this is used to create an array of Files in that directory and how each File in turn is transferred to a collection (ArrayList) of FileFacade objects. Note how the collection is set up as a request attribute called *fileList*.

12. Now look at the source for FileFacade.java (same solution directory as the servlet source code). Note how this is a bean that "wrappers" a genuine java.io.File object, with the express purpose of exposing three properties: *size* (of file), *directory* (is the file in fact a directory?), and *nameAndPath* (the full name of the file). This will make it easier to write EL in the tag file in the next stage of the exercise.

Write the Tag File

13. Create a file called fileBrowser.tag directly in directory /WEB-INF/tags (create the directory as necessary).
14. Include a `taglib` directive to reference the JSTL core tag library.
15. Define two attributes for the tag (in attribute directives) with the names *initDir* and *size*. *initDir* represents the directory that the tag file operates on. *size* indicates whether or not the "size" column should appear in the displayed table.
16. Now use the `<c:import>` core library action to invoke the URL /FileBrowser, which will cause the FileBrowserServlet to process the request. Within `<c:import>`, pass a parameter (using `<c:param>`) with a value of `${initDir}`—the directory the servlet should operate on.
17. Include a table with two columns, with the headings "Name" and "Size." Use `<c:if>` and the `${size}` attribute to include only the Size column if it is requested.
18. Use `<c:forEach>` to iterate over the request attribute *fileList* set up by the servlet. Pull each object in the collection (a FileFacade object) back into a variable called *file*.
19. Within the `<c:forEach>` loop, display the file's full name (with the *nameAndPath* property on file) and (if requested) the file's size.
20. Optionally, detect whether the file is a directory or not. When it is a directory, set the displayed name up as a hyperlink back to the JSP fileBrowser.jsp, forwarding the link directory name as the `initDir` parameter.

Create, Deploy, and Test a WAR File

21. Zip up your context directory in a WAR file, and deploy this to your server.
22. Test with a URL such as

```
http://localhost:8080/ex0903/fileBrowser.html
```

23. Supply an initial directory name (e.g., C:\Documents and Settings\All Users), and click the submit button.
24. The solution page is shown in the following illustration. If you have included hyperlinks to other directories, check to see that they work.

Show Files in Requested Directory (using Tag File)

Directory: C:\Documents and Settings\David

Name	Size
C:\Documents and Settings\David\.WASRegistry	59
C:\Documents and Settings\David\Application Data	N/A
C:\Documents and Settings\David\Cookies	N/A
C:\Documents and Settings\David\Desktop	N/A
C:\Documents and Settings\David\Favorites	N/A
C:\Documents and Settings\David\IBM	N/A
C:\Documents and Settings\David\Local Settings	N/A
C:\Documents and Settings\David\My Documents	N/A
C:\Documents and Settings\David\NetHood	N/A
C:\Documents and Settings\David\NTUSER.DAT	1835008
C:\Documents and Settings\David\NTUSER.DAT.LOG	1024

CERTIFICATION OBJECTIVE

Tag Hierarchies (Exam Objective 10.3)

Given a scenario, write tag handler code to access the parent tag and an arbitrary tag ancestor.

The good thing about this exam objective is that you have already worked on it. In the last section of Chapter 8, you learned about iteration tags, following a card dealing example. Within that example, you saw how an inner tag could make use

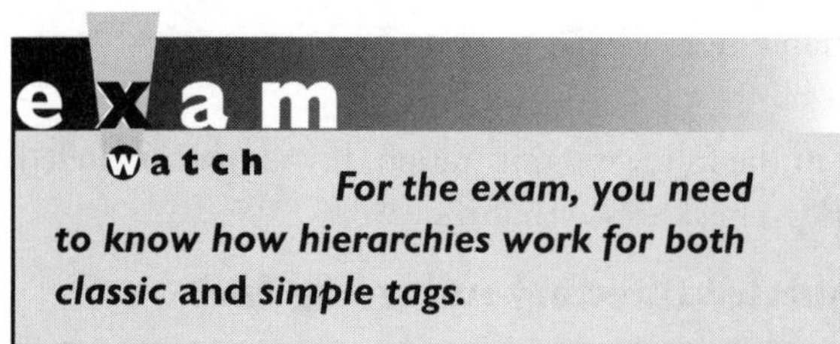

For the exam, you need to know how hierarchies work for both classic and simple tags.

of methods in an outer tag. This chapter will round out your knowledge on this topic. In the Chapter 8, you considered how you could access parent tags (and parents of parents) in the classic tag model. This section shows you how the simple tag model can also access members of a simple tag hierarchy, and how you can even mix simple and classic tags together in the same hierarchy.

Tag Hierarchies

Instead of having a practical example (such as card dealing), we're going to strip hierarchies back to their bare essentials in this section. You'll meet both a classic tag and a simple tag that have only a single purpose: to display the name of their parent. You'll see that *name* is an attribute of the tags. Then you'll see the tags embedded in all combinations:

- Simple within simple
- Classic within classic
- Simple within classic
- Classic within simple

You'll see how this works in three out of the four cases, but how one case (in which a classic tag is embedded inside a simple tag) proves to be problematic. However, the JSP container provides a solution, which we will explore.

The Big Picture

The entirety of this example is available in the CD in /sourcecode/ch09/examp0904.war. You may want to deploy and run the code first of all. All the source code is available in the WAR file, so not all of this is reproduced in the pages that follow. Once deployed, run the code using a URL such as

```
http://localhost:8080/examp0904/nestingTags.jsp
```

This should produce a page in your browser similar to that shown in Figure 9-4.

We'll explore each of the five cases illustrated one by one.

FIGURE 9-4 Experiment with nesting tags

Nesting Tags Example Output

Simple within Simple	My name is: outerSimple; my parent's name is: No parent My name is: innerSimple; my parent's name is: outerSimple
Classic within Classic	My name is: outerClassic; my parent's name is: No parent My name is: innerClassic; my parent's name is: outerClassic
Simple within Classic	My name is: outerClassic; my parent's name is: No parent My name is: innerSimple; my parent's name is: outerClassic
Classic within Simple (Broken)	My name is: outerSimple; my parent's name is: No parent My name is: innerClassic; my parent's name is: No parent
Classic within Simple (Fixed)	My name is: outerSimple; my parent's name is: No parent My name is: innerClassic2; my parent's name is: outerSimple

Simple within Simple

The JSP code that produces the "simple within simple" output in Figure 9-4 is as follows:

```
<mytags:nestingSimple name="outerSimple">
  <mytags:nestingSimple name="innerSimple" />
</mytags:nestingSimple>
```

You can see that there is an outer occurrence of a tag called nestingSimple, with a name attribute of `outer`. There is an inner occurrence of the same tag—this time without a body—called `inner`. The outer occurrence has no parent, so it displays the following:

```
My name is: outerSimple; my parent's name is: No parent
```

The inner occurrence does have its own name ("innerSimple"), and we would expect its parent to be "outerSimple." Again, this performs as expected. The next line of output in the web page is

```
My name is: innerSimple; my parent's name is: outerSimple
```

So far, so good.

The crucial code to accomplish this output in the `doTag()` method of the tag handler (which extends SimpleTagSupport) goes as follows:

```
String bodyMessage;
JspTag parent = getParent();
if (parent instanceof NestingSimpleTag) {
  NestingSimpleTag nst = (NestingSimpleTag) parent;
  bodyMessage = nst.getName();
} else {
  bodyMessage = "No parent";
}
bodyMessage = "My name is: " + getName() + "; my parent's name is: " +
bodyMessage + "<br />";
```

Just as for classic tags (as implemented in TagSupport), so any SimpleTag (as implemented in SimpleTagSupport) has a `getParent()` method. Note that this returns not a Tag, but a JspTag—useless by itself, for it has no methods. However, we suspect that the parent might be an instance of NestingSimpleTag—if it is, we can cast the parent reference to a NestingSimpleTag and get hold of its name. The rest is finagling with the String output (the code to send the String to the associated page output Writer has been omitted).

Classic within Classic

The code for a classic tag to retrieve its classic parent is hardly any different. Here's the highly predictable JSP code first of all:

```
<mytags:nestingClassic name="outerClassic">
  <mytags:nestingClassic name="innerClassic" />
</mytags:nestingClassic>
```

The relevant code in the `doStartTag()` method of the tag handler (which extends TagSupport) looks like this:

```
String bodyMessage;
Tag parent = getParent();
if (parent instanceof NestingClassicTag) {
  NestingClassicTag nct = (NestingClassicTag) parent;
  bodyMessage = nct.getName();
} else {
  bodyMessage = "No parent";
}
```

Since this is a Tag (not a SimpleTag), the `getParent()` method retrieves a Tag rather than a JspTag—a subtle difference, but one that proves important later. And this time, the code tests for an instance of a NestingClassicTag rather than a NestingSimpleTag—naturally enough. The output is just as expected for the outer and inner invocations:

```
My name is: outerClassic; my parent's name is: No parent
My name is: innerClassic; my parent's name is: outerClassic
```

Simple within Classic

What happens, though, when we embed our nestingSimple tag in our nestingClassic tag, as in the following JSP code?

```
<mytags:nestingClassic name="outerClassic">
  <mytags:nestingSimple name="innerSimple" />
</mytags:nestingClassic>
```

The desired output is clear enough:

```
My name is: outerClassic; my parent's name is: No parent
My name is: innerSimple; my parent's name is: outerClassic
```

Our tag handler code won't quite work as it stood before. We need some additional code to make the right cast to a classic tag:

```
String bodyMessage;
JspTag parent = getParent();
if (parent instanceof NestingSimpleTag) {
  NestingSimpleTag nst = (NestingSimpleTag) parent;
  bodyMessage = nst.getName();
} else if (parent instanceof NestingClassicTag) {
  NestingClassicTag nct = (NestingClassicTag) parent;
  bodyMessage = nct.getName();
} else {
  bodyMessage = "No parent";
}
```

This allows the code to call the `getName()` method on the right sort of tag—nothing more than this. The important part is that the `getParent()` call doesn't change. Even though we are in simple tag handler code, `getParent()` still retrieves the classic tag handler instance parent: as a JspTag. That's no problem because classic tag handler instances are all Tags—and in JSP 2.0, Tag inherits from JspTag. JspTag, as we have seen before, is the common ancestor for both classic and simple tags. So this works.

Classic within Simple (Broken)

Only one combination to go—a classic tag trying to find a simple parent, as in this JSP code:

```
<mytags:nestingSimple name="outerSimple">
  <mytags:nestingClassic name="innerClassic" />
</mytags:nestingSimple>
```

The naïve approach to making our nestingClassic tag find a nestingSimple parent is to write a mirror image of the adaptations we made to our simple tag handler code, which looks like this:

```
String bodyMessage;
Tag parent = getParent();
if (parent instanceof NestingClassicTag) {
  NestingClassicTag nct = (NestingClassicTag) parent;
  bodyMessage = nct.getName();
} else if (parent instanceof NestingSimpleTag) {
  NestingSimpleTag nst = (NestingSimpleTag) parent;
  bodyMessage = nst.getName();
} else {
  bodyMessage = "No parent";
}
```

However, this doesn't work. It doesn't break at run time; instead, we're told that the innerClassic tag has no parent, which is simply untrue:

```
My name is: outerSimple; my parent's name is: No parent
My name is: innerClassic; my parent's name is: No parent
```

Why doesn't the test `(parent instanceof NestingSimpleTag)` prove true? Consider that we are in an implementation of Tag and so the `getParent()` method has a return type of Tag, not JspTag. NestingSimpleTag can *never* be an instance of Tag—it's in the wrong hierarchy, as the following illustration shows.

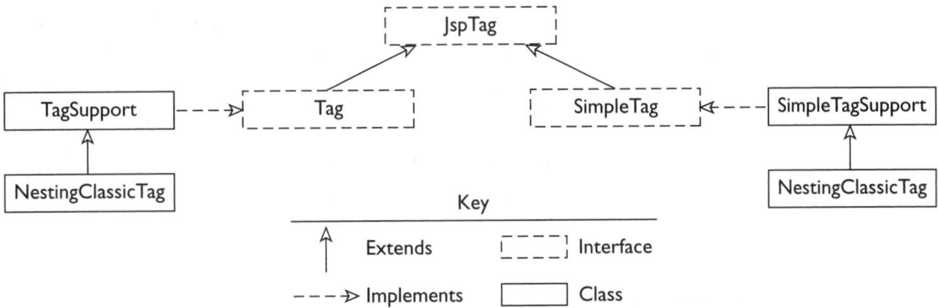

So what does `getParent()` return? Maybe **null** because classic tags perhaps can't detect simple parents? On the contrary—the JSP container has an ace up its sleeve. One step ahead of our tag handler, it detects the mixed hierarchy and shrouds the NestedSimpleTag object in a TagAdapter instance. The process is as follows:

- The JSP container calls `doTag()` on `mytags:nestingSimple` (the outer—simple—tag).
- The `doTag()` method chooses to process the body of the simple tag (by calling the `JspFragment.invoke()` method).
- The body of the simple tag contains `mytags:nestingClassic` (the classic tag)—so the JSP container exercises the classic model life cycle on this tag.
- The classic model life cycle includes a call to `setParent()` for the classic tag. The JSP container knows the parent is a simple tag. However, `setParent()` will only accept a Tag as a parameter—and simple tag is a JspTag, not a Tag.
- The JSP container gets out of the dilemma by creating an instance of TagAdapter, which is of type Tag. The JSP Container passes the simple tag to the TagAdapter's one-argument (and only) constructor.
- Now the JSP container calls `setParent()` on the classic tag, passing in the TagAdapter instance.
- When—later—the code in the classic tag calls `getParent()`, the method returns this TagAdapter instance.
- In a moment, we'll see what methods the classic tag can use from TagAdapter to get at the real parent: the simple tag.

The TagAdapter is a class that you don't need to instantiate in your own code—it's there for the JSP container. The TagAdapter is a "wrapper" around the simple tag. You encountered this kind of behavior before in the SCJP exam, in the java.io library. Recall that if you have a byte stream, but need to deal with characters, you can pass your byte stream to the constructor of an InputStreamReader. Thereafter, you deal with the character-oriented InputStreamReader—though under the covers, this is manipulating the original stream of bytes. So with the TagAdapter—it allows the JSP container code to deal with simple tags as classic tags in situations where there is no alternative.

Classic within Simple (Fixed)

Armed with this information, we can set about making NestedClassicTag work properly (which is done in the nestingClassic2 tag, with tag handler class NestedClassicTag2). TagAdapter has two useful methods:

- `getAdaptee()` returns the wrappered-up JspTag (i.e., your simple tag instance).
- `getParent()` returns the adaptee's parent (by running `getAdaptee().getParent()`). If *that* parent isn't an instance of a Tag, then it in turn is wrappered up as a TagAdapter, then returned from this method.

exam watch

The TagAdapter class also contains a number of deliberately useless methods. Because TagAdapter implements the Tag interface, it includes all the classic life cycle methods: `setPageContext()`, `setParent()`, `doStartTag()`, `doEndTag()`, and `release()`. These mustn't be called directly—by you or the JSP container. To do so results in an UnsupportedOperationException in all cases.

So back in our classic tag handler: `getParent()` returns—in these circumstances—an instance of TagAdapter. Given that, we can use the `getAdaptee()` method to fix our code, as follows:

```
String bodyMessage;
Tag parent = getParent();
if (parent instanceof NestingClassicTag2) {
  NestingClassicTag2 nct = (NestingClassicTag2) parent;
  bodyMessage = nct.getName();
} else if (parent instanceof TagAdapter) {
  JspTag simpleParent = ((TagAdapter) parent).getAdaptee();
  if (simpleParent instanceof NestingSimpleTag) {
```

```
      bodyMessage = ((NestingSimpleTag) simpleParent).getName();
    } else {
      bodyMessage = "No parent";
    }
  } else {
    bodyMessage = "No parent";
  }
```

If the parent is a classic tag, nothing has changed—we test for an instance of the classic tag class (true, there has been a name change to NestingClassicTag2—to differentiate it from the broken original). Next, the code—suspecting a simple tag as parent—tests for `getParent()` returning an instance of TagAdapter. If it has, the simple tag is extracted from the TagAdapter by using the `getAdaptee()` method. The output from this is a JspTag, and finally this instance can be tested to see if it is the tag we're hoping for, the NestingSimpleTag. When this code is run, the output is fixed, as shown:

```
My name is: outerSimple; my parent's name is: No parent
My name is: innerClassic2; my parent's name is: outerSimple
```

exam watch

Just as TagSupport has a `findAncestorWithClass()` method, so SimpleTagSupport has a method of the same name. It has some important differences, though. For one thing, it returns a JspTag rather than a Tag: It's intended to hunt down simple classes. For another (and in keeping with this), any TagAdapter found in the hierarchy is not taken at face value—instead, the simple tag it contains (obtained with `getAdaptee()`) is compared with the class passed in as the second parameter to the `findAncestorWithClass()` method. Check out the API documentation for chapter and verse.

EXERCISE 9-4

Tag Hierarchies

In this exercise you will build a version of the card dealing example that you first met in Chapter 8. This will give you a good feel for classic tag hierarchies (to complete the picture, in the lab at the end of the chapter, you'll convert this example to use a mixed hierarchy with classic and simple tags).

For this exercise, create a web application directory structure under a directory called ex0904, and proceed with the steps for the exercise. There's a solution in the CD in the file sourcecode/ch09/ex0904.war.

Copy the CardDealingTag Code from the Solution

1. The main custom action (code in the CardDealingTag class) contains mostly the "business" method for the card dealing solution. Rather than attempt to recreate this yourself, copy it from the solution code WAR file to a directory called /ex0904/WEB-INF/classes/webcert/ch09/ex0904.
2. Copy the source file CardDealingTag.java to /ex0904/WEB-INF/src/webcert/ch09/ex0904.
3. Open the source file. Note the following methods:

   `doStartTag()`—this shuffles the card every time it's invoked, and returns EVAL_BODY_INCLUDE to ensure that the body is processed.

   `doAfterBody()`—this continues to loop until all cards are "dealt" (as indicated by the currentCard value).

   `dealCard()`—this is the method that must be called to "deal" cards from the pack and will be called by child tag handlers you will write.

Write Child Tag Handler Classes

4. Create two Java source files in your context directory, under a suitable package directory in /WEB-INF/classes, called CardTag.java and CardTag2.java.
5. Have CardTag extend TagSupport. Override the `doEndTag()` method. This should use `getParent()` to get hold of the parent tag, and cast this to a CardDealingTag reference. Call the `dealCard()` method on the `CardDealingTag()` instance so that one card is dealt. `dealCard()` returns a String holding the card name — output this to the Writer for the page context object.
6. Have CardTag2 extend TagSupport as well. Copy the code from `CardTag.doEndTag()` into CardTag2. Change the code so that instead of using `getParent()`, it uses `TagSupport.findAncestorWithClass()` to return a reference to the parent CardDealerTag.

Write the Tag Library Descriptor File

7. Create a TLD file called mytags.tld in /WEB-INF/tags (create the directory as necessary).
8. Declare three tags called cardDealer, card, and card2. These reference (respectively) the CardDealerTag, CardTag, and CardTag2 classes. The body content of cardDealer should be set to JSP, and for card and card2 should be set to empty.

Reference the TLD in the Deployment Descriptor

9. Place a `<jsp-config>` element in web.xml, which defines a mapping from taglib URI http://www.osborne.com/taglibs/mytags to a location of /WEB-INF/tags/mytags.tld.

Define a JSP Document to Use the Tags

10. Create a JSP document called cardGame.jspx directly in the ex0904 context directory.
11. Include the following "boilerplate" namespace declarations for your own tag library, JSP standard actions, and the JSTL core library:

```
<html xmlns:mytags="http://www.osborne.com/taglibs/mytags"
  xmlns:jsp="http://java.sun.com/JSP/Page"
  xmlns:c="http://java.sun.com/jsp/jstl/core">
```

12. Include the following standard actions to ensure HTML rather than XML output to your browser:

```
<jsp:output omit-xml-declaration="true" />
<jsp:directive.page contentType="text/html" />
```

13. Create an HTML table with four columns. Include table headings labeled Player 1 through to Player 4.
14. Surround the main table row with opening and closing cardDealer tags.
15. In each of the four cells for the main table row, include a self-closing card tag.

Create, Deploy, and Test a WAR File

16. Zip up your context directory in a WAR file, and deploy this to your server.
17. Test with a URL such as

```
http://localhost:8080/ex0904/cardGame.jspx
```

18. The solution output is shown in the following illustration. Each refresh of the browser should result in a newly shuffled deal.

Bridge Hand

Player 1	Player 2	Player 3	Player 4
Three of spades	Eight of spades	Nine of hearts	Ten of hearts
Six of clubs	Four of spades	Queen of hearts	Four of clubs
Four of hearts	Queen of spades	Ten of clubs	Nine of spades
Two of spades	Queen of diamonds	King of hearts	Two of clubs
Three of hearts	Jack of diamonds	Five of diamonds	Jack of hearts
Nine of clubs	Ace of spades	Ace of clubs	Seven of spades
Ten of diamonds	King of diamonds	Ten of spades	Ace of diamonds
Eight of clubs	King of clubs	Two of hearts	Five of spades
King of spades	Six of hearts	Jack of spades	Seven of hearts
Six of spades	Jack of clubs	Four of diamonds	Nine of diamonds
Ace of hearts	Three of diamonds	Seven of diamonds	Five of clubs
Five of hearts	Seven of clubs	Two of diamonds	Three of clubs
Eight of hearts	Queen of clubs	Eight of diamonds	Six of diamonds

19. Now amend cardGame.jspx (you can, if you wish, amend the deployed copy under Tomcat; otherwise, change the document in your context directory, remake the WAR, and redeploy it).
20. Change one of the card tags to be surrounded by a `<c:if>` action like this:

```
<c:if test="${true}"><mytags:card2 /></c:if>
```

The test will always be true, so the `<c:if>` is spurious. However, it separates the <mytags:card> action from its proper parent (`<mytags:cardDealer>`) in the hierarchy.

21. Retest the document. You should get a ClassCastException, like this:

HTTP Status 500 -

---

type Exception report

message

description The server encountered an internal error () that prevented it from fulfilling this request.

exception

```
org.apache.jasper.JasperException: org.apache.taglibs.standard.tag.rt.core.IfTag
	org.apache.jasper.servlet.JspServletWrapper.service(JspServletWrapper.java:373)
	org.apache.jasper.servlet.JspServlet.serviceJspFile(JspServlet.java:295)
	org.apache.jasper.servlet.JspServlet.service(JspServlet.java:245)
	javax.servlet.http.HttpServlet.service(HttpServlet.java:802)
```

root cause

```
java.lang.ClassCastException: org.apache.taglibs.standard.tag.rt.core.IfTag
	webcert.ch09.ex0904.CardTag.doEndTag(CardTag.java:30)
	org.apache.jsp.cardGame_jspx._jspx_meth_mytags_card_1(org.apache.jsp.cardGame_jspx:194)
```

22. Now change the tag enclosed in the `<c:if>` to `<mytags:card2>`. When you retest this time, the page should work. This is because `<mytags:card2>` uses the `findAncestorByClass()` method and is not sensitive to intervening actions in the hierarchy.

CERTIFICATION SUMMARY

In this chapter you started by learning about accessing implicit variables in tag handler code. You saw that this involved gaining a thorough knowledge of methods on the PageContext class that provide equivalent instances to the JSP's implicit variables, such as `getRequest()` for *request*.

You also revised the topic of attributes and PageContext: Any attribute in any scope can be manipulated through the PageContext object.

You went on from there to explore the simple tag model. You saw that simple tags implement the SimpleTag interface or, more usually, extend the SimpleTagSupport class, which provides useful default implementations of methods. You learned all about the simple tag life cycle and maybe agreed that although it is not that simple, it removes a lot of the complexity that goes with classic tags. You learned that a new simple tag gets created for every invocation (no pooling as there is—potentially—for classic tags), so instance variables are safe to use. You saw that `setJspContext()` is the first life cycle method to be called, and this provides the tag handler with a JspContext object—very like a PageContext (which is JspContext's subclass). You saw that a call to `setParent()` followed—passing in a JspTag reference (as opposed to a Tag for the equivalent classic tag method). You saw that attributes are set after this (much as classic tags), followed by a call to setJspBody, providing something called a JspFragment to your simple tag. You then learned that `doTag()` is called and that this can write directly to page output and cause the body to be executed using the `JspFragment.invoke()` method. You finally learned that even though `doTag()` has no return value, you can skip the rest of the page by throwing a SkipPageException.

Next you saw that simple tags can be written without any Java source—in the form of tag files. You saw that tag files are written very much like JSP pages (though without any Java syntax—only template text, actions, and EL allowed). You saw that tag files must have a .tag extension and are normally placed in /WEB-INF/tags or a subdirectory thereof. You learned that the JSP container generates simple tag source code from a tag file and compiles this into a class that then functions just as a handcrafted simple tag.

You learned that tag file source shares some directives in common with JSPs (`<%@ taglib %>`, `<%@ include %>`), has one that it doesn't share (`<%@ page %>`), and has three directives all of its own (`<%@ tag %>`, `<%@ attribute %>`, `<%@ variable %>`). You learned that the attribute and variable directives have attributes very similar to subelements of the `<attribute>` and `<variable>` elements in a tag library descriptor. You also saw that the tag directive has several attributes in common with the JSP page directive, but also has some attributes (such as *body-content*) that reflect subelements of the `<tag>` element in a TLD.

In the final section of the chapter, you revisited the subject of tag file hierarchies. You saw that both TagSupport and SimpleTagSupport have identically named methods for retrieving instances of tag handlers: `getParent()`, for retrieving an immediate parent in the hierarchy, and `findAncestorWithClass()`, for retrieving a tag handler somewhere farther up the hierarchy of the class identified in the parameter.

However, you learned that there are subtle differences—Tags and SimpleTags do not belong to the same class hierarchy (although they do both have JspTag as their ultimate parent). Tag hierarchy methods return Tags. SimpleTags return JspTags, and a SimpleTag can never be a Tag. You saw that to stop a fatal collision where a classic tag has a simple parent, simple tags may be cloaked in a TagAdapter, which presents the SimpleTag as a classic Tag.

TWO-MINUTE DRILL

Tags and Implicit Variables

- In tag handler code, implicit variables are available through methods on the PageContext object.
- The PageContext object is handed to the tag handler code in the `setPageContext()` method.
- For ServletRequest *request*, use `PageContext.getRequest()`.
- For ServletResponse *response*, use `PageContext.getResponse()`.
- For Writer *out*, use `JspWriter.getOut()`. (JspWriter is the superclass for PageContext.)
- For HttpSession *session*, use `PageContext.getSession()`.
- For ServletConfig *config*, use `PageContext.getServletConfig()`.
- For ServletContext *application*, use `PageContext.getServletContext()`.
- For Object *page*, use `PageContext.getPage()` (it's usually a Servlet).
- For PageContext *pageContext*—that is the PageContext object passed to the tag handler through the setPageContext() method.
- For Exception exception, use `PageContext.getException()`.
- `PageContext.getException()` will return **null**, unless the enclosing JSP page is marked as an error page (`isErrorPage="true"`) and the JSP container has redirected to this page as the result of an error.
- PageContext can be used to access attributes in all scopes.

The "Simple" Custom Tag Event Model

- Simple tags implement the SimpleTag interface or extend the SimpleTagSupport class.
- An instance of a simple tag is created for each run-time use.
- Simple tag life cycle methods are called in sequence by the JSP container. None of the methods produce return codes.
- Following construction, `setJspContext` is called to provide a context object (in much the same way that `setPageContext` is called for a classic tag).
- Next: `setParent()`—passing a reference to a JspTag.

- Next: `setXXX()` methods for attributes.
- Next: `setJspBody()`—passing in a JspFragment representing the JSP code within the body of the tag (called only if there is a body).
- Next: `doTag()`. All looping, body processing, and other page output occurs within this method.
- Normal exit from `doTag()` allows the JSP container to process the remainder of the page.
- A SkipPageException thrown from `doTag()` makes the JSP container skip the rest of the page.
- JspFragment is not like BodyContent. BodyContent represents evaluated content, buffered. JspFragment is content that hasn't been evaluated yet (so no need for a buffer).

The Tag File Model

- Tag files are simple tags whose source is in JSP-syntax form.
- Tag files must have a .tag extension (or .tagx if they are XML documents).
- Tag files are kept in /WEB-INF/tags or a subdirectory of /WEB-INF/tags.
- A JSP page using a tag file has access to it through a tag library directive: The tagdir attribute is used instead of uri—for example,

```
<%@ taglib prefix="mytags" tagdir="/WEB-INF/tags" %>
```

- Tag files may also be kept in a JAR file in /WEB-INF/lib.
- Tag files within a JAR must reside in the /META-INF/tags directory (or a subdirectory of this).
- Tag files within a JAR are only accessible if declared in a `<tag-file>` element in a tag library descriptor (TLD).
- The `<tag-file>` element in the TLD has two subelements: `<name>` and `<path>`.
- `<name>` must contain a name unique across all tag files, tags, and EL functions contained in the TLD.
- `<path>` must begin with /META-INF/tags.
- Tag files have limitations on body content: `empty`, `tagdependent`, or `scriptless`.

- The fourth value for body content—JSP—is disallowed in tag files (as for all simple tags).
- `scriptless` is the default.
- To set another value for body-content, use the `tag` directive:

```
<% tag body-content="tagdependent" %>
```

- Tag files have three directives that may only occur in tag files: `tag`, `attribute`, and `variable`.
- The `tag` directive is like the page directive in the JSP (and has four attributes in common with it—`language`, `import`, `pageEncoding`, and `isELIgnored`).
- The `attribute` directive is like the `<attribute>` element within a TLD.
- The `variable` directive is like the `<variable>` element within a TLD.
- At run time, Java source is generated for a SimpleTag from the tag file source and compiled into a class file.

Tag Hierarchies

- Tag has a `getParent()` method, implemented in TagSupport.
- `getParent()` retrieves the immediate parent of a tag—if there is one.
- `getParent()` returns a Tag reference, which can be cast to something more appropriate if specific methods are needed.
- SimpleTag also has a `getParent()` method, implemented in SimpleTagSupport.
- `getParent()` in SimpleTag also returns its immediate parent, if there is one.
- However, `SimpleTag.getParent()` returns a JspTag, so it can accommodate both simple or classic tag parents.
- As `Tag.getParent()` can accommodate only Tags, any simple tag higher in the hierarchy is "cloaked" by the JSP container in an instance of TagAdapter.
- `TagAdapter.getAdaptee()` returns the simple tag wrappered by the TagAdapter instance (as a JspTag reference—which you can cast as needed).
- TagSupport has a **static** method called `findAncestorWithClass()`.
- To this method, you pass in the Tag instance to start from (usually *this*) and the Class whose type should match a tag handler instance in the hierarchy.

- `TagSupport.findAncestorByClass()` returns a Tag reference—this could be a TagAdapter.
- SimpleTagSupport also has a static `findAncestorByClass()` method, which works in identical fashion, except that it receives a JspTag to start from (not a Tag), and returns a JspTag reference.
- When using `SimpleTagSupport.findAncestorByClass()` methods, where TagAdapters are encountered, the class comparison is to `TagAdapter.getAdaptee()` (not directly to the class of the TagAdapter instance).

SELF TEST

The following questions will help you measure your understanding of the material presented in this chapter. Read all the choices carefully because there might be more than one correct answer. Choose all the correct answers for each question.

Tags and Implicit Variables

1. Given the following JSP and tag handler code, what is the result of accessing the JSP? (Choose one.)

JSP Page Source

```
<%@ taglib prefix="mytags" uri="http://www.osborne.com/taglibs/mytags" %>
<html><head><title>Questions</title></head>
<body><p><% session.setAttribute("first", "first"); %>
<mytags:question01 />
${second}
</p></body></html>
```

Tag Handler Code for <mytags:question01 />
(imports missing, but assume they are correct)

```
public class Question01 extends TagSupport {
  public int doStartTag() throws JspException {
    Writer out = pageContext.getOut();
    try {
      out.write("" + pageContext.getAttribute("first"));
    } catch (IOException e) {
      e.printStackTrace();
    }
    pageContext.setAttribute("second", "second", PageContext.SESSION_SCOPE);
    return super.doStartTag();
  }
}
```

A. first first

B. second second

C. first second

D. second first

E. first null

F. null second

G. null null

2. Which of the following snippets of code, if inserted into the `doStartTag()` method of a tag handler class extending TagSupport, would compile? (Choose three.)

   A.

   ```
   pageContext.getSession().getId();
   ```

   B.

   ```
   pageContext.getRequest().getAttributeName();
   ```

   C.

   ```
   pageContext.getHttpResponse().getBufferSize();
   ```

   D.

   ```
   pageContext.getPage().getServletName();
   ```

   E.

   ```
   pageContext.getException().getStackTrace();
   ```

   F.

   ```
   pageContext.getExpressionEvaluator();
   ```

3. Identify true statements about the *exception* implicit object in tag handler code. (Choose two.)

   A. It can be obtained through the page context's `getError()` method.

   B. The JSP page housing the tag must have page directive isErrorPage set to true for exception to be non-null in the tag handler code.

   C. The JSP page housing the tag must have page directive errorPage set to true for exception to be non-null in the tag handler code.

   D. The page context's `getError()` method return type is java.lang.Throwable.

   E. The page context's `getException()` method return type is java.lang.Throwable.

   F. The exception implicit object has a `getLocalizedMessage()` method.

4. The following is an extract from a tag handler class that implements the Tag interface. Given the code in the `doStartTag()` method, what else is likely to be true for the tag handler to compile and run successfully? (Choose three.)

```
// ...all necessary imports supplied...
public class Question04 implements Tag {
  public int doStartTag() throws JspException {
    HttpServletRequest request = pageContext.getRequest();
    request.setAttribute("myattr", "myvalue");
    return Tag.SKIP_BODY;
  }
  // ...Other methods and instance variables defined...
}
```

A. pageContext should be defined as an instance variable of type PageContext.

B. The method `pageContext.getRequest()` should be replaced with `pageContext.getServletRequest()`.

C. The `setPageContext()` method must initialize a value for pageContext.

D. A cast needs to be inserted in the `doStartTag()` code.

E. The `release()` method should set pageContext to **null**.

F. A scope parameter should be provided to the `request.setAttribute()` method call.

5. Which of the following methods are available in the java.servlet.jspPageContext class? (Choose three.)

   A. getPageScope

   B. getServletConfig

   C. include

   D. getErrorData

   E. getError

   F. getApplication

The "Simple" Custom Tag Event Model

6. For a tag implementing the SimpleTag interface, which of the following method sequences might be called by the JSP container? (Choose two.)

   A. setParent, setPageContext, setJspBody

   B. setParent, setJspContext, doInitBody

   C. setJspContext, setAnAttribute, doTag

   D. setPageContext, setParent, doTag

E. setJspBody, doAfterBody, doTag

F. setJspContext, setParent, doTag

7. Which of the following techniques causes the JSP container to skip the rest of the page after processing a custom action implementing the SimpleTag interface? (Choose one.)

   A. Returning Tag.SKIP_PAGE from the `doEndTag()` method

   B. Returning −1 from the `doPage()` method

   C. Returning −1 from the `doTag()` method

   D. Returning Tag.SKIP_PAGE from the `doTag()` method

   E. Throwing a SkipPageException within the `doTag()` method

   F. Throwing a JspException from the `doPage()` method

8. Consider the following JSP page code and SimpleTag code. What is the output from tag `<mytags:question08>` to the requesting JSP page? You can assume that all necessary deployment descriptor and tag library descriptor elements are set up correctly. (Choose one.)

JSP Page Code:

```
<%@ taglib prefix="mytags" uri="http://www.osborne.com/taglibs/mytags"
%>
<html><head><title>Question08</title></head>
<body><p><mytags:question08>a</mytags:question08></body>
</html>
```

SimpleTag Tag Handler Code for <mytags:question08>:

```
import java.io.IOException;
import java.io.StringWriter;
import javax.servlet.jsp.JspException;
import javax.servlet.jsp.tagext.JspFragment;
import javax.servlet.jsp.tagext.SimpleTagSupport;
public class Question08 extends SimpleTagSupport {
  public void doTag() throws JspException, IOException {
    JspFragment fragment = getJspBody();
    StringWriter sw = new StringWriter();
    for (int i = 0; i < 3; i++) {
      fragment.invoke(sw);
      String s = "b" + sw;
      sw.write(s);
      fragment.invoke(null);
    }
  }
}
```

A. aaa

B. bababa

C. babaabaaa

D. baabaaabaaaa

E. No output

9. Identify true statements about tag declarations in tag library descriptors from the following list. (Choose three.)

   A. The element `<simpletag>` is used to differentiate actions following the simple tag model from the classic tag model.

   B. A tag whose `<body-content>` is declared as JSP must follow the classic tag model.

   C. Separate tag library descriptor files must be used to separate classic and simple tag declarations.

   D. A simple tag has a default `<body-content>` of scriptless.

   E. Simple tags are commonly declared with a `<body-content>` of scriptless.

   F. If a simple tag is declared with a `<body-content>` of "empty," the JSP container makes one less method call on the simple tag handler class.

10. Consider the following JSP page code and SimpleTag code. What is the output from tag `<mytags:question08>` to the requesting JSP page? You can assume that all necessary deployment descriptor and tag library descriptor elements are set up correctly. (Choose one.)

JSP Page Code:

```
<%@ taglib prefix="mytags" uri="http://www.osborne.com/taglibs/mytags"
%>
<%@ taglib prefix="c" uri="http://java.sun.com/jsp/jstl/core" %>
<html><head><title>Question 10</title></head>
<c:set var="counter">1</c:set>
<body><p><mytags:question10>
<c:forEach begin="${counter}" end="3">${counter}</c:forEach>
</mytags:question10></p></body>
</html>
```

SimpleTag Tag Handler Code for `<mytags:question08>`:

```
package webcert.ch09.questions09;
import java.io.IOException;
import javax.servlet.jsp.JspContext;
import javax.servlet.jsp.JspException;
import javax.servlet.jsp.tagext.SimpleTagSupport;
public class Question10 extends SimpleTagSupport {
```

```
  public void doTag() throws JspException, IOException {
    JspContext context = getJspContext();
    int i = Integer.parseInt("" + context.getAttribute("counter"));
    for (; i < 4; i++) {
      context.setAttribute("counter", new Integer(i));
      getJspBody().invoke(null);
    }
  }
}
```

A. No output

B. 111 222 333

C. 1 2 3

D. 123 123 123

E. 111 22 3

F. 22 3

The Tag File Model

11. From the list, identify correct techniques to make tag files available in a JSP page or JSP document. (Choose two.)

A.

```
<%@ taglib prefix="mytags" uri="/WEB-INF/tags/mytags.tld" %>
```

B.

```
<%@ taglib prefix="mytags" taglocation="/WEB-INF/tags" %>
```

C.

```
<html xmlns:mytags="http://www.tags.com/tags">
```

D.

```
<html xmlns:mytags="urn:jsptagdir:/WEB-INF/tags/">
```

E.

```
<%@ taglib prefix="mytags" tagdir="/WEB-INF/tags" %>
```

F.

```
<%@ taglib prefix="mytags" tagdir="/WEB-INF/tags/mytags.tld" %>
```

12. What is the result of accessing the following tag file? (Line numbers are for reference only and should not be considered part of the tag file source.) (Choose one.)

```
01 <%@ taglib prefix="c" uri="http://java.sun.com/jsp/jstl/core" %>
02 <c:set var="character">65</c:set>
03 <c:forEach begin="1" end="10" varStatus="loopCount" >
04 <% char c = (char)
Integer.parseInt(pageContext.getAttribute("character").toString());
05 pageContext.setAttribute("displayCharacter", new Character(c));
07 %>
08 ${displayCharacter}
09 <c:set var="character">${character + 1}</c:set>
10 </c:forEach>
```

A. Translation error at line 1

B. Translation error at line 4

C. Translation error at line 9

D. Run-time error at line 9

E. Output from tag file of A B C D E F G H I J

13. Which of the following are directives you might find in a tag file? (Choose three.)

A. page

B. tag

C. variable

D. import

E. attribute

F. jspcontext

G. scope

14. (drag-and-drop question) In the following illustration, match the numbered options on the right with the concealed lettered portions of the JSP page and tag file, such that the output from accessing the JSP page is as follows:

```
Body: 1 Tag File: 2 Body: 1 Tag File: 3 Body: 1 Tag File: 4
```

JSP Source

```
<%@ taglib prefix="mytags" tagdir="/WEB-INF/tags" %>
<%@ taglib prefix="c"
uri="http://java.sun.com/jsp/jstl/core" %>
<html><head><title>Question 14</title></head>
<[ A ] var="counter" value="1" />
<body><mytags:question14 counter="${counter}">
  Body: [ B ]
</mytags:question14></body></html>
```

Tag File Source for /WEB-INF/tags/question14.tag

```
<%@ taglib prefix="c"
uri="http://java.sun.com/jsp/jstl/core" %>
<%@ [ C ] name="counter" %>
<c:forEach begin="[D]"end="[E]"
varStatus="loopCounter">
  [ F ]
   Tag File: ${counter + [ G ]}
</c:forEach>
```

1	1
2	2
3	3
4	4
5	tag
6	attribute
7	variable
8	c:set
9	loopCounter
10	loopCounter.count
11	loopCounter.index
12	<jsp:attribute />
13	<jsp:doBody />
14	<jsp:invoker />
15	${counter}
16	${counter + 1}
17	${counter + loopCounter}

15. Which of the following is a valid location for a tag file? (Choose one.)
   - A. Directly in the context directory
   - B. Directly in the /WEB-INF directory
   - C. In any subdirectory of /WEB-INF
   - D. In /WEB-INF/tags or a subdirectory beneath /WEB-INF/tags
   - E. In a JAR file in /WEB-INF/lib, under the /META-INF/tags directory
   - F. C and D
   - G. D and E

Tag Hierarchies

16. Consider the following hierarchy of actions. `<c:if>` is from the JSTL core library, and `<a:tagA>` and `<a:tagB>` are classic custom actions.

```
<a:tagA>
  <c:if test="${true}">
    <a:tagB />
  </c:if>
</a:tagA>
```

What options does tagB have for obtaining the enclosing instance of tagA? (Choose one.)

A. Use `TagSupport.findAncestorWithClass()`

B. Invoke `getParent().getParent()`.

C. Use `SimpleTagSupport.findAncestorWithClass()`

D. A, B, and C

E. A and B only

F. B and C only

17. Which of the following could not be returned by either of the `getParent()` methods in the JSP class libraries? (Choose two.)

A. An instance of a JSTL `core` library tag handler

B. An instance of a JSTL `xml` library tag handler

C. An instance of an HTML tag

D. An instance of an XML template tag in a JSP document

E. An instance of BodyTagSupport

F. An instance of SimpleTagSupport

18. What methods can you execute on the reference myAncestor at ??? in the code snippet below? (Choose two.)

```
JspTag myAncestor = SimpleTagSupport.findAncestorWithClass(MyTagClass);
myAncestor.???
```

A. `notifyAll()`

B. `setParent()`

C. `doStartTag()`

D. `doEndTag()`

E. `doAfterBody()`

F. `clone()`

G. `hashCode()`

19. (drag-and-drop question) Consider the `doStartTag()` method shown in the following illustration. The tag for this tag handler will always have a parent, which could obey the simple or classic model. Complete the code by matching numbered options from the right with the concealed letter options, such that the code will successfully identify and print out whether the parent is simple or classic (you may need to use some numbered options more than once).

```
public int doStartTag() {
  [ A ] enclosing = getParent();
  if (enclosing instanceof [ B ]) {
    [ C ] enclosingSimple =
      ([ D ]) enclosing;
    JspTag simpleTag =
      enclosingSimple.[ E ];
    System.out.println("Simple parent: " +
      simpleTag.getClass().getName());
  } else {
    System.out.println("Classic parent: " +
      [ F ].getClass().getName());
  }
  return Tag.[ G ];
}
```

1	`Tag`
2	`TagSupport`
3	`SimpleTag`
4	`SimpleTagSupport`
5	`TagAdapter`
6	`TagAdaptee`
7	`getAdapter()`
8	`getAdaptee()`
9	`enclosing`
10	`enclosingSimple`
11	`simpleTag`
12	`EVAL_BODY`
13	`EVAL_BUFFERED_BODY`
14	`EVAL_BODY_INCLUDE`

20. What strategies might a parent tag use to get hold of a child tag handler instance? (Choose two.)

   A. Classic model: Child gets hold of parent and provides the parent with its own reference to the child. Parent uses the reference in `doAfterBody()` method.

   B. Classic model: Child gets hold of parent and provides the parent with its own reference to the child. Parent uses the reference in `doStartTag()` method.

C. Simple model: Child gets hold of parent and provides the parent with its own reference to the child. Parent uses the reference after a call to `JspFragment.invoke()`.

D. Simple model: Child gets hold of parent and provides the parent with its own reference to the child. Parent uses the reference after `doTag()` method completes.

E. Parent tag uses `TagSupport.findDescendantWithClass()`.

F. Parent tag uses `this.getChild()`.

LAB QUESTION

Before you finish shuffling cards altogether, attempt the following moderately difficult undertaking. Take the solution code from Exercise 9-4, and convert the CardDealingTag to a simple tag. Leave Card and Card2 as classic tag handlers. You'll need to make some adjustments, though, to cope with having a simple tag handler as a parent.

SELF TEST ANSWERS

Tags and Implicit Variables

1. ☑ **F** is the correct answer: The output is null second. In the JSP a session attribute called *first* is set to a value of "first." Although the tag handler code attempts to retrieve an attribute called "first," it uses the `pageContext.getAttribute()` method without supplying a scope parameter—hence, the code looks in page scope and retrieves a null reference that is output to the page within the code. Still in the tag handler code, another attribute called *second* is set up with a value of "second"—again in session scope. Back in the JSP, EL is used to output the attribute. Because EL uses `findAttribute()` under the covers, the JSP searches through all scopes until finding the `second` attribute.
   ☒ **A**, **B**, **C**, **D**, **E**, and **G** are incorrect according to the reasoning in the correct answer.

2. ☑ **A**, **E**, and **F** are the correct answers. **A** returns the ID for a session. **E** prints the stack trace for an exception object. Of course, the exception object will be **null** unless this tag handler is called from a JSP error page. So you might get a run-time error (NullPointer Exception), but the question is about compilation. **F** is correct, for there is a method called `getExpressionEvaluator()` on the pageContext object (not that you are likely to need it very often).
   ☒ **B** is incorrect because there is a ServletRequest method called `getAttributeNames()`, but not one called `getAttributeName()`. **C** is incorrect; although ServletResponse has a getBufferSize method, to get the ServletResponse object from PageContext, you should use (just) `getResponse()` (there is no `getHttpResponse()` method). **D** is incorrect; although the page implicit variable is likely to be a servlet object (with a `getServletName()` method), the `getPage()` method returns java.lang.Object, so some casting is necessary before using servlet methods.

3. ☑ **B** and **F** are the correct answers. **B** is correct because only error pages (designated by `isErrorPage` set to true) have an exception implicit variable. This is then available to the tags used in the page as a non-null object available through the pageContext object. **F** is correct because all exception objects have a `getLocalizedMessage()` method, for they must implement java.lang.Throwable. This has little to do with web coding, but don't forget that the SCWCD exam assumes you can remember things from the SCJP exam!
   ☒ **A** is incorrect—the PageContext object doesn't have a `getError()` method. This also rules out answer **D**. **C** is incorrect because although there is a page directive errorPage, it's for pages to specify a *separate* page as their chosen error page to divert to when things go wrong. The actual page with the errorPage directive won't have an exception implicit object available.

E is incorrect: Although PageContext has a `getException()` method (the one you do use to get hold of the exception implicit object), it returns java.lang.Exception—not java.lang .Throwable.

4. ☑ **A**, **C**, and **D** are the correct answers. **A** is correct because—as this is a direct implementation of the Tag interface (not an extension of TagSupport)—you need to do the work to set up a pageContext variable. **C** is also correct because having set up the pageContext variable, `setPageContext()` is the appropriate method for supplying a value. **D** is correct because `pageContext.getRequest()` returns a ServletRequest, not an HttpServletRequest (but a cast to HttpServletRequest is likely to work in an HTTP environment).
   ☒ **B** is incorrect: The method name (`getRequest()`) is already correct, so should not be changed. **E** is incorrect—there's nothing wrong with setting pageContext to **null**, but it doesn't contribute to making the code compile and run correctly. **F** is incorrect: `request.setAttribute()` sets an attribute in request scope—you can't adjust the scope to something else.

5. ☑ **B**, **C**, and **D** are the correct answers. All these methods (`getServletConfig`, `include`, and `getErrorData`) are available on PageContext.
   ☒ **A** is incorrect: PageContext has a `getPage()` method and a static **int** value defined of PageContext.PAGE_SCOPE, but the method `getPageScope()` is made up and meaningless. **E** is incorrect: There is a `getException()` method that you can legitimately call when a tag is located within a JSP error page, but there is no `getError()`. **F** is incorrect: Although there is an implicit variable called *application* in JSPs, the correct way to access this through the PageContext object is through the getServletContext method.

The "Simple" Custom Tag Event Model

6. ☑ **C** and **F** are the correct answers. **C** is correct because `setJspContext()` is always the first method to be called for a SimpleTag. Next is `setParent()`, missing in this sequence, and it will be bypassed if this tag doesn't have a custom action for a parent. Next comes attribute setting—so `setAnAttribute()` is a plausible method call. Next is `setJspBody()`, again missing in this sequence, but bypassed by the JSP container if the SimpleTag doesn't have a body. Finally, the JSP container does call `doTag()`. **F** is correct because `setJspContext()`, `setParent()`, and `doTag()` is a plausible sequence for a tag with no attributes and no body.
   ☒ **A** is incorrect because SimpleTags do not have a `setPageContext` method, and even if they did, it wouldn't come after `setParent()` (setting of contexts is the first thing to happen). **B** is incorrect because `setJspContext()` should come before `setParent()`, and SimpleTags do not have a `doInitBody()` method. **D** is incorrect because—although the order

is plausible—SimpleTags have a `setJspContext()` method, not `setPageContext()` (as for classic tags). Finally, **F** is incorrect because SimpleTags do not have a `doAfterBody()` method.

7. ☑ **E** is the correct answer. To make the JSP container skip the rest of the JSP page, throw a SkipPageException (subclass of JspException) from the `doTag()` method of a SimpleTag. You can do this anyway and should rethrow the exception if it originates from any enclosed custom actions.
☒ **A** is incorrect for SimpleTags (this is the correct technique for classic tags, but of course, simple tags do not have a `doEndTag()` method). **B** and **F** are incorrect because there is no such method (in the simple or classic tag model) as `doPage()`. **C** and **D** are incorrect because the `doTag()` method returns nothing (**void**), so any attempt to return an integer literal or constant will result in a compilation error.

8. ☑ **A** is the correct answer. All the work that the code does using the java.io.StringWriter goes nowhere. When `JspFragment.invoke(null)` is executed at the end of the **for** loop, however, the contents of the body (the letter *a*) are output to the JspWriter associated with the page. This happens three times within the loop—hence, `aaa` is output to the page from the tag.
☒ **B**, **C**, **D**, and **E** are incorrect according to the reasoning in the correct answer.

9. ☑ **B**, **E**, and **F** are the correct answers. **B** is correct because simple tags are not allowed JSP content: `scriptless`, `tagdependent`, and `empty` are the only valid values for a simple tag's `<body-content>`. **E** is correct because the most common use of simple tag handler code is to manipulate attributes that are accessed by EL variables in the body of the action—and for the EL variables to be interpreted, the only valid setting is scriptless. **F** is correct: If `<body-content>` is declared as empty, the JSP container will not call the `setJspBody()` method on the simple tag handler class.
☒ **A** is incorrect as there is no such element as `<simpletag>`; the `<tag>` element is used to declare both classic and simple tags. **C** is also incorrect, for simple and classic tags can be mixed freely in the same tag library descriptor file—as long, of course, as their names are unique. **D** is incorrect, though almost right—there is no default for simple tags (though as discussed in the correct answer **E**, `scriptless` is a common choice).

10. ☑ **E** is the correct answer. First a page attribute is set up in the JSP called `counter`, with a value of 1. This is retrieved in the tag handler code into the **int** value *i*. On entry to the **for** loop, the page attribute *counter* is set to the value of *i*, so it remains at 1. Then the body of the action is invoked. This executes a `<c:forEach>` loop beginning at the current value of *counter*, and ending at 3. So the `<c:forEach>` loop executes three times, printing *counter* (with a value of 1) three times, through the EL syntax `${counter}`. Back now to the **for** loop in the tag handler code: second iteration. *i* is incremented to 2, so the attribute *counter* is incremented to

2. The body is invoked again, and the `<c:forEach>` loop outputs "2" twice. Repeat the process, and "3" is output once. So the entire output is: 111 22 3.
☒ A, B, C, D, and F are incorrect following the reasoning in the correct answer.

The Tag File Model

11. ☑ D and E are the correct answers. D looks strange but is the namespace convention for declaring a tag file directory in a JSP document (the namespace doesn't have to be declared in an `<html>` opening tag but is usually declared in the root element for the document). E is the right way to reference a tag file directory in a conventional `taglib` directive.
☒ A is incorrect—it depicts the correct way to declare a tag library descriptor, not a directory for tag files. B is incorrect because `taglocation` is a made-up attribute for the `taglib` directive. C is incorrect because the value for the namespace is not a URN for a tag directory. Finally, F is incorrect because the *tagdir* attribute must reference a directory, not a TLD file.

12. ☑ B is the correct answer. A translation error occurs as soon as the JSP scriptlet begins at line 4. You are not allowed to embed scriptlets or scriptlet expressions (or any other sort of direct Java language syntax) in a tag file.
☒ A and C are incorrect because all remaining syntax in the tag file is correct apart from the presence of the scriptlet. D is incorrect because the tag file will never be run. E is incorrect because you will never get output—although if you transfer this code to a normal JSP file, it will produce the output shown.

13. ☑ B, C, and E are the correct answers: tag, attribute, and variable are the three possible directives present in a tag file.
☒ A is incorrect: The `page` directive is valid in JSPs, not tag files—where the tag file replaces it (and shares many of the same attributes). D is incorrect: `import` is not a directive, but an attribute of the tag directive. F is incorrect—although a tag file has an associated JspContext, jspcontext is not a directive. Finally, G is incorrect—*scope* is an attribute of the variable directive.

14. ☑ A maps to 8 (`c:set`), B maps to 15 (`${counter}`), C to 6 (`attribute`), D to 1 (the figure 1), E to 3 (the figure 3), F to 13 (`<jsp:doBody>`), and G to 11 (`loopCounter.index`). The key things to note about the code: `${counter}` in the JSP file is independent of `${counter}` in the tag file. However, as the body is re-executed three times (through placing `<jsp:doBody>` in the `<c:forEach>` loop in the tag file), the original value of `${counter}` (a value of 1) is passed through as the initial value for the attribute named *counter* on each occasion.
☒ All other combinations are incorrect.

15. ☑ G is the correct answer. Tag files can live directly in the /WEB-INF/tags directory (or any subdirectory of it) or can be packaged with a JAR file. The directory in the JAR file must be /META-INF/tags (or a subdirectory of this), and the JAR file must be located in /WEB-INF/lib.
☒ A is incorrect: Tag files in the context directory will just be treated as web content. **B** and **C** are incorrect: /WEB-INF and any arbitrary subdirectory of /WEB-INF won't do according to the specification. **F** is wrong, for it includes one incorrect location. **D** and **E** are correct locations—but because both are correct, one choice on its own is not a correct answer to the question.

Tag Hierarchies

16. ☑ **D** is the correct answer. All the techniques listed in answers **A**, **B**, and **C** are viable. `TagSupport.findAncestorWithClass()` is a natural approach: You would pass as parameter the class for `<a:tagA>`. `getParent().getParent()` is viable in this circumstance—this technique will return the grandparent tag `<a:tagA>`. However, unless you can be very sure of the tag hierarchy, it's not a great approach. What may come as a surprise is that `SimpleTagSupport.findAncestorWithClass()` works in the context of classic tags. In fact, it's more flexible than `TagSupport.findAncestorWithClass()`—it returns a JspTag rather than a Tag. This means that the method can be used to find both simple and classic tags in the hierarchy (whereas `TagSupport.findAncestorWithClass()` is restricted to classic tags only).
☒ **A**, **B**, **C**, **E**, and **F** are incorrect according to the reasoning in the correct answer. (**A**, **B**, and **C** are correct approaches, but because all three are correct, you have to select answer **D**.)

17. ☑ **C** and **D** are the correct answers. Tags that qualify as template text—whether XML or HTML—are not part of the JSP custom tag hierarchy accessible through methods such as `getParent()`.
☒ **A**, **B**, **E**, and **F** are incorrect answers. All are instances of objects that implement JspTag and mostly Tag as well—so all are possible to recover with one of the two `getParent()` methods (provided in the Tag and SimpleTag interfaces).

18. ☑ **A** and **G** are the correct answers. Because the JspTag interface has no methods of its own (it is only a marker interface), then the only methods available in a JspTag reference are those on java.lang.Object. Hence, `notifyAll()` and `hashCode()` would be valid method calls.
☒ **B**, **C**, and **D** are incorrect, for all are methods in the Tag interface, which is a subinterface of JspTag. **E** is incorrect because `doAfterBody()` is a method in the IterationTag interface, yet farther down the hierarchy. **F** is incorrect, for although `clone()` is a method on Object, it is protected— only **public** methods are available to call on a local reference.

19. ☑ **A** maps to **1** (Tag); **B**, **C**, and **D** map to **5** (TagAdapter); **E** maps to **8** (`getAdaptee()`); **F** maps to **9** (the variable *enclosing*); and **G** maps to **14** (the return value EVAL_BODY _INCLUDE—beware of fake constants in the answers!).
☒ All other combinations are incorrect.

20. ☑ **A** and **C** are the correct answers. **A** is correct, for `doAfterBody()` will be executed after the evaluation of the body that contains the child tag. **C** is correct because by calling the `invoke()` method, the parent tag forces execution of the body containing the child tag, which sets the reference to the child tag that it needs.
☒ **B** is incorrect because the body (containing the child tag) hasn't yet been evaluated, so the child tag cannot have set a reference for the parent tag to use. **D** is incorrect because there is no life cycle method invoked on a simple tag after the `doTag()` method completes. **E** and **F** are incorrect because the methods are made up: There are no parent-to-child methods. This is a pity, but obvious when you consider that a JSP is processed in strict sequence, so parent tags always come before child tags.

LAB ANSWER

Deploy the WAR file from the CD called lab09.war, in the /sourcecode/chapter09 directory. This contains a sample solution. You can call the initial document with a URL such as:

```
http://localhost:8080/lab09/cardGame.jspx
```

The output should be no different from before—see Exercise 9-4 for an illustration.

10

J2EE Patterns

CERTIFICATION OBJECTIVES

- Intercepting Filter Pattern
- Front Controller Pattern
- Model View Controller Pattern
- Business Delegate Pattern
- Service Locator Pattern
- Transfer Object Pattern
- ✓ Two-Minute Drill
- Q&A Self Test

In this final chapter of the book, we move from the "micro" level of individual servlet and tag APIs to the "macro" level of designing entire systems. You leave the low-level world of servlet containers and the tag life cycle API, and embrace some altogether bigger notions on how a J2EE system should be constructed.

This comes about because the SCWCD exam includes questions on six design patterns. A design pattern is like an architectural blueprint for solving some common problem, and J2EE applications exhibit a whole range of common problems that have been solved hundreds of times before. So when you encounter your own J2EE design issues, you may not have to think for yourself, but instead adopt an off-the-shelf design pattern.

The questions in this area are much more like those you find in the first stage of the Sun Certified Enterprise Architect (SCEA) examination. At first sight, this may seem like a soft topic. How difficult can big design ideas be compared to knowing low-level APIs? But proceed with caution: This is an area that often lets SCWCD exam candidates down, and it accounts for nearly 10 percent of the questions. Design patterns are not fluffy, easy things—you can't afford to be woolly in your grasp on them. So with that stern warning in mind, read on.

Core J2EE Patterns

You have probably encountered design patterns before in your work as a Java developer. Even if you haven't read the legendary design patterns book, you will have used at least one pattern.[1] You don't believe me? You can't have got this far in your Java career without using the java.util.Iterator interface. This is a living embodiment of the iterator design pattern documented in the Design Patterns book. As you'll recall, java.util.Iterator keeps the specifics of what kind of collection you are dealing with at arm's length, while allowing you to traverse the contents of the collection. If you compare this with the pattern in the GoF book, you'll find that this description of java.util.Iterator matches the goals for the iterator pattern.

Patterns are not confined to the lowest levels of a computing language. Good design ideas can be found at any level—indeed, some of them work at several levels (from fiddly components to enormous building blocks). J2EE boasts its own set of design patterns, targeted at solving problems working with J2EE-size components,

[1]See *Design Patterns—Elements of Reusable Object-Oriented Software*, by Gamma, Helm, Johnson, and Vlissides [Addison Wesley]. The authors are often referred to as the Gang of Four—abbreviated GoF—and their magnum opus referred to as the GoF book.

so the building blocks involved might be servlets, JavaServer Pages, and Enterprise JavaBeans as well as other support classes. The motivation for discovering and documenting J2EE patterns is the same as for patterns elsewhere. Your problem needs a solution. Chances are that somebody else has hit your problem (or one very like it) before. If they've taken the trouble to document that solution, you can adopt it: either as a ready-made solution or as one that requires a little adaptation.

Elements of a Pattern

In this chapter I've tried to cover everything you need to know to do well with the SCWCD design patterns questions, but I do have only 60 or so pages at my disposal. If you want to broaden and deepen your design exploration, you should know that the "bible" for J2EE design patterns is a book called *Core J2EE Patterns: Best Practices and Design Strategies* (by Alur et al., published by Sun Microsystems). Five out of the six design patterns required for the SCWCD exam were first defined in this book. You'll find the content of the core patterns book on the Sun web site:

```
http://java.sun.com/blueprints/corej2eepatterns/Patterns/
```

Just one unfortunate thing: At least at the time of writing, the free resources on the web site are aimed at J2EE 1.3, whereas the SCWCD is pitched at J2EE 1.4. Fortunately, the patterns world moves a little more slowly than the rate of API evolution, so most of what the web site covers is absolutely germane to your SCWCD studies. However, if you want the absolute latest information, you'll need to purchase the second edition of the book (revised for J2EE 1.4).

The features of design patterns are described according to a set of headings that act as a template for each pattern. This set of headings is not standard between champions of design patterns. So what the GoF book calls "implementation," the Core J2EE Patterns book calls "strategies," and so forth. The Core J2EE Patterns book talks in terms of

- **Context**—where in the J2EE environment you are likely to encounter a need for the pattern
- **Problem**—an account of the design problem that a developer needs to solve
- **Forces**—motivations and justifications for adopting the pattern
- **Solution**—how the design works, both in structural terms (depicted with UML diagrams) and implementation terms (often backed up with example code)
- **Consequences**—what are the pros and cons when the pattern is applied

My "template" for describing the patterns will be simpler than this. Here is what I will describe:

- How each pattern works, with reference to a concrete example
- The benefits (and, sometimes, drawbacks) of using the pattern
- Particular scenarios when it might be appropriate to adopt the pattern

I've found this approach gets you to the heart of the exam objectives quicker than any other. Your task in the exam is not to be able to implement a design pattern (even though understanding the implementation clearly helps). You'll see from the wording of the exam objectives that you have to match benefits and scenarios to specific patterns.

A Road Map for J2EE Patterns

First of all, Sun's J2EE patterns are based on a tiered approach to application development. Of course, Sun wouldn't claim to have invented this idea, but has sensibly adopted it as the best approach to separating out concerns and responsibilities: an aspect of object orientation in the large. The five tiers are depicted in Figure 10-1, together with the J2EE (and other) components you are likely to find in each.

FIGURE 10-1 Tiers for Application Development

Client Tier	Presentation Tier	Business Tier	Integration Tier	Resource Tier
Swing	JSPs	EJBs	JDBC	Databases
Other apps	Servlets	Other business objects	JMS	Topics, queues
Applets	HTML		Enterprise information system connectors	Enterprise information systems
"Thick clients"	GIFs			

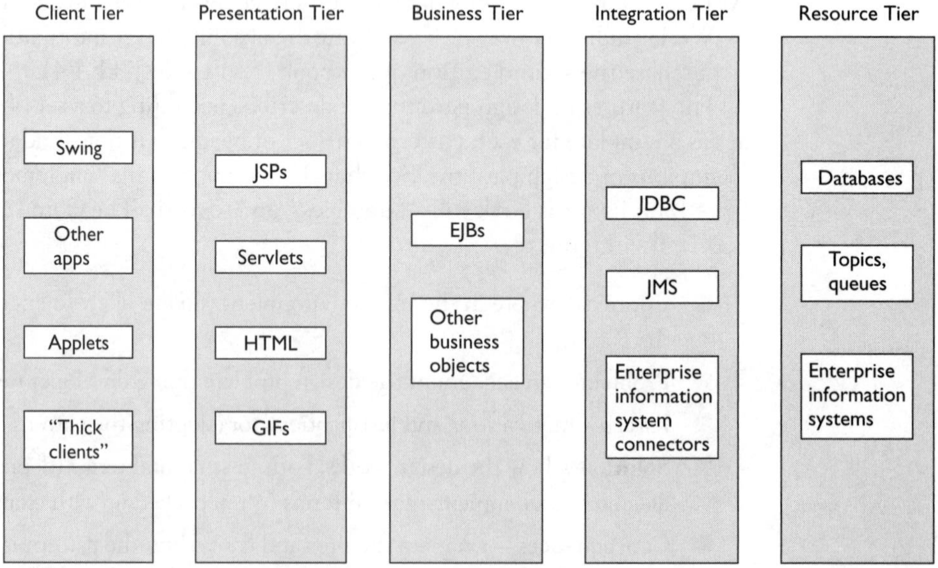

You'll be familiar with many of the components depicted in the presentation tier. However, we haven't touched on components in the business tier: They haven't impinged at all on what you have needed to learn for the SCWCD—until now. The principal J2EE business component is the Enterprise JavaBean, or EJB. Fortunately, you don't need any great expertise in its use; that's the subject of a whole separate certification exam (the Sun Certified Business Component Developer Exam, or SCBCD). You do need a token idea, though, of what Enterprise JavaBeans are, and the issues they present.

To start off with, Enterprise JavaBeans are designed to be self-contained business components. That doesn't mean they constitute a single Java class: An Enterprise JavaBean is composed of a number of classes, some written by developers, some generated. However, a particular Enterprise JavaBean—maybe representing some business entity such as "Customer"—can be considered as a unit in its own right.

Just as servlets run in a servlet container, so EJBs run in an Enterprise JavaBean container. You can't make an EJB with the *new* keyword, any more than you'd consider doing the same for a servlet: The container supplies the life cycle. Whereas you fire an HTTP request to make use of a servlet in a servlet container, you execute JNDI (Java Naming and Directory Interface) code to get hold of the services an EJB can offer within its EJB container.

Originally, EJBs were designed to be independent, so independent that they did not even have to run in the same JVM as the client code using them. In the past, this meant that every use of an EJB involved a remote method call using Java's Remote Method Invocation (RMI) protocol. This doesn't have to be the case anymore when EJBs are co-located in the same JVM as the client using them. However, EJBs are to be treated with respect because they do a lot for you (not least of which is masking network concerns); they are heavyweight components. You might pay a price in performance for naïve use of EJBs.

The preceding paragraphs made a very minimalist introduction to a very big topic, but it is important to understand that EJBs are a primary force in driving some of the patterns you encounter for the SCWCD (Business Delegate, Service Locator, and Transfer Object).

Having understood tiers and components, the next thing to consider is where the design patterns fit. Figure 10-2 shows the tiers again, but this time with the six design patterns superimposed. (You may also want to reference the diagram on the Sun web site that shows how all the J2EE core patterns fit together: That's at the Sun URL referenced a little earlier in the chapter.)

You can see from Figure 10-2 that the patterns you are concerned with live within or straddle different tiers, and often work in combination with one another. Here's a

FIGURE 10-2

How the J2EE Patterns Fit Together

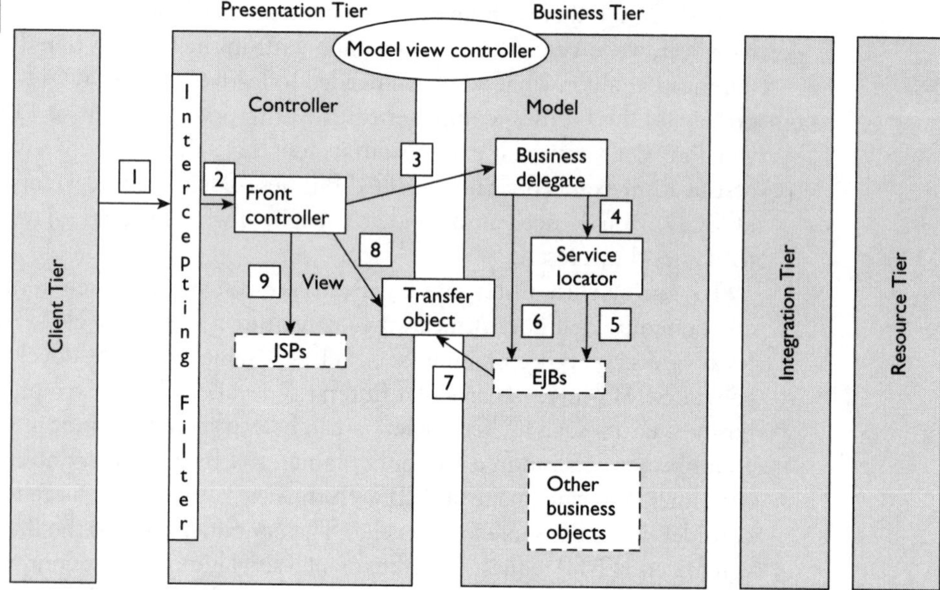

brief explanation of each of the six patterns so that you have a road map for the rest of the chapter.

- Intercepting Filter: used to check or transform a request or a response.
- Front Controller: a "gateway" for all requests—can be used to check requests and control navigation centrally.
- Model View Controller: used to keep presentation and business concerns independent. The model holds the business data, the view presents the data, and the controller mediates between the two.
- Business Delegate: used to provide a friendly front end to business-level APIs (especially when those APIs involve Enterprise JavaBeans).
- Service Locator: used to locate services (!), which usually means executing highly technical code to get back references to resources such as Enterprise JavaBeans and JMS queues.
- Transfer Object: encapsulates the data returned from complex business objects (usually EJBs again).

There is a whole flow of control among these different patterns. Figure 10-2 shows how they might typically collaborate, tracing the flow of a request through the application. A request is trapped by an Intercepting Filter (1 in Figure 10-2)—if the filter allows it, the request passes on to a Front Controller (2). The Front Controller makes use of a Business Delegate to obtain business data (3). The Business Delegate uses a Service Locator (4) to find the business component it needs (5)— often an EJB. The Business Delegate requests data (6), which it gets back in the form of a Transfer Object (7), and returns this to the Front Controller. The Front Controller takes what it needs from the Transfer Object (8), then forwards to an appropriate JSP (9) (which—in all likelihood—uses data originating from the Transfer Object). Where does Model View Controller fit in? That's the collection of components represented by the JSP (for the view), the Front Controller (evidently the controller!), and the Business Delegate (fronting the business model).

A Working Example

This chapter is underpinned by a working example that uses all six patterns in its construction. There are no Enterprise JavaBeans within the example, for they require an Enterprise JavaBean container to support them (like the open source JBoss: See http://www.jboss.org). At this stage of your SCWCD exam preparation, coming to terms with an EJB container is a bridge too far. So instead, I have implemented the integration tier of the example using Java Remote Method Invocation (RMI). This introduces quite a few of the issues associated with EJBs but doesn't require additional software (beyond the J2SDK) to make it run.

Figure 10-3 shows how the application fits together and indicates which classes embody J2EE patterns. Some of the classes actually reflect the name of the pattern. There's a danger in this: You might think that one pattern = one class. Whereas that can be the case, it doesn't do justice to the full story. Even if only one class is involved, that class must cooperate in the right way with other classes and do a particular job to count as an implementation of a pattern.

The idea of the example application is to display information about the six patterns for SCWCD. The application has only two working screens: home.jspx and pattern.jspx. home.jspx displays a menu, from which you can select the pattern you want information about (Figure 10-4). On selecting a pattern, you see a detail screen with information about the pattern (Figure 10-5).

For such a simple application, the supporting architecture is very ornate, but the complexity is there to illustrate how to apply the six patterns. Let's consider how the application works, with reference to Figure 10-3. We'll start with the back end: the resource tier. The "database" of pattern information is represented by a simple properties file, called patternsDB.props. The PatternLoader class is arguably part of both the integration and business tiers. It contains a method to load the contents

FIGURE 10-3 How the Working Example Implements J2EE Patterns

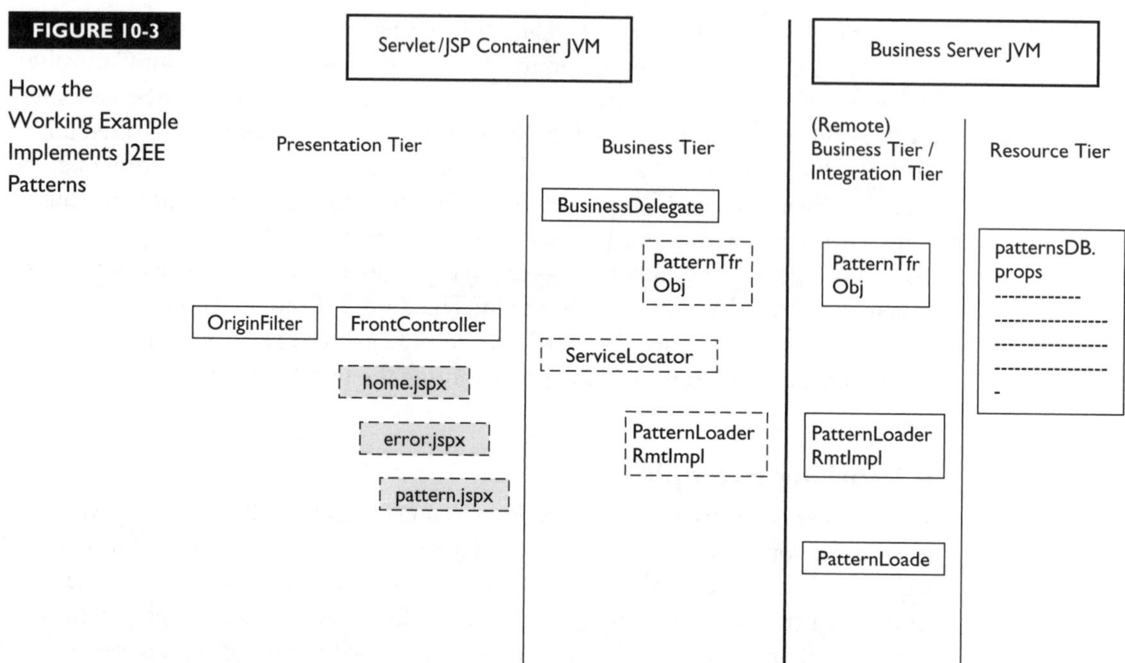

FIGURE 10-4 The Working Example Home Page

J2EE Patterns Examples: Home Page

○	Intercepting Filter
○	Front Controller
○	Model View Controller
○	Business Delegate
○	Service Locator
○	Transfer Object
Show Pattern Details	Show Exercise Solution

of the "database" into an internally held java.util.Properties object, using simple file input/output for connectivity to the data (in a real production system, you might expect to see JDBC code connecting to a relational database). PatternLoader also contains the first of our patterns: Transfer Object. It provides a "getData" method that returns a PatternTfrObj, which encapsulates all the data about one pattern. We'll see later why this is an advantage.

FIGURE 10-5 The Working Example Detail Page

J2EE Pattern: Intercepting Filter

Home Page

Name:	Intercepting Filter
Description:	Intercepting Filter pre-processes requests and post-processes responses, applying loosely coupled filters.
Benefits:	1. Centralizes control 2. Filters should be swappable (they are loosely coupled) 3. Filter chains are declared, not compiled 4. Reuse of code for common actions
Drawbacks:	1. Inefficient sharing of information between filters (potentially)

To make PatternLoader more EJB-like, it's wrapped up in a remote implementation class called PatternLoaderRmtImpl. The idea is that the web application will run within Tomcat and be forced to access this part of the business tier through remote calls. PatternLoader and its remote implementation run in an entirely separate JVM, launched with Java's `rmiregistry` command—we'll see more of that in the deployment instructions later.

Let's now come at the application from the other direction. First I make a request for the main screen of the application from my browser. The request is intercepted by the OriginFilter class. This is the key player in the Intercepting Filter J2EE pattern, and is a bona fide class implementing the Filter interface and declared as a filter in the deployment descriptor. Its purpose is to guard the borders of the application, turning away requests from any host of origin it doesn't like (in this case, it's set up to allow only requests from the localhost with IP address 127.0.0.1, but you can adjust this by changing the relevant initialization parameter within the web.xml filter declaration).

If the request gets past the border guard, it goes to a servlet called FrontController (named after the J2EE pattern it supports). Front Controller determines from parameters passed whether this is a request for a specific pattern or not. If not, it forwards to the home menu page, home.jspx. A selection from this page goes back to Front Controller—this time with a named pattern as parameter. This prompts FrontController to do a deal more work. It passed the pattern name requested to the BusinessDelegate class (our next J2EE pattern). BusinessDelegate checks to see if it has information about the pattern in its own data cache. If not, it sees if it has a reference to a remote PatternLoader object. If not, it calls on the ServiceLocator (next pattern) class to find the remote PatternLoader object. Once armed with a remote PatternLoader object, BusinessDelegate uses it to return a PatternTfrObj (the Transfer Object). Now the explanations have met in the middle. This is the point where our survey of the presentation and business tiers meets the earlier exploration of the resource, integration, and (remote) business tiers.

We'll revisit the application in detail when explaining the purpose of the different J2EE design patterns. It would be a good idea to deploy the application at this point. The WAR file is in the CD in /sourcode/ch10/lab10.war. Deploy this WAR file in the normal way; then access the home page with a URL such as the following:

```
http://localhost:8080/lab10/controller
```

You should see the screen we saw earlier in Figure 10-4—the application home page. However, when you select one of the patterns and click the "Show Pattern Details" button, you'll see an application error screen (Figure 10-6). This is because the remote layers of the application haven't yet been started up. To bring these to life, take the following steps:

1. Start *two* command windows. In both command windows, change the current directory to /WEB-INF/classes within the deployed application directory (e.g., <Tomcat Installation Directory>/webapps/lab10/WEB-INF/classes).
2. In the first command window, execute the command `rmiregistry`. No parameters—just as printed. If the command is not recognized, make sure that you have the /bin directory of your J2SDK installation in your path (so if we're talking MS-DOS, adjust the PATH environment variable). This is the Java command that starts off your Remote Method Invocation Registry, which listens (by default) on port 1099. If successful, the command just hangs there, not giving much appearance of doing anything—don't worry about it!
3. In the second command window, execute the command `java webcert.ch10.lab10.RemoteBusinessServer`. The result should be a message saying "Pattern Loader bound in RMI Registry." Again, the command appears to hang in midair—leave it to do its stuff.
4. Now return to your browser, and try again to access a pattern through the main menu. This time, you should see a detail screen as in Figure 10-5.
5. When you have finished with the application, just abort the two command windows (CTRL-C and EXIT in MS-DOS terms).

FIGURE 10-6 The Working Example Error Page

With luck, RMI will be familiar to you from your previous programming experience (though it's not a mandatory part of the SCJP exam). Don't worry if not: It's certainly not central to the explanation of patterns—I've included it to give more of a sense of a "real" full-blown J2EE application. We'll revisit some of the technicalities when explaining the Transfer Object pattern at the end of the chapter.

CERTIFICATION OBJECTIVE

Intercepting Filter Pattern (Exam Objectives 11.1 and 11.2)

Given a scenario description with a list of issues, select a pattern that would solve the issues. The list of patterns you must know are: ***Intercepting Filter****, Model-View -Controller, Front Controller, Service Locator, Business Delegate, and Transfer Object.*

Match design patterns with statements describing potential benefits that accrue from the use of the pattern, for any of the following patterns: ***Intercepting Filter****, Model -View-Controller, Front Controller, Service Locator, Business Delegate, and Transfer Object.*

Let's start with some good news—you have learned all about the Intercepting Filter design pattern already. The kindly designers of J2EE have built the Intercepting Filter pattern directly into J2EE architecture. You learned all about Filters and FilterChains in Chapter 3, and how these could be used to "pre-process" a request for a web resource, or "post-process" the response. These interfaces and classes (together with the life cycle support for them in a servlet container) are the concrete embodiment of the Intercepting Filter pattern.

Intercepting Filter Pattern

The Intercepting Filter pattern works in the following way. A filter manager intercepts a request on its way to a target resource. From the content of the request (usually from its URL pattern), the filter manager calls on the help of a filter chain object, which creates the filter objects needful to the request (if they haven't been created already). The filter chain also dictates the correct sequence of filters to apply (hence the name: filter chain). The filter chain object infers the appropriate sequence from some information in the request: As we've seen with the "official" filter mechanism, the basis for this is the request's URL pattern.

So in Figure 10-7, we see that a request is made for the file /resources/resource1 .html. This request is grabbed by a FilterManager object, which builds a FilterChain object. The FilterChain object holds references to the matching filters, which the FilterManager determines by matching up the request URL to the URL mappings for each of the five available filters. From these, it selects one of the following choices:

FIGURE 10-7

A Request's Route Through Filters

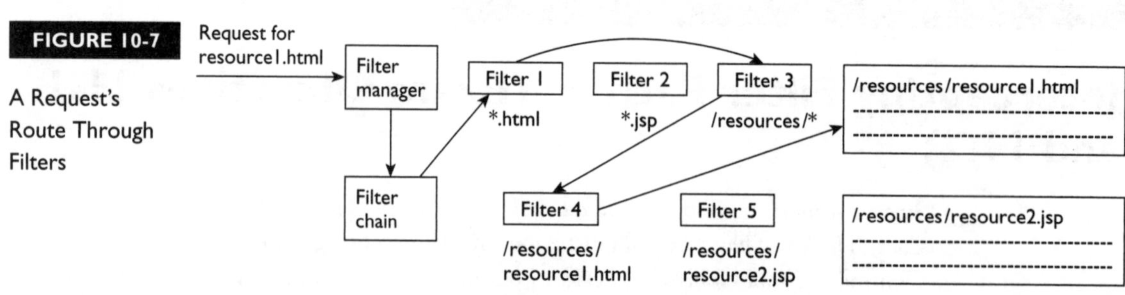

FIGURE 10-8 Another Request Routing Through Filters

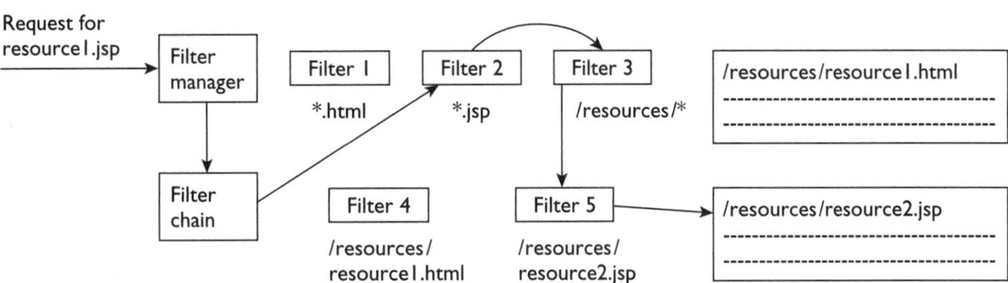

- Filter 1: because of the extension match (*.html)
- Filter 3: because of the path match (/resources/*—anything whose path begins with /resources)
- Filter 4: because of the exact match (/resources/resource1.html)

See if you can work out the logic for the filter selection in Figure 10-8, when /resources/resource2.jsp is requested.

I am being very prescriptive here in saying that this J2EE pattern works by URL matching. If you write code for a customized Intercepting Filter, you might use some other criteria altogether for the selection of filters in the chain. It is just that in this case, the J2EE pattern has to be implemented in your application server because it's a mandatory part of the servlet specification—and the servlet specification goes with URL matching (and servlet naming) as the basis for filter selection.

How Is Intercepting Filter Used in the Example Application?

The example application uses a filter called OriginFilter. This is specified in the deployment descriptor as follows:

```
<filter>
  <filter-name>OriginFilter</filter-name>
  <filter-class>webcert.ch10.lab10.OriginFilter</filter-class>
  <init-param>
    <param-name>origin</param-name>
    <param-value>127.0.0.1</param-value>
  </init-param>
</filter>
<filter-mapping>
  <filter-name>OriginFilter</filter-name>
  <servlet-name>FrontController</servlet-name>
</filter-mapping>
```

You can see that the filter has an initialization parameter called "origin" that holds an Internet address as a value—the one for the local host, 127.0.0.1. The implementing class has the following filter logic:

```
public void doFilter(ServletRequest request, ServletResponse
response,
            FilterChain chain) throws IOException,
ServletException {
  String origin = request.getRemoteHost();
  String mustMatch = config.getInitParameter("origin");
  if (origin.equals(mustMatch)) {
    chain.doFilter(request, response);
  } else {
    sendErrorPage(response, origin);
  }
}
```

The code performs a simple check, getting hold of the Internet address associated with the incoming request and comparing this with the initialization parameter setup on the filter in the deployment descriptor. If the two match, the filter chain is used to invoke the next item in the chain (`chain.doFilter()`), which is the FrontController servlet (there are only two things in the chain: the filter and the servlet).

Why Use Intercepting Filter?

What you see in the example code is a typical use of a filter: to perform an authentication check. In this case, the code is only allowing approaches from one particular server. When we first discussed filters in Chapter 3, you saw that you could harness them for a range of purposes—including but not limited to auditing, security, compressing, decompressing, and transforming request and response messages. I apply two tests when deciding whether some or other functional requirement should be placed in a filter:

1. Is the requirement discrete?
2. Is it common to more than one type of request (and/or response) from my web application?

For test 1, I define "discrete" as whether or not the filter can perform its work independently of other considerations. If other filters are placed before or after, will the current filter remain unaffected? For test 2, I may not want to apply my filter globally, but if it's executing logic that is specific to one particular resource, then perhaps the code belongs with that particular resource, not in a filter. Filters are meant to be more general purpose.

Possible reasons for using a filter are limited only by your imagination. Here are some scenarios where you might want to do some processing on the request before letting it loose on the targeted resource:

- You want to check something about the origin of the request. This might be the type of device making the request (laptop or iPod?).
- You might want to detect how the request is encoded, and maybe re-encode it before it reaches the core of your application.

These are "inbound" reasons for using a filter. What about "outbound" possibilities—things you might want to do to the completed response before returning it to the requester? You might

- Translate the response in some way—to make it more intelligible to another computer system or to a human.
- Tag your response in some general way—perhaps adding a copyright notice.

There's nothing stopping you from using a servlet to carry out any of the above tasks. The very worst case would have every servlet in your application embedding copied and pasted logic to perform common filtration actions (count yourself lucky if you have never witnessed this kind of bad practice!). A much better approach is to dedicate a servlet as a "gateway" to your application—this is like the Front Controller pattern we'll be considering next. This gateway (or controller) servlet could examine the request, perform whatever actions are required (using helper classes or other included servlets as necessary), then permit access to the actual requested resource. There are some drawbacks to this approach, however:

- You have to design the approach yourself. You might end up by reinventing the elegant wheels of the existing filter mechanism.
- It's easy to overburden your "gateway" servlet with too many responsibilities. At worst, your servlet will contain a burgeoning series of nested checks.
- Depending on your design, you'll need to change servlet code to add new filter logic or alter the sequence of the filter chain.

The official list of benefits (or at least, consequences) of using the Intercepting Filter pattern are as follows:

- Control is centralized for chosen activities (like encryption) but in a loosely coupled way (the encryption happens independently of anything else going on around it).
- Filters promote the reuse of code. It's easy to plug a filter in where you want it (as it presents a standard interface) so that there's no barrier to including it in your web application.
- Including a filter doesn't involve recompilation: Everything is controlled from the deployment descriptor, declaratively. You can juggle your filter order without recourse to javac (though dependent on your application server, you might have to remake and redeploy your WAR file).

The only real identified drawback for filters is this: Information sharing between filters is likely to be inefficient. You may well need to reprocess an entire request or entire response all over again in each filter in the chain. Imagine a multipart request—that's a POST with a load of file attachments. Suppose that these are composed of a random mixture of documents and spreadsheets and that you have one filter dedicated to automatic translation of the documents and another filter to verify the technical integrity of the formulae in the spreadsheets. Each filter would have to read through the entire request, with the document filter ignoring spreadsheet attachments and the spreadsheet filter needlessly churning through documents. However, to flip-flop between the two filters as each attachment type was recognized would constitute a violation of each filter's independence from the other.

EXERCISE 10-1

Intercepting Filter Pattern

Consider how you would use the Intercepting Filter pattern to fulfill the following requirement: A company keeps information on the sales of goods from certain of its suppliers. These are accessible through the company's extranet and are currently produced through servlets whose response is delivered in plain-text, comma-delimited format. Some of their suppliers (readily identifiable through the host component of their requesting machines) are more sophisticated and would like the files delivering for a trial period ready-translated into an agreed XML format.

What are the benefits of the approach you use versus placing the same logic in a combination of servlets and JSPs?

If you run the working example that accompanies this chapter, select the Intercepting Filter pattern radio button option, and click the "Solution to Exercise" button, you'll find a discussion of the above scenario. The URL to launch the working example is likely to be

```
http://localhost:8080/lab10/controller
```

CERTIFICATION OBJECTIVE

Front Controller Pattern (Exam Objectives 11.1 and 11.2)

Given a scenario description with a list of issues, select a pattern that would solve the issues. The list of patterns you must know are: Intercepting Filter, Model-View-Controller, ***Front Controller****, Service Locator, Business Delegate, and Transfer Object.*

Match design patterns with statements describing potential benefits that accrue from the use of the pattern, for any of the following patterns: Intercepting Filter, Model-View -Controller, ***Front Controller****, Service Locator, Business Delegate, and Transfer Object.*

The essence of Front Controller is that it acts as a centralized point of access for requests. There are many responsibilities Front Controller may take on. As a gateway, it might control access through authentication and authorization rules. It may delegate to business processes. Almost invariably, it plays a crucial role in controlling (screen) flow through an application. In this next section, we'll consider how Front Controller works, the benefits it provides, and some scenarios for which it is well suited.

The Front Controller Pattern

Like Intercepting Filter, Front Controller is another presentation tier pattern. The main difficulty in answering questions about Front Controller is, in fact, distinguishing it from the Intercepting Filter pattern, for both have a lot in common. If you look back at Figure 10-1, though, you can see that Front Controller is embedded deeper within the presentation layer; Intercepting Filter is more at the fringes (as its name implies).

The pattern works by having an object (the Controller object) as the initial point of contact for requests to a web application (after those requests have made it past any en route filters!). The controller may validate the request according to any criteria it chooses. It may also extract information from the request that determines which page to navigate to next.

on the job

The prime example of a Front Controller that you are likely to encounter in your working life is the framework Struts. This uses what the Core J2EE Patterns book terms the "multiplexed resource mapping strategy." What this boils down to is this: The URL mapping *.do maps to a master servlet (acting as a Front Controller). Dependent on what is before the .do, the master servlet delegates to a class of type Action. So thisaction.do might map onto a class called ThisAction, and thataction.do to ThatAction.

How Is Front Controller Used in the Example Application?

Front Controller is best understood by example. In our application, the Front Controller pattern manifests itself in a single servlet called FrontController. This FrontController confines itself strictly to navigational issues. Here is the complete code for the servlet class (excluding package and import statements):

```
public class FrontController extends HttpServlet {
  public static final String[] patternNames = { "interceptingFilter",
    "frontController", "modelViewController", "businessDelegate",
    "serviceLocator", "transferObject" };
  private BusinessDelegate businessDelegate = new BusinessDelegate();
  protected void doGet(HttpServletRequest request,
    HttpServletResponse response) throws ServletException, IOException {
    // Sort out link back to controller servlet
    String actionLink = request.getContextPath() + request.getServletPath();
    request.setAttribute("actionLink", actionLink);
    // Sort out the action required
    String patternName = request.getParameter("patternChoice");
    String page;
    if (isPatternNameRecognized(patternName)) {
      try {
        setPatternAttributes(patternName, request);
        page = "/pattern.jspx";
      } catch (PatternNotFoundException pnfe) {
        // Application error handling: masks remote error
        request.setAttribute("patternName", pnfe.getPatternName());
        page = "/error.jspx";
      }
    } else {
      page = "/home.jspx";
    }
    // Forward to required page
```

```
27      RequestDispatcher rd = getServletContext().getRequestDispatcher(page);
28      rd.forward(request, response);
29    }
30    protected boolean isPatternNameRecognized(String patternName) {
31      for (int i = 0; i < patternNames.length; i++) {
32        if (patternNames[i].equals(patternName)) {
33          return true;
34        }
35      }
36      return false;
37    }
38    protected void setPatternAttributes(String patternName,
39      ServletRequest request) throws PatternNotFoundException {
40      PatternTfrObj pto = businessDelegate.findPattern(patternName);
41      // translate value object properties to request attributes
42      request.setAttribute("patternName", pto.getName());
43      request.setAttribute("patternDescription", pto.getDescription());
44      request.setAttribute("patternBenefits", pto.getBenefits());
45      request.setAttribute("patternDrawbacks", pto.getDrawbacks());
46    }
47  }
```

The purpose of the code is to navigate to a page displaying the correct pattern information or, if no specific pattern is requested, to display the menu (home) page. Here's a breakdown of what the code does:

- In lines 02 to 04, a String array is declared as a constant. Called patternNames, it holds the names by which the six J2EE patterns in this chapter are known internally to the application.
- In line 05, FrontController declares an instance of a class called BusinessDelegate. We'll explore this class fully later in the chapter. It serves to front the business logic that FrontController needs—namely, getting hold of business objects that contain J2EE pattern information.
- The `doGet()` method begins at line 06. In lines 09 and 10, the FrontController servlet sorts out a URL to point back to itself. This is built dynamically from the context path and the servlet path, avoiding any literal hardcoding. Then the URL is made available as a request attribute (called `actionLink`) that can be accessed in the JSP "views"—avoiding JSPs having to hard-code any URL that may later change.
- In line 12, FrontController determines if there is a request parameter available called `patternChoice`, and stores the value as the local variable `patternName`.

- The remaining logic in the **doGet()** method is concerned with navigating to the right page. The major determining factor is whether of not the **patternName** passed is recognized or not. At line 14, the **doGet()** method calls **isPatternRecognized()** (lines 30 to 37), which takes the value of the **patternName** local variable, and compares this with the valid values for pattern names in the String array **patternNames**. Even if **patternName** is **null** (intentionally not passed), **isPatternRecognized()** won't fail, but will simply return **false**.
- If **patternName** is not recognized (or **null**), the name of the page to navigate to is set to the home page (line 24).
- If **patternName** is recognized, **doGet()** calls the **setPatternAttributes()** method (line 16). This method uses the BusinessDelegate object to return an object representing pattern data (line 40). The object returned is of type PatternTfrObj—a manifestation of the TransferObject pattern that we discuss at the end of the chapter. The **setPatternAttributes()** method then transfers the attributes of the PatternTfrObj object to a set of request attributes (lines 42 to 45).
- Back at line 17—after a successful call to **setPatternAttributes()**—the name of the next page to navigate to is set to be the pattern detail page (pattern.jspx).
- Line 18 catches a possible exception from **setPatternAttributes()**, the business error PatternNotFoundException. This doesn't originate from **setPatternAttributes()**—it's passed on from the BusinessDelegate object if an error occurs. We'll see later that the BusinessDelegate class masks any "technical" errors and translates them to this "application" exception.
- If a PatternNotFoundException is thrown, the **doGet()** method sets up an error page name to forward to (line 21).
- Finally in the **doGet()** method, at lines 27 and 28, a RequestDispatcher object is used to forward to whichever of the three pages has been determined by the foregoing logic.

The net result is that the three JSP documents in the application (home.jspx, pattern.jspx, and error.jspx) have nothing in the way of hard-coded navigation information. Here's a short extract from home.jspx:

```
<form action="${actionLink}">
  <table border="1">
    <tr>
```

```
      <td><input type="radio"
        name="patternChoice" value="interceptingFilter" /></td>
      <td>Intercepting Filter</td>
    </tr>
...
```

You can see that the target action for the HTML form is derived from an EL variable actionLink—which ties back to the request attribute set up in the controller so that all requests link back to the controller. From this short extract, you can also see that the parameter value for the pattern name comes from a value on a radio button.

Why Use Front Controller?

The reasons you might want to use Front Controller are numerous:

- *Central control of navigation.* Instead of allowing one JSP to directly link to another, you plant logical links in your JSPs instead—sending you via the Front Controller, which makes the ultimate decision about forwarding to the next JSP.
- *Central control of requests.* You might want this control so that you can easily track or log requests.
- *Better management of security.* With centralized access, you can cut off illegal requests in one place. Authentication and authorization can also be centralized (but only worry about this if declarative security, as discussed in Chapter 5, isn't enough for you. Better to have security embedded in your deployment descriptor than in code—even when that code is centralized in a Front Controller!).
- *To avoid embedding control code within lots of separate resources.* This is an approach that easily leads to a copy-and-paste mentality.

And the drawbacks? The Core J2EE Patterns book points out that the pattern can lead to a single point of failure. Given, though, that your Front Controller is likely to be implemented as a servlet, you can always mitigate this by distributing your application, as long as your application server supports this. And as servlets are by their nature multithreaded, it is not as if your Front Controller should be a bottleneck allowing only one request through at a time.

exam watch

If you are asked to match the pattern for a scenario that contains the words "managing the workflow," then the answer is very likely to be Front Controller.

It is very easy to overload a servlet acting as a Front Controller with too many responsibilities and too much code. The answer is to ensure that Front Controller, wherever necessary, delegates to appropriate helper classes. If you want to go further with this (beyond what the SCWCD exam requires), take a look at the View Helper pattern.

When Do You Choose a Front Controller Instead of an Intercepting Filter?

It's often hard to tell which pattern to use—Front Controller or Intercepting Filter. The Core J2EE Patterns book identifies these two patterns as complementary: "Both Intercepting Filter and Front Controller describe ways to centralize control of certain types of request processing, suggesting different approaches to this issue." You can't really argue with that statement, but it does leave you wondering which approach is suitable for which requirement. It's often a matter of experience and taste—which is less clear-cut than you would like in face of the SCWCD exam! The following Scenario and Solution table may help you to get a feel for which pattern is appropriate and when.

SCENARIO & SOLUTION	
Controlling the flow of navigation from one page to another	Front Controller (as we've seen)
Converting responses from one form of XML to another	Intercepting Filter (as long as there is a general way of translating the XML for many different responses)
Zipping up the response	Intercepting Filter
Executing different blocks of business logic dependent on a parameter in the request	Front Controller (dispatching to other classes that contain the business logic)
Stopping a request dead in its tracks if your application dislikes its encoding	Intercepting Filter
Enforcing J2EE authentication and authorization (as per Chapter 5 on security)	Neither Intercepting Filter nor Front Controller. You want to protect individual components declaratively in the deployment descriptor as far as possible.
Enforcing custom authentication or authorization rules	Depends: could be Intercepting Filter or Front Controller. Use Intercepting Filter if these are "blanket" rules, applying to all (or most) resources. If authentication and authorization needs to be closer to business logic, use Front Controller.

EXERCISE 10-2

Front Controller Pattern

Would the Front Controller pattern help with the following requirement? List the pros and cons of adopting the approach. A company has a medium-sized web application that is undergoing extensive enhancement. The company realizes that the JavaServer Pages in the application should be reorganized into different directories relating to subsystems within the application, but that this will upset the many embedded links within the current pages. Because the company is working on all aspects of the pages, changing the links is not a big deal—but the company would like to protect itself from URL volatility in JSPs in the future.

If you run the working example that accompanies this chapter, select the Front Controller pattern radio button option, and click the "Solution to Exercise" button, you'll find a discussion of the above scenario. The URL to launch the working example is likely to be

```
http://localhost:8080/lab10/controller
```

CERTIFICATION OBJECTIVE

Model View Controller Pattern (Exam Objectives 11.1 and 11.2)

Given a scenario description with a list of issues, select a pattern that would solve the issues. The list of patterns you must know are: Intercepting Filter, ***Model-View-Controller,*** *Front Controller, Service Locator, Business Delegate, and Transfer Object.*

Match design patterns with statements describing potential benefits that accrue from the use of the pattern, for any of the following patterns: Intercepting Filter, ***Model-View -Controller,*** *Front Controller, Service Locator, Business Delegate, and Transfer Object.*

Model View Controller doesn't quite fit with the other five patterns on the list for the SCWCD exam. It sits at a higher level than the others. You combine several J2EE patterns to make up a Model View Controller architecture, some of which are on our exam hit list (such as Front Controller and Business Delegate) and some of which are not (View Helper and Dispatcher View).

Model View Controller isn't just a J2EE pattern—it has a far longer pedigree going back to the heydays of the object-oriented language SmallTalk. If you explore web sites dedicated to discussions of patterns (they exist!), you will find more disagreement and controversy about the definition of Model View Controller (MVC) than almost any other pattern. But don't be daunted—this section of the chapter will pick out the incontrovertible bits that you need for the SCWCD.

Model View Controller

The main motivation for using MVC is to separate your presentation logic from your business logic. The idea is to have a "controller" component that mediates between the two—something we have already explored in the preceding section on the Front Controller pattern. You can see the Model View Controller pattern depicted in Figure 10-9.

The view is far from unintelligent—your view code may be the most complex part of your application (all the more reason not to tangle it up with business logic). Figure 10-9 indicates two principle responsibilities for the view:

- To detect each user action (like a mouse click or an ENTER keypress) and transmit it to the controller component

FIGURE 10-9

The Model View Controller Pattern

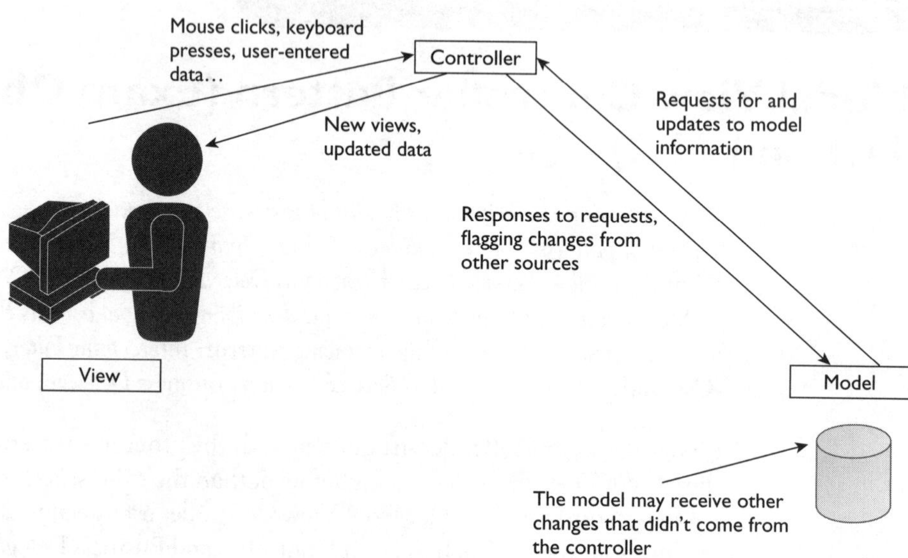

- To receive information back from the controller and organize this appropriately for the recipient

The view can range in complexity from some text on a screen and a gray button or two to a fully interactive display resplendent with color. Indeed, different circumstances may demand entirely different views.

From our previous discussion of the Front Controller pattern, you can predict the likely responsibilities of the controller:

- To supply the view with the information it needs—usually by obtaining information from the underlying model
- To interpret user actions and take appropriate actions—usually updating the model and switching view (or both)
- To receive changes from the model that come from other sources, and update views as appropriate

That third and last responsibility causes some problems in the web browser environment—see the nearby On the Job comments.

Finally, what are the model's responsibilities? Easy: to look after the underlying data. It must respond to requests for information and update from the controller. It must (or should) inform the controller of external changes to the data that didn't arrive through the controller.

What I've described here is the scale at which Model View Controller works in J2EE terms—at application level. You should be aware, though, that MVC can be found at the micro as well as the macro level. Swing components have the same idea: a visual component, the view (like a JTable); an underlying representation of the data, the model (JTableModel); and the Swing framework acting as controller mediating between the two.

But because our focus is J2EE web applications, we need to consider where we are likely to find the constituent parts of MVC. To start with, where is the view? Typically, the view is represented by a JavaServer Page. At run time, though, it's really the web browser that acts as the view component. It's not literally the JSP you interact with—that's been translated to pure HTML and delivered to your browser. When you type in text and click buttons, you are using the browser, which sends the results back to the controller component in your design. This is something of an academic point, for it is ultimately the JSP that dictates the availability of those text fields and buttons. So in design and development terms, the JSP is the view.

exam watch

There is nothing stopping you from having other components for views—you don't have to have a JavaServer Page. A pattern is a "logical" design, with several possible physical implementations. A servlet could act as a view component (though has the disadvantage of embedding HTML in code, which we discussed much earlier in the book). Maybe your aim is to present a graphical chart that allows client-side interaction (reordering columns, changing line colors). In these circumstances, an applet may be a good choice. When you meet questions on the exam, don't be too narrow in your interpretation of what a view can be. A view may not even be graphic—just because your client is another business application running silently in batch mode, it can still have a view on your system.

Look out for any of these scenarios—they probably indicate use of the Model View Controller pattern:

- ***When you see the words "presenting data in different ways"***
- ***When the presentation changes dependent on user feedback***
- ***When the data has to be presented to different types of users***

We've already seen (in J2EE terms) that an appropriate choice for a controller component is often a servlet (with assistant classes where necessary). The model is composed—more often than not—of Enterprise JavaBeans (though there are good reasons why we might want to place some classes in between our controller and the Enterprise JavaBeans, as we'll see with the Business Delegate and Service Locator patterns).

on the job

In an ideal world, changes to the model from other sources would result in updates to the appropriate views. Suppose you have a web page where you are viewing volatile stock quotes. Your J2EE application has a real-time feed from another application, which updates quote figures every 30 seconds, so the model data is always up to date. Ideally, you would like the model to be able to tell the controller "I've changed." Then the controller could update the view.

If your view client was a Swing application with a permanent connection to the controller, this could be achieved easily. The trouble is that the web is a connection-less world. Unless you press the refresh button in your browser, you won't see the latest figures. Consequently, you are more or less reliant on a browser client "pulling" fresh changes from the controller. In the cruel

real world, you may have to fudge the illusion of the controller "pushing" to the client by inserting some tawdry bit of script in your web page to cause an auto-refresh at given intervals.

How Is Model View Controller Used in the Example Application?

The example application for this chapter separates out model, view, and controller in ways that you have probably already guessed. Here they are anyway:

- The view consists of three JSP documents: home.jspx, pattern.jspx, and error.jspx. These views are more or less dumb consumers of request attributes—they aren't very clever (so all the better for later maintenance).
- The controller is the FrontController class, which we have already examined in some detail. We have seen how it uses logic to direct to the different JSP documents, and how it populates those request attributes required by the views.
- The model is the BusinessDelegate class, and everything behind it. We'll explore this in the later patterns.

Why Use Model View Controller?

Imagining this question asked out loud at a design patterns conference, I can almost hear the collective sharp intake of breath. MVC is such a sacred pattern that you are practically obligated to use it in every circumstance—whether you are adding a Swing widget to a screen design or putting together a complex J2EE architecture for an investment bank.

Perversely, though, I'll start this section by exploring some reasons for not adopting MVC. By its nature, MVC increases the number of moving parts in your application. There is more overall complexity. Very few of the examples in this book (present chapter notably excepted!) use a Model View Controller design. This could be down to bad design choices on my part, but I prefer to claim that MVC would have just got in the way of explaining other concepts. The undoubted benefits of MVC are outweighed by the complexity it brings.

Teaching examples are a special case, though. What about real J2EE applications that avoid MVC? One of the JSTL libraries contains custom actions dedicated to SQL (database access functionality). This library has a host of useful facilities for embedding database access directly in your JavaServer Page. But hang on—because the JavaServer Page is normally the view, and the database is ultimately a model, where is the controller? You could perhaps use some JSPs with embedded SQL actions separate from JSPs representing the view, and have controlling logic separating them. But this seems perverse: You lose the convenience of embedding an SQL tag right in an HTML table where you want it, and you still end up putting the model code inside a JavaServer Page. It doesn't feel like the purpose for which the JSTL SQL library was intended.

Therefore, many J2EE architects would avoid using the JSTL SQL components altogether, just because they fundamentally violate MVC rules. I would say that it depends on the job at hand. If you have a one-developer project, where the developer has good web design and Java skills, then the SQL components might be ideal for getting a quick-and-dirty version of your application into existence. Later you might choose to re-architect the system along cleaner lines.

So after that exploration of when not to use Model View Controller, let's enumerate the reasons for using it:

- You want to reduce dependencies between the view code and the business model code. That way,
  - You can graft on additional views much more easily (so you might have a web client and a Swing client showing alternative views of the same model data).
  - You can change the view without affecting the business model, and vice versa.
  - The controller is the only volatile component that might be affected by changes at either end.
- You are using a framework that has MVC built into it. Struts is a very popular framework. If you are in a development team that uses it, you are forced into a set of programming standards that abide by MVC rules.
- You want the maintenance benefit that comes from separating the layers. Expert Java programmers can concentrate on the controller and model ends of the application. Web designers (potentially, nondevelopers) can concentrate on the JSP view side of things. Alternatively, if you are using a fancy graphical view, expert Swing Java programmers can concentrate on the visual aspects and be freed up from most concerns about model access.

EXERCISE 10-3

Model View Controller Pattern

Consider again the company featured in the first exercise, 10-1. It had an extranet application executing business logic to manufacture comma-delimited files or XML for various suppliers. A further requirement arises. Some consumers of the same data don't want file downloads: They need a view of the data presented in a simple web page with an HTML table. How could Model View Controller be integrated into the application to fulfill this requirement, without disturbing the way that existing users of the system work?

If you run the working example that accompanies this chapter, select the Model View Controller pattern radio button option, and click the "Solution to Exercise" button, you'll find a discussion of the above scenario. The URL to launch the working example is likely to be

```
http://localhost:8080/lab10/controller
```

CERTIFICATION OBJECTIVE

Business Delegate Pattern (Exam Objectives 11.1 and 11.2)

Given a scenario description with a list of issues, select a pattern that would solve the issues. The list of patterns you must know are: Intercepting Filter, Model-View-Controller, Front Controller, Service Locator, ***Business Delegate****, and Transfer Object.*

Match design patterns with statements describing potential benefits that accrue from the use of the pattern, for any of the following patterns: Intercepting Filter, Model-View -Controller, Front Controller, Service Locator, ***Business Delegate****, and Transfer Object.*

Model View Controller damps down the destructive aspects of change that ripple through the presentation tier. What, though, if you want to insulate your presentation tier more fully from the effects of volatility at the model end? Enter the Business Delegate Pattern, which creates a buffer zone for business APIs.

Business Delegate Pattern

The Business Delegate pattern works by placing a layer in between a client (possibly a Front Controller object) and a business object. That way, even when business object interfaces change, it may well be possible to absorb the change within the business delegate object—without changing the interface that this presents to its clients.

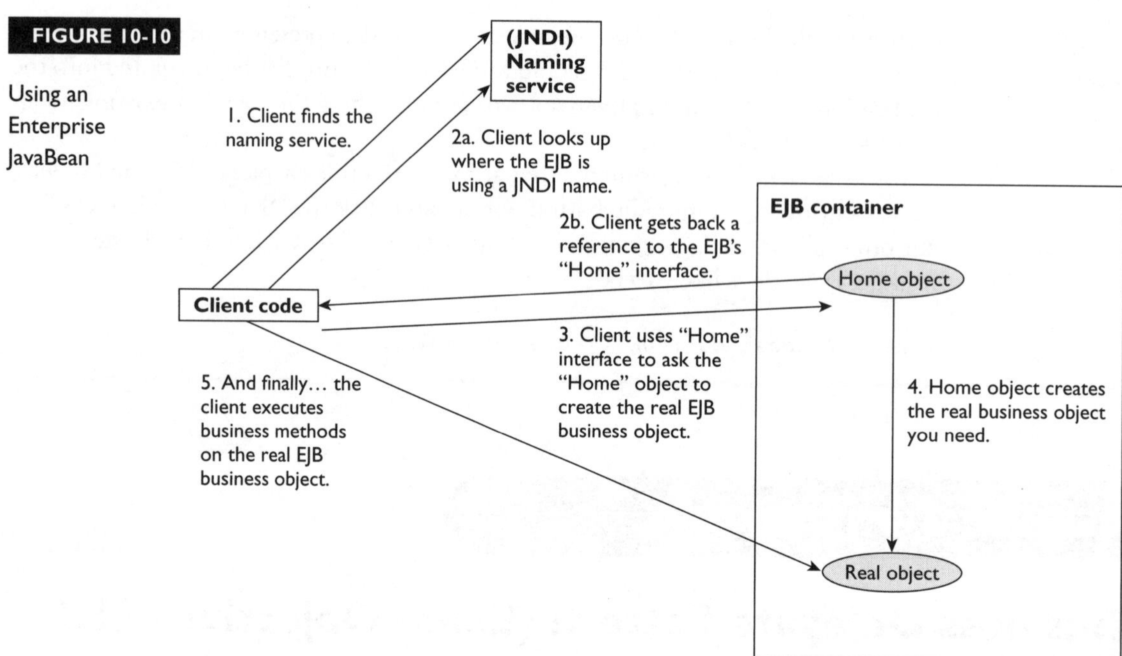

FIGURE 10-10 Using an Enterprise JavaBean

It's not just about change. The other service a Business Delegate typically provides is encapsulation of all the ugly details that might be involved in getting hold of the business object in the first place, and coping with any errors thrown up. Without turning this chapter into an EJB tutorial, consider the process shown in Figure 10-10. This shows (in slightly simplified form!) a typical process involved in executing a business method on an Enterprise JavaBean.

There are three independent processes running. First is our client-side code. Second is the "Naming Service"—like a phone directory, which translates names to references to objects. Third is the EJB container. These three processes may run as threads inside the same JVM, within separate JVMs on the same physical computer, or on three separate computers. The actual implementation doesn't matter, as long as you get the idea that what's going on here is a big deal. There is plenty of potential for breakdown in the message passing between the three participants.

Figure 10-10 describes the process involved in obtaining the bean. The code to achieve this (not shown here) is not so *very* frightening—it distills down to a half a dozen lines of code, doubled or tripled by whatever mechanics you put in place to catch the many exceptions that might result—RemoteExceptions (even where the network is all local to one machine), CreateExceptions (because something goes wrong in the EJB creation mechanics), and so on. However, the code involved is not beginner material: You need to know plenty about EJBs to handle them successfully. Given that there is a parallel certification exam dedicated to EJBs alone, you can believe that gaining the knowledge is a long and painful process. Already you have a motive for burying this code in a layer of its own and giving your Java web application developers a simpler API for accessing business data (after all, they have enough to think about—witness the thickness of this book!).

That's not all of it, though. We mentioned exceptions above. The process of looking up the name of your EJB involves JNDI (Java Naming and Directory Interface) code. This can kick up some pretty intimidating exceptions just by itself—InterruptedNamingExceptions and NameNotFoundExceptions, to name but two. These may be important for support developers trying to diagnose a problem with your application, but you may want some friendlier business-type exception to pass through the presentation tier and ultimately drive whatever nonthreatening message shows to the user of the application. And we haven't even started on EJB exceptions.

Still that's not all. There are vendor-specific issues. Surely, J2EE (including the JNDI and EJB) specifications involve standard interface calls, such that your code is portable from one application server to another? Well, yes they do—but there may still be vendor-specific details. Let's pick on JNDI again to furnish an example. As Figure 10-10 shows, the long road to an EJB business method call begins with finding your JNDI Naming Service. This involves getting hold of a JNDI object called an InitialContext. The parameters for getting hold of the InitialContext (which host to look up, which port, etc.) do vary from one platform to another. How to feed the parameters to the calling code (directly or via properties files) varies as well.

With luck, you are getting the idea that it might be a good idea to confine some of this code to easily accessible regions of your web application. And that is, of course, where the Business Delegate pattern comes in. It is used to

- Encapsulate EJB (and other complex business object access) code
- Encapsulate JNDI code (but often defers to the Service Locator pattern for that—see the next section of the chapter)
- Present simple business interfaces to presentation-tier clients
- Cache (sometimes) the results of expensive calls on business objects

Finally in this description, where does the Business Delegate belong? Because it has the name "Business" within it, you would assume the business tier. In physical terms, though, the classes involved are likely to remain close to your presentation code (the EJB server itself is potentially remote). Perhaps for this reason, it's described as a *client-side* business abstraction and often regarded as belonging to the (physical) presentation tier.

The presence of the acronym "EJB" in an exam question scenario is very likely to imply the use of Business Delegate. However, EJBs are not the only kind of business object that can be fronted by the Business Delegate pattern. Be sensitive to other possibilities and phrases that describe systems for managing information: "business rules" and "stored procedures," for example.

How Is Business Delegate Used in the Example Application?

The example application has a class called BusinessDelegate that exhibits most of the Business Delegate pattern features. Here is the code for the BusinessDelegate class (minus package statement and imports):

```
public class BusinessDelegate {
  Map patternCache = new HashMap();
  ServiceLocator serviceLocator = new ServiceLocator();
  PatternLoaderRmtI patternLoader;
  public PatternTfrObj findPattern(String patternName)
    throws PatternNotFoundException {
    // Is the pattern already in the cache?
    PatternTfrObj pattern = findCachedPattern(patternName);
    // Not in cache: use remote object
    if (pattern == null) {
      if (patternLoader == null) {
        patternLoader = serviceLocator.findPatternLoader();
      }
      try {
        pattern = findRemotePattern(patternName);
      } catch (RemoteException re) {
       // Print the stack trace for internal diagnosis
        re.printStackTrace();
        // Re-throw an "application" exception
        throw new PatternNotFoundException(patternName);
      }
      patternCache.put(patternName, pattern);
    }
    return pattern;
  }
  protected PatternTfrObj findCachedPattern(String patternName) {
    return (PatternTfrObj) patternCache.get(patternName);
```

```
28    }
29    protected PatternTfrObj findRemotePattern(String patternName)
30      throws RemoteException, PatternNotFoundException {
31      System.out.println("Making expensive call to remote API...");
32      delay(3000);
33      if (patternLoader == null) {
34        throw new PatternNotFoundException(patternName);
35      }
36      return patternLoader.getData(patternName);
37    }
38   protected void delay(int millis) {
39      try {
40        Thread.sleep(millis);
41      } catch (InterruptedException ie) {
42      }
43    }
44 }
```

Here are the Business Delegate pattern features that this class implements:

- Its main business method begins at line 05: **`findPattern()`**. This returns a business object — of type PatternTfrObj — given a named pattern passed as a parameter. So the first point is that this class exposes a business method for use by classes in the presentation tier (in this case, the FrontController class).
- In line 02, BusinessDelegate declares a local cache (a HashMap)—for pattern business objects. Because pattern information doesn't change very much (at all!) in the example application, having a cache makes a great deal of sense. So at line 08 in the **`findPattern()`** method, the code first looks for the business object in the cache — only if it doesn't find it there will it execute calls to real remote business services. Note that at line 22, after doing a remote call to find a pattern, there is code to place that pattern in the cache.
- At line 15, BusinessDelegate calls its own method—**`findRemotePattern()`**— beginning at line 29. This calls the real business method on the real remote object. The real remote object (of type PatternLoaderRemoteImpl) is very much like an Enterprise JavaBean: You have to go through RMI to get hold of its methods. Consequently, **`findRemotePattern()`** might throw a RemoteException. Just to emphasize the expense and remoteness of making the call, the method throws in an arbitrary 3-second delay — this is so you can tell the difference when information comes out of the cache, which has no such built-in artificial delay.

- If the `findRemotePattern()` method fails to find a pattern, it throws a business-type exception: PatternNotFoundException (at line 34).
- There's still the possibility that RemoteException will be thrown—so back in the calling code, the call to `findRemotePattern()` is couched in a try-catch block. You can see how—in lines 17 to 20—the contents of the RemoteException are printed in the stack trace for later diagnosis. Then—at line 20—the application-friendly PatternNotFoundException is thrown for the benefit of the presentation code.
- One thing the BusinessDelegate doesn't do is contain code to find the remote business object in the first place (which involves JNDI code and other nastiness). Instead, it defers to a helper class called ServiceLocator, declared at line 03 and used at line 12. We will explore that in a subsequent part of the chapter devoted to the Service Locator pattern.

So you can see this BusinessDelegate class does most of what you would expect from the Business Delegate pattern: It encapsulates difficult-to-handle business objects, has its own cache for performance gains, and translates technical errors to application errors.

Why Use Business Delegate?

By now, most of the reasons for using Business Delegate have been exposed. Here's a summary:

- To reduce coupling between clients in the presentation tier and actual business services, by hiding the way the underlying business service is implemented.
- To cache the results from business services.
- To reduce network traffic between a client and a remote business service.
- To minimize error handling code (particularly network error handling code) in the presentation tier.
- Substituting application-level (user-friendly) errors for highly technical ones.
- If at first the business service doesn't succeed, the Business Delegate class might choose to retry or to implement some alternative API call to recover a situation. A business service failure doesn't immediately have to be passed on to a client.
- Make naming and lookup activities happen within the Business Delegate—or code that the Business Delegate uses (see Service Locator).

- To act as an adapter between two systems (B2B-type communication—where a visible GUI isn't involved). The delegate might interpret incoming XML as a business API call.

EXERCISE 10-4

Business Delegate Pattern

This time, you are managing a project to build a new web application to extend the functionality of an existing legacy COBOL system. The COBOL system has a number of programs that offer stable, well-tested business services and whose code you don't want to duplicate or change. There are Java APIs to handle calls to COBOL, but you know that they are tricky to write and use and that they throw a multitude of obscure exceptions, and you have at your disposal only a single developer skilled in their use—and he spends most of his days supporting existing systems. How could the Business Delegate pattern help the project and the future support of your new web application?

If you run the working example that accompanies this chapter, select the Business Delegate pattern radio button option, and click the "Solution to Exercise" button, you'll find a discussion of the above scenario. The URL to launch the working example is likely to be

```
http://localhost:8080/lab10/controller
```

CERTIFICATION OBJECTIVE

Service Locator Pattern (Exam Objectives 11.1 and 11.2)

Given a scenario description with a list of issues, select a pattern that would solve the issues. The list of patterns you must know are: Intercepting Filter, Model-View-Controller, Front Controller, ***Service Locator****, Business Delegate, and Transfer Object.*

Match design patterns with statements describing potential benefits that accrue from the use of the pattern, for any of the following patterns: Intercepting Filter, Model-View -Controller, Front Controller, ***Service Locator****, Business Delegate, and Transfer Object.*

The Service Locator pattern often acts in conjunction with the Business Delegate. We already discussed Business Delegate as a way of offloading the "technical" aspects of calling business APIs—you use a Business Delegate to do this instead of letting presentation code perform this task directly. What Service Locator does is to allow a Business Delegate class to further offload the most gruesome aspects of Business Service access code, which is normally the sleight of hand involving looking up the business service in the first place and getting some kind of reference to it. Thereafter, the Business Delegate can happily call APIs on the business object. So Service Locator encapsulates the mysteries of finding business objects (services).

The Service Locator Pattern

Service Locator is like a subset of Business Delegate—you might even include "service locator" code in methods within your "business delegate" class. It's a valid implementation of the pattern. However, I prefer the obvious separation of different classes—even in the small-scale example application that accompanies this chapter.

The main reason for using the Service Locator pattern is to avoid duplication of code that gets references to business resources (services) you need to use. To start the ball rolling, you most often use JNDI (Java Naming and Directory Interface) code, and this can easily proliferate across all kinds of clients. Furthermore, the operation of looking up some resource in a JNDI-compliant naming and directory service is expensive, so if the results of retrieving the resource can be cached rather than repeated, there is a performance saving to be had.

If you look at the J2EE Core Patterns book (or web site on line), you'll see that there are lots of specific "strategies" for the Service Locator pattern that have mainly to do with the particular kind of J2EE resource Service Locator is after. You might be after Enterprise JavaBeans. Or JMS (Java Messaging Service) objects. Or other things not mentioned: legacy programs in Enterprise Information Systems, or Java Mail, or URL factories. I boldly suggest that the specifics of these don't matter at all. The general principle holds true in all cases. Your Java code needs to get hold of a reference to a business service. That's code you will want to isolate.

How Is Service Locator Used in the Example Application?

Let's see how the ServiceLocator class in the example application contains the pattern features. At first sight, it doesn't look like much—here's the class (minus package and import statements):

```
public class ServiceLocator {
  PatternLoaderRmtI patternLoader;
```

```
03   public PatternLoaderRmtI findPatternLoader() {
04     if (patternLoader == null) {
05       initializePatternLoader();
06     }
07      return patternLoader;
08   }
09   protected void initializePatternLoader() {
10     try {
11       // Needless 6-second delay to make the point that looking up
12       // a remote registry might be expensive.
13       System.out.println("Making expensive call to naming registry...");
14       delay(6000);
15       patternLoader = (PatternLoaderRmtI) Naming
        .lookup("rmi://localhost/patternLoader");
16     } catch (MalformedURLException e) {
17       e.printStackTrace();
18     } catch (RemoteException e) {
19       e.printStackTrace();
20     } catch (NotBoundException e) {
21       e.printStackTrace();
22     }
23   }
24   protected void delay(int millis) {
25     try {
26       Thread.sleep(millis);
27     } catch (InterruptedException ie) {
28     }
29   }
30 }
```

The first and only public method in the class is called `findPatternLoader()`, and it returns a business object of type PatternLoaderRemoteI. The real work to get hold of this object occurs in the protected method `initializePatternLoader()`, but notice that if the class has gone to the trouble of executing this method already, it keeps hold of the reference (lines 04 to 07).

Within `initializePatternLoader()`, you first of all find an artificial delay built in (lines 13 and 14). This is not part of the Service Locator pattern—your real application architecture is unlikely to need any artificial delays! It makes the point that the reference-finding process can be a lengthy one (if the delay wasn't there, you wouldn't notice the difference between cached calls and remote calls when running all the example components on your desktop PC). The real work is done at line 15. This uses a JNDI class called Naming to look up the remote business object in the RMI Registry. You can see from the stack of catch clauses that follow (lines 16 to 22) that there is plenty of potential for disaster.

If the JNDI call works, the code casts the object returned to the type of business object expected: a PatternLoaderRemoteI reference. This is held as an instance variable in the class, so there is no need to repeat the JNDI call.

At last the business of finding is done: The result (for clients—the BusinessDelegate class in our case) is an already found reference to a business object. Hiding RMI code like this may seem trivial. However, it makes the point that you can easily trap this code in one place. Inasmuch as this is a simulation of EJB use (without the need for an EJB container), take a look back at Figure 10-10. The Service Locator encapsulates the steps numbered 1 to 3 on the figure: everything from finding a naming service to getting hold of the remote object. This leaves the Business Delegate to concentrate solely on step 5: executing business methods on the remote object once found.

So when you come to writing classes that deal not with simple RMI objects but with bigger business components—such as EJBs—you are likely to be grateful to the Service Locator pattern.

Why Use Service Locator?

The reasons for using the Service Locator pattern are these:

- To hide JNDI (or similar) code that gets hold of a reference to a service. Even though JNDI code is pure, portable Java, the parameters fed into JNDI code can be vendor-specific, so locating all these details in one place (rather than leaking them all over your business objects) is desirable if you want to port your application later with minimum hassle.
- By locating JNDI (or similar) code in one place—or a few places—you avoid copying and pasting technical calls across many business objects.
- To minimize network calls—the Service Locator can decide which JNDI calls need to be made and when it has appropriate references to remote objects already. This can, of course, improve performance.

EXERCISE 10-5

Service Locator Pattern

Consider the scenario from the previous exercise, where you used the Business Delegate pattern to front calls to legacy COBOL programs. How could the Service Locator pattern be used to further ease the maintenance of your web application?

If you run the working example that accompanies this chapter, select the Service Locator pattern radio button option, and click the "Solution to Exercise" button, you'll find a discussion of the above scenario. The URL to launch the working example is likely to be

```
http://localhost:8080/lab10/controller
```

CERTIFICATION OBJECTIVE

Transfer Object Pattern (Exam Objectives 11.1 and 11.2)

Given a scenario description with a list of issues, select a pattern that would solve the issues. The list of patterns you must know are: Intercepting Filter, Model-View-Controller, Front Controller, Service Locator, Business Delegate, and ***Transfer Object****.*

Match design patterns with statements describing potential benefits that accrue from the use of the pattern, for any of the following patterns: Intercepting Filter, Model-View -Controller, Front Controller, Service Locator, Business Delegate, and ***Transfer Object****.*

The idea of the Transfer Object pattern is to encapsulate data—usually the data that would be available inside a complex (and possibly remote) object, such as an Enterprise JavaBean (EJB). The class representing a Transfer Object is a very simple thing, but what goes on around it is moderately profound and complex, and that's what we'll explore in this final section on J2EE design patterns.

The Transfer Object Pattern

Structurally, the object representing a Transfer Object is very simple. It's a Java Bean—not an Enterprise JavaBean—just a bean. And a bean only in the sense that is has a bunch of properties that can be accessed with `set` and `get` methods.

The idea of a Transfer Object is that it holds the data returned from a more complex business object, such as an Enterprise JavaBean. You may well ask a question: Wouldn't it be more straightforward to deal with the EJB business object directly? Why bother with additional objects? To understand that, let's consider client code that deals with a type of EJB called an Entity EJB. It's a big simplification, but more often than not, an Entity EJB represents a single row on a table (and has attributes to match). Let's consider a fashion retailing example. Suppose that we have a database table to record information about dresses—one row per dress. And suppose we tie an Entity EJB definition to this table, as shown in Figure 10-11.

You see how the attributes of the EJB (each with their own getters and setters) map on to equivalent table fields—fashionSeason to FSHN_SEASON, and so on. Let's consider what might happen if you had hold of the EJB and executed the `getSizeRange()` method. This might well be a remote call across the network. Because EJBs are often designed to disguise the JDBC database access details from you, your EJB might (under the covers) generate some JDBC SQL SELECT statement to get hold of the individual piece of information you are after: the size range for the dress. Now suppose that you want to get hold of the dress color. You make a call to `getColor()`, which goes remotely across the network and instigates a new and separate JDBC SQL SELECT statement to get hold of the color attribute from the same table row.

It should be said at this point that no sane EJB container vendor manages SQL access in such a naïve way. However, you should be getting the message that access

FIGURE 10-11

An EJB Mapping to a Database Table

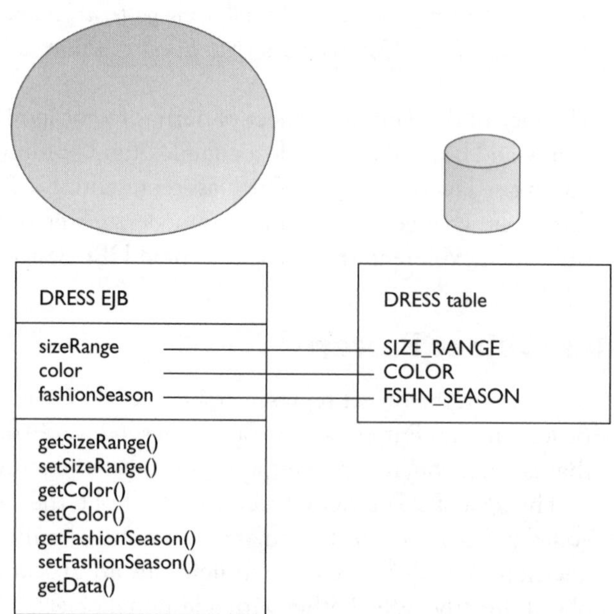

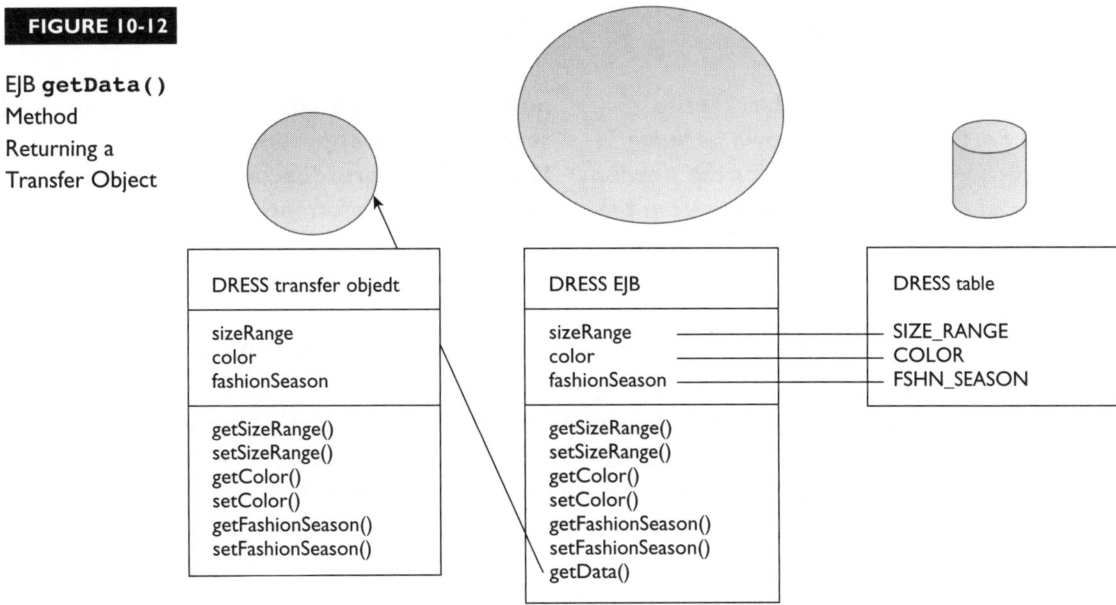

FIGURE 10-12 EJB `getData()` Method Returning a Transfer Object

to separate attributes in this piecemeal fashion can be expensive in networking and processing terms. The answer? To get hold of all the attributes you need together. Place in the EJB a `getData()` method that returns all three attributes at once—color, fashion season, and size range. `getData()` returns an object—a transfer object—that has all attributes of the EJB but none of the complexity. You might not want to know abut the fashion season for your particular call to `getData()`, but it's far cheaper to collect all the data you're likely to need in one hit and pass it back in one package—as shown in Figure 10-12.

Classes for Transfer Objects are always implement Serializable so that they can be returned from remote method calls.

You can even apply the same principle in reverse. A client may want to update this row on the Dress table through the system. A client can make changes to its own copy of the transfer object, then pass this back to the Enterprise JavaBean via a `setData()` method. That gives the EJB code the opportunity to execute a single SQL update statement for all the changed attributes in one hit, instead of updating each attribute in turn.

exam watch

Transfer Object is the design pattern formerly known as Value Object (if you were around for the previous version of J2EE, or are upgrading from the previous version of the SCWCD). Almost none of the details have changed—it just seemed a more appropriate name to the J2EE pattern gurus (because it's to do with the transfer of information).

How Is Transfer Object Used in the Example Application?

Bearing in mind that the example application doesn't use actual EJBs, you still get the full Transfer Object pattern rendered for your money. The simulation EJB is the class called PatternLoader. Rather than connecting to a database, this class maps on to a properties file in the file system, which loads into a Properties object. PatternLoader has its own `getData()` method, which returns a PatternTfrObj (Pattern Transfer Object). This takes data from the Properties object and populates attributes on the PatternTfrObj by calling appropriate getter methods. For brevity, the code isn't shown here—the source is, of course, available in the solution code.

You can follow the PatternTfrObj back through the system. BusinessDelegate makes the call to the `getData()` method. It passes the transfer object back to FrontController. As we've seen, FrontController strips the values into request attributes, which are then used by the JavaServer Pages. Alternatively, the PatternTfrObj could have been made directly available with the JSP as a bean (using the `<jsp:useBean>` custom action, for example).

The example application doesn't go as far as providing a `setData()` method on PatternLoader, whereby an updated version of the PatternTfrObj could be passed back in order to update the underlying properties file.

Why Use Transfer Object?

Having seen how the Transfer Object pattern works and where it fits, we just need to give some thought to why you would employ the pattern. These are the benefits:

- Transfer Objects simplify your life on the client side. You avoid direct dependence on potentially complex business objects and deal instead with relatively simple bean-like objects.

- You avoid the expense of repeated interaction with remote business objects. This occurs when you accumulate dribs and drabs of data from those business objects by a series of expensive remote calls. Better to pass all the data you are likely to need in one remote "hit." This may seem profligate if you never use some of these attributes, but this is likely to be a small overhead compared even to one unnecessary network call.

There are some real drawbacks to using the Transfer Object pattern, however. A Transfer Object is likely to duplicate code—notably in the attributes and getter and setter methods that shadow those of its associated Enterprise JavaBean (or other business component). That said, there are ways to mitigate this. You could consider coupling the Transfer Object and business component by having the business component extend the Transfer Object and so inheriting its attributes and getter and setter methods. Alternatively, you might have a tool available to generate Transfer Object code directly from your business component. These strategies are not that palatable, though, just because they tie together an object deep in the model with an object that is used—potentially—on the fringe of the presentation layer. You could imagine adding a fresh attribute to the EJB, regenerating the code for the associated Transfer Object, and forgetting to revisit a particular client using the Transfer Object (because it had no particular reason to use the new attribute).

Transfer Objects can also go stale. Vendors of EJB containers go to great lengths to ensure that EJBs keep up to date with changes from multiple users of the EJB. As soon as you copy the data from the EJB as you do with the Transfer Object, you have an object bouncing around your system with data that will inevitably get out of date. This may not matter very much, especially when you are only reading data. However, you may not be able to remain complacent over multiple user update issues. You may happily update values in the Transfer Object you are using. Yet in the meantime, someone may have sneaked up and updated the underlying business component. When you press the update button, what should happen? Should the old values in your Transfer Object (as well as your changes) overwrite the changes from the other user—which you were never aware of? Or should your changes be rejected? To protect against this, you may introduce complexity into your code—by adding some form of version control or locking to your system. When you deal directly with EJBs, you could end up attempting to solve problems that EJB container designers have already solved.

EXERCISE 10-6

Transfer Object Pattern

For this exercise, we'll stick with the web application tied to legacy COBOL programs that has dominated the previous two exercises. The COBOL program update routines will disallow your update to a row on a table, if this row has been updated by another user since you read the record for update. How could you use Transfer Objects to integrate with this mechanism?

If you run the working example that accompanies this chapter, select the Transfer Object pattern radio button option, and click the "Solution to Exercise" button, you'll find a discussion of the above scenario. The URL to launch the working example is likely to be

```
http://localhost:8080/lab10/controller
```

CERTIFICATION SUMMARY

In this chapter you surveyed around a quarter of the J2EE core patterns catalogue, concentrating on the six J2EE patterns you need to know for the SCWCD exam.

You started by thinking about patterns in general—and how they supply a logical design solution to a particular design problem. You examined

- Intercepting Filter—and saw that this is a logical description of the Filter mechanisms you met in Chapter 3. You learned that Intercepting Filter can be used to manipulate or validate requests and responses on their way into or out of a web application. You saw that filters can be independent and loosely coupled, with a chain controlling the passage from one to another. You learned that a principal benefit of a filter chain like this is the avoidance of conditional code to fulfill the same function copied and pasted around several points of entry to your application.
- Front Controller—you learned that this is used as a gateway into a web application and can be used as a point where a request is authenticated before passing on to real resources within the application. You also saw that navigation

can be greatly simplified by adopting Front Controller. If all links lead to the Front Controller, you appreciated how navigation might be controlled by logical links.

- Model View Controller—you saw that this is a bit less specific than the other patterns; it describes how to separate out presentation logic and business logic, then interpose a controller to mediate between them. You saw that in J2EE terms, the View might be represented by JSPs, the controller by a class or classes implementing the Front Controller pattern, and the model by a Business Delegate (or at least, fronted by classes representing the Business Delegate pattern). You learned how the view sends user actions to the controller, and how the controller translates these into actions against the model. You learned that this separation of concerns can help in practical project terms—allowing developers with different skills to concentrate on components matched to their area of expertise.
- Business Delegate—you learned that this can be used as a translation layer between a client wanting to use business routines (like a Front Controller) and the business routines themselves. You further learned that the motive for this is to hide some of the complexity that might come with business routines—for example, where these involve calling methods on Enterprise JavaBeans. You saw also that changes to business routines need not necessarily result in changes to the interface that a Business Delegate exposes to its clients—so in this way, the presentation layer has an element of protection from volatility in the model layer.
- Service Locator—you saw that this is effectively a helper to the Business Delegate pattern. You learned that it is often the case in J2EE applications that just finding the resources you want to use can be an expensive business, involving calls to a naming service through JNDI. You saw how a Service Locator can encapsulate this often complex code, and also cache references to business objects once found.
- Transfer Object—the last pattern you met, this encapsulates data in a simple bean-like way. You learned that the idea of a Transfer Object is to return many items of data at once, instead of making repeated calls to (potentially) remote methods to get attributes one at a time. You saw how this can decrease network traffic, and—by giving the client a simple object to deal with—reduce the complexity of client code.

TWO-MINUTE DRILL

Intercepting Filter Pattern

- ❑ Allows each incoming request (and outgoing response) to be pre-processed (or post-processed).
- ❑ Acts as the first port of call—before accessing a requested resource.
- ❑ Involves a filter chain of loosely coupled filters.
- ❑ A filter manager constructs each filter chain based on information in the incoming request—most often the URL pattern used—so each request can have a unique filter chain associated with it.
- ❑ Possible uses for filters include (but are not limited to): auditing, transforming, compressing, decompressing and re-encoding.
- ❑ Because filters are deliberately loosely coupled (order of execution may even not matter), they are bad at sharing information efficiently.

Front Controller Pattern

- ❑ Acts as a centralized request handler.
- ❑ Can be used as a central initial point for authentication, authorization, auditing, logging, and error handling.
- ❑ May make decisions on content handling—based on the requesting client (is it a laptop or a wireless device?).
- ❑ Can be used to centralize error handling.
- ❑ Very often used for the flow of control through views in an application.
- ❑ Should delegate business processes to other classes (perhaps implementing the Business Delegate pattern).
- ❑ Can make the management of security and navigation much easier.
- ❑ Can be used to centralize code that would otherwise be duplicated around many separate resources.

Model View Controller Pattern

- ❑ Is a pattern not just defined within J2EE: It can be found on a smaller scale in (for example) Swing components.

- ❑ Separates out data (the model) from the presentation of data (the view), by having a controller object interposed between the model and the view.
- ❑ In J2EE terms, the view is often represented by JSPs and the model by business components (like EJBs—fronted by Business Delegates), and the controller is often a servlet (conforming to the Front Controller pattern).
- ❑ The controller selects which view to display.
- ❑ The controller can embed security functionality—maybe disallowing some requests from the view.
- ❑ This pattern can lead to a cleaner approach to application design, for concerns are separated.
- ❑ This pattern can even suit projects where different developers have different expertise—some developers may concentrate on business logic in the model and others on presentation in the view JSPs.

Business Delegate Pattern

- ❑ An abstraction of the business layer, this pattern hides business services.
- ❑ This pattern presents
  - ❑ a route into business services that stays constant even if the underlying business services change in minor ways
  - ❑ simpler access to business services
- ❑ Most often, this pattern is used to stop presentation code from accessing EJBs directly.
- ❑ The complexity of EJB method calls is encapsulated in the Business Delegate.
- ❑ May also cache the results of calling underlying business APIs.
- ❑ By reducing business API calls—which are often networked—a Business Delegate can reduce network traffic.
- ❑ May also cope with failing business services through retry and recovery code, passing on failures to the presentation layer only when there is no other option.
- ❑ May simplify the errors arising from business API calls, translating these to more application-oriented messages.

Service Locator Pattern

- Is used to find references to business services in the first place.
- May take some of the load off the Business Delegate pattern.
- Typically encapsulates calls to naming service (JNDI) routines.
- May cache references to business objects, avoiding unnecessary repeated JNDI calls.
- Reduces the need to have JNDI code at many points in the application—wherever a business object must be found.
- Can help with application server migration; because some details of JNDI are inevitably vendor-specific, it reduces the places where code needs to change.

Transfer Object Pattern

- Is used to encapsulate data returned from a business service (usually from an EJB).
- All (or a meaningful subset) of the attributes on a business object are collected together in a transfer object.
- Takes the form of a simple bean, with get and set methods.
- Is usually the return type for a `getData()` method on an EJB.
- The `getData()` method transfers the EJB attributes to the Transfer Object.
- Is usually the input parameter to a `setData()` method on an EJB.
- The `setData()` method takes attribute values on a Transfer Object, and updates these on the EJB.
- Reduces the need for separate API calls to get individual attributes from a remote business object.
- May contain stale data at variance with the originating business object (because the business object has been updated by another user).
- May duplicate attribute definition and getter/setter methods from the EJB (or other business object) with which it is associated.

SELF TEST

The following questions will help you measure your understanding of the material presented in this chapter. Read all the choices carefully because there might be more than one correct answer. The number of correct choices to make is stated in the question, as in the real SCWCD exam.

1. Which of the following patterns can reduce network overhead? (Choose one.)

   A. Model View Controller
   B. Business Delegate
   C. Service Locator
   D. Transfer Object
   E. All of the above
   F. B, C, and D above

2. Which pattern insulates the presentation client code from volatility in business APIs? (Choose one.)

   A. Business Delegate
   B. Service Layer
   C. Service Delegate
   D. Service Locator
   E. Model View Controller
   F. Business Service Locator

3. A company has a message queuing system, accessible with complex Java APIs. The company wants a new web application but also wants to minimize the specialized knowledge required to write business code that accesses the queuing system. Which J2EE patterns might best help the company with this problem? (Choose two.)

   A. Front Controller
   B. Front Director
   C. Business Controller
   D. Service Locator
   E. View Controller
   F. Business Delegate

4. From the following list, choose benefits that are usually conferred by the Transfer Object pattern. (Choose two.)

   A. Reduces network traffic

   B. Packages data into an accessible form

   C. Decreases client memory use

   D. Reduces code dependencies

   E. Simplifies EJB development

5. A company wants to structure its development department on specialist lines so that web designers can concentrate on page layout and Java developers can concentrate on business API development. Which pattern should the company use in application development to best support its organizational aims? (Choose one.)

   A. Service Locator

   B. View Helper

   C. Intercepting Filter

   D. Model View Controller

   E. Front Controller

   F. View Controller

6. From the following list, choose benefits that are usually conferred by the Service Locator pattern. (Choose two.)

   A. Acts as a wrapper around business API calls

   B. Reduces strain on the Business Delegate pattern

   C. Encapsulates naming service code

   D. Bridges gaps to non-Java (web services aware) platforms

   E. Caches business data

7. Which of the following patterns might best be used to reject requests from a host machine with "uk" in its domain name? (Choose one.)

   A. Front Controller

   B. Business Delegate

   C. Authentication Guard

   D. Request Analyzer

   E. Intercepting Filter

   F. Service Locator

8. From the following list, choose benefits that are usually conferred by the Model View Controller pattern. (Choose two.)

   A. Insulation from volatility in business APIs
   B. Reduced EJB code
   C. Better graphical representation of information
   D. Decreased code complexity
   E. Separation of concerns
   F. Better project management

9. Which of the following patterns might be used to dispatch a view containing an application-friendly error message? (Choose one.)

   A. Business Delegate
   B. Front Controller
   C. Model View Controller
   D. View Controller
   E. Business Handler

10. From the following list, choose benefits that are usually conferred by the Business Delegate pattern. (Choose two.)

    A. Presentation code stability
    B. Less JNDI code
    C. Less layering
    D. Better business models
    E. Simplified EJB code
    F. Better network performance

11. Which scenario below could best use Transfer Object as a solution? (Choose one.)

    A. An application needs to have its navigation rationalized—at the moment, JSPs have URLs pointing to other JSPs, and the naming is nonstandard throughout.
    B. Some developers inexperienced with EJBs are having trouble calling business routines throughout a large application.
    C. An application appears to have hit a bottleneck when using some EJBs. On analysis, it appears that there are numerous method calls to retrieve individual attributes.
    D. An application appears to have hit a bottleneck through excessive calls to the JNDI naming service fronting an RMI registry.

12. From the following list, choose benefits that are usually conferred by the Front Controller pattern. (Choose three.)

    A. Imposes JSPs as views
    B. Reduces network traffic
    C. Adds a single point of failure
    D. Acts a gateway for requests to the system
    E. Centralizes control of navigation
    F. Reduces complexity of links in JSPs

13. Which of the patterns below will definitely reduce the lines of code in an application? (Choose one.)

    A. Front Controller
    B. Front View
    C. Model View Controller
    D. Intercepting Filter
    E. None of the above

14. From the following list, choose reasonable applications for the Intercepting Filter pattern. (Choose one.)

    A. Re-encoding request or response data
    B. Unzipping uploaded files
    C. Authenticating requests
    D. Invalidating sessions
    E. All of the above
    F. A, B, and C above
    G. A and B above

15. Which of the patterns below might reduce the lines of code in an application? (Choose one.)

    A. Business Delegate
    B. Service Locator
    C. Intercepting Filter
    D. All of the above

LAB QUESTION

Write your own application that uses all the patterns in this chapter. Of course, you have been working with my solution to this throughout the chapter.

SELF TEST ANSWERS

1. ☑ **F** is the correct answer. Business Delegate can reduce network overhead by caching results of executing business methods (where appropriate). Service Locator can cache references to remote objects to avoid making repeated networked calls to (mostly) JNDI code. Transfer Object collects together lots of data that might otherwise be garnered by repeated network calls.
   ☒ **A** is incorrect—Model View Controller is about the separation of concerns and doesn't directly address any network issues. **B**, **C**, and **D** are all patterns that contribute to reducing network overhead, but no one of these answers is correct on its own. **E** is incorrect because MVC is included in the list.

2. ☑ **A** is the correct answer—Business Delegate wraps business APIs. If the business APIs change, it may be unnecessary to change the interfaces that Business Delegate offers to clients in the presentation tier.
   ☒ **B**, **C**, and **F** are incorrect are they are made-up pattern names. **D** is incorrect—Service Locator is used by Business Delegate, so it shouldn't be directly exposed to presentation client code. **E** is incorrect because the Model View Controller doesn't specify how the Controller (the presentation client code in the question) should be kept at arm's length from the model.

3. ☑ **D** and **F** are the correct answers. The Service Locator pattern can be used to isolate the code that finds references to the objects that give access to the queuing system. The Business Delegate pattern can be used to translate simple method calls (used by the business code) into the complex method calls required by the queuing system.
   ☒ **A** is incorrect: Front Controller doesn't address complexity at the model end. **B**, **C**, and **E** are incorrect because they have made-up or incomplete pattern names.

4. ☑ **A** and **B** are the correct answers. Transfer Object can reduce network traffic by encouraging a call to one coarse-grained method instead of repeated calls to lots of fine-grained remote methods. Transfer Object also packages data in a convenient and simple bean-like form.
   ☒ **C** is incorrect—potentially, bulky Transfer Objects could increase client memory usage rather than reducing it. **D** is incorrect—Transfer Object doesn't reduce code dependencies; it permeates several layers, so it increases them instead. **E** is incorrect—the Transfer Object pattern implies increased work at the EJB development end: to define Transfer Objects and supply `getData()` and `setData()` methods, for example.

5. ☑ **D** is the correct answer. Model View Controller helps separate presentation and business concerns in a design sense, and this can support the organization of projects in the way described.

☒ **A** is incorrect—Service Locator is a refinement of the Java development side. **B** is incorrect—there is a pattern called View Helper, but it's a refinement of Model View Controller, so it's not central to the issue at hand. The same goes for answer **E**, Front Controller. **C** is incorrect—Intercepting Filter is independent of separating view and model development management. Finally, **F** is wrong—there is no such thing as the View Controller pattern.

6. ☑ **B** and **C**. The Service Locator pattern is often used in conjunction with Business Delegate, to take from it the responsibility of encapsulating naming service code.
   ☒ **A** is incorrect—wrapping business API calls is actually the responsibility of the Business Delegate pattern. **D** is incorrect, for there is nothing particular about Service Locator regarding web services. There is potential for using a Service Locator to front the finding of a web service, but it's not a benefit that can be described as being "usually conferred" by the pattern. Finally, **E** is incorrect—again, it's Business Delegate that may cache business data. Service Locator can cache things—usually references to remote objects that don't then have to be looked up again through the naming service.

7. ☑ **E** is correct. An Intercepting Filter could be used to check the remote host and block the request before it gets any farther into the application.
   ☒ **A** is incorrect, though certainly possible—a Front Controller could perform this task. However, for this particular sort of blanket authentication, I would judge that Intercepting Filter is a better choice—and the question wanted the best pattern. **C** and **D** are incorrect, for the names are made up. **B** and **F** are correct pattern names, but not right at all for this task.

8. ☑ **E** and **F**. Model View Controller is all about separation of concerns: different components dedicated to different aspects. Though a more contentious claim, Model View Controller can also lead to better project management, for different specialists (graphics programmers, business API experts) can concentrate on their own areas.
   ☒ **A** is incorrect—Business Delegate leads to insulation from business API volatility. **B** is incorrect—MVC has nothing to say about the amount of EJB code. **C** is incorrect—MVC doesn't dictate how information is represented graphically. It might improve as a result of separating concerns, but that's a by-product—not a stated benefit of the pattern. **D** is incorrect, for MVC might actually increase code complexity because it is a more complex framework to work within than simple JSPs accessing data with JSTL SQL custom actions, for example.

9. ☑ **B** is correct. Front Controller is used to dispatch to views in general—so it is the best choice for redirecting to an error page.
   ☒ **A** is incorrect—although Business Delegate might return an application-friendly exception from one of its methods, it shouldn't be used to dispatch to a view. **C** is incorrect—Model View Controller is not specific enough (it's the controller part we are interested in only). **D** and **E** are incorrect, for they are not valid pattern names.

10. ☑ **A** and **F** are the correct answers. The primary reason for using the Business Delegate pattern is to bring about presentation code stability. Presentation code is insulated from direct use of business APIs. Also, Business Delegate often brings about better network performance by caching data and avoiding calls to remote business objects if they don't need to be repeated.
☒ **B** is incorrect, for JNDI code is typically reduced by adopting the Service Locator pattern. **C** is incorrect, for Business Delegate introduces another layer into your code, so it increases layering. **D** is incorrect—nothing can improve business models except better analysis! **E** is incorrect, for Business Delegates—although they are liable to use EJBs—don't have any necessary effect on the way EJBs are coded.

11. ☑ **C** is the correct answer. Transfer Object could be used to collate the individual attributes on the EJB, so only one networked method call would be required to return all the attributes in one go.
☒ **A** is incorrect: Front Controller is used to rationalize navigation. **B** is incorrect—Business Delegate is used to encapsulate (and minimize) EJB method calls. **D** is incorrect—Service Locator is used to encapsulate (and minimize) JNDI calls.

12. ☑ **D**, **E**, and **F** are the correct answers. The Front Controller pattern does act as a gateway for requests, and it should be used to centralize control of navigation. It is also likely to reduce the complexity of links in JSPs; those links should all point to the Front Controller (preferably through an attribute set flexibly by the Front Controller itself).
☒ **A** is incorrect because the Front Controller pattern doesn't insist that you have to have JSPs for the view element: applets, Swing clients, or even other applications are valid view clients for the Front Controller. **B** is incorrect, for Front Controller makes no claim to reduce network traffic. **C** is incorrect—although Front Controller may become a single point of failure, this is hardly a benefit conferred by the pattern; it's more of a drawback.

13. ☑ **E** is the correct answer. None of the patterns listed will unequivocally decrease the number of lines of code in an application. Some may actually increase the lines of code (even though the code is likely to be in a much better organized state).
☒ **A** is incorrect—Front Controller may initially increase the number of components and lines of code. It could reduce navigation code where this is embedded in many different places, but not necessarily. **B** is incorrect—Front View doesn't exist. **C** is incorrect—again, Model View Controller may increase code, especially when first introduced. **D** is incorrect, for Intercepting Filter may just fulfill an additional requirement in the application. It may reduce code where it takes over from code that has been copied and pasted into many separate points of entry into an application.

14. ☑ **E** is the correct answer. All the applications listed in answers **A** through to **D** are reasonable applications for the Intercepting Filter pattern. Re-encoding and unzipping tasks

are the classic province of filters. It is reasonable to use a filter to perform some form of authentication. Equally, you might use a filter to invalidate a session—perhaps as the result of an authentication or authorization check.

☒ A, B, C, D, F, and G are incorrect answers based on the reasoning in the correct answer.

15. ☑ D is the correct answer—all of the above. Because the question (rephrased from question 13) is which patterns *might* reduce code, then all the patterns listed could do this. Business Delegate can ultimately reduce code by locating EJB method calls in one place. Because an EJB method call will have many lines of code just for exception handling, these multiply when distributed across all the presentation code that might make EJB method calls. Service Locator can reduce code in the same way, mainly for JNDI method calls. Finally, Intercepting Filter (as noted in question 13 as well) may reduce code by locating some functionality in one place that might otherwise be copied into (for example) all the servlets in an application.

☒ A, B, and C are incorrect answers according to the reasoning in the correct answer.

LAB ANSWER

The lab answer is in the CD at sourcecode/ch10/lab10.war. This is the example application that was used throughout the chapter—detailed instructions on its deployment can be found at the beginning of the chapter.

A

About the CD

The CD-ROM included with this book comes complete with MasterExam, the electronic version of the book, and the solution code for the exercises in the book. The software is easy to install on any Windows 98/NT/2000/XP computer and must be installed to access the MasterExam feature. You may, however, browse the electronic book and solution code directly from the CD without installation. To register for a second bonus MasterExam, simply click the Online Training link on the Main Page and follow the directions for the free online registration.

System Requirements

Software requires Windows 98 or higher and Internet Explorer 5.0 or above and 20 MB of hard disk space for full installation. The electronic book requires Adobe Acrobat Reader.

Installing and Running MasterExam

If your computer CD-ROM drive is configured to auto run, the CD-ROM will automatically start up upon inserting the disk. From the opening screen you may install MasterExam by pressing the *MasterExam* button. This will begin the installation process and create a program group named "LearnKey." To run MasterExam use START | PROGRAMS | LEARNKEY. If the auto run feature does not launch your CD, browse to the CD and click the "LaunchTraining.exe" icon.

MasterExam

MasterExam provides you with a simulation of the actual exam. The number of questions, the types of questions, and the time allowed are intended to be an accurate representation of the exam environment. You have the option to take an open-book exam, including hints, references, and answers; a closed-book exam; or the timed MasterExam simulation.

When you launch MasterExam, a digital clock display will appear in the upper left-hand corner of your screen. The clock will continue to count down to zero unless you choose to end the exam before the time expires.

Electronic Book

The entire contents of the Study Guide are provided in PDF. Adobe's Acrobat Reader has been included on the CD.

Solution Code

The solution code is supplied as a collection of WAR files. Full instructions on the installation and use of WAR files can be found in Appendix B.

Help

A help file is provided through the help button on the main page in the lower left-hand corner. An individual help feature is also available through MasterExam.

Removing Installation(s)

MasterExam is installed to your hard drive. For *best* results for removal of the programs, use the START | PROGRAMS | LEARNKEY | UNINSTALL options to remove MasterExam.

Technical Support

For questions regarding the technical content of the electronic book, source code, or MasterExam, please visit www.osborne.com or email customer.service@mcgraw-hill.com. For customers outside the 50 United States, email international_cs@mcgraw-hill.com.

LearnKey Technical Support

For technical problems with the software (installation, operation, removing installations), please visit www.learnkey.com or email techsupport@learnkey.com.

B

General Exercise Instructions

The exercises in the book almost all involve building and deploying web applications. This appendix tells you what you will need to complete the exercises and covers

- What software you need and where to get it
- How to create a directory structure for your web applications and where to put the files you create
- How to set up your environment to compile Java source
- Where to put other files related to your web applications
- How to package your web applications
- How to deploy your web applications on the Tomcat application server
- How to make the supplied solutions work and how to inspect the source code

Downloading and Installing Software

There are three things you will need:

1. Java2 Standard Edition (J2SDK), version 1.4.2
2. Java2 Enterprise Edition (J2EE), version 1.4
3. Tomcat application server

When you download the Java2 Enterprise Edition (item 2 in the preceding list), you will have the opportunity to download the J2SDK (item 1 in the list) at the same time. So if you don't already have J2SDK 1.4.2, this might be a good option for you. Both of these pieces of software are available from Sun:

- J2SDK 1.4.2: http://java.sun.com/j2se/1.4.2/index.jsp
- J2EE 1.4: http://java.sun.com/j2ee/1.4/download.html#sdk

You should download

- All of J2SDK 1.4.2.
- Only the Platform API Documentation for J2EE 1.4 (include J2SDK 1.4.2 as well if you have not downloaded this separately). You won't need Sun's Application Server or the J2EE 1.4 SDK examples for the purposes of this book (though you're welcome, or course, to download everything anyway).

Follow Sun's download and installation instructions for your platform (this is a very straightforward process).

Tomcat is a freely available, open-source application server from Jakarta Project, part of the Apache Source Foundation. It also (still) advertises itself as the official reference implementation for Java Servlet and JavaServer Pages technologies. This may seem a little at odds with Sun's J2EE site, which now supplies its own application server (Sun Java System Application Server Platform Edition 8.1 at the time of writing). I've chosen to go with Tomcat for the purposes of this book. My opinion is that it's been around longer, has better documentation, and is a bit easier to use than the Sun equivalent. And since it seems to retain its status as an official reference implementation (so should behave exactly as the examiners expect), I'm happier recommending it. Of course, you can choose to do your own thing—use the Sun reference implementation instead, or perhaps a commercial application server like BEA's Weblogic or IBM's WebSphere. However, you'll have to adapt the instructions here and elsewhere in the book to suit. While I take care to point out when a description is server specific (so not part of the exam syllabus) as opposed to core J2EE behavior, this appendix and the exercise instructions rather assume that Tomcat is your deployment platform.

Tomcat can be downloaded by taking a link from the product's home page, which is http://jakarta.apache.org/tomcat/index.html. Version 5.0.n is the best to use for your exam preparation. I've used 5.0.27 in this book, but also cross-checked all the solution code on Tomcat 5.5. The reason for not using Tomcat 5.5 is that you should ideally run it on a 1.5.0 JDK (without exploiting any of the new language features). However, if you do decide to use Tomcat 5.5, you can adapt it to run on J2SE 1.4.2, but you will need to pay careful attention to the release notes (particularly the file RUNNING.txt). In all events, Tomcat is easy to install—just follow its simple installation instructions.

Creating a Directory Structure for Web Applications

As discussed in Chapter 2, J2EE web applications adhere to a fairly strict directory structure. Here's how I suggest you organize directories to perform the exercises in the book.

1. Create a top-level directory for all your exercise work, for example, C:\WebCert.
2. Within this, create a directory that represents the chapter and exercise number within the chapter as you come to it. The convention I follow throughout (in the solution files as well) is exCCEE, where "ex" is constant,

"CC" is the number of the chapter (01 for Chapter 1, 02 for Chapter 2, etc.), and "EE" is the number of the exercise (01 for the first exercise in a chapter, 02 for the second, and so on). So the first exercise in the sixth chapter has a dedicated directory called C:\WebCert\ex0601. This is equivalent to the context directory in the deployed web application. You can use the same naming convention for the context directory as I do—but do something different if you want to deploy your own code and the solution code side by side on the Tomcat server.

3. Within this, create a WEB-INF subdirectory (e.g., C:\WebCert\ex0601\WEB-INF).
4. With the WEB-INF subdirectory, create three subdirectories: classes, lib, and src: C:\WebCert\ex0601\WEB-INF\classes, C:\WebCert\ex0601\lib, and C:\WebCert\ex0601\src in our example. The following illustration shows the complete example structure.

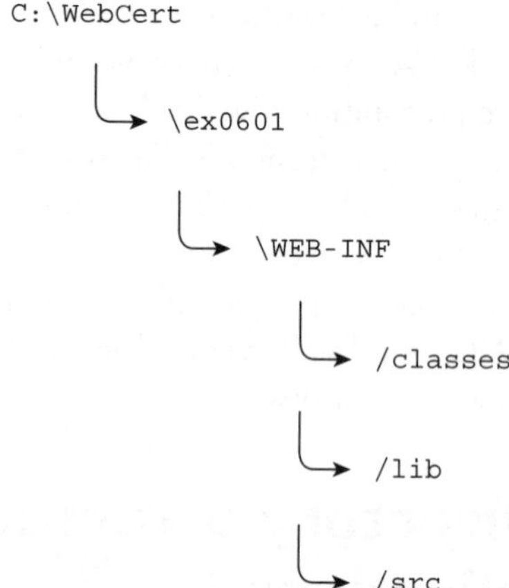

You'll place Java source for servlets and any supporting classes in the WEB-INF\src subdirectory for a given exercise's context directory. If you are using package names, you'll need to create the relevant subdirectories under WEB-INF\src to support these. My solution files follow this package structure: webcert.chCC.exCCEE, where CC is the chapter number and EE is the exercise number within the chapter (zero prefixed). Therefore, the last element of the package name is the same as the context directory. You can use the same naming convention or use your own.

When I say "if you are using package names," it's not really an option in J2EE 1.4. The so-called "default package" is disallowed—and quite right, too. Whatever

Java source you're writing, there's no excuse for not providing a package structure! Although some JSP containers will let you get away with using the default package, I suggest you get into good habits from the start. As a bonus for me telling you this, note that the package name topic might come up in the exam!

Compiling Java Source

Having placed your web application source in the relevant directory, compiling from a command line is no different from normal Java projects. First change to the src directory for the web application you're working on. For example,

```
cd C:\WebCert\examp0401\WEB-INF\src
```

Since most of what you will be doing relies on servlet technology, however, you will have to ensure that the base J2EE servlet packages are available on your class path. These will live with your Tomcat installation in <tomcat-installation-directory>/common/lib/servlet-api.jar. For example, on my Windows machine, I set the classpath as follows:

```
set classpath=.;C:\Java\jakarta-tomcat-5.0.27\common\lib\
servlet-api.jar
```

To compile a Java source file (servlet or otherwise),

- Switch to the src directory under WEB-INF for the context directory for the exercise or lab.
- Enter a compilation command in the form

```
javac your/package/structure/YourServlet.java -d ..\classes
```

By using `-d ..\classes`, the compiled class files will be placed in the classes directory under WEB-INF.

Other Files

Any other files you need to create for the exercise should be placed in the web application directory structure as indicated by the exercise instructions. For example,

- web.xml—the web application deployment descriptor—will live directly in the WEB-INF directory.
- JavaServer Pages will normally live in the context directory of your web application directory structure (the one above WEB-INF, e.g., ex0601).

Packaging Web Applications

So you have your compiled code and other related files. The next thing you need to do is to package up your web application for deployment on a suitable server such as Tomcat. To do this, you use the `jar` utility to create a java archive, with the subtle difference that you call the resulting file a .war file (web archive). Web archive files are fully described in Chapter 2, but for now all you need to know is how to create one.

Suppose the name of the exercise context directory is ex0601. On a command line, navigate to the directory above this (C:\WebCert). Then enter the following:

```
jar cvf0 ex0601.war ex0601
```

This creates an archive file called ex0601.war in C:\WebCert, which contains the full contents of the C:\WebCert\ex0601 directory (including all the sub-directories and files within them).

Deploying Web Applications on Tomcat

Under Tomcat, deploying is the easy part. You'll need to follow the Tomcat documentation so you are at least familiar with starting and stopping the Tomcat server and looking at the Tomcat server console. Beyond that, the default behavior of Tomcat (for a new installation) is to automatically deploy web applications. All you have to do is to put the .war file you just created in the right place, which is <tomcat installation directory>/webapps. With the Tomcat application server started, you will see two things happen. First, messages appear in the console to denote that your application is being installed, as shown in the following illustration:

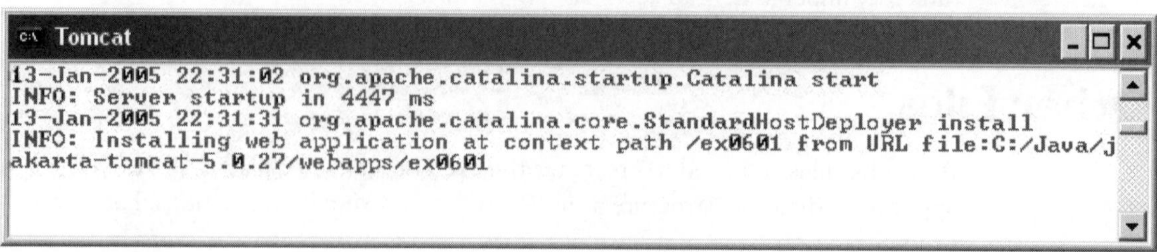

Second, your .war file is "un-jarred" (unzipped) into its own directory structure under <tomcat installation directory>/webapps. The structure will mirror exactly the one you built in your development area C:\WebCert.

At this point, your application is ready to run. Again by default, Tomcat listens for your requests on port 8080 on the PC on which it is installed. Assuming you are running your browser on the same PC, you can access resources in your web application with a URL such as the following:

```
http://localhost:8080/<context name>/<resource name>
```

Therefore, if the context is ex0601 and the resource you want to access is called lifecycle.jsp, then the URL would be

```
http://localhost:8080/ex0601/lifecycle.jsp
```

If you get an HTTP 404 (page not found) error in your browser, then check the following:

- You spelled everything correctly, including using the correct upper- and lowercase letters.
- You have an appropriate `<servlet-mapping>` in web.xml (see Chapter 2).
- The application deployed correctly: There are no errors in the Tomcat server console window.
- The resource you're after has actually been expanded into the directory.

An HTTP 500 error indicates a Java problem running your servlet or server page—the error may show up in your browser window, or you may need to look for errors in the Tomcat server console window.

Tomcat is smart about recognizing when a .war file has been updated. Therefore, if you re-deploy a new .war to the webapps directory, overwriting one with an earlier date, Tomcat will elegantly close the current version of the application and deploy the new one.

In some of the earlier exercises, you bypass the steps of making and deploying the WAR file. On Tomcat, you can get away with copying the working directory structure for your application to the webapps directory. After a server restart, Tomcat will recognize your new application. However, this is more of a workaround until you are comfortable with WAR file creation—later exercises (from around Chapter 3) expect you to make WAR files from your working directories and deploy them, instead of copying your working directories directly to the Tomcat webapps directory.

Solution Code

The solution code for each of the exercises and the labs can be found on the CD. There's a .war file for almost every one (for the handful where this isn't true, the exercise is not directly code based). Deploying the solution code follows the same pattern as for your own code: Place each .war file as needed in <tomcat-installation-directory>/webapps. The .war will automatically expand and deploy. Look in the directory structure (under WEB-INF/src) for the accompanying Java source code, wherever appropriate.

Using Your Own IDE

What I've outlined here uses the most basic, but most commonly available development tooling — the command line facilities of the J2SDK. There is no compulsion to do this. If you are already familiar with an integrated development environment that supports servlet and JavaServer Page development and deployment, by all means use it. I freely confess that I haven't used the J2SDK in preparation of this book: I worked with the open-source Eclipse Java IDE, in combination with a plug-in called Lomboz, which facilitates J2EE web application development. Lomboz is freely available from http://www.objectlearn.com.

There are dangers in using an IDE to learn a technology for certification — their ease-of-use features sometimes obscure what you need to know for an exam. For example: IBM's Rational Application Developer has a sophisticated graphical user interface for manipulating the information in the web deployment descriptor, web.xml. For the exam, though, you must be familiar with web.xml in its naked, textual form. (And much to the credit of IBM Rational Application Developer, you have the choice to switch to a "source level" view of web.xml and edit it as a text file in tandem with the GUI approach.)

Some certification books take a purist approach and suggest that you avoid IDEs altogether for technology-learning purposes. I take a more pragmatic stance — do whatever you're comfortable with. Use the tools if you're already familiar with them and you're aware of the areas where the tools do too much for you. If you don't use tools already, or would rather avoid them while learning, work at ground level with a text editor and the J2SDK.

Glossary

Absolute Path A path describing where a file is located, described from the root of the file system. The ServletContext object has a method called `getRealPath()` that returns an absolute path from a partial path pointing to a resource within a web application.

Absolute URL A URL that fully describes the path to a resource, including protocol and host information—for example, `http://mywebhost:9080/mywebapp/myresource.jsp`.

Action JavaServer Pages contain actions that are elements in the page source expressed in XML syntax. During translation of the JavaServer Page, an action is transformed into Java source code placed in the `_jspService()` method of the generated servlet. An action has an opening tag, closing tag, and body (in some cases, the body is absent). Actions are grouped into standard actions (which must be supported by a J2EE-compliant JSP container) and custom actions (which share the syntax and mechanisms of standard actions, but are optionally present within a JSP container or web application). Custom actions are frequently referred to as custom tags.

application An implicit variable, available within JavaServer Page source, which represents the ServletContext object for a web application.

Application Scope The available lifetime for attributes associated with an entire web application—from the point where a web application starts up to the point where the web application is stopped (these points often coincide with application server startup and shutdown).

Application Server A body of software that is capable of running J2EE applications. An application server can be expected to have at least the following features:

- The ability to respond to different kinds of requests from different kinds of clients
- The ability to return responses
- A web container for housing web applications
- An EJB container for providing life cycle support to Enterprise JavaBeans
- Other services: naming support (JNDI), database access support (JDBC), security support, and so on

Commercial application servers include IBM WebSphere and BEA WebLogic. Open-source application servers include Tomcat, JBoss, and Apache Geronimo.

Attribute A piece of information held as a name and a value. Attributes occur in two main places in web applications:

1. When attaching information to any of the four scopes in a web application: page, request, session, or application. Methods exist to read and write attributes that comprise a name (any String) and a value (any kind of Object).
2. Within XML (including the XML used to describe JSP actions) and HTML, attributes are frequently found in the opening tags of elements. These take the form name="value" (for example, `<c:set var="myVariable">myValue</c:set>`).

Authentication The process of validating a "principal" to a computer system. Principal is a general term meaning either a human user or another computer system. The principal supplies credentials to the security component of the target computer system, which accepts or rejects them according to its internal rules. Web applications have four types of authentication available: BASIC, FORM, DIGEST, and CLIENT-CERT.

Authorization After authentication has taken place, the process of authorization determines which resources a principal is allowed to use within a computer system. Web applications allow administrators to associate target resources with given roles. If a principal belongs to the given role, access is granted to the protected resource.

BASIC A form of authentication. BASIC authentication operates at the point where a principal first makes a request for a protected resource within a web application. The application server returns an HTTP response demanding credentials in the form of a user ID and password (typically, a browser will pop up a dialog box for the user to type these in). The user ID and password are only weakly encoded when transmitted back to the application server. Consequently, BASIC authentication should be used in conjunction with SSL.

Body In an HTML element or XML element (including JSP actions), the part that comes between the opening and closing tag. Here is an HTML example: <p>**This is the body of the paragraph element in HTML**</p>.

Business Delegate A design pattern that suggests providing a layer between presentation components and business components. This layer can perform several useful functions such as dealing with complex business component APIs, and their exceptions; simplifying the interface presentation code needs to make use of business services; and implementing retry and recovery code in the event of business service failure.

CGI *See* Common Gateway Interface.

Classic Tag Handler The original JavaServer Page standard for tag handler code. Classic tag handlers have a relatively complex life cycle, with a number of methods called by the JSP container in response to events such as processing the opening tag, the body, and the closing tag.

CLIENT-CERT A very secure form of authentication. On requesting a secure resource in a web application, the application server demands a digital certificate from the client. If the client returns a digital certificate that matches those known to the application server, authentication is granted.

Common Gateway Interface (CGI) One of the original standards for providing dynamic content within web pages. The standard defines how a World Wide Web server can interact with a program. Typically, the result of running such a program is to return data within web page output. Java web applications represent an improvement on CGI in performance and maintainability.

config An implicit object available within a JavaServer page of ServletConfig type, capable, for example, of returning initialization parameters associated with the JavaServer Page.

Container A piece of software that provides life cycle support to J2EE components. An application server typically contains several containers: a web container to run servlets and JavaServer Pages and an EJB container to run Enterprise JavaBeans.

Context The part of a URL that uniquely separates one web application from another installed on the same web application server.

Context Root The location of the top-level directory that houses one individual web application.

Cookie A short file (usually just a string of text) that can accompany an HTTP request or HTTP response. Used to pass information between clients and servers in web applications. Often, this information is for tracking purposes—to attach a session ID to a series of unrelated requests, for example.

Custom Action *See* Action.

Custom Tag *See* Action.

Declaration In a JavaServer Page, a declaration is a piece of code that contains complete method definitions (and—though not recommended—class or instance data members). The code is included within the servlet source file generated from the JavaServer Page source.

Declarative Security Security that is imposed by declaring information within a web application's deployment descriptor, rather than in program code.

DELETE This HTTP method deletes a resource at a target URL. Understandably, most web servers disallow execution of this method.

Deployment Descriptor A file used within a J2EE module to define its characteristics. For a web application, the deployment descriptor defines resource (servlet) names, resource mappings, security definitions, listeners, filters, welcome pages, error pages, dependent resources, and many other things. The deployment descriptor for a web application *must* be called web.xml and *must* be placed directly in the WEB-INF subdirectory.

Design Pattern A design blueprint for solving a particular problem within a computer application. Design patterns are most commonly associated with the object-oriented community. There is a set of design patterns exclusively associated with J2EE applications.

DIGEST A secure form of authentication, which unfortunately doesn't enjoy widespread support on web servers and within browser clients. A digest comprises a highly encrypted form of client credentials, which are useless to any third party who intercepts them. The challenging server receiving such credentials can, however, compare the encrypted digest with its own database of encrypted digest information, thereby allowing a user access to a protected resource.

Directive Directives can be placed within JavaServer Pages to control a number of aspects about the generation of the servlet source representing the JavaServer Page source. A good example is the `<%@ include ...%>` directive, which incorporates the contents of another file within the JavaServer Page at translation time. In their original syntax, directives can be recognized by the `<%@` characters at their beginning. There are now preferred XML equivalent syntaxes for directives used within a JavaServer Page.

Distributable A web application can be labeled as distributable by including the `<distributable />` element within the deployment descriptor. This indicates to the application server that the web application need not be confined to one JVM. If the application server supports distributable behavior, it may maintain multiple running copies of the web application across separate JVMs. This is usually for reasons of failure: If one of the web applications fails in one of the JVMs, the other copies will still run. One implication of distributable web applications is that session data for an individual user should be duplicated to all JVMs. The user can then experience continuity of service and no loss of data, even if a JVM terminates unexpectedly.

Document Type Definition (DTD) A file used to validate an XML file. The earlier servlet specification (level 2.3) defined DTDs for the deployment descriptor web.xml and tag library descriptor files.

DTD *See* **Document Type Definition.**

EJB *See* **Enterprise JavaBean.**

EL *See* **Expression Language.**

Element In XML and HTML, the fundamental building block, potentially comprising a starting tag (with attributes), a body, and a closing tag. For example:

```
<p class="fancy">This is an element</p>
```

Enterprise JavaBean (EJB) An Enterprise JavaBean is a J2EE business component. EJBs need an EJB container (typically part of a larger application server) to support their life cycle and other requirements.

Entity Bean A kind of EJB that is associated with persistent data—data that doesn't go away even when the application server containing the EJB is shut down. This typically means that an entity bean is associated with a relational database table (though any other form of persistent storage is acceptable as far as the J2EE specification is concerned). An application server provides its own mechanisms for mapping the properties of an entity bean to elements of the persistent storage mechanism (such as tuples in a relational table).

Error Page A page defined with the deployment descriptor for a web application. The page can be associated with an HTTP error code (such as 404: page not found) or a Java exception (such as javax.servlet.ServletException). If the defined HTTP error code or Java exception occurs within a request, the corresponding error page is displayed to the user.

exception An implicit object available in a JavaServer Page that is designated as an error page (by setting the isErrorPage of a page directive to a value of true). The exception object is of type java.lang.Throwable and therefore might be used, for example, to obtain stack traces.

Expression Within a JavaServer Page, an expression is a piece of Java code that results in direct output to the response.

Expression Language (EL) An entire syntax independent of the Java language. EL can be placed in JavaServer Pages to display the output of simple expressions. EL is a preferred alternative to using Java language syntax in normal expressions.

Extended Markup Language (XML) A standard for writing text files to contain data in a structured way. Data is held between opening and closing tags. Tags can be nested inside one another in a hierarchical fashion. XML is used for all the key configuration files in a web application, such as the deployment descriptor file and tag library descriptors. XML (or XML-like syntax) is also used for much of JavaServer Page syntax. JSP documents are JavaServer Pages written entirely in XML.

Filter An object within a web application that can manipulate a request before it reaches the desired resource, and/or change a response before it is returned to the requester. Typical uses for filters include auditing, logging, transforming, encrypting, de-encrypting, and enforcing security rules.

Filter Chain A filter chain is produced when a request hits the outskirts of a web application. The filters that are applicable to the request (as determined by URL mapping) comprise the filter chain, and are ordered according to their order of appearance in the deployment descriptor.

`<form>` In HTML, a form can be defined to receive data input from a user. The importance for web applications is that the named fields within the form (defined with HTML tags such as the `<input>` tag) result in request parameters that can be interpreted by servlets and JavaServer Pages.

FORM A type of authentication used by web containers as a cosmetic improvement on BASIC authentication. As an alternative to the browser dialog box, a web page is presented for user ID and password entry.

Forward If one resource (JSP or servlet) forwards to another, it is giving responsibility to the other resource for returning a response. Forwarding actions are usually implemented by a RequestDispatcher object.

Front Controller A design pattern whereby a component (usually a servlet) acts as a gateway for requests. This component usually takes responsibility for centralized actions, especially controlling navigation between resources.

GET An HTTP method that requests the return of a resource from a specified URL.

HEAD An HTTP method that requests the header information (metadata) for a resource from a specified URL. HEAD should return everything that is returned by GET, except for the resource itself.

HTTP Methods An HTTP method is a mandatory component of an HTTP request. There are seven bona fide HTTP methods that can be associated with HTTP requests: GET, POST, PUT, DELETE, HEAD, OPTIONS, and TRACE.

HttpSession Objects implementing the javax.servlet.http.HttpSession interface are created within web containers to overcome the connectionless nature of HTTP. They act as a repository of data that needs to be remembered between requests from an individual user's browser session.

HyperText Markup Language (HTML) The language used to construct web pages. Although primarily used for formatting text, HTML defines some tags that control interactivity in the web client. *See* **`<form>`**.

HyperText Transfer Protocol (HTTP) A high-level communications protocol situated above Transmission Control Protocol and Internet Protocol (TCP/IP). HTTP is the conduit for most requests on the Internet. The protocol works through requests and responses. Communication between two computers is not meant to be continuous: An interaction typically lasts for one request and one response (it's a connectionless protocol). A whole layer of servlet design (in the javax.servlet.http package) is dedicated to the interpretation and control of HTTP requests and responses. Each HTTP request contains an HTTP method, which can be trapped by a servlet method: GET by `doGet()`, POST by `doPost()`, and so on.

Idempotent An action that can be repeated without causing any additional changes. Therefore, "read-only" actions such as an HTTP GET are idempotent. However, idempotent methods are not restricted to "read-only." An HTTP PUT, which places a file on the remote server, is also thought of as idempotent because even when the action is repeated for the same file, the end result will be the same as after the first action. The only nonidempotent method is, in fact, POST. (The idempotent methods are GET, PUT, DELETE, OPTIONS, TRACE, and HEAD.)

Implicit Objects In the context of JavaServer Pages, implicit objects are local variables within the `_jspService()` method. Each one represents a significant object in the servlet environment. There are nine in all: *request*, *response*, *out*, *config*, *application*, *session*, *page*, *pageContext* and *exception* (all are defined within this glossary). Implicit objects can be used directly by page authors in, for example, Java scriptlets. Implicit objects are also used liberally by the web container as it generates (nonscriptlet) servlet code for a JavaServer Page.

Implicit Variables *See* **Implicit Objects**.

Include The process of including another resource within the including resource's response output. Within web applications, this can be achieved in several ways. An include directive will include other resources in a static way, at the point where a JavaServer Page is translated into servlet source. Other forms of include, such as the `include()` method on a RequestDispatcher object and the JavaServer Page `<jsp:include>` custom action, include resources in a dynamic way as each request is run.

Intercepting Filter A design pattern that describes an intercepting layer for trapping incoming requests and/or decorating (changing) outgoing responses. This design pattern is built into the servlet specification in a standard way. *See* **Filter**.

ISO (International Standards Organization) A body responsible for setting international standards. Character sets for encoding text are described by ISO standards. Of particular relevance to web applications is ISO-8859-1, the default Latin 1 encoding used for HTTP messages.

Java Archive File (JAR) A ZIP format file that contains any artifacts needed for a Java application. Within the context of the web application, a JAR file might contain classes that support the activity of other components such as JavaServer Pages.

Java Message Service A Java standard API (within J2EE) for communicating in a standard way over messaging middleware (e.g., IBM's MQSeries).

Java Naming and Directory Interface (JNDI) A standard within J2EE for locating resources that may be distributed over different JVMs and different computers within a network.

Java Virtual Machine (JVM) Software used to run Java code. A JVM transforms Java bytecode (class files) into executable statements for the target platform.

Java2 Enterprise Edition (J2EE) A set of Java technologies that augments the standard edition (J2SE). Primarily, J2EE brings together numerous standards and interfaces defining the behavior for enterprise applications written in Java. Some of the more important standards include servlets, JavaServer Pages (JSPs), Enterprise JavaBeans (EJBs), Java Naming and Directory Interface (JNDI), and Java Messaging Service (JMS).

JavaBean A simple standard for writing a Java class as an easily reusable component. JavaBeans are especially important for certain JSP custom actions—`<jsp:useBean>`, for example.

JavaServer Page (JSP) A text file consisting of native HTML or XML with embedded elements for dynamic content. The embedded elements can consist of script (typically in Java code), XML-like "tags," or a simple expression language (EL). JSPs usually have a .jsp file extension. Once installed in a web container, JavaServer Pages are subject to a "translation phase" that turns the entire JSP source into a Java servlet class.

JDBC JDBC describes Java's standard set of APIs for database access. The letters—officially—don't stand for anything.

JMS *See* **Java Message Service**.

JSP *See* **JavaServer Page**.

JSP Container *See* **Container**.

JSP Document A form of JavaServer Page source written entirely in XML syntax and often used to output XML files. JSP documents often have a .jspx file extension.

J2EE *See* **Java2 Enterprise Edition**.

JVM *See* **Java Virtual Machine**.

Listener An interface defining methods that can be called by a servlet container when some event occurs. Objects implementing some Listener interface or other can be declared in the web deployment descriptor. The servlet container manages a large range of events. Examples include adding, changing, or removing attributes; starting up or shutting down a web application; and moving a session from one JVM to another in a distributed application.

Local Variables Variables declared within a method or received as parameters to a method. These are of particular interest to web component developers because they are thread safe and are therefore a much better alternative to (say) servlet instance variables. Implicit objects are all defined as local variables in the `_jspService()` method.

MIME (Multipurpose Internet Mail Extensions) An Internet standard that defines message formats. Originally developed for email systems, but also embraced by browsers and web servers. The format is very flexible and extensible because MIME messages can embrace many different file types.

MVC (Model View Controller) A design pattern, which originated in the Smalltalk community, that separates display logic from the underlying data affecting the display.

OPTIONS An HTTP method that returns information about all the HTTP methods allowed for a target resource.

out An implicit object, of type javax.servlet.jsp.JspWriter, used for writing to the response associated with a JavaServer Page.

page An implicit object, of type java.lang.Object, that represents a JavaServer Page. Not typically used directly by JavaServer Page authors.

pageContext An implicit object, of type javax.servlet.jsp.PageContext, that acts as a "master" implicit object for its enclosing JavaServer Page. Most other implicit objects are derived from *pageContext*. Furthermore, *pageContext* is used to store attributes that exist in Page Scope.

Page Scope The scope within a JSP from the point where the request is received by that JSP, up to the end of the user request (or until an enclosing JSP or servlet is reached if this comes sooner).

Pattern *See* **Design Pattern**.

POST An HTTP method that sends data to be processed on a target web server. The results of a POST may be (and often are) of an "updating" nature—perhaps to some underlying database. Consequently, the POST method is not regarded as idempotent, nor is it safe: Users who launch a POST request should be made aware that they may be held accountable. POST has an advantage over GET in that any associated data is sent in the body of the HTTP request, not as part of the Query String. Consequently, data sent with the POST method can be of any length.

Programmatic Security Enforcing security rules through lines of code. J2EE prefers declarative security, but defines APIs to allow the inclusion of programmatic security where required.

PUT An HTTP method that places a resource at a target URL. This can be used as a mechanism for uploading files, although most servers disallow it, because any resource already on the server at the location designated by the target URL will be overwritten.

Query String A string suffixed to a URL that contains request parameters, and separated by a question mark from the rest of the URL. During execution of an HTTP GET method, form data is appended as request parameters to a query string.

Relative Path A path to a resource expressed in partial terms, such as an absolute path, but with information missing from the beginning. Web applications recognize two kinds of relative paths. Relative paths beginning with a forward slash (/) are interpreted as being relative to the context root of the web application. Relative paths without an initial forward slash are interpreted as relative to the location of the resource containing the relative path.

Relative URI A partial URL. A relative URI typically misses information from the beginning that would be present in an absolute URL, such as the protocol and host name. *See also* **Relative Path**.

request An implicit object, almost always of type javax.servlet.http.Http ServletRequest, that represents the HTTP request made to a JavaServer Page.

RequestDispatcher A RequestDispatcher object can be used to involve other objects (aside from the requested resource) in the production of a response to the user. It can either forward to other resources or include other resources within the current resource's output.

Request for Comments (RFC) A series of documents that have evolved into standards for the Internet, maintained by the Internet Engineering Task Force

(IETF: http://www.ietf.org). An RFC may begin as a suggestion and, if popular enough, be adopted as a concrete standard.

Request Parameter A piece of information with a name and a value passed within an HTTP request.

Request Scope The scope marked out by a single request to a web application—from the request's interception by a web application to its fulfillment.

response An implicit object, almost always of type javax.servlet.http.HttpServletResponse, that represents the HTTP response returned from a JavaServer Page.

RFC *See* **Request for Comments.**

Schema Definition File (XSD File) An XML file that provides rules about the way another XML document should be constructed. Such an XML file typically has a .xsd extension. In J2EE 2.0, key XML files (such as deployment descriptors and tag library definition files) are now validated against schema definition files. In J2EE 1.2, those same key XML files were validated against document type definition (DTD) files. Schema definition files are often referred to as XSD files.

Scope In web applications, the lifetime of variables (attributes) associated with different life cycle objects: page, request, session and context (application).

Scriptlet A piece of Java code embedded in a JavaServer Page. The code is placed directly in the `_jspService()` method of the servlet generated from the JavaServer Page source.

Service Locator A design pattern that works in conjunction with the Business Delegate design pattern. A Business Delegate component may offload certain responsibilities to a Service Locator—most notably, the code needed to find business services. This is usually (but doesn't have to be) JNDI code.

Servlet A Java program that can receive requests and provide responses to a range of clients. Most implementations of servlets provide for HTTP requests, typically originating from a web browser, and return HTTP responses, often in the form of web pages. A servlet needs a servlet container in which to run.

ServletConfig A Java object, of type javax.servlet.ServletConfig, created at the point where a servlet is instantiated. Its main role is to give the servlet access to initialization parameters defined in the deployment descriptor.

Servlet Container *See* Container.

ServletContext A Java object, of type javax.servlet.ServletContext, created at the point where a web application is started. Its role is to hold information and give access to APIs that pertain to the web application as a whole.

Session A series of interlinked requests.

session An implicit object that contains information about a connected series of requests to a web application (requests are usually deemed to be connected if they originate from the same browser session).

Session Scope The scope for attributes attached to the same session, thereby permitting a longer duration than the scope of an individual request.

Simple Tag An innovation in JSP 2.0 that simplifies the code needed for a tag handler. The number of life cycle events is radically reduced—effectively, responsibility for processing most tag events is handed back to the tag handler developer.

SSL (Secure Sockets Layer) A cryptographic protocol designed to provide secure communications on the Internet. It runs beneath protocols such as HTTP, but above the base TCP/IP transport layer.

Standard Action *See* Action.

Tag *See* Action.

Tag File A JSP-like file that is turned into a simple tag when deployed and used in a JSP container.

Tag Handler The Java class file that supports the operation of a custom tag placed in a JSP. Tag handler developers must select from among a number of possible interfaces when writing a tag handler class. The chosen interface determines the nature and number of life cycle methods that the JSP container calls within the tag handler class. Tag Handlers can be broadly subdivided into classic tag handlers and simple tag handlers.

Tag Library Descriptor (TLD) An XML file that defines the characteristics of custom elements that can be placed in JavaServer Pages. Traditionally, this means custom tags, but TLDs can now also be used to define other elements as well, including listeners, EL functions, and tag files.

taglib Directive A directive within a JavaServer Page that makes the listeners, EL functions, and custom tags within a tag library descriptor available as actions for use within the page.

Thread Safety Servlets are multithreaded by nature. Therefore, within a given servlet container, the same instance of a servlet may have several threads running within its `service()` method simultaneously. This means that local variables are much preferred for use within servlets.

TRACE An HTTP method that follows a request from its destination for the purpose of seeing if the request has been changed en route.

Transfer Object A design pattern that advises the use of simple JavaBean objects as parameters to and return types from remote Enterprise JavaBean methods. The purpose of this is to reduce and amalgamate the number of remote network calls required to return information from (or pass information to) an EJB object. This pattern was formerly known as the "value object" pattern in previous J2EE versions.

Translation In the context of JavaServer pages, the process that turns JavaServer page source into Java servlet source and then compiles this source into a servlet class.

Translation Unit An amalgam of a JavaServer Page, any pages statically included in that page, and any pages statically included in those pages (to the end of the static inclusion tree). The entire unit of JavaServer Page source that results is translated into one servlet.

Uniform Resource Indicator (URI) The generic name for a means of uniquely identifying a resource within the World Wide Web.

Uniform Resource Locator (URL) A string that targets a resource on the Internet, consisting of a protocol (e.g., http), host name (e.g., www.osborne.com), port number (e.g., 80), optional path (e.g., /myfiles), and file name (e.g., index.html, welcome.jsp). A URL is a specific type of URI.

URL Rewriting A way of associating all requests having to do with a given session, whereby some unique session ID is appended to all the URLs used in all the requests in the application. Cookies are a preferable way of achieving this aim, but not all client browsers permit the use of cookies.

Value Object *See* **Transfer Object**.

WAR File *See* **Web Archive**.

Web Application In J2EE terms, a web application is a deployable collection of web resources. It comprises many kinds of resources, including servlets, JavaServer Pages, and custom tags. It also supports Java classes, HTML pages, images (GIFs and JPEGs), and a deployment descriptor file. A web application obeys rigid rules about the formation of its directory structure and is often zipped for deployment into a WAR file. *See* **WEB-INF**.

Web Archive (WAR) A file in Java archive (zipped) format that contains all the artifacts comprising a web application.

Web Module A synonym for web application. Web modules are one of several kinds of J2EE modules (EJB modules are another). Several modules (of the same or different types) may be shipped together as part of the same enterprise application.

web.xml *See* **Deployment Descriptor**.

WEB-INF A special subdirectory within a web application. It contains artifacts to support the working of the web application: Servlet classes, support classes, and tag libraries should all live within WEB-INF or appropriate subdirectories (/WEB-INF/classes for servlet and support classes and /WEB-INF/lib for components within

JAR files). An application server must not allow direct access to /WEB-INF or its subdirectories.

Welcome Page A page defined for a web application that will be displayed when no specific resource in the application is requested (because the requesting URL contains only the context root for the web application).

XML *See* **Extended Markup Language**.

XSD *See* **Schema Definition File**.

INDEX

Italic page numbers indicate material in tables or figures. Page numbers followed by n refer to a footnote.

SYMBOLS

A

B

E

F

G

Q

R

S

T

U

V

W

X

Z

LICENSE AGREEMENT

THIS PRODUCT (THE "PRODUCT") CONTAINS PROPRIETARY SOFTWARE, DATA AND INFORMATION (INCLUDING DOCUMENTATION) OWNED BY THE McGRAW-HILL COMPANIES, INC. ("McGRAW-HILL") AND ITS LICENSORS. YOUR RIGHT TO USE THE PRODUCT IS GOVERNED BY THE TERMS AND CONDITIONS OF THIS AGREEMENT.

LICENSE: Throughout this License Agreement, "you" shall mean either the individual or the entity whose agent opens this package. You are granted a non-exclusive and non-transferable license to use the Product subject to the following terms:

(i) If you have licensed a single user version of the Product, the Product may only be used on a single computer (i.e., a single CPU). If you licensed and paid the fee applicable to a local area network or wide area network version of the Product, you are subject to the terms of the following subparagraph (ii).

(ii) If you have licensed a local area network version, you may use the Product on unlimited workstations located in one single building selected by you that is served by such local area network. If you have licensed a wide area network version, you may use the Product on unlimited workstations located in multiple buildings on the same site selected by you that is served by such wide area network; provided, however, that any building will not be considered located in the same site if it is more than five (5) miles away from any building included in such site. In addition, you may only use a local area or wide area network version of the Product on one single server. If you wish to use the Product on more than one server, you must obtain written authorization from McGraw-Hill and pay additional fees.

(iii) You may make one copy of the Product for back-up purposes only and you must maintain an accurate record as to the location of the back-up at all times.

COPYRIGHT; RESTRICTIONS ON USE AND TRANSFER: All rights (including copyright) in and to the Product are owned by McGraw-Hill and its licensors. You are the owner of the enclosed disc on which the Product is recorded. You may not use, copy, decompile, disassemble, reverse engineer, modify, reproduce, create derivative works, transmit, distribute, sublicense, store in a database or retrieval system of any kind, rent or transfer the Product, or any portion thereof, in any form or by any means (including electronically or otherwise) except as expressly provided for in this License Agreement. You must reproduce the copyright notices, trademark notices, legends and logos of McGraw-Hill and its licensors that appear on the Product on the back-up copy of the Product which you are permitted to make hereunder. All rights in the Product not expressly granted herein are reserved by McGraw-Hill and its licensors.

TERM: This License Agreement is effective until terminated. It will terminate if you fail to comply with any term or condition of this License Agreement. Upon termination, you are obligated to return to McGraw-Hill the Product together with all copies thereof and to purge all copies of the Product included in any and all servers and computer facilities.

DISCLAIMER OF WARRANTY: THE PRODUCT AND THE BACK-UP COPY ARE LICENSED "AS IS." McGRAW-HILL, ITS LICENSORS AND THE AUTHORS MAKE NO WARRANTIES, EXPRESS OR IMPLIED, AS TO THE RESULTS TO BE OBTAINED BY ANY PERSON OR ENTITY FROM USE OF THE PRODUCT, ANY INFORMATION OR DATA INCLUDED THEREIN AND/OR ANY TECHNICAL SUPPORT SERVICES PROVIDED HEREUNDER, IF ANY ("TECHNICAL SUPPORT SERVICES"). McGRAW-HILL, ITS LICENSORS AND THE AUTHORS MAKE NO EXPRESS OR IMPLIED WARRANTIES OF MERCHANTABILITY OR FITNESS FOR A PARTICULAR PURPOSE OR USE WITH RESPECT TO THE PRODUCT. McGRAW-HILL, ITS LICENSORS, AND THE AUTHORS MAKE NO GUARANTEE THAT YOU WILL PASS ANY CERTIFICATION EXAM WHATSOEVER BY USING THIS PRODUCT. NEITHER McGRAW-HILL, ANY OF ITS LICENSORS NOR THE AUTHORS WARRANT THAT THE FUNCTIONS CONTAINED IN THE PRODUCT WILL MEET YOUR REQUIREMENTS OR THAT THE OPERATION OF THE PRODUCT WILL BE UNINTERRUPTED OR ERROR FREE. YOU ASSUME THE ENTIRE RISK WITH RESPECT TO THE QUALITY AND PERFORMANCE OF THE PRODUCT.

LIMITED WARRANTY FOR DISC: To the original licensee only, McGraw-Hill warrants that the enclosed disc on which the Product is recorded is free from defects in materials and workmanship under normal use and service for a period of ninety (90) days from the date of purchase. In the event of a defect in the disc covered by the foregoing warranty, McGraw-Hill will replace the disc.

LIMITATION OF LIABILITY: NEITHER McGRAW-HILL, ITS LICENSORS NOR THE AUTHORS SHALL BE LIABLE FOR ANY INDIRECT, SPECIAL OR CONSEQUENTIAL DAMAGES, SUCH AS BUT NOT LIMITED TO, LOSS OF ANTICIPATED PROFITS OR BENEFITS, RESULTING FROM THE USE OR INABILITY TO USE THE PRODUCT EVEN IF ANY OF THEM HAS BEEN ADVISED OF THE POSSIBILITY OF SUCH DAMAGES. THIS LIMITATION OF LIABILITY SHALL APPLY TO ANY CLAIM OR CAUSE WHATSOEVER WHETHER SUCH CLAIM OR CAUSE ARISES IN CONTRACT, TORT, OR OTHERWISE. Some states do not allow the exclusion or limitation of indirect, special or consequential damages, so the above limitation may not apply to you.

U.S. GOVERNMENT RESTRICTED RIGHTS: Any software included in the Product is provided with restricted rights subject to subparagraphs (c), (1) and (2) of the Commercial Computer Software-Restricted Rights clause at 48 C.F.R. 52.227-19. The terms of this Agreement applicable to the use of the data in the Product are those under which the data are generally made available to the general public by McGraw-Hill. Except as provided herein, no reproduction, use, or disclosure rights are granted with respect to the data included in the Product and no right to modify or create derivative works from any such data is hereby granted.

GENERAL: This License Agreement constitutes the entire agreement between the parties relating to the Product. The terms of any Pu[illegible] Order shall have no effect on the terms of this License Agreement. Failure of McGraw-Hill to insist at any time on strict compliance with this License Agreement shall not constitute a waiver of any rights under this License Agreement. This License Agreement shall be construed and governed in accordance with the laws of the State of New York. If any provision of this License Agreement is held to be contrary to law, that provision will be enforced to the maximum extent permissible and the remaining provisions will remain in full force and effect.